WX154 CLt

CLINICAL RISK MANAGEMENT

To both Angelas and Tony

CLINICAL RISK MANAGEMENT

Edited by

CHARLES VINCENT

Senior Lecturer
Department of Psychology,
University College London

Publishing
Group

© BMJ Publishing Group 1995

All rights reserved. No part of this publication may be reproduced,
stored in a retrieval system, or transmitted, in any form or by any
means, electronic, mechanical, photocopying, recording and/or
otherwise, without the prior written permission of the publishers.

First published in 1995 by the BMJ Publishing Group,
BMA House, Tavistock Square,
London WC1H 9JR

British Library Cataloguing in Publication Data

A catalogue record for this book is available from the British Library

ISBN 0-7279-0947-9

Typeset, printed, and bound in Great Britain by
Latimer Trend & Company Ltd, Plymouth

Contents

Acknowledgements

This book has its roots in a programme of research carried out at University College over the past 10 years, initially with Bob Audley and Maeve Ennis. Many of the ideas underlying and guiding my approach to risk management were developed with them. More recently I have worked with and been generously funded by North Thames Region developing research and training in risk management. I would particularly like to thank Sheila Adam, Pippa Bark, Fiona Moss, Angela Jones, and Laura Olivieri for their constant encouragement and good humour. I also thank the authors of all the chapters for patiently enduring the editing process and responding to my many requests. Mary Banks, Diana Blair-Fish, Basil Haynes, and Deborah Reece at the *BMJ* were splendidly efficient and tolerant of the book's ever increasing size. Special thanks must go to Pam La Rose for calm and capable assistance with all aspects of the book.

Contributors

Judith Allsop
Professor of health policy and associate director,
Social Sciences Research Centre,
South Bank University,
London, UK

Gordon Bannister
Consultant orthopaedic surgeon,
Medical School Unit,
Southmead Hospital,
Bristol, UK

Pippa Bark
Clinical Risk Unit,
Department of Psychology,
University College London,
London, UK

R W Beard
Professor and head of department,
Department of Obstetrics and Gynaecology,
St Mary's Hospital Medical School,
London, UK

G E von Bolschwing
Attorney, chief executive officer,
Professional Risk Management Group,
Long Beach, California 90815, USA

CONTRIBUTORS

Henry Brown
Solicitor,
Penningtons,
Dashwood House,
69 Old Broad Street,
London, UK

Roger V Clements
Consultant gynaecologist and obstetrician,
111 Harley Street,
London, UK

Peter Dear
Consultant and senior lecturer in neonatal medicine,
St James' University Hospital,
Leeds, UK

Gordon Dickson
Dean, Faculty of Health,
Glasgow Caledonian University,
Glasgow, UK

Bridgit Dimond
Barrister-at-law,
16 Highfields,
Llandaff,
Cardiff, UK

Robert Dingwall
Professor and head,
School of Social Studies,
University of Nottingham,
University Park,
Nottingham, UK

James Drife
Professor of obstetrics and gynaecology,
Academic Unit of Obstetrics and Gynaecology,
University of Leeds,
Leeds, UK

P Driscoll
Senior lecturer in accident and emergency medicine,
Hope Hospital,
Salford,
Manchester, UK

Paul Fenn
Norwich Union professor of insurance studies,
School of Management and Finance,
University of Nottingham,
University Park,
Nottingham, UK

Jenny Firth-Cozens
Principal research fellow in clinical audit,
Department of Psychology,
University of Leeds,
Leeds, UK

J Fothergill
Consultant in accident and emergency medicine,
St Mary's Hospital,
London, UK

Hazel Genn
Professor of socio-legal studies,
Faculty of Laws,
University College London,
London, UK

John Hickey
Commercial director,
Medical Protection Society,
London, UK

Orley Lindgren
Cofounder and director,
Quality Risk Management Ltd,
Professional Risk Management Group and
Institute for Medical Risk Studies,
Sausalito, California 94965, USA

M Lipsedge
Consultant psychiatrist,
Department of Psychiatry,
Guy's Hospital,
London, UK

Don Harper Mills
Medical director,
Professional Risk Management Group,
Long Beach, California 90815, USA

Laura L Morlock
Professor of health finance and management,
The Johns Hopkins University School of
Hygiene and Public Health,
Baltimore,
Maryland 21205, USA

Fiona Moss
Consultant physician,
Central Middlesex Hospital,
London, UK

Linda Mulcahy
Senior research fellow,
Social Sciences Research Centre,
South Bank University,
London, UK

Graham Neale
Consultant physician,
Addenbrooke's NHS Trust,
Box 133,
Cambridge, UK

A M O'Connor
Risk manager,
Maternity Directorate,
St Mary's Hospital NHS Trust,
London, UK

Yvonne Peters
Executive director of nursing and quality,
Llandough Hospital and Community NHS Trust,
Sully Hospital,
Sully,
South Glamorgan, UK

James Reason
Professor of psychology,
Department of Psychology,
University of Manchester,
Manchester, UK

Isabel M Sanderson
Consultant to Independent Medico–Legal Services,
66 Queens Road,
Wimbledon,
London, UK

Jonathan Secker-Walker
Medical director,
Merrett Health Risk Management Ltd
Honorary senior lecturer,
Department of Surgery,
Rayne Institute,
University College London,
London, UK

Arnold Simanowitz
Chief executive,
Action for Victims of Medical Accidents,
Bank Chambers,
1 London Road,
Forest Hill,
London, UK

P J B Smith
Consultant urological surgeon,
Bristol Royal Infirmary,
Bristol, UK

CONTRIBUTORS

R Touquet
Consultant in accident and emergency medicine,
St Mary's Hospital,
London, UK

Charles Vincent
Senior lecturer,
Department of Psychology,
University College London,
London, UK

Idris Williams
Professor of general practice,
Department of General Practice,
Nottingham University Medical School,
Queens Medical Centre,
Nottingham, UK

Michael Wilson
Consultant anaesthetist,
Department of Anaesthetics,
Royal United Hospital,
Combe Park,
Bath, UK

Introduction

CHARLES VINCENT

Risk management was initially primarily considered as a means of controlling litigation, which has been a major worry for clinicians in the United States for over 20 years and a growing problem in Britain in the past decade. In the United States malpractice costs were over $1 billion a year by 1985 and were continuing to rise[1]; early risk management strategies were dominated by attempts to reform the legal system and reduce the costs of compensation. Gradually the need to consider the underlying clinical problems became apparent and the term risk management came to include strategies to reduce the incidence of harm and improve the quality of care. Crucially it began to also include positive efforts to care for injured patients and respond to their needs rather than simply treating them as potential litigants.

The narrow view of risk management, at worst both negative and defensive, holds that its aim is primarily to protect the hospital from claims, with little regard for the origins of those claims or for the wellbeing of the patients concerned. The more positive, broader view of risk management, hopefully apparent throughout this book, is that it is fundamentally a particular approach to improving the quality of care, which places special emphasis on occasions on which patients are harmed or disturbed by their treatment. Dealing with complaints and litigation is of course an important aspect of this overall project.

Risk management is developing in a receptive climate in Britain. With the growth of clinical audit it is now commonplace to review the structure, process, and outcomes of treatment, although few audits examine adverse outcomes in any detail. In Britain, as in the United States, the rising rate of litigation has also been a major stimulus to the development of risk management. Now that trusts are carrying the liability for claims made against them, albeit with the assistance of the Central Negligence Scheme, they have a strong inducement to reduce the level of claims made against them.

However, in the anxiety and occasional hysteria about the costs of litigation the principal problem is often overlooked. Many more patients are injured or traumatised by their treatment than ever even consider legal action. These incidents are referred to as adverse events (unintended injury to patients) or medical accidents. Adverse events should be the targets of risk management, not the litigation to which they sometimes give rise. It is the scale of injury to patients, not the costs of litigation, that is the primary justification for investment of time and resources in risk management. To understand this it is necessary to consider the scale of the underlying problem.

The nature and frequency of adverse events

Adverse events are much more common than is generally realised, occurring in the United States in almost 4% of admissions. For 70% of these patients the resulting disability is slight or shortlived, but in 7% it is permanent and 14% of patients die as a result of part of their treatment.[23] On the assumption that the rate of injury is broadly comparable we can estimate the numbers of adverse events in a European context.

In England alone there are about 8 million admissions to hospital a year, suggesting about 320 000 adverse events, 40 000 deaths, and 20 000 cases of permanent disability—before even considering primary care. In a medium sized district general hospital with 50 000 admissions a year this would suggest 1850 adverse events, including 75 deaths and 37 cases of permanent disability each year—each in some way a result of the treatment they received. This is clearly a major problem, irrespective of the level of litigation a trust may experience.

The cost of adverse events

The current cost of litigation is variously estimated at between £100 and 150m a year.[4] This is less than 0·5% of the NHS budget (£37 billion) and some have suggested that litigation is not worth all the attention being lavished on it.[1] Others argue that risk management is only important in specialties such as obstetrics, in which claims can be large enough to destabilise a trust (even with the assistance of the Central Negligence Scheme). It is certainly arguable that the cost of litigation does not warrant substantial investment in risk management, given that clinicians are in any case always striving to avoid adverse outcomes. The calculations become rather different when the costs of adverse events are considered, rather than the costs of litigation.

In the Harvard study[2] there were about seven times as many adverse events as claims for compensation, and about 14 adverse events for every paid claim. Any adverse event involves costs to the patient, staff, and the organisation. For instance, a recent case of damage to the ureter was settled out of court for a substantial sum, tens of thousands of pounds, but not one to worry the finance director of the health authority concerned. (The case preceded trust status.) However, the patient concerned had seven additional operations, each necessitating a stay in hospital of 10 days, and numerous additional investigations and outpatient appointments. The financial costs to the NHS in terms of use of resources and reduced efficiency are unknown, but probably vastly greater than the immediate costs of litigation. Most importantly, in financial terms, there are huge costs in the form of increased disability payments and other benefits which are likely to far outweigh the costs to individual hospitals.

Adverse events also involve a huge personal cost to the people involved, both patients and staff. Many patients suffer increased pain, disability, and psychological trauma and may experience their treatment as a terrible betrayal of trust. They may become depressed, angry, and bitter, and their problems are often compounded by a protracted adversarial legal process. Staff may experience shame, guilt, and depression after making a mistake and litigation and complaints impose an additional burden. A doctor whose confidence has been impaired will probably work less effectively and efficiently. At worst they may abandon medicine as a career.

The need for risk management is therefore acute, although how it should best be approached is less easy to determine. Risk management programmes aim to: (a) reduce the frequency of preventable adverse events; (b) reduce the chance of a claim being made after an adverse event; (c) control the costs of claims that are made; and (d) minimise the damage caused by early identification of adverse events, using either staff reports or a systematic screening of records. Reports of serious incidents are made before claims are initiated, and while memories are still fresh. The reports are used to create a database to identify common patterns and prevent future incidents. Ideally patients and relatives are also informed about adverse incidents and action is taken to minimise both the physical and psychological trauma.

Aims and structure of the book

The aim of this book is to stimulate and guide the development of clinical risk management in Britain and elsewhere. Risk management in Britain, and in many other countries, is still in its infancy. Although there is a wealth of experience to draw on in the United States, there is very little useful and practical literature available outside that country. The book provides an overview of the major themes and principles underlying clinical risk management but will also act as a handbook and source of reference for clinicians and managers. Risk management has many facets and several different disciplines are represented. Doctors, nurses, lawyers, psychologists, economists, and others have all brought their own perspectives to bear.

The book is divided into three sections. The first, Principles of Risk Management, provides essential background material for the more practical chapters that follow. This section partly relies on experience in the United States, where clinical risk management has been developed over the past 15–20 years. The second chapter provides a perspective from industry and insurance, and outlines the systems that have been developed to manage risks in those settings. Industry has again provided an excellent test bed for the development of accident analysis, and this approach to accidents and safety has many important implications for medicine. Chapters follow on the need to consider how behaviour can be changed, a problem which has bedevilled audit and attempts to "close the audit loop" (see "changes come about as a result of audit information"). Later chapters consider how risk management should be integrated into other quality initiatives, the financial background to litigation, and finally the evaluation of risk management. Evaluation in the United States has lagged well behind the enthusiastic implementation of risk management. In Britain we have the opportunity to build evaluation in from the beginning to discover if risk management is an effective approach to quality and, if so, which components are most useful.

In the second section experienced clinicians discuss the main areas of risk to patients in their particular specialty. Each chapter identifies high risk patient groups and procedures and discusses common causes of injury to patients and suggests how the various problems might be remedied. Adverse events of all kind are considered, not just those that lead to litigation. As many of the authors point out, risk is inherent in the practice of medicine, and a single chapter can only highlight the most important areas in each specialty. The clinical authors have all written in a way that can be understood by those with a non-clinical background.

Studies of accidents in other areas have led to a much broader understanding of accident causation, with less focus on the individual who makes an error and more on pre-existing organisational factors that provide the context in which errors occur. With this in mind clinicians were asked to discuss not only errors that are made, but also the background circumstances which predispose to errors and accidents.[5] Thus the background causes of adverse events will include the characteristics of the patient and their condition, but may also involve such factors as the use of locums, communication and supervision problems, excessive workload, educational and training deficiencies, and so on.[6] Safety programmes in industry have found that it is most effective to examine and change these background conditions, rather than exhorting people not to make errors. People do not, after all, intend to make errors and it is often pointless to chastise them for doing so. Each chapter makes specific recommendations for the management of risk within that specialty.

The third section concerns the implementation of risk management. The early chapters describe the systems and management structures that are needed for reporting and analysis of adverse events and the development of risk management protocols to reduce risk in clinical settings. Later chapters cover the response to adverse events. Here we should note that the term risk management has been extended to what would, in other contexts, be termed crisis management or disaster recovery. Clinical risk management is unusual in that the accident victims may be cared for in the same, or a similar, setting to that in which the accident occurred. They will be cared for by the same professions, and perhaps the same people, as those involved in the original injury. The continuing care of the injured patient must be considered as an integral part of risk management, especially as the original trauma is often made worse by insensitive handling after the event. Some litigation arises primarily because of poor communication, when patients have unrealistic expectations or misunderstand the nature of their treatment. The care of injured patients, the sensitive handling of complaints, the support of staff involved in litigation and serious incidents are all an integral part of clinical risk management. The last chapter considers the efficient and effective handling of claims. It is an axiom of risk management, or should be, that justified claims should be settled quickly with the minimum of distress to patients and staff and the minimum of legal expenses. Conversely unjustified claims may be defended with all necessary statements, documentation to hand, and in the knowledge that risk management programmes are in place to minimise the chances of accidental injuries to patients.

Twenty six chapters and an introduction may already seem a sufficient burden on the reader, even though the book is designed partly as a work of reference. The decision to restrict the legal aspects to a single chapter on the management of claims is deliberate. Risk managers of course need to understand basic medical negligence law, but this is available elsewhere. Several other areas could have been covered, or will need to be covered when risk management is further developed. The clinical section has concentrated on the specialties at high risk of litigation, but there is no reason that the principles of risk management, as a quality initiative, cannot be applied to any specialty. There may also be much to be gained from the systematic investigation of near misses, and iatrogenic effects of treatment, as well as incidents that may lead to litigation. It is not yet clear how closely clinical risk management needs to be linked to the management of health and safety in the workplace. Certainly, health and safety and clinical risk management are separate responsibilties, but safe clinical practice requires a safe environment in which staff themselves are not placed at risk. A generally inadequate safety culture may certainly predispose to clinical errors.

From litigation to risk management

The negative aspects of litigation, especially the costly and time consuming adversarial procedures, are clear to everyone involved. Nevertheless, a positive side is emerging. Litigation has continued to draw attention to the immense problems faced by patients who are harmed by their treatment, it has led to studies that have disclosed the numbers of people involved, and it has now led to risk management. To begin to use complaints as a form of feedback and to focus on adverse events as revealing deeper problems in an organisation requires a fundamental shift in attitude in many hospitals and practices. This book suggests that such a shift would bring widespread benefits. Risk management offers the chance to turn a potentially disastrous downward spiral of litigation and mistrust into a focused quality initiative targeted at the avoidable injuries that do so much harm to patients and staff alike.

1 Dingwall R, Fenn P. Is risk management necessary? *International Journal of Risk and Safety in Medicine* 1991;2:91–106.
2 Hiatt HH, Barnes BA, Brennan TA, *et al*. A study of medical injury and medical malpractice: an overview. *N Engl J Med* 1989;321:480–4.
3 Morlock L. *The evaluation of risk management programmes*. Chapter 7, this volume.
4 Ham C, ed. *NHS handbook*. Tunbridge Wells: JMH Publishing, 1995.
5 Reason JT. *Understanding adverse events: the human factor*. Chapter 3, this volume.
6 Vincent CA, Ennis M, Audley RJ, eds. *Medical accidents*. Oxford: Oxford University Press, 1993.

I: Principles of risk management

1 Clinical risk management: experiences from the United States

DON HARPER MILLS, G E von BOLSCHWING

While a major goal of clinical risk management today is to improve patient care, the concept and development of risk management generally have evolved out of the litigation process and continue to do so. How should injuries that lead to litigation be compensated, managed or prevented, or both? The answers depend on the risks involved: What is the risk of injury? How severe are injuries when they occur? Can they be modified once they occur? Do the modifications impart cost savings? Can the injuries be prevented in the first place? Does the cost of prevention exceed the value of the injuries themselves? Do social costs have to be considered? These questions apply to any industry in which injury litigation is a recurring theme. Health care is a prime example. Studies in California[1] and New York state[2] have shown that injuries and adverse outcomes from health care occur often enough to warrant concern even without litigation: about 4% of patients in acute care hospitals incur injuries and adverse outcomes of medical and clinical management sufficient to cause substantial financial impact through prolonged hospital stay, readmission, surgery, reoperation, special clinical treatment, or even death. About a quarter of these outcomes occur under circumstances that could lead to successful litigation in the United States should the affected patients or their relatives decide to sue. That only a small percentage of them actually sue (about 10%) is of little solace, because the cost of their lawsuits is already a social burden, and the situation could get worse. Since we cannot always change or control social structure, including the tendency to sue, solutions will have to be found in antecedent factors, hence the need for risk management.

Published technical books describing standard risk management structure and function abound. We will not duplicate those efforts; rather, we want to tell of our personal experiences as we have participated in the growth and development of risk management related to health care in the United States. Most of these experiences have not previously been published, and we feel they may be particularly germane to the United Kingdom at a time when risk management is just beginning to become an important factor in health care.

History of risk management in the United States

We found that the focus of risk management at any time depends greatly on the content of current lawsuits. Before the 1960s most litigation concerning medical injury involved complaints against hospitals and their nursing staff (as opposed to their medical staff). Doctors were rarely the primary targets because the legal profession was not sufficiently sophisticated to confront the judgmental decision making that forms the basis of clinical management. Thus, when a risk management programme was developed for the hospital industry in the mid-1950s attention was directed towards patients' falls, treatment errors, patient misidentifications, retained operative sponges, and the like.[3] Since the largest hospital litigation losses at that time arose from retained sponges, initial efforts were devoted to that problem. Analysis indicated that the methods of counting sponges during surgery was ineffective, even though universally followed. A third sponge count at the time of skin closure was recommended and adopted and was followed by a precipitous drop in retained sponges and resultant claims. Interestingly, a similar analysis of instrument counting procedures concluded that, although adding a terminal count might prevent retention of some instruments, prolonging surgery unduly would be counterproductive. Balancing risks and benefits therefore became a key element in the development of clinical risk management.

Incident reporting systems

Except for reported claims, there was no database to help to determine where the management problems lay and which of these

4

was important. One of the first incident reporting systems was inaugurated for the California Hospital Association. It merely asked nurses to report unusual events occurring to and around patients—that is, events that were inconsistent with good nursing management. The resulting database disclosed that patients' falls out of bed were much too frequent. Bed rails were purchased, but these proved more of a hazard than a solution. Patients determined to get out of bed would do so anyway, only to find that the drop to the floor was much farther than before, producing more severe injuries. Lowering the beds so that the falls would be less severe only aggravated the nurses, who had to care for patients in stooping positions. Nurses' complaints of back strain led to the creation of high–low beds, which allowed the nurses to crank up the beds for attending to patients and then crank them down to avoid excessive injuries from falls. This development was the forerunner of the electrically controlled beds we have today.

Another problem at the time was losing patients when they were transported to radiology, surgery, or some other specialised care unit. Patients became separated from their charts (medical records), and, because they were often sedated no one could determine where they belonged. The frequency of lost patients was recorded by the incident reporting system and led to the introduction of wrist band identifiers. But patients going to surgery still became lost occasionally because anaesthetists would cut off the wrist bands to facilitate vascular access. The bands were subsequently loosened to avoid that necessity, and anaesthetists were counselled on the need for retaining them.

The incident reporting system also became a product of litigation in the United States, serving as an early warning system for potential claims, as well as for finding problems before they were bad enough to cause claims. Injuries sustained by patients falling out of bed prompted lawsuits and solutions. Losing patients in the hospital rarely caused injuries but needed to be avoided; similarly, treatment errors rarely caused injuries, but they too needed to be avoided just to prevent an unusual toxic or allergic reaction. From unpublished data in our files for 1980–2, the incidence of treatment errors was 0·54/100 patient days in participating California hospitals whereas that of actual treatment reactions was only 0·03/100 patient days. According to the medical insurance feasibility study in California in 1977, 85% of drug reactions were transient in nature.[1]

As malpractice litigation increased during the 1960s and early 1970s, attorneys representing patients became more experienced in managing issues of clinical care and the emphasis on liability shifted from the hospital and nursing staff to primarily doctors. But during this transition, risk management programmes lagged behind, continuing to address problems associated with hospitals and nursing and rarely focusing on those associated with doctors. Doctors allowed hospitals to accumulate data about non-clinical issues but often resisted the development of information about their own clinical conduct, even though they had functioning tissue committees and surgical case review committees. (These committees of medical staff review appropriateness of indication for surgery and complications.) It was not until the mid-1970s, with the California medical insurance feasibility study,[1] that the development of databases involving clinical problems became a reality. The concept that generic screens could flag adverse outcomes made this transition possible. This study measured the frequency of patients' injuries and adverse outcomes arising from health care management, much as did the New York study in the late 1980s.[2] To facilitate the search for these injuries and outcomes special criteria were developed to screen patients' charts. Of the 20 original criteria, only 11 proved necessary to identify virtually all of the injuries and outcomes: criterion 1, admission in the previous six months; criterion 3, admission for conditions suggesting prior failure or adverse result of treatment; criterion 4, trauma incurred in hospital; criterion 8, return to surgery; criterion 10, unplanned removal of an organ or part during surgery; criterion 11, acute myocardial infarction during this admission; criterion 12, wound infection; criterion 13, neurological deficit occurring during admission; criterion 14, death in hospital; criterion 15, length of stay exceeding the 90th percentile for the region; and criterion 20, any other unlisted complication of clinical management.

Generic screens were intended to serve as indicators for the possibility that adverse outcomes from medical or clinical management had occurred. That is, if a patient was returned to surgery, that chart needed to be examined to see what adverse outcome, if any, was responsible (such as postoperative infection, postoperative haemorrhage, or some other complication related to the previous surgical management). Also, the transfer of a patient from a non-intensive unit to an intensive care unit creates the presumption that something might have gone wrong; therefore, the chart should be examined to see what adverse outcome, if any, was responsible. That a patient's chart was flagged by a generic screen, therefore, did not mean that an actual adverse outcome had occurred; it merely meant that certain outcomes might be present and the chart needed to be examined for those possibilities. Yet a tendency developed in the United States to regard return for surgery and unanticipated transfers to intensive care units as ultimate adverse outcomes.[4] In our opinion this was accumulation of ineffective information. These criteria identified 16 486 occurrences (79%) in 20 864 charts; yet, only 7% of these occurrences were shown by peer review to represent clinically caused injuries and adverse outcomes. Such a high sensitivity/low specificity may be good enough for research to establish baselines, but it is not efficient enough for prospective risk management. If a patient returned to surgery for peritonitis after an appendicectomy the return would be reported first on the generic screen, later followed by an examination of that chart to see if an adverse outcome was responsible. Taking the case that it was a burst appendiceal stump, the case should be added to other similar cases which could later be reviewed as a group. If this hospital had only one burst stump over 12 months, that episode would not be considered important in terms of quality management. However, if there had been six such occurrences a surgical problem probably existed and deserved attention with a view to prevention. The development of this scenario required three stages: a flagging system, a chart analysis for adverse outcomes, and the audit of the group of adverse outcomes. Today, with the utilisation of more refined indicators by departments, the data gathering can be simplified by combining the first and second stages into a single outcome measuring system. The initial flagging system should have identified the burst stump directly.

Overcoming resistance to reporting

We encountered resistance in expanding risk management from hospital and nursing care to include outcomes of clinical management. Doctors not only became protective when their own information was being screened for quality analysis and management but they also tended to find many reasons for not reporting their own adverse outcomes. We therefore chose nurses to do this reporting. They were already proficient in reporting non-clinical problems on their old incident report, and since clinical reporting did not involve assessment, cause, or conduct they were fully capable of identifying current adverse outcomes sufficiently to comply with our reporting requirements. But knowing that doctors themselves tended not to report these outcomes, nurses complained that they were being required to do the work of others. They considered that doctors should do their own reporting. So we had to meet with doctors and nurses together to try to solve the riddle of data gathering on a reasonably concurrent basis. We established hotlines for reporting incidents by telephone. Doctors preferred this method to writing reports, particularly when the outcomes were serious. We found that doctors used the hotline primarily to find out what they should do. Thus we piggybacked the data gathering system on requests for information. Of course, additional time and effort are required for hospitals to maintain adequately trained staff to respond to such hotline calls, but where this has been done risk management has improved, both for the care of injured patients, and for developing information for protecting yet uninjured patients. Once the nurses realised that doctors were participating in the reporting system, albeit only orally, they became less reticent in complying with the written reporting requirements.

Managing injured patients

An injured patient is one who has experienced some form of injury or adverse outcome either as a result of custodial or nursing management or as a result of clinical practice. Once a mechanism to identify such patients is in place, the next action is to minimise the injuries. For example, if a patient fell and sustained a fracture we need to evaluate that fracture and ensure appropriate management; if a patient developed a postoperative deep venous thrombosis and a pulmonary embolism we need to ensure that appropriate anticoagulation has been undertaken to avoid the next, and possibly fatal, embolism. Someone should monitor the process of identifying and managing these adverse outcomes and, when necessary, obtain clinical consultation to ensure that appropriate action is taken. Many hospitals in the United States did not have ongoing systems to carry out these functions. As early as 1963 a review of 1000 malpractice cases disclosed that at least 5% of adverse outcomes were worsened by subsequent problems with management (such as inadequate management of postoperative

8

wound infections).[6] These additional complicating factors have to be avoided.

In addition to minimising injuries, we need to tell patients what happened and what will be done. Whether an adverse outcome is a result of bad clinical care or merely a calculated risk of modern medicine, doctors tend to become silent and defensive when it occurs. They have been told over the years not to confess to patients for fear of litigation, and therefore they tend not to talk to patients at all about adverse outcomes. This is counterproductive. In the United States many injured patients go to lawyers simply to find out what happened—an unnecessary and costly investigative approach. It would be much better for doctors to sit with their patients and talk about what happened and what will be done medically and surgically. If liability is involved, now is the time to begin to consider some form of compensation. But the purpose of this communication is not for litigation, it is primarily to satisfy patients' clinical uncertainty. Yet, communications such as this will go far to preclude expensive litigation.

Managing malpractice claims

Decades ago all malpractice claims were defended with determination. Few claimants succeeded because attorneys representing them were incapable of ferreting out the real issues; obtaining medical advice and experts; and proving negligence, causation, and damages; but they have learnt well subsequently. Total resistance is no longer an appropriate manoeuvre for claims or risk management, particularly for public entities (county or state hospitals in the United States). These institutions may be embarrassed by such tactics taken against the very population they serve. Serious and meritorious claims can and should be resolved, often without entering into formal litigation.

Managing claims before or during litigation requires risk managers to utilise in house consultations. For instance, cases involving adverse outcomes from fractures will almost always be decided by what the radiographs show. These should be gathered and delivered to the chief of the orthopaedic department for a review to describe the initial fractures, to determine how well they were managed, and to ascertain whether the outcomes should have been different. Although the chief might have an interest in protecting his or her staff, utilising this help in evaluating claims allows for both departmental interaction and the implementation

9

of whatever preventive means might surface from the evaluation. This method therefore entails both awareness and participation of the institution in the claims management process. If the chief thinks that the case is "clean" the claims manager or risk manager may still seek independent consultation that avoids conflicting interests to ensure that the assessment has been appropriate. This process should not be put in the hands of solicitors. They are not trained for this purpose and they may not know how to ask appropriate questions. Solicitors and barristers are trained to conduct litigation; they may not be good claims managers.

Risk managers need to view medical and legal issues in malpractice litigation in a way that makes sense to doctors. To talk about duty, breach of duty, and proximate cause often leaves doctors bewildered. Thus we have learnt to approach these concepts differently. In clinical negligence there are two types of adverse outcomes.

The first type of adverse outcome is a new abnormal condition (such as an allergic reaction) caused by doing something to or for the patient (such as prescribing a drug). A set of medical issues pertain to this type of outcome, a breakdown in any one of which may result in liability for the doctor: (1) Was the drug or procedure calculated to be effective for its intended use for this patient (technology assessment, for example, North American Symptomatic Carotid Endarterectomy Trial Collaborators[7])? (2) Was it adequately indicated at this time (appropriateness, for example, McGlynn et al[8])? (3) Was the doctor competent to perform the procedure (credentialling, for example, Langsley[9])? (4) Was valid consent obtained from the patient? (5) Was the procedure or prescription properly performed? The incident reporting system should disclose what procedures or drugs are causing undue problems, and the case analyses should identify which issues are involved. Groups of cases can then be subjected to clinical audit for quality improvement.

Lack of valid consent from the patient is a frequent allegation in clinical negligence cases in the United States.[10] It does not fit into the usual category of clinical negligence in that it is not a professional judgment or performance issue. Rather, it is a doctor–patient communication problem. Did the doctor disclose sufficient information for the patient to make a personal decision to proceed? Not only is the doctor required to balance risks and benefits in deciding to recommend the procedure (involving categories (1) and (2) above) but he or she must then allow the

10

patient to make a similar judgment, though at a non-clinical level. The usual lawsuit in the United States stems from experiencing a complication of the procedure which the patient alleges he or she would have refused had the risk of that complication been adequately disclosed. Doctors in the United States have been slow to realise their obligations of disclosure, finding it difficult to switch from paternalism to accepting patients' autonomy. The duty to disclose the risks of a beneficial procedure sometimes seems antithetic to the desire to help the patient. Fortunately, we have been able to define most lack of consent cases by emphasising the need for the procedure (benefit to the patient) and by establishing that most reasonable patients would have accepted the risks had these been disclosed. But we have not been able to cope successfully with consent cases based on misinformation (as opposed to lack of information)—that is, if doctors downplay the risks, they place themselves in an almost indefensible position should the patient sue, even though the sole intent was to benefit the patient.

The second type of adverse outcome is a worsening or prolonging of the patient's disease or condition caused by a lack of timely intervention (that is, a failure to do something). The medical or legal issues for such adverse outcomes are different. (1) Was the lack of diagnosis or misdiagnosis reasonable? (2) Did the doctor accumulate enough information before making a diagnostic or therapeutic decision? If the database was adequate the doctor may have a right to be wrong, but if it was insufficient the misdiagnosis is probably not defensible, medically or legally. Examples are (a) not performing a rectal examination in acute appendicitis (the patient went on to experience rupture of the appendix and died from sepsis) and (b) not performing a spinal fluid examination in acute meningitis (the patient developed severe, permanent neurological sequelae because of delayed treatment). We found that the audit for problems of misdiagnosis may be more fruitful if it is focused on the status of the database, rather than on the misdiagnosis alone.

What we have just described are forms of system errors that may be remedied if there has been adequate data gathering, analysis, and action. But episodic errors also exist. These are instances of clinical negligence that occur regularly but seem to defy prediction and therefore prevention. The problem has not been lack of analytical ability, but the failure to accumulate enough information about the occurrence of episodic errors. Lawsuits alone do not supply enough information to permit analysis of these episodes, so

11

we have had to fold in the cumulative data from incident reports to establish trends and to permit auditing, which seems to be satisfactory, but only when the incident reporting system is equal to the task.

Few doctors know how to analyse clinical negligence cases well. They are not trained to appreciate the credibility factors or the types of evidence most meaningful to judges. Nor are they conversant with the types of system errors we have been talking about. Solicitors and barristers may have similar shortcomings unless they are extraordinarily skilled in this field. The risk or claims manager, therefore, has a role to oversee the evaluation of claims and to ensure that consulting doctors are focused appropriately. It is inefficient and insufficient for a solicitor or claims manager simply to provide a medical record to a consulting reviewer without guidance. A factual determination of what happened in the case must be carried out before asking consulting experts to evaluate the defendant's conduct. This preparation often includes the use of in house consultation with departmental chiefs.

Preventing the next injury

In working on preventing adverse outcomes, risk management becomes a subset of quality assurance. As we found out in the mid-1970s, most adverse outcomes are not related to clinical negligence. In the sentinel California study 4·65% of patients in acute care hospitals developed adverse outcomes from their management, of which only 17% were caused by negligence.[1] In real numbers, out of three million admissions annually in California, 140 000 adverse outcomes occurred, only 23 000 of which were due to clinical negligence. Efforts at prevention therefore focused on a much greater population than the liability cases. But even so, this comprises less than 5% of admissions; this is an outlier population, and some people complain that focusing on this group is an inefficient way of improving quality of care.[11] Although we agree that continuous quality management is an appropriate route to improve the quality of care, we have to realise that when particular adverse outcomes lead to litigation they exact substantial expense. This alone deserves attention. Even if adverse outcomes are not a major quality problem they are certainly a cost control problem. Some episodes are eggregious enough to demand instant reaction whereas others may wait for trends to be identified. The degree of clinical responsiveness often depends on the points of view of the institution's administrator. In California some hospital administrators will hesitate to pay damages for an injury clearly negligently caused unless steps are in place to prevent such an episode from recurring. But the way to prevent recurrence may not be apparent from solitary episodes. The risk manager is therefore in a position of having to satisfy both the administration and the doctors. It is not often a good idea to delay settling a damage case just because we cannot immediately produce methods to prevent recurrence.

Predicting problems

Prediction should be high in the vocabulary of risk managers. They should be clinically aware of the progress in medical science to predict when and where problems may arise. Once closed chest cardiac massage proved effective in the early 1960s, we began to worry about the concept of coronary care units, where patients could be salvaged from cardiac electrical failures. The first units were small and not all hospitals had them. We were concerned about the survival of patients with heart attack admitted to hospitals without such units (that alone prompted the rapid development of coronary care units in many hospitals). But we were more concerned about the small units that were in operation. How would decisions be made to discharge patients prematurely to make room for new patients who had greater priorities? Rather than wait to allow these problems to be decided ad hoc, we recommended the development of protocols which identified known criteria for admission, retention, and discharge from these units. Most hospitals developed these protocols early, and they proved effective. Although some patients who were excluded from continuous care owing to limited space in the units developed fatal cardiac arrhythmias in unmonitored rooms, we had very few lawsuits. Attorneys who represented the families of deceased patients admitted that the protocols contributed to the decisions for refusing their representation.

Prediction was again effective when the immune globulin to prevent maternal sensitisation in mother/fetus Rh incompatibility was developed. We knew this globulin was to be universally available in southern California by 15 June 1968; therefore, we flooded the medical media to prepare physicians and hospitals for this eventuality. Thereafter, only a few children developed

13

erythroblastosis fetalis from lack of administration of immune globulin.[12]

Occasionally ethical dilemmas are deposited at the risk manager's doorstep. In the United States Jehovah's witnesses have the right to refuse blood transfusion, even if that refusal entails a risk of immediate death, and even if the patient is a pregnant woman. But some doctors feel morally and ethically impelled to override these refusals if transfusions would alter the outcomes. Other doctors feel that it is only ethical and moral to abide by the patient's wishes, with today's emphasis on autonomy. Neither group can be condemned, nor should they be. But the mere fact that both are "correct" prompts the recognition of a special obligation of that group which feels compelled to treat over objection. Since there are others who feel just as strongly the other way, the group that "must treat" needs to refer these patients elsewhere for management. Risk management is involved in developing lists of physicians who will accept patients under these circumstances.

Interpreting and implementing court decisions

Risk management in the United States must often interface between courts and the health care system, and it has the obligation to be the caregivers' legal interpreter. The rules for civil liability, which includes clinical negligence, are controlled by the legislatures and courts of the individual states. Risk managers must therefore monitor legislative enactments and the state court opinions to interpret these for the hospitals and doctors in their particular state. In California we learnt in 1958 that doctors and nurses have the same direct obligation to serve their patients.[13] This should not seem earth shaking, but it required nurses to intervene to protect patients from doctors' misactions. The appellate court opinion arose from a postpartum maternal death caused by exsanguination from a cervical laceration. The nurses were aware that the mother was not responding to the doctor's ministrations but failed to intervene. The court held the doctor and the nurses responsible. This case accelerated the development of chains of command that now exist in most hospitals. Time and again risk managers had to explain to nurses and doctors that knowledgeable hospital staff have the duty to act. They cannot sit by knowing a patient may be injured. Their duty to intercede exceeds the rights of doctors to make mistakes, even non-negligent mistakes.

14

Many of the important court decisions affecting doctors' obligations arise from problems of communication. As we stated previously, doctors are not prone to be particularly informative to their patients. Courts therefore accepted the task of developing duties of communication for them. In Truman versus Thomas doctors were told that they had to warn patients of the downside risks when they refuse recommended procedures.[14] That case involved a woman who refused successive annual Pap (Papanicolaou) smears and developed advanced cervical cancer. She complained that the doctor should have told her why it was important not to refuse (and the court agreed). The impact of this case has been far reaching. Diabetic patients with infected foot ulcers must be told why they should not refuse admission for intensive care. Even patients who leave hospitals against medical advice must be warned of the consequences.

Various court decision have affected doctors' duty to warn patients of the danger of driving motor cars while taking sedative drugs[15] or if they have brittle diabetes[16] and to warn an identified potential victim of a psychiatric patient's stated intent to harm that person.[17] The risk manager's task is not only to disseminate these principles but also to devise means to document warnings whenever given. Patients who drive under the influence of sedatives or tranquillising drugs who become involved in motor car accidents may claim that they were unaware of the dangers. Doctors have to prove that the warning was given, but they complain that they are already overburdened with menial recording tasks. However, in this case a stamp would suffice ("sedative warning given") if placed in an appropriate part of the chart at the time of the patient's visit.

One obligation for communication does not include patients directly. The Joint Commission on Accreditation of Healthcare Organisations (JCAHO) requires doctors to talk with one another in evaluating and improving clinical care systems and in carrying out credentialling processes. These functions are enforced with varying degrees of success by hospitals seeking accreditation. Doctors have worried about these communications, fearing they may be developing information that patients' solicitors can use against them. These clinical care judgments are "built in" expert opinions that would greatly facilitate the prosecution of malpractice lawsuits. In the 1950s and early 1960s we thought that judges would understand that quality assurance activities were essential to improving care and that, since communications about these activities were not directly involved in any particular patient's day to day care, they would be considered irrelevant and inadmissible in a malpractice case.[18] A California appellate court proved us wrong, and the floodgates were opened for patients' solicitors to go on fishing expeditions in the entire clinical audit system for whatever evidence or opinions might be beneficial to their claims.[19] Doctors threatened to close down the audits unless they were assured that their activities would not rebound against them. There was a danger that medical audit would be reduced to examining non-threatening issues only. Risk management investigations into individual, potential lawsuits would not be impeded because of the attorney–client confidentiality and work-product rules; however, injury prevention and other programmes to improve clinical care would be devastated. The California Legislature responded by reversing the appellate court's decision with section 1157 of the California Evidence Code. This new law made proceedings and documents of quality care committees non-discoverable in legal proceedings. It has withstood attacks by the plaintiffs' bar,[20] and most other states have now followed suit. These legislative changes are now the mainstay of doctors' cooperative ventures into quality improvement.

Conclusion

What we have described here has been drawn from decades of firsthand experience in medical and clinical risk management. We have not always succeeded, but we have found most of the essentials, as follows. (1) To succeed in the larger arena of clinical risk management, doctors must be involved, both individually and as a group. They need to participate in gathering data and finding problems; they need to improve their skills in analysing evidence; and they need to communicate more readily with their patients. (2) The risk manager has fundamental obligations (*a*) to control lawsuits in his or her jurisdiction (gathering evidence, seeking appropriate analysis, helping solicitors and barristers, but always keeping control over each claim); (*b*) to monitor injured patients, making every effort to minimise their injuries and keeping them informed; (*c*) to help in data gathering and analysis for preventing injury; and (*d*) to predict the clinical effects of new medical and legal changes in health care. Risk management is thus a complex endeavour.

16

Mr Jack J Fulton, hospital administrator and lawyer, was the first special representative for the California Hospital Association's risk management programme, beginning in the mid-1950s. He was responsible for most of the early examples cited in this paper, and we appreciate his review and guidance.

1 Mills DH, ed. *Report on the medical insurance feasibility study.* San Francisco: Sutter Publications, 1977.
2 Brennan TA, Leape LL, Laird NM, *et al.* Evidence of adverse events and negligence in hospitalized patients. *N Engl J Med* 1991;**324**:370–6.
3 Ludlam JE. A personal history of the California hospital association insurance program. In: Dunlap HB, ed. *Fifty years.* Glendale, California: Bright Publishers, 1991:176–96.
4 Sanasaro PJ, Mills DH. A critique of the use of generic screens in quality assessment. *JAMA* 1991;**265**:1977–81.
6 Mills DH. Medical lessons from malpractice cases. *JAMA* 1963;**183**:1073–7.
7 North American Symptomatic Carotid Endarterectomy Trial Collaborators. Beneficial effect of carotid endarterectomy in symptomatic patients with high-grade carotid stenosis. *N Engl J Med* 1991;**325**:445–53.
8 McGlynn EA, Naylor CD, Anderson GM, *et al.* Comparison of the appropriateness of coronary angioplasty and coronary artery bypass graft surgery between Canada and New York State. *JAMA* 1994;**272**:934–40.
9 Langsley DG. Medical competence and performance assessment, a new era. *JAMA* 1991;**266**:977–80.
10 Mills DH. Whither informed consent? *JAMA* 1974;**229**:305–10.
11 Kritchevsky SB, Simmons BP. Continuous quality improvement, concepts and applications for physician care. *JAMA* 1991;**266**:1817–23.
12 Mills DH. Medical legal aspects of RhoGam. *Maternal and Child Health* 1968; **1**:18–9.
13 Goff v Doctors General Hospital of San Jose. *Pacific Reporter, Second Series* 1958;**333**:29 (California).
14 Truman v Thomas. *California Reporter* 1980;**165**:308.
15 Kaiser v Suburban. *Pacific Reporter, Second Series* 1965;**398**:14 (Washington).
16 Myers v Quesenberry. *California Reporter* 1983;**192**:583.
17 Tarasoff v Regents. *California Reporter* 1976;**131**:334.
18 Tissue committee of a hospital staff. *California Medicine* 1961;**95**:264–6. Judd v Park Avenue Hospital. *New York State Reporter, Second Series* 1962;**235**:843.
19 Mills DH. Medical peer review: the need to organise a protective approach. *Health Matrix, Journal of Law-Medicine* (Case Western Reserve University School of Law) 1991;**1**:67–76.
20 Mills DH. Protecting medical peer review, the case for confidentiality. *Los Angeles Lawyer* 1993;**15**:23–5.

2 Principles of risk management

GORDON DICKSON

Risk is part of everyday life. Many ordinary activities—driving a car, going out in a thunderstorm, walking under a scaffold—carry a definite, although very small, risk. And, moreover, few would want to live in an entirely risk free world—where the outcome of every action would be known in advance and life would be predictable and dull. Risk brings excitement and an edge to life. For some—for example, those who climb mountains or explore or drive formula one racing cars—this excitement takes them to the limits of endurance and daring. But in taking risks the consequences may be damaging or destructive. When this happens and the dice fall the wrong way excitement gives way to distress. It is this "downside" or cost of risk which is the subject of this chapter.

In day to day activities we seek to minimise risk—by wearing seat belts, locking houses, and insuring property. And even in risky sports such as formula motor racing the chance of the downside of a risky action actually happening pushes us to increase our level of certainty as much as possible by controlling the environment and thus our exposure to risk. Each move to reduce risk has costs. Risk management has an important role in striking the balance between the cost of risk and risk reduction.

Meaning of risk management

Risk management is a mechanism for managing exposure to risk that enables us to recognise the events that may result in unfortunate or damaging consequences in the future, their

18

severity, and how they can be controlled. A working definition of risk management that applies generally and not specifically to health care could be: the identification, analysis, and economic control of those risks which can threaten the assets or earning capacity of an enterprise.

Several important points emerge from this definition.

(1) The threefold approach to risk management is quite evident. Risks must be *identified* before they can be measured, and only after their impact has been assessed can we decide what to do with them.

(2) The eventual control mechanism, whatever it is, must be *economic*. There is no point in spending £10 to control a risk which can only ever cost you £5. There will always be a point where spending on risk control has to stop.

(3) The definition mentions *assets and earning capacity*. These assets can of course be physical or human. They are both important, and risk management must be seen to have a part to play in both. However, risks do not only strike at assets directly, and for this reason the definition mentions the earning capacity of an enterprise.

(4) The definition uses the word *enterprise* rather than a more restrictive word such as company or manufacturer. Risk management has its origins in manufacturing or process industries, but the principles are just as applicable in the service sector as the manufacturing sector and are of equal importance in the public and private sectors of the economy. Reference to "earning capacity" does not automatically imply the private sector and the profit motive.

(5) Finally, the definition is couched in terms which support the expected objectives of the enterprise. Risk management should be viewed as a positive way of helping operational managers to achieve their objectives. It is by identifying, measuring, and controlling risk that assets, earning capabilities, and hence the objectives of the enterprise will be secured.

Risk management has its origins in manufacturing and process industries, in which the need to respond to health and safety issues and to fluctuations in the insurance market have influenced its development. This paper is about the general principles of risk management. The application of risk management to health care will be discussed in other papers.

Identifying risk

Identifying risk starts from a broad view posed by the question how can the assets or earning capacity of the enterprise be threatened? This does not place any constraint on the type of risks we are seeking to identify as we need to be unblinkered and identify a wide range of ways that an organisation may be impeded in achieving its objectives.

Looking at any enterprise or organisation in this way is difficult. Ideally we need an open roof and gantry through which, unseen, we could observe all components of our enterprise. From such a vantage point we could identify what was done where and by whom; identify processes in one department that were potentially dangerous to adjacent departments; see the interaction between sections of the organisation; identify points of possible conflict; and look for concentrations of processes and any dependencies between departments. By looking down on our own operation we would also see outside the organisation itself and notice if our work threatened the surrounding area or if a neighbour threatened us.

How can we get this type of insight into our organisation? A structure to formalise the task of risk identification is needed, and a range of identification tools can be used. Flow charts, fault trees, hazard and operability studies, hazard indices, physical inspections, and many others are all available to help those charged with the responsibility of risk identification. These techniques merit a text in their own right. Many will sound unfamiliar to those who work in health care.

General principles of risk identification

The following points represent the general principles of risk identification regardless of the technique used.

(1) One particular method of identification is unlikely to cover all the problems of risk posed in any organisation or situation. Using one or two particular techniques to the exclusion of all others is not good practice, and a combination of methods is considered a thorough approach.

(2) Some methods suit certain situations. Flow charts, for example, are appropriate tools for identifying risk in a process that involves goods, services, materials, or people moving through several different stages. When flow is not the main activity, as in an office, other risk identification tools may be appropriate.

Matching the method to the perceived risks is important. Firm guidelines for doing this are not available, but risk managers are helped by a clear understanding of the organisation.

(3) Understanding the organisation and its work fully is greatly helped if as many people as possible within the organisation but outside the risk management department are consulted. Before embarking on risk identification a risk manager should identify all those who could be of help.

(4) A large scale risk identification exercise will always disclose risks. But however well the task has been done, further risks will emerge in the following weeks and months. Thus a continuing programme of risk identification is crucial for monitoring the continued identification of new risks, and such a programme entails careful planning.

(5) Accurate record keeping is an important component of risk identification. The form of record keeping should be agreed at the start of the programme and the relevant data must be recorded so that they are easy to refer to later.

(6) The task of risk identification must be carried out with financial realism—there is little point in spending £100 to identify a risk that can only ever result in a £10 loss.

Task of risk identification

Individual managers within an organisation are busy managing finance, production, marketing, or sales. Focusing on identifying risk needs to be a stated part of someone's function. In many organisations a risk manager may have been appointed for this task, but in others, which may be too small to employ a risk manager, risk identification should be clearly stated as part of someone's job description. The importance of this is illustrated by a real event.

In 1974 a catastrophic explosion occurred at Flixborough, a large chemical manufacturing plant in the United Kingdom. Before the explosion a set of chemical reactors had been removed for repair, and to keep production flowing a dog-leg pipe had been installed around the damaged reactor. A flange used to connect this pipe did not prove strong enough, and the result was the explosion. The official inquiry into the facts surrounding the explosion makes interesting reading for those involved in risk management. One passage from that report reads: "The key post of works engineer was vacant and none of the senior personnel, who were chemical engineers, were capable of recognising the existence of what in essence was a simple engineering problem." It seems that nobody had the specific task of asking how the changes in the plant had altered the risks inherent in its operation.

Need for clear organisational objectives

Risk management exists to support an enterprise in achieving its objectives. For risk to be identified effectively these objectives need to be clearly stated. Although self evident, often such objectives either do not exist or are known to only a few. Those responsible for identifying risk must understand fully what the organisation hopes to achieve. It is these expectations that are at risk.

Risk analysis

Once a risk is identified the next task is to *measure its impact* on the enterprise, which entails quantitative analysis. Much has been written about quantitative analysis, but there are three important general points.

The detail of past events is a good starting point for analysis of what might happen in future. A loss experience can yield interesting information on the trend and pattern of losses. Information technology has greatly improved the ability to analyse losses. With complete and accurate storage of data, useful information about trends and patterns of losses can be obtained.

Losses should be considered in terms of their impact on the organisation. In a very basic way we can identify the "layers" of losses. A bottom layer is characterised by high frequency and low severity. In insurance this layer is often referred to as the pound swapping layer, as the losses are predictable and the insurer and the insured know that losses in this region are likely to occur. The insured pays a premium and in due course the inevitable losses are met. But from the insured's point of view, the insurer has to meet expenses and make a profit on the transaction. The top layer holds losses of very high severity but low frequency. These are the losses whch, if they occurred, might destroy an organisation. The middle layer of losses are those of medium severity and moderate frequency. Expressing losses in terms of these layers helps to understand the impact of losses and the financial decisions about risk that may have to be taken.

Finally, an analysis of loss may need to be presented as a report. Thus it is essential that losses or potential losses, the impact of risk, are expressed in a way that is understood by all those involved—for example, finance managers, general managers, or lay directors. Communication of such findings is important. We could, for example, express our employee injury costs in terms of lost service, to provide perspective.

Risk control

The final part of the process of managing risk is *economic* control. The importance of economic control can be illustrated by the example of a corner shop so protected that the risk of fire was reduced to an absolute minimum, but if the associated costs represented a large percentage of the shop's turnover the degree of protection would be uneconomic. Therefore the steps to reduce risk must be financially reasonable. There are three aspects of risk control; loss reduction, risk retention, and risk transfer.

Reduction

A loss control programme starts with loss reduction—that is, a strategy to reduce as far as possible the impact of losses. The risk must be as low as possible. Rushing to control losses through insurance, without exhausting all possible ways of reducing the impact of the loss on the organisation, should be resisted. Loss reduction can be done either before or after an event has happened.

Pre-loss reduction entails those steps taken by the risk manager once a risk has been identified and before a loss has been incurred. For example, the instructions issued with a product are a form of pre-loss reduction. The manufacturer has identified a risk of injury to the consumer if the product is used in a certain way and has issued instructions in the hope that such injury can be avoided.

Post-loss reduction entails those steps that the risk manager believes will reduce the impact of the loss once the event has taken place. For example, the use of fire sprinkler systems once a fire or suspected fire has been detected are intended to reduce drastically the impact of any fire.

Risk managers require particular skills and understanding of both the physical means by which risk can be controlled and a knowledge of the processes within the organisation. In a real sense they must integrate all the pieces of information from the various sources to arrive at the optimum solution.

Retention

Once a risk has been identified and reduced as far as possible further decisions about managing the risk are needed. Before transferring the risk, which will incur the costs of insurance, we need to consider whether the risk can simply be retained.

Expected losses in the pound swapping or bottom layer will be expensive to transfer to the insurers, who will want the cost of claims and their own expenses and profit to be met. Such losses may well be suitable for retention. Knowledge of risk financing mechanisms is essential; risk managers will not want to expose their organisation to an intolerable level of loss nor spend money on insurance which may not be justified.

Not all decisions about retaining risk are taken voluntarily by risk managers. In some cases the retention of risk may be involuntary. For example, a limited capacity may exist for a certain form of risk and the risk manager may consequently be left carrying some risk. In other cases the cost of the cover may simply be prohibitive, thus forcing the risk manager to consider an alternative approach.

Transfer

The final step of a loss control programme is risk transfer. Essentially, the risk is transferred to another party, possibly through wording a contract so that any risk is left with the other party, but the most common form of risk transfer is insurance.

From the risk manager's point of view insurance is simply *a risk transfer mechanism*. The insurance premium is a loss today but relieves the risk manager and the organisation of the uncertainty of the timing and cost of future losses. The great benefit of insurance is that *loss costs are mostly fixed*. Budgeting is easier as losses are smoothed over the year rather than occurring at random.

Managing risk management

Implementing a risk management programme is an organisational and managerial function. Figure 2.1 illustrates the processes by

Figure 2.1 *Corporate risk management chart.*

which risk management can be implemented and includes the steps of risk identification, analysis, and control. But first is the task of developing the risk management philosophy and writing the risk management statement.

The risk management philosophy should be the one clear statement of where the organisation stands on the issue of risk and its management and is often expressed as a *risk management statement.* The process of generating the philosophy should involve several executives within the organisation and could represent good public relations for the risk management department. Deciding a corporate philosophy towards risk brings several distinct advantages, as shown next.

(1) The long term objectives of risk management are thought out by the organisation. The organisation has declared what it believes to be the optimum approach with the information available and in this way is seen to have a positive attitude to risk rather than a reactive attitude.

(2) Declaring a philosophy focuses attention on the work of the risk management department. The organisation is likely to have a declared philosophy in several of its activities— from marketing to product design, investment to

25

diversification—and placing a risk management philosophy alongside all these others could heighten the profile of risk management and bring with it an increased awareness of risk itself.

(3) The philosophy can also act as a useful benchmark against which to measure the effectiveness of the risk manager and the department. Without a philosophy it becomes difficult for risk managers or their bosses to know if they are performing satisfactorily. The task of measuring effectiveness would become very subjective.

(4) The philosophy represents the organisation's view of the management of risk and is essential for long term planning and for the evolution of risk management within the organisation as a whole. A philosophy may be described as permanent in the sense that it is the corporate view, but it should not be inflexible.

Risk management statement

The risk management statement outlines the policy of the organisation towards the problem of risk. It is not a manual in the sense of describing how something is done, and ideally, it should be brief and to the point, as illustrated by the two examples (boxes 1 and 2). The statement in the first example is relatively brief and represents one style of statement. Slanted towards the objectives and work of the department—for example, in its terms "identify activities," "measure impact," "take reasonable steps," "purchase insurance"—it is "objective centred." But although focused on objectives, it is also quite wide in its remit. It does not in any way restrict the actions of the risk manager or the risk management department, and the liberal use of such phrases as "loss producing events," "reasonable," and "economically attractive" gives the risk manager a good measure of flexibility. The statement follows fairly closely the three main steps in risk management of *identification*, *analysis*, and *control*. But care needs to be exercised with the use of this type of language if it is to be read and understood by people outside risk management. The sample statement in the second example has a different style. It is very brief and avoids specifics but emphasises the coordinating role of the risk manager and the department. Clearly, statements can be written in many different ways, and each organisation should decide on the style most suited to it and its general corporate structure.

Box 1—Sample risk management statement

Example 1: Imperial Machines plc
It is the policy of this company to take all reasonable steps in the management of pure risk, to ensure that the company is not financially or operationally disrupted.

In implementing this general philosophy, it is the philosophy of the company to:

1 Identify those activities which have or may give rise to loss producing events
2 Measure the impact of potential loss producing events on the company and its subsidiaries
3 Take reasonable physical or financial steps to avoid or reduce the impact of potential losses
4 Purchase insurance for those risks which cannot be avoided or reduced further, always retaining risk where this is economically attractive

---

These written statements are valuable for several reasons, as follows.

(1) The statement is a way of communicating the philosophy of the company as far as risk management is concerned. The best philosophy in the world will be of no value if it is not communicated to those who are meant to implement it.

Box 2—Sample risk management statement

Example 2: Associated Plant Limited
The risk management department is responsible for implementing all risk management activities. It has specified responsibilities in the area of:
Risk identification
Risk evaluation
Insurance

The department will act in an advisory capacity in the areas of:
Physical loss prevention

The department will coordinate the activities of safety, occupational health, and other related matters

---

(2) The statement can also encourage an element of corporate discussion around the problems of risk and its management. Provided the discussion is constructive, that is good.

(3) The statement will probably show the lines of authority. It will state who is responsible for certain aspects of risk management, and it can also be used to indicate areas of risk management that are the responsibility of others outside the risk management department. For example, the statement may make it clear that all acquisitions are to be reported to the risk manager by divisional general managers.

Risk management report

Most organisations produce a range of yearly in house reports—on research and development, marketing, new products, advertising, changes in the organisation, acquisitions and mergers, etc. Similarly, the annual risk management report would cover a whole range of risk management related problems.

There is a wide diversity of style and use of such reports. Each organisation has to produce reports which fit with the general image of the organisation as a whole, and this is true also for the risk manager's report. Three different contents pages, giving some idea of the possible contents of a risk management report are outlined in box 3. Format A seems to concentrate on the insured/uninsured distinction whereas format B features the philosophy and has more general divisions and format C has used the type of risk itself as a means of structuring the report. Hence the same information can be easily contained in each of these reports, the style that suits a particular organisation is a matter of judgement.

The value of these reports is as follows.

(1) The reports are excellent public relations documents, providing an opportunity for risk managers to put forward a "good" image of their function and the work of their departments. This is useful as much of the year will have been spent dealing with people after loss or other traumatic experience.

(2) The very discipline and work needed to prepare the report may disclose otherwise hidden information and may be valuable in itself.

(3) The report can act as a good educational tool for the risk manager. The essence of risk management often lies in communicating the message of risk, and the report is an

---

Box 3—Sample formats of risk management report

Format A
Summary
Highlights of the year
Loss analysis
    Insurance claims
    Uninsured losses
Premiums paid
Intergroup comparisons
Conclusions

Format B
The risk management department
Corporate risk management philosophy
Implementing the philosophy
Review of loss producing events
Risk financing analysis
Five year comparisons
The next five years
Summary of major points

Format C
Introduction
Property risks
Pecuniary risks
Liability risks
Transport risks
Major incidents summary
Expected changes
Conclusions

---

opportunity to put across ideas in a document that has a chance of being read.

(4) The report may indicate to other managers their comparative success or failure within the organisation. The risk manager has an overview and is able to report on the range of losses sustained within the organisation, which will be reflected in the figure for the departments or divisions.

Conclusion

This paper describes some of the principles of risk management. Rooted in the industrial and manufacturing sectors, some of the terms used and the economic analysis may be unfamiliar in clinical work. But risk management is very much concerned with people. Relationships and the ability to create and sustain them are essential for effective risk management. The principles of risk management have a broad applicability for health care and can be used to reduce the risks of harm to patients and health care staff and to make hospitals as safe as possible.

Further reading

Published work in risk management tends to be specific and technical. Readers interested in further reading may wish to contact the Institute of Risk Management, the professional education body in risk management in the United Kingdom, which can offer several textbooks on various aspect of the subject. (Institute of Risk Management, 6 Lloyds Avenue, London EC3N 3AX.)

3 Understanding adverse events: human factors

JAMES REASON

A decade ago, very few specialists in human factors were involved in the study and prevention of medical accidents. Now there are many. Between the 1940s and 1980s a major concern of that community was to limit the human contribution to the conspicuously catastrophic breakdown of high hazard enterprises such as air, sea, and road transport; nuclear power generation; chemical process plants, and the like. Accidents in these systems cost many lives, create widespread environmental damage, and generate much public and political concern.

By contrast, medical mishaps mostly affect single individuals in a wide variety of healthcare institutions and are seldom discussed publicly. Only within the past few years has the likely extent of these accidental injuries become apparent. The Harvard medical practice study found that 4% of patients in hospital in New York City in 1984 sustained unintended injuries caused by their treatment. For New York state this amounted to 98 600 injuries in one year and, when extrapolated to the entire United States, to the staggering figure of 1·3 million people harmed annually—more than twice the number injured in one year in road accidents in the United States.[1][2]

Since the mid-1980s several interdisciplinary research groups have begun to investigate the human and organisational factors affecting the reliability of healthcare provision. Initially, these collaborations were focused around the work of anaesthetists and intensivists,[3][4] partly because these professionals' activities shared much in common with those of more widely studied groups such

31

as pilots and operators of nuclear power plants. This commonality existed at two levels.

- At the "sharp end" (that is, at the immediate human–system or doctor–patient interface) common features include uncertain and dynamic environments, multiple sources of concurrent information, shifting and often ill defined goals, reliance on indirect or inferred indications, actions having immediate and multiple consequences, moments of intense time stress interspersed with long periods of routine activity, advanced technologies with many redundancies, complex and often confusing human–machine interfaces, and multiple players with differing priorities and high stakes.[5]
- At an organisational level these activities are carried on within complex, tightly coupled institutional settings and entail multiple interactions between different professional groups.[6] This is extremely important for understanding not only the character and aetiology of medical mishaps but also for devising more effective remedial measures.

More recently, the interest in the human factors of health care has spread to a wide range of medical specialties (for example, general practice, accident and emergency care, obstetrics and gynaecology, radiology, psychiatry, surgery, etc). This burgeoning concern is reflected in several recent texts and journal articles devoted to medical accidents[7-9] and in the creation of incident monitoring schemes that embody leading edge thinking with regard to human and organisational contributions.[9] One of the most significant consequences of the collaboration between specialists in medicine and in human factors is the widespread acceptance that models of causation of accidents developed for domains such as aviation and nuclear power generation apply equally well to most healthcare applications. The same is also true for many of the diagnostic and remedial measures that have been created within these non-medical areas.

I will first consider the different ways in which humans can contribute to the breakdown of complex, well defended technologies. Then I will show how these various contributions may be combined within a generic model of accident causation and illustrate its practical application with two case studies of medical accidents. Finally, I will outline the practical implications of such models for improving risk management within the healthcare domain.

32

Human contribution

A recent survey of published work on human factors disclosed that the estimated contribution of human error to accidents in hazardous technologies increased fourfold between the 1960s and 1990s, from minima of around 20% to maxima of beyond 90%.[10] One possible inference is that people have become more prone to error. A likelier explanation, however, is that equipment has become more reliable and that accident investigators have become increasingly aware that safety-critical errors are not restricted to the "sharp end". Figures of around 90% are hardly surprising considering that people design, build, operate, maintain, organise, and manage these systems. The large contribution of human error is more a matter of opportunity than the result of excessive carelessness, ignorance, or recklessness. Whatever the true figure, though, human behaviour—for good or ill—clearly dominates the risks to modern technological systems—medical or otherwise.

Not long ago, these human contributions would have been lumped together under the catch all label of "human error". Now it is apparent that unsafe acts come in many forms—slips, lapses and mistakes, errors and violations—each having different psychological origins and requiring different countermeasures. Nor can we take account of only those human failures that were the proximal causes of an accident. Major accident inquiries (for example those for Three Mile Island nuclear reactor accident, *Challenger* (space shuttle) explosion, King's Cross underground fire, *Herald of Free Enterprise* capsizing, *Piper Alpha* explosion and fire, Clapham rail disaster, *Exxon Valdez* oil spill, Kegworth air crash, etc) make it apparent that the human causes of major accidents are distributed very widely, both within an organisation as a whole and over several years before the actual event. In consequence, we also need to distinguish between active failures (having immediate adverse outcomes) and latent or delayed action failures that can exist for long periods before combining with local triggering events to penetrate the system's defences.

Human errors may be classified either by their consequences or by their presumed causes. Consequential classifications are already widely used in medicine. The error is described in terms of the proximal actions contributing to a mishap (for example, administration of a wrong drug or a wrong vessel unintentionally severed during surgery, etc). Causal classifications, on the other hand, make assumptions about the psychological mechanisms implicated in generating the error. Since causal or psychological classifications are not widely used in medicine

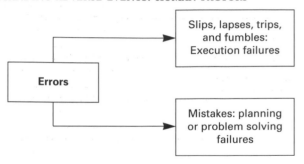

Figure 3.1   *Distinguishing slips, lapses, and mistakes.*

(though there are notable exceptions, see Gaba,[4] Runciman *et al*[9]) a brief description of the main distinctions among types of errors and their underlying rationale is given below.

Psychologists divide errors into two causally determined groups (see Reason[11]), as summarised in figure 3.1.

Slips and lapses versus mistakes: the first distinction

Error can be defined in many ways. For my present purpose an error is the failure of planned actions to achieve their desired goal. There are basically two ways in which this failure can occur, as follows.

- The plan is adequate, but the associated actions do not go as intended. The failures are failures of execution and are commonly termed slips and lapses. Slips relate to observable actions and are associated with attentional failures. Lapses are more internal events and relate to failures of memory.
- The actions may go entirely as planned, but the plan is inadequate to achieve its intended outcome. These are failures of intention, termed mistakes. Mistakes can be further subdivided into rule based mistakes and knowledge based mistakes (see below).

All errors involve some kind of deviation. In the case of slips, lapses, trips, and fumbles, actions deviate from the current intention. Here the failure occurs at the level of execution. For mistakes, the actions may go entirely as planned but the plan itself deviates from some adequate path towards its intended goal. Here the failure lies at a higher level: with the mental processes involved in planning, formulating intentions, judging, and problem solving.

Slips and lapses occur during the largely automatic performance of some routine task, usually in familiar surroundings. They are almost

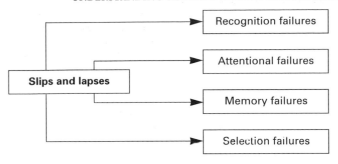

Figure 3.2   *Varieties of slips and lapses.*

invariably associated with some form of attentional capture, either distraction from the immediate surroundings or preoccupation with something in mind. They are also provoked by change, either in the current plan of action or in the immediate surroundings. Figure 3.2 shows the further subdivisions of slips and lapses; these have been discussed in detail elsewhere.[11]

Mistakes can begin to occur once a problem has been detected. A problem is anything that requires a change or alteration of the current plan. Mistakes may be subdivided into two groups, as follows.

- Rule based mistakes, which relate to problems for which the person possesses some prepackaged solution, acquired as the result of training, experience, or the availability of appropriate procedures. The associated errors may come in various forms: the misapplication of a good rule (usually because of a failure to spot the contra-indications), the application of a bad rule, or the non-application of a good rule.

- Knowledge based mistakes, which occur in novel situations where the solution to a problem has to be worked out on the spot without the help of preprogrammed solutions. This entails the use of slow, resource limited but computationally powerful conscious reasoning carried out in relation to what is often an inaccurate and incomplete "mental model" of the problem and its possible causes. Under these circumstances the human mind is subject to several powerful biases, of which the most universal is confirmation bias. This was described by Sir Francis Bacon more than 300 years ago. "The human mind when it has once adopted an opinion draws all things else to support and agree with it."[12] Confirmation bias or "mindset" is particularly evident when trying to diagnose what has gone wrong with a malfunctioning system. We "pattern match" a possible cause to the

35

available signs and symptoms and then seek out only that evidence that supports this particular hunch, ignoring or rationalising away contradictory facts. Other biases have been discussed elsewhere.[11]

Errors versus violations: the second distinction

Violations are deviations from safe operating practices, procedures, standards, or rules. Here, we are mostly interested in deliberate violations, in which the actions (though not the possible bad consequences) were intended.

Violations fall into three main groups.

- Routine violations, which entail cutting corners whenever such opportunities present themselves
- Optimising violations, or actions taken to further personal rather than strictly task related goals (that is, violations for "kicks" or to alleviate boredom)
- Necessary or situational violations that seem to offer the only path available to getting the job done, and where the rules or procedures are seen to be inappropriate for the present situation.

Deliberate violations differ from errors in several important ways.

- Whereas errors arise primarily from informational problems (that is, forgetting, inattention, incomplete knowledge, etc) violations are more generally associated with motivational problems (that is, low morale, poor supervisory example, perceived lack of concern, the failure to reward compliance and sanction non-compliance, etc)
- Errors can be explained by what goes on in the mind of an individual, but violations occur in a regulated social context
- Errors can be reduced by improving the quality and the delivery of necessary information within the workplace. Violations require motivational and organisational remedies.

Active versus latent human failures: the third distinction

In considering how people contribute to accidents a third and very important distinction is necessary—namely, that between active and latent failures. The difference concerns the length of time that passes before human failures are shown to have an adverse impact on safety. For active failures the negative outcome is almost immediate, but for latent failures the consequences of human actions or decisions can take a long time to be disclosed, sometimes many years.

The distinction between active and latent failures owes much to Mr Justice Sheen's observations on the capsizing of the *Herald of Free Enterprise*. In his inquiry report, he wrote:

> At first sight the faults which led to this disaster were the . . . errors of omission on the part of the Master, the Chief Officer and the assistant bosun . . . But a full investigation into the circumstances of the disaster leads inexorably to the conclusion that the underlying or cardinal faults lay higher up in the Company . . . From top to bottom the body corporate was infected with the disease of sloppiness.[13]

Here the distinction between active and latent failures is made very clear. The active failures—the immediate causes of the capsize—were various errors on the part of the ships' officers and crew. But, as the inquiry disclosed, the ship was a "sick" ship even before it sailed from Zeebrugge on 6 March 1987.

To summarise the differences between active and latent failures:

- Active failures are unsafe acts (errors and violations) committed by those at the "sharp end" of the system (surgeons, anaesthetists, nurses, physicians, etc). It is the people at the human system interface whose actions can, and sometimes do, have immediate adverse consequences
- Latent failures are created as the result of decisions, taken at the higher echelons of an organisation. Their damaging consequences may lie dormant for a long time, only becoming evident when they combine with local triggering factors (for example, the spring tide, the loading difficulties at Zeebrugge harbour, etc) to breach the system's defences.

Thus, the distinction between active and latent failures rests on two considerations: firstly, the length of time before the failures have a bad outcome and, secondly, where in an organisation the failures occur. Generally, medical active failures are committed by those people in direct contact with the patient, and latent failures occur within the higher echelons of the institution, in the organisational and management spheres. A brief account of a model showing how top level decisions create conditions that produce accidents in the workplace is given below.

Aetiology of "organisational" accidents

The technological advances of the past 20 years, particularly in regard to engineered safety features, have made many hazardous systems largely proof against single failures, either human or mechanical.

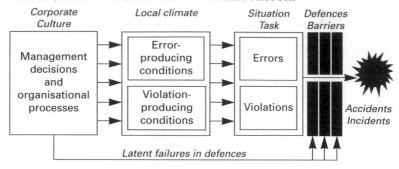

Figure 3.3   *Stages of development of organisational accident.*

Breaching the "defences in depth" now requires the unlikely confluence of several causal streams. Unfortunately, the increased automation afforded by cheap computing power also provides greater opportunities for the insidious accumulation of latent failures within the system as a whole. Medical systems and items of equipment have become more opaque to the people who work them and are thus especially prone to the rare, but often catastrophic, "organisational accident." Tackling these organisational failures represents a major challenge in medicine and elsewhere.

Figure 3.3 shows the anatomy of an organisational accident, the direction of causality being from left to right. The accident sequence begins with the negative consequences of organisational processes (that is, decisions concerned with planning, scheduling, forecasting, designing, policy making, communicating, regulating, maintaining, etc). The latent failures so created are transmitted along various organisational and departmental pathways to the workplace (the operating theatre, the ward, etc), where they create the local conditions that promote the commission of errors and violations (for example, understaffing, high workload, poor human equipment interfaces, etc). Many of these unsafe acts are likely to be committed, but only very few of them will penetrate the defences to produce damaging outcomes. The fact that engineered safety features, standards, controls, procedures, etc, can be deficient due to latent failures as well as active failures is shown in the figure by the arrow connecting organisational processes directly to defences.

The model presents the people at the sharp end as the inheritors rather than as the instigators of an accident sequence. This may seem as if the "blame" for accidents has been shifted from the sharp end to the system managers. But this is *not* the case for the following reasons.

- The attribution of blame, though often emotionally satisfying, hardly ever translates into effective countermeasures. Blame implies delinquency, and delinquency is normally dealt with by exhortations and sanctions. But these are wholly inappropriate if the individual people concerned did not choose to err in the first place, nor were not appreciably prone to error.
- High level management and organisational decisions are shaped by economic, political, and operational constraints. Like designs, decisions are nearly always a compromise. It is thus axiomatic that all strategic decisions will carry some negative safety consequences for some part of the system. This is not to say that all such decisions are flawed, though some of them will be. But even those decisions judged at the time as being good ones will carry a potential downside. Resources, for example, are rarely allocated evenly. There are nearly always losers. In judging uncertain futures some of the shots will inevitably be called wrong. The crux of the matter is that we cannot prevent the creation of latent failures; we can only make their adverse consequences visible before they combine with local triggers to breach the system's defences.

These organisational root causes are further complicated by the fact that the healthcare system as a whole involves many interdependent organisations: manufacturers, government agencies, professional and patient organisations, etc. The model shown in figure 3.3 relates primarily to a given institution, but the reality is considerably more complex, with the behaviour of other organisations impinging on the accident sequence at many different points.

Applying the organisational accident model in medicine: two case studies

Two radiological case studies are presented to give substance to this rather abstract theoretical framework and to emphasise some important points regarding the practice of high tech medicine. Radiological mishaps tend to be extensively investigated, particularly in the United States where these examples occurred. But organisational accidents should not be assumed to be unique to this specialty. An entirely comparable anaesthetic case study has been presented elsewhere.[14 15] Generally, though, medical accidents have rarely been investigated to the extent that their systemic and institutional root causes are disclosed, so the range of suitable case studies is limited. Box 1 describes details of the first case study.

Several latent failures contributed to this accident.

- The Canadian manufacturer had not considered it possible that a technician coud enter that particular sequence of keyboard commands within the space of eight seconds and so had not tested the effects of these closely spaced inputs
- The technician had not been trained to interpret the error signals
- It was regarded as normal practice to carry out radiation treatment without video or sound communication with the patient
- Perhaps most significantly, the technician was provided with totally inadequate feedback regarding the state of the machine and its prior activity.

This case study provides a clear example of what has been called "clumsy automation."[3][16][17] Automation intended to reduce errors created by the variability of human performance increases the probability of certain kinds of mistakes by making the system and its current state opaque to the people who operate it. Comparable problems have been identified in the control rooms of nuclear power plants, on the flight decks of modern airliners, and in relation to contemporary anaesthetic work stations.[17] Automation and "defence in depth" mean that these complex systems are largely protected against single failures. But they render the workings of the system more mysterious to its human controllers. In addition, they permit the subtle build up of latent failures, hidden behind high technology interfaces and within the interdepartmental interstices of complex organisations.

The second case study (Box 2) has all the causal hallmarks of an organisational accident but differs from most medical mishaps in having adverse outcomes for nearly 100 people. The accident is described in detail elsewhere.[18]

The accident occurred as the result of a combination of procedural violations (resulting in breached or ignored defences) and latent failures.

Active failures

- The area radiation monitor alarmed several times during the treatment but was ignored, partly because the doctor and technicians knew that it had a history of false alarms

Box 1: Therac-25 accident at East Texas Medical Centre (1986)

A 33 year old man was due to receive his ninth radiation treatment after surgery for the removal of a tumour on his left shoulder. The radiotherapy technician positioned him on the table and then went to her adjoining control room. The Therac-25 machine had two modes: a high power "x ray" mode and a low power "electron beam" mode. The high power mode was selected by typing an "x" on the keyboard of the VT100 terminal. This put the machine on maximum power and inserted a thick metal plate between the beam generator and the patient. The plate transformed the 25 million volt electron beam into therapeutic x rays. The low power mode was selected by typing "e" and was designed to deliver a 200 rad beam to the tumour.

The intention on this occasion was to deliver the low power beam. But the technician made a slip and typed in an "x" instead of an "e". She immediately detected her error, pressed the "up" arrow to select the edit functions from the screem menu and changed the incorrect "x" command to the desired "e" command. The screen now confirmed that the machine was in electron beam mode. She returned the cursor to the bottom of the screen in preparation for the "beam ready" display showing that the machine was fully charged. As soon as the "beam ready" signal appeared she depressed the "b" key to activate the beam.

What she did not realise—and had no way of knowing—was that an undetected bug in the software had retracted the thick metal protective plate (used in the x ray mode) but had left the power setting on maximum. As soon as she activated the "b" command, a blast of 25 000 rads was delivered to the patient's unprotected shoulder. He saw a flash of blue light (Cherenkov radiation), heard his flesh frying, and felt an excruciating pain. He called out to the technician, but both the voice and video intercom were switched off.

Meanwhile, back in the control room, the computer screen displayed a "malfunction 54" error signal. This meant little to the technician. She took it to mean that the beam had not fired, so reset the machine to fire again. Once again, she received the "malfunction 54" signal, and once more the reset and fired the machine. As a result, the patient received three, 25 000 rad blasts to his neck and upper torso, although the technician's display showed that he had only received a tenth of his prescribed treatment dose. The patient died four months later with gaping lesions on his upper body. His wry comment was: "Captain Kirk forgot to put his phaser on stun."

A very similar incident occurred three weeks later. Subsequently, comparable overdoses were discovered to have been administered in three other centres using the same equipment.

Box 2—Omnitron 2000 accident at Indiana Regional Cancer Centre (1992)

An elderly patient with anal carcinoma was treated with high dose rate (HDR) brachytherapy. Five catheters were placed in the tumour. An iridium-192 source (4·3 curie, 1·6 E + 11 becquerel) was intended to be located in various positions within each catheter, using a remotely controlled Omnitron 2000 afterloader. The treatment was the first of three treatments planned by the doctor, and the catheters were to remain in the patient for the subsequent treatments.

The iridium source wire was placed in four of the catheters without apparent difficulty, but after several unsuccessful attempts to insert the source wire into the fifth catheter, the treatment was terminated. In fact, a wire had broken, leaving an iridium source inside one of the first four catheters. Four days later the catheter containing the source came loose and eventually fell out of the patient. It was picked up and placed in a storage room by a member of staff of the nursing home, who did not realise it was radioactive. Five days later a truck picked up the waste bag containing the source. As part of the driver's normal routine the bag was then driven to the depot and remained there for a day (during Thanksgiving) before being delivered to a medical waste incinerator where the source was detected by fixed radiation monitors at the site. It was retrieved nearly three weeks after the original treatment. The patient had died five days after the treatment session, and in the ensuing weeks over 90 people had been irradiated in varying degrees by the iridium source.

- The console indicator showed "safe" and the attending staff mistakenly believed the source to be fully retracted into the lead shield
- The truck driver deviated from company procedures when he failed to check the nursing home waste with his personal radiation survey meter.

Latent failures

- The rapid expansion of high dose rate brachytherapy, from one to 10 facilities in less than a year, had created serious weaknesses in the radiation safety programme
- Too much reliance was placed on unwritten or informal procedures and working practices

- There were serious inadequacies in the design and testing of the equipment
- There was a poor organisational safety culture. The technicians routinely ignored alarms and did not survey patients, the afterloader, or the treatment room after high dose rate procedures
- There was weak regulatory oversight. The Nuclear Regulatory Commission did not adequately address the problems and dangers associated with high dose rate procedures.

This case study illustrates how a combination of active failures and latent systemic weaknesses can conspire to penetrate the many layers of defences which are designed to protect both patients and staff. No one person was to blame; each person acted according to his or her appraisal of the situation, yet one person died and over 90 people were irradiated.

Principled risk management

In many organisations managing the human risks has concentrated on trying to prevent the recurrence of specific error and violations that have been implicated in particular local mishaps. The common internal response to such events is to issue new procedures that proscribe the particular behaviour; to devise engineering "retro-fixes" that will prevent such actions having adverse outcomes; to sanction, exhort, and retrain key staff in an effort to make them more careful; and to introduce increased automation. This "anti-personnel" approach has several problems.

(1) People do not intend to commit errors. It is therefore difficult for others to control what people cannot control for themselves.
(2) The psychological precursors of an error (that is, inattention, distraction, preoccupation, forgetting, fatigue, and stress) are probably the last and least manageable links in the chain of events leading to an error.
(3) Accidents rarely occur as the result of single unsafe acts. They are the product of many factors: personal, task related, situational, and organisational. This has two implications. Firstly, the mere recurrence of some act involved in a previous accident will probably not have an adverse outcome in the absence of the other causal factors. Secondly, so long as these underlying latent problems persist, other acts—not hitherto

regarded as unsafe—can also serve to complete an incipient accident sequence.

(4) These countermeasures can create a false sense of security.[3] Since modern systems are usually highly reliable some time is likely to pass between implementing these personnel related measures and the next mishap. During this time, those who have instituted the changes are inclined to believe that they have fixed the problem. But then a different kind of mishap occurs, and the cycle of local repairs begins all over again. Such accidents tend to be viewed in isolation, rather than being seen as symptomatic of some underlying systemic malaise.

(5) Increased automation does not cure the human factors problem, it simply changes its nature. Systems become more opaque to their operators. Instead of causing harm by slips, lapses, trips, and fumbles, people are now more prone to make mistaken judgements about the state of the system.

The goal of effective risk management is not so much to minimise particular errors and violations as to enhance human performance at all levels of the system.[3] Perhaps paradoxically, most performance enhancement measures are not directly focused at what goes on inside the heads of single individuals. Rather, they are directed at team, task, situation, and organisational factors, as discussed below.

Team factors

A great deal of health care is delivered by multidisciplinary teams. Over a decade of experience in aviation (and, more recently, marine technology) has shown that measures designed to improve team management and the quality of the communications between team members can have an enormous impact on human performance. The aviation psychologist Robert Helmreich (one of the pioneers of crew resource management) and his colleagues at the University of Texas analysed 51 aircraft accidents and incidents, paying special attention to team related factors.[19] Box 3 summarises their findings, where the team related factors are categorised as negative (having an adverse impact upon safety and survivability) or positive (acting to improve survivability). The numbers given in each case relate to the number of accidents or incidents in which particular team related factors had a negative or a positive role.

This list offers clear recommendations for the interactions of medical teams just as much as for aircraft crews. Recently, Helmreich and the anaesthetist Hans-Gerhard Schaefer studied

44

Box 3—Team related factors and role in 51 aircraft accidents and incidents*

Team concept and environment for open communications established (negative 7; positive 2)

Briefings are operationally thorough, interesting, and address crew coordination and planning for potential problems. Expectations are set for how possible deviations from normal operations are to be handled (negative 9; positive 2)

Cabin crew are included as part of the team in briefings, as appropriate, and guidelines are established for coordination between flight deck and cabin (negative 2)

Group climate is appropriate to operational situation (for example, presence of social conversation). Crew ensures that non-operational factors such as social interaction do not interfere with necessary tasks (negative 13; positive 4)

Crew members ask questions regarding crew actions and decisions (negative 11; positive 4)

Crew members speak up and state their information with appropriate persistence until there is some clear resolution or decision (negative 14; positive 4)

Captain coordinates flight deck activities to establish proper balance between command authority and crew member participation and acts decisively when the situation requires it (negative 18; positive 4)

Workload and task distribution are clearly communicated and acknowledged by crew members. Adequate time is provided for the completion of tasks (negative 12; positive 4)

Secondary tasks are prioritised to allow sufficient resources for dealing effectively with primary duties (negative 5; positive 2)

Crew members check with each other during times of high and low workload to maintain situational awareness and alertness (negative 3; positive 3)

Crew prepares for expected contingency situations (negative 28; positive 4)

Guidelines are established for the operation and disablement of automated systems. Duties and responsibilities with regard to automated systems are made clear. Crew periodically review and verify the status of automated systems. Crew verbalises and acknowledges entries and changes to automated systems. Crew allows sufficient time for programming automated systems before manoeuvres (negative 14)

When conflicts arise the crew remains focused on the problem or situation at hand. Crew members listen actively to ideas and opinions and admit mistakes when wrong (negative 2)

* After Helmreich et al[19]

team performance in the operating theatre of a Swiss teaching hospital.[20] They noted that "interpersonal and communications issues are responsible for many inefficiencies, errors, and frustrations in this psychologically and organisationally complex environment."[8] They also observed that attempts to improve institutional performance largely entailed throwing money at the problem through the acquisition of new and ever more advanced equipment whereas improvements to training and team performance could be achieved more effectively at a fraction of this cost. As has been clearly shown for aviation, formal training in team management and communication skills can produce substantial improvements in human performance as well as reducing safety-critical errors.

Task factors

Tasks vary widely in their liability to promote errors. Identifying and modifying tasks and task elements that are conspicuously prone to failure are essential steps in risk management.

The following simple example is representative of many maintenance tasks. Imagine a bolt with eight nuts on it. Each nut is coded and has to be located in a particular sequence. Disassembly is virtually error free. There is only one way in which the nuts can be removed from the bolt and all the necessary knowledge to perform this task is located in the world (that is, each step in the procedure is automatically cued by the preceding one). But the task of correct reassembly is immensely more difficult. There are over 40 000 ways in which this assemblage of nuts can be wrongly located on the bolt (factorial 8). In addition, the knowledge necessary to get the nuts back in the right order has to be either memorised or read from some written procedure, both of which are highly liable to error or neglect. Such an example may seem at first sight to be far removed from the practice of medicine, but medical equipment, like any other sophisticated hardware, requires careful maintenance—and maintenance errors (particularly omitting necessary reassembly steps) constitute one of the greatest sources of human factors problems in high technology industries.[11]

Effective incident monitoring is an invaluable tool in identifying tasks prone to error. On the basis of their body of nearly 4000 anaesthetic and intensive care incidents, Runciman et al at the Royal Adelaide Hospital (see Runciman et al[9] for a report of the first 2000 incidents) introduced many inexpensive equipment

Table 3.1 *Summary of error producing conditions ranked in order of known effect (after Williams[22])*

Condition	Risk factor
Unfamiliarity with the task	($\times$ 17)
Time shortage	($\times$ 11)
Poor signal:noise ratio	($\times$ 10)
Poor human system interface	($\times$ 8)
Designer user mismatch	($\times$ 8)
Irreversibility of errors	($\times$ 8)
Information overload	($\times$ 6)
Negative transfer between tasks	($\times$ 5)
Misperception of risk	($\times$ 4)
Poor feedback from system	($\times$ 4)
Inexperience not lack of training	($\times$ 3)
Poor instructions or procedures	($\times$ 3)
Inadequate checking	($\times$ 3)
Educational mismatch of person with task	($\times$ 2)
Disturbed sleep patterns	($\times$ 1·6)
Hostile environment	($\times$ 1·2)
Monotony and boredom	($\times$ 1·1)

modifications guaranteed to enhance performance and to minimise recurrent errors. These include colour coded syringes and endotracheal tubes graduated to help non-intrusive identification of endobronchial intubation.[21]

Situational factors

Each type of task has its own nominal error probability. For example, carrying out a totally novel task with no clear idea of the likely consequences (that is, knowledge based processing) has a basic error probability of 0·75. At the other extreme, a highly familiar, routine task performed by a well motivated and competent workforce has an error probability of 0·0005. But there are certain conditions both of the individual person and his or her immediate environment that are guaranteed to increase these nominal error probabilities (table 3.1). Here the error producing conditions are ranked in the order of their known effects and the numbers in parentheses indicate the risk factor (that is, the amount by which the nominal error rates should be multiplied under the worst conditions). Notably, three of the best researched factors—namely, sleep disturbance, hostile environment, and boredom—carry the least penalties. Also, those error producing factors at the top of the list are those that lie squarely within the organisational sphere of influence. This is a central element in the present view of organisational accidents. Managers and administrators rarely, if

47

Table 3.2 *Violation producing conditions, unranked*

Conditions
Manifest lack of organisational safety culture
Conflict between management and staff
Poor morale
Poor supervision and checking
Group norms condoning violations
Misperception of hazards
Perceived lack of management care and concern
Little elan or pride in work
Culture that encourages taking risks
Beliefs that bad outcomes will not happen
Low self esteem
Learned helplessness
Perceived licence to bend rules
Ambiguous or apparently meaningless rules
Rules inapplicable due to local conditions
Inadequate tools and equipment
Inadequate training
Time pressure
Professional attitudes hostile to procedures

ever, have the opportunity to jeopardise a system's safety directly. Their influence is more indirect: top level decisions create the conditions that promote unsafe acts.

For convenience, error producing conditions can be reduced to seven broad categories: high workload; inadequate knowledge, ability or experience, poor interface design; inadequate supervision or instruction; stressful environment; mental state (fatigue, boredom, etc); and change. Departures from routine and changes in the circumstances in which actions are normally performed constitute a major factor in absentminded slips of action.[23]

Compared with error producing conditions, the factors that promote violations are less well understood. Ranking their relative effects is not possible. However, we can make an informed guess at the nature of these violation producing conditions, as shown in table 3.2, although in no particular order of effect.

Again, for causal analysis this list can be reduced to a few general categories: lack of safety culture, lack of concern, poor morale, norms condoning violation, "can do" attitudes, and apparently meaningless or ambiguous rules.

Organisational factors

Quality and safety, like health and happiness, have two aspects: a negative aspect disclosed by incidents and accidents and a positive

48

aspect, to do with the system's intrinsic resistance to human factors problems. Whereas incidents and accidents convert easily into numbers, trends, and targets, the positive aspect is much harder to identify and measure.

Accident and incident reporting procedures are a crucial part of any safety or quality information system. But, by themselves, they are insufficient to support effective quality and safety management. The information they provide is both too little and too late for this longer term purpose. To promote proactive accident prevention rather than reactive "local repairs" an organisation's "vital signs" should be monitored regularly.

When a doctor carries out a routine medical check he or she samples the state of several critical bodily systems: the cardiovascular, pulmonary, excretory, neurological systems, and so on. From individual measures of blood pressure, electro-cardiographic activity, cholesterol concentration, urinary contents, reflexes, and so on the doctor makes a professional judgement about the individual's general state of health. There is no direct, definitive measure of a person's health. It is an emergent property inferred from a selection of physiological signs and lifestyle indicators. The same is also true from complex hazardous systems. Assessing an organisation's current state of "safety health," as in medicine, entails regular and judicious sampling of a small subset of a potentially large number of indices. But what are the dimensions along which to assess organisational "safety health?"

Several such diagnostic techniques are already being implemented in various industries.[24] The individual labels for the assessed dimensions vary from industry to industry (oil exploration and production, tankers, helicopters, railway operations, and aircraft engineering), but all of them have been guided by two principles. Firstly, they try to include those organisational "pathogens" that have featured most conspicuously in well documented accidents (that is, hardware defects, incompatible goals, poor operating procedures, understaffing, high workload, inadequate training, etc). Secondly, they seek to encompass a representative sampling of those core processes common to all technological organisations (that is, design, build, operate, maintain, manage, communicate, etc).

Since there is unlikely to be a single universal set of indicators for all types of hazardous operations one way of communicating how safety health can be assessed is simply to list the organisational factors that are currently measured (see table 3.3). Tripod-Delta,

Table 3.3 *Measures of organisational health used in different industrial settings*

Oil exploration and production	Railways	Aircraft maintenance
Hardware	Tools and equipment	Organisational structure
Design	Materials	People management
Maintenance management	Supervision	Provision and quality of tools and equipment
Procedures	Working environment	Training and selection
Error enforcing conditions	Staff attitudes	Commercial and operational pressures
Housekeeping	Housekeeping	Planning and scheduling
Incompatible goals	Contractors	Maintenance of buildings and equipment
Organisation	Design	Communication
Communication	Staff communication	
Training	Departmental communication	
Defences	Staffing and rostering	
	Training	
	Planning	
	Rules	
	Management	
	Maintenance	

commissioned by Shell International and currently implemented in several of its exploration and production operating companies, on Shell tankers, and on its contracted helicopters in the North Sea, assesses the quarterly or half yearly state of 11 general failure types in specific workplaces: hardware, design, maintenance management, procedures, error enforcing conditions, housekeeping, incompatible goals, organisational structure, communication, training, and defences. A discussion of the rationale behind the selection and measurement of these failure types can be found elsewhere.[25]

Tripod-Delta uses tangible, dimension related indicators as direct measures or "symptoms" of the state of each of the 11 failure types. These indicators are generated by task specialists and are assembled into checklists by a computer program (Delta) for each testing occasion. The nature of the indicators varies from activity to activity (that is, drilling, seismic surveys, transport, etc) and from test to test. Examples of such indicators for design associated with an offshore platform are listed below. All questions have yes/no answers.

- Was this platform originally designed to be unmanned?
- Are shut off valves fitted at a height of more than 2 metres?
- Is standard (company) coding used for the pipes?
- Are there locations on this platform where the deck and walkways differ in height?
- Have there been more than two unscheduled maintenance jobs over the past week?
- Are there any bad smells from the low pressure vent system?

Relatively few of the organisational and managerial factors listed in table 3.3 are specific to safety; rather, they relate to the quality of the overall system. As such, they can also be used to gauge proactively the likelihood of negative outcomes other than coming into damaging contact with physical hazards, such as loss of market share, bankruptcy, and liability to criminal prosecution or civil laws suits.

The measurements derived from Tripod-Delta are summarised as bar graph profiles. Their purpose is to identify the two or three factors most in need of remediation and to track changes over time. Maintaining adequate safety health is thus comparable with a long term fitness programme in which the focus of remedial efforts switches from dimension to dimension as previously salient factors improve and new ones come into prominence. Like life, effective safety management is "one thing after another." Striving for the best attainable level of intrinsic resistance to operational hazards is like fighting a guerrilla war. One can expect no absolute victories. There are no "Waterloos" in the safety war.

Summary and conclusions

(1) Human rather than technical failures now represent the greatest threat to complex and potentially hazardous systems. This includes healthcare systems.

(2) Managing the human risks will never be 100% effective. Human fallibility can be moderated, but it cannot be eliminated.

(3) Different error types have different underlying mechanisms, occur in different parts of the organisation, and require different methods of risk management. The basic distinctions are between:

- Slips, lapses, trips, and fumbles (execution failures) and mistakes (planning or problem solving failures). Mistakes are divided into rule based mistakes and knowledge based mistakes
- Errors (information-handling problems) and violations (motivational problems)
- Active versus latent failures. Active failures are committed by those in direct contact with the patient, latent failures arise in organisational and managerial spheres and their adverse effects may take a long time to become evident.

(4) Safety significant errors occur at all levels of the system, not just at the sharp end. Decisions made in the upper echelons of the organisation create the conditions in the workplace that subsequently promote individual errors and violations. Latent failures are present long before an accident and are hence prime candidates for principled risk management.

(5) Measures that involve sanctions and exhortations (that is, moralistic measures directed to those at the sharp end) have only very limited effectiveness, especially so in the case of highly trained professionals.

(6) Problems of human factors are a product of a chain of causes in which the individual psychological factors (that is, momentary inattention, forgetting, etc) are the last and least

manageable links. Attentional "capture" (preoccupation or distraction) is a necessary condition for the commission of slips and lapses. Yet its occurrence is almost impossible to predict or control effectively. The same is true of the factors associated with forgetting. States of mind contributing to error are thus extremely difficult to manage; they can happen to the best of people at any time.

(7) People do not act in isolation. Their behaviour is shaped by circumstances. The same is true for errors and violations. The likelihood of an unsafe act being committed is heavily influenced by the nature of the task and by the local workplace conditions. These, in turn, are the product of "upstream" organisational factors. Great gains in safety can be achieved through relatively small modifications of equipment and workplaces.

(8) Automation and increasingly advanced equipment do not cure problems associated with human factors, they merely relocate them. In contrast, training people to work effectively in teams costs little, but has achieved significant enhancements of human performance in aviation.

(9) Effective risk management depends critically on a confidential and preferably anonymous incident monitoring system that records the individual, task, situational, and organisational factors associated with incidents and near misses.

(10) Effective risk management means the simultaneous and targeted deployment of limited remedial resources at different levels of the system: the individual or team, the task, the situation, and the organisation as a whole.

1 Brennan TA, Leape LL, Laird NM, Herbert L, Localio AR, Lawthers AG, et al. Incidence of adverse events and negligence in hospitalized patients: results from the Harvard medical practice study 1. *New Engl J Med* 1991;**324**: 370–6.

2 Leape LL, Brennan TA, Laird NM, Lawthers AG, Localio AR, Barnes BA, et al. The nature of adverse events in hospitalized patients: results from the Harvard medical practice study II. *New Engl J Med* 1991;**324**:377–84.

3 Cook RI, Woods DD. Operating at the sharp end: the complexity of human error. In: Bogner MS, ed. *Human errors in medicine.* Hillsdale, New Jersey: Erlbaum, 1994:255–310.

4 Gaba DM. Human error in anesthetic mishaps. *Int Anesthesiol Clin* 1989;**27**: 137–47.

5 Gaba DM. Human error in dynamic medical domains. In: Bogner MS, ed. *Human errors in medicine.* Hillsdale, New Jersey: Erlbaum, 1994:197–224.

6 Perrow C. *Normal accidents,* New York: Basic Books, 1984.

7 Vincent C, Ennis M, Audley RJ. *Medical accidents.* Oxford: Oxford University Press, 1993.
8 Bogner MS. *Human error in medicine.* Hillsdale, New Jersey: Erlbaum, 1994.
9 Runciman WB, Sellen A, Webb RK, Williamson JA, Currie M, Morgan C, *et al.* Errors, incidents and accidents in anaesthetic practice. *Anaesth Intensive Care* 1993;**21**:506–19.
10 Hollnagel E. *Reliability of cognition: foundations of human reliability analysis.* London: Academic Press, 1993.
11 Reason J. *Human error.* New York: Cambridge University Press, 1990.
12 Bacon F. In: Anderson F, ed. *The new Organon.* Indianapolis: Bobbs-Merrill, 1960. (Originally published 1620.)
13 Sheen. *MV Herald of Free Enterprise. Report of court No 8074 formal investigation.* London: Department of Transport, 1987.
14 Eagle CJ, Davies JM, Reason JT. Accident analysis of large scale technological disasters applied to an anaesthetic complication. *Canadian Journal of Anaesthesia* 1992;**39**:118–22.
15 Reason J. The human factor in medical accidents. In: Vincent C, Ennis M, Audley R, eds. *Medical accidents.* Oxford: Oxford University Press, 1993: 1–16.
16 Wiener EL. *Human factors of advanced technology ("glass cockpit") transport aircraft.* Moffett Field, California: NASA Ames Research Center, 1989. Technical report 117528.
17 Woods DD, Johannesen JJ, Cook RI, Sarter NB. *Behind human error: cognitive systems, computers, and hindsight.* Wright-Patterson Air Force Base, Ohio: Crew Systems Ergonomics Information Analysis Center, 1994. (CSERIAC state of the art report.)
18 NUREG. *Loss of an iridium-192 source and therapy misadministration at Indiana Regional Cancer Center, Indiana, Pennsylvania, on November 16, 1992.* Washington, DC: US Nuclear Regulatory Commission, 1993. (NUREG-1480.)
19 Helmreich RL, Butler RA, Taggart WR, Wilhem JA. *Behavioral markers in accidents and incidents: reference list.* Austin, Texas: University of Texas, 1994. (Technical report 94-3; NASA/University of Texas FAA Aerospace Crew Research Project.)
20 Helmreich RL, Schaefer H-G. Team performance in the operating room. In: Bogner MS, ed. *Human errors in medicine.* Hillsdale, New Jersey: Erlbaum, 1994.
21 Runciman WB. Anaesthesia incident monitoring study. In: *Incident monitoring and risk management in the health care sector.* Canberra: Commonwealth Department of Human Services and Health, 1994: 13–5.
22 Williams J. A data-based method for assessing and reducing human error to improve operational performance. In: Hagen W, ed. *1988 IEEE Fourth Conference on Human Factors and Power Plants.* New York: Institute of Electrical and Electronic Engineers, 1988:200–31.
23 Reason J, Mycielska K. *Absent-minded? The psychology of mental lapses and everyday errors.* Englewood Cliffs, New Jersey: Prentice-Hall, 1982.
24 Reason J. A systems approach to organisation errors. *Ergonomics* (in press).
25 Hudson P, Reason J, Wagenaar W, Bentley P, Primrose M, Visser J. Tripod Delta: proactive approach to enhanced safety. *Journal of Petroleum Technology* 1994;**46**:58–62.

4 Tackling risk by changing behaviour

JENNY FIRTH-COZENS

As the millennium approaches, the rate of change that takes place in every aspect of our lives at times seems overwhelming. Organisations are advised to change or become defunct: to alter their goals and their behaviours constantly to raise production, to take notice of new advances, and to provide new services. Because organisations are no more than the people within them, each member of staff has to be ready to change his or her behaviour in response to the organisation's current aims and standards. In terms of the need to ensure quality in its widest sense—and within this, to avoid risk or to manage its consequences—staff need to be able to change or maintain their behaviour to produce safe procedures and good outcomes. This inevitably entails perceiving potential risks, devising and following systems which eliminate or minimise these risks, and developing approaches which reduce the effects of accidents when they do occur.

The types of changes that are required of people within risk management are, at their most general, the same as those required of them in any other sphere of organisational life. One way they can be categorised usefully is according to how easy it is to anticipate the cause and effects of the risk involved.[1]

Risks with a clear recognised antecedent, process, and outcome

Such risks might happen with the purchasing of supplies or, clinically, with much of the work of pathology laboratories, where a specimen arrives, is analysed in response to specific requests, and the results are communicated to the referrer. The current emphasis on getting research findings into clinical practice[2]—for example, the use of steroids in preterm births—comes within this risk reducing category of behaviours. In this "closed" system of organisational behaviour, the consequences of any failures are known or easy to anticipate, and the behaviours that need to be encouraged in staff are therefore those that will become habitual, procedures specified in protocols and fully incorporated within the process.

Areas of risk with a probable cause, a usual process, and a probable outcome

An example would be an outpatient's appointment for a specialist opinion on optimum asthma treatment. In this group, behaviours and outcomes are more flexible than in the closed systems of change, but are contained as well as possible. The "contained" changes necessary to manage risks within this group require some ability to anticipate events outside of the routine and to alter course where necessary. Most procedures within clinical care are a combination of the closed and the contained systems. For example, a surgical operation entails a firmly closed system of risk avoidance in terms of sterile services and various routines in the theatre to avoid infection, to ensure safe anaesthesia, and so on. Alongside this a contained system will need to be able to respond to the purely clinical but not always controllable aspects of the disease, the equipment, the patient, and the staff.

Risks associated with open ended change beyond control of the organisation

These types of risk cannot readily be anticipated, and so the process for considering them and dealing with their consequences cannot be accurately planned. Many of the latent factors which will turn them into accidents or even disasters are already in place within the organisation.[3] Such events might include the casual remark of a junior health minister about the extent of salmonella poisoning in eggs, which had such dire effects on the poultry industry. Within the health service as a whole, the rise of babysnatchers and the actions of healthcare workers deliberately harming patients, as in the case of Beverly Allitt, represent unforeseen and open ended change. The creation of fundholding practices and the introduction of new technologies such as minimal access surgery might be seen as occurring largely within this area since the final consequences are far from clear.

The most obvious recent clinical example is the appearance of HIV as a disease to be treated within health care—one which was unpredictable. It is a condition from which health care workers can also suffer, a factor which was ignored for years, as if illnesses could only be transmitted in one direction. Although this is something which is still evolving in terms of its consequences for every level of the service, not least the patients, it is increasingly becoming part of a contained or even closed system of change. Major trauma incidents happening locally involve this need for open ended behavioural change as well as some background anticipation and planning of the type entailed in contained change, as discussed earlier.

This chapter considers ways to encourage appropriate behavioural change for these different categories.

Good habits

Closed change—known risks, known consequences, and known ways to avoid both—is a manager's dream. With so much that is fixed, all that needs to be done is to ensure that people acquire and carry out the behaviours to bring about what is required. The more systematic and automatic these behaviours can become, the greater the chance of avoiding risks. Bringing this about requires learning that lasts: something that is theoretically possible to achieve through a system of rewards and punishment; through the modelling of behaviours by others trusted and admired; and by group influences.

Before we can change anyone's behaviour in the way that we wish, we have to be clear exactly what it is that we want, and then to communicate this accurately to those who have to change, not in terms of vague requests (for example, "reduce infection" or "write legibly" or "medicate appropriately") but in terms of the precise behaviours required. As in every other facet of management, good communication is the key without which all else fails.[4] The goals in management cannot be presumed to be the same as those at the coalface (and vice versa) although they should be, because a divided organisation is rarely a safe one.[5] Managers need to be

57

sure that they are not saying that they want one thing, such as quality, while actually punishing staff for not achieving another—such as efficiency—which might run counter to it, and create a culture in which no one knows when they have done well.

Rewards for doing it right

Most species, including humans, tend to do those actions that are rewarded and not to do those that are not; this is the basis for most of our learning. In general, rewards work better than punishments, although there should always be clearly understood punishments in the form of sanctions to be used as a last resort.[6] To create changed behaviour through rewards—something that should be the basis of all employment—we need to know what it is that individual subjects find rewarding. For doctors, this is often presumed to be money (hence Bevan's remark about stuffing their mouths with gold). In reality, once people get beyond the financial threshold where they have sufficient to meet their everyday requirements, other rewards such as interest, participation, status, excitement, social support, praise, and so on, may be more relevant. These higher level needs are more individual, so people with a preference for novelty might find any element of risk reducing routines eventual anathema and might even introduce new procedures to liven up the working day. Not recognising this individuality in the case of rewards (or punishments) leads to naive presumptions such as that all doctors respond well to money or all nurses respond to praise for their attention to duty.

In reality, rewards for reducing risk are rare, perhaps because it is much easier to reward an attribute (such as productivity) than the absence of something (such as complaints). To counteract this it is better to see error as a part of productivity or general clinical effectiveness, and to reward accordingly. Clinical audit, with its positive methodology of criteria based audits of good practice and its emphasis on feedback and change[7] is a good move towards this type of learning, rather than simply counting sentinel or adverse events. Until now, when things have gone wrong, greater emphasis has been put on punishment, certainly for front line staff. Because the analysis of disasters in every other industry has shown that operational workers are only the tip of the iceberg in terms of causing accidents, and that management decisions and systems are always involved and are often more crucial,[38] any system of rewards and sanctions to aid learning should be directed equally towards management, perhaps by those who commission or contract for health care.

Certainly the potential sanction of legal claims in itself has acted in the United States as a prompt for the creation of protocols. For example, Karca and Holbrook describe a protocol to ensure that a diagnosis of myocardial infarction is considered and procedures followed even when symptoms do not include chest pain.[9] Those physicians showing good audit results in terms of adopting the protocol are rewarded with a 20% discount on their malpractice premiums.

In terms of bringing about desired behavioural change of this type it is important that we do not inadvertently reward a behaviour that we want to limit. For example, Kerr suggested that doctors are rewarded for what he called "type 1" errors (labelling a well person sick) by being seen as taking a sound, conservative approach clinically; by increased income in private work; and by "a stream of steady customers who, being well in a limited physiological sense, will not embarrass the doctor by dying abruptly".[10]

A second form of learning involves the acquisition of conditioned responses, so a common means of risk avoidance is to teach people to respond appropriately to a signal that is distinct from the normal routine. This is the basis of crash calls, of particular sounds and displays on monitors, flags or general practitioners' notes, and so on. Its effectiveness for inducing appropriate action will depend not just on the rewards and threats attached, but also on the frequency of the signal. If the signal comes too rarely then the response may fade away; if it comes too often staff can adapt to it, no longer seeing or hearing the signal unless it has a saliency that maintains its effect.

For example, a primary care practice did an excellent audit on the use of non-steroidal anti-inflammatory drugs after finding that more than half of its patients receiving them were seriously anaemic. Through discussion of criteria, flagging the notes, and feeding back results the practice team successfully reduced the use of these drugs to almost zero. However, on re-audit the team realised that the numbers of patients receiving these drugs had, within a year, risen almost to the level they were at before the audit started. The flagging system alone was insufficient to maintain the change in behaviour, and other influences such as fresh rewards or a "noisier" stimulus—were needed.

Model characters

A third means of learning is to model behaviour on that of another, usually someone who is respected or in authority.[11] A randomised control trial that used opinion leaders in this way showed it to be a more effective means of gaining adherence to guidelines than the feedback of data that is a part of clinical audit.[12] The guidelines concerned the management of women with previous caesarean sections and aimed to increase vaginal births. After two years the rates in the audit group were the same as controls, whereas the group using the two opinion leaders had results 46% and 85% higher.

The problem of using modelling to encourage changes in behaviour lies in the fact that such charismatic seniors are not always present in the lives of junior staff[13]; their influence might not always be in the required direction; and if they move jobs or retire, there are inevitable difficulties for those who follow in finding ways to exert similar influences.[14] Moreover, unless great efforts are made against it, strong charismatic leaders can create dependency in group members, which goes against the necessity within risk management of people having individual authority to question the right route.

Power of the group

The group (for example, a clinical team) is a powerful influence in terms of changing its members' behaviour. Humans are sociable creatures and so the group's power probably depends largely on the rewards it provides to those who keep its rules, and the potential threat of isolation for those who do not. However, the influence of groups is not always in the way that we might hope. Early social psychological experiments showed, for example, that groups could pressure a single dissenter into conforming to manifestly bizarre decisions, although often secretly holding the same opinion about what was right.[17] Moreover, decisions of a group have been shown to be significantly more extreme than the mean of the individual decisions of its members.[18] Often, this "risky shift" entails a move towards increasing risk (as in the Bay of Pigs fiasco or the Watergate scandal) but it can also be towards caution, depending upon the culture of the organisation, the power of the group's leader, and so on.

Because of the power of groups to influence the individual (perhaps even the one who understands best the risk involved) and

60

to move in ways which might not always be appropriate—either too risky or too cautious—they need to be tied very firmly into management or peer review systems so that an "outsider" to the group has the chance and the authority to review standards and behaviours, and work with the group on necessary changes. In this sense, the move to bring audit out from a secret activity conducted behind closed doors and create links with provider and purchaser management is a necessary one.

The group should provide accurate data, and report when things go wrong—and the code of loyalty which exists within it may help or stop this happening. For example, in a review of nurses' reporting of errors which either harmed patients or put them at risk, 91% said that they would report such an incident, but only around half actually did so.[19] Menninger emphasises the need to develop systems beyond self reporting by group members,[20] and describes a study of risk management in Kansas in which only 36% of those interviewed over a wide range of units were comfortable in reporting their concerns about colleagues; in fact, 10% said that they would not report concerns at all (W C Rein *et al*, unpublished data).

Education

Apart from developing other systems of discovering errors, the reluctance to report can only be changed by the development of a culture in which such groups believe that it is better to report accidents and incidents than not. This may be achieved with an ongoing educational system that uses these events as a vehicle for learning rather than for discipline.

The general importance of continuing medical education in changing the behaviour of clinicians has been shown including some positive results in terms of patient improvement.[21] Traditional methods of education and of training for risk usually use verbal (spoken or written) ways of assessment to make sure that the lessons have been learnt. A review of the evidence for this, however, suggests that in practice people can act correctly but cannot answer questions about what it is they are doing; others can say what they should do (perhaps because they have had verbal instruction in this) but not actually do it.[22] This has great implications for the educational side of risk management: assessment of learning must cover verbal and, in particular, practical evidence that a necessary skill or procedure is able to be performed.

Grouping the strategies

On the whole we humans take the easiest path, and the best habituated behaviours can slip away without continuous attention; for example, facets of driving behaviour become much more risky within weeks of passing the test, despite the rewards of personal safety and the potential punishment of legal sanctions. Because there is a natural tendency for people, even in areas of risk, typically to seek the way of least effort,[8] changing and then maintaining a behaviour in these closed areas where cause and effect are known precisely might best be achieved by a deliberate use of various learning strategies. Firstly, what needs to be learned (perhaps from a research finding, by team consensus, or from risk analysis) must be accurately and clearly specified and an appropriate training given to staff who are involved. We can also consider the politics of change by getting on board influential and respected leaders to take the issues forward and help to maintain the behaviours, remembering, however, that the flag they carry needs to be handed on rather than simply stuck in the corner of the storeroom. At the same time, steps need to be taken to give individual authority rather than dependency, so that staff can report areas where improvements seem possible.

Figure 4.1, based on a model about the links between audit and research,[15] shows the ways that behaviour can be developed to avoid risk, in particular in situations where we know the causes and consequences of particular risks. It starts with a research finding or local consensus, followed by local guidelines or protocol.[16] Staff need to be educated in their use, and their practice in terms of the guidelines then monitored by audit. Change management is necessary at every stage, using methods discussed throughout the chapter.

Contained change

This area involves the behaviours needed when the causes and consequences are probable rather than known. Through diagnosis and resulting treatments, the aim of medical care is to reduce those probabilities as far as possible, so that actions can become closed rather than merely contained. In practice, it could be argued that most clinical care will fall within this category because little has been researched,[23] and because both patients and staff, being

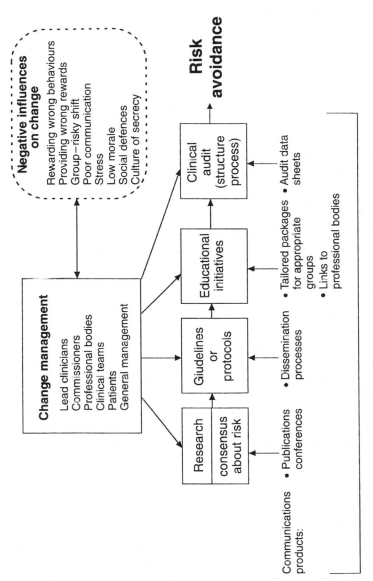

Figure 4.1   *Influences on risk.*
(*Based on a model about the links between audit and research.*[15])

individuals and so always to some extent unpredictable, will rarely behave in a purely robotic manner.

Nevertheless, all that has been said earlier in terms of changing behaviour in closed systems applies equally to contained change. The difference is that we are not asking for precise responses, but for responses within a range, for guidelines rather than protocols. The main difference from closed change is that this calls for a distinct form of education; one where problem solving is central, where innovation and creativity are encouraged within certain limits; and where error is used as central to the learning process. Certainly this is not the way that one would sum up the key elements of medical education as we know it, where coping with uncertainty is taught more as a philosophical aside than as a core curriculum. Within other high risk industries, the advice that is generally given is to provide opportunities to test hypotheses and to learn by trial and error. For example, Rasmussen, discussing the need to curtail adaptation to stimuli, says: "adaptation can only be constrained by the once-in-a-while experience gained when crossing the tolerance limits, ie, by the experience of errors or near-errors. Some errors, therefore, have a function in maintaining a skill at its proper level."[8] In situations such as this, the requirements for recovery from the effects of error become all the more important.

Of course, this trial and error learning is much more difficult to see as acceptable in medicine than in other skilled activities, primarily because of the involvement of patients; unless, of course, they too are brought into the process and exposed to the same uncertainties that face the clinician, a move that is taking place successfully in some areas of care.[24] By adopting this method of education for contained change for all clinically involved staff both at undergraduate and postgraduate levels, the feedback on error becomes useful rather than at present—often so negative that cover ups are inevitably rewarded and the foundations laid for more serious incidents in the future.

Open ended change

This area contains the type of changes in behaviour which are necessary to meet events that are unpredictable, perhaps random, the causes and consequences of which are unknown. In organisations as a whole, these are the events which throw visions and strategic plans off course, sometimes curtailing activity, sometimes adding new opportunities. In addition to these events, which may occur at any time, we struggle with those that happened in the past, with consequences still being played out in ways which remain unpredictable; for example, minimal access surgery as a potentially positive event, and Ben Zito's murder as the type of clearly negative event which may have still greater repercussions for parts of the community care programme. Within health care these open ended events are far from rare, so, in reality, we are playing out several all the time alongside our usual contained and closed changes which themselves will often be affected by open ended changes.

Open ended change is central to chaos theory, which shows that "systems driven by certain types of perfectly orderly laws are capable of behaving in a manner that is random and therefore inherently unpredictable over the long term at a specific level."[1] In terms of organisations Stacey argues that long term forecasts and even simulations are impossible, and small events can escalate alongside or into major ones. However, that does not negate long term planning with steps outlined along the way, so long as this involves recognition of the fact that we do not know the outcome, and that at any time the steps might have to change. It makes the planning of short term actions important, but based on the ability both to make good decisions and to alter course as necessary.

How we decide what is necessary is in turn based on creating a culture of good intelligence—or communication—in which new events such as previously unencountered accidents or problems can be discussed in a widely representative forum, and actions put into place to discourage any escalation of risk. This comes back to the need to create a culture and a system of communication where error becomes a vital signal—not something to be punished or covered up.

Humans can adapt to uncertainty by their ability to look ahead and to conjecture, to hypothesise, and to plan. So long as they work within the context that uncertainty is fundamental, there are means to encourage sound decision making, including that concerning risk, which allows for the necessary flexibility; for example, a variety of decision analysis techniques,[25] or scenario planning[26] which involve groups working out the detailed strategies of imagined events.

What stops the change necessary for management of risk?

The outline described, on methods to bring about behavioural change, contains both implied and specific ways that can stop change happening; for example, by not rewarding change accurately, or by loyalty to the group outweighing organisational loyalty, or by poor (or absent) communication. Figure 4.1 outlines these and others. The section that follows contains two other, more general issues which can hinder or even stop change coming about. One involves blocks that might occur to perceiving risk in the first place and the other relates to the individual factors which can make change in favour of risk management less likely to occur.

Failure to perceive the risk

Human efficiency is lowered considerably when people are asked to do two things at once, both of which require accuracy and attention[27]—for example, attending to clinical care and watching for risk. Therefore, if risk is separated out from the rest of the job instead of being an integral part of it, both clinicians and managers are less likely to perceive it accurately because it becomes something distinct from the main thrust of their jobs. One way to tackle this problem is to have separate people—safety officers or risk assessors—to do the job of inspecting for risk. Often, however, the organisational culture can stop this working well. Risk may be seen as macho and heroic, whereas safety is soft, and a split-off function can cause the problem of all the responsibility and anxiety being located in the risk manager, and all the danger and excitement being located in the general management and medical staff. The reluctance of physicians, for example, to participate in risk management activities has been noted in the United States.[28] On the other hand, the benefits of including clinicians in decision making about the perception and reporting of risk is described by Morlock and Malitz in terms of the reduction of malpractice claims.[30] In hospitals without high levels of interventions, the procedure of notifying the clinical chief of incidents was a significant predictor of a lower level of claims. They conclude that "This pattern could be interpreted as an indication that formalized medical staff controls may be of particular importance in settings less likely to have the staff experience and specialized work routines that merge over time in hospitals with higher volumes of services."

66

This organisational splitting of perception about safety and threat is a "social defence" against the anxiety created in any high risk environment. Hirschhorn,[29] using a psychodynamic approach to the workplace, described what was happening: "After exploring the relationship between the safety workers on the one hand and the line workers and managers on the other, I concluded that the latter controlled their anxiety by 'blaming the messenger', the safety inspectors, for the bad news, rather than paying attention to their findings. Instead of identifying closely with the inspectors' work and seeing safety issues from their point of view, workers and managers scapegoated the inspector." He was referring to a situation in a nuclear power plant!

Good leadership will include being able to see such splits occurring and to rectify them by spreading responsibility for risk more widely as part of a general quality system. Hirshhorn's recommendations for dealing with safety, far from giving responsibility to one group or one individual, involve bringing the entire organisation together to work on safety issues.[5] An alternative—one which overcomes our difficulty in doing two high demand tasks at once—is to hand one member of a clinical team the task of observing for risk rather than participating, a role that must revolve around the entire team if the "scapegoat scenario" is not to occur.

Individual propensity to risk

Individual differences will also play their part in making people more or less susceptible to particular risks. Some can be changed; others simply need recognising so that they can be compensated for as far as possible. These differences stem from personality, from past experience, and from current psychological and physiological states.

There is no clear evidence within medicine that certain personalities are more likely to have accidents than others. There are various findings, however, which suggest areas for future research. For example, a review by McManus and Vincent gives some evidence that people with an extrovert, aggressive personality have a propensity for road traffic accidents.[31] It also gives data showing that women are less likely to be sued in medical claims and to be involved in road traffic accidents than men. My own longitudinal study of young doctors, followed up for 10 years since they were students, shows that women are significantly more self

67

critical than men; that doctors who report making mistakes are more self critical than those who do not; and that those who reported having difficulties with patients are less self critical than those who did not report such difficulties.[32][33] It may be that there is a personality characteristic which predisposes people to take the blame, and therefore the responsibility, early on in risky situations and so be more likely to avoid more serious risks; at the other end of the range, there may be a rather arrogant, aggressive, outwardly blaming character who cannot see his or her responsibility so easily and so is inevitably more likely both to take less care and, perhaps also to get into confrontation with patients after accidents have happened.

In terms of change, whereas it is not useful to individuals to continually blame themselves for what goes wrong,[34] it is possible to teach people through cognitive exercises how to control their attributions from being constantly external (or internal) to being more central.[35] I have suggested this in terms of getting on better with difficult patients or with senior doctors,[33] but it may also affect the perception of risk and help people deal with accidents once they have happened.

Other personality characteristics worth considering in terms of change include those outlined in inventories such as the Myers–Brigg type indicator,[36] which is based upon Jungian type theory and contains at least one dimension important to the decision making surrounding risk. This dimension concerns how people get their data for making decisions—at one end being those who attend to and use the here and now, the detail, and the concrete—and at the other end those who constantly go beyond the data to what they can make out of them, and to the future. Whereas the first group should perhaps take the lead in a closed change area, the second group would be useful in considering the areas of open ended change. The best teams use diversity well[37] and it would be most important to have both types of people involved so that neither the detail nor the possibilities are overlooked.

Past experiences can also affect people's attitudes to risk. A physician whose patient died six days after a simple operation might from then on choose to err on the side of caution and keep patients in hospital too long. The more that personal information can be appreciated and not exploited, the more it is possible to support people to change in ways that are difficult for them. For example, psychiatric staff who have had a traumatic childhood, or who are currently in crisis, might be more likely to be a party to boundary violations such as striking up a sexual relationship with a patient.[20] A good team can help individual members to overcome their difficulties, and not put others at risk.

Being aware of the current life events of colleagues—especially major ones such as death or divorce—is also important in terms of the links between stress and accidents. Although there is no clear evidence linking risk taking behaviour with stress—in fact, it might be that we take more risks when we are happy[38]—there seems little doubt now that both stress and exhaustion increase the chances of error.[39] This is supported by the finding that stress management courses reduce significantly both medication errors and claims.[40] It is clear from this that people can be changed both by such brief interventions, and by more intensive counselling interventions[41] in ways which can reduce risk.

In terms of tiredness, we know that almost every major disaster, as well as single driver road traffic accidents, happen in the early hours of the morning.[42] This is a time when junior doctors and general practitioners are often at their lowest ebb and most susceptible to accidents. Here are three accounts describing this:

> If I am asked to treat/advise on patient care after midnight my entire goal is to solve the problem with the least amount of effort to myself as long as there are no professional repercussions.

> Tiredness—missing a life threatening complication which I would have picked up if not exhausted. Luckily it was picked up in time.

> Been asleep for half an hour, request for a visit a long way away; patient's parents refuse to come to surgery (though easy to do). I get grumpy and try to be "in–out" as quickly as possible when there. I didn't fully examine the child and missed a potentially serious physical sign. The child taken to own general practitioner in the morning and sent to hospital.

Procedures must be developed to help decision making and actions at that time of night, which take into account exhaustion rather than pretending that it is only something experienced by those who are not up to scratch. Similar ones could be introduced for practitioners receiving treatment,[43] or those with respiratory virus infections,[44] as these also reduce performance.

Conclusions

The potential for individual and organisational change in terms of risk is very real. In putting it into practice, it is important, first, to consider the type of change required, and then to use several methods to take into account the differences that exist within and between organisations. Against the backdrop of tight routines, there needs to be a coexisting system which encourages open debate about new situations, outside influences, and anticipated and experienced difficulties. Such a system calls for communication that is genuinely two way and a management willing to accept its possible role when things go wrong and to learn from the experience alongside their staff.

Above all, there is a need for individuals and teams to experience belonging first and foremost to the organisation rather than feeling and using barriers—them and us, doctors and nurses, managers and clinicians, those concerned with risk and the rest—splits which will lie as dynamite for future sparks. While there are divisions like this, responsibility and blame can be shifted elsewhere.[5] Any organisational structure put in place for risk must ensure therefore that such splits, if present, are healed rather than institutionalised.[5]

1 Stacy RD. *The chaos frontier.* London: Butterworth–Heinemann, 1991.
2 Haines A, Jones R. Implementing findings of research. *BMJ* 1994;**308**:1488–92.
3 Reason J. The contribution of latent human failures to the breakdown of complex systems. *Philos Trans R Soc Lond Biol* 1990;**327**:475–84.
4 Kreps GL. *Organizational communication.* New York: Longman, 1990.
5 Hirschhorn L. The psychodynamics of safety. In: Hirschhorn L, Barnett CK, eds. *The psychology of organizations.* Philadelphia: Temple University Press, 1993:143–63.
6 Donaldson LJ. Doctors with problems in the NHS workforce. *BMJ* 1994;**308**: 1277–82.
7 Jewell D. Setting standards: from passing fashion to essential clinical activity. *Quality in Health Care* 1992;**1**:217–8.
8 Rasmussen J. Human error and the problem of causality in analysis of accidents. *Philos Trans R Soc Lond Biol* 1990;**327**:449–62.
9 Karca A, Holbrook J. The Massachusetts emergency medicine risk management program. *QRB* 1991;**17**:287–92.
10 Kerr S. On the folly of rewarding A, while hoping for B. *Academy of Management Journal* 1975;**18**:769–82.
11 Lefkowitz MM, Blake RR, Mouton JS. Status factors in pedestrian violation of traffic signals. *Journal of Abnormal and Social Psychology* 1955;**51**:704–6.
12 Lomas J. Enkin M, Anderson GM, Hannah WJ, Vayda E, Singer J. Opinion leaders vs audit and feedback to implement practise guidelines: delivery after previous cesarean section. *JAMA* 1991;**265**:2202–07.
13 Allen I. *Doctors and their careers: a new generation.* London: PSI, 1994.
14 Salaman G. An historical discontinuity: from charisma to routinization. *Human Relations* 1977;**30**:373–88.
15 Firth-Cozens J, Ennis W. Marriage guidance: the relationship between research and clinical audit. *Health Services Journal* 10 August 1995: 24–5.
16 Grimshaw J, Russell T. Effect of clinical guidelines on medical practice: a systematic review of rigorous evaluations. *Lancet* 1993;**342**:1317–22.

17 Asch SE. Effects of group pressure upon the modification and distortion of judgements. In: Guetzkow H, ed. *Groups, leadership and men: research in human relations.* New York: Russell and Russell, 1963.

18 Pruitt DG. Choice shifts in group discussion: an introductory review. *J Pers Soc Psychol* 1971;20:339–60.

19 Cerrato PL. What to do when you suspect incompetence. *RN* 1988;51:36–41.

20 Menninger WW. Identifying, evaluating and responding to boundary violations: a risk management program. *Psychiatric Annals* 1991;21:675–80.

21 Davis DA, Thomson MA, Oxman AD, Haynes RB. Evidence for the effectiveness of CME: a review of 50 randomized controlled trials. *JAMA* 1992; **268**:9.

22 Broadbent DE. Effective decisions and their verbal justification. *Philos Trans R Soc Lond Biol* 1990;**327**:493–502.

23 Sheldon TA. Quality: link with effectiveness. *Raising Quality in the NHS: What progress. Quality in Health Care* 1994; 3(suppl): 541–5.

24 Mulley A. Outcomes research: implications for policy and practice. In: Delamothe T, ed. *Outcomes into clinical practice.* London: *BMJ Publishing Group* 1994:13–27.

25 Covello VT. Decision analysis and risk management decision making: issues and methods. *Risk Analysis* 1987;7:131–9.

26 Hadridge P. Tomorrow's world. *Health Service Journal* 1995;**105**:18–20.

27 Anderson JR. *Cognitive psychology and its implications.* San Francisco: Freeman, 1985.

28 Hudson T. Hospitals find ways to integrate risk management functions. *Hospitals* 1992;**66**:32, 34–6.

29 Hirshhorn I. *The workplace within: psychodynamics of organizational life.* Cambridge, Massachusetts. MIT Press, 1988.

30 Morlock LL, Malitz FE. Do hospital risk management programs make a difference?: relationships between risk management program activities and hospital malpractice claims experience. *Law and Contemporary Problems* 1991; 54:1–22.

31 McManus C, Vincent C. Selecting and educating safer doctors. In: Vincent C, Ennis M, Audley RJ, eds. *Medical accidents.* New York: Oxford University Press, 1993:80–105.

32 Firth-Cozens J. Sources of stress in women junior house officers. *BMJ* 1990; **301**:89–91.

33 Firth-Cozens J. Stress in Doctors: A longitudinal study. *Report prepared for Department of Health, Research and Development Initiative on Mental Health of the NHS Workforce.* London: Department of Health, 1994.

34 Firth-Cozens J. Women Doctors: In: Firth-Cozens J, West M, eds. *Women at work.* Milton Keynes: Open University Press, 1991:131–142.

35 Layden MA. Attributional style therapy. In: Antaki C, Brewin CR, eds. *Attributions and psychological change.* London: Academic Press, 1982:63–82.

36 Quenk NL. *Beside ourselves: our hidden personality in everyday life.* Palo Alto: CPP Books, 1993.

37 Firth-Cozens J. Building teams for effective audit. *Quality in Health Care* 1992; 1:252–5.

38 Mann L. Stress, affect and risk taking. In: Yates JF, ed. *Risk-taking behaviour.* Chichester: Wiley, 1992:202–30.

39 Firth-Cozens J. Stress, psychological problems, and clinical performance. In: Vincent C, Ennis M, Audley RJ, eds. *Medical accidents.* New York: Oxford University Press, 1993:131–49.

40 Jones JW, Barge BN, Steffy BD, Fay LM, Kunz LK, Wuebeker LJ. Stress and medical malpractice: Organizational risk assessment and intervention. *J Appl Psychology* 1988;4:727–35.

41 Firth-Cozens J, Hardy G. Occupational stress, clinical treatment and changes in job perceptions. *Journal of Occupational and Organization Psychology* 1992; **65**:81–8.
42 Folkard S. Circadian performance rhythms: some practical and theoretical implications. *Philos Trans R Soc Lond Biol* 1990;**327**:543–53.
43 Nicholson AN. Medication and skilled work. *Philos Trans R Soc Lond Biol* 1990; **327**:513–8.
44 Smith AP, Respiratory virus infections and performance. *Philos Trans R Soc Lond Biol* 1990;**327**:519–28.

5 Risk management: financial implications

ROBERT DINGWALL, PAUL FENN

The financial impact of litigation on the NHS and the British medical profession has been a matter of increasing concern since the mid-1980s, although it has almost certainly been much exaggerated. The objective of this chapter is to consider the available evidence on the real cost of litigation to the NHS, to review the institutional responses which have taken place, and to comment briefly on some of the alternatives to litigation which have been proposed.

Medical negligence litigation in the United Kingdom

Although litigation against doctors has always been a theoretical possibility—the earliest recorded cases in England go back to the 14th century[1]—it was not seen as a major issue of financial concern for English healthcare providers until the 1980s. Before the establishment of the NHS, doctors were liable for their negligence as individuals and took individual action to protect their position by joining a medical defence organisation (MDO). The foundation of the MDOs between 1885 and 1902 grew out of a different concern—namely, the treatment of doctors appearing in criminal trials and coroners' courts and initially insurance against the costs of negligence actions was a minor part of their activities.[2]

Litigation and the NHS

When the NHS was set up, it was originally intended that, as employers, regional hospital boards and local authorities should assume the liability for all hospital and community medical staff, just as they did for all other employees. This position, of vicarious liability, predominates among corporate bodies where it is recognised that negligence is generally a matter of organisational rather than individual failures. This arrangement was not popular with the doctors, who argued that their professional reputation was at stake in allegations of negligence and were worried that their employer might settle claims, for economic reasons, that they would want to resist. The Ministry of Health also seem to have been unhappy about the prospects of litigation between employers and doctors over the allocation of liability. The eventual outcome was an agreement embodied in the 1954 Circular HM(54)32. This allowed employed doctors to retain their individual liability, although they were required to belong to an MDO as a term of their contract of employment. The defence of any claim would be coordinated between the MDO and the doctor's employer and they would aim to reach a mutually acceptable allocation of the costs of defence and settlement. As self employed independent contractors, general practitioners retained their historical position of individual liability.

The costs of this system were relatively low. There were few claims: the Royal Commission on Civil Liability and Personal Injury, using data supplied by the MDOs for 1974 and 1975, estimated that about 500 negligence claims were made per year of which 170 were settled out of court, with 25 going to trial.[3] Of these, five led to awards in favour of the plaintiff. The total value of compensation paid was about £1m, although it is not clear whether this includes the NHS share. Subscription rates for MDOs rose slowly in line with general levels of inflation in the economy. In 1978, for example, they were £40 per year.

Litigation in the 1980s

Sometime in the period 1978–80, the situation changed radically. It is not possible to put a more precise date on this change or to be entirely clear about its causes. However, the experience of the NHS during the 1980s can be clearly documented. We reviewed all the available closed claim records in the Oxford Region for the period 1974–88, a series of 470 cases. Although we have some reservations about the completeness of the series for the years before 1980, the general trends are supported by other evidence including our own postal survey of regional legal advisers in 1987, which yielded usable data from five other regions, studies by Bowles and Jones[4] and Hawkins and Paterson,[5] and MDO annual reports. In summary, these data suggest that the frequency of claims increased by about 500% and their average severity adjusted for inflation, the cost of settling successful claims, by about 250%. The success rate of claims seems to have fallen from about 40% at the time of the Royal Commission's studies to about 25% in the 1980s. This work also drew attention to the wide annual fluctuations in claim frequency and severity at both district and regional level. These posed problems for sensible financial management, particularly since health authorities, as Crown Bodies, were not allowed to take out insurance but had to meet these costs from current revenue. We also reported on the distribution of liability by specialty. Five specialties—obstetrics/gynaecology, orthopaedics, accident/emergency, general surgery, and anaesthetics—accounted for two thirds of the claims and just over half of the total costs in the Oxford Region over the period studied.[6-8]

The rising costs of the system were reflected in rising MDO subscriptions. These had reached £1080 per year by 1988, an increase of 2700% in a decade. Even allowing for the sharp inflation of the late 1970s and early 1980s, this was a steep rise and posed growing problems for pay determination. The actual costs to the profession should not be exaggerated, though: MDO subscriptions were fully reimbursable practice expenses for general practitioners and were explicitly acknowledged as an element in pay calculations by the Review Body on Doctors' and Dentists' Remuneration. The real problem related to NHS pay structures because the MDO subscriptions represented a powerful cost push at a time when the government was trying to hold back public sector pay. This component tended to edge doctors above the "going rate", risking claims for comparable gross increases from other groups.

The "crisis" of 1989

As a result of complaints from the review body and the profession, the Department of Health adopted an interim solution of partial direct reimbursement of MDO subscriptions for the years 1986 and 1987. Membership of an MDO was taken out of salary calculations by requiring health authorities to reimburse two thirds of the cost for staff working exclusively for the NHS. There was considerable uncertainty about the definition of exclusiveness, which gave rise to several anomalies. These were further compounded when the MDOs announced that they intended to charge differential subscription rates in 1989 reflecting their assessment of the relative losses generated by different specialties. This was partly a response to the growing evidence of interest from commercial insurers in "cherry picking" low risk specialties by offering coverage at lower rates than the MDOs. Differential premiums, whether paid to MDOs or to other insurers, threatened to cause further disruption to the NHS remuneration system by introducing a demand for matching salary differentials between specialties. The Department of Health also seems to have been concerned about the administrative problems for health authorities of dealing with new insurers who had less experience of the peculiar workings of the medical liability market and whose long-term commitment might be uncertain.

Despite the high level of professional concern, the crucial pressures for change in the system of response to medical negligence claims seem to have been these administrative difficulties. This is reflected in the Department of Health's proposal in March 1989 to proceed with the introduction of a form of Crown indemnity from 1 July 1989. This was an entirely unexpected move but it was the one which made most sense for the NHS. It avoided the uncharted waters of an alternative system, which would almost certainly be more expensive, removed a source of grievance from the medical profession at a time when far more radical upheavals were about to begin, and might even lead to some minimal administrative savings from removing the partial duplication of effort between health authorities and MDOs in defending claims.

NHS indemnity

In fact, the consultation period on the 1989 proposals took rather longer than the Department had allowed and a decision on what was now called NHS Indemnity was not finally announced until November 1989 for implementation from 1 January 1990. District health authorities would take over responsibility for the defence of all new and existing claims from that date. Some of the costs would initially be met by a transfer of reserves from the MDOs, but the burden would then fall wholly on the employing authorities. The MDO reserves were actually used to set up a central pool for meeting 80% of a district's costs above £300 000 on an individual claim. To monitor this scheme, the Department asked authorities to send in quarterly and annual returns of current and outstanding claims during 1990–1.

In October 1990, it was announced that liability would be transferred to trusts and directly managed units, as the actual employers of medical staff, from 1 April 1991. Claims relating to events before that date would continue to be managed by health authorities under the established financial arrangements using regional and former MDO reserves. New claims would fall as a direct cost on the unit's operating budget. The Department of Health indicated in further guidance issued in February 1991 that it expected that the costs of negligence should be charged back to the relevant clinical area and built into its prices rather than being treated as a general overhead on the whole unit. Regions would operate an interest bearing loan scheme to smooth out cash flow disruptions from large settlements.

When seeking to evaluate NHS indemnity, it is important to distinguish these two different models. The first year adopted a pattern characteristic of NHS traditions, whereas the second and subsequent years have assimilated NHS indemnity to the philosophy of the internal market. In effect, the economic analysis of tort as a mechanism designed to provide appropriate incentives for loss prevention has been directly incorporated into the logic of the system. Units with high litigation costs will be obliged to charge higher prices, losing business to competitors who are more successful at managing their risks or delivering better quality services.

The first year's experience

In February 1991, we were awarded a grant by the Nuffield Provincial Hospitals Trust to update our previous work on NHS claims, with a view to producing more accurate estimates of the total cost of the present system and a database that would allow for more realistic costing of alternative proposals. The project began by renewing contacts with the regions who had assisted the earlier work. However, they held less information than had been the case in 1988. The Department of Health were proposing to publish their own analysis of year I claims and refused us access to the districts' annual returns. We therefore contacted the districts directly, requesting a copy of the return, which was then reviewed for completeness and followed up by telephone if necessary. By these means, we obtained data from 110 out of 190 districts. Ideally, these included: (1) The number of claims outstanding on 31 March 1991. (2) The number of cases settled during the period 1 April 1990–31 March 1991, with health authority costs and damages reported in four bands: Under £100 000; £100–200 000; £200–300 000; over £300 000. (3) Total cost of settlements and awards, distinguishing the authority's costs from payments of costs and damages to plaintiffs, and an estimate of the total costs attributable to negligence by doctors as opposed to other members of staff.

By January 1992, the Department of Health had decided that they were not going to analyse and publish the 1990–1 data and that they were, in fact, going to discontinue central monitoring altogether. They did, however, agree to give us access to their data: although the quality was poorer, this did allow us to extend the sample in several important respects. We eventually had some information for 142 districts.

The findings from this study are reported in more detail elsewhere.[9] In summary, we used various assumptions to extrapolate from the available data and produce estimates of claim volumes and costs for England as a whole. The total number of closed claims was estimated as about 1600, with a stock of about 22 000 open claims. New claims were running in the region of 6000 a year. These figures are consistent with a slow upward drift of claims rather than the explosive growth of the early and mid-1980s. Indeed, if it were possible to take out the possible effects of changes in the legal aid rules for claims relating to injuries to children, which would have the effect of bringing forward claims that might otherwise have been deferred, we might be seeing very little real growth at all. The direct cost to the NHS in 1990–1 is estimated to be around £52m (including a notional 20% administrative loading). To put NHS indemnity in perspective, it can be compared with the operating expenditure of English health authorities in the same financial year, £15·426 billion. This would suggest that negligence costs about 0·4% of total health authority expenditure.

Our broad conclusion was that NHS indemnity, in its first year, had little or no impact on the frequency or severity of claims. Medical negligence remained a minor irritant to most districts with a relatively low average level of losses, around £234 000 per district per year. A few outliers had much more severe problems, but there was a statistically significant relation between a district's size, measured by the number of medical staff employed, and its claim

78

rate. Districts with higher losses tended to be larger and busier with higher rates of admission to hospital and more obstetric activity. Although the data on new claims were limited, they showed no indication of a sharp upward trend. We found that the frequency of new claims per 100 000 population had increased from the 10 estimated for 1986–7 to 12·11 per 100 000 population, an increase of about 20% in five years.

It is important to emphasise the modest scale of medical negligence litigation as a financial problem for the NHS. There has been a good deal of alarmist talk, which mainly reflects the confusion and uncertainty within the service arising from the limitations of its own financial information systems in this area. This is well illustrated by the events of the spring of 1994. In February, the deputy finance director of the NHS Management Executive made a speech to a closed meeting at which, according to a report in *The Observer* (27 February 1994), he asserted that negligence costs were expected to reach £125m in 1993–4. The consultation document on the mutual insurance scheme gave a rival estimate of £75m when this was published in March. In the same month, a parliamentary answer by Dr Brian Mawhinney, minister of state at the Department of Health, reported final returns to the Department for 1990–1 and near final returns for 1991–2. The first of these relates to the year described in our study: it confirms a final cost of £53·2m, well within our range. A total of 1618 claims were reported, also within our estimate, but this is slightly misleading as one region failed to make this return: the true figure is probably around 1700, suggesting a slight undershoot in our data. The provisional 1991–2 figures are £51·3m from 1751 claims. Since then the figures have been more difficult to collect as a result of the structural changes in the NHS. Indications are that there has been some increase in overall costs, but not to the extent forecast earlier.

Although there might be other grounds for being concerned about the adequacy of institutional responses to medical negligence and about the efficiency and effectiveness of the tort system as an instrument for compensation and accountability, there is no evidence of an acute economic crisis for the NHS.

Financial Implications of litigation

The more extreme predictions of an explosion in litigation and a sharp increase in costs do not seem to have been fulfilled. From the standpoint of local NHS managers, the situation has probably become more complex as they have acquired new responsibilities for claim management and the smaller financial units now bearing claims will face cash flow problems from annual fluctuations in claim settlements. On the other hand, the Mk 2 version of NHS indemnity has produced a system of allocating liability which is philosophically consistent with the rest of the restructuring package. Litigation has been turned into a market signal for investments in quality improvement and risk management.

It is, however, a notoriously ineffective signal, as litigation is not related in any simple way to the quality of service offered. At a minimum, it is also affected by the distribution of the propensity to sue, the willingness of victims to bring claims forward, and by their access to the legal system. The latter reflects the victim's knowledge of effective routes for pursuing claims, such as their ability to identify a solicitor with adequate skills in this specialised legal area and their ability to resource a claim, particularly with the decreasing availability of legal aid for civil cases. The few claims experienced by any unit in a given year makes it very difficult to make appropriate investments in prevention, even assuming that much reliance can be placed on the validity of the data which they represent. The average district received about 37 new claims per year in 1990–1, of which no more than one third will eventually lead to some admission of liability and payment: it seems unlikely that most trusts will be receiving more than a handful of new claims each year.

This makes it hard for trust finance managers to behave as rational insurers. We have encountered some who are clearly significantly overestimating their future liabilities by setting aside funds to meet every claim received in full, without discounting this sum by an assessment of the claim's chances of success. Such judgements are crucial skills for commercial insurers. Their premium rates are set to produce the amount of money thought to be required to meet the company's estimated liabilities. If the estimates are too high, rates are set too high and the company loses business. The same error in the NHS leads to money being unnecessarily diverted from current patient care.

These problems may be eased by the development of a "clinical negligence scheme for trusts", using the provisions of the NHS and Community Care Act 1990. The timetable for the implementation of this has now been scheduled for 1 April 1995, having slipped from the original target of 1 April 1994, which is a good illustration of the complexity of the problems involved in its design. The details of the scheme have recently been confirmed in outline. Trusts are to be permitted, but not required, to contribute to the scheme, which operates as a mutual fund, financed on a "pay as you go" basis. Members will be entitled to payment from the fund in the event of a successful claim arising from an incident after the trust joined the scheme. Claims arising from previous activity must be dealt with under existing arrangements. Consequently, initial contributions will start low, and increase over the years as the volume of valid claims grows. In the absence of accurate claims data, contributions will be set by reference to a trust's scale of operations, its case mix, and its risk management procedures. Significant excess levels (below which trusts must self insure) are to be incorporated, with excesses for the largest trusts being as high as £100 000. According to our own data, very few claims are in excess of that figure. The scheme will develop a comprehensive database of claims and settlements which can be used to encourage good practice in risk management. This development should (in the long run) smooth out the cash flow problems, although the success of the scheme and the quality of its claims data will depend critically on the extent to which trusts actually join. If only the high risk trusts find it attractive, the fund will experience an adverse selection of risks, and will be forced to drive up contributions, which will mean even fewer trusts retaining membership.

The centralisation of claims management under this system seems likely to be financially neutral in its impact on the total of NHS expenditure. There should be some gains from a build up of claims management experience and, in the longer term, from better risk management information. Victims of medical injury should find a more consistent approach, although this may be outweighed by the greater remoteness of the scheme and, perhaps, a reduced sensitivity to local conditions in settlement negotiations.

The real question, though, is whether we should be satisfied with such a minimalist approach. The inequities and intrinsic inefficiencies of the tort system as a means of compensation are well recognised.[10] It has often been compared to an obstacle race which many are deterred from entering at all and which erects more and more ingenious barriers to all but the luckiest and most determined of personal litigants. These obstructions and distortions also undermine its value as a method of achieving quality improvements or controlling professional standards. Because the impact of litigation is seen to be arbitrary, the profession's response is often to regard defendants as unfortunate rather than incompetent.

It is not, in fact, difficult to design systems which would be more effective in compensating victims and produce more useful information for quality purposes. However, most of them have the disadvantage of being considerably more expensive and of leaving some of the areas of inequity untouched.

No fault schemes

Most of the professional and political interest in reform has been concentrated on the introduction of some version of the no fault schemes currently operating in Sweden and Finland. The BMA and the Royal College of Physicians have both proposed no fault approaches, and the members of parliament Harriet Harman and Rosie Barnes introduced reform bills in the 1987–92 Parliament while the Labour Party included a no fault scheme as a manifesto commitment in 1992.[11-13] The details of these packages vary but what they have in common is the desire to remove one of the major hurdles from tort claims—namely, the need to prove that someone was at fault. It must be stressed that there is still an important obstacle in the need to prove a causal relation between an adverse event and a medical intervention and to exclude the possibility that the event was an uncommon but natural outcome of the course of the disease or injury.

The Swedish model is actually not very different in structure from the proposed NHS mutual fund. The Patient Insurance Scheme is run by a consortium of private insurers. Since its inception as a scheme for public hospital care in 1975, its coverage has expanded to include virtually all providers in the country. The relevant comparison here, however, is with the hospitals owned by the county councils. Each council pays an annual premium related solely to its population and the insurers pay out under five main headings: treatment injuries; injuries caused by incorrect diagnosis; injuries arising from hospital acquired infections; injuries caused by accidents in the course of treatments; and, a new category, unreasonably severe injuries arising from relatively common illnesses or conditions (Espersson, conference, 1992).

In 1992, the Swedish scheme generated about 65 new claims per 100 000 population, mostly from hospitals, of which roughly 36% were accepted for payment. Applying the same rates to the United Kingdom would imply a potential of about 11 000 paid claims per year, some seven times the present level. A Swedish model could pay compensation to many more injured people. The scheme has also been effective in generating risk management information, although its administrators concede that they have been slow to make systematic use of this.

The system also seems to be inexpensive. This was certainly a reason for BMA enthusiasm in the early 1980s. However, further investigation has shown that costs are kept down because of the very high level of public social welfare provision in Sweden.[14] People who are unable to work because of short term illness have their income replaced up to a level of about 80–90%, and long term disability pensions are paid at about 65% of previous earnings. The comparable schemes in the United Kingdom rarely replace more than about 45% of previous income. As a result, a United Kingdom scheme based on Swedish levels of compensation would seriously undercompensate victims of medical injuries relative to what a few might get from the tort system or what the levels of perceived need might be. Our best estimate is that a United Kingdom scheme which sought to place victims in the same position as the Swedish scheme relative to other citizens and with comparable restrictions would increase costs to between £235m and £350m per year.[15] There would, of course, be benefits to the NHS from the fuller reporting of adverse outcomes, to the profession from the dilution of the adversarial environment encouraged by tort claims, and to the injured patients who received compensation. Against this, one can reasonably ask how far it is appropriate to use money voted for health care to provide social insurance.

It is also important to recognise that a significant no fault scheme would also introduce an important new source of inequity. As the Spastics Society have pointed out, payment would still depend on establishing a causal link between exposure to medical intervention and some injury.[16] This would mean treating people who were disabled as a result of a genetic accident, aging, or the ordinary progress of a disease very differently from those who could ascribe their disability to medical treatment. It is not immediately obvious why one group should be thought of as more deserving than another. In fact, this has not been a big issue in Sweden, partly because the top up received by the medically injured is relatively small. It did, however, emerge as a concern in New Zealand, where medical injuries were dealt with as part of a national no fault scheme covering all accident victims.

Accident Compensation Corporation

New Zealand abolished tort claims for personal injury in 1972 and replaced them with what in effect was a national no fault scheme administered by a public agency, the Accident Compensation Corporation (ACC), for all personal injury financed by levies on employers, the self employed, and motor vehicle owners with a contribution from general taxation. Most medical injuries fell within the scope of the scheme. The ACC could pay income replacement up to about 80% of previous earnings, lump sum compensation, and the costs of additional medical treatment resulting from the accident. There was growing concern about the discrepancy between the support available to people falling within the legal definition of an accident and those disabled from natural causes, who had to rely on a less generous social security system. Eventually a New Zealand Royal Commission on Social Policy was led to propose in 1988 that there should be some restriction on ACC benefits and enhancement of disability support to bring the two more closely into line. This development was overtaken by a sharply deteriorating economic situation and by the election of a National Party government committed to the reduction of the substantial net of public welfare in New Zealand. The national government secured the passage of legislation in the 1991–2 parliamentary session which substantially modified the ACC scheme and which, on some interpretations, would virtually eliminate the right of injured patients to claim and oblige them to rely as before on tort actions (Vennell, conference, 1992). It is not yet clear how this has worked out in practice.

The New Zealand approach also indicates some of the possible disadvantages of no fault systems. There was considerable concern in the country about whether it was actually diluting standards of medical care, particularly in the wake of the revelations about the failure to treat women with positive cervical smears in Auckland in 1988 in the interests of a controlled trial of different interventions. Although it is not obvious that the decisions of the doctors concerned would have been different under different liability rules, this case was widely taken to be symptomatic of a cavalier attitude towards patients' rights in the New Zealand medical profession. The chairman of the ACC expressed concern in the corporation's 1991 annual report that doctors made an insufficient contribution to the scheme in relation to the costs of compensating medical injuries. In fact, the same report suggested that medical injuries were costing about NZ$5m per year against a total expenditure of NZ$1·2 billion, which hardly seems to amount to a serious problem but the attitude is indicative of the extent to which public support for medical no fault had been eroded by the failure to develop adequate systems of accountability.

This must remain a concern for any no fault system or any move to replace tort by more comprehensive social security provision. Indeed it may be the strongest argument for tolerating a degree of injustice between different classes of disabled people in the way that the Swedes seem to. A Swedish type no fault scheme could be seen as a way of paying for information about quality and risk, encouraging people to report adverse occurrences in the hope that preventive systems can be improved. It may not matter too much that individual doctors are not called to account directly by the scheme. The information which is fed back to hospitals now seems to be taking a form that would highlight problems in a specialty to the administration and prompt them to make their own inquiries. More to the point, in an organisational environment as complex as that of modern health care the objective should be to devise systems of working which limit the damage that any one individual failure can inflict by routine checks, monitoring, and fail safes. The problem of the maverick doctor is often really a problem of weak organisation. Nevertheless, we must also acknowledge that the costs of adopting a Swedish model would be very large indeed and would require a political direction and level of economic performance which are not consistent with recent United Kingdom experience and which the Swedes themselves are not confident of maintaining.

Conclusion

It is important for trust managers to think very carefully about the cost effectiveness of major investments in risk management, if these are seen mainly as intended to reduce litigation costs. On its own, litigation is a rare event in the life of a trust with costs that are likely to be relatively trivial. If a trust is finding claims a problem, then it is likely that something fairly obvious is wrong. Even then, it is important to exclude the possibility that the problem is actually one of financial management, caused by something like an incorrect reserving policy, rather than a clinical or organisational problem. The most frequent types of claim are relatively cheap to settle and prevention is usually a matter of creating conditions that do not require staff to cut corners on well established safety procedures. The best defence of an expensive claim is often a system of record keeping that ensures the integrity and security of the data needed to resist the allegations of negligence. It is, in fact, highly questionable whether it is worth most trusts making heavy investments in risk prevention. It is also not yet clear whether most trusts will decide to join the clinical negligence scheme, given the cross subsidisation which is inevitable in the early years of the scheme.

It must be stressed that this analysis approaches risk management purely in terms of litigation prevention. The calculation may be different if it is seen in terms of quality improvement. Clearly, there are both social and economic benefits to be gained from reducing untoward outcomes, lowering cross infection rates, encouraging less invasive surgery, and so on. To get some idea of the scale of these benefits, we know from the Harvard Medical Practice Study that there are 370 "adverse events" per 10 000 admissions to hospital in New York State. If this were to be replicated in the United Kingdom, it would imply a total of 235 000 adverse events each year. Of these, some 35 000 are serious iatrogenic injuries, on the basis of the Harvard figures. Given that we have argued in this paper that the number of paid claims per year in England was in the region of 1600 in 1990–1, this indicates the extent to which litigation is only the tip of the risk management iceberg. After all, those adverse events which do not lead to a claim may still provide pointers to the way in which the quality of health care can be improved. Moreover, even when litigation does not occur, adverse events may often result in a financial cost to the NHS. There are administrative costs involved in dealing with complaints, there are costs involved in dealing with the clinical consequences of adverse events, and the patient's duration of stay may be unnecessarily prolonged. Although it is impossible to estimate the full cost of these factors in the absence of better United Kingdom data on adverse events and their consequences, it is clear that the financial return to risk management should be seen as far more than the cost of averted litigation.

Finally, however, it should be borne in mind that improvements in risk management are not costless. In an ideal world, every patient would leave hospital with the predicted outcome. But the costs of achieving that, especially in the face of the natural variability in the human organism, may well deprive us of the possibility of making other private and social investments of an equally desirable kind. Trust managers have a responsibility to consider the opportunity costs of quality improvements just as carefully as any other proposed change of development.

1 Dingwall R, Fenn P. *Quality and regulation in health care*. London: Routledge, 1992.
2 Hawkins C. *Mishap or malpractice*. Oxford: Blackwell, 1985.
3 *Royal Commission on Civil Liability and Compensation for Personal Injury*, Cmnd 7054. London: HMSO, 1978.
4 Bowles R, Jones P. A health authority's experience. *New Law Journal* 1989;**139**: 119–23.
5 Hawkins C, Paterson I. Medicolegal audit in the West Midlands: analysis of 100 cases. *BMJ* **295**:1533–6.
6 Dingwall R, Fenn P. Is risk management necessary? *International Journal of Risk and Safety in Medicine* 1991;2:91–106.
7 Fenn P, Dingwall R. The tort system and information: some comparisons between the UK and the US. In Dingwall R, Fenn P, eds. *Quality and regulation in health care*. London: Routledge, 1992.
8 Ham C, Dingwall R, Fenn P, Harris D. *Medical negligence: compensation and accountability*. London: Kings Fund, 1988.
9 Fenn P, Hermanns D, Dingwall R. Estimating the cost of compensating victims of medical negligence. *BMJ* 1994;309:389–91.
10 Harris DR, Maclean M, Genn H, *et al. Compensation and support for illness and injury*. Oxford: Oxford University Press, 1984.
11 British Medical Association. *Report of the working party on no-fault compensation for medical injury*. London: BMA Publishing Group, 1983.
12 British Medical Association. *Working party report on no-fault compensation*. London: BMA Publishing Group, 1991.
13 Royal College of Physicians. *Compensation for adverse consequences of medical intervention*. London: Royal College of Physicians, 1990.
14 Ham C, Dingwall R, Fenn P, Harris D. *Medical negligence: compensation and accountability*. London: Kings Fund, 1988.
15 Fenn P, Hermanns D, Dingwall R. Estimating the cost of compensating victims of medical negligence. *BMJ* 1994;**309**:389–91.
16 Lamb B, Percival R. *Paying for disability—no fault compensation: panacea or Pandora's box*. London: Spastics Society, 1992.

6 Risk management and quality of care

FIONA MOSS

> An honest concern about quality, however genuine, is not the same as methodical assessment based on reliable evidence.[1]

Risk management is about reducing the likelihood of errors. Its particular aims are to reduce errors that are costly in terms of damage, discomfort, disability, or distress to an individual and to limit financial loss to an organisation. Risk management achieves this through detecting, reporting, and correcting actual or potential deficiencies in the process of care that, however small, could lead to significant and costly mistakes. Risk management programmes therefore involve all aspects of work, production, and interactions within an organisation—and in health care this includes looking beyond clinical care. An established and well run risk management programme contributes towards providing hospital care that is free of mistakes and makes a clear contribution to healthcare quality. The benefits to patients of care in a hospital in which treatment can be guaranteed to be as safe as possible are obvious. But risk management is only one of a clutch of programmes in which the aim is to improve quality of care, and reducing harm is only one aspect of healthcare quality. Linking risk management programmes with other quality initiatives will help to develop a coherent approach to quality improvement within a hospital or practice.

This paper will explore some of the ideas and definitions of quality of care and examine the particular contribution of risk management and that of other quality initiatives to improving different aspects of healthcare quality.

88

Quality of care: what does it include?

Healthcare quality is much more than a matter of technical or professional performance, but it is difficult to sum up the individual components of good quality care. Much care is to some extent a series of compromises, trade offs, and choices, made, in the best circumstances, by properly informed patients guided by knowledgeable healthcare professionals in safe and comfortable surroundings. Good quality care incorporates appropriate and competent technical care with opportunities for patients to make choices and to discuss concerns and fears, and it should result in an outcome appropriate to the problem. Even this long and cumbersome description excludes some important aspects of good quality care, such as fairness and access, and assumes much in the phrase "competent technical care" and says little about the organisation of care.

Classifying quality of care

Three classifications provide a useful framework for discussing quality of health care. The first, the basis of much work on quality improvement, is Donabedian's classification of health care into its structure, process, and outcome components as targets for quality assessment.[2] The second is the six dimensions of quality described by Maxwell as part of a discussion on the need for an integrated quality improvement programme based on methodical assessment (box 1).[1] The third, also from the work of Donabedian, considers health care in three parts: the technical aspects of care, the

---

Box 1—Dimensions of quality

- Effectiveness
- Efficiency
- Appropriateness
- Acceptability
- Access
- Equity

---

interpersonal aspects of care, and the amenities or the environment in which health care is provided.[3] Of course, these classifications overlap, but each approaches the definition of quality of care differently and together they provide a more complete picture than each alone. By combining structure, process, and outcome with the six dimensions of quality a structure emerges that can be used to compile a series of questions about the quality of, say, an intensive care unit (box 2).[4]

Structure, process, and outcome

The *structure* of care describes the resources that combine to deliver care and includes all aspects of the environment of the hospital, clinic, or practice premises where patients are seen and treated. Structure includes the number of grades of staff as well as the number of beds, the number and configuration of clinics, and the availability and standard of equipment and other items necessary for delivering health care. Clearly, some aspects of structure, although desirable, are not crucial for good quality care and, conversely, bad care is quite possible within a well equipped hospital.

The *process* of care refers to all the events, procedures, and actions included in the health care received. This includes assessments such as clinical examinations and investigations, clinical interventions such as prescription of a drug or an operation as well as outpatient appointments, and the processes of nursing care and therapy. The interpersonal aspects of care may also be considered part of the process of care.

The *outcome* of health care is any change in a patient's health status attributable to a healthcare intervention and includes restoration of function, relief of symptoms, and improvement in life expectancy. Improving health—either current or future—is a central aim of health care. Knowing what works or what is effective is important to individual patients and to healthcare providers, purchasers, and policy makers. Measurement of outcomes is of crucial importance to assessing health care and attempts to improve effectiveness and efficiency. Outcomes might seem to be a measure of the sum of all that goes into health care—an outcome less than expected might indicate poor quality care. However, measuring outcome is not always straightforward; a change in health status of an individual must be directly attributable to a healthcare intervention to be classed as an outcome of health care—that is, a direct causal link must exist between the result and the intervention.[5]

Assessing outcomes of clinical interventions has mostly been described by healthcare professionals and expressed largely in terms of physiological or other technical measures. Thus the outcome of the use of inhaled steroids in patients with troublesome nocturnal

90

Box 2—Assessing quality in an intensive care unit (from Maxwell[4])

	Structure	Process	Outcome
Effectiveness	Staffing level and skills Equipment Access to theatres, etc	Workload (volume of patients treated) Compliance with protocols, where relevant Data based peer review Infection and complications rates	Survival rates compared with similar units for matched cases
Acceptability	Is setting frightening or reassuring? What provision for relatives (privacy for counselling, overnight accommodation)?	Is explanation to relatives required and recorded in notes?	Is there follow up of patients and relatives to obtain their opinions and suggestions for improvement?
Efficiency	Avoidance of extravagance in structure, equipment, and staffing	Throughput, staffing, etc Admission and discharge arrangements	Costs for comparable cases
Access		How many patients suitable for admission have to be refused because the unit is full?	What happens to patients refused or delayed admission because the unit is full?
Equity		Is there any evidence of bias in who is admitted or how they are treated?	Is there any evidence of bias in outcomes?
Relevance	Bearing in mind other needs, is this service an appropriate use of resources at the current activity and expenditure level?		How much difference does the unit make to survival and health status, and for whom?

asthma is understood technically in terms of change in the morning peak expiratory flow rate. But what matters for the patient may not be so much this criterion but a reduction in symptoms and undisturbed sleep.

Measuring the outcome of a clinical intervention implies assessment of a change in health status. Some measures of health status are condition specific—for example, changes in blood glucose concentration in diabetes. Generic measures express changes in health status that apply to any condition and describe three domains of wellbeing: physical functioning, mental health, and social function. The development and validation of health status questionnaires such as the SF 36 questionnaire[6] offer a means of comparing outcomes across specialties. The use of health status measures permits an understanding of the impact of clinical interventions on patients' wellbeing and, when used alongside conventional clinical and physiological measures, adds to the information on effectiveness of interventions.

Dimensions of quality

Effectiveness is the extent to which a healthcare intervention, when used in routine practice, achieves the desired outcome.[7] From all perspectives—those of patients, providers, and purchasers—promoting the use of effective interventions and limiting the use of ineffective ones is an important focus for quality improvement programmes. However, evidence exists that some patients are treated with ineffective interventions and others who would benefit from specific effective treatments do not receive them. One example of the use of ineffective care is the continued use of dilatation and curettage for women under 40 with menstrual problems, for whom this procedure is unlikely to have any benefit. Among patients not always receiving effective interventions are those admitted with acute myocardial infarction, some of whom do not receive β blockers and aspirin, which reduce the risk of infarction.[8]

Appropriate care has been defined as ". . . the selection, from the body of interventions that have been shown to be efficacious for a disorder, of the intervention that is most likely to produce the outcomes desired by the individual patient."[9] Again, there is evidence that interventions are at times used inappropriately. One example is the use of coronary artery surgery in coronary artery disease; in one health region in the United Kingdom 16% of

92

Box 3—Additional criteria for appropriateness of an intervention*

Availability of technical skills and resources to allow intervention to be performed to a high standard

Intervention performed in a manner acceptable to the patient

Patient to have adequate information about the range of effective interventions

Patient to be fully informed of and to be involved in discussions about likelihood of adverse outcomes

Patient's preferences to guide choice of intervention

Patient's preferences should reflect both primary outcome and perceptions of potential adverse outcomes

* From working group report[9]

---

coronary artery bypass surgery, assessed retrospectively by a panel of experts, was found to be inappropriate.[10]

Good quality care must be *acceptable*. The working group who defined the appropriateness of care quoted above emphasised the importance of the individuality of the patient, the social and cultural context, and the availability of healthcare resources when considering appropriateness of health care. Appropriate care goes further than just medicotechnical concerns and must include a measure of acceptability to the patient and to society (box 3). Thus the assessment of the appropriateness of coronary artery surgery referred to above may have underestimated its level of inappropriate use as the study examined appropriateness from only a medicotechnical perspective and did not investigate patient choice or other criteria.

Assessing the acceptability of care is difficult. No mechanism exists for routine collection of information about the acceptability of interventions to individual patients. The weight an individual places on risks of treatment and likelihood of a treatment working is not always predictable. And societal attitudes to acceptability of care are not always explicit. A recent case reported widely in the British press of a 10 year old girl who had experienced a relapse of leukaemia after a bone marrow transplant illustrates the tensions that may emerge when differences exist between the acceptability of an intervention as perceived by an individual (represented by the girl's father and his legal advisers) and by society (represented by the purchasers of care). The purchasing authority, having taken medical advice, refused payment for further transplantation, estimated at £75 000, as there was judged to be only a minimal chance that treatment would be successful. Its view was that the girl should be made as comfortable as possible and not given active treatment. But the girl wanted to pursue active treatment. The case went to the Appeal Court, which ruled in the purchasing authority's favour.[11][12]

Acceptability of care to an individual may be as much about the interpersonal aspects of care as the technical task of delivering care. Healthcare professionals need to be good at communicating if patients are to be able to make choices and to decide what is to them acceptable. Allowing people to make choices requires respect and sensitivity.

Access to care, in terms of waiting lists, is perhaps the most easily measured of all the dimensions of quality and in the United Kingdom has become a matter of political concern. Debated in the media, access to care as defined by waiting lists for operations and for first outpatient appointments has a greater profile than other aspects of quality of care. The patients' charter has set out standards that may help improve the way that hospitals manage waiting for appointments within hospital clinics.[13] The easy availability of data on waiting lists may give undue weight to one aspect of quality at the expense of others. This is illustrated by a case of a child who had been waiting for 12 months to have an ear operation that became public in the run up to the general election in 1992 in the United Kingdom. The political furore and media discussion that followed focused on access to care and paid little attention to consideration of more pertinent issues, such as the appropriateness of the procedure.[14]

Equity is about fairness and assuring that healthcare delivery is related to need and is a specific aspect of access to care. In the United Kingdom the health care provided by the NHS is based on equitable principles and is free at the point of delivery. Access to care is related to need and not, for example, to ability to pay. This contrasts with much health care in the United States. But equity has a wider application than just the system of health care and within the health service in the United Kingdom examples of inequity can be found. People whose first language is not English may have a restricted access to advice and care, unrelated to need, if they are unable to explain their problems fluently to the doctor because of lack of interpreting services. The introduction of fundholding for some general practices has led to concern that the patients of fundholding general practitioners may get preferential access to some aspects of hospital care as their doctors control budgets for elective care. And studies in both the United Kingdom and United States have shown that women with coronary artery disease are less likely than men with similar disease to have coronary angiography or surgery.

Interpersonal and technical aspects of care

The third classification of the quality of care includes a distinction between interpersonal and technical aspects of care. Practitioners require skills in both in order to deliver good quality care. Being able to discuss the risks and benefits of interventions and describe possible outcomes is a prerequisite if patients are to make informed choices. Technical competence is crucial but alone will not guarantee good quality care.

Systematic approaches to quality

The range of questions encompassed in the notion of the quality of care—from details of the effectiveness of technical interventions to equity and respect—indicate the enormity of the task of its assessment. Risk management deals with only some of the dimensions of quality and targets adverse events and aims at reducing errors. A quality improvement programme that relied only on risk management might reduce risk and result in a safer hospital but would not, for example, tackle issues such as effectiveness or appropriateness of care. Each quality programme has a particular perspective and a contribution to different aspects of the quality of care.

A jungle of terminology and the differing functions and origins of programmes that focus on the quality of care have made this seem a perplexing area to many healthcare professionals. I shall describe quality programmes briefly in three broad categories: quality assurance, quality improvement, and clinical audit. Although each may have a different emphasis they all entail a systematic approach to assessing quality of care.

Quality assurance

Quality assurance, which has had greater prominence in the United States than the United Kingdom, tends to rely on measurement of indicators of performance. Broadly, quality assurance systems rely on external inspection. One aim is to guarantee that an organisation meets predefined standards and may be described as a checking mechanism. In the United States since the 1950s external monitoring agencies have accredited hospitals and monitored the quality of care. The system is complex and is a mix of private and public organisations whose objectives include cost containment as well as quality improvement.[15 16]

External quality assessment and accreditation have not been a major feature of health care in the United Kingdom. But examples of mechanisms for external checks on quality do exist and include the quality assurance system for chemical pathology; the Health Advisory Service, set up to inspect services for long stay elderly and mentally ill patients; the confidential enquiry into maternal mortality; and the confidential enquiry into perioperative deaths conducted by the Royal Colleges of Anaesthetists and Surgeons.[17]

The confidential enquiry into perioperative deaths (CEPOD) has had an important impact on the organisation of emergency surgery particularly on procedures performed out of hours. By focusing on possibly avoidable serious events this enquiry is similar to the process of risk management. Futhermore, it is based on a reporting system—another important element of risk management. Local risk management programmes should work closely with those involved in CEPOD.

Clinical audit

The introduction of medical and then clinical audit into the United Kingdom health service in 1990[18 19] represented a fundamental change in approach to the quality of clinical care. Until then the approach in hospitals was rarely systematic. Discussion about methodical approaches to quality assessment was limited to groups of enthusiasts. But backed up with specific central funding of £48m annually medical audit very quickly became part of the contractual commitment for hospital doctors and a near mandatory activity for general practitioners. In the definition of audit included in the Department of Health's documents medical audit was described as a *professional* activity. At first, audit was apparently only for doctors. But this inward approach changed and medical audit was superseded by clinical audit, which has a wider remit by including the work of all healthcare professionals.

The principles of clinical audit are described in the notion of the audit cycle.[20] Using the best evidence available—from scientific publications or nationally agreed standards or locally agreed codes of practice—local practice is measured and compared with the agreed standards. Appropriate sampling methods and sample size are necessary to ensure that the data give an accurate view of the aspect of care being examined. After discussion of the results with the relevant healthcare professionals any difference between the agreed observed standards is analysed and attempts are made to find the reason for any difference so that changes can be made with a view to improve practice.[21] Thus a quantitative approach is used to gain a picture of the standard of care. But the action needed to change practice is often less clear, which may explain why audits often fail to change practice and improve quality.

The success of this servicewide implementation of clinical audit in improving patient care has not been formally evaluated, and the benefit of this investment is not known.[22] Nevertheless, clinical audit is now established in the United Kingdom as the focus of quality assessment in hospital practice. Most hospitals have audit meetings, designated audit officers or facilitators, and a programme of topics for audit. Direct central funding for audit has now been passed to the purchasing authorities. Audit continues as a provider function, but purchasers can now add some external pressure by including quality statements in contracts and asking for audits of specific topics.

Quality improvement

The essential features of quality improvement are that it is largely an internal mechanism; that it is reflective and not punitive or defensive; that it relies on learning and improving; and that it is based on an understanding of the needs of the customer and on good evidence. Compared with quality assurance, quality improvement does not primarily set out to determine whether care is substandard or not or whether it meets a set standard, but it is a more dynamic approach to quality that relies on systematic analyses of the processes of work—quantitative or qualitative that are considered and used by those doing the work to improve what they do. All healthcare professionals and all who work in health care should be involved; quality improvement is not a specialty or discipline in its own right. To bring about change those involved in quality improvement must not only undertake methodical study but also understand how their organisation works and what motivates change.

Some readers will identify in this a description of continuous quality improvement and others might recognise it as total quality management. Much has been written about the development of total quality management in industry and its relevance to health care. In health care, quality is almost exclusively focused on clinical quality; there is a tendency to disassociate managerial and clinical activity within quality improvement. In total quality management the idea of quality improvement is linked to the notion that quality is a characteristic of the whole organisation. This approach to quality improvement was developed by American experts asked by Japanese industrialists to advise about improving Japanese industrial production processes. These advisors, among them W Edwards Deming and Joseph M Duran, understood that documenting the technical quality or specifications of components on a production line would not alone produce lasting improvement in production quality. They approached quality improvement from a much wider perspective. Drawing from a wide range of disciplines, they advocated the development of an approach to quality improvement that involves everyone in the organisation as part of a continual drive to do better. Box 4 shows some of the characteristics of total quality management. Although total quality management may sound like jargon to people working in health care and its industrial origins may provoke resistance, it is an approach which could be applied to the National Health Service.[24][25]

Some of the characteristics of total quality management are similar to those of risk management—for example, examining the processes of care rather than individual performance for explanations of flaws or errors. Others, in particular the emphasis on measurement, are in line with the principles that underpin audit. The need to develop an integrated approach to quality and its improvement and to avoid separating those programmes that within one organisation aim at improving the quality of care would be in keeping with total quality management.

Comparing the contributions of risk management and clinical audit

Risk management and clinical audit focus on different aspects of the quality of care and are complementary, not alternative, programmes. Structure is more often a topic for risk management

---

Box 4—Some characteristics of total quality management*

Making customers' needs a priority for everyone
Defining quality in terms of customer needs
Recognising the existence of internal customers and suppliers
Examining the process of production rather than individual performance for explanations of flaws or poor quality
Using sound measurement to understand how to improve quality
Removing barriers between staff and promoting effective teamwork
Promoting training for everyone
Involving the whole workforce in the task of improving quality
Understanding that quality improvement is a continuous process

* From Moss and Garside[23]

---

that clinical audit. Safety depends on good, well maintained equipment, and hospitals should have a mechanism to detect faulty equipment. Staffing also affects the quality of care. The national confidential enquiry in perioperative deaths highlighted the risks of operations being done by surgeons of inappropriate seniority for the tasks they are asked to do. Buildings also need to be safe, well maintained, and to provide the appropriate environment for patients and for staff.

Much audit activity is about the process of care, which is relatively easy to measure. The importance of the process of care is its relation to outcome and the presupposition of a relation between the appropriate use of an effective intervention and a favourable outcome. Both (in)effective and (in)appropriate care interventions may be a focus for audit. By setting standards and measuring care against them the degree to which care meets those standards can be assessed. An example is the use of thrombolytic therapy for people with myocardial infarction—an intervention of established benefit. Reasonable targets for audit, as process markers of good quality care, are the rate and timing of administration of thrombolytic therapy. Many hospitals, through the audit process, know the proportion of patients admitted with myocardial infarction who receive thrombolytic therapy and the delay between arrival in hospital and receiving this treatment. This information, used properly, can help a hospital to improve this aspect of care.[26]

In contrast, effectiveness and appropriateness are not prime targets for risk management programmes, although questions about

99

these aspects of quality may be asked when an untoward event has occurred. Sometimes the process of care is a trigger for risk management, but the targets are unexpected activity and indicators of problems with care. For example, a need for a patient to return to theatre after an operation or a greater than predicted blood transfusion after a caesarean delivery are interventions that might indicate that something had not gone according to plan.

The government white paper *Working for Patients* included outcomes within the working definition of medical audit.[27] In reality using outcome for audit is difficult. Problems of case mix, different perspectives on outcome, the need for large numbers to make sense of small changes, and the importance of medium and long term outcomes which may be difficult to collect at discharge have thwarted attempts to audit outcome. For to act as a lever for change a link with process is needed, Some outcomes are most usefully measured some time after the intervention so that both collecting the data and communicating them to the healthcare professionals who initiated the intervention may not be straightforward.

Unwanted outcomes or adverse outcomes are important triggers in risk management. Unexpected death or a complication from an intervention warrants investigation. Each specialty will have its own series of such outcomes—for example, a poor Apgar score of a newborn baby, neonatal death, or any death after an elective operation.

Most instances of care that patients find unacceptable are probably unreported and are unlikely to be disclosed by any of the quality improvement initiatives. Acceptability of care is not a usual focus for audit but may be detected through risk management programmes, in some cases passing through the clinical complaints process. One study of clinical complaints found that most complaints were seldom about a clinical problem alone; most also included some dissatisfaction with personal treatment.[28]

Continuous quality improvement

Firm links between clinical and managerial activity are necessary if risk management or clinical audit is to be effective. All these initiatives depend on organisational support and the cooperation and the involvement of all staff. An organisation that works through the principles of continuous quality improvement will be responsive to the demands of both audit and risk management and enable links between these and other similar programmes. A workforce receptive to the notion of continuous quality improvement is likely to adopt a positive attitude to the reporting systems that are part of risk management. Some features of good quality care—allowing patient choice, assuring equity, and providing information—are difficult to measure and rarely assessed. But these aspects of quality will be integral to organisations whose functions are based on the principles of continuous quality improvement because of the emphasis on the needs of their customers and the importance given to training of all staff. The success of risk management may depend on the adoption of the principles of continuous quality improvement.

Conclusions

Good quality care is more than either average care or simply care free of mistakes. No single technology that purports to improve the quality of care can encompass the many dimensions of quality. Some aspects of quality are more easily targeted by audit and others by risk management; and some are unlikely to be the focus of either programme. In the United Kingdom the development of clinical risk management is being introduced after the implementation of clinical audit. With their separate funding and perhaps their aim at primarily different groups within the health service there is a risk that clinical audit and risk management will develop separately, but should be linked through good organisational support.

1 Maxwell R. Quality assessment in health. *BMJ* 1984;**288**:1470–2.
2 Donabedian A. Evaluating the quality of medical care. *Millbank Memorial Fund Quarterly* 1066;**44**:166–206.
3 Donabedian A. *The definition of quality and approaches to its assessment.* Ann Arbor, Michigan: Health Administration Press, 1980.
4 Maxwell R. Dimensions of quality revisited: from thought to action. *Quality in Health Care* 1992;**1**:171–7.
5 Shanks J, Frater A. Health status, outcome, and attributality: is a red rose red in the dark? *Quality in Health Care* 1993;**2**:259–62.
6 Brazier JE, Harper R, Jones NMB, O'Cathain A, Thomas KJ, Usherwood T, *et al.* Validating the SF-36 health survey questionnaire: new outcome measure for primary care. *BMJ* 1992;**305**:160–4.
7 Hopkins A. *Measuring the quality of medical care.* London: Royal College of Physicians of London, 1990.
8 Eccles M, Bradshaw C. Use of secondary prophylaxis against myocardial infarction in the north of England. *BMJ* 1991;**302**:91–2.

9 What do we mean by appropriate health care? Report of a working group prepared for the Director of Research and Development of the NHS Management Executive. *Quality in Health Care* 1993;2:117–23.

10 Gray D, Hampton JR, Bernstein SJ, Kosekoff J, Brook R. Audit of coronary angiography and bypass surgery. *Lancet* 1990;**335**:1317–20.

11 Mullin J. Leukaemia girl loses court fight. *Guardian* 11 March 1995:1.

12 Mihill C. Guideline plea for rationing treatment. *Guardian* 11 March 1995.

13 Collins C. Implementing the patient's charter in outpatient services. *BMJ* 1993; **302**:1396.

14 Black N. Jennifer's ear: airing the issues. *Quality in Health Care* 1992;1:213–4.

15 Wareham NJ. External monitoring of quality of health care in the United States. *Quality in Health Care* 1994;3:97–101.

16 Wareham NJ. Changing systems of external monitoring of quality of health care in the United States. *Quality in Health Care* 1994;**3**:102–6.

17 Buck N, Devlin HB, Lunn JN. *Report of a confidential enquiry into perioperative deaths.* London: Nuffield Provincial Hospitals Trusts, 1988.

18 Department of Health. *Medical audit in the family practitioner services.* London: HMSO, 1990. (HC(FP) 90(8).)

19 Department of Health. *Medical audit in the hospital and community services.* London: HMSO, 1991. (HC 91(2).)

20 Russell IT, Wilson BL. Audit: the third clinical science? *Quality in Health Care* 1992;**1**:51–5.

21 Crombie IK, Davies HTO. Missing link in the audit cycle. *Quality in Health Care* 1993;2:47–8.

22 Buxton M. Achievements of audit in the NHS. *Quality in Health Care* 1994; **3**(suppl):S31–4.

23 Moss F, Garside P. The importance of quality: sharing responsibilities for improving patient care. *BMJ* 1995;**310**:996–1000.

24 Berwick DM, Enthoven A, Bunker JP. Quality management in the NHS: the doctor's role. I. *BMJ* 1992;**394**:235–9.

25 Berwick DM, Enthoven A, Bunker JP. Quality management in the NHS: the doctor's role. II. *BMJ* 1992;**304**:304–8.

26 Nee PA, Gray AJ, Martin MA. Audit of thrombolysis initiated in an accident and emergency department. *Quality in Health Care* 1994;2:29–33.

27 Secretaries of State for Health, Wales, Northern Ireland, and Scotland. *Medical audit. Working paper 6.* London: HMSO, 1989.

28 Bark P, Vincent C, Jones A, Savory J. Clinical complaints: a means of improving quality of care. *Quality in Health Care* 1994;**3**:123–32.

7 Evaluation of clinical risk management programmes

LAURA L MORLOCK

There is widespread agreement that a principal goal of clinical risk management programmes must be to reduce the frequency of preventable adverse events that may lead to liability claims. The route is through implementing activities designed to identify and decrease the risks of patient injury associated with clinical care.[1-3] Important objectives of risk management also include decreasing the number of claims and controlling the costs of claims that do emerge, through both the prompt identification and follow up of maloccurrences, and improving communications between providers and patients. Risk management programmes also try to finance risk through the most economical methods.[1]

Clinical risk management programmes are regarded by many in the public policy and health care communities as a promising approach to medical liability issues. Such programmes, however, have rarely been evaluated with respect to their effectiveness in actually decreasing the frequency of liability claims, lowering the amount of claim payments, or reducing the number of patient injuries associated with medical care. To some degree this is because many programmes are recent. An even more important factor, however, is the difficulty in showing an impact on claims frequency or payments due to the typical patterns involved in emergence and resolution of liability claims.

It is characteristic of medical liability claims that there may be a considerable time lag between an episode of patient care

103

and notification that an injury has occurred due to alleged negligence. Data, for example, from a large professional liability insurer, the St Paul Companies, suggest that on average, about 30% of claims are filed in the year of treatment, 30% in the year after treatment, 25% in the third year, 7% in the fourth year, and 8% five or more years later.[4] For providers and insurers this pattern has often resulted in a "long tail" of exposure to unfiled liability claims, which once filed, usually require additional months or years to close—particularly if a jury trial is needed for resolution. In Maryland, for example, claims require on average about two years from the patient care incident to claim filing, and on average, a further two years for resolution. As a consequence, particular risk management strategies once in place will typically require, due to claims emergence patterns, at least two to three years to achieve a demonstrated impact on claims frequency, and an additional two to three years for a measurable effect on claim payments (including privately negotiated settlements and arbitration or jury awards).

In addition, risk managers often express frustration with their attempts to document the results of their efforts to prevent adverse events. The central issue, in the words of one risk manager is "how to measure what *didn't* happen, and how to demonstrate that it was my programme that was responsible for it not happening." Two evaluation designs are appropriate for considering this issue. Firstly, trends can be examined within one's own institution in the numbers and types of adverse events, claims, and payments, and comparisons made between periods before and after the implementation of specific risk management strategies. Such an approach obviously must take into consideration any differences over time in the institution mix of patients, services provided, or other changes that affect exposure to the risk of adverse events or claims. Although claims, and especially claim payments, must usually be viewed as long term outcomes, it may be possible to identify shorter term indicators (such as specific types of complaints) that can be used to predict subsequent claims.

This approach cannot control, however, for environmental factors such as legal reforms or population changes, that may result in increases or decreases in claiming behaviour. Thus a useful second strategy is to compare one's own institution over time with the experience of a relevant peer group. Currently, however, there is substantial variability among institutions with

104

respect to systems for identifying adverse events, the types of data collected, and data collection procedures.[5] Differences are also likely to exist in how claims—and claim payments—are defined, making comparisons across institutions often hazardous.

Despite the considerable challenges, evaluating the effectiveness of risk management programmes is critical to focus efforts on those activities likely to be the most beneficial, and to show the value of such activities in containing costs and improving the quality of patient care. Such an evaluation is dependent on identifying and measuring the degree of risk exposure, the processes designed to manage risk, and the outcomes that indicate the extent to which benefits attainable through risk management activities are actually achieved. Outcome measures generally involve the monitoring of adverse patient events, liability claims, and claim payments. The best evidence available on the frequencies and relations among these three indicators is discussed in the next section.

Subsequent sections focus to evaluate hospital based risk management programmes, and current issues critical to the evaluation of risk management in clinical settings.

Relations among adverse patient events, filed claims, and claim payments

Most information on medical liability claims comes from closed claim studies, which by definition are limited to those patient injuries (and alleged injuries) that have resulted in demands for compensation. There is little evidence available on the frequency with which injuries to patients actually occur during the course of medical treatment, or the extent to which these injuries are the result of provider error.

Results from the only large scale studies that are available strongly suggest that the number of injuries to patients likely to be due to the negligence of health care providers is far larger than the numbers of medical liability claims filed by health care consumers. To a considerable degree it has been these findings that have generated interest in the potential of clinical risk management programmes for reducing the number of preventable adverse events in patient care, in addition to helping prevent or control the filing of medical malpractice claims. Such an approach has the potential for improving the quality of medical services as well as aiding in the containment of costs of health care.

The California medical insurance feasibility study

The first comprehensive investigation of these issues was the medical insurance feasibility study conducted during the mid-1970s under the auspices of the California Medical Association and the California Hospital Association.[6] The study was prompted by a widely held belief within the healthcare community that most bad outcomes of medical and surgical management were litigated successfully by plaintiff attorneys regardless of whether they involved provider negligence.

The purpose of the California study was to determine the cost and feasibility of a no fault compensation system by conducting a detailed examination of the frequency, severity, and characteristics of patient disabilities resulting from health care management. The study was designed and implemented by Don Harper Mills, John Boyden, and David Rubsamen with the assistance of a team of medical consultants coordinated by Charles Jacobs of InterQual Inc. The study sample consisted of 23 hospitals selected to be representative of all California acute care hospitals in terms of size, region, ownership, and teaching status. From these institutions a sample of 20 864 medical records was selected to represent all California hospital discharges during 1974 with respect to age, sex, race, and payment source.

To help identify injuries related to medical care that might be eligible for compensation, 20 screening criteria were developed that represented adverse incidents of major significance such as the following: patient admitted for condition suggesting potential prior failure or adverse results of medical management; death during stay in hospital; hospital incurred trauma; adverse drug reaction; unplanned return to the operating room; temperature of 38·5°C or greater on last full day before, or day of, discharge.

The initial screening by medical chart reviewers identified those hospital admissions in which patient had experienced one or more adverse incidents as defined by the screening criteria. The screened medical records were examined next by physicians and physician attorneys to determine whether a potentially compensable event (PCE) had occurred. Such an event was defined as an incident resulting in temporary or permanent disability, most probably caused by health care management, that either led to the index admission to hospital, prolonged the stay in hospital, or resulted in substantial treatment after leaving hospital. Charts containing a PCE were then further evaluated by a panel of experienced physician attorneys to determine the likelihood of an adverse jury decision if the incident had resulted in a claim litigated to court verdict.

The investigators concluded that 970 out of the 20 864 medical records examined (4·65%) contained information indicative of a patient disability caused by healthcare management. It was further estimated that 17% of these iatrogenic injuries (or 0·8% of the total) would probably have resulted in a jury finding of provider liability under the tort system then in place. The remaining 83% were judged to derive from adverse events produced by the normal risk of medical treatment. These results imply, however, that one out of every 126 patients admitted to California hospitals in 1974 experienced, either prior to or during the stay in hospital, a significant injury due to probable negligence (as legally defined) which was judged to have been suitable for compensation if it had resulted in a malpractice claim. Although these problems were detected in the medical charts of patients in hospital, it is important to note that one third of the adverse events actually had occurred outside of the sample hospitals, usually in physicians' offices and clinics. The effects, however, were severe enough to result in admission to hospital.

Due to restrictions placed on the study to safeguard confidentiality, investigators were not able to determine how many of the patients injured in adverse events actually filed malpractice claims. This number has been estimated, however, by Danzon,[7] who compared the 1974 injury information with aggregate claims data for California available from a national survey of all liability claims closed during July 1975–December 1978. Danzon restricted her analysis to adverse events in hospitals, and compared the number of claims relative to the number of injuries by age of the injured party, severity of the injury, and type of medical error.[8]

Although during this period California had one of the highest frequencies of claims per physician and claims per capita in the nation, results from Danzon's analysis suggest that at most one in 10 of the patients experiencing an injury due to error actually filed a malpractice claim.[7] Danzon notes that this proportion is likely to be an overestimate as it assumes that all of the injuries due to probable error in the California study were identified through the medical record review. Of the claims filed, only about 40% resulted in payment to the claimant, leading Danzon to conclude that at most one in 25 injuries to patients because of probable negligence resulted in compensation through the medical malpractice system.

A comparison of types of injuries resulting from error with characteristics of claims filed and claims paid suggested that claim filing was more likely for permanent than for temporary injuries, and lowest for incidents resulting in death. Age of the injured party seemed to be a significant predictor of claim payment. The probability of an injury due to error resulting in a paid claim was three times more likely for younger (aged 20 to 44) than for older (greater than 65) age groups. With respect to the types of medical errors resulting in claims, the analysis indicated that errors of performance, rather than errors of judgment or diagnosis, seemed to be both the primary cause of injuries and the principal allegation in claims. As Danzon and others have noted, iatrogenic injuries due to omissions in healthcare management or diagnostic errors may be as common, but less visible and harder to detect—whether by patients, plaintiff attorneys, or research investigators.

The Harvard study of adverse events in New York hospitals

A more recent investigation of the frequency of adverse occurrences among patients in hospital used a methodology similar to that developed during the California study.[9-11] An interdisciplinary team of Harvard researchers reviewed 30 195 randomly selected records of patients in hospital in 1984 in 51 randomly selected acute care, general hospitals in New York State. In the first phase of the study all records were screened for the presence of an adverse event. This was done by trained nurses or medical records administrators who used 18 screening criteria. Records meeting the screening criteria were then reviewed independently by two physicians who identified adverse events and instances of probable negligence. Adverse events were found to have occurred in the treatment of 3·7% of those in hospital, and 27·6% of these adverse events (or 1·02% of the total) were judged to have resulted from negligence.

The overall statewide estimate of the ratio of adverse events caused by negligence to malpractice claims resulting from care delivered during the index year was 7·6:1. The investigators note that this relative frequency overstates the chances that a negligent adverse event resulted in a claim, as most of the events in the sample for which claims were filed did not meet the study's definition of adverse events due to negligence. Of the 280 patients who had adverse events due to medical negligence as defined by

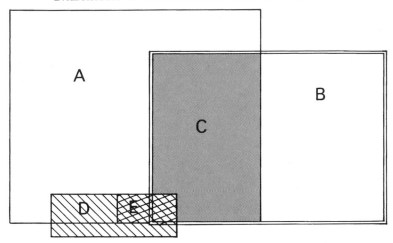

Figure 7.1 *Relations among patient injuries, provider errors, and malpractice claims. A = incidence of patient injuries; B = incidence of errors during medical care; C = patient injuries due to errors during medical care; D = filed malpractice claims; E = filed claims resulting in claimant compensation.*

the study protocol, only eight (about 3%) filed malpractice claims. The researchers conclude that medical malpractice litigation rarely compensates patients injured by medical negligence and infrequently identifies, and holds providers accountable for substandard care.[11]

Adverse events, claims, and payments: summary

Figure 7.1 summarises the available evidence on the relation among patient injuries associated with medical care, provider errors, and malpractice claims. Area A represents all medical injuries among patients in hospital, estimated on the basis of the California and New York studies to be in the range of 3·7–4·7% of all patient admissions. Area B represents the incidence of all errors by health care providers, the extent of which is unknown.

To be compensated through the legal system for medical malpractice, it must be established that there has been a breach in the appropriate standard of care, injury to the patient eligible for compensation, and a causal connection between the provider's negligence and the patient's injury.[12] Area C defines injuries due to provider error that would constitute negligence as legally defined. Theoretically, these are "actionable" injuries under the tort system

109

of liability that should result in the payment of compensation if claims are filed. The overlap of area A and area C constituted 17% of area A, or 0·79% (1 per 126) of all patients admitted to acute care institutions in California in 1974. Applying the same rate to national hospital admissions data suggests that during that year about 260 000 patients in the United States experienced injuries due to errors in the delivery of medical care. The New York study estimated "actionable" injuries as 27·6% of adverse events or 1·02% of all patients admitted to acute care institutions in New York in 1984.

Area D in Figure 7.1 represents the number of malpractice claims filed. Based on Danzon's analysis, at the height of the malpractice crisis in the mid-1970s at most 10% of the injuries due to provider errors in California resulted in filed claims. The New York study suggests that an even smaller percentage of adverse events due to error result in medical malpractice claims, and that many of the claims that do occur are not associated with treatment that was judged to be negligent. A recent study of the litigation process by Farber and White may aid in the interpretation of this pattern.[13] Study findings suggest that many patients who experience injuries during treatment file claims in an effort to determine whether the care they received was of high quality because they are often unable to obtain this information outside of the litigation process. In this study most patients dropped their claims after learning more information about their treatment.

As indicated by area E, about 40% of the claims in Danzon's study of California cases resulted in payment to the claimant, suggesting that during this period about one in 25 patients who experienced an injury due to medical care error received compensation. Similar data from the New York study are not yet available, but a national study by the US General Accounting Office of a sample of claims closed in 1984 indicates that a similar percentage (43%) of claims closed with payment.[34]

Implications for risk management activities and evaluation

The clinical risk management process is usually considered to have four basic components: event identification and reporting; evaluation of risk through event analysis; risk treatment which may include clinical, patient relations and legal aspects; and risk prevention activities.[3] As the previous discussion has indicated, most adverse patient events—including those incidents that result in liability claims—are most likely to occur as part of the "normal risk" of medical treatment rather than provider error. In these cases, good patient and provider communication regarding factors contributing to the event may be the key to decreasing the probability of a claim. If, on the other hand, it has been determined or is strongly suspected that the injury is due to provider error, the patient (or family member) can be informed as rapidly as possible of treatment plans, as well as the waiver of charges and financial restitution if considered appropriate. The timely identification and resolution of patient complaints, as well as prompt attention to and compensation for justifiable claims, is thought to reduce the costs of defence and possibly the size of settlements and awards. Thus the timely identification of adverse events is critical, whether or not provider error is likely to be a factor.

An equally important objective of most systems for the detection of adverse events is to accumulate and analyse reliable information in a manner that facilitates the identification of trends and possible problem areas.[23] Such information can provide a focus for risk prevention and quality management efforts, as well as a means of measuring their effectiveness.

Measurement issues

Measuring outcomes: adverse events, claims, payments, and expenses

Adverse events

As early as the 1950s and 1960s, most hospitals in the United States had in place some type of administrative reporting system for adverse incidents involving patients or visitors. These early, traditional incident reporting systems have been credited with identifying risks and facilitating improvements in several problem areas.[14] Such reports were of limited value for risk management or liability insurers, however, as they rarely included injuries related to medical or surgical care that were the most likely to generate significant claims or suits. (See chapter 1 for a more detailed discussion of these early systems.)

The failure of traditional incident reporting systems to capture the clinical incidents that led to the greatest risk exposure for liability claims resulted in the design of alternative approaches to data gathering that would facilitate detection of these important adverse events. Occurrence screening and occurrence reporting were two such strategies for clinical adverse event detection that were based on criteria developed and knowledge gained by investigators during the California study.

Occurrence screening strategies flag adverse events through the review of either all or a percentage of medical charts, using generic criteria (such as the presence of a medication error or nosocomial infection), or specialty or service specific criteria (such as incorrect sponge count during surgery) for more focused review. Most approaches to occurrence screening use a two step methodology in which explicit screening criteria are used in an initial review by trained staff, followed by physician (and sometimes attorney) review of those cases identified as having unanticipated and undesirable outcomes.

This strategy is widely regarded as an effective and valid method of identifying adverse clinical occurrences, including events resulting from substandard care and that potentially merit compensation. But screening—particularly using generic criteria—is also viewed as costly and inefficient due to the large number of "false positives" that are often identified during the initial chart review.[5 15]

Efforts to consider this issue have generated several strategies that result in more targeted detection activities. One approach has been to replace or supplement the generic hospital-wide outcome criteria with more focused screens that are developed specifically for specialties or services perceived to be at high risk for adverse events.[16] The Joint Commission on Accreditation of Healthcare Organisations (JCAHO), for example, has developed focused screens for the review of obstetrics, anaesthesia, and other higher risk services, as well as its hospitalwide quality indicators.[17] Evaluations of focused occurrence screens suggest much higher levels of agreement (interrater reliability) among trained data retrieval staff when the medical charts of patients with selected problems or diagnoses are reviewed using focused screens than when generic criteria are used to screen all medical records.[18 19]

Screening methods for the identification of patient risk factors have also been used in attempts to increase the efficiency and utility of occurrence screening tools. In the JCAHO methodology, for example, data are collected not only on adverse events, but also on patient risk factors and other factors that may influence outcomes.[17]

The general goal of many organisations that rely on some form of occurrence screening for monitoring and evaluation purposes has been to try to develop over time an abbreviated list of "high yield" screens. These are indicators that permit high levels of agreement on the presence or absence of an adverse event during the screening phase, and that experience indicates are likely to identify relevant patient problems or to result in high potential for liability claims. This approach seems inevitably to require experimentation and a fairly lengthy iterative process within the particular practice setting or organisation.[20] The continuing refinement of the approach is also required as new technologies are introduced and as changes in patient care reduce potential risk in areas targeted for improvements.

Efforts to reduce the high costs and inefficiency associated with the two stage method of screening many medical charts also led to the development of occurrence reporting. In this approach, generic or service specific criteria are developed for the reporting of significant adverse clinical events by physicians and other health care providers.[221] There is a growing medical literature documenting and comparing the effectiveness of various approaches to significant clinical adverse event detection,[20–23] and some empirical evidence that the "early warning" provided by timely event detection can help facilitate the claims resolution process.[24]

To be most useful for targeting and evaluating risk management activities, the number of adverse events should be analysed, and trends over time displayed, according to the type of occurrence, location of the event, severity of the injury, time of day, and shift on which the incident occurred, as well as the relevant characteristics of the patients and staff concerned.[225] As more organisations begin to collect this type of information, it may become possible to identify particular problem areas not only through the analyses of trends with time within the organisation, but also through comparisons with peer institutions.

Currently there are substantial efforts among hospitals, multihospital systems, and accrediting bodies to develop comparable adverse event information that should help facilitate meaningful comparisons and better interpretation of data. Both the JCAHO and The Maryland Hospital Association, for example, have developed core sets of "clinical indicators" that can be commonly defined and that will permit meaningful comparisons among hospitals with similar characteristics.[17 26]

Liability claims

Analyses of the frequency and types of medical liability claims have long been used to target risk management efforts. An early example is a study conducted by the National Association of Insurance Commissioners (NAIC) of all medical malpractice claims closed by United States insurers during 1975–8.[8] The NAIC study, as well as more limited data from individual insurers, provided an initial information base supporting the development of both quality assurance and risk management programmes targeted towards physicians in hospital settings, particularly those involved in obstetrics and other surgical specialties and anaesthesiology. The more recent analysis by the United States General Accounting Office of a national sample of claims closed by United States insurers in 1984 also suggested the appropriateness of this focus.[27]

Although an important objective of risk management programmes is to decrease the frequency and reduce the consequences of medical liability claims, evaluating the effectiveness of efforts to accomplish these goals presents challenges. Of fundamental importance—whether examining trends with time within the same institution, or comparing claim patterns across multiple institutions—is ensuring comparability by resolving the following issues:

Defining whether a claim has occurred A claim is most often defined as a demand for monetary compensation for an injury due to alleged provider negligence. It is important to note, however, that this definition is not used uniformly either by institutions or insurers, due to several factors. Often a file may be established by an institution or an insurer after the identification or notification of an adverse event in the absence of a demand for compensation from a patient or attorney. These files may facilitate investigating and tracking adverse events thought likely to eventually result in demands for payment. When such files are established, however, sometimes may be a reflection of the provider's type of liability coverage. Claims made liability insurance policies cover only those claims filed in the policy year, regardless of the date of injury. By contrast, occurrence based policies cover all claims arising from incidents during the policy year, regardless of the date that payment is requested (that the claim is filed).[12] A health care provider or institution insured under a claims made policy is particularly likely to notify its liability insurer of such events in order to have the

114

incidents covered under the current policy in the likelihood that payments are eventually demanded. The presence of these "warning files" may or may not be included in both open and closed claim frequency statistics, creating uncertainty regarding the validity of comparisons across institutions and time periods.

Distinguishing between incidents and defendants Ambiguity is also created by a lack of uniformity regarding whether claims are defined in terms of the incident (event) that resulted in the alleged injury, or in terms of the providers—including individuals and institutions—named as defendant(s). A claim for payment resulting from a single adverse incident may include multiple defendants, whose liability coverage may be provided by different insurers. Medical liability claims filed in the Maryland legal system, for example, include on average, two or three defendants. If, in a multiple defendant case, each defendant is counted as one claim (as is most often the case in liability insurer data bases), claim frequency obviously will be higher than in data systems in which claims are counted in terms of incidents.

It is also important to note that statistics generated from defendant based claims will weight the characteristics of each incident (such as location where the incident occurred) by the number of defendants involved who are present in the data base. It may facilitate different types of analyses if defendants and incidents are tracked and analysed in separate data files. Comparisons with time or across institutions must use a standard definition, whether incident based or defendant based.

Selecting claims from the most appropriate time frame Evaluations of the effectiveness of risk management activities for improving claims experience must select claims from the most appropriate time frame in order to analyse possible changes in claim frequency and characteristics. The date used to classify claims may be based on the period in which any of the following events occurred: incident resulting in the claim; awareness of the event by the provider/institution; notification of the insurer that the incident occurred; patient complaint; receipt of demand for compensation; filing of claim/suit; claim resolution through private settlement, arbitration award, or jury verdict.

If the objectives of particular risk management efforts are to decrease claim frequency by reducing the number of adverse events, then it is critical to examine only those claims resulting from

115

incidents occurring during the period in which the risk management activities were in place. As noted previously, accomplishing this objective may require a long time frame to capture all claims emerging from a particular incident year. The amount of time required to observe claims emergence will typically depend on several factors, including the type of care provided (for example, claims in obstetrics typically emerge more slowly than claims resulting from anaesthesia), as well as laws governing the statute of limitations for filing claims within the jurisdiction. It is worth noting that assigning a date to "when the incident occurred" is not always a straightforward matter, particularly when the allegation involves an error of omission (for example, failure to diagnose breast cancer) and the patient and provider relations extended over a relatively long time period.

Claim payments and expenses

Evaluating the effectiveness of risk management activities with respect to changes in claim payments with time, or by comparison with similar institutions, involves many of the same issues associated with the analysis of claim frequency. In addition, the following issues may be relevant:

- Comparisons with time should be made in "constant dollars" (for example, deflated to 1990 dollars) in order to take into consideration general or medical price inflation that is likely to influence liability claim payments
- The distribution of claim payments is likely to be highly skewed due to the presence of one or more very large awards or settlements. Because the presence of such "outliers" is likely to have a disproportionate influence on evaluation results, it may be desirable to "cap" claim payments at a certain level for purposes of the analysis, or to include very large payments in a separate analysis
- In evaluations of the effectiveness of risk management activities during a given period, it will often be the case that some of the claims resulting from incidents during that time frame are still open. It is common among liability insurers and self insured institutions to use reserve amounts to estimate payments for claims that are still open at the time of the analysis. This is generally preferable to omitting open claims from the analysis, but it is important to update the analysis as actual payment data become available.

Expenses

A frequent objective of risk management programmes is to reduce the costs of claims management. Evaluating the effectiveness of these efforts requires tracking the direct costs involved in managing each claim, whether or not the claim resolves with compensation to the claimant. Liability insurers commonly track allocated loss adjustment expenses, which include the following costs: attorney's fees, expert medical testimony, providing evidence such as medical examination of the claimant and necessary laboratory tests, obtaining and compensating witnesses, subpoenas and court fees, and document reproduction.[12] They do not include "overhead" costs of the liability insurer or risk management staff such as salaries or space costs.

Allocated loss adjustment expenses are likely to be less for claims that are filed shortly after the alleged incident, for claims in which there was rapid identification of the adverse (early warning), and for claims in which a resolution is attained relatively rapidly. Because these three factors are so important in determining allocated loss adjustment expenses, and may be important in influencing claim outcomes, risk management programmes are likely to want to assess their effectiveness in terms of their ability to reduce the average time to claims emergence or to increase the proportion of claims for which they received "early warning," as well as to reduce the time required for claim resolution.

Other outcome measures

There are various other outcome measures that can potentially be used to assess the effectiveness of risk management. For some institutions, reducing or stabilising the amount paid in liability insurance premiums may be viewed as a key longer term outcome. Others have suggested that in addition to preventing claims, hospital risk management programmes may help create better public relations and patient satisfaction, improve the institution's ability to attract and retain medical and other staff, and aid in compliance with regulatory and accreditation standards.[29]

Although quantifying the impact of risk management activities is likely to be difficult, it may be useful for programmes to document and try to track the results of their efforts in these areas.

Measuring the degree of risk exposure

To make meaningful comparisons of risk management outcome

117

indicators over time or across institutions, it is necessary to take into consideration variation in levels of activity that create exposure to the risk of adverse events or claims. Most often, the numbers of adverse events and claims are related to the most appropriate activity level indicator such as number of occupied beds, patient days, admissions, or ambulatory visits. Then, for a given period, ratios are calculated of outcomes (such as numbers of incidents or claims) to levels of activity.[25] It is often desirable to develop additional ratios of outcomes to activity levels for high risk locations such as obstetrics or emergency departments. As knowledge is gained regarding the predictors of adverse events and claims within the institution of the insuring entity, it may be possible to develop more sensitive indicators of risk exposure than general activity level measures. For example, The St Paul Fire and Marine Insurance Company, the largest liability insurer of United States hospitals, has now developed indicators of risk exposure based on actual inpatient diagnoses and types of outpatient visits, and intends to use these measures in establishing liability insurance premiums instead of relying on numbers of occupied beds and outpatient visits.[30]

Comparisons across hospitals must consider not only differences in activity levels—particularly in high risk areas—but also variability in other factors that are known to be associated with higher levels of adverse events or claims. In the United States, for example, there are significant regional, as well as urban–rural differences in the liability claims experiences of physicians and hospitals.[7][31] Luft et al, in an analysis of 212 hospitals in California, found that claims expenses were significantly higher for children's specialty hospitals, those with large intensive care units and newborn intensive care units, and institutions owned by "for profit" companies.[32] Other factors such as teaching status, surgery volumes, and staffing patterns had no significant effect, with the exception of whether the hospital had under contract a physician with responsibility for serving as a liaison officer with the medical staff. The presence of such an arrangement was associated with significantly lower claim costs. A study of 51 New York hospitals by Brennan et al found that by comparison with community hospitals, university hospitals had higher adverse event rates, but lower rates due to negligence.[33] Rural location and size were also associated with lower rates of adverse events.

In addition, there is a growing medical literature which suggests that, at least for some procedures and diagnoses, higher volumes are associated with better quality outcomes.[34][35] Thus greater activity levels, particularly in high risk areas, may be associated with greater *numbers* of adverse events and claims, but they may also result in lower adverse event and claim *rates*.

Measuring risk management programmes and processes

A very useful guide for developing process and outcomes measures for programme self assessments has been developed by the American Society for Healthcare Risk Management.[25] This self assessment manual suggests several process measures that can be used to evaluate risk management activities in five programme areas: risk management programme organisation, risk identification and analysis, loss prevention, risk financing, and claims management. The manual helps risk managers identify the activities that occur or that should occur within each programme component, and suggests potential process and outcome measures for assessing the effectiveness of each activity. For example, in the programme activity area of loss identification, the risk manager can indicate whether an incident reporting form exists, and if reporting procedures are in place. Suggested process measures might include reporting rates, such as number of incidents per patient day or per occupied bed; whereas the associated outcome measure might determine the percentage of actual claims identified soon after the alleged adverse event.

Previous evaluations of risk management effectiveness

As noted earlier, there is little empirical evidence regarding the degree to which hospital risk management activities actually result in a more positive malpractice claims experience. One attempt to document the effectiveness of risk management efforts in anaesthesiology has been conducted by the Risk Management Foundation of the Harvard Medical Institutions. This study reported on a project begun in 1983 in which chiefs of anaesthesiology at the Harvard teaching hospitals formed a committee to investigate strategies for minimising accidents, errors, and patient injuries associated with anaesthesia.[36] The committee developed clinical standards for monitoring patients during anaesthesia based on a review of case summaries from previous malpractice claims. The standards were then implemented throughout the Harvard system in the spring of 1985.

The average loss per anaesthesia related claim during the decade before the establishment of this programme was about $153 000; during the 33 month period after implementation of the programme the average cost per claim was about $34 000. The savings resulted in a reduction of liability insurance premiums of about one third for anaesthesiologists in the Harvard system.

The relations between hospital wide risk management activities and subsequent claims experience have been examined in a study of 40 community hospitals in Maryland.[37] Due to the time often required after incidents occur for claims to emerge and resolve, it was decided to use the earliest systematic information available on hospital risk management activities—a 1980 survey of all hospitals in the state conducted by the state hospital association. Survey responses included information on the role of the governing board in risk management activities, risk management programme components, hospital policies for handling adverse medical incidents, and educational programmes offered by the hospital in quality assurance and risk management. Forty seven hospitals returned usable questionnaires to the hospital association. To limit the analysis to a relatively homogeneous sample, responses were only used from the group of 40 general acute care medical/surgical hospitals, representing 82% of all such institutions in the state.

The professional liability experience of each hospital was assessed through data on claims resulting from hospital based incidents (whether or not the hospital was named as a defendant) that occurred during 1980–2, and that were completely resolved by the end of 1987. Information on claims filed in the legal system was available from the files of the state's health claims arbitration office, and from the court files in Maryland's 24 jurisdictions. Information on claims settled privately, either before filing in the legal system or during the formal claims resolution process, was obtained from 13 liability insurance carriers who provided around 85% of the professional liability insurance available in the state during the study period. All claims information was aggregated to the hospital level, and the following indicators of medical liability claims experience were constructed for each hospital: total number of filed claims per 100 beds, number of filed claims settled privately per 100 beds, number of filed claims per 100 beds that received a verdict favouring the claimant, total dollars awarded in the court system per bed, and total dollars in private settlements per bed.

These indicators were examined for all claims arising from hospital based incidents, and separately, for only those claims in which hospitals were named as defendants.

Claims experience was adjusted for hospital differences in risk exposure by including information in the analysis on the number of beds in a hospital, as well as the volume of services provided in high risk locations. Both Maryland and national United States data indicated that during this period hospital related claims were most likely to result from incidents during surgical and obstetric procedures and from occurrences in emergency departments and patient rooms.[8 27] Information on the volume of services delivered during 1980–2 was obtained for each hospital from the state hospital reporting system. Data from this system were obtained for each hospital on the total number of surgical minutes (the total amount of time that operating suites were in use), the total number of obstetric procedures, and the number of emergency department visits. Hospitals were ranked on each of these dimensions, and the three ranks were averaged to form a combined indicator of the likelihood that a claim would be filed (exposure to claim risk). Hospital size was taken into consideration by dividing each of the malpractice claims experience indicators by the average number of beds set up and staffed during 1980–2 in each hospital.

Results indicate that after adjusting for differences in exposure to claim risk, the total number of claims experienced was lower in institutions that had implemented in hospital programmes regarding physician and nurse responsibilities in quality assurance and risk management. Both the number of claims in which defendants were found liable and the total amount of dollars awarded in damages were significantly less in hospitals that by 1980 had established a governing board oversight committee for quality assurance and risk management, that included information on risk management in regular reports sent to the governing board, and that had a formal policy indicating that clinical chiefs must be notified of adverse medical incidents. In addition, the number of claims in which defendants were found liable was significantly lower for hospitals that had formal policies indicating whether patients or families should be informed of medical errors, and specifying who had responsibility for communicating such information.

It is important to note that there are corresponding strengths and limitations, or "trade offs", associated with each of the major features of this study design. A major strength is the relatively long

121

follow up period which allowed for the emergence and resolution of most claims resulting from incidents close in time to when the risk management programme activities were measured. A corresponding disadvantage with this approach, however, is that by definition, this strategy becomes a historical analysis that cannot take into consideration what might be more timely and state of the art risk management programme activities.

In addition, this study included only a few hospitals in a single state. The advantage of such an approach is that it facilitates comparisons of hospitals with and without particular risk management programme activities by, in effect, controlling for (or holding constant) some legal, regulatory, and other state specific factors that might affect claiming behaviour or the claims resolution process. The inclusion of only one state, however, obviously may limit generalisability of the results. A third strength of the study is the ability to take into consideration through statistical controls several indicators of each hospital's exposure to claims risk. This represents a relatively new area of inquiry, however, and there is little guidance available on the most appropriate patient and provider related indicators that should be used in analyses of claims experience.

Although it is important to acknowledge the limitations inherent in this study's evaluation design, the findings have provided some of the first evidence available for several key tenets in the literature on clinical risk management. These include the importance of educating clinicians regarding their role in risk management efforts; formalising channels of communication that can facilitate early intervention if needed with patients and families following adverse medical events; and establishing a strong organisational structure for using information on unanticipated adverse occurrences.

Possible lessons from the American experience

Perhaps the most important lessons that have been learned from the past 30 years of experience in the United States with these issues are the following:

● The number of medical liability claims filed represents only a small fraction of the number of adverse events in patient care that are likely to be due to provider errors, and it is common for such claims to be filed several years after such events occurred. Therefore, efforts to improve patient safety and the quality of medical care, as well as to reduce the number of claims likely to result from negligent care, must depend on some system for the identification and analysis of adverse events without depending on claim filing to provide notice of such incidents

- Of all claims filed, the great majority are likely to result from adverse events unrelated to provider errors. This pattern also suggests the importance of a system of early identification and analysis that can trigger risk management efforts, including appropriate communication with injured patients and family members

- Evaluating the effectiveness of risk management strategies will typically involve the examination of trends over time within one institution, cross sectional comparisons among institutions, and the examination of trends over time across multiple institutions. The last approach has the strongest evaluation design in that it may help control for environmental or temporal factors (such as legal reforms or population changes) that may influence claiming behaviour. Any of these evaluation designs, however, require uniformity in definitions, as well as methods for considering variation over time or across institutions in the exposure to claim risk

- Although monitoring at the level of a single institution may be optimal for identifying individual providers with a history of serious adverse events or liability claims who should be flagged for further review, comparisons of larger data bases with multiple institutions are likely to be of greater utility in identifying suboptimal procedures or patterns of care.

Current issues in risk management evaluation

Risk management programmes in health care are currently in a period of experimentation, in which there are various approaches both for the detection of adverse patient events and for how to use such information. There are few empirical studies reagrding the efficacy of alternative approaches, either as mechanisms for the "early warning" of claims activity or in terms of their usefulness for reducing claims or improving the quality of patient care.

Among the issues which must be further investigated are the relative advantages of "broad based" clinical incident reporting, more focused reporting, and occurrence screening approaches to detection of adverse event; as well as how improvements can be made in the use of information available through these strategies for the management and prevention of malpractice claims.

An area of intense controversy within the medical profession has been whether the development of guidelines or standards for clinical performance will result in decreased or increased malpractice claims activity.[31 38] The careful monitoring of this issue must be another area of high priority for healthcare risk managers.

To date, most approaches to detection of adverse events and other risk management strategies have been hospital based efforts. At the same time that risk managers have been developing more sophisticated approaches to hospital based issues and problems, an increasing number of services are rapidly moving outside the hospital setting.[39] A continuing challenge is likely to be the design, implementation, and evaluation of risk management strategies appropriate for the entire continuum of care settings.

Partial support for this review was provided by the Agency for Health Care Policy and Research, the Public Health Service, Department of Health and Human Services under Grant Number 1 RO1 HS06735.

1 Bader and Associates Inc. *Patient safety manual: a guide for hospitals and physicians to a systematic approach to quality assurance and risk management.* 2nd ed. Chicago: American College of Surgeons, 1985.

2 Orlikoff JE, Vanagunas AM. *Malpractice prevention and liability control for hospitals.* 2nd ed. Chicago: American Hospital Publishing Inc, 1988.

3 Kilduff R. Clinical risk management—a practical approach. Chicago: InterQual Inc, 1985.

4 American Medical Association Special Task Force on Professional Liability and Insurance. *Professional liability in the 80s. Report I.* Chicago: American Medical Association, 1984.

5 US Congress, Office of Technology Assessment. *The quality of medical care: information for consumers.* Washington DC: US Government Printing Office, 1988.

6 Mills DH, ed. California Medical Association and California Hospital Association. *Report on the medical insurance feasibility study.* San Francisco: Sutter Publications, 1977.

7 Danzon PM. *Medical malpractice: theory, evidence and public policy.* Cambridge: Harvard University Press, 1985.

8 National Association of Insurance Commissioners. Malpractice claims: medical malpractice closed claims, 1975–8. Brookfield, WI: National Association of Insurance Commissioners, 1980.

9 Brennan TA, Leape LL, Laird NM, *et al.* Incidence of adverse events and negligence in hospitalized patients: results of the Harvard medical practice study I. *N Engl J Med* 1991;324:370–7.

10 Leape LL, Brennan TA, Laird N, *et al.* The nature of adverse events in hospitalized patients: results of the Harvard medical practice study II. *N Engl J Med* 1991;324:377–84.

11 Localio AR, Lawthers AG, Brennan TA, *et al.* Relation between malpractice claims and adverse events due to negligence: results of the Harvard medical practice study III. *N Engl J Med* 1991;**325**:245–51.

12 Department of Health and Human Services. *Report of the task force on medical liability and malpractice.* Washington, DC: DHHS, 1987.

13 Farber HS, White MJ. Medical malpractice: An empirical examination of the litigation process. Cambridge MA: The National Bureau of Economic Research Working Papers Series (Working paper No 3428), 1990.

14 Morlock LL, Lindgren O, Mills DH. Malpractice, clinical risk management, and quality assessment. In: Goldfield N, Nash D, eds. *Providing quality care: the challenge to clinicians.* Philadelphia: American College of Physicians, 1989.

15 Sanazaro PJ, Mills DH. A critique of the use of generic screening in quality assessment. *JAMA* 1991;**265**:1977–81.

16 Craddick JW. *Medical management analysis series.* Vol II: *Improving quality and resource management through medical management analysis.* Rockville MD: Medical Management Analysis International Inc, 1987.

17 Joint Commission on Accreditation of Healthcare Organisations. IMsystem general information. Oakbrook Terrace IL: JCAHO, 1995.

18 Panniers TL, Newlander J. The adverse patient occurrences inventory: validity, reliability, and implications. *Qual Rev Bull* 1986;**12**:311–5.

19 Schumacher DN, Parker B, Kofie V, Munns JM. Severity of illness index and the adverse patient occurrence index. *Med Care* 1987;**25**:695–704.

20 Sicher CM, Sisters of Mercy Health Corporation. *Approaches to patient care assessment in a multihospital system.* Chicago: Joint Commission on Accreditation of Healthcare Organisations, 1987.

21 American Hospital Association. *Medical malpractice task force report on tort reform and compendium of professional liability early warning systems for health care providers.* Chicago: American Hospital Association, 1986.

22 Vanagunas A, Halleen N. CHRPP complete study of concurrent monitoring. *Occurrence* 1986;**1**:1–5.

23 Nadzam DM, Turpin R, Hanold L, White R. Data driven performance improvement in health care: The Joint Commission's indicator measurement system. *Joint Commission Journal of Quality Improvement* 1993;**19**:492–500.

24 Lindgren OH, Christensen R, Mills DH. Medical malpractice risk management early warning systems. *Law and Contemporary Problems* 1991;**54**:23–41.

25 American Society for Healthcare Risk Management. *ASHRM risk management self-assessment manual.* Chicago: American Hospital Association, 1991.

26 Maryland Hospital Association. *Guidebook for quality indicator data: a continuous improvement model.* Lutherville MD: Maryland Hospital Association, 1990.

27 United States General Accounting Office. *Medical malpractice: characteristics of claims closed in 1984.* Washington DC: GAO, 1987.

28 Danzon PM. The frequency and severity of medical malpractice claims: new evidence. *Law and Contemporary Problems* 1986;**49**:57–84.

29 Hudson T. Objective measures prove value of risk management. *Hospitals* 1991; **64**:34–40.

30 St Paul Medical Services, St Paul Fire and Marine Insurance Company. *1994 Hospital Update.* St Paul, MN: St Paul Medical Services, 1994.

31 US Congress, Office of Technology Assessment. *Defensive medicine and medical malpractice.* Washington, DC: US Government Printing Office, July 1994. (OTA II 602).

32 Luft HS, Katz PP, Pinney DG. Risk factors for hospital malpractice exposure: implications for managers and insurers. *Law and Contemporary Problems* 1991; **54**:43–64.

33 Brennan TA, Hebert LE, Laird NM, *et al.* Hospital characteristics associated with adverse events and substandard care. *JAMA* 1991;**265**:3266–9.

34 Luft HS, Hunt SS. Evaluating individual hospital quality through outcome statistics. *JAMA* 1986;**255**:2780–4.
35 Luft HS, Garnick DW, Mark DH, McPhee SJ, *et al. Hospital volume, physician volume, and patient outcomes. Hospital volume.* Ann Arbor MI: Health Administration Press, 1990.
36 Holzer JF. Liability insurance issues in anesthesiology. *Int Anesthesiol Clin* 1989; **27**:205–12.
37 Morlock LL, Malitz FE. Do hospital risk management programs make a difference?: relationships between risk management program activities and hospital malpractice claims experience. *Law and Contemporary Problems* 1991; **54**:1–22.
38 Brennan TA. Practice guidelines and malpractice litigation: Collision or cohesion? *J Health Polit Policy Law* 1991;**16**:67–85.
39 Stoeckle JD. The citadel cannot hold: technologies go outside the hospital, patients and doctors too. *Milbank Q* 1995;**73**:3–17.

II: Reducing risk in clinical practice

8 Reducing risk in obstetrics

JAMES DRIFE

Maternity care is changing. In 1994 the government accepted an expert report called *Changing Childbirth*,[1] which recommended giving women more choice in their care. In future more care will probably be provided by midwives without direct medical supervision. Some midwives foresee an increase in home deliveries; others want to encourage a return to small maternity units run by general practitioners; still others advocate midwifery group practices independent of doctors.

These changes are not a response to increasing obstetric litigation but are the result of pressure from consumer groups and midwives. Many obstetricians and general practitioners are apprehensive about the trend, fearing that dismantling the established system—even partially—will compromise its high standards of safety for mothers and babies.

Therefore anyone setting out to reduce risk in obstetrics in the late 1990s faces a challenging task. He or she will receive conflicting advice from obstetricians, general practitioners, midwives, and consumer groups and will have to work with a system in which no individual manager or group of clinicians has overall control. Nevertheless, a time of change represents an opportunity for introducing new ways of reducing risk.

Risk reduction requires identification and analysis of patterns of risk, followed by improvements in clinical practice focused on the problem areas.[2] In obstetrics we can identify risk areas in current practice but we can only guess at the risks of the proposed changes. Improvements directed towards risk reduction will have to be implemented in conjunction with changes that are already in progress.

In Britain almost all mothers now survive pregnancy, as do 99% of babies. Between 1935 and 1985 the British maternal mortality rate fell from 1 in 200 pregnancies to 1 in 10 000 pregnancies, and the perinatal mortality rate from 60 per 1000 to under 10 per 1000. These dramatic improvements in safety have led to a change in people's expectations. Women now want childbirth to be an emotionally rewarding experience. Nevertheless, almost all women put safety at the top of their list of priorities.

Women also know that caesarean section is no longer an operation fraught with risk, and for more and more women "choice" means freedom to request a caesarean delivery. Such women are underrepresented in consumer groups, which tend to blame obstetricians for the steady rise in Britain's rate of caesarean section—now about 15% and showing no sign of levelling off. Research on women's views through "decision analysis" discloses that women are willing to opt for caesarean section at lower levels of risk than many obstetricians thought.[3]

Current pattern of care

Pregnancy care can be divided into three parts: antenatal care, intrapartum care, and postnatal care. Currently, these are resourced according to tradition rather than logic.

Antenatal care

Much effort is put into antenatal care, which is usually shared between hospital, general practitioner, and community midwife. Clinic visits are monthly in the first two thirds of pregnancy and more frequent thereafter, so that a healthy woman may make more than a dozen visits to the clinic. This traditional pattern is not based on scientific evidence,[4] and some obstetricians contend that it is of dubious benefit.[5]

At each visit the mother is checked for complications such as diabetes and hypertension. Fetal growth is checked by palpation of the uterus, though this misses about a quarter of cases of growth retardation. The fetal condition can be more accurately checked by cardiotocography, ultrasound measurements, and blood flow

130

assessment. These require the mother to spend time in the ultrasound or fetal assessment unit: they are therefore not used routinely but only in cases of high risk.

Care in labour

Almost all British babies are born in National Health Service (NHS) hospitals, and around 70% are delivered by midwives. Home delivery accounts for less than 1% of births in Britain and private obstetric practice for very few. Intrapartum care is crucially important to reducing risk but is often provided by staff under stress because of limited resources and minimal consultant support.

Fetal monitoring during labour

The fetal condition in labour is assessed through the fetal heart rate, auscultated by the midwife every 15 minutes. She also observes the colour of the amniotic fluid, which is normally clear but turns green if the fetus releases meconium (bowel contents)—a possible sign of lack of oxygen. This is one of the reasons for artificial rupture of the membranes early in labour, though some women refuse this as they feel it makes labour unnatural. Abnormalities of fetal heart rate or amniotic fluid are the traditional signs of "fetal distress", a vague term which lacks a single precise definition.

Electronic fetal monitoring, in widespread use for over 20 years,[6] entails continuous recording of the fetal heart rate. Signs of fetal distress are reduced heart rate variability, a rate that is too fast or too slow, or decelerations that are not synchronous with uterine contractions.

These abnormalities, however, are not diagnostic of fetal distress. Even with the most sinister abnormalities there is only a 50% chance that the fetus is deprived of oxygen. Thus if electronic fetal monitoring is the sole guide to fetal condition, unnecessary caesarean sections or instrumental deliveries will be done. Electronic fetal monitoring was intended as a screening test to decide which babies should be assessed by fetal blood sampling.

Fetal blood sampling is technically more difficult than electronic fetal monitoring, entailing inserting a tubular instrument through the cervix, stabbing the baby's scalp with a guarded blade, collecting a blood sample and analysing it in a machine which has to be carefully maintained. Not every unit that uses electronic fetal monitoring has access to fetal blood sampling.

131

Electronic fetal monitoring is important in high risk labour, but its use in low risk labour has been controversial. A large study of electronic fetal monitoring in low risk cases in Dublin in 1985 showed that the rate of stillbirths in the monitored group was no different from that in the unmonitored group.[7]

Nevertheless, nowadays a woman in the low risk category is often checked with a short interval of electronic fetal monitoring on admission to the labour ward. A normal trace is reassuring. Newer ways of assessing the fetal condition are being investigated,[8] but electronic fetal monitoring is likely to be the mainstay of intrapartum assessment for many years.

Instrumental delivery and caesarean section

Rates of caesarean section and instrumental delivery can vary widely between hospitals. For example, in 1983 the rate of forceps delivery was 6·5% in one Dublin hospital, 16·3% in a neighbouring hospital, and 21% in Birmingham Maternity Hospital; perinatal mortality rates in all three hospitals were similar.[9] Of course, different hospitals serve different populations, some with a high proportion of patients from ethnic minority groups, but this is unlikely to explain such wide variations in clinical practice.

Rates of forceps delivery fell sharply in the late 1970s in British hospitals, but rates of caesarean section rose steadily from 6–7% in the mid-1970s to 10–15% in the early 1990s.[10] At the same time perinatal mortality fell but not necessarily as a consequence of more caesarean sections.[11] As O'Driscoll and Foley pointed out, in the National Maternity Hospital in Dublin perinatal mortality fell during the 1970s with no increase in the rate of caesarean section.[12]

Postnatal care

The lying in period has been greatly reduced over the years. The community midwife has a statutory duty to visit women for 10 days after delivery but postnatal care is the Cinderella of the service: much of the morbidity of pregnancy occurs after delivery but little of it is recognised by health professionals.[13]

Standardisation of practice

Obstetric management varies between consultants and between hospitals. Case notes also vary, though there are now moves to standardise maternity notes throughout England. Many British hospitals have labour ward guidelines. There is no national protocol because consensus would be hard to achieve, particularly regarding the balance between "natural childbirth" and "active management". Some midwives dislike protocols, thinking that they limit individual judgement, and some doctors fear that national guidelines would make it easier for plaintiffs to sue hospitals.

Effective Care in Pregnancy and Childbirth, a landmark book published in 1989, applied science to the debates about different styles of practice. It attempted to review all published and, indeed, unpublished trials of obstetric management.[14] With a continuously updated database in electronic form, and including lists of interventions of established effectiveness, those that are unproved, and those that are definitely ineffective; it has been called "the most important book in obstetrics to appear this century".[15]

Staffing

Midwives

Community midwives are usually attached to one or more groups of general practitioners. Hospital midwives work shifts which may change during a woman's labour, and most women are delivered by a midwife they have never met before. Flexible schemes have been introduced, such as the "domino" scheme, in which the community midwife accompanies the woman to hospital and supervises the delivery and her return home a few hours later.[16]

General practitioners

To qualify for the "obstetric list" a general practitioner must have completed a six month training post in a maternity hospital. Most general practitioners want to be involved in antenatal care but only a few in intrapartum care.

Hospital doctors

Hospital medical staffing is hierarchical, and the most junior doctor is first on call. He or she will have been qualified for at least a year but may have only a few months' obstetric experience. Larger obstetric units also have a resident middle grade doctor—usually a registrar with several years' obstetric experience. There is a limit on the number of registrar posts in the United Kingdom. Some registrars are doctors from overseas, mainly from the Commonwealth although more are coming from Europe. The Royal College of Obstetricians and Gynaecologists has urged that no registrar should have duties on more than one site simultaneously.

Consultants are on call from home at night, and their involvement in the labour ward during the day is variable. The royal college now recommends that all labour wards should have dedicated consultant sessions, but as yet this recommendation has been implemented patchily. Some consultants carry out a labour ward round every morning but there is no official requirement for this.

Relationships between health professionals

Midwives are independent practitioners but are bound by the Midwives' Rules to call a doctor when they judge this necessary.[17] An experienced midwife in hospital may have to call an inexperienced doctor. Usually this does not cause problems, but sometimes midwives are required to call a doctor unnecessarily because of hospital policy.[18] Conversely, a midwife may be frustrated by a doctor who does not respond appropriately to her concerns: yet she may be reluctant to "go over the head" of a junior doctor to a more senior doctor.

Audit in obstetrics

For many years obstetricians led the way in audit. Confidential enquiries into maternal deaths have been systematically carried out for over 40 years to identify and correct avoidable factors. National reports are published every three years.[19] Most maternity hospitals hold regular meetings at which doctors and midwives review cases of stillbirth and neonatal death, again with the aim of improving practice to prevent similar future events. As obstetric care has improved, however, these meetings have become less useful, and it has been suggested that hospitals should discuss "near misses", in which the mother has been at risk or the baby has been delivered in poor condition.[20] Identifying such cases consistently is difficult,[21] and "near miss" meetings are not yet widespread.

Complaints and litigation

Litigation is increasing in obstetrics.[22] Obstetric and gynaecological claims comprised around 20% of the workload of the Medical Protection Society before NHS indemnity: of these, 40% were obstetric claims.[23] The Medical Defence Union in the mid-1980s opened 9000 new files a year, of which some 600 related to obstetrics and gynaecology.[24]

Obstetric cases may involve very large settlements. A child who requires constant nursing and who has a normal expectation of life may be awarded over £1m in damages, and the resultant publicity may encourage other people towards litigation. Such large awards give the impression of serious clinical incompetence, even though a case may be settled because of a minor lapse in care.

Causes of litigation (box 1)

Stillbirth or handicap may arise from congenital abnormality, complications before labour, premature delivery, or lack of oxygen in labour. At present, premature delivery is almost impossible to predict and prevent but to some extent the other causes are theoretically preventable.

Box 1—Obstetric outcomes leading to litigation

Congenital abnormalities
Antepartum or intrapartum stillbirth or neonatal death
Mental handicap ("brain damage")

Congenital abnormalities

Congenital abnormalities could be reduced by prepregnancy counselling (for example, to improve diabetic control or give vitamin supplements to prevent spina bifida) or by prenatal diagnosis followed by termination of pregnancy. Prenatal diagnosis is now offered routinely in antenatal clinics in the form of an ultrasound scan—usually at 19 weeks' gestation—to detect fetal anomalies. The range of anomalies that can be detected is steadily increasing, but district hospitals may not match the standards of tertiary referral centres.

A woman who has an abnormal baby may blame the hospital for not offering her the appropriate test or not referring her to a tertiary centre. It has been suggested that blood testing for Down's

135

syndrome should be offered to all pregnant women,[25] but the decision to do so has financial and ethical implications. A decision not to offer testing to all women may be made by a committee of doctors or managers, or both.

Antepartum causes of stillbirth

Death in utero before labour sometimes has a specific cause such as maternal diabetes or infection. When a stillbirth occurs maternity hospitals have a protocol of tests on the baby and mother but, nevertheless, a cause may not be identified. Growth retardation may be recognised after delivery but, as mentioned, its diagnosis before delivery can be difficult.

Intrapartum stillbirth

Uncommon in modern practice in Britain, occasional cases of intrapartum stillbirth still occur: it has been suggested that a rate of one in 1000 deliveries is an "irreducible minimum." Human error is often to blame. There may be failure to recognise abnormalities in fetal heart rate which seem glaringly obvious in retrospect. Nevertheless, some obstetric disasters are hard to predict and cannot be prevented.

Handicap

As far as litigation is concerned handicap is more important than stillbirth. A large proportion of cases of mental handicap (often misleadingly called "brain damage") are due to genetic causes—that is, the problem lies in abnormal development of the brain and not in outside influences. Prenatal diagnosis has only a limited role—for example, counselling before pregnancy may detect a risk due to consanguineous marriage, and tests can detect Down's syndrome during pregnancy, but other types of mental handicap cannot be detected by ultrasound or other tests during pregnancy.

Birth injury due to forceps can cause mental handicap if intracranial bleeding occurs, but direct injury is unlikely to be a cause without such bleeding. Intrapartum hypoxia is often blamed for causing mental handicap or cerebral palsy, but in fact less than 10% of cases of cerebral palsy are due to asphyxia.[26] Nevertheless, whatever the cause of the child's disability, a coincident abnormality may be evident on the cardiotocograph; if it was not acted on a court may link it with the child's subsequent condition and award damages to the child.

"Brain damage"

In cases of mental handicap the condition of the child in the days after birth may be crucial. The newborn baby is routinely assessed by the Apgar score, which notes the baby's colour, tone, breathing, heart rate, and response to stimulation but has little prognostic value. Taking a sample of blood from the umbilical cord and measuring its oxygen tension and pH gives a more accurate assessment but is not routine practice.

A better guide to prognosis is the baby's condition in the first days after delivery. Abnormal neurological signs may amount to hypoxic–ischaemic encephalopathy, a condition characterised by fits, excessive muscular tone, and poor feeding ability.[27 28] Ultrasound scans may show signs of bleeding within the brain and later cavitation due to lack of oxygen. It can be hard to tell whether such deprivation of oxygen occurred during or before labour.

Freeman and Nelson[29] suggested that if "brain damage" is due to asphyxia four questions should be answered positively:

(1) Is there evidence of pronounced and prolonged intrapartum asphyxia?
(2) Did the infant show signs of moderate or severe hypoxic–ischaemic encephalopathy during the newborn period, with evidence also of asphyxial injury to other organ systems?
(3) Is the child's neurological condition one that intrapartum asphyxia could explain?
(4) Has the assessment been sufficient to rule out other conditions?

Deficiencies in care

Ennis and Vincent, reviewing 64 cases that came to litigation over stillbirth, perinatal or neonatal death, or other problems, identified three main concerns: inadequate fetal heart monitoring, mismanagement of forceps delivery, and inadequate supervision by senior staff.[30] In addition, women reported that sometimes staff were unsympathetic and gave too little information.[31]

Murphy *et al* carried out a study in which the intrapartum cardiotocographic records of severely asphyxiated babies were compared with those of healthy infants.[32] Investigators unaware of the clinical outcome agreed that abnormalities were present in the traces of 87% of the asphyxiated infants and 29% of the controls. They diagnosed severe abnormalities in 61% of the asphyxiated infants and 9% of the controls. Fetal blood sampling was indicated in 58% of cases in the asphyxia group but was actually carried out in only 16%. The response of staff to the abnormalities was slow, and the authors of this study concluded that "the interpretation of cardiotocographic records during labour continues to pose major problems for practising clinicians".

In a study of the training of obstetric senior house officers in teaching hospitals and district general hospitals Ennis found that most of these doctors received only one or two hours' teaching a week and some received even less.[33] Half of the doctors had had no formal training in interpreting or recognising abnormal or equivocal cardiotocograms. When questioned at the end of their jobs about training in the use of forceps, 23% of the senior house officers said they had had no training, and 35% of the remainder thought their training had been less than adequate. In a study of general practitioner trainees' views on hospital obstetric training Smith found that less than 40% believed at the end of their six months' training that they were competent to perform a simple forceps delivery, most believing that longer training was necessary for a general practitioner who wished to provide care in labour.[34]

Reducing risk

"The real answer to the question 'How to avoid medicolegal problems in obstetrics and gynaecology' is good practice and good communication."[35] Good practice is the best form of defence, and several improvements are necessary (box 2).

Focusing care

Resources need to be directed to where they are needed most. This applies, for example, to senior medical staff. Much of their time and attention has been devoted to antenatal care, on the basis that many problems during labour are predictable and preventable,

Box 2—Checklist for risk reduction

Equipment	—No obsolete monitors
	—Fetal blood gas equipment available
Staffing	—Minimal use of agency and "bank" staff
	—Workload includes time to talk to patients
Consultants' role	—Dedicated sessions in delivery suite
	—Sessions dedicated to training
Junior doctors' training	—Introductory training at start of post
	—Regular *protected* teaching sessions
	—Occasional "fire drill" exercises
	—Regular formal feedback on quality of training
Junior doctors' work	—Guidelines on routine and emergency practice
	—Formal handovers between shifts
	—Support from senior doctors and midwives
Midwives' work	—Regular training sessions on fetal monitoring
	—Clear definition of role vis a vis senior house officers
	—Senior midwife has access to duty consultant
Staff communication	—Regular delivery suite meetings
	—Teambuilding social occasions
Communication with patients	—Regular feedback from patients' advocates
	—Consultant promptly notified of problems
	—Explanations are consultant's responsibility

leading to "cattle market" antenatal clinics, and a detraction from intrapartum and postnatal care. The approach has raised patient expectations but has not abolished medicolegal problems. Most litigation arises from events in labour, and most dissatisfaction

139

arises from postnatal care (box 3). Strategies for risk reduction should focus on both these areas, but particularly on care in labour.

Box 3—Focusing care

- Most litigation arises from events in labour
- Most unhappiness arises from postnatal care

Equipment

Fetal monitoring equipment is often used long after it has become obsolete. The danger is that staff learn to mistrust unreliable equipment, making them slow to react to genuine abnormalities. An inventory of monitoring equipment should be maintained and there should be planned programmes of replacement.

Fetal blood sampling equipment should be available in all units that use electronic fetal monitoring. It is prone to technical problems and requires careful daily maintenance.

Consultant involvement in delivery

The royal college has recommended that new consultant contracts should in future include sessions in the delivery suite. The Department of Health is reducing the long hours worked by junior doctors in "hard pressed" specialties and consultant posts are being created to reduce the workload on the juniors. It will be far from easy, however, to ensure that these initiatives actually change working practices in hospital, as the pressures on consultants to delegate their duties in the labour ward will continue. The current NHS reforms may lead to closer scrutiny of doctors' work patterns, and this may enable consultants to avoid being drawn away from the delivery suite by other duties.

Training of junior doctors

The need for better training of senior house officers is becoming glaringly apparent. As NHS managers become more aware of the importance of risk management, pressure to improve training will increase. There has been excessive complacency in British hospital practice that learning by osmosis is adequate for junior doctors: the recent studies reviewed above disclose how far training is falling short of what is needed.

A distinction is needed between "teaching" (often directed towards future practice or examinations) and "training" to do the job in hand. The immediate need for risk management is to ensure that senior house officers are trained in interpreting cardiotocograms and in the procedures they are expected to undertake unsupervised.

Resources for teaching are now being identified more clearly and should in future be better directed as postgraduate deans' control budgets. It has been suggested that attitudes towards general practitioner training should change and that only those vocational trainees who wish to contribute to intrapartum care should be specially trained to do so.[36]

Specific requirements

(1) Training of new senior house officers should include an introductory session to orient them to the organisation of the hospital and to its clinical guidelines. Most hospitals already hold such sessions.

(2) Presently, teaching sessions for junior staff are often poorly attended due to pressure of clinical work. Arrangements should be in place to ensure that such sessions are not interfered with by other commitments.

(3) Some emergencies, such as major haemorrhage or eclampsia, occur so infrequently in most hospitals that staff do not get regular experience in dealing with them. Hospitals should have protocols to guide staff dealing with obstetric emergencies, and it may be helpful to hold irregular "fire drill" exercises to test how well these protocols work.

(4) There should be formal mechanisms for reviewing the effectiveness of training. District tutors of the royal college should liaise with postgraduate deans and hospital managers to ensure that weaknesses in training are identified and remedied.

Doctors' work

Guidelines

As mentioned above, most hospitals have guidelines for managing routine cases and emergencies. These should be regularly reviewed and updated.

Handovers

With the new restrictions on junior doctors' working hours, hospitals are introducing partial shifts and split weekends, increasing the need for formal handovers between medical teams at the start of each shift. Traditionally, such handovers have been part of nursing and midwifery practice: they should now be part of routine medical practice in the delivery suite.

Support

A problem that has received little attention is that a doctor managing a patient for a prolonged period may sometimes not notice signs that later seem obvious and important. This problem may be reduced by shorter shifts, as a new team will review problems with fresh eyes. It could also be tackled by the junior doctor reporting regularly to a senior doctor (perhaps by telephone) and by ensuring that the midwifery staff can speak directly to the duty consultant if they have any concerns.

Midwives' work

Antenatal care

Schemes are being introduced to standardise antenatal care while allowing it to be shared appropriately between midwife, hospital clinic, and general practitioner. These should include clear guidelines, agreed between midwives and doctors, about when medical referral is required.

Care in labour

In the delivery suite the use of electronic fetal monitoring seems likely to continue even if midwives gain more autonomy and run sections of the delivery suite without doctors in attendance. Many midwives do not feel comfortable with interpreting cardiotocograms, and better training is required to teach them which types of pattern require further investigation. Such training should not be provided as a "one off" session but should include regular revision and updating.

Some hospitals are relying increasingly on staff from a "bank" or a nursing agency. The dangers of this trend should be obvious: ensuring that temporary staff are adequately trained in the hospital's procedures is impossible, and reliance on them should be kept to an absolute minimum.

Relationships between midwives and doctors

Ideally, labour should be supervised by an experienced midwife who has immediate support from an experienced doctor.[37] The place of the inexperienced doctor in the labour ward will become more and more that of a trainee, learning from senior doctors and midwives.[36]

Generally, consultants and midwives have good working relationships, particularly in the private sector. To provide this level of cover in the NHS will require increased resources from health authorities, who will need to be educated that increased investment in experienced staff will save money in claims as well as providing a better service for women.

Specific measures

As mentioned, the senior midwife on duty should have direct access to the consultant on call.

The relationship between midwives and junior doctors can be made less difficult by having guidelines which define as clearly as possible their roles and responsibilities in each particular hospital. These guidelines should, of course, be drawn up by the consultants and midwives together.

Regular meetings should be held to review the work of the delivery suite. The atmosphere in perinatal mortality meetings and "near miss" meetings can be tense, and it is better to hold regular meetings to discuss interesting cases and matters of current concern as well as cases which have a poor outcome.

"Team building" is necessary in the delivery suite as in any other organisation where staff need to interact under pressure. Social occasions have an important part to play in this process. They occur infrequently, however, because doctors socialise with doctors and midwives with midwives. This problem needs to be recognised and addressed.

Communication with patients

The importance of a good rapport with the woman and her partner is now recognised, and communication is being given a higher priority by doctors as well as midwives. "The best protection for the doctor remains the one of talking to the patient and recording an outline of what is said."[38] Good communication is essential once a problem has arisen, but good rapport with women throughout pregnancy and labour will create a sound basis for full explanations if anything goes wrong.

Good communication as a routine

Midwives and doctors often feel offended if it is suggested that they are poor communicators. They protest that such skill is fundamental to their job. Nevertheless, they receive little feedback on these skills and often do not realise how they are perceived by women and their partners.

The delivery suite has the dual function of dealing with life threatening emergencies and creating a relaxed atmosphere for normal childbirth. These functions do not easily mix. Efficiency may be perceived as abruptness, and communication problems are likely to be worse if staff are under pressure. Communication takes time, and therefore adequate numbers of staff must be on duty.

There is a need for sessions providing feedback to staff from patients' advocates, who can tactfully identify any shortcomings in attitudes to women and their partners. This is particularly important in units dealing with a high proportion of patients from ethnic minorities.

Communication in problem cases

If a problem does arise, whether or not it is thought likely to lead to litigation, it should be notified as soon as possible to the consultant—ideally the woman's own consultant but if not, the consultant on duty. Whenever possible, explanations to the woman and her relatives should be given by the consultant, in conjunction with other staff as necessary. This is not to say that consultants are always the best communicators, but litigation sometimes arises because the woman feels the problem has not been taken seriously at a senior level.

A single explanation may not be enough, and it may be necessary for the same doctor to see the couple again to answer further questions. More often, however, the couple will ask the same questions of different members of staff. It is helpful if a note is made of what the patient has been told, so that unnecessary confusion can be avoided.

Conclusion

Pessimists will conclude that the current trend towards making care of pregnancy more relaxed is a recipe for disaster and that if we lose the safety first philosophy of the past 50 years we shall have slipshod care and more litigation as a consequence. Optimists, however, will contend that many of our current problems in obstetrics have resulted from too rigid a hierarchy, unrealistic expectations of the benefits of medicalisation, and a poor relationship with our clients—all of which could be improved by the changes now being implemented.

I belong to the optimistic group. Although *Changing Childbirth* was not inspired by the principles of risk management, it could well be a significant initiative in reducing risk—but only if its principles are implemented with care and cooperation among the health professionals involved.

1 Department of Health. *Changing childbirth*. London: HMSO, 1993.
2 Capstick B. Risk management in obstetrics. In: Clements RV, ed. *Safe practice in obstetrics and gynaecology: a medico-legal handbook*. Edinburgh: Churchill Livingstone, 1994:405–16.
3 Thornton JG. Measuring patients' values in reproductive medicine. *Contemporary Reviews in Obstetrics and Gynaecology* 1988;1:5–12.
4 Chamberlain G. Organisation of antenatal care. *BMJ* 1991;302:647–50.
5 Hall M. Is routine antenatal care worthwhile? *Lancet* 1980;ii:78–80.
6 Beard RW, Filshie GM, Knight CA, Roberts GM. The significance of the changes in the continuous fetal heart rate in the first stage of labour. *J Obstet Gynaecol Brit Commonw* 1971;78:865–81.
7 MacDonald D, Grant A, Sheridan-Pereira M, Boylan P, Chalmers I. The Dublin randomized controlled trial of intrapartum fetal heart rate monitoring. *Am J Obstet Gynecol* 1985;152:524–39.
8 Johnson N, Johnson V, Fisher J, Jobbings B, Bannister J, Lilford R. Fetal monitoring with pulse oximetry. *Br J Obstet Gynaecol* 1991;98:36–41.
9 Drife JO. Operative delivery—clinical aspects. In: Chamberlain GVP, Orr CJB, Sharp F, eds. *Litigation in obstetrics and gynaecology: proceedings of the fourteenth study group of the Royal College of Obstetricians and Gynaecologists*. London: RCOG, 1985:255–64.
10 Derom R, Patel NB, Thiery M. Implications of increasing rates of caesarean section. In: Studd J, ed. *Progress in obstetrics and gynaecology*. Vol 6. Edinburgh: Churchill Livingstone, 1988:175–94.
11 Friedman EA. The obstetrician's dilemma: how much fetal monitoring and cesarean section is enough? *N Engl J Med* 1986;315:641–3.
12 O'Driscoll K, Foley M. Correlation of decrease in perinatal mortality and increase in caesarean section rates. *Obstet Gynecol* 1983;61:1–5.
13 Glazener CMA, MacArthur C, Garcia J. Postnatal care: time for a change. *Contemporary Review of Obstetrics and Gynaecology* 1993;5:130–6.
14 Chalmers I, Enkin M, Keirse MJNC. *Effective care in pregnancy and childbirth*. Oxford: Oxford University Press, 1989.
15 Paintin DB. Effective care in pregnancy and childbirth. *Br J Obstet Gynaecol* 1990;97:967–9.
16 Smith LFP, Jewell D. Roles of midwives and general practitioners in hospital intrapartum care, England and Wales, 1988. *BMJ* 1991;303:1443–4.

17 Drife JO. Disciplining midwives. *BMJ* 1988;**297**:806–7.
18 McKee M, Priest P, Ginzler M, Black N. Can out of hours work by junior doctors in obstetrics be reduced? *Br J Obstet Gynaecol* 1992;**99**:197–202.
19 Department of Health. *Report on confidential enquiries into maternal deaths in the United Kingdom 1988–1990.* London: HMSO, 1994.
20 Barron SL. Audit in obstetrics. *Br J Obstet Gynaecol* 1991;**98**:1065–7.
21 Drife JO. Maternal "near miss" reports? *BMJ* 1993;**307**:1087.
22 Chamberlain G, Orr C, eds. *How to avoid medico–legal problems in obstetrics and gynaecology.* London: RCOG, 1990.
23 Brown ADG. Accidents in gynaecological surgery—medico–legal. In: Chamberlain GVP, Orr CJB, Sharp F, eds. *Litigation in obstetrics and gynaecology: proceedings of the fourteenth study group of the Royal College of Obstetricians and Gynaecologists.* London: RCOG, 1985.
24 Symonds EM. Litigation in obstetrics and gynaecology. *Br J Obstet Gynaecol* 1985;**92**:433–6.
25 Wald N, Cuckle S. Some practical issues in the antenatal detection of neural tube defects and Down's syndrome. In: Drife JO, Donnai D, eds. *Antenatal diagnosis of fetal abnormalities.* London: Springer Verlag, 1990:45–57.
26 Lamb B, Lang R. Aetiology of cerebral palsy. *Br J Obstet Gynaecol* 1992;**99**: 176–7.
27 Hall DMV. Birth asphyxia and cerebral palsy. *BMJ* 1989;**299**:279.
28 Hull J, Dodd K. What is birth asphyxia? *Br J Obstet Gynaecol* 1991;**98**:953–5.
29 Freeman J, Nelson K. Intrapartum asphyxia and cerebral palsy. *Pediatrics* 1988; **82**:240–9.
30 Ennis M, Vincent CA. Obstetric accidents: a review of 64 cases. *BMJ* 1990; **300**:1365–7.
31 Vincent CA, Martin T, Ennis M. Obstetric accidents: the patient's perspective. *Br J Obstet Gynaecol* 1991;**98**:390–5.
32 Murphy KW, Johnson P, Moorcraft J, Pattinson R, Russell V, Turnbull A. Birth asphyxia and the intrapartum cardiotocograph. *Br J Obstet Gynaecol* 1990;**97**: 470–9.
33 Ennis M. Training and supervision of obstetric senior house officers. *BMJ* 1991;**303**:1442–3.
34 Smith LFP. GP trainees' views on hospital obstetric vocational training. *BMJ* 1991;**303**:1447–50.
35 Clements RV. Litigation in obstetrics and gynaecology. *Br J Obstet Gynaecol* 1991;**98**:423–6.
36 Pogmore JR. Role of the senior house officer in the labour ward. *Br J Obstet Gynaecol* 1992;**99**:180–1.
37 Drife JO. My grandchild's birth. *BMJ* 1988;**297**:1208.
38 MacDonald RR. In defence of the obstetrician. *Br J Obstet Gynaecol* 1987;**94**: 833–5.

9 Reducing risk in paediatrics and neonatal intensive care

PETER DEAR

No area of medical practice is free of the risk of causing harm to patients. Even taking a clinical history may compel the patient to consider aspects of their life that are painful. Medical practice cannot be pursued according to the aphorism "first do no harm" but rather is practised along the less absolutist path of doing more good than harm. Before performing any investigation or treatment it is always necessary to assess the balance of risks and benefits. For the paediatrician the magnitude of both the benefits and risks of practice is higher than for most other clinicians so that the implications of getting the balance wrong are generally greater. This is particularly true in the case of very young children, in whom every aspect of investigation and treatment is difficult and in whom the consequences of any harm done may have to be borne for a lifetime. The most extreme example is neonatal intensive care.

From the medicolegal point of view paediatricians are in double jeopardy. Firstly, a doctor or health authority can be sued for medical negligence until the child reaches 21 years of age, or indeed any age if the child is so disabled that a state of independence is never reached. Secondly, eligibility for legal aid is based on the child's earnings and therefore easily obtained if there seems to be a prima facie case. The need for paediatricians to be risk conscious in the interests both of their patient and themselves is obvious. Although the stakes are high, paediatricians are clearly not expected

147

to perform at a higher level than other doctors. They, like others, are expected to take all reasonable precautions to avoid inflicting preventable and foreseeable harm on their patients and to communicate effectively when there has been a misadventure. Recognising the main areas of risk is an essential prerequisite for their prevention and this chapter is devoted to just that in relation to paediatric practice. The first section of the chapter considers general areas of risk, common to almost all paediatric practice, and the second section considers a selection of risks related to neonatal medicine.

Areas of risk in general paediatric practice

Children have in common the facts that they are small, generally uncooperative, difficult to evaluate medically, and mostly have parents who watch over them and guard their best interests. These features alone create potential problems for the doctor attempting to provide a high quality of care and to stay out of court. Some barriers to these endeavours as well as some possible solutions are discussed.

The need for specialisation

Paediatricians are often heard to say, usually in conversation with clinicians in non-paediatric specialties, that "children are not simply small adults". Although now a cliché, this vitally important message is by no means redundant in the current state of organisation of medical services for children in this country.

It is the first and most important step in reducing clinical risk in paediatric practice to ensure that medical care for children is provided by clinical staff with appropriate training and experience of specialist techniques, in purpose designed acccommodation. A good illustration of the risks associated with not doing so was provided by the recent confidential enquiry into perioperative deaths in relation to paediatric anaesthesia and surgery. No similar investigation has yet been conducted into other areas of hospital care for children but it is likely that similar findings would be obtained—for example, in paediatric intensive care, paediatric accident and emergency attendances, and so on. This is a matter of health care planning and organisation and it is the responsibility of all those engaged in this activity to ensure that these initial conditions for risk reduction in paediatric practice are met. To

148

persist with the surgical example, when every child who needs an operation sets out from a children's surgical ward in the company of its parents and a paediatrically trained nurse to be anaesthetised by a paediatric anaesthetist and operated on by a paediatric surgeon in a designated paediatric operating theatre we will have got it right.

An extension of this line of argument to subspecialisation within paediatric medicine is also appropriate to a consideration of risk reduction. Paediatrics has been slower than adult medicine in recognising the place of the specialist. The general paediatrician is certainly able to deal effectively with most problems but as the body of scientific knowledge on which paediatric practice is based continues to expand, and in the face of increasing public awareness and expectation, the doctor who does not know when to refer is increasingly vulnerable. A possible solution to this might be to form closer links between central and peripheral units so that the care of children with less common problems can be shared rather than devolved. In that way the best interests of the child can be combined with professional interest.

Communication with parents

One of the peculiar features of paediatric practice is the tripartite relationship between the doctor, the child, and the parents. Although most experienced paediatricians regard this as one of the more interesting and challenging aspects of their specialty there is an unfortunate tendency among less experienced doctors to regard parents as mere accessories. To an extent this may reflect the insecurity of the doctor in dealing with non-dependent adults who often seem to want to know an awful lot about what is going on. It is, however, in the best interests of both the child and the doctor for the parents to be thoroughly well informed on every point including an understanding of the risks as well as the benefits that might be associated with the investigation and treatment to be undertaken. In relation to avoiding litigation, as opposed to simply providing good care, communication with parents about high risk procedures, particularly on the intensive care unit, will pay dividends. Parents embarking on legal action do so for a variety of motives but a recurring theme is a feeling that they have not received adequate explanation and that they are victims of a cover up. We cannot prevent parents from suing us because the public provision for handicapped children is lamentably inadequate but we can prevent them from suing us because we did not talk to them.

Child protection

Most children are fortunate enough to have parents who try to meet their needs and guard their interests. An extremely unfortunate minority inherit parents who have no interest in them or in some way abuse them. This distortion of the expected parent and child relationship is difficult for health professionals to come to terms with but when it goes undetected children are put at great risk.

Child abuse, in any one of its varied forms, is much more likely to be suspected by clinical staff specialising in the care of children than by those not doing so. Some doctors and nurses outside paediatric practice just do not seem to be able to accept that so many apparently normal parents do such terrible things to their offspring. Until we achieve the ideal of having all children in hospital cared for by children's nurses, hospitals should at least ensure that there is good liaison between departments such as the orthopaedic ward and the accident and emergency department and the paediatricians. Each district has a designated doctor for child protection who will be a useful source of advice. There should be a low threshold for consulting the Child Protection Register whenever suspicions are aroused. The register is held by Social Services and a child's name can be added or removed only as a result of a decision reached by a case conference. The child's name remains on the register as long as there is a current child protection plan in operation. As well as the names of children who have been officially placed on the register the registry keeps a log of the names of children about whom there have been enquiries.

Particularly difficult to recognise are cases of emotional deprivation and cases of what has become known as Munchausen syndrome by proxy.[1] Children may be repeatedly poisoned, suffocated, or subjected to innumerable, unnecessary investigations in the pursuit of an organic disease. The parent responsible is often highly inventive and plausible. The only way that the risks associated with this and other forms of child abuse can be minimised is for clinical staff caring for children to be fully aware of such possibilities and to become suspicious when there are features of the case that do not seem right. These are difficult cases that may demand

150

considerable expertise to unravel but there are plenty of sources of expert advice; by far the most common reason for children to remain at risk from their own parents is that the problem remains unsuspected. Continuing medical and nursing education have a vital part to play here as in so many other areas of risk reduction.

The possibility that children might be at risk of deliberate harm perpetrated by healthcare professionals was recently thrown into sharp focus by the Beverly Allitt affair. The recommendations of the Clothier committee should reduce the risk of a recurrence of this tragedy but only if the recommendations are implemented in full and monitored in every hospital providing clinical services for children. The main recommendations concern more stringent assessment of the physical and mental health of nurses caring for children; better access to paediatric pathology services; improved reporting of untoward incidents and better collating of reports; better implementation of the recommendations of the Department of Health report *Welfare of children and young people in hospital*.

Handover and continuity of care

Young children cannot explain that they have already had their evening medication or that they are supposed to be fasting before surgery. As a result they are so much more vulnerable to the risks of mishap through failures of communication. Nurses are generally good at handover but doctors are generally not and the changes in training and working patterns that are being inflicted (with scant regard for the needs of patients) are bound to make matters worse. Handover rounds between junior staff are a crucial component of any risk reduction strategy and it is incumbent on senior staff to insist that they be done and to demand the resources required to enable them.

Cross infection

Too many children admitted to hospital acquire infection from other children as the result of inadequate isolation facilities or poor prevention measures such as hand washing. It is a serious deficiency in the service when a baby admitted for a minor operation contracts a major respiratory illness such as bronchiolitis from the baby in the adjacent bed or when a child with cystic fibrosis acquires a problematic organism such as *Pseudomonas cepacia* for the first time, in hospital. The current recommendation is for 50% of all children's beds to be in cubicles but this is probably an

151

underprovision. The problem with more cubicles is that more nurses are generally required to look after them but the costs of unnecessary morbidity generated by cross infection may well outweigh this. Perhaps there is an unusually useful role for the health economist here.

Prescribing for children

One of the many benefits associated with children receiving their medical care in dedicated facilities from specialist staff is that such an arrangement goes a long way towards ensuring that children receive appropriate medication for their age, by an appropriate route, and in an appropriate dosage. Those who only occasionally prescribe for children are much more likely to make errors. Unfortunately, our knowledge of paediatric pharmacology, particularly in the younger age groups, lags well behind our knowledge of adult pharmacology, partly because of the ethical and technical difficulties involved in studying children but partly because it is generally a commercially less attractive area. Growth and maturation bring about immense changes in drug distribution and metabolism and to ensure efficacy and avoid toxicity it is essential for those prescribing drugs for children to consult a good paediatric vademecum. Unfortunately, it is still not uncommon to find young children prescribed inappropriate medications by non-paediatricians and such occurrences are usually indefensible.

Record keeping

This is such an important topic that no doubt it is discussed many times in this book. Two particular points need to be made about record keeping in paediatrics. The first is the importance of recording normal findings and it relates particularly to the screening examinations that are part of normal child health surveillance. There is a natural tendency when writing notes to concentrate on the abnormal findings but failure to record the fact that an infant's hips examined normally at 1 week of age can create a serious problem if dislocation is diagnosed later on. Such considerations are usually more relevant to medicolegal matters than to the quality of patient care but are hardly the less weighty for that.

The other important consideration is the fact that all children under 5 years of age now have a personal health record held by their parents. This contains (or would if it was completed properly by the professionals) important information that, in some circumstances, it might be deemed negligent not to have discovered. A note about drug allergy for example!

Follow up

The need to organise appropriate follow up is common to all branches of medicine. The need to take steps to ensure that it takes place is peculiar to specialties such as paediatrics, in which the patients cannot be expected to take responsibility for their own actions. If a child fails to attend for a hearing test after meningitis or is discharged on heavy medication for asthma and does not attend for review it is the responsibility of the medical staff concerned to do something. Sometimes just informing the general practitioner will be enough but on other occasions it will be necessary to pursue the family with the aid of the health visitor or social services.

Follow up of the results of tests is another aspect of this. It is especially important in paediatrics when a battery of tests may be requested at once to avoid repeated venepuncture. The results of every test performed must be seen and signed by somebody and not just filed in the notes. An abnormal test result that was not pursued is difficult to explain.

Neonatal medicine

Neonatal medicine is unquestionably one of the most venturesome areas of medical practice, for patients and doctors alike. It is also one of the few specialties in which a mistaken diagnosis can have serious legal implications for doctors in another specialty. I refer here to the consequences for obstetricians of a false diagnosis of birth asphyxia. This section begins by considering that particular issue and then goes on to consider some of the commoner hazards associated with intensive care of the newborn.

The diagnosis of birth asphyxia

The diagnostic label "birth asphyxia" (or "birth trauma") should be used with great care. A considerable proportion of litigation against obstetricians is started on the basis of a mistaken diagnosis of birth asphyxia. In these cases it is usually the paediatric staff who have used the term inappropriately and usually without realising the potential repercussions.

153

The term "birth asphyxia" is likely to be used as a diagnostic term when babies present with one or more of the following features:

- Obstetric evidence of "fetal distress." Usually in the form of fetal heart rate abnormalities on the cardiotocograph
- Poor condition at birth. Usually described by low Apgar scores and the need for resuscitation
- A metabolic acidosis in umbilical cord blood or blood taken soon after birth. (Metabolic acidosis occurs when the cells of the body try to generate energy in the absence of sufficient oxygen.)
- A neurological illness during the first few days of life, characterised by irritability, seizures, and abnormalities of consciousness level, posture, and muscle tone.

When such an illness is genuinely the result of acute asphyxial brain injury it is properly termed a "postasphyxial" or "hypoxic/ischaemic" encephalopathy. When the cause is less certain the implication-free term "neonatal-encephalopathy" is more appropriate.

Although these features are indeed the hallmark of intrapartum asphyxia, it is also true that any one of them (and some combinations of them) may have a different aetiology. It is only when all of the evidence is taken together and alternative explanations have been excluded by appropriate investigation that the diagnosis of birth asphyxia can be made with reasonable confidence. Even when that situation is reached, however, it does not necessarily follow that any subsequent disabilities are the result of birth asphyxia. The fetus with a serious intrinsic abnormality of the nervous system or one with antepartum damage to the central nervous system may not be able to cope with the stresses imposed by birth and may present many of the features of an asphyxiated baby without necessarily having been damaged further in the process. Such babies may, for example, appear very floppy and unresponsive at birth, to the extent of requiring ventilatory support, and may then go on to exhibit a host of abnormal neurological features.

In most cases of cerebral palsy associated with problems at birth and in the neonatal period, appropriate investigation, including brain imaging and a search for metabolic disorders, usually allows the formation of a reasonably clear view on the likelihood of the cerebral palsy being due to intrapartum asphyxia.[2] Too often,

154

though, the necessary analytical thinking and investigation is performed as part of the medical litigation process and by the time it is concluded that a child's disabilities are probably due to something other than intrapartum asphyxia a good deal of stress has been imposed on all those concerned and a good deal of public money has been wasted. It is the responsibility of all paediatricians to avoid the false attribution of the term "birth asphyxia" and to hold such discussions with parents as are necessary, sometimes in conjunction with colleagues in obstetrics, to convey as clear a picture as possible of the likely cause of the child's problems.

It seems likely that less than 20% of cerebral palsy is due to asphyxial brain injury acquired intrapartum (which is a helpful perspective) but it is unlikely that we will ever be able to prevent all of these cases from occurring.[34] The public at large is not as acutely aware as are obstetricians and neonatologists of the hazards associated with birth. It is sometimes necessary to confess that a baby has been damaged by intrapartum asphyxia that could not have been prevented, other than by a prior caesarean section for which there was no indication.

Resuscitation

It is possible to predict most instances when resuscitation of the newborn might be required but it is not, and never will be, possible to predict them all. At present about 7% of babies needing resuscitation are born normally at term. This means that every birth must be attended by someone capable of assessing an asphyxiated baby, establishing a clear airway, and giving effective bag and mask ventilation. This is the key to neonatal resuscitation and the vast majority of asphyxiated babies need no more than lung inflation and improved arterial oxygenation to recover fully. For the benefit of readers who are not paediatricians it should be pointed out that drugs are rarely needed during resuscitation of the newborn and the trappings of the adult resuscitation scene such as cardiac monitors and defibrillators are redundant. When the birth occurs in hospital it is reasonable to expect that someone with the ability to intubate and provide advanced resuscitation if necessary will be available within five minutes. For births taking place outside a hospital with resident paediatric cover this will not usually be possible and this constitutes an area of small, but finite, risk. Women choosing to give birth under such circumstances should be fully informed about what will and will not be available

155

in the event that an unexpectedly asphyxiated baby is born. They should not be encouraged to believe that giving birth at home is as safe as doing so in hospital; it can never be so.

Neonatal intensive care

Despite the associated high mortality and morbidity neonatal intensive care is rarely the subject of litigation. This may be mainly because the hazardous nature of the undertaking is explicit, and different from childbirth which is perceived to be a normal process that should have a normal outcome. Yet paediatricians can take some of the credit by effectively communicating with parents and involving them in decision making and aspects of care. We must not become complacent, though, as the climate may change and there is invariably room for improvement. This section deals with aspects of some of the commonest avoidable mishaps.

Hypoglycaemia

All newborn infants are liable to become hypoglycaemic if they do not receive adequate nutrition. Some infants are particularly predisposed to do so because of reduced endogenous nutrient stores, increased glucose utilisation, disordered metabolism, or endocrine imbalance. Most important among these are the small for gestational age infant and the infant of a diabetic mother. Hypoglycaemia of sufficient severity and duration can cause irreversible brain injury—through mechanisms believed to be similar to those occurring during hypoxia—leading to mental retardation and cerebral palsy. It is thought that only symptomatic hypoglycaemia is likely to damage the brain. The symptoms of hypoglycaemia are too subtle and varied, however, especially in the immature or sick infant, to be relied on and adherence to biochemical limits is a safer approach. A particularly difficult situation is hypoglycaemia after birth asphyxia when it is impossible to disentangle the contributions from the two possible causes of abnormal neurological signs.

Recent research suggests that to be on the safe side the blood glucose concentration should be maintained above 2·7 mml/l.[56] Efforts should be made to meet the nutritional needs of every infant but those known to be at increased risk of hypoglycaemia should receive regular monitoring of blood glucose concentration by a stick test; as ever, with documentation of the results! If the blood glucose concentration falls below 2·7 mmol/l other than transiently, steps must be taken to bring it to a safer level by whatever means necessary. Too often there is procrastination. In circumstances of appreciable clinical risk an intravenous infusion should be set up and the concentration of glucose should be increased until normoglycaemia is achieved. If that means a central venous catheter and 20% dextrose so be it! Untreated, sustained hypoglycaemia in the newborn is absolutely unacceptable.

Neonatal sepsis

Newborn infants, particularly those born prematurely, have poor defences against infection and yet are exposed to a wide variety of potentially pathogenic microorganisms during early postnatal life. The rapidity with which an infected infant can deteriorate and the non-specific nature of the presenting signs make sepsis a very serious threat. Among the most notorious pathogens are group B *Streptococci*, *Staphylococcus aureus*, *Listeria*, *Haemophilus influenzae*, and *Escherichia coli*. All are capable of causing the death of a previously well infant within 24 hours. Delays in the diagnosis and treatment of neonatal sepsis are all too common and it is incumbent on all maternity units to ensure that their staff are well trained in recognising the early signs of neonatal infection. Loss of signs of wellbeing in any young infant should raise the suspicion of sepsis and always merits a careful clinical appraisal. Among presenting features demanding urgent evaluation are grunting or moaning respiration, lack of interest in feeding, pallor, mottling of the skin, and loss of muscle tone. By no means do all babies presenting with such signs have an infection but the penalties for delayed diagnosis and treatment are so severe as to demand a screening approach that emphasises sensitivity over specificity. That is, it is preferable to make false positive diagnoses of sepsis than to make false negative ones. An unnecessary septic screen and a 48 hour course of antibiotics is the price that some babies have to pay for the safety of others.

Vascular access procedures

Securing and maintaining safe vascular access is a challenging task in all young children but nowhere more so than in neonatal intensive care. No type of vascular access is totally free of risk and a complete list of possible adverse events is too frightening to contemplate. It would certainly include the loss of limbs and sudden death from perforation of the myocardium. Vascular access is often essential, however, and all that can be asked is that appropriate measures are taken to minimise the risk of serious complications.

Arterial lines

Gaining and maintaining arterial access is an essential component of neonatal intensive care. In any objective appraisal of risks and benefits, catheterisation of the umbilical artery with a catheter bearing a continuous reading oxygen electrode has to be best value. Locating the tip of the catheter in the lower thorax possibly has fewer complications than placing it at the bifurcation of the aorta but both approaches have their advocates. Placing the catheter tip anywhere between these locations is taboo. A well recognised hazard of umbilical artery catheterisation in very immature babies is burning of the skin by the fluid used to clean the periumbilical area. This is especially likely to occur if excess cleaning fluid soaks into the bedding and remains in contact with the skin of the back and buttocks. As a precaution the minimum amount of fluid should be used and the baby's bedding should be replaced after the procedure. Regular checks must be made of the circulation to the buttocks and lower limbs and these should be documented. Any non-transient compromise of the circulation should trigger the immediate removal of the catheter under virtually all circumstances. Catheters in the umbilical artery will often continue to function for many weeks but should be removed once the baby's condition is sufficiently improved for the benefits to become outweighed by the risks. There are no hard and fast rules.

Next in order of preference is the radial artery cannula. This does not have the benefits of continuous oxygen monitoring but does allow continuous arterial blood pressure monitoring and frequent arterial sampling. Before catheterising the radial artery it is mandatory to ensure that the correponding ulnar artery is able to maintain a satisfactory circulation to the hand by using what has become known as Allen's test. This is widely known to paediatricians and does not require description here. In common with the catheter in the umbilical artery, and every other form of arterial line, if there is more than a transient compromise of the circulation the line should be removed. There may occasionally be circumstances in which the benefits of maintaining arterial access are thought to outweigh a significant risk of ischaemic injury to the tissues but these are few and far between and in such

158

circumstances it would be wise to share a discussion of the risks and benefits with the parents.

All other sites of arterial access are less desirable than the two outlined although ulnar arteries, brachial arteries, femoral arteries, posterior tibial arteries, and superficial temporal arteries are all acceptable sites when necessary as long as careful monitoring for complications is undertaken and documented.

Whichever artery is cannulated it is absolutely vital to ensure that vasoactive drugs such as adrenaline and dopamine are *never* infused through an arterial line. The consequences can be disastrous.

Venous access

Venous access is generally far less problematic than arterial access but by no means free from potentially serious complications. The main risks associated with peripheral venous access are those related to leakage of the infusion fluid into the tissues. Large extravasated volumes of any fluid are capable of causing ischaemic tissue injury but quite small volumes of some fluids are notorious for causing tissue necrosis. Among the worst offenders are solutions containing calcium, some antibiotics, and concentrated glucose solutions. All infusion sites should be inspected at least hourly and some form of simple documentation of this process must be undertaken. Once again, no documentation may be interpreted as a lack of observation.

Retinopathy of prematurity (damage to the developing retina of the eye)

The development and growth of the blood vessels of the retina is normally an antenatal event but after preterm birth it occurs postnatally, particularly in the peripheral retina, which is the last part to be reached by the advancing tide of capillaries. The retinopathy of prematurity (ROP) is a disorder of vascularisation and the main, but not the only, factor predisposing to ROP is an excessively high oxygen tension (Po_2) in arterial blood. Meticulous control of arterial Po_2 below 10 kpa until retinal vascularisation is complete will prevent the development of significant ROP in the vast majority of susceptible infants. To achieve this aim arterial Po_2 must be monitored carefully in all babies of less than 32 weeks gestation receiving supplemental oxygen, especially during their period of intensive care. By far the best way to do this is to use an umbilical artery catheter with a continuous reading Po_2 electrode but regular intermittent sampling of arterial blood supported by some form of continuous non-invasive monitoring is an acceptable alternative. It is not sufficient to rely on pulse oximetry, transcutaneous Po_2 monitoring, or capillary blood gas sampling alone and a claim of medical negligence would be difficult to defend if appreciable ROP occurred in the absence of attempts to secure some form of direct arterial Po_2 monitoring. It is of course not always possible to achieve arterial access but it is always possible to make a determined effort to do so and to record these efforts in the notes.

As babies improve and move out of intensive care their vulnerability to ROP generally declines and less intensive monitoring of Po_2 is appropriate even if oxygen treatment is continued on account of chronic lung disease. This is just as well as arterial access may be difficult to maintain for prolonged periods. The emphasis at that stage is on the prevention of hypoxia and pulse oximetry is now the best technique for this.

In addition to taking appropriate steps to try to prevent ROP it is also now essential to ensure that babies at risk of it are screened by an opthalmologist so that those few babies who develop progressive ROP despite primary prevention measures can benefit from retinal treatment with either cryosurgery or laser. Current recommendations are that all babies born at less than 1500 g birthweight or 31 weeks gestation should be screened from 6 to 7 weeks postnatal age.[7] If abnormalities are noted repeated examinations are required to check for progression to severe disease and to determine when treatment is indicated. Such screening and treatment can substantially reduce the expected rate of severe visual impairment and scrupulous efforts at primary prevention coupled with an effective screening programme make blindness from ROP an extremely rare event. Unfortunately, screening for ROP requires considerable ophthalmological skill, patience, and experience and it may be difficult to offer an effective screening programme to every at risk infant. It is unlikely that failure to screen could be successfully defended if potentially treatable visual impairment developed. This represents a major area of risk for many hospitals in the United Kingdom at the present time, particularly as financial considerations are encouraging tertiary referral units to return babies to their hospital of origin as quickly as possible. If preventable blindness occurs as a result of this policy it will turn out to have been a very false economy in every respect.

160

Conclusions

There are probably more specific risks in paediatric practice than there are words in this chapter and so I have been highly selective. The more general issues are as usual the most important ones and the following check list reiterates some key points:

- Children should be cared for in designated children's wards, outpatient clinics, accident and emergency departments, operating theatres, and so on. They should not share accommodation with adult patients. Apart from permitting a "child oriented" physical environment, including suitable cross infection measures, the segregation of children's services helps to ensure that child and family centred care can be developed and sustained. This usually means good communication, a holistic approach to the child's needs, and the early detection of disturbed family relationships

- Children should be cared for and treated by healthcare professionals specialising in paediatrics. This includes medical, nursing, and paramedical staff. In this way the risk of children coming to harm out of ignorance is minimised

- The recommendations of key advisory documents such as the *report of the Clothier committee* and the *welfare of children and young people in hospital* should be implemented. There is a great measure of risk reduction implicit in many of the recommendations contained in these reports

- Effective child protection procedures should be in place and arrangements for educating staff and publicising networks of communication should be established and kept up to date

- Adequate medical and nursing notes should be maintained as a permanent record of the high quality of care provided and as a means of ensuring effective transfer of information between professionals. The parent held record is a part of this

- As well as providing good quality care, communicating with parents is vital. Not the transatlantic approach of detailing every conceivable potential hazard but rather showing a willingness to explain and, when appropriate, sharing decision making. Parents generally have a right to know exactly what is going on and are probably less likely to embark on legal action if they think that they were partners with the staff in the care of their child than if they are treated in a high handed and paternalistic manner.

Reports advising on aspects of health care for children

Welfare of children and young people in hospital. London: HMSO, 1991.

Children first. A study of hospital services. London: Audit Commission, 1993.

Working together. Under the Children Act 1989. London: HMSO, 1991.

Management models in established combined or integrated child health services. London: British Paediatric Association, 1992.

Outcome measurements for child health. London: British Paediatric Association, 1992.

Parent held and professional records used in child health surveillance. London: British Paediatric Association, 1993.

Purchasing health services for children and young people. London: British Paediatric Association, 1994.

References

1 Meadow R. Munchausen syndrome by proxy. *Arch Dis Child* 1982;**57**:92–8.
2 Freeman JM, Nelson KB. Intrapartum asphyxia and cerebral palsy. *Paediatrics* 1988;**82**:240–9.
3 Blair E, Stanley FJ. Intrapartum asphyxia: a rare cause of cerebral palsy. *J Paediatr* 1988;**112**:515–9.
4 Stanley FJ. The aetiology of cerebral palsy. *Early Hum Dev* 1994;**36**:81–8.
5 Lucas A, Morley R, Cole T. Adverse neurodevelopmental outcome of moderate neonatal hypoglycaemia. *BMJ* 1988;**297**:1304–8.
6 Koh TH, Eyre JA, Aynsley-Green A. Neural dysfunction during hypoglycaemia. *Arch Dis Child* 1988;**63**:1386–8.
7 Fielder AR, Levene MI. *Arch Dis Child* 1992;**67**:860–7.

10 Clinical risk management in anaesthesia

JONATHAN SECKER-WALKER,
MICHAEL WILSON

Health care is a risky business; clinical risk management is a system which helps reduce avoidable risk to patients and staff, which enhances the quality of care for future patients by identifying areas of risk and by changing practice, and which at the same time protects the financial assets of a healthcare institution. Clinical risk management has been defined by Runciman as the cost effective reduction of risk to levels perceived to be acceptable to society.[1]

What are the risks associated with anaesthesia?

General anaesthesia entails keeping the patient unconscious, providing adequate analgesia, and relaxing the patient's muscles to facilitate surgery. All these processes may, to a greater or lesser degree depending on the depth of anaesthesia, deprive patients of their respiratory reflexes. Hence safeguarding the patient's airway from the mouth to the lungs and maintaining adequate ventilation is a major component of a general anaesthetic procedure.

According to Utting, the commonest reason for anaesthetists in the United Kingdom contacting the Medical Defence Union, comprising 52% of its reports, was because they had damaged their patient's teeth during anaesthesia.[2] More recently, Aitkenhead analysed the 150 claims to the union between 1989 and 1990 and

163

Table 10.1 *Proportion of serious injuries leading to actual or threatened litigation among 150 claims, 1989–90*

	%
Brain or spinal cord damage	23·8
Death in postoperative period	17·0
Awareness during general anaesthesia	12·2
Death during anaesthesia	11·6
Pain during regional anaesthesia	7·5
Peripheral nerve damage	4·1
Fetal death	1·4
Suxamethonium pains	1·4
Miscellaneous injuries	21·1
(fractured ribs, tissued infusions, pneumothorax, and laryngeal damage)	

listed the pattern of more serious injuries leading to actual or threatened litigation (table 10.1).

Allegations of painful awareness, accounting for about 12% of this review series,[3] continue to be an appreciable problem, perhaps because press coverage has alerted patients to its possibility. The incidence of painful awareness has been reported to be of the order of 0·01% during elective general surgery.[4] Among 2000 anaesthetic incident reports Osborne *et al* found 16 cases of awareness, six due to a syringe swap in which the muscle relaxant suxamethonium was given to a conscious patient and three due to low concentrations of volatile agents; in the remaining seven cases no cause was obvious.[5] Painful awareness is usually accompanied by hypertension and tachycardia, and such signs should alert the anaesthetist to the possibility that the patient is not fully anaesthetised. Such experiences can lead to post-traumatic stress syndrome for patients, for whom early recognition and counselling are advisable. Denial by the anaesthetist of the possibility of awareness during the postoperative visit usually makes the situation considerably worse. In a review of five recent legal cases involving plaintiffs complaining of being awake and in pain during some part of the operation settlements for the plaintiff ranged from £15 000 to £100 000.[6] The commonest causes related to insufficient induction agent (thiopentone), no volatile agent being given, no hyperventilation and low percentages of nitrous oxide, and the error of not checking that the vaporiser is full.

The immediate postoperative period is potentially dangerous for anaesthetised patients: of the deaths and cases of brain damage in Aitkenhead's review no less than 47·8% occurred in the

Box 1—Commonest critical incidents in anaesthesia

Breathing circuit disconnection
Inadequate gas flows
Syringe swap
Gas supply problems
Disconnected intravenous line
Malfunction of laryngoscope
Premature extubation
Circuit misconnection
Hypovolaemia
Problem with endotracheal tube

postoperative period.[3] Cooper *et al* used collections of critical incidents in anaesthesia to investigate human errors and equipment failure.[7] They showed that 82% of preventable incidents involved human error and only 14% equipment failure. However, the proportion for human error is increased by many breathing system disconnections, which might equally well have been classed as equipment failure. Evidently, poor equipment design was partially involved with many of the human errors. Cooper *et al* also described the 10 commonest critical incidents, of which 70% were related to failure to ventilate the lungs with oxygen (box 1).[8] Webb *et al* in an analysis of 2000 incidents showed that the five commonest incidents, comprising 40% of the total, were all related to ventilatory problems,[9] and the same pattern applied to recovery wards, in which over two thirds of critical incidents related to ventilation of patients.[10]

Frequency of risks

Reliable estimates of the frequency of risk are difficult to obtain, since although death is absolute and measurable, those deaths whose cause is considered to be totally or partially due to anaesthesia are often a subject of debate and the arguments based on imperfect information. Furthermore, the numerator is small and there is often uncertainty about the accuracy of the denominator. Therefore the many differing reported rates of mortality and anaesthesia should be accepted with caution. The report of the Confidential Enquiry into Perioperative Deaths (CEPOD), for example, indicates that only three deaths out of nearly half a million were entirely due to anaesthesia whereas anaesthesia was partly implicated in one death in 1300 deaths.[11]

The reported incidence of complications in anaesthesia depends on definitions, classification, and the enthusiasm of the reporters. The risks change from year to year and country to country as anaesthetic practice alters and adapts. Various values for risk have been reported[12 13] and it is probably less than 0·5%. What matters most is the situation in individual hospitals at a particular time.

Reducing risk

Risk may be reduced by three strategies, as follows.

- Identifying the causes of accidents and errors and developing preventive measures
- Adopting procedures associated with less risk
- Using monitors to give early warning of trouble, thus allowing the anaesthetist to recover the situation before harm befalls the patient

Identifying causes of accidents and errors and developing preventive measures

Accidents may be caused by human error, equipment failure, and some kinds of organisational failure.

Human error

An anaesthetist has to obtain information about the physiological state of the patient and the progress of the anaesthetic from observing the patient, the monitors, and the anaesthetic machine, the information from which is used to make decisions about the anaesthetic. Any required change will necessitate an action, such as adjusting a control, which must be correctly executed to achieve the desired end. Consequently, human errors may occur during the observation (input), decision making, or action (output) stages.

Input and output errors can be minimised by good equipment design. Advances in the design of monitors have eliminated many subjective errors and introduced a range of important measurements not previously available. A new generation of anaesthetic monitors using computer technology can integrate and display physiological information and raise alarms when predetermined limits are transgressed. The overall aim is to provide

166

information that is easily assimilated, thus reducing the risk of mental overload; unfortunately false alarms are still very common with current monitoring equipment.[14] This usually means repeating the observation or acquiring other confirmatory evidence, or both,[15 16] by direct observation of the patient or from other monitors.

Traditionally, constant vigilance is expected of the anaesthetist,[16 17] yet it is clear that continuously maintaining total alertness and vigilance is not possible, as confirmed by critical incident studies.[17] Well designed equipment and physiological monitors trigger a return to total vigilance at appropriate times. Critical incident studies also suggest that there may be an advantage in changing anaesthetists during a long procedure.[18]

When making decisions the anaesthetist has to decide not only *whether* something is wrong but also *why*. The monitors indicate which vital signs are abnormal, but the anaesthetist must piece the various items of information together and choose a hypothesis that will lead to the correct action. Often the anaesthetist will follow some, perhaps unconscious, mental rule and select the most common explanation that matches the situation. Known as frequency gambling,[19] this approach usually provides a correct solution, although not always.[20] Abstract reasoning will be required to solve a novel problem. This knowledge based behaviour is slower and requires more effort. Anaesthetists need to be taught to question their decisions because clinging to false hypotheses or an inappropriate rule is a well known cause of accidents. This dangerous form of "keyhole" thinking[19 21 22] is especially common in particular circumstances,[23] when disastrous decisions may be adhered to, irrationally and tenaciously, despite conflicting evidence. Anaesthetists need to be aware of this danger and must be prepared to listen to other opinions. The House of Lords recently upheld a conviction for manslaughter on the grounds that it constituted gross negligence (and hence a criminal offence) for an anaesthetist to have failed to recognise a ventilator circuit disconnection which led to a patient's death.

Equipment failure

Since faulty equipment rarely causes serious accidents[21 24 25] or critical incidents[7 8 26] there is the risk of complacency. Disconnections in the breathing systems carrying oxygen and anaesthetic to the patient are frequent and if undetected can cause death.[7 8 26-28] But latterly, with the increasing use of disposable breathing systems, this incident seems less common. None the less some form of disconnection warning device is essential.

Various national and international standards organisations have taken an important lead in improving equipment safety.[27] In the United Kingdom the Medical Devices Directorate[24] has an important role in developing these standards, evaluating equipment, and approving manufacturers, also being responsible for investigating accidents associated with medical devices and issuing hazard notices and safety action bulletins to warn other users.

Organisational failure

Hospitals should provide a safe environment for anaesthesia with well designed and equipped anaesthetic, operating, and recovery rooms. The importance of skilled help—operating department assistants or anaesthetic nurses, recovery nurses, and more senior anaesthetic help (when required)—has already been emphasised in many mortality surveys.[11 25 29] Hospital managers require proof that investment in safety is worthwhile; however, as Brahams pointed out, those who plead lack of cash may regret their decision when a case comes before the courts.[30]

Too few appropriate staff, poor departmental organisation, or insensitive management may lead to fatigue, lack of sleep, hunger, frustration, excessive workload, and poor morale, all of which probably decrease performance.[16] Although experience and common sense support this view, satisfactory experimental evidence is hard to find and in surveys the number of incidents attributed to these factors is few.[8 11 26]

Adopting procedures associated with less risk

Whenever possible, adopting techniques that avoid known risks has obvious advantages. For example, the complications of failed intubation (which include death) will not arise if anaesthetic techniques are chosen which do not require tracheal intubation. Furthermore, it is wise to choose techniques that are "fail safe"[23]; a spontaneously breathing patient will survive a disconnection whereas a paralysed patient may die.

Monitoring and recovery procedures

When something does go wrong during an anaesthetic a chain of events is initiated which may lead to harm and, in an extreme

168

situation, to cardiac arrest, an event which could be detected by a single monitor (an electrocardiograph). However, investing in several monitors that can detect different stages in the propagation of an incident is more sensible (a disconnected ventilator may be detected, for example, by falls in inspiratory pressure, tidal volume, end tidal partial pressure of carbon dioxide, and oxygen saturation before the electrocardiogram becomes flat). Different types of monitor cover a range of possible incidents. Consequently if an incident is detected early enough harm may be avoided by the speedy implementation of some recovery procedure. For example, Gaba et al discussing techniques to interrupt evolving anaesthetic accidents, pointed out that 93% of the critical incidents recorded by Cooper et al[8] were successfully managed.[15] Early detection allows more time to initiate recovery procedures and reduces the likelihood of an incident leading to harm.[15 31] Factors affecting the recovery sequence have been analysed by Galletly and Mushet.[32]

Prompt corrective action may not allow much time for thought and some incidents may occur so rarely that little experience is gained in handling them. Taking the appropriate recovery action is essential because an incorrect response may precipitate another incident,[21] which may have even more serious consequences. For these reasons there is much to recommend having readily available a set of *Anaesthesia Action Plans.*[33] Such a strategy represents a shift to rule based behaviour rather than the slower knowledge based behaviour. Ideally, decisions about emergency procedures should be made in advance, at leisure, with the benefit of collective wisdom, and incorporated into the department's standard operating procedures. Both DeAnda and Gaba[20 21] and Schwid and O'Donnell[22] using an anaesthesia simulator provided a valuable training tool and also insight into the way anaesthetists deal with critical incidents. Proceeding further, Gaba et al have encouraged specific training in crisis management in anaesthesia.[34]

Managing risk

A risk management programme in anaesthesia should aim at identifying areas of risk before a patient is harmed and it needs to continuously review, and where necessary improve, various aspects of anaesthesia delivery (box 2).

Box 2—Aspects of delivery of anaesthesia

1 Equipment and monitoring policies
2 Adverse incident reporting systems
3 Medical records
4 Communication and informed consent
5 Operating theatre procedures
6 Supervision of junior staff and locums
7 Locums
8 Recovery room
9 Continuing medical education, maintenance of skills
10 Consideration of risks associated with new techniques
11 Damage limitation

Equipment and monitoring policies

Many departments of anaesthesia have agreed policies for purchasing equipment and deciding the appropriate level of monitoring. Conformity of equipment and monitors decreases the risk of junior anaesthetists being confronted with unfamiliar tools in the middle of the night. Furthermore, a sensible budgetary approach is required to ensure regular servicing of the equipment and a rolling replacement programme, which, if not performed, may lead to patient harm or sudden cancellation of operating lists resulting in inconvenience to patients and loss of revenue to the provider. Enlightened trust status may encourage such budget management, which was usually lacking under previous administrations. Aitkenhead estimated that an anaesthetic machine costing £25 000 discounted over a 10 year period would add £4 to the cost of each operation[35]; anaesthetic work stations that include full integral monitoring and computerised record keeping cost twice as much, but even this would be a tiny proportion of an operation's total cost. There is increasing evidence to convince managers that compliance with minimum monitoring standards does improve the safety of anaesthesia.[36] The Australian incident monitoring study of 2000 incidents, showed that the role of monitors in aiding patient safety was thoroughly vindicated.[9 37] Tinker et al reviewed 1175 anaesthetic related malpractice claims between 1974 and 1988[38]: among the 1097 claims with sufficient information available for the reviewers to make a judgement,

170

31·5% of negative outcomes—the worst rated—would have been prevented by additional monitors. Pulse oximetry and capnometry were judged the most useful monitors. Since minimal standards for anaesthesia have been adopted in the United States the cost of malpractice claims against anaesthesiologists has decreased by about two thirds and in the Harvard group of hospitals insurance premiums for anaesthesiologists have fallen by 40% and are now less than for a urologist or gynaecologist.[39]

A common cause of incidents is failure to understand how to use the equipment.[7 8 26 40] This is no surprise; one survey disclosed that 48% of anaesthetists use new equipment without reading the instruction manual.[41] Some manuals are ignored because they are excessively long and poorly written. Sometimes, because of urgency or other force of circumstance there is no opportunity for training, and it is regrettable that hospitals commonly fail to ensure that sufficient time is devoted to training.

Another common cause of incidents is failure to check equipment before use[7 8 26 40 42]: between 30% and 41% of anaesthetists perform no checks and, of those who do, few follow the guidelines of the Association of Anaesthetists.[43] Seemingly the risk of serious injury is perceived as being so small that the effort is not seen to be justified, a view strengthened by the knowledge that trivial equipment related incidents are a daily occurrence which are almost always detected and rectified—a very dangerous attitude.

The anaesthetist is held legally responsible for the functioning of the equipment he or she uses and the drugs given. Apart from the checks of the machine and monitors, other danger areas that need special attention are unlabelled syringes, running repairs to equipment (especially components of the airway), drugs drawn up by other staff, and the vaporiser that looks full but is actually empty, which is one cause of painful awareness. All new staff and locums should receive training on the equipment used by the department and should be provided with protocols for equipment checks.

Procedures to ensure that hazard warning notices and safety action bulletins issued by Medical Devices Directorate are received and read by relevant staff are the resposibility of the hospital managers and the clinical director. In a recent survey of southwest England only 66% of consultant anaesthetists and 33% of junior anaesthetists were moderately confident that they had seen relevant notices.[41]

Adverse incident reporting systems

An integral part of any risk management programme is the reporting of adverse incidents since the collection and interpretation of such data allow patterns of particular or repeated events to be identified. A suitable system will facilitate the mapping of the distribution of incidents within the hospital and is described in greater detail by Lindgren et al.[44] Although complete computerised hospital adverse incident reporting systems are still fairly uncommon in the United Kingdom, anaesthetic audit systems have been recording critical incidents and complications in many hospitals for some years. To be of use, serious or repeated incidents must be investigated and recommendations made to reduce the likelihood of recurrence. The Australian incident monitoring study (AIMS) recommends that a non-culpable culture that encourages reporting of critical incidents is essential if the full potential of incident analysis as a means of identifying risk is to be realised and that this should include accepting anonymous reports.[45] The relation between hospitalwide adverse incident reports and critical incident monitoring in anaesthesia needs to be agreed to avoid unnecessary data collection; incidents in which patients may have suffered actual harm should always be reported to the central risk management system.

Medical records

The risk of litigation may be reduced by maintaining high quality anaesthetic records. If the plaintiff has been granted legal aid the hospital will have to pay its own costs of a court case even when it wins. In the High Court this may amount to £100 000. Properly kept anaesthetic records will reduce the chance of the expert witness for the plaintiff, when reviewing the notes, alleging that as a matter of probability (without evidence to the contrary) the cause of, say, brain damage was a hypoxic episode and may prevent the case coming to court. Meticulous notes detailing drug doses and vapour concentrations may help to defend against allegations of awareness.[46] The development of modern complete monitoring systems allows continuous printouts of information monitored, with the ability for the information monitored, with the ability for the anaesthetist to mark drugs and events on the same chart. These printouts provide valuable evidence of exactly what took place at what time, but it is important to note artifacts and add any necessary explanation.

Communication and informed consent

Good communication with patients is a crucial part of clinical practice and one of the most effective means of preventing litigation when patients believe that something has gone wrong. Doctors who seem hurried and uninterested are at risk of being sued even if they practice good quality medicine.[47] For the anaesthetist this communication needs to start with the preoperative visit. Furthermore, patients now expect to give "informed" consent to the procedures carried out. Lord Bridge, considering the case of Mrs Sidaway versus the Board of Governors of the Bethlem Royal Hospital in the House of Lords, stated in his judgement, "When specifically questioned by a patient of apparently sound mind about risks involved in a particular treatment proposed, a doctor's duty must, in my opinion, be to answer both truthfully and as fully as the questioner requires."[48] Lord Scarman in a minority judgement in the same case felt that the doctor should be liable "where the risk is such that in the court's view a prudent person in the patient's situation would have regarded it as significant."[48] There have recently been increasing numbers of legal cases concerning informed consent, many of which have been won by the plaintiff.

In view of the high incidence of complaints to the Medical Defence Union it is prudent to warn patients about the possibility of damage to their teeth, particularly to teeth that are already loose and in patients with capped or crowned teeth. Similarly, if regional analgesia is proposed the possibility of pain or discomfort (accounting for 7·5% of claims to the Medical Defence Union) should be discussed and the patient reassured about the action the anaesthetist would take.[46] If the patient is clearly unhappy at the prospect and there is no strong contraindication for general anaesthesia it is probably wiser to opt for a general anaesthetic. Consent for the use of suppositories for postoperative analgesia should always be sought from the patient preoperatively.[49] If general anaesthesia with concurrent regional analgesia is proposed it is important to explain this to the patient (or their parent): a patient expecting general anaesthesia who in addition suffers an inadvertent spinal tap or neurological damage is likely to feel upset and angry. A report of the preoperative visit and the issues discussed should always be made in the patient's notes.

Operating theatre procedures

Each operating theatre should have strict procedures for checking the patient, the intended operation, and the consent form. The operating list should be clearly displayed with the patients' names, hospital numbers, and intended operation. The order of the operating list should be altered only for emergencies and patients should be accompanied by their notes, any relevant radiographs or electrocardiograms, and results of blood tests. Skilled help for the anaesthetist should be available throughout 24 hours.[11 25 29] Good operating theatre procedures should ensure that trained staff routinely protect patients against injury to eyes, nerves, and skin and from diathermy burns. In addition, training for staff in lifting and handling patients is an important safeguard against back injury, a common cause of staff sickness which may lead staff to sue their employer.

Supervision of junior staff

Failure to supervise junior anaesthetists is a common factor in anaesthetic accidents. Reports by Lunn and Mushin[50] and the later CEPOD reports[11 25] indicate that perioperative mortality is to some degree related to the supervision of trainees in anaesthesia, especially in very sick or elderly patients or patients admitted as emergencies. Cooper showed that lack of supervision was the single most commonly associated factor in anaesthetic mishaps[7] and Gannon that inadequate supervision was a factor in 32% of anaesthetic deaths.[51] The CEPOD report of 1987 recommended that a consultant should be responsible for all elective lists.[11] Medical audit databases can provide useful information as to the degree of supervision and types of cases that juniors are undertaking, which can also be used for their training logbook.

Clinical directors of departments of anaesthesia are responsible for ensuring that the service provided for each operating list is given by appropriately qualified anaesthetists and that junior staff are aware of guidelines and rules, especially when to call for help. A common cause for concern is lack of induction courses for staff (especially locums) joining departments. Training of young anaesthetists should emphasise the value of "safe" anaesthetic practice in reducing risk to the patient and of being alert to the possibility of awareness.

Locum cover

Locums are commonly involved in medicolegal problems. Often hired in haste to fill gaps in staffing cover, frequently for a weekend,

174

their credentials may not be fully checked. Some doctors remain locums because of difficulty in securing a recognised post and tend to pass from one short term job to another. They may encounter considerable difficulty in keeping their postgraduate training up to date. It is important that the consultant responsible for obtaining locums vets their qualifications and experience, and he or she *must* make checks with a previous employer.[52] Too often this task is left to a very junior medical staffing officer. The degree to which junior staff locums may be left unsupervised should be decided by the clinical director and made explicit to the person responsible for drawing up the rota. Special care needs to be taken with locum consultants who will be left without supervision.

Recovery rooms

The use of recovery rooms, provided they are appropriately staffed and equipped, should lead to fewer accidents occurring in the immediate postoperative period, and recovery rooms should be available to receive all postoperative patients 24 hours a day.[11 25] The precipitate return of a patient to a surgical ward, where the degree of patient supervision may be much less, owing to inadequate staffing and the consequences of skill mix reviews in the interests of economy, does place sick postoperative patients at risk of complications going unrecognised, and the anaesthetist may be criticised for allowing discharge to the ward too early. High dependency units or the postanaesthetic recovery (PAR) rooms used in many North American hospitals, where patients stay for considerable periods after major surgery before returning to the ward, have much to commend them. They have the added advantage of allocation of an anaesthetist to the facility, enabling cardiorespiratory instability to be treated and proper pain relief maintained, and in addition, postoperative complications are more likely to be accurately recorded than in the ward.

Continuing medical education

The importance of postgraduate education and training has been a feature in published work related to adverse events in anaesthesia. A risk management programme should keep under review the opportunities and funding available to staff for continuing education.

The royal colleges are all developing continuing medical education schemes for consultants, requiring a set number of hours of approved study in order to retain the right to teach. It is not clear, at this point, what sanctions will apply for failure to comply.

The current position as regards the Calman recommendations for staff in training[53] is also unclear. The proposals for the hours that junior doctors may work; new style training posts, meaning significant reductions in the availability and numbers of junior staff; an official ceiling on the numbers of non-consultant career grades; and a shortage of available potential consultants will all tend to make anaesthetic staffing increasingly difficult to maintain and hamper opportunities for time allowed for junior staff to attend courses for specialist diplomas, in house postgraduate meetings, and training in practical anaesthesia.

The job description and contract of consultants in the NHS do not encourage flexibility of interpretation. Accreditation entails demonstrating broad skills across the anaesthetic range. However, after appointment to a consultant post an anaesthetist may be contractually required to cover the same operation lists for years making it difficult to maintain skills in subspecialties which require constant practice, especially in small children, thoracic and vascular surgery, emergency neurosurgery, neonatal care, and cardiac surgery. Many such cases are referred to regional centres but a patient reasonably expects that the anaesthetist is appropriately skilful for their particular condition. Clinical directors bear the responsibility of ensuring that operating sessions are covered by doctors with appropriate specialist competence. Frequently on-call work is split into subspecialty rotas such as those for small children, obstetrics, and intensive care. Postgraduate training should be available to consultants to promote their maintenance of necessary experience and skills, including advanced trauma (ATLS) and cardiac life support (ACLS) courses. This may require flexibility in the weekly timetable and, in smaller hospitals, the opportunity to practise in larger postgraduate centres.

Evaluating risks associated with new techniques

Anaesthesia has to adapt to changing surgical requirements, and hazards that may be peculiar to a new operation or anaesthetic technique need to be considered. In the early days of laparoscopy patients were occasionally anaesthetised solely with a mask and spontaneous ventilation, with inevitably serious consequences. Laser surgery to the lower respiratory tract to relieve the dyspnoea of bronchial tumour is a procedure potentially fraught with hazard, and laparoscopic cholecystectomy has cardiovascular effects on older patients under general anaesthesia that might not have been expected.[54] Such procedures need consideration, discussion, and evaluation by senior anaesthetists before a protocol is developed and junior staff left unsupervised.

Damage limitation

Even in the best hospitals accidents will continue to happen, and the organisation needs to develop policy as to how to cope with a patient who has been harmed and who is angry or with the relatives. Denial and secrecy usually lead to an increasingly vindictive victim whereas honesty, discussion, and offers of support may defuse the situation before lawyers become involved.

Patients who have suffered anaesthetic awareness need counselling and understanding, and it is essential that nurses in whom the patient may confide always inform the anaesthetist involved as soon as possible.

Admitting to an accident need not automatically include admission of any negligence. Patients are often very anxious that their bad experience will not be suffered by others and seek reassurance that the hospital has learnt from the event. Early support for the patient by staff mature enough to deal with the situation is important, as is support for the doctor or nurse, who usually feels very deeply about the accident and whose feelings are all too often ignored.

A recent study suggests that many senior doctors suffer high levels of stress, both anxiety and depression.[55] Other studies have found similar problems in junior doctors.[56 57] Psychological ill health often leads to excessive alcohol use or drug dependency. These are conditions which are dangerous for patients in any doctor but can be quickly lethal in an anaesthetist. To turn a blind eye on a troubled colleague does no one any good. There are procedures to help sick doctors before patients are harmed, in particular the three wise men procedure,[58] the mechanism of which should be clearly understood by all medical and senior nursing staff. Additionally, professional help for a sick anaesthetist can be provided by the confidential Counselling Service for Anaesthetists based at the Association of Anaesthetists' headquarters.

To most anaesthetists the issues discussed in this chapter will be familiar, and yet in the hurly-burly of modern hospital life it is often difficult for the clinical director and his or her colleagues to

177

find the time to review risk factors regularly and remind and educate new and current staff about methods to reduce avoidable risk. Such regular review—perhaps three monthly—might become the responsibility of a particular consultant and could, like clinical audit, become a part of regular postgraduate training programmes in order to promote a continuing improvement in patient safety.

1 Runciman WB. Risk assessment in the formulation of anaesthesia safety standards. *Eur J Anaesthesiol* 1993;**10**(suppl 7):26–32.
2 Utting JE. Pitfalls in anaesthetic practice. *Br J Anaesth* 1987;**59**:877–90.
3 Aitkenhead AR. Risk management in anaesthesia. *Journal of the Medical Defence Union* 1991;**4**:86–90.
4 Jones JG. Memory of intraoperative events. *BMJ* 1994;**309**:967–8.
5 Osborne GA, Webb RK, Runciman WB. Patiet awareness during anaesthesia: an analysis of 2000 incident reports. *Anaesth Intensive Care* 1993;**21**:653–4.
6 Payne JP. Awareness and its medicolegal implications. *Br J Anaesth* 1994;**73**: 38–45.
7 Cooper JB, Newbower RS, Kitz RJ. An analysis of major errors and equipment failure in anesthesia management considerations for prevention and detection. *Anesthesiology* 1984;**60**:34–42.
8 Cooper JB, Newbower RS, Long CD, *et al.* Preventable anesthesia mishaps. *Anesthesiology* 1978;**49**:399–406.
9 Webb RK, Van Der Walt JH, Runciman WB, *et al.* Which monitor? An analysis of 2000 incident reports. *Anaesth Intensive Care* 1993;**21**:529–42.
10 Van Der Walt JH, Webb RK, Osborne GA, *et al.* Recovery room incidents in the first 2000 incident reports. *Anaesth Intensive Care* 1993;**21**:650–2.
11 Buck N, Devlin HB, Lunn JN. *Report of a confidential enquiry into perioperative deaths (CEPOD).* London: Nuffield Provincial Hospitals Trust/King's Fund, 1987.
12 Tiret L, Desmonts J-M, Hatton F, *et al.* Complications associated with anaesthesia—a prospective survey in France. *Canadian Anaesthetists Society Journal* 1986;**33**:336–44.
13 Cohen MH, Duncan PG, Pope WDB, *et al.* A survey of 112 000 anaesthetics at one teaching hospital. *Canadian Anaesthetists Society Journal* 1986;**33**:22–31.
14 McIntyre JWR. Alarms in the operating room. *Can J Anaesth* 1991;**38**:951–3.
15 Gaba DM, Maxwell M, DeAnda A. Anesthetic mishaps: breaking the chain of accident evolution. *Anesthesiology* 1987;**66**:670–6.
16 Gaba DM. Human error in anesthetic mishaps. *Int Anesthesiol Clin* 1989;**27**: 137–47.
17 Newbower RS, Cooper JB, Long CD. Failure analysis—the human element. In: Gravenstein JS, Newbower RS, Ream AK, *et al*, eds. *Essential non-invasive monitoring in anaesthesia.* New York: Grune and Stratton, 1980:269–82.
18 Cooper JB, Long CD, Newbower RS, *et al.* Critical incidents associated with intraoperative exchanges of anesthesia personnel. *Anesthesiology* 1982;**36**: 456–61.
19 Reason J. *Human error.* New York: Cambridge University Press, 1990.
20 DeAnda A, Gaba DM. Role of experience in the response to simulated critical incidents. *Anesth Analg* 1991;**72**:308–15.
21 DeAnda A, Gaba DM. Unplanned incidents during comprehensive anesthesia simulation. *Anesth Analg* 1990;**71**:77–82.

22 Schwid HA, O'Donnell D. Anesthesiologist's management of simulated critical incidents. *Anesthesiology* 1992;76:495–501.

23 Hawkins FH. *Human factors in flight.* Aldershot: Gower Technical Press, 1987.

24 Barton A. 'Alarm signals' over warning signs? *Anaesthesia* 1991;46:809.

25 Campling EA, Devlin HB, Hoile RW, et al. *Report of the national confidential enquiry into perioperative deaths 1990.* London: Nuffield Provincial Hospitals Trust/King's Fund, 1987.

26 Craig J, Wilson ME. A study of anaesthetic misadventures. *Anaesth* 1981;36: 933–6.

27 Thompson PW. Safer design of anaesthetic machines. *Br J Anaesth* 1987;59: 913.

28 Currie M. A prospective survey of anaesthetic critical events in a teaching hospital. *Anaesth Intensive Care* 1989;17:403–11.

29 Department of Health, Welsh Office, Scottish Home and Health Department, and DHSS, Northern Ireland. *Report on confidential enquiries into maternal deaths in the United Kingdom 1985–1987.* London: HMSO, 1991.

30 Brahams D. Anaesthesia and the law. Monitoring. *Anaesthesia* 1989;44:606–7.

31 Schreiber P, Schreiber J. *Anesthesia system risk analysis and risk reduction.* Telford, Pennsylvania: Drager, 1987.

32 Galletly DC, Mushet NN. Anaesthesia system errors. *Anaesth Intensive Care* 1991;19:66–73.

33 Eaton JM, Fielden JM, Wilson ME. *Anaesthesia action plans.* 2nd ed. Maidenhead, Berkshire: Abbott Laboratories, 1994.

34 Gaba DM, Howard SK, Fish KJ, et al. Anesthesia crisis resource management training. *Anesthesiology* 1991;75:A1062.

35 Aitkenhead AR. Risk management in anaesthesia. *Healthcare Risk Management Bulletin* 1992;2:4–5.

36 Eickhorn JH. Prevention of intraoperative anesthesia accidents and related severe injury through safety monitoring. *Anesthesiology* 1989;70:572–7.

37 Morgan CA, Webb RK, Cockings JA, et al. Cardiac arrest—an analysis of 2000 incident reports. *Anaesth Intensive Care* 1993;21:626–37.

38 Tinker JH, Dull DL, Caplan RA, et al. Review of 1175 anesthesia related malpractice claims between 1974 and 1988. *Anesthesiology* 1989;71:541–6.

39 Taylor TH, Goldhill DR. Standards and audit. In: *Standards of care in anaesthesia.* Oxford: Butterworth-Heinemann, 1992:170.

40 Kuman V, Barcellos WA, Mehta MP, et al. An analysis of critical incidents in a teaching department for quality assurance. A survey of mishaps during anaesthesia. *Anaesthesia* 1988;43:879–83.

41 Weir PM, Wilson ME. Are you getting the message? A look at the communication between the Department of Health, manufacturers and anaesthetists. *Anaesthesia* 1991;46:845–8.

42 Chopra V, Bovill JG, Spierdijk J, et al. Reported significant observations during anaesthesia: a prospective analysis over an 18 month period. *Br J Anaesth* 1992; 68:13–7.

43 Mayor AH, Eaton JM. Anaesthetic machine checking practices: a survey. *Anaesthesia* 1992;47:866–8.

44 Lingren O, Secker-Walker J. Incident reporting systems: early warning for the prevention and control of clinical negligence. Chapter 20, this volume.

45 Runciman WB, Sellen A, Webb RK, et al. Errors, incidents and accidents in anaesthetic practice. *Anaesth Intensive Care* 1993;21:506–19.

46 Aitkenhead AR. Awareness during anaesthesia: what the patient should be told. *Anaesthesia* 1990;45:351–2.

47 Hickson G, Clayton EW, Entman SS, et al. Obstetricians' prior malpractice experience and patients' satisfaction with care. *JAMA* 1994;272:1583–7.

48 Sidaway v Board of Governors of the Bethlem Royal and the Maudsley Hospital [1985] 2 WLR 480.

49 Mitchell J. A fundamental problem of consent. *BMJ* 1995;**310**:43–6.
50 Lunn JN, Mushin WW. *Mortality associated with anaesthesia.* London: Nuffield Provincial Hospitals Trust, 1982.
51 Gannon K. Mortality associated with anaesthesia. *Anaesthesia* 1991;**46**:962–6.
52 Atkinson RS. The problem of the unsafe anaesthetist. *Br J Anaesth* 1994;**73**: 29–30.
53 Department of Health. *Hospital doctors: training for the future. Report of the Working Group on Specialist Medical Training.* London: HMSO, 1993.
54 Bromley LM. Does minimal access cholecystectomy require simple anaesthesia? *Clinical Risk* 1995;**1**:18–21.
55 Caplan RP. Stress, anxiety, and depression in hospital consultants, general practitioners, and senior health service managers. *BMJ* 1994;**309**:1261–3.
56 Valko RJ, Clayton PJ. Depression in the internship. *Diseases of Nervous System* 1975;**36**:26–9.
57 Reuben DB. Depressive symptoms in medical house officers. Effects of level of training and work rotation. *Arch Intern Med* 1985;**145**:286–8.
58 Department of Health. *Prevention of harm to patients resulting from physical or mental disability of hospital or community medical or dental staff.* London: DoH, 1982. (HC (82) 13.)

11 Clinical risk management: urology and general surgery

P J B SMITH

By its very nature an operation is a hazardous affair. The surgical insult to the body combined with the stress of life support systems caused by anaesthesia will always be a risk for any patient requiring surgery. This risk is directly proportional to any pre-existing medical disorders, particularly those of the circulatory and cardiorespiratory systems. Nevertheless, a wide variety of clinical situations require surgical intervention. Any associated recognisable risks are "calculated risks" and in that respect, if that is realised, they are normally clinically acceptable.

Before attempting any operation a surgeon should be satisfied that the choice of surgical treatment is correct and therefore the natural hazards of surgery and any attendant anaesthesia are acceptable. A surgeon must be aware that the operation is but the middle part of overall surgical management, which will also include a preoperative assessment and postoperative care.

At any one of these three stages of surgical management a surgeon must realise the acceptable risks to which the patient may be exposed. Furthermore the patient should, to a reasonable extent, also be aware of the nature and incidence of such risks. It is to be remembered that not only each operation but also each patient will be different. A surgeon should choose the correct level of explanation consistent with the patient's ability to understand any attendant risks, but at the same time not be unnecessarily alarmist in their description.

181

Similarly, when problems arise during surgery or in the postoperative period, it is important that where possible the patient and, if necessary, the relatives, have an understanding of the nature of those complications and the treatments being provided.

The risks of any surgical intervention on any patient can be broadly divided into generalised and specific. Generalised risks relate to abnormal stresses on vital functions, in particular the cardiac and respiratory systems. These risks are mainly associated with the necessary attendant anaesthesia required for most operations. Although an anaesthetist is required to give a professional opinion on the suitability or otherwise of a patient requiring surgery, it remains the ultimate responsibility of the surgeon whether to proceed with such surgery or not. The other generalised area of morbidity of surgical procedures lies within the circulatory system. In both the arterial and venous parts of that system intraoperative and postoperative changes may result in ischaemia (reduced blood supply), necrosis (death from lack of blood supply), or, specifically in the case of the venous system, the development of thromboses (intravascular blood clots) with either local or central (blockage of pulmonary circulation) complications.

Specific risks concern surgical procedures that may interfere with other organs at the site of an operation. These structures, not necessarily associated with the operative manoeuvre itself, are at risk if the surgical anatomy of the procedure is not adequately displayed. On occasion complications associated with disease or previous surgery may interfere with normal surgical anatomy and increase the difficulty of the operation, and hence the risk to adjacent organs.

Finally, surgery of the urinary tract or the gastrointestinal tract carries a high incidence of secondary sepsis within the operative field. This may subsequently complicate a patient's recovery or interfere with the natural healing of tissues associated with that urological surgery.

Ultimately, as in all aspects of medical and surgical care, much will depend on the professional skill of the clinician. Unlike any other branch of medicine surgery requires the learning of two disciplines. The first is the necessary knowledge of the background of diseases requiring surgical care. The second is the development of the optical and manual skills required to perform operations. In this respect surgeons have to be the equivalent of "physicians who operate." Inevitable variations between these two clinical skills will exist in any one surgeon at any one time.

Ideally, all operations should be performed by consultants. In practice this would, within a generation, lead to the virtual collapse of British surgical practice. An essential component of a consultant surgeon's professional responsibility is the necessary training of junior doctors. Surgery, in all its aspects, is a practical subject. There is no substitute for the real world of surgical management in the training of surgeons. Routine operations performed by competent surgeons should not result in unacceptable injuries to patients. Competent surgeons are either those whose training is complete (consultants) or those in training but directly (within the operating theatre or outpatient environments) supervised by competent surgeons.

Surgical training must necessarily teach both medical and operative skills. This training commences in undergraduate life. It is no coincidence that British medical schools award two medical degrees, one for medicine and one for surgery. Initially a surgeon's training involves the acquiring of knowledge of overall surgical management. To this is gradually added the technical ability to perform operations as part of treatment. Both the intellectual and practical training of a surgeon require constant supervision. It represents a long tradition of apprenticeship training. Junior surgeons should only be allowed to undertake operations and, indeed, make decisions on the use of such operations when those concerned with their training are satisfied that they are competent in both aspects. At all times a surgical trainee must be under the supervision of a consultant surgeon. This need not necessarily always be direct (in person). Indeed, in a busy hospital within the United Kingdom such one to one continuous supervision would be impossible.

In emergency surgery the stakes are raised. The optimum level of direct care by consultants cannot be maintained 24 hours a day. Thus in the night time performance of emergency surgery care has to be taken to limit the number of operations to an absolute minimum and then only to perform them if a senior opinion can be obtained by way of an on call consultant. Wherever possible, emergency surgery should be performed in daylight hours when the fully working and on site consultant support is available. Inevitably there will be situations when this cannot be achieved. The level of competence of surgeons in these night time hours must therefore be less, and the "acceptability" of risks is correspondingly increased.

Notwithstanding the high standards of surgical care that exist in the United Kingdom there are areas of urology and general surgery where specific risk related procedures exist and surgical hazards may be encountered.

Urology

Urology is one of the oldest branches of surgery. It was the first surgical specialty to undertake minimally invasive surgery, by way of transurethral surgery to the bladder and prostate. Urology carries a high diagnostic bias with various radiological and endoscopic procedures being designed to provide the maximum of preoperative information and, hence, diagnosis. The development of modern optical systems and the use of video linked training, particularly in transurethral surgery, have maintained a high standard of urological care in the United Kingdom.

Transurethral surgery

Patients undergoing transurethral surgery, most commonly prostatectomy, are usually elderly and thereby liable to have coexisting circulatory and cardiorespiratory problems. They require careful preoperative assessment and equally careful anaesthesia. The use of the urethra for surgical access makes them at risk from urinary tract infection and on occasions blood born infections during or immediately after transurethral procedures. This is particularly so if the preoperative urine is already infected. To reduce this risk of possibly life threatening sepsis patients should have an immediate preoperative urine culture. If the result is either not available or the test not feasible then it is considered best to protect such patients from the risk of infection by a "single shot" of intravenous antibiotic before any transurethral surgery.

Sexual dysfunction

Loss of erectile function is a recognised but uncommon complication of prostatectomy.[1] In this respect, as for any operation performed on an elderly man, it may occur as part of an overall steady diminution in libido, accelerated by the psychogenic factors of major surgery in this age group. There is no specific mechanical interference with erectile function from routine transurethral resection of the prostate. Patients who are sexually active should,

184

however, be warned before a prostatectomy that there may be a diminution in libido and with that some loss of erectile function.

It is important in the preoperative assessment of patients awaiting transurethral prostatectomy to indicate the inevitable occurrence of retrograde ejaculation as a result of such a resection. Retrograde ejaculation does not destroy the ejaculatory reflex or the relating sensation. However, the patient should be warned that little if any ejaculate may appear at the external urethral meatus. It will subsequently wash out with the next void of urine. Men who are sexually active and, although admittedly in only a few cases, concerned about their fertility, should be warned in advance of this disturbance of ejaculatory function that a prostatectomy involves.

The use of preoperative information sheets for patients undergoing prostatectomy may be of assistance in establishing these sexual facts. These allow the patients to consider such matters for private discussion, where a formal consultation might be either embarrassing or inappropriate.

Urinary incontinence

Urinary incontinence after a transurethral resection is rare.[2] It should not occur in a routine procedure performed by a competent surgeon. Such incontinence is due to damage of the external sphincter during that procedure. The anatomical distribution of the prostate and the known and established endoscopic appearances and manoeuvres of transurethral surgery should prevent such sphincter damage. There are, however, instances, such as previous prostate surgery or malignant prostate disease, when the anatomy of the posterior urethra and within that the prostate and external sphincter, are sufficiently disturbed for the surgeon to inadvertently and therefore in risk terms acceptably, extend the resection into the sphincter system. Thus patients with previous prostate surgery and with known carcinoma of the prostate should be warned that full urinary control after their transurethral surgery cannot be guaranteed.

Another cause of prostatectomy incontinence is the "unmasking" of an irritable bladder syndrome—namely, a primary detrusor muscle instability. The preoperative existence of this abnormality should be considered in patients with pronounced symptoms of frequency and urgency disproportionate to any obstructive symptoms present (hesitancy, slow stream, and terminal dribbling). In these patients it is best to undertake urodynamic studies to assess the proportions of obstructive and irritable symptoms before embarking on a prostatectomy. If these tests show a predominantly irritable rather than obstructive picture surgery may not be appropriate.

Such situations require careful consideration because a degree of bladder instability is also associated with straightforward obstruction. If doubt exists as to the precise mixture of obstructive and irritable symptoms the patient should be warned of the possibility of postprostatectomy frequency, urgency, and even urge incontinence.

Haemorrhage

A major risk to the patient undergoing transurethral surgery is haemorrhage. Although an ever present risk in any operation, bleeding can be particularly difficult to deal with during and after transurethral surgery. In the event of serious haemorrhage facilities should always be available for patients to be returned to theatre for further endoscopic surgery and haemostasis. If necessary, open exposure with packing of the bleeding area may be needed. For this reason transurethral surgery should ideally only be performed during "daylight hours" with the facilities of a postoperative recovery area and, if needed, easy access to an intensive therapy unit.

Perforation

Perforation of the prostate capsule is a relatively common event in transurethral surgery. Provided it is identified and any associated bleeding controlled, no immediate harm will come from such a perforation. The use of prophylactic antibiotic cover and the maintenance of catheter drainage in the postoperative period will be sufficient to "cure" such perforations. In most cases, provided any associated bleeding is controlled, it is possible to complete the operation, despite the presence of such a perforation.

Care is needed in any transurethral surgery in relation to the risk of extravasation of irrigant fluid into the tissues surrounding the prostate. The presence of small amounts will cause no immediate harm. Continuous reabsorption of increasing quantities can, however, over a period of time, induce a potentially life threatening fluid overload of the circulation. This, the so called transurethral resection syndrome,[3] can be dangerous in that it may induce cerebral oedema and lead to circulatory failure. If significant

186

extravasation of irrigant fluid has occurred it is important to complete the operation as quickly as possible even if this is only half done. It is always easy to revisit the operative site some weeks later to complete the surgery.

If a patient shows the postoperative signs of such a fluid overloaded by way of restlessness, disturbance of circulation, and signs of cerebral oedema, it is important to shift that fluid from the tissues into the circulation and from there via the kidneys into urine. This is achieved by the use of rapid intravenous infusions of hypertonic solutions.

Prostate cancer

Prostate cancer has become an increasingly complex condition to manage.[4] This is because the development of a tumour marker, prostate specific androgen, has allowed for the early diagnosis of this disease in an increasing number of men. However, the biology of prostate cancer is still not fully understood. What is known is that all men if they live long enough will develop malignant cells within their prostate. The question remains at what stage do these malignant cells constitute a threat to the patient's life and thereby indicate a need for treatment.

Palliative treatment of advanced prostate disease by way of transurethral surgery for the local cancer and androgen suppression for metastatic cancer is most effective. In over 80% of patients such hormone treatment will give an adequate urological response for two to five years.

It is, however, in the younger man, a situation somewhat arbitrarily suggested at less than the age of 65, that difficulties arise. In these men a raised prostate specific androgen should cause concern for the diagnosis of early, localised prostate cancer. That in turn should trigger the performance of a prostate ultrasound examination and simultaneous guided needle biopsy. If these tests prove positive then consideration should be given to radical (curative) treatment either by way of surgery or radiotherapy. All patients should be aware of the specific risks of such radical treatments. These are incontinence and impotence from radical prostatectomy and proctitis from radical radiotherapy. Any "young" man with localised prostate cancer needs to contribute to the decision on its treatment. The surgeon must be aware of the need to assess separately each case of localised prostate cancer no matter what the age or general condition of the patient.

187

Stone disease

The past 10 years have seen a revolution in the management of urinary tract stones through the development of endoscopes to extract stones from the ureter and stone machines to shatter stones within the renal pelvis of the kidney.[5] These developments have been so successful that the previous formal open operations of stone surgery (pyelolithotomy, nephrolithotomy, or ureterolithotomy) have all but disappeared.

A patient presenting with a diagnosis of urinary tract stone disease should be investigated to show the site, size, and number of stones.

Stones in the lower half of the ureter can be extracted by endoscopic means, sometimes with preliminary in situ destruction using special probes applied directly to the stone under endoscopic vision. Any endoscopy of the ureter associated with stone extraction carries the risk of damaging the ureteric wall. This may cause a perforation and thereby allow urine to leak into the surrounding tissues. If untreated this extravasated urine can result in a profound reaction around the ureter which, because of its tenuous blood supply, may partially necrose and develop a fibrous contracture (stricture). For this reason, when doubt exists as to the state of the ureter after endoscopic surgery, a temporary indwelling fine, hollow, plastic stent should be inserted to protect the ureter. This stent has the effects of directly draining urine from the kidney above to the bladder below and at the same time "splinting" the damaged ureter, to allow for the healing process to occur.

Stones in the upper ureter and renal pelvis are accessible to endoscopy but the complication rate of ureteric injury is much greater. A ureteroscope should only be used in the upper ureter by an experienced urologist and then only under radiographic control. This ideal situation is not always possible and therefore stones in the upper ureter are normally best treated by their upward dislodgement into the renal pelvis, the collecting system of the kidney, with the simultaneous insertion of an indwelling ureteric stent maintaining their presence in the kidney.

Stones in the renal pelvis, either original or displaced from the ureter, are best treated by a lithotripter (stone machine). This technique results in the fragmentation of those stones sufficient for their subsequent easy passage as debris in the urine. This will occur in over 80% of patients.

An alternative treatment for stones in the renal pelvis is percutaneous nephrolithotomy. This follows the same broad

188

principle as endoscopy treatment of stones in the lower ureter but with the important difference that access to the stone has to be through a track through the loin and, more importantly, the vascular tissues of the kidney substance. There is a significant risk of renal haemorrhage either during or after a percutaneous nephro- lithotomy. Even in the most experienced of surgical hands, kidney stones, and in particular sizeable fragments thereof, may be difficult to remove complete via a nephroscope.

Open renal surgery is now rarely required. It is, however, an option that the patient with an extensive kidney stone (for example, staghorn kidney) should still consider. An initial exploration by open surgery may be indicated if this can result in the removal of the greater bulk of the stone, thus leaving any remnants to be treated by stone machine.

In summary, the lithotripter remains the treatment of choice for most kidney stones. If percutaneous surgery is considered, the patient should be advised of the risks of kidney bleeding and the possible failure of complete stone extraction compared with the virtual bloodless nature and high success rate of the stone machine. Percutaneous nephrolithotomy, when indicated, should only be performed by an experienced urologist. Primary treatment by open exploration of kidney or ureter for stone disease should only be performed in special circumstances with the patient's clear understanding that lithotripter or endoscopic treatments have already been considered.

Vasectomy

The final group of urological patients at appreciable clinical risk of complication are those undergoing the relatively simple (in technical terms) operation of vasectomy. Men who undergo this operation may do so at the behest of their wives or partners for whom further pregnancy would cause physical, mental, or social distress. In other words, many men are having the operation for their wife's or partner's sake. This puts a degree of psychological pressure on them, such that if complications occur these are doubly miserable. It should also be remembered that men undergoing vasectomy are essentially fit and that any complication that arises will again be distressful in the disturbance of that prevasectomy fitness, particularly if this results in time off work.

It is essential before a vasectomy that the man should understand that there are complications in such scrotal surgery.[6] About 1 in

189

10 men may, as a result of vasectomy, have problems of scrotal bruising including haematoma formation, scrotal sepsis including an infected haematoma and, occasionally, a debilitating post-vasectomy pain syndrome. These complications do not relate to the performance of the operation. They represent the inevitable risk of vasectomy surgery in and around the nervous and vascular tisues of the scrotum.

Vasectomy is one of the most effective methods of preventing further parenthood but it has a failure rate.[7] A man undergoing vasectomy and his wife or partner should understand this. They should understand that the failure rate occurs either at an early stage before the vasectomy is completed or, more perplexingly, at a much later stage, sometimes years after the operation. This phenomenon is called late spontaneous recanalisation of vas.

General surgery

Vascular surgery

Vascular surgery is a surgical specialty with inherent risks both of complications and failure. This is due to the obvious risk to all related tissues through interference with their blood supply. Some risks are to an extent inevitable because the vascular disease process requiring surgery is itself already part way to threatening the viability of local tissues.

Carotid artery surgery carries an appreciable risk, estimated in the order of 5%, of producing major postoperative cerebrovascular accidents, in particular stroke.[8] Despite its relative rarity this complication is obviously highly relevant. Patients and, if needed, their relatives, should be warned of this risk before agreeing to carotid artery surgery.

The surgery of thoracic aneurysms runs the risk of interfering with the blood supply of the adjacent spinal cord through coincidental damage to the small spinal arteries.[9] The same risk will apply to major intrathoracic aortic reconstruction for congenital anomalies. The risk is sufficient to require a warning to patients and, if necessary, their relatives, especially of children. Its potential occurrence requires a total clinical justification for any such aortic surgery.

Peripheral limb ischaemia requiring femoropopliteal bypass is a common surgical situation. Failure rates of up to 10% can occur in such surgery.[10] These are due to thrombosis within the bypass or its distal arterial circulation. If postoperative occlusion of blood supply to the lower limb occurs this may result in the need for amputation. Patients undergoing peripheral vascular surgery need to be warned both of the possible failure of the procedure and, should ischaemic complications occur, the existence of that threat of amputation.

Any extensive dissection of an abdominal aorta and pelvic blood vessels for arterial disease or adjacent lymph node dissection runs the risk of damage to the virtually invisible, lumbar and pelvic autonomic nervous tissues. In men who are active sexually, and, in particular, younger men to whom fertility is important, damage to the autonomic nerves in these areas may impair sexual function.[11] This is particularly so in the case of surgical trauma to the sympathetic nerves, which can result in ejaculatory failure and the loss of orgasmic sensation. This in turn would be likely to impair overall erectile function and with that cause a disturbance of libido. Sexually active men undergoing extensive abdominal vascular or lymph node surgery should be warned of the possibility of such sexual side effects. In relation to any failure of ejaculation and any resultant effect on fertility, the question of preoperative sperm retrieval should be discussed beforehand.

Head and neck surgery

In surgery of the head and neck areas, there are two classic operative procedures which carry significant risks to the peripheral nervous system. The first of these, thyroidectomy, represents a threat through the well known anatomical relations of the recurrent laryngeal nerve to the blood supply of the thyroid. Damage of the nerve either by its crushing or division during the ligation of the vascular pedicles of the thyroid will result in a partial laryngeal palsy, and with that permanent hoarseness and noticeable voice impairment.[12] The risk is greater in the presence of infiltrative, either benign or malignant, disease of the thyroid. In particular the risk exists when the surgical anatomy and associated surgical dissection are complicated by the fibrosis of previous surgery in the same area A meticulous technique in the case of such surgically complicating features is mandatory in any thyroid procedure. Preoperative and postoperative inspection of the vocal cords by the anaesthetist is recommended.

The other nerve at risk in surgery of the head and neck is the facial nerve as it passes between the elements of the parotid gland. In surgery of the parotid gland (for example, for removal of a tumour) great care is required in the dissection so as to prevent damage to this nerve. Such damage, if it occurs, will result in a facial nerve palsy with appreciable cosmetic disadvantage, ophthalmic problems, and difficulties in mastication due to spillage of saliva. Dissection of the parotid gland requires a high level of surgical expertise and experience. It is mandatory to use a nerve stimulator during such dissection so as to identify and protect the branches of the facial nerve as they pass through the operative field of the parotid dissection.[13]

Gastrointestinal surgery

Surgery of the gastrointestinal tract represents the major area of emergency surgery. The acute abdomen remains a singular surgical challenge.[14] Medical audit has shown convincingly that the surgical management of acute abdominal disease is best performed by experienced surgeons during "daylight" hours. This provides the patient with the maximum benefit of appropriate surgical, anaesthetic, and nursing skills. A careful preoperative assessment with, if necessary, fluid replacement and antibiotic prophylaxis should be established. This gives maximum support to surgeon and anaesthetist in the performance of any laparotomy, and within that any subsequent gut surgery.

The provision of properly constructed junior doctor rotas with appropriate consultant cover providing clinical support and postgraduate training and supervision is essential. An increasing number of hospitals provide a specific emergency session within daylight hours to deal with all but the most acute surgical emergencies that present in the night time period. A few hours of preoperative treatment and the provision of fresh surgical skills in an up and running surgical environment may make all the difference between success and failure in the management of acute abdominal emergencies.

Any patient undergoing emergency or elective reconstructive surgery of the intestine, and in particular of the large intestine, needs to be warned beforehand of the possibility, and on occasion probability, of the need for an intestinal stoma (colostomy) as part of such surgery. This warning should be given even though in the preoperative phase this may be considered unlikely.

Extensive gut surgery within the pelvic cavity may inadvertently, but on occasion inevitably, cause considerable damage to the pelvic autonomic nervous system as it lies in the side wall of the pelvis. This is a particular risk in colorectal surgery for malignant disease when wide margins of dissection are required to ensure a successful cancer curing procedure. In such situations there may be postoperative disturbance of bladder function. This is due to interference with the synchronised balance of bladder function by way of its being a passive filling reservoir alternating with an active muscular pump. Post-operative disturbance of bladder function may be short term. However, so common is this urological complication that any patient undergoing major pelvic surgery should have a period of catheter drainage and thereafter careful monitoring of bladder function on removal of that catheter.

Disturbance of bladder function by way of postoperative retention is particularly common in women whose thin walled and poorly contractile bladders are particularly susceptible to relatively minor interference with normal bladder reflexes. Similarly, men in an age group with early prostatic obstruction may be "tipped into" urinary difficulties by way of coincidental pelvic autonomic nerve damage. Such situations are classically seen after abdominoperineal excision of the rectum. Again, careful and, if necessary, prolonged catheter drainage will help to obviate damage to the bladder by prolonged overdistention and thereby save some patients from developing chronic urinary retention.[15]

Hernia and varicose vein surgery

Two of the commonest, albeit in themselves minor, surgical operations—varicose vein surgery and hernia repair—represent low risk procedures.

It is important to warn all patients undergoing varicose vein surgery that the surgery is designed to treat the existing varicosities but cannot prevent further (not strictly recurrent) varicosities appearing within the same venous circulation. Modern methods for the management of varicose veins carry little risk. Any surgery represents no more risk than that associated with such minor operations—namely, bruising and infection at the site of the incision. However, care must be exercised during dissection of the saphenofemoral junction in those operations requiring removal of the long saphenous vein.[16] Only surgeons with the necessary experience and expertise, or those in training supervised by such a surgeon, should undertake this part of a varicose vein procedure. Any damage to the adjacent femoral nerve would have serious consequences for lower limb function.

Hernia surgery also carries a risk of recurrence. It is important that patients are warned of this. Many surgical techniques are available for this operation.[17] A surgeon will have a particular preference based on his personal experience. It would be reasonable for a surgeon to advise a patient of the basic design of the hernia operation and to indicate the existence of other techniques. Within the operation itself there are the usual risks of bleeding, haematoma formation, and sepsis.

Particularly in those techniques which use non-absorbable material it is important to stress to a patient that infection of such a hernia operation site might require the removal of that non-absorbable material should chronic wound sepsis occur. In the same way any non-absorbable material used should be inserted with an appropriate level of surgical hygiene, local antiseptics, and with consideration at least to the use of prophylactic antibiotics (usually by way of a "one shot" injection at the time of surgery).

Cholecystectomy

Removal of the gallbladder is one of the commonest procedures in general surgery. The operative technique for this procedure has changed dramatically in the past few years with the introduction of laparoscopic surgery. This is still probably the commonest and most successful of the so called "key hole" surgical procedures. As with all laparoscopic surgery there are risks involved separate from those which are inherent in any routine (open) surgical removal of a gallbladder.[18] Of these risks the greatest is damage to the adjacent common bile duct. Laparoscopic surgery has if anything reduced the risk of injury to the common bile duct due to the better visualisation of the surgical anatomy of the operative site intrinsic in the endoscopic technique. There does need to be a period of learning, however, in the technique of laparoscopic surgery in general and laparoscopic cholecystectomy in particular. During this learning period a surgeon should always be in a position to abandon the laparoscopic technique should difficulties—for example, troublesome bleeding—arise and proceed to perform a routine open procedure. With the growing expertise and experience among surgeons performing laparoscopic cholecystectomy the need for such open procedures will steadily diminish.

Laparoscopic techniques are, however, still to an extent experimental. Patients should be advised that the alternative of an open procedure is available and may indeed be required if the laparoscopic exposure is inadequate.

In general terms the development of laparoscopic techniques is to be encouraged. The significant reduction in operative morbidity associated with the minimal access involved in such surgery is to everyone's benefit, especially that of the patient. However, surgeons developing these innovative procedures must remain constantly aware of the need for care, particularly in the control of bleeding and with that the maintenance of good exposure of the operative field. Unlike the open procedure, in which direct control of bleeding and, if necessary, rapid enlargement of the operative field can be undertaken, laparoscopic surgery must proceed more carefully.

All surgical techniques have to start somewhere. There is no doubt that laparoscopic surgery is here to stay. An increasing range of operations are now available for this technique. The principle of selecting a laparoscopic technique remains the same—namely, that the operative manoeuvre itself must be as effective as that performed by the traditional open method. The advantage of laparoscopic surgery lies solely, but most importantly, in the significant reduction in operative morbidity and with that, hospital stay associated with the absence of an incision in the abdominal wall.

Overall risks of surgery

There are two areas of overall risk which all surgeons and sometimes their patients need to be aware.

The first of these is the postoperative development of a deep vein thrombosis. Certain operations and certain patients seem to be at much greater risk of this complication than others. These operations include major abdominal procedures requiring prolonged postoperative bed rest, and orthopaedic procedures, particularly those involving the lower limbs. The risk is particularly so in patients who have had a history of deep vein thrombosis.

The life threatening risk of a deep vein thrombosis is the development of a pulmonar embolus due to the release into the circulation of a portion of clot. This causes lung damage and with that heart frailure. Less serious but for the patient most miserable, is the development of localised impairment of venous circulation

195

in the affected area. Thus chronic leg pain and swelling may be long term sequelae of deep vein thrombosis.

Prophylactic anticoagulant treatment is essential for patients at risk from deep vein thrombosis. For high risk situations this is best provided by the use of heparin in that this gives greater control of anticoagulation during the perioperative period. Patients thus anticoagulated or those already on anticoagulation with warfarin or aspirin will be at risk from bleeding during any surgical procedure. That risk would need to be offset against the risk of any disturbance of anticoagulation through temporary cessation of anticoagulants. On balance, unless there is a serious risk of haemorrhage during surgery, patients with current anticoagulant therapy, a history of deep vein thrombosis, or with operations known to have an increased risk of such thrombosis, should have anticoagulant cover both during and for a period after their surgery. A low risk of thrombosis from surgery is best treated by the use of compression stockings combined with early postoperative mobilisation of the patient.

The other general risk relates to the potential infection of nonabsorbable materials. Although mention has been made previously to specific situations such as in hernia repairs, non-absorbable materials are used in many other surgical procedures. Thus vascular and urological prostheses need to be protected from accidental contamination by bacteria during the perioperative period, and through that the development of chronic sepsis of the prosthesis and surrounding tissues.

It is impossible to eliminate completely the risk of secondary infection of prostheses. It is, however, possible to reduce that risk by the use of a meticulous surgical technique, the provision of antisepsis, particularly in skin preparation, and finally, perhaps most importantly, by the use of prophylactic antibiotics at the time of surgery.

Conclusions

Whatever the future development of surgery both surgeons and their patients will need to accept the continued presence of risks. A reasonable proportion of such risks are acceptable, being calculated both before and during operations. Without taking such risks surgery will either never be attempted or worse still would be abandoned. These risks are largely recognised and their existence may need to be made clear to patients as part of the pre-operative management of their surgical conditions.

Thus patients undergoing transurethral prostatectomy should know of the occurrence of retrograde ejaculation, the occasional diminution in libido, loss of erectile function, as well as the very rare incidence of urinary incontinence. The risks of haemorrhage, capsular perforation, or transurethral resection syndrome are essentially those of an intraoperative nature and need not be discussed with the patient beforehand. In the postoperative period if such complications occurred they should be explained.

The management of prostate cancer requires an intelligent debate between the patient and surgeon as to the best means of managing this increasingly complex biological/pathological condition.

Stone disease of the urinary tract is now almost universally dealt with by a lithotripter. Only in special circumstances, and then only with the full understanding and agreement of the patient, should either percutaneous or open renal surgery be undertaken. Endoscopic extraction of a ureteric stone runs the risk of ureteric injury and the patient should normally be protected against this by the use of an indwelling ureteric stent.

In vascular surgery the risk of a stroke after carotid artery procedures needs to be understood by the patient and, if necessary, their relatives. During surgery of the thoracic aorta there is serious risk of spinal cord injury and paralysis. Only if such surgery is needed should that risk be taken. Peripheral vascular disease is increasingly and most successfully treated by surgical means, particularly femoropopliteal bypass. This operation carries a risk of thrombosis and with that, a possible need for amputation. Extensive perivascular dissection in the abdominal cavity and pelvis carry the risk of interfering with the autonomic nervous system, particularly that part concerned with sexual function in young men. It may also cause disturbance of bladder functions.

Surgery of the abdominal contents is most critically associated with emergency surgery. Only competent surgeons or those in training and supervised by competent surgeons should undertake emergency procedures. These operations are best done in a specified emergency environment and preferably within daylight hours.

The common and simple hernia and varicose vein procedures both carry the risk of failure. Such failure can occur regardless of the surgical competence.

Laparoscopic surgery for cholecystectomy has opened the way for a wide range of minimally invasive procedures. The surgical principles of good exposure of surgical anatomy, still apply within that operation. The necessary learning experience for laparoscopic techniques requires time and patience. A close supervision of trainees is needed in this burgeoning surgical area.

A deep vein thrombosis causes miserable local symptoms but most worryingly can, through the development of an embolus, cause life threatening disturbance of respiratory and cardiac function. Patients at risk should be treated with anticoagulants both before surgery and in the postoperative period. Those already on anticoagulants should be carefully assessed as to the need of surgery and within that the balance between the risks of haemorrhage in association with anticoagulants or thrombosis and pulmonary embolus in the absence of such anticoagulants. Where possible the patient and relatives should be included in such a debate.

Finally, surgery has always carried the risk of infection and within that, in recent times, infection of foreign body materials, particularly prostheses. The use of careful antisepsis and a meticulous surgical technique combined with the use of prophylactic antibiotics will usually protect the patient from such sepsis.

Notwithstanding all these problems surgery within the United Kingdom remains a generally safe and highly effective aspect of clinical care. Although risks have to be taken these should be carefully calculated such that if they are realised they are acceptable. The current trust between surgeons and patients in relation to this calculation of risk factors remains one of the cornerstones of success in British surgical practice.

1 Hargreave TB, Stephenson TP. Potency and prostatectomy. *Br J Urol* 1983;**55**: 564–7.
2 Zafar K, Mieza M, Staper P, Singh V. Post prostatectomy incontinence. *Urology* 1991;**28**:483–8.
3 Whitfield H, Kirby R, eds. *Textbook of genitourinary surgery* 1st ed. Edinburgh: Churchill Livingstone, 1985:416–8.
4 Bullock N, Sibley G, Whitaker R, eds. *Essential urology.* 2nd ed. London: Churchill Livingstone, 1994:255–60.
5 Keen G, Farndon J, eds. *Operative surgery and management.* 3rd ed. Oxford: Butterworth-Heinemann, 1994:525–39.
6 Randall PE, Ganguli L, Marcusson RW. Wound infection following vasectomy. *Br J Urol* 1983;**55**:564–7.
7 Philp T, Guillebaud J, Budd D. Complications of vasectomy: review of 16 000 patients. *Br J Urol* 1983;**55**:564–7.

8 European carotid surgery trialists' collaborative group MRC European carotid surgery trial, interim results for symptomatic patients with severe (70–90%) or mild (0–20%) carotid stenosis. *Lancet* 1991;**337**:1235–43.

9 Keen G. Spinal cord injury associated with surgery of the descending aorta. In: Hadfield J, Hobsley M, Treasure T, eds. Current surgical practice. Vol 5. London: Edward Arnold, 1990:260–9.

10 Keen G, Farndon J, eds. *Operative surgery and management.* 3rd ed. Oxford: Butterworth-Heinemann, 1994: 562–3.

11 Weinstein MH, Machleper HI. Sexual function after aorta–iliac surgery. *Ann Surg* 1975;**181**:787–90.

12 Keen G, Farndon J, eds. *Operative surgery and management.* 3rd ed. Oxford: Butterworth-Heinemann, 1994:345–7.

13 Rintouil RF, ed. *Textbook of operative surgery.* 7th ed. Edinburgh: Churchill Livingstone, 1986:263–7.

14 Dudley H, ed. *Hamilton Bailey's emergency surgery.* 11th ed. Bristol: Wright, 1986:259 411.

15 Keen G, Farndon J, eds. *Operative surgery and management.* 3rd ed. Oxford: Butterworth-Heinemann, 1994:808–17.

16 Jamieson C, James Y, eds. *Rob and Smith's operative surgery–vascular surgery.* 5th ed. London: Chapman and Hall Medical, 1994:552–92.

17 Burmand KG, Young AE, eds. *The new Aird's companion in surgical studies.* 3rd ed. London: Churchill Livingstone, 1992:860–4.

18 Zucker KA, ed. *Surgical laparoscopy.* 1st ed. St Louis: Quality Medical Publishing Inc, 1991:311–42.

12 Risk management in orthopaedic surgery

GORDON BANNISTER

The modern practice of orthopaedic surgery continues to be heavily influenced by its roots. The specialty evolved from Huw Owen Thomas, the medically qualified son of a long line of north Wales bone setters. Thomas was a general practioner in Liverpool and every Sunday morning he treated the disadvantaged poor of the city free of charge. The principal conditions that he faced were neglected industrial trauma and tuberculosis. He was a keen advocate of rest, and had a smithy behind his surgery, where metal splints were made in which he immobilised his patients for months or years. His nephew was Robert Jones, who learnt from his uncle and secured a consultant surgeon's post at one of the Liverpool hospitals.

At that time trauma was managed either by general practitioners or by junior medical staff, who treated patients brought to hospital as casual (hence casualty) attenders. As the surgeons gained seniority they relinquished their trauma commitment for elective work and Jones was one of the few senior surgeons in the country with good trauma training. He enhanced this as medical officer to the Manchester Ship Canal Company, and in 1917 was appointed director of military orthopaedics, introducing the Thomas splint for open femoral fractures, and reducing the mortality from 80% to 20%. After the first world war he set up country orthopaedic hospitals on south west facing slopes, for the dual purpose of rehabilitating injured soldiers and treating tuberculosis in children.

Because of Jones's success in managing trauma, care of injuries has remained the responsibility of orthopaedic surgeons in Britain. Infection in bones and joints is extremely difficult to eradicate,
200

even in the antibiotic era, and the fear of infecting patients dictated that open operative intervention be avoided when at all possible. The philosophy of treatment was splintage, in a position where if the joint stiffened it would be useful. Fractures were allowed to unite (knit) short, rather than risk infection from the internal fixation that would have ensured a more anatomical reduction. Treatment was protracted. Children were kept in hospital for years. The least risky method of avoiding shortening was traction (applying a pull to the broken bone). The operative procedure required to set this up was sufficiently simple to be undertaken by very junior staff. Nurses could take an orthopaedic nursing certificate by completing a two year course in their late teens before definitive general nursing training, and were skilled in the application of plaster and splints and the management of traction. With such a slow process of management of musculoskeletal disorders, relatively few consultant staff could supervise large numbers of patients who required to be visited on no more than a monthly basis.

In the second half of the 20th century tuberculosis became less prevalent and osteoarthritis presented more often. In 1960 John Charnley published his first paper on total hip replacement, and the same year some surgeons on the continent formed a group (AO Group) to develop internal fixation techniques, so that fractures could be fixed in their anatomical position and joint movement encouraged. This group of Swiss surgeons developed a standardised set of instruments manufactured to extremely high specification, and they and Charnley instituted classes in fracture management and hip replacement respectively. By the mid-1970s total hip replacement was being offered in most large centres and by 1980 the AO system of fracture management was widely adopted.

There followed an explosion of new technology and techniques, which transformed orthopaedic surgery from being a supervisory to an operative specialty. Arthroscopy (looking inside a joint with an illuminated miniature telescope) of the knee, first for diagnosis then for therapeutic purposes, was followed by arthroscopy of the shoulder, ankle, wrist, and hip. External fixators with varying pin configurations and frames, that were first static, then dynamic, were introduced. Wide excisions of the knee and elbow and their replacement by metallic hinges, designed by individual surgeons and made up by the local hospital instrument maker, were replaced by biomechanical analysis and surface replacement, with

201

considerably increased technical demands on the surgeon's ability to align his prostheses and handle soft tissue. Throughout the 1980s injuries to the long bones (femur, tibia, humerus, radius, and ulna) were progressively stabilised by closed intramedullary (down the marrow cavity of the bone) nailing and increasingly stable fixation devices for the spine became available, requiring either interlaminar wiring or intrapedicular (within the bone at the side of the spine) screws.

This increasing knowledge was accompanied by the development of specialist journals in rheumatoid surgery, the hand, knee, foot and ankle, paediatric orthopaedics, the hip, spine, shoulder, and elbow, with societies at national, continental, and international levels. The effect of this has been apparent to people in general and in orthopaedic wards. No longer are patients seen in the streets wearing raised shoes or limping with deformed malunions (bones that have knitted in the wrong alignment). Traction is a relatively rare sight in orthopaedic wards. Potential benefits of hip replacement are common knowledge among the population who see its provision as the yardstick of health care.

Inevitably, this burgeoning knowledge has outstripped the resource, both of the surgeon and the health service. No one surgeon can reasonably have mastered all the techniques described. Historically, Robert Jones carried out 20 cases in an operating list (although many of these were closed procedures), there were two tables in the theatre, plasters were applied by well trained nursing staff, a supporting team of junior staff gave the anaesthetics and closed wounds, and there was no constraint on the time the list finished.

Changes in hospital practice have been slower than the specialty. There is a constant shortage of operating time, as a result of which trauma has traditionally been carried out either in the evening or at night. It has been impossible for consultants to keep up with the demand placed on them. Waiting lists have become long and, at times, the potential of the specialty has not been fully realised. This has been particularly apparent in trauma management.

Trauma management

Staniforth reviewed 755 fractures (broken bones) seen for personal injury reports by 33 surgeons.[1] There was morbidity in

Table 12.1 *Points of risk*

Initial hospital assessment	Diagnosis General medical state
Orthopaedic management	Functional assessment Appropriateness of available treatment
Information to patient	Nature of condition Natural history of condition Influence of intervention Price of intervention Risks and nature of complications

Intervention	Timing
	Execution Calibre of surgeon
	                      Theatre staff support
	                      Equipment
	                      Theatre quality

Rehabilitation	Calibre and numbers of ward staff Ward equipment Physio and occupational therapy Social work
Follow up	Goals Timing

50% of cases. In 30% this was inevitable, but in 20% potentially preventable. Half the preventable morbidity was severe and half of it was missed before referral to an orthopaedic surgeon. Twenty five per cent related to poor operations, 40% to poor non-operative management, and 10% to inadequate equipment. Langkamer and Ackroyd examined the management of displaced forearm fractures, noting non-union in 10%, delayed union in 22%, and poor surgical technique in 30%.[2]

Although there is a wide variety of specialties in orthopaedic surgery, there is a common theme to the risks encountered (table 12.1). Risks occur at the point of referral, in the assessment of the patient, in explanation of the condition, and in the therapeutic intervention proposed, in the technical performance of the intervention, and rehabilitation after it. As my expertise is in hip surgery, the risks involved in two conditions affecting the adult hip will be considered as an illustration. These are proximal femoral hip fracture and hip replacement.

Hip fracture

Proximal femoral fracture (hip fracture)

Proximal femoral fracture is a common condition with widespread risk. Patients with such fractures occupy between a third and half of all acute orthopaedic beds. They present particular problems in that they are commonly elderly and have a wide variation in functional state, life expectancy, and personal expectations. Fractures themselves behave differently, bone stock is poor, and in intracapsular (breaks within the hip joint itself) fractures the blood supply is disrupted, preventing union or causing late avascular necrosis of the head (death of the head because its blood supply has not recovered from the fracture) if union takes place. Most proximal femoral fractures are sustained against a background of deteriorating general health and independence. Twenty per cent of patients die as inpatients and 37% succumb within a year of the fracture. Some 50% of patients fail to regain their previous mobility and 16% require to be rehoused in nursing homes.[3] At any one time, some 28% of patients with proximal femoral fractures occupying an acute hospital bed have completed their medical treatment and are awaiting discharge.[4] Having completed their treatment, patients who have sustained a proximal femoral fracture have a risk of between six and 10 times that of an age and sex matched population of sustaining another one. The protracted bed occupancy reflects in the cost of health care. May *et al* estimated that a QUALY (cost of a year of quality adjusted independent life) for proximal femoral fracture is 15 times that of total hip replacement.[5]

Such poor results engender nihilism in the face of a heavy elective and long bone fracture workload. The management of proximal femoral fractures in elderly patients is usually delegated to junior staff. Surgery is often carried out on emergency lists, after the patient has been starved, the operation cancelled, and the patient starved again. The incidence of infection, pressure areas, and medical complications is high, and even in the finest centres the results of surgery can be so poor that it has been temporarily abandoned for conservative non-operative management.[6]

Whereas the outcome of proximal femoral fracture is undisputed, the associated causes are hard to define because they are multifactorial. These causes are inherent in the population at risk and associated with the hospital episode. We examined the

204

Table 12.2 *Predetermined risk in proximal femoral fracture*

Variable	Increased risk factor
	Death in hospital
Male sex	× 4
Aged >80	× 2
Admission from residential or nursing home	× 2
Bed bound	× 9
	Duration of hospital stay
Aged >80	× 2
	Ability to walk again
Male sex	× 2
	Need for more sheltered housing
Housebound before	× 2
Use of Zimmer frame	× 4

population features, hospital management, and outcome in 142 patients with proximal femoral fracture, admitted to our own institution over a one year period.[3] Patients were managed traditionally within an out of hours emergency operating service run by junior staff. They were nursed on a ward with high turnover of nursing staff of reduced seniority, a patient population of increasingly high dependence, and a multitiered management structure, heavily involved in forward planning, delegating patient care to its most inexperienced personnel. Ten variable were identified. Four of these related to the hospital episodes and this was reflected in the duration of stay in hospital. Delay to operation, development of broken pressure areas, wound infection, and reoperation were all associated with prolonged admission. These four complications accounted for 30% of the total bed days throughout the entire year and 55% of this was associated with non-medical delay to surgery, 20% with broken pressure areas, 18% with infection, and 7% with reoperation. Non-medical delay to surgery often involved starvation throughout the afternoon and evening and cancellation late at night, with repetition of the episode the next day. There was an 11% incidence of broken pressure areas and 6% of infection.

The 2% reoperation rate was not associated with seniority of surgical staff. The predetermined risk (table 12.2) includes male sex, advancing age, independence as measured by residential situation, and mobility before admission. Sex, age, residential state, and mobility increase the risks of death in hospital by factors of

Table 12.3   *Hospital induced risk factors*

	Death in hospital
Non-medical delay to surgery	× 2

	Duration of hospital stay
Broken pressure areas	× 2
Infection	× 2
Non-medical delay to surgery	× 1·1

four, two, two, and nine respectively. Advancing years double the duration of stay in hospital, men die or walk and have double the chance of retaining their preaccident mobility on discharge, and being housebound or requiring the use of a Zimmer frame increases the need for nursing home placement by two and four times.

The hospital induced risk factors (table 12.3) relate to non-medical delay in hospital, which, apart from being associated with prolonged bed occupancy, doubles the risk of death if it exceeds two days and the stay in hospital is doubled by broken pressure areas and infection. Non-medical delay to surgery is caused by inadequate operating theatre time for trauma. Such delay can almost always be avoided by daily trauma lists on which fractures admitted the day before can be given a time in the same way as an elective case.

The mortality after proximal femoral fracture is associated with bronchopneumonia in about 40% of cases, cardiac failure and myocardial infarction in 24%, and pulmonary embolism in 14%.[7] The most striking hospital variable to be associated with this is non-medical delay to surgery and bronchopneumonia. When surgery is delayed by more than 24 hours from admission, mortality from bronchopneumonia increases by a factor of five. Using two of four principal variables, it is possible to predict the mobility after one year and need for rehousing with an accuracy of 78% and 92% respectively (tables 12.4 and 12.5). The chances of regaining mobility are increased by 50% if patients are either admitted from their own homes or are under 80 years of age, and the need for rehousing in nursing or residential homes is doubled in women over 80 and trebled in those able to walk only with a frame before fracture.

Although risk management is most obviously directed to avoiding morbidity, there is a wider duty of health services to the population they serve and whose taxes they consume. A hospital bed occupied by a patient unable to regain independence after a proximal femoral fracture, and waiting for long term residential placement, is a

Table 12.4 *Probability of regaining mobility**

	Independent or stick	Admit from home	Aged <80 years	Male
Independent or stick	64	76	80	96
Admitted from home		72	83	100
Aged <80 years			73	88
Male sex				83

* Probability table for surviving patients, independently mobile or using a stick at time of admission, regaining their preinjury level of mobility at one year. Probability figures are for two variables combined (expressed as a percentage). Thus the chance of regaining mobility is 64% if patients are walking independently or with a stick before fracture. If, in addition, they were admitted from their own homes, this rises to 76%, or were under 80 years 80%, or were male 96%.

bed denied to another patient who might benefit from surgical management of a treatable condition.

Community care has attracted increasing interest and the need to rehabilitate elderly patients for return to their own homes has been recognised since the 1960s in both Stoke-on-Trent and Hastings, where orthogeriatric rehabilitation units were set up. The type of patient to benefit from these facilities is the one who has been admitted from their own home, but already has impaired function or whose recovery after surgery seems slow. The considerable enthusiasm shown for such services may relate more to the release of acute orthopaedic beds than any long term benefit in the patient populations. Scandinavian series have shown that rehabilitation units prolong hospital admission, whereas this is reduced by early discharge.[89] Only one controlled trial has shown any benefit from a rehabilitation programme, and this was related to particularly poor results in its control group.[10] Our own

Table 12.5 *Probability of requiring nursing or residential home accommodation at one year**

	Female sex	Aged >80 years	Uses a frame to mobilise
Female sex	53	63	90
Aged >80 years		61	89
Uses a frame to mobilise			88

* Probability table for all patients, irrespective of preinjury residence, requiring residential or nursing home accommodation at one year, related to mobility, age and sex. Probability figures are for two variables combined (expressed as a percentage). Thus the chance of requiring rehousing in a residential or nursing home within a year is 53% if the patient is female. If, in addition, she is over 80 years this rises to 63%, or walked with a frame before fracture 90%.

207

experience,[11 12] comparing adjacent hospitals in the Bristol area, has mirrored that of Scandinavia. In these studies, two similar health districts admitting patients with comparable levels of disability adopted different discharge policies. In one hospital, appropriate patients were transferred as quickly as was practical to a dedicated rehabilitation unit, whereas in the other an experienced ward sister assessed patients on admission and arranged their early discharge to either a community hospital or nursing home. The mean duration of stay at the hospital with a rehabilitation unit was 31 days, and that with the early discharge policy 18, including the time spent at community hospitals. Mortalities were comparable and slightly more patients from the hospital with the early discharge policy had retained their independence after one year, but the differences in occupancy of hospital beds between the two districts realised the potential funding for 100 primary hip replacements.

Surgical risks

Most of the medical literature on proximal femoral fractures considers union and surgical complications.

Intracapsular (within the hip joint) fractures are at risk of disruption of the blood supply to the proximal fragment and have high rates of non-union. Extracapsular (outside the hip joint) fractures are more unstable, more painful, cause greater blood loss, have higher union rates, higher mortality, and more prolonged pain after fixation.

Intracapsular fractures

Intracapsular fractures may be undisplaced or displaced. If an undisplaced fracture is treated by bed rest or traction, 10% will become displaced. If undisplaced fractures are fixed in situ, 95% unite and the reoperation rate is 3% (table 12.6).[13 14] Displaced fractures were treated by traction, plasters, or splinting to the opposite leg until the introduction of the trifin nail (nail with three fins to prevent rotation) in 1931,[15] after which union rates rose to about 60%. Fractures unite better if they are properly reduced, and increasingly well with stabilisation. A double implant resists rotational instability (shear or twisting) better than a single one.[16 17] None the less, regardless of the configuration of fracture reduction or metalwork implanted for stabilisation, reoperation rate is 31%, which is 10 times that of an undisplaced fracture treated in the same manner.

Table 12.6 *Management of intracapsular hip fractures*

Type of fracture	Treatment	Fracture union (%)	Reoperation (%)
Undisplaced	Traction	85	0
	Screws	95	3
Displaced	Traction	24	31
	Unreduced and fixed	44	14
	Reduced Trifin nail	53	31
	Reduced sliding screw	72	31
	Reduced double screw	75	31
	Hemiarthroplasty		14
	Hip replacement		14

Failure to diagnose an undisplaced fracture places the patient at risk of displacement and a considerably worse result. Medical students are taught that hip fractures lie in a shortened and externally rotated position. Few family practitioners have been exposed to any further training in orthopaedics before becoming primary health care physicians. Failure to x ray a painful hip in an old lady may result in loss of the opportunity for simple and effective percutaneous screw fixation and early return to the community, by allowing the fracture to displace and become a more difficult management problem.

Union of displaced intracapsular fractures is both age and disease related

Patients over the age of 84 have a non-union rate of 50%, whereas under the age of 50 this falls to 25%.[14] Non-union in rheumatoid patients is 20% in undisplaced fractures and 60% in displaced.[18]

Even when the fracture has united, patients remain at risk; 16% of undisplaced fractures and 25% of displaced develop avascular necrosis and late segmental collapse between 18 months and 3·5 years after fracture. Of these, about 30% require further surgical intervention.[14] Thus retaining the patients' femoral head after a displaced intracapsular hip fracture places them at risk of failure of reduction in about 15%, non-union in between 25% and 50%, and surgery some years later in between 5% and 8% of cases.

An alternative to retaining the head is to fashion a new joint (arthroplasty) with replacement either of the head (hemiarthroplasty) or the whole joint (total hip arthroplasty).

209

Table 12.7   *Extracapsular fractures*

Fixation device	Reoperation rate (%)
Dynamic hip screw	6
Gamma nail	12
Enders nails	41

Replacement hemiathroplasty dislocates in about 4%, of whom 60% succumb. This is probably representative of the quality of patient, and both mortality and dislocation are higher in mentally infirm patients. Although the combined literature suggests that a surgical approach influences dislocation rates after proximal femoral fracture, the only controlled trial on this subject showed no difference between anterior and posterior approaches.[19] Hemiarthroplasty is a reliable procedure unless the patient is active and long living. The friction of metal on cartilage is 100 times that of cartilage on cartilage, and acetabular erosion results in revision to hip arthroplasty in 20% of survivors after five years.[20][21]

Primary total hip replacement avoids the risk of acetabular erosion, but the risk of dislocation rises to 11%. The only controlled trial of reduction and fixation, hemiarthroplasty, and hip replacement showed the lowest reoperation rate, and best results came from total hip replacement in an unselected population over the age of 65.[22]

Extracapsular fractures (table 12.7)

The commonest extracapsular fracture is trochanteric. Union is the rule. The fracture, therefore, can be managed conservatively or operatively. The only randomised prospective controlled trial[6] showed superior function after six months, better anatomical results, and shorter stay in hospital in a group of patients treated with a dynamic hip screw than in those with skeletal traction. The dynamic hip screw has a lower complication rate than the gamma nail[23] or Enders nails.[24] The principal complication of dynamic hip screw fixation is cutting out as a result of failure to place the screw centrally. The fixation failure rate in implants placed centrally on both anteroposterior and lateral planes was 8% compared with 28% of those placed posteriorly or anterosuperiorly.[25] Infection is the second principal complication, which is reduced by a factor of three by parenteral prophylactic antibiotics.[26]

210

Table 12.8   *Complications of total hip replacement*

Complication	%
Shaft fracture	1
Nerve palsy	1
Infection	2
Dislocation	4
Aseptic loosening (10 years)	10
Death (6 months)	1·5

In subtrochanteric fractures the dynamic hip screw again has clear advantages over other devices, with half the non-union rate reported when intramedullary and AO plates are used.[21]

Risk factors in total hip replacement

During the 30 years since its introduction, total hip replacement has justified its reputation as one of the major advances in postwar medicine. Its provision has expanded from specialist centres to district general hospitals. The seniority of the surgeon carrying out the procedure has declined as output has increased. Public expectation and demand for the procedure has escalated and the provision of the operation is now an intrinsic part of health care politics.

Although 93% of total hip replacements continue to give satisfactory service after 10 years, there are several complications, the risk of which may be predetermined or potentially avoidable (table 12.8).

Intraoperative shaft fracture (table 12.9) occurs in about 1% of cases and gives satisfactory results in only 33%.[27] The risk is trebled in thin bone of rheumatoid patients and when endosteal bone lysis has weakened the femoral shaft, which fractures on revision.

Some 1·3% of cases sustain a nerve injury of which 80% involve the sciatic nerve and, in particular, its common peroneal component. About 25% of nerve palsies are delayed and are presumably the result of compression by postoperative haematoma.

Table 12.9   *Shaft fracture in total hip replacement*

	%	Risk factor
Primary hip replacement	1	
Rheumatoid patients	3	3
Revisions	3	3

Table 12.10   *Nerve palsy in total hip replacement*

	%	Risk factor
Uncomplicated primary hip replacement	1·3	
Congenital hip dysplasia	5·2	4
Revisions	3·2	2·5

Of the remainder, it seems that the commonest association is in attempting to regain leg length in congenitally dislocated or dysplastic hips, or while exploring the scarred anatomy at revision hip arthroplasty. Historically, total hip arthroplasty was carried out by detaching the trochanter and clinical nerve palsies are associated with this more often than by non-trochanteric detaching approaches. This association is further reinforced by asymptomatic nerve palsy, as shown by nerve conduction studies, which commonly show abnormalities after the transtrochanteric approach, but very much less so after access by anterior or posterior routes. Nerve palsy is one of the most disabling complications of total hip replacement, as the deficit is permanent in 43% of cases (tables 12.8, 12.10).[28]

Infection

The adjuvant effect of implanted foreign material is such that whereas it would require about 1m organisms to infect subcutaneous tissue, the presence of a cemented hip arthroplasty reduces that inoculum to 10. In a series of hip arthroplasty operations infection rates as high as 11% were recorded,[29] although the current risk is nearer 2% because of reduced inoculum and host resistence enhanced by antibiotics. The latest report of the Medical Research Council prospective controlled trial on ultraclean air indicates the immense advantages of combining antibiotic prophylaxis, ultraclean air, and body exhaust suits (table 12.11).[30] The presence of operating theatre personnel creates turbulence around the wound and flora from medical and nursing staff contaminate wounds unless the staff are suitably attired with occlusive theatre clothing. Infection rates as low as 0·06% are recorded when antibiotic prophylaxis, ultraclean air, and body exhaust suits are combined. Omission of body exhaust suits raises this figure by an order of magnitude and failure to use antibiotics, clean air, or occlusive clothing increase the risk of deep prosthetic infection by a factor of 57. Infection is a catastrophe both for the

Table 12.11   *Infection in joint replacement*

Antibiotics	Ultra clean air	Body exhaust suits	Infection rate (%)	Risk factor
+	+	+	0·06	1
+	+	−	0·7	× 12
+	−	−	0·8	× 13
−	+	+	0·9	× 15
−	+	−	1·6	× 27
−	−	−	3·4	× 57

patient and the health care accountant, and no combination of preventative measures is more expensive than the cost of treating an infection. Broad spectrum antibiotics confer some advantage (table 12.12) and antibiotic loaded acrylic cement, used alone,[31] produced infection rates that were a quarter those achieved with systemic antistaphylococcal antibiotics. Once infected, about 80% of total hip replacements can be successfully reimplanted, with satisfactory results in some 75% of cases.

Leg length discrepancy

About 35% of patients who undergo total hip replacement perceive a leg length differential at the end of the procedure.[32] If leg length discrepancy exceeds 0·5 cm, 65% of patients notice the difference, and the prevention of this seems to depend on the surgeon. Thirteen per cent of cases were lengthened by more than 5 mm when consultants undertook the procedure, whereas when surgery was carried out by trainees this was three times greater.

Dislocation

The general dislocation rate is about 3%, but can be significantly higher (table 12.13). Predictably, revision surgery for instability is complicated by a dislocation rate of over 25%, but patients over the age of 80 undergoing primary hip arthroplasty, those

Table 12.12   *Antibiotic prophylaxis*

No antibiotics	Cloxacillin or flucloxacillin	Broad spectrum	Infection rate (%)	Risk factor
+	−	−	2·3	× 5·75
−	+	−	0·7	× 1·75
−	−	+	0·5	× 1·2

Table 12.13   *Dislocation*

Treatment	Dislocation (%)	Risk factor
Revision for instability	25·7	× 10·7
Primary total hip replacement in over 80 years	15·00	× 6·3
Reimplantation after Girdlestone	13·6	× 5·7
Revision hip replacement	13	× 5·4
Old fracture	12·5	× 5·2
New fracture	8·5	× 3·5
Primary total hip replacement by posterior approach	5·8	× 2·4
Primary total hip replacement	2·4	1

reimplanted after Girdlestone arthroplasties, revisions, and fractures, all have significantly higher risks of dislocation. In early series of hip replacements, the posterior approach doubled the risk of dislocation. About 16% of dislocations are the result of prosthetic malalignment,[33] the others being a function of soft tissue laxity or failure of the patient to appreciate the constraints of a hip replacement. The highest recorded rate is 15% in primary hip replacement in patients over the age of 80.[34] This became chronic in 10% in a centre in which the general rate was 20% of that figure and reflected the inability of octogenerians to remember postoperative instructions.

Death

About 1·5% of patients with hip replacements die within six months. In the Bristol series 24% of deaths resulted from pulmonary embolism and 3·4% of a population of 1162 hip replacements required readmission for venous thrombosis.[35]

Venous thrombosis is extremely common after total hip replacement, suggesting that were its incidence reduced, fewer patients would die of pulmonary embolism. To this end, several studies have been carried out using venous thrombosis as a marker of the efficacy of the intervention. Only one prospective controlled trial has assessed death and with full anticoagulation the mortality within the two groups was comparable, because those who were given anticoagulants died of bleeding, rather than thrombotic complications.

The classic model of venous thrombosis is a clot that propagates and dislodges on the 10th postoperative day, but this only partially explains pulmonary embolism after hip replacement. In our own series half of the deaths from pulmonary embolism occurred within

214

two days of surgery, suggesting that antithrombotic therapy is likely to be less effective in preventing death than reducing veno-graphically demonstrable thrombus after 10 days.

There has been a considerable amount of enthusiasm for low molecular weight heparins on the basis of venographic studies. Of the available interventions it would seem that foot or calf pumps are probably superior. No study has shown a significant reduction in pulmonary embolism, let alone death, and more work is required before risk factors in this area can be properly evaluated.

Aseptic loosening

By far the most common complication of total hip replacement is aseptic loosening. Hip replacement never became a feasible operation until polymethylmethacrylate bone cement was used. When cemented hip arthroplasties began to loosen, cement was incriminated and there was a return to cementless implants.

In a study of almost 6000 hip revisions 78% of revisions resulted from aseptic loosening and of these 78% involved the stem.[36]

There is little difference in revision rates of uncemented and cemented cups, but the uncemented stem has generally given results inferior to the cemented stem.[37] Cementless hip arthroplasty seems to be highly dependent both on the surgeon and prosthetic design. The world literature up to 1989 showed that whereas 9% of cemented hip arthroplasties are revised by five years, some 30% of uncemented had come to the same fate. For general use, it seems that cemented stem fixation is the wiser option. Within the range of designs for cemented stem replacement, traditional designs or minor modern variations of them seem to offer half the rate of revision of some later modifications. Dall et al showed a five times greater revision rate in the second generation roundback Charnley stem than in the narrow first generation flatback.[38] Value added modifications introduced by instrument houses do not seem to have translated the increased cost of implant design to patient benefit.

Aseptic loosening is associated not only with implant design, but with surgical technique. In cemented hip replacement 21% of replacements inserted by good technique revised compared with 69% of those implanted poorly.[39] Consultants in my own unit are twice as likely to implant a femoral stem with good technique as unsupervised trainees.

215

Summary

Risk management in orthopaedic surgery

The risks to patient, doctor, and institution can be reduced by expertise at all levels. Expertise is dependent on past and continuing experience. A surgeon with a low volume training and faced with a difficult technical procedure is likely to expose his patient to a greater risk than if he had already accumulated wide experience and kept it up with regular exposure to the condition being treated.

Training

The amount of experience required during training relates very much to the ability of the trainee to take on and master new problems. This ability is heavily dependent on previous training received.

At present, the duration of courses in undergraduate training in orthopaedics varies, goals are not defined and, when defined, are often not achieved. For students about to enter clinical practice, skills dealing with patients are of the essence. A working knowledge of the subject needs to be applied by simple history taking and examination. These skills need to be taught by experienced senior staff in groups small enough for teaching to be interactive. Good undergraduate education requires a high input of staff senior enough to be assured in their teaching, and with sufficient time to be able to enthuse their subject.

Some 43% of orthopaedic outpatient referrals are considered inappropriate.[40] The variable standard of referral by family practitioners reflects their training. Senior house officer posts in the accident and emergency department or elective orthopaedic units are not appropriate for general practitioner training, where concentrated outpatient experience and education is required. There is a continuing conflict between the needs of services and the escalating demands for training in junior doctor hospital posts. Posts with a high input of outpatient training need to be created to satisfy the requirements of future generations of general practitioners.

Orthopaedic trainees will shortly be exposed to no more than six years of training, with an on duty rota of no more than one in five.[41] Previous training programmes have been blighted by large volumes of routine operations with little supervised training. At present, 5% of trauma and 15% of elective operating carried out by junior staff is supervised by more senior personnel. Residents will need to acquire graded experience with considerably more supervision and a critical volume of more specialised work to become effective at the specialist level.

All training requires consultant time. Consultant time is finite. There must, inevitably, be conflict between the targets imposed by managers and the longer term needs for service.

Supervision and staffing levels

Traditionally, consultants have supervised senior registrars and registrars who, in turn, have supervised senior house officers. The ethic of teaching must be inbuilt in medical education at the earliest possible stage. There are now severe time constraints on the hours of junior hospital doctors, particularly at senior level. The requirement to pass specialist fellowship exit examinations and publish to enhance curricula vitae erodes the willingness of senior trainees to educate their juniors. The expressed aim at present is to create a consultant based service, but this would require 35 new consultant posts to be created every year and even at this rate it would take 30 years to double the present consultant establishment. A temporary increase in the number of orthopaedic trainees would either mean that their training would be further diluted, or existing consultants would have to devote more time to it, seeing fewer patients.

Organisation of departments and consultant time

Training, supervision, and service are all dependent on the consultant staff. Funding for further consultant posts will not realise additional staff unless there are sufficiently trained surgeons to fill them. Orthopaedic surgery will remain a shortage specialty for the foreseeable future and it is essential that consultant time be employed to maximum benefit of patient and trainees. This can be achieved by rationalising trauma services and minimising paperwork, which includes statements of need for replacement equipment and long hours of correcting typing errors that result from secretarial support that reflects the salaries paid. Long committee meetings are a further erosion of time that could be more usefully spent.

217

Avoiding delays to surgery

The patient admitted as an emergency requiring urgent surgery does better if that surgery is performed by a fresh surgeon in daylight hours, at a time for which the patient could be properly prepared. This can be achieved by adequate provision of theatre time and its efficient use. Much theatre time is wasted at changeover. If there are insufficient porters to collect the patients, not enough anaesthetic support staff to allow safe induction, and insufficient recovery beds operations cannot proceed smoothly. Operating theatres work best with teams who regularly operate together. Efficient operating requires adequate equipment and expertise in its use. Operating records need to be legible and preferably typed. This requires sufficient secretarial support.

Communication with staff

With ever reducing hours for junior hospital doctors the three tier team of consultant, middle grade, and house officer is often broken up. The effects of this need to be minimised by handover. Ideally, handover takes place before the day's work, but with the limitations of junior hospital doctor hours this either impinges on off duty time or means that the day's work starts later. For most of the time care of patients will be in the hands of doctors other than their own team. Records need to be legible and typed. Clear records both aid patient care and assist in the management of complaints, which inevitably occur despite the very best practice.

Communication with patients

Few patients will be completely cured of the symptoms with which they present to an orthopaedic outpatient clinic or an accident department. Most medical negligence claims result from poor communication. Most British patients are very understanding if a mistake takes place, provided it is properly explained. Informed consent requires time and knowledge. This particularly applies in the outpatient department and the British Orthopaedic Association recommends that 20 minutes be allowed for a new patient and 10 minutes for subsequent consultations, if taken by consultants and twice that amount of time if taken by junior staff.

Many of the risks in orthopaedic surgery are inherent in the patient and the condition with which they present. Improved risk management in orthopaedic surgery requires education, investment in which will only be returned in the medium term.

1 Staniforth P. Trauma morbidity audit—a multisurgeon study. *J Bone Joint Surg* 1991;**73B** (suppl II): 175–6.
2 Langkamer VG, Ackroyd CE. Internal fixation of forearm fractures in the 1980s: lessons to be learned. *J Bone Joint Surg* 1990;**72B**:530–1.
3 Fox HJ, Pooler J, Prothero D, Bannister GC. Factors affecting the outcome after proximal femoral fractures. *Injury* 1994;**25**:297–300.
4 Robbins JA, Donaldson LJ. Analysing stages of care in hospital stay for fractured neck of femur. *Lancet* 1984;ii:1028–9.
5 May PC, Mahendren V, Habib K. Are costs per qualy a useful orthopaedic tool? *J Bone Joint Surg* 1991;**73B** (suppl 1):70.
6 Hornby R, Grimley-Evans J, Vardon V. Operative or conservative treatment for trochanteric fracture of the femur? *J Bone Joint Surg* 1989;**71B**:618–23.
7 Perez JV, Warwick DJ, Case CP, Bannister GC. Death after proximal femoral fracture: an autopsy study. *Injury* 1995;**26**:237–40.
8 Ceder L, Thorngren KG, Wallden B. Prognostic indicators and early home rehabilitation in elderly patients with hip fractures. *Clin Orthop* 1980;**152**:173–84.
9 Jensen JS, Tondevold E, Sorensen PH. Social rehabilitation following hip fractures. *Acta Orthop Scand* 1979;**50**:777–85.
10 Reid J, Kennie DC. Geriatric rehabilitative care after fractures of the proximal femur: one year follow up of a randomised clinical trial. *BMJ* 1989;**299**:25–6.
11 Hubble M, Little C, Prothero D, Bannister GC. Predicting the prognosis after proximal femoral fracture. *Ann R Coll Surg Engl* 1995 (in press).
12 Fox HJ, Hughes SJ, Pooler J, Prothero D, Bannister GC. Length of hospital stay and outcome after femoral neck fracture—a prospective study comparing the performance of two hospitals. *Injury* 1993;**24**:464–6.
13 Bentley G. Impacted fractures of the neck of the femur. *J Bone Joint Surg* 1968;**50B**:551.
14 Barnes R, Brown JT, Garden RS, Nicoll EA. Subcapital fractures of the femur. *J Bone Joint Surg* 1976;**58B**:2–24.
15 Smith-Petersen MN, Cave EF, Van Gorder GW. Intracapsular fractures of the neck of the femur treated by internal fixation. *Arch Surg* 1931;**23**:715–59.
16 McQuillan WM, Abernethy PJ, Guy JG. Subcapital fractures of the neck of the femur treated by double-divergent fixation. *Br J Surg* 1973;**190**:859–66.
17 Christie J, Howie CR, Armour PC. Fixation of displaced subcapital femoral fractures. *J Bone Joint Surg* 1988;**70B**:199–201.
18 Bogoch E, Quellette G, Hastings D. Failure of internal fixation of displaced femoral neck fractures in rheumatoid patients. *J Bone Joint Surg* 1991;**73B**:7–10.
19 Sikorski JM, Barrington R. Internal fixation versus hemi-arthroplasty for the displaced subcapital fracture of the femur. *J Bone Joint Surg* 1981;**63B**:357–61.
20 Maxted MJ, Denham RA. Failure of hemi-arthroplasty for fractures of the neck of the femur. *Injury* 1984;**15**:224–6.
21 Parker MJ, Pryor GA. *Hip fracture management.* Oxford: Blackwell Scientific Publications, 1993.
22 Skinner PW, Riley D, Ellery JJ, Beaumont TA, Coumine R, Shafighian B. Displaced subcapital fractures of the femur: a prospective randomised comparison of internal fixation, hemi-arthroplasty and total hip replacement. *Injury* 1989;**20**:291–3.

23 Bridle SH, Patel AD, Bircher M, Calvert PT. Fixation of intertrochanteric fractures of the femur: a randomised prospective comparison of the gamma nail and the dynamic hip screw. *J Bone Joint Surg* 1991;**73B**:330–4.

24 Jensen JS, Sonne-Holm S, Tondevold E. Unstable trochanteric fractures: a comparative analysis of four methods of internal fixation. *Acta Orthop Scand* 1980;**51**:949–962.

25 Davis TRC, Sher JL, Horsman A, Simpson M, Porter BB, Checketts RG. Intertrochanteric femoral fractures: mechanical failure after internal fixation. *J Bone Joint Surg* 1990;**72B**:26–31.

26 Ericson C, Lidgren L, Lindberg L. Cloxacillin in prophylaxis of postoperative infections of the hip. *J Bone Joint Surg* 1973;**55A**:808–13.

27 Barrington TW, Johannson JE, McBroom RJ. Fractures of the femur complicating total hip replacement. In: Ling RSM, ed. *Complications of total hip replacement*. Churchill Livingstone 1984:30–40.

28 Schmalzreid TP, Amstutz HC, Dorey FJ. Nerve palsy associated with hip replacement. *J Bone Joint Surg* 1991;**73A**:1074–80.

29 Patterson FP, Brown CS. The McKee–Farrar total hip replacement. *J Bone Joint Surg* 1972;**54A**:257–75.

30 Lidwell OM. Air antibiotics and sepsis in replacement joints. *J Hosp Inf* 1988; **11**(C):18–40.

31 Josefsson G, Lindberg L, Wiklander B. Systemic antibiotics and gentamicin containing bone cement in the prophylaxis of post-operative infections in total hip arthroplasty. *Clin Orthop* 1981;**159**:194–200.

32 Sarangi PP, Bannister GC. Leg length discrepancy after total hip replacement. *Hip International* 1995 (in press).

33 Woo RGY, Morrey BF. Dislocation after total hip arthroplasty. *J Bone Joint Surg* 1982;**64A**:1295–306.

34 Newington DP, Bannister GC, Fordyce M. Primary total hip replacement in patients over 80 years of age. *J Bone Joint Surg* 1990;**72B**:450–2.

35 Warwick D, Williams MH, Bannister GC. Death and thromboembolic disease after total hip replacement. *J Bone Joint Surg* 1995;**75B**:6–10.

36 Malchau H, Herberts P, Ahnfelt L. Prognosis of total hip replacement in Sweden. Follow up of 92 675 operations performed 1978–1990. *Acta Orthop Scand* 1993;**63**:497–506.

37 Havelin LI, Espehaug B, Vollset SE, Engesaeter LB. Early aseptic loosening of uncemented femoral components in primary total hip replacement. *J Bone Joint Surg* 1995;**77B**:11–17.

38 Dall DM, Learmonth ID, Solomon MI, Miles AW, Davenport JM. Fracture and loosening of Charnley femoral stems: comparison between first-generation and subsequent designs. *J Bone Joint Surg* 1993;**75B**:259–65.

39 Bannister GC. *Fixation of the femoral component in total hip replacement* [MD thesis]. Bristol: University of Bristol, 1993.

40 Roland MO, Porter RW, Mathew JG, Redden JF, Simonds GW. Improving care: a study of orthopaedic outpatient referrals. *BMJ* 1991;**302**:1124–8.

41 British Orthopaedic Association. *Consultant staffing requirements for an orthopaedic service in the National Health Service*. London: British Orthopaedic Association, January, 1995.

13 Risk management in accident and emergency medicine

P DRISCOLL, J FOTHERGILL,
R TOUQUET

The objectives of this chapter are to understand how mistakes happen in accident and emergency medicine and to discuss means by which these can be prevented or their effect minimised.

Accident and emergency medicine is a relatively new specialty with the first 30 consultants being appointed in 1974. Although the number of these senior doctors has increased to about 230, accident and emergency departments remain largely staffed by inexperienced senior house officers working in shifts and changing jobs every six months. Furthermore, 44 departments, seeing over 20 000 attendees a year, still do not have an accident and emergency consultant.

As the specialty has matured, expectations of what it can provide have increased. Consequently the pressure felt by overstretched accident and emergency staff can be very great because of all the hospital specialties, their's sees and treats the greatest number of patients. Indeed the amount is larger than the total number seen in the outpatient department.[1 2] The open door access 24 hours a day further exacerbates the situation by helping to produce a vast range of presenting conditions.

Therefore, although accident and emergency departments vary considerably in shape and size, all will have as a minimum the following three key clinical sectors for both adults and children:

Table 13.1   *Reasons for common claims in accident and emergency in the North West Regional Health Authority*

Nature	%
Missed fracture	42
Misdiagnosis	9
Poor fracture management	7
Nerve, tendon, or ligamental injury	6
Poor wound healing and missed foreign body	5
Missed dislocation	3

- A resuscitation room for seriously ill or injured patients
- Cubicles or rooms for patients who need to lie down on a trolley
- Cubicles or rooms for patients who can walk.

Around 60% of patients attending accident and emergency departments in the United Kingdom are in the last category. They generally have soft tissue conditions or skeletal problems and, once treated, over 90% will be able to go home. By contrast, patients in the first two categories have a higher chance of requiring admission. Furthermore they take longer to categorise and use a greater amount of both human and technical resources.

Nature and frequency of errors

When these pressures of the large and heterogeneous patient population are considered it is not surprising that mistakes occur. As with any department there are many more "near miss" episodes than full blown errors. Nevertheless both usually involve a combination of inexperience, inattention, distraction, and poor communication leading to missed diagnosis or inappropriate treatment.

In practice accident and emergency medicine has a high incidence of complaints and medical negligence cases.[3-5] Figures from the North West Regional Health Authority place it third in the league table of incidence of claims made against specialties. Table 13.1 lists the commonest claims. Nationally over half concern radiology, usually pertaining to a missed fracture or dislocation. Misdiagnosis in other clinical situations occur less often but can have much more serious consequences. The most worrying of these are the patients who are inappropriately discharged because their

222

Table 13.2 *Common misdiagnosis of life threatening conditions*

Life threatening condition	Misdiagnosis
Subarachnoid haemorrhage	Non-specific headache; migraine
Myocardial infarction	Indigestion; angina
Pulmonary embolus	Indigestion; angina
Ectopic pregnancy	Period pain; salpingitis
Abdominal aortic aneurysm	Renal colic; pancreatitis
Gastrointestinal perforation	Gastroenteritis

underlying life threatening condition has been missed (table 13.2).

To offset the rise in the number and amount of claims, the defence society subscriptions were increased each year. Eventually by 1990 they became so expensive that crown indemnity was introduced (NHS Circular, HC (89) and HC(FC)(89)22). As this meant that medical negligence claims where now the responsibility of the hospital trust, it became essential that both managers and clinical NHS staff developed a risk management strategy.

To facilitate this process it is helpful to first consider how mistakes occur.

Anatomy of a mistake

Mistakes made in accident and emergency rarely result from a single error (figure 13.1). Usually there is an interplay between human, environmental, and equipment factors which increase the chances of an error happening.

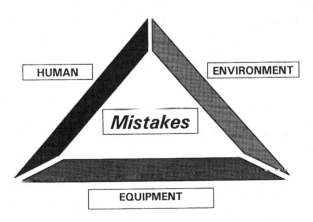

HUMAN

ENVIRONMENT

Mistakes

EQUIPMENT

Figure 13.1 *Factors behind clinical mistakes.*

223

Human factors

Experience and training

A particular skill required by accident and emergency personnel is the ability to correctly prioritise, or triage, patients so that the sickest can be treated first. This also applies to the individual so that the most dangerous condition takes priority. As with other skills this is best learnt from experienced staff and constructive feedback. When these are lacking large errors can occur whereby whole groups of patients may be allowed to deteriorate before it becomes apparent that they require urgent attention.

Another essential skill is the ability to manage critically ill patients. As this can be difficult, the chances of errors occurring increase if inexperienced staff are left unsupervised.[6 7] Indeed studies in the past have shown that junior doctors lack even the rudimentary knowledge and skills to manage these types of patients.[8 10] It is therefore worrying that there are still accident and emergency departments where junior doctors work without adequate experienced cover. In 1992 the British Orthopaedic Association reported that only 38% of the departments in Scotland and 82% in England and Wales had a consultant in charge. Furthermore 66% had no intermediate training posts.[11]

This lack of supervision not only allows mistakes to occur but also limits any educational benefit for the personnel involved. Staff learn best by acquiring knowledge and skills and then applying them in a safe and supportive environment. In this way the effect of their actions can be assessed. A lack of feedback, however, allows inappropriate actions to develop into bad habits. These in turn tend to be handed on from one member of staff to another.

Shift patterns

Emergency physicians commonly work 12 hour shifts in the United States. In the United Kingdom, shifts vary between eight and 24 hours. It is well established that the speed, accuracy, and reaction times in carrying out tasks is best when a person's core temperature is highest; however, the 24 hour temperature curves differ between people. For example, those who prefer to go to bed early and get up early have their temperature peak usually before noon. By contrast, those who prefer to work at night have their temperature peak later in the day. These cycles can be profoundly affected by shiftwork.

As the shift gets longer it becomes progressively more difficult for the circadian rhythm to adjust. In addition there is a tendency to fatigue and this becomes more pronounced the longer the shifts are. For example, it may encompass the last few hours of a 12 hour shift, especially if the person is on a new night rotation when alertness is already reduced. Interestingly, at the beginning of shifts certain tasks are also carried out less effectively, especially by inexperienced staff. For example, radiological interpretation by junior staff is more likely to be faulty at the beginning and end of the shift than in the middle.

Studies have also shown an adverse effect of shiftwork on physical and mental health and cognitive and manual performance.[12 13] This is most pronounced when the rotations last less than three weeks.[14] A further insult occurs if the shift rotation is in a counterclockwise rotation, because the biological clock is totally disrupted. Changes in shifts are another important cause of variation in the functional ability of staff. Indeed in the United States they are cited as a major cause of stress and dissatisfaction in accident and emergency medicine and the principle reason for the annual loss from the specialty of 12%.[12]

The shift system also means that some patients will not have been completely managed by the time the doctor or nurse has to leave. Consequently the departing staff need to hand over the patient's continuing care to other personnel. This process is susceptible to errors. For example, a clinician may fail to reassess a patient handed on by a colleague. In doing so there is danger of perpetuating an error made by the departing doctor.

Physical tiredness

Working in accident and emergency departments can be physically tiring. Personnel need to remain on their feet for many hours as they move around the department assessing and treating the constant stream of patients. Therefore without proper organisation, personnel may become exhausted especially by the end of a shift in a busy, large department. This, in turn, can lead to errors of judgement.

Alertness

Box 1 lists the major factors effecting the doctors' alertness in the department (these are discussed in greater detail in chapter 3). Alertness to subtle abnormalities is dulled if they only occur rarely. For example, a common complaint presenting to accident and

225

> ## Box 1—Factors effecting alertness
> - Circadian rhythm
> - Total sleep time the night before
> - The amount of recent slow wave sleep
> - Regularity of the sleep schedule
> - Regularity of the work schedule

emergency is a painful, swollen ankle after an inversion injury. Most of these patients will have ligamental sprain, with only the minority having a fracture. Nevertheless, most will require a radiograph so that skeletal damage can be excluded.[15] As a result doctors can become less alert because they will have to inspect many normal radiographs; their mind may already be made up before looking at the film. It follows that unless they maintain a disciplined systematic approach to examining these patients and their radiographs, mistakes will occur.[15 16]

Kadzombe and Coals have shown that complaints are at their highest when senior house officers are in their last month in the department.[3] Although further work is needed to confirm this finding, it may reflect both misplaced confidence and a fall in alertness during the final month of the doctor's attachment.

Stress

Accident and emergency medicine has stresses that occur above and beyond those found in other branches of clinical medicine. Accident and emergency doctors deal with excessive patient loads and treat people, with incomplete information, for conditions which vary from the trivial to the immediately life threatening. Furthermore they are continuously having to negotiate with the admitting team as well as being aware of the medicolegal issues of each patient they see. The high incidence of drug misuse by accident and emergency residents themselves in the United States is probably a reflection of the levels of stress faced by these doctors.[17–19]

In addition accident and emergency doctors routinely have to manage several patients at once. Although these patients may cover a wide variety of conditions and clinical severity, the doctor will be expected to move smoothly from one patient to another so that their management can be continued. Needless to say, with an increase in patient numbers and clinical severity, there is a greater risk of mistakes being made. These usually take the form of omissions—for example, incomplete documentation, inadequate investigations, or lack of reassessment. There is, however, potential for a total mix up whereby patients' histories are written in the wrong notes and inappropriate treatment prescribed.

Patients attending accident and emergency departments are themselves sometimes difficult for inexperienced staff to deal with. Many patients are anxious and agitated by delays. When drunkenness and drug misuse is added to this, verbal and sometimes physical aggression towards staff can result. As a consequence stress in personnel will increase.

Accident and emergency medicine is a human activity. It is therefore important to be aware that the doctors and nurses working in the department carry the emotional upheavals experienced both inside and outside the workplace. Although most health care professionals learn to detach themselves from these issues, occasionally they cannot. Bereavement and illness of a loved one are obvious examples. This lack of detachment will interfere with the health care provider's performance. The break up of relationships also provides a powerful distracting force. Compared with married non-clinicians, doctors who are married have a higher incidence of divorce, troubled marriages, and drug and alcohol misuse.[20] (On the other hand, it has been shown that married medical students and residents experience fewer symptoms of stress and depression than their unmarried counterparts.[21]) When long term relationships are ending, the emotional ramifications are usually protracted and it is during this phase that performance can vary.

Communication

There are many examples of poor communication considerably increasing the risk of mistakes. Not listening to patients or not understanding them means that making a correct diagnosis is dependent on the physical examination. When this happens conditions are likely to be missed and incorrect management decisions made. Failures of communication also occur between medical and nursing staff especially when discussions are carried out by telephone. Not only does this allow mistakes to be perpetuated, it also introduces conceptual errors because medical staff differ in what they consider terms such as "exhaustion", "cyanosis", "pallor", and "sickness" to mean.

Environment and equipment

Environmental factors can alter the physical comfort of personnel working in the accident and emergency department (box 2). In doing so, they will effect concentration time and lead to quicker decision making. If the adverse environmental features are only present in a particular area of the department, then personnel will try to avoid working there. Furthermore, as well as rapid decision making, there is less inclination to go back into the area to review the patient.

Box 2—Common environmental factors in accident and emergency affecting performance

Noise   Departmental acoustics
         Background noise from staff and patients
         Intercoms
         Building alterations
Light   Flickering
         Inadequate
Space   Confined
         Exposed (for example, gynaecological cubicles)
Smell

Faulty, inadequate, or absent equipment also lead to a poor clinical performance and so increase the risks of mistakes being made. For example, lack of standard equipment such as auroscopes, ophthalmoscopes, and page writing 12 lead ECG machines leads to staff taking short cuts and not undertaking a sufficiently detailed examination.

Risk management: human factors

It follows that personnel in charge of the emergency department should organise it so that risk factors do not occur in combination. In this way, the chances of a mistake happening are considerably reduced. A major aspect in attempting to achieve this is to establish an appropriate number of trained staff in departments which are well laid out, organised, and fully supported by other specialties and services.[2]

Table 13.3 *Recommended medical staffing of accident and emergency departments*

No of new patients	Consultants	Middle grade	Senior house officers
20 000	1	2	6
35 000	2	4	7
65 000	3	5	13

Appropriate number and type of staff

The NHS has always been organised so that young doctors and nurses consolidate learning by clinical apprenticeship. If hospitals stopped using inexperienced people, they could not staff their departments and the junior staff could never learn. The long term interests of patients as a whole are therefore best served by this system. Nevertheless the ratio of more senior to junior staff must improve to provide adequate supervision. Furthermore, NHS purchasers increasingly expect there to be adequate middle grade (career registrars or senior registrars, staff grade doctors, or associate specialists) and consultant supervision of junior staff in accident and emergency departments.

Table 13.3 gives the recommendations of the British Association for Accident and Emergency Medicine on staffing levels. It is strongly advised that there is one senior house officer for each 5000 patients attending annually, with a minimum compliment of six to maintain 24 hour cover by shiftwork. To try and achieve some of these guidelines the Joint Planning Advisory Committee has advised the Department of Health that there should be an increase of 72 new consultant posts by the end of 1995.[2]

Staffing levels less than this will lead to a deterioration in service due to lack of supervision, teaching, audit, and time available to spend with each patient. In addition, it will lead to prolongation of the waiting times, which aggravates the situation. Therefore for overall patient care, it is essential that accident and emergency departments have adequate senior cover (table 13.3).[2 22] Unfortunately this is not cheap and hospital trusts may express concern at the costs. The counter argument is that the cost is considerably less than the financial penalty that may result from a medical negligence claim.[11]

By a combination of identifying mistakes and acting as a source of information and advice, the immediate availability of experienced staff helps to prevent errors occurring. Although this is particularly noticeable in cases of critically ill patients,[23 24] it also extends to the

229

less severely injured. For example, apparently innocent lacerations to the hand or wrist could overlie more severe damage which, if missed, could result in profound morbidity.[11 25 26]

Children and elderly people represent two groups of patients well recognised for presenting staff with both puzzling and potentially dangerous diagnostic dilemmas.[28 29] To help prevent mistakes, a systematic assessment needs to be carried out by experienced personnel with early recourse to investigative tools such as plane radiography and ultrasonography.[28] Other diagnostic aids need to be available to staff because they have a role in certain situations such as the assessment of abdominal pain and interpretation of electrocardiograms.[30–32]

Training

This should take place at a formal and informal level. A formal or planned teaching programme for the medical staff is essential (box 3).

Box 3—Components of the formal teaching programme

- Departmental introduction
- Departmental medical guidance notes
- Induction course
- Regular teaching

New senior house officers should not be expected to see patients as soon as they arrive for work on their first day. Time must be spent teaching them the departmental organisation, local management protocols, and essential practical skills. They must also be told clearly the tasks and roles expected of them. Not only are these essential factors in ensuring work satisfaction, they also enhance team work and reduce stress.[19] This teaching is helped greatly if the doctors are given copies of the department's medical guidance notes. Several units achieve this by giving all new members of staff a filofax with the departmental policies and protocols printed inside (figure 13.2).

Experience has shown that trying to cram too much teaching into the first day is counter productive. Instead it should be considered part of an ongoing training programme which will last the entire duration of the doctor's stay in the department.

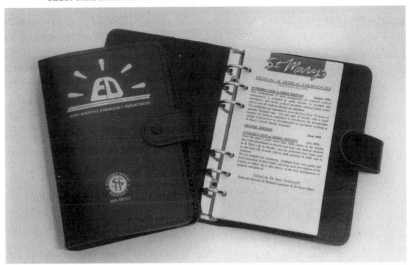

Figure 13.2   *Filofax with departmental protocols*

Nevertheless those conditions that are most serious or most common must be covered sooner rather than later. Examples of these core topics include all types of resuscitation,[27][33-36] ischaemic heart disease,[37] asthma,[38][39] musculoskeletal problems, tendon injuries,[25] wounds,[40] bleeding in pregnancy,[41] and investigations, especially radiology.[16][42-44]

Teaching sessions after the first day should be held at least weekly and the time protected (that is, the doctors should not be clinically on duty). A way forward is to dedicate two to four hours a week as paid "protected education time". As an accident and emergency department cannot close for staff training, adequate staffing arrangements are essential so that somebody is doing the teaching while another person sees patients. Attendance at the formal teaching sessions must be compulsory and part of the doctors' contracted hours of work.

An integral part of the teaching of senior house officers is the induction course.[45] All new senior house officers working in the department must attend this within the first month of their attachment. Usually they are run at a regional level and aim to cover the common presenting clinical problems, national protocols, and training in resuscitation skills. How this formal training programme is put into effect will depend on staffing numbers and local expertise.

Informal teaching takes place at several levels (box 4). Training in the actual situation enables junior doctors to be taught about clinical problems as they occur. During these sessions, advice on communication, prioritisation, documentation, and how to avoid distractions can be given along with basic clinical training including history taking and examination.[26] This teaching is the responsibility of both the consultants and other middle grade staff. Only by having enough staff can this service be provided throughout the day and evening.

Box 4—Components of the informal teaching programme

- Teaching during real situations
- Logbook
- Feedback
- Mentor system

It is important to ensure that the educational aims are met. This can come from constructive feedback during informal teaching sessions or audit. Allocating each doctor a senior accident and emergency doctor to act as a mentor also helps. An additional method is to give staff logbooks to fill in. This enables the doctors and their mentor to see how they are progressing and which areas still require attention.

It needs to be remembered that doctors working in the department on a locum basis may not have had the opportunity to benefit from this educational system. Furthermore, they will not have undergone a formal selection procedure. As a consequence these members of staff can have a greater potential for making mistakes. The most sensible solution to this problem is to have an adequate staffing level to start with. This may not always be possible, however, and many departments reduce these risks by only using doctors who have previously worked full time in the department.

Staff organisation and shift patterns

When a department has the correct number of adequately trained senior house officers they can be built into a team, with two rotated each month to cover for those who are away. Senior house officers appreciate their rotas being done by the consultant personally. It is brought home to the junior doctors how important it is to turn up for work on time and this breeds team spirit and self respect. Members of a happy team of accident and emergency doctors will be more responsive to patients' needs (reducing the likelihood of complaints) and also be more likely to help each other, minimising the chance of mistakes. The incidence of doctors' sickness usually declines in this situation, reducing the costs of locums, and so leaving more funds for reasonable staffing levels.

Having departments of sufficient size such that doctors are never working on their own reduces tiredness and stress and enables peer stimulation and security. Tiredness can also be minimised by carefully planned shift patterns and by good departmental organisation.[19] For example, it is strongly recommended that the optimum shift rotation is in a clockwise direction with at least a month between rotations to allow for circadian stabilisation.[12] It is important to match peaks in patient arrivals with appropriate numbers of both medical and nursing staff.

Senior personnel must watch for mistakes particularly at the beginning and end of shifts when the chances of them occurring are highest. Furthermore all medical personnel should be made aware of how their performance will vary during the day so that they can be extra vigilant. Shifts must be arranged with an hour's overlap between the doctor who is leaving and the one who is starting work so that the handover of patients is not hurried. The doctor or nurse on a new shift should assess all the patients in their area of responsibility who still require investigation or treatment. In this way errors of judgement made by the outgoing team are not perpetuated. Furthermore, any deterioration in the patient's condition can be detected at an early stage.

Personal work load organisation

Doctors working in accident and emergency need to be taught to organise their work load into manageable tasks. They should concentrate on what they are doing and aim to complete as much as possible before taking on another problem. On those occasions when the task is interrupted by an emergency, the doctor is strongly advised to review the situation from the beginning when returning to the patient.

Breaks are essential for both physical and mental recuperation. Therefore senior staff must ensure that personnel take time for meals as well as a break from the intensity of the department. Rotating personnel to different parts of the department is also a good idea because it prevents staff becoming stale due to seeing the same types of conditions for long periods.

The doctor or nurse on a new shift should assess personally all the patients in their area of responsibility who still require investigation or treatment. In this way errors of judgement made by the outgoing team are not perpetuated. Furthermore any deterioration in the patient's condition can be detected at an early stage.

Errors resulting from mixing up patients are best prevented by training doctors to complete any documentation during the consultation or immediately afterwards. A personal self linking name stamp for each accident and emergency doctor facilitates clarity and responsibility because signatures are often difficult to read and senior house officers change jobs every six months. Having the nursing staff aware of each patient in their area of responsibility also helps because it reduces the chances of inappropriate treatment.

Communication

Communication skills can be taught, particularly by using videoed consultations or role play with actors. This training is now widespread in general practice but is not yet an accepted part of medical or nursing training in accident and emergency medicine. Nevertheless some departments are running pilot training schemes.

Communication with patients

In the drive to perfect clinical and diagnostic skills, the human side of practising medicine must not be forgotten. One of the commonest causes of complaint is poor communication.[35] Furthermore failures in communication are usually an important aspect in all types of complaints, including those primarily dealing with missed diagnosis and classification with treatment.[3] To improve communication with patients, Hill listed several recommendations (box 5).[46]

The initial impression given to the patient is vital. Not only will this effect the consultation but it will also encourage the patient to complain if they are dissatisfied with the treatment. Furthermore when giving advice, the clinician must ensure that the patient understands the instructions and can carry them out.

Box 5—Key points on communication with patients

- Listen and ensure that you understand what the patient is saying
- Ensure that patients and relatives understand what you are saying
- Before any procedure, explain carefully why and what you are doing
- Do not speak down to patients either figuratively or literally
- Control your own emotions
- Avoid unintended communication such as disparaging asides
- Do not criticise previous advice or treatment unless you have all the facts

---

It is important that the patient is fully informed before they are asked to consent to a particular procedure. Indeed if this is not done the doctor could be considered negligent if they went on to develop a complication after the treatment. The number of possible misadventures after most medical procedures is legend but the chances of some of them occurring is very remote. It is therefore considered essential that the patient is told about complications with a greater than 10% of occurring. Other possibilities should be discussed if the patient asks or the doctor considers it appropriate in that particular case.[47]

There are several reasons for patients leaving against medical advice and the most common are misunderstanding, anger, fear, and loss of control.[48] As these patients are potentially putting their own health at risk, as well as that of others, it is important that they are persuaded to stay. Often timely explanation, reassurance, and involvement of friends and relatives can help to prevent the patient leaving. It is their right, however, to refuse treatment, provided they are able to fully understand the risks they are facing. In these situations it is important that the clinician documents advice given and has this witnessed by a senior member of staff (box 6).[48]

When patients are incapable of comprehending the risks, they can be restrained and retained in the department pending a Section 2 by an approved psychiatrist and social worker or relative. An NHS trust, as an employer, has a duty to protect staff and therefore must provide the necessary security staff. This is especially so now that many more psychiatric patients are managed in the community

235

Box 6—Crucial documentation on patients leaving against medical advice

- Reasons why the patient was thought to be competent
- The patient's reason for leaving
- What management has been recommended and its risk and benefits
- The reasonable alternative approaches to care which have been discussed
- The risks associated with leaving which have been discussed
- Confirmation that the patient can return after a change of mind

---

and attend accident and emergency departments out of normal working hours.

Communication with hospital medical staff

As discussed previously, great potential for mistakes exists when patients are handed on to other health care professionals. To try and prevent such errors Hill suggests that certain key facts must be born in mind (box 7).[46]

Obviously care must be taken that the notes are both legible and comprehensible. This can be helped greatly by having structured accident and emergency cards which prompt the doctor to elicit certain pieces of information. This concept has been used for many years in the documentation of trauma resuscitations[49] and figure 13.3 gives an example. More recently documentation sheets for other conditions such as head injuries have also been developed.[50]

Irrespective of which type of documentation sheet is used, it is also advisable to hand over directly any vital clinical details. Consequently the clinician is not dependent on the receiving doctor

---

Box 7—Key points on communication with health care professionals

- Write legible and comprehensible notes
- Pass on in person any clinically vital pieces of information
- Provide sufficient clinical details when requesting investigations
- Only accept second opinions if the patient has been seen
- Verbal instructions on further management must be supplemented by written notes

---

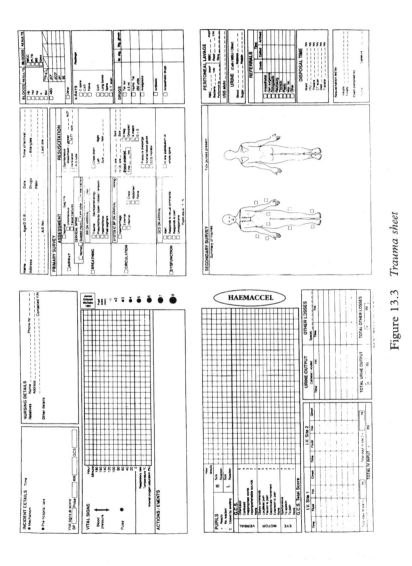

Figure 13.3 *Trauma sheet*

237

reading the notes. This discipline is an important element in preventing errors resulting from the "hand over" of patients between doctors.

Communication between doctors is also helped if the one initiating the exchange is clear what is required by a colleague. It is important that only unambiguous terms and phrases are used. For example, after a head injury the individual components of the Glasgow coma score should be given rather than their sum total. This gives a clearer assessment of the patient and reduces the chances of misinterpretation. Similarly the accident and emergency doctor must provide clear and appropriate clinical information when requesting any investigation. This enables the investigating team to contribute much more in excluding of diagnosing specific conditions.[51][52]

Occasionally patients can be so ill or injured that they have to be transferred rapidly through the department with only a limited assessment and investigation. Examples of this include the tender abdominal aortic aneurysm or the patient with multiple injuries who is haemodynamically unstable. In these circumstances it is important that the accident and emergency staff document what has and what has not been carried out and that the receiving team are fully aware of this.

Communication with the community

Good communication must also extend into the community. For example the patient's general practitioner must be informed if the patient is not ill enough to be admitted but doubt remains as to the cause of the condition. Several departments have computerised systems which enable letters to be generated automatically. Although the letter can be given to the patient to hand to the general practitioner, only about 60% will arrive.[53] It is therefore preferable to post the letter and, in appropriate cases, to phone the general practitioner and discuss the management with them.

Communication by telephone

Telephone communication between accident and emergency personnel and patients is becoming more common in the United Kingdom.[54] These advice lines provide patients with a fast and convenient source of medical help. For the department it represents a method of reducing patient attendance. As the doctor or nurse cannot see the patient, however, there is always a risk that errors of judgement may occur. To help reduce the chances of this happening it is essential that certain safeguards are in place (box 8).

Box 8—Safeguards for accident and emergency telephone advice lines

- Only experienced clinical accident and emergency personnel should be involved
- The time and date of the call must be recorded
- The patient's name, phone number, and complaint must be recorded
- The staff involved and the advice given must be recorded
- All advice should comply with the standard treatment of care
- All telephone records must be regularly assessed

Performance and stress

During a single shift staff may be exposed to a wide range of emotions and be expected to provide the appropriate response in each case. This continuous adaptation can lead to emotional fatigue which will be manifested as irritability, anxiety, depression, or a blunted affect. Critical incident debriefing can go some way to reducing emotional stress. It is therefore important that seniors are sensitive and supportive to the emotional thresholds of personnel in the department. Taking time to listen is an important first step. Without this, the staff will develop low levels of alertness, physical fatigue, and eventually absenteeism, and the chances of the doctor or nurse making a mistake are increased.

Risk management: environment

The layout of the department should be optimised so that staff are not uncomfortable or cramped while working. Equipment must be adequate, checked regularly, and positioned so that it is close to the patients. The accident and emergency consultant must also ensure that distracting and intrusive environmental conditions are kept to a minimum. Occasionally this is unavoidable, such as during structural alterations. Other sources—for example, the volume of departmental intercoms—should be adjusted so they get the message over but allow people to carry on working.

Lighting has to be adequate and non-flickering. It has been found that exposure to bright light (for example, 10 000 lux) shifts the temperature curve, affects the subjective assessment of alertness, and improves cognitive performance.[12] The actual level required, however, varies with the activity. High levels are required for patient assessment, surgical procedures, and radiological interpretation.

Departmental organisation

Triage

This process enables patients to be sorted into categories of increasing urgency. In this way personnel and equipment can be used most effectively. Furthermore, the staff's awareness will be heightened before seeing the urgent cases because of the prior warning made by the person triaging the patient.

Once triage is introduced, staff soon find it an essential element in the department's overall organisation. Incorrect triage will result in the patient going to the wrong part of the department to be seen by the wrong person. When this happens the chances of a mistake increases. To overcome this, three rules need to be obeyed:

- Triage **Must** be carried out by experienced staff
- Triage **Must** be repeated
- Triage **Must** be audited.

The risk of incorrect triage will be reduced by having only experienced staff carrying it out. Furthermore, it is important to realise that the patient's condition can change with time. It is therefore essential that triage is carried out several times during the stay in the department. This also helps to minimise the effect of any initially incorrect triage decisions. Auditing triage enables the sensitivity and specificity to be assessed and appropriate training or adjustments to be made.

Departmental protocols

The aim of these is to force a course of action which is considered to be the most appropriate by the senior members of the department, hospital, or indeed specialty. Protocols cover aspects of patient management, data interpretation, and radiological assessment and minimise risks of mistakes. The "10 commandments of emergency radiography" show one such system of good practice (box 9).[44]

Box 9—The 10 commandments of accident and emergency radiology

(1) Treat the patient, not the radiograph
(2) Take a history and examine the patient before requesting a radiograph
(3) Request a radiograph only when necessary
(4) Never look at a radiograph without seeing the patient; never see the patient without looking at the radiograph
(5) Look at every radiograph, the whole radiograph, and the radiograph as a whole
(6) Re-examine the patient when there is an incongruity between the radiograph and the expected findings
(7) The rule of twos: two views, two joints
(8) Take radiographs before and after procedures
(9) If a radiograph does not look quite right, ask and listen: there is probably something wrong
(10) Ensure that you are protected by fail safe mechanisms

Another example of good practice is not discharging patients until the social situation has been determined. This ensures that patients with missed fractures can return to hospital if the condition does not improve.

All the people working in the department should be aware of these policies and, ideally, have a personal copy. Compliance with these protocols and their effectiveness can be audited.

Referral procedures

An accident and emergency department cannot work in isolation from the rest of the hospital. Key support staff must be on site 24 hours a day to provide experienced medical and surgical back up as well as all the appropriate investigations.[2] This process is helped greatly by the accident and emergency consultant having developed with these specialties an inpatient referral system of particular patient groups. Where appropriate this must include generally accepted recommendations (box 10).

The accident and emergency consultant must establish a robust system of outpatient referral to ensure follow up of appropriate cases. In this way the initial treatment can be assessed and

241

> ## Box 10—Patient groups with generally accepted referral recommendations
>
> - Head injuries[55 56]
> - Asthmatics[38]
> - Suspected acute myocardial infarction[37 57]
> - Pulmonary embolism[11]
> - Injuries in children[11]
> - Sexual assault[58]

continuing management can be provided. A common example is the referral of fractures and dislocations to the hospital's orthopaedic clinic. Links with other specialties, including general practice, is also desirable. Feedback from these specialists is an important element in the training of accident and emergency doctors.[59]

Children

Around 20% of those attending accident and emergency departments are children under the age of 16, with a disproportionately high number of patients who are under 5. Senior house officers may have little postgraduate experience in paediatrics, and yet they must be able to identify those few children with early, possibly extremely subtle, signs of serious illness from the majority who will have only minor complaints. It is therefore vital not only that senior house officers receive formal teaching in paediatrics, but that a second opinion is readily available from middle grade and consultant accident and emergency staff as well as from paediatric registrars and consultants.

A joint statement produced in 1988 by the British Paediatric Association, the British Association of Paediatric Surgeons, and the Casualty Surgeons Association (now the British Association for Accident and Emergency Medicine) laid down the minimum requirements for children in accident and emergency departments.[60] These requirements include a consultant paediatrician who has responsibility for liaison with the consultant in accident and emergency medicine as well as a liaison health visitor to facilitate communication between the accident and emergency department and the community. The accident and emergency consultants must ensure that there is good liaison between their department, the paediatricians, and the community. When funding for a liaison health visitor is not provided by the commmunity there is a risk of serious consequences to the care of children attending accident and emergency departments. This is because an isolated problem may not assume its correct importance when viewed without all the other information relating to the child's social circumstances and previous health record.

Liaison and community support

Many accident and emergency doctors are junior and do not have experience of working in the community. Therefore the creation of specialist therapy posts brings into departments expertise which not only provides a higher standard of initial care but also provides for follow up in the community. If the therapist is concerned the patient may be referred back to a more experienced accident and emergency doctor. Examples are the occupational therapist, the psychiatric liaison nurse, and the alcohol health worker. Such therapists are particularly of use for the repeat attender who may well have problems which have not been recognised at the time of the individual attendances.

Transfer of patients

To facilitate a smooth transfer, it is important to ensure that the receiving facility and personnel have been contacted. If a transfer to another hospital is envisaged, the clinicians must also decide on the most suitable method of transportation and how the patient should be stabilised and prepared for the journey.[61-65]

All aspects of the patient's airway, breathing, and circulation must be reassessed before the patient leaves and appropriate adjustments made. For example, the patient who tolerates an oropharyngeal airway should be intubated and ventilated so that the airway can be protected and hypoxia and hypercarbia prevented. All cannulae, catheters, tubes, and drains must be secured.

Monitoring during the transfer period must be continued to ensure that ventilation and tissue perfusion are adequate. During transit, the patient needs to be accompanied by appropriately trained and equipped staff to enable them to monitor any ventilatory perfusion problems and intervene if necessary. All the medical and nursing notes, radiographs, blood tests, identifying labels and, if appropriate, consent forms must also be taken with the patient.

Upon arrival the transfer team must hand over to the personnel who will be in charge of the patient's definitive care. In this way important events during transfer as well as a summary of the initial resuscitation can be provided.

Near misses

These are situations when several risk factors are present but they are of insufficient magnitude or number for a mistake to occur. It is our opinion that there are many more near misses than full blown mistakes. Consequently they may represent an invaluable source of information on how errors are occurring in the department as well as indicating ways on how they can be avoided.

Unfortunately, near misses are difficult to detect and are therefore rarely recorded. A system which has been used with effect in clinical practice is the anonymous documentation of clinical incidents. Certain specialties have enhanced this system by employing a "risk management" officer to specifically assess near misses so that lessons can be learnt before a patient is affected. It would be interesting to see if the introduction of such a system into emergency medicine would have a beneficial effect. In the meantime departments will have to continue to rely on other time honoured ways of detecting near misses, namely:

Return visits

Special attention must be given to patients who return with the same condition because it is no better or has worsened. Studies have shown that 9–20% of these patients have conditions missed on their first visit and initial care had been inappropriate in 5–23% of cases.[66-68] These people must be completely reassessed and any investigation reviewed to make sure that a mistake has not occurred. Ideally such patients should be seen by a doctor more senior than a senior house officer while they are in the department or, if this is not possible, referred to the next accident and emergency review clinic.

Review clinics

Most accident and emergency departments run review clinics to which senior house officers refer patients for follow up of specific

244

conditions (for example, burns) or for review by a senior doctor for confirmation of their diagnosis. At the present time, however, few departments have enough staff to provide 24 hour senior cover. Consequently these clinics tend to be used to provide a second opinion. When used in this way they provide a safety net for the patient (and junior staff) as well as giving the senior staff a chance to informally assess medical management and record keeping by the referring staff.

Quality control

No matter how good an accident and emergency department is, errors will occur, It is therefore important that a quality control system is in place which can identify errors quickly so that patients can be recalled and any harm minimised. As there are several aspects of work which must be routinely checked (box 11), adequate staffing levels are essential.

Box 11—Accident and emergency activities subjected to routine quality control

- Radiology
- Electrocardiography
- Telephone advice records
- Laboratory results
- Children and elderly patients
- Discharge summaries

Most missed diagnoses in the accident and emergency department result from misinterpretation of radiographs.[51] Error rates of 2·8–35% have been found but this number can be reduced when a system is set up whereby all radiographs are reported on by radiologists.[69-75] It is important that all emergency radiographs must be reviewed by an experienced radiologist within three working days. To enable this to be done, there must be an adequately completed request card (see earlier) and the accident and emergency doctor's radiological opinion. Should an abnormality have been missed, the radiologist can then rapidly inform the accident and emergency department so that the patient can be recalled. Cases in which a normal appearance was

245

misinterpreted as being abnormal should also be identified in this quality control system. In this way, a resource of false positive and negative radiographs are collected which can be used to teach the medical staff in the department.

A similar quality control system for all electrocardiography carried out in the department is also essential.[10][11][76] As with radiographs, this is particularly important when the investigation is carried out on patients who are subsequently discharged. A system also needs to be in place for assessing the telephone advice records, discharge summaries, and all laboratory results returned to accident and emergency.[77] The laboratory results must be checked and acted on before filing. Unfortunately there is usually a considerable gap between the time the patient was in the department and when the discharge letter is written by the in house team. Nevertheless, analysis of these reports by senior accident and emergency personnel provides important feedback as well as pointers for quality control.

All patients under 16 or over 65 who have been discharged from the department must be followed up by a health visitor liaison officer. As both groups are particularly sensitive to poor social situations it is important to determine if they and their relatives are coping, if any new symptoms have developed, and that their general practitioners know of their plight.

Complaints

An essential aspect of quality control is analysis of the complaints against the department. They have a frequency of around 0·2–0·4 per 1000 new patients seen and cover a wide range of quality issues including communication and diagnostic and therapeutic matters.[3-5][78] Considering these issues will lead to improvements in the quality of care as well as reducing the risk of mistakes. Once a mistake is identified by the quality control system, it should be studied so that the reasons for it can be determined. The lessons learnt from this can then be fed back into the appropriate part of the departmental system to reduce the chances of this error occurring again.

Audit

This is an important element in departmental quality control. It entails both the setting of standards and an assessment to see if these are being met. The reasons for any shortfall from the desired standards should then be determined and appopriate changes made to the system. Subsequent analysis can then be carried out to ascertain if the modifications have helped move the actual practice closer to the desired standards.

The Major Trauma Outcome Study (MTOS) represents a national based audit system.[79] Highly effective audit can also be carried out at a local level.[41 75 80 81] The number and depth of clinical topics covered depends on the administrative resources available but all should be quantifiable, repeatable, and relevant to accident and emergency.[82] The choice of clinical topics audited depends on the incidence of the particular condition, its morbidity, and its mortality. Examples include resuscitation attempts, the "door to needle time" for treatment with streptokinase, and the management of asthma. Triage decisions and record keeping must also be audited often as inaccurate initial patient assessment can have serious consequences.

Departmental and hospital medical guidance notes, along with clinical protocols, should be used as a basis for clinical audit. When audit highlights difficulties in the provision of clinical care or outmoded protocols it may be appropriate to update them. In this way doctors and nurses throughout the hospital can develop a feeling of ownership for clinical protocols which, as a result, are more likely to be adhered to.

Integrated care pathways are a relatively new natural progression from clinical audit. They are protocols for the management of patients with particular conditions (for example, asthma) which are available at the patients' bedside to inform and guide them, the doctors, nurses, and all other health care professionals on the likely plan for their care during their stay in hospital. Overall patient care involves management, resources, and a multidisciplinary team. Scrutiny of integrated care pathways for areas in which a patient's care does not follow the anticipated route is a helpful form of audit which may highlight areas of risk in an accident and emergency department.

Most departments now regularly audit the clinical recordkeeping of their nursing and medical staff. This is most valuable if a structured audit form is used so that individual feedback can be given in areas of good and poor practice. Figure 13.4 gives an example of a simple systematic card audit. It is important to note not only that the patient contact stages are correctly done, but also which are done inappropriately. Staff will then have clear objectives and an improvement with subsequent audit can be shown. It is

St Mary's A&E Department random CARD & COMPUTER AUDIT

Dr _____

A&E card numbers	Date	Diagnosis
1._____	_____	_____
2._____	_____	_____
3._____	_____	_____
4._____	_____	_____
5._____	_____	_____

CARDS	DONE	NOT DONE	NOT DONE appropriately	DONE inappropriately
1]Date & Time seen				
2]Satisfactory history				
3]Satisfactory exam				
4]Appropriate Ix				
5]Results recorded				
6]Diagnosis recorded				
7]Management approp				
8]Referral Doc & time				
9]Legible				
10]Sign & Stamp				
COMPUTER				
11]Clinical details				
12]Ix results				
13]approp Letter				

Figure 13.4   *Random card and computer audit form*

otherwise easy for junior medical and nursing staff to view audit as a negative experience.

It is very important that all the recommendations made are documented so that follow up audits can ascertain whether these policies have been carried out and whether their execution has had the effect of improving the service to patients.

Conclusions

- Mistakes in the accident and emergency department rarely result from one catastrophic error
- The chances of a mistake being made are high because a catalogue of human, environmental, and equipment problems coexist

- People responsible for running accident and emergency departments must reduce the chances of human mistakes by adequate training, staffing, and optimal shift patterns

- Accident and emergency staff should be provided with an environment and equipment which facilitates effective and efficient work

- By appropriate departmental organisation, people responsible for running accident and emergency departments must ensure that human, environmental, and equipment problems do not occur in combination

- Finally it is important that a good quality control system is present to minimise the effect of any mistake as well as to investigate why it occurred.

1 Wilson D. The development of accident and emergency medicine. *Community Medicine* 1980;2:28–35.
2 National Audit Office. *NHS accident and emergency departments in England. Report by the Controller and Auditor General.* London: HMSO, 1992.
3 Kadzombe E, Coals J. Complaints against doctors in an accident and emergency department: A 10 year analysis. *Arch Emerg Med* 1992;9:134–42.
4 Hunt T, Glucksman M. A review of 7 years of complaints in an inner-city accident and emergency department. *Arch Emerg Med* 1991;8:17–23.
5 Reichl M, Sleet R. Complaints against accident and emergency departments: current trends. *Arch Emerg Med* 1990;7:246–48.
6 Royal College of Surgeons of England. *Report of the working party on the management of major trauma.* London: Royal College of Surgeons of England, 1988.
7 Dearden C, Rutherford W. The resuscitation of the severely injured in the accident and emergency Department—a medical audit. *Injury* 1985;16:249–52,
8 Skinner D, Camm J, Miles S. Cardiopulmonary resuscitation skills of pre-registration house officers. *BMJ* 1985;290:1549–50.
9 Morris F, Tordoff S, Wallis D, Skinner D. Cardiopulmonary resuscitation skills of pre-registration house officers: five years on. *BMJ* 1991;302:626–7.
10 Guly U, Sammy I, Driscoll P. Arrythmia recognition and management: A need for improvement. *European Journal of Emergency Medicine* 1995 (in press).
11 Touquet R, Fothergill J, Harris N. Accident and emergency department; the specialty of accident and emergency medicine. In: Powers M, Harris N, eds. *Medical negligence.* London: Butterworths, 1994:615–46.
12 Whitehead D. Using circadian principles in emergency medicine scheduling. In: Andrew A, Pollack M, eds. *Wellness for emergency physicians.* Dallas: American College of Emergency Physicians, 1995:8–13.
13 Smith-Coggins R, Rosekind M, Hurd S, Buccino K. Relationship of day versus night sleep to physician performance and mood. *Ann Emerg Med* 1994;24: 928–34.
14 Coleman R. *Wide awake at 3:00 am.* New York: Freeman and Co, 1986.
15 Stiell I, Greenberg G, McKnight B, *et al.* Decision rules for the use of radiographs in ankle injury: refinement and prospective validation. *JAMA* 1993;269: 1127–32.

16 Nicholson D, Driscoll P. *ABC of emergency radiology.* London: BMJ Publishing Group, 1995.
17 McNamara R, Margulies J. Chemical dependency in emergency medical residency programs: perspective of the program disorder. *Ann Emerg Med* 1994; **23**:1072–76.
18 Hughes P, Baldwin D, Sheehan D, *et al.* Resident physician substance abuse by speciality. *Am J Psychiatry* 1992;**149**:1348–54.
19 Heyworth J, Whitley T, Allison E, Revicki D. Predictors of work satisfaction among SHOs during accident and emergency medicine training. *Arch Emerg Med* 1993;**10**:279–88.
20 LeWinter J. The medical family. In: Andrew A, Pollack M, eds. *Wellness for emergency physicians.* Dallas: American College of Emergency Physicians, 1995: 14–6.
21 Kelner M, Rosenthal C. Postgraduate medical training, stress and marriage. *Can J Psychiatry* 1986;**31**:22–4.
22 British Association of Accident and Emergency Medicine. *Medical staffing: accident and emergency departments.* London: British Association of Accident and Emergency Medicine, 1993.
23 Driscoll P, Vincent C. Variation in trauma resuscitation and its effect on outcome. *Injury* 1992;**23**:111–5.
24 Driscoll P, Vincent C. Organising an efficient trauma team. *Injury* 1992;**23**: 107–10.
25 Guly H. Missed tendon injuries. *Arch Emerg Med* 1991;**8**:87–91.
26 Guly H. Medico–legal problems in accident and emergency departments. *Journal of the Medical Defence Union* 1993;**2**:36–9.
27 Advanced Life Support Group. *Advanced paediatric life support: a practical approach.* London: BMJ Publishing Group, 1993.
28 Caesar R. Dangerous complaints: The acute geriatric abdomen. *Emergency Medicine Reports* 1994;**15**:190–202.
29 Dove A, Dave S. Elderly patients in the accident department and their problems. *BMJ* 1986;**292**:807–9.
30 De Dombal F. Computers, diagnosis and patients with abdominal pain [editorial]. *Arch Emerg Med* 1992;**9**:267–70.
31 Stonebridge P, Freeland P, Rainey J, Macleod D. Audit of computer aided diagnosis of abdominal pain in accident and emergency departments. *Arch Emerg Med* 1992;**9**:271–3.
32 Wilson D, Wilson P, Walmsley R, Horrocks J, DeDombal F. Diagnosis of acute abdominal pain in the accident and emergency department. *Br J Surg* 1977; **64**:250–4.
33 Driscoll P, Skinner D. Initial assessment and management. In: Skinner D, Driscoll P, Earlam R, eds. *ABC of major trauma.* 2nd ed. London: BMJ Publishing Group, 1995 (in press).
34 Driscoll P, Gwinnutt C, Jimmerson C, Goodall O, eds. *Trauma resuscitation: the team approach.* London: MacMillan, 1993.
35 Advanced Life Support Group. *Advanced cardiac life support: a practical approach.* London: Chapman and Hall Medical, 1993.
36 European Resuscitation Council. *Guidelines for resuscitation.* Belgium: European Resuscitation Council Secretariat, 1994.
37 National heart attack alert program co-ordinating committee 60 Minutes to Treatment Working Group. *Emergency department: rapid identification and treatment of patients with acute myocardial infarction.* Washington: US Department of Health and Human Resources, 1993.
38 British Thoracic Society and others. Guidelines for the management of asthma. *BMJ* 1993;**306**:776–82.
39 Karras D. Asthma: current therapeutic strategies and comprehensive patient management. *Emergency Medicine Reports* 1994;**15**:170–80.

40 Wardrope J, Smith J. *The management of wounds and burns.* Oxford: Oxford University Press, 1993.
41 Gilling-Smith C, Zelin J, Touquet R, Steer P. Management of early pregnancy bleeding in the accident and emergency department. *Arch Emerg Med* 1988;**5**: 133–8.
42 Royal College of Radiologists. *Making the best use of the department of clinical radiology: guidelines for doctors.* 2nd ed. London: Royal College of Radiologists, 1993.
43 Craig J. *Pitfalls in diagnostic radiology.* London: The Medical Protection Society, 1993.
44 Touquet R, Driscoll P, Nicholson D. Teaching in accident and emergency medicine—10 commandments of accident and emergency radiology. *BMJ* 1995; **310**:642–5.
45 Tachakra S, Beckett M. An induction course for casualty officers. *British Journal of Accident and Emergency Medicine* 1987;**2**:8–10.
46 Hill G. *A&E risk management.* London: The Medical Defence Union, 1991.
47 Sidaway v Board of Governors of the Bethlem Royal and the Maudsley Hospital (1985). 2 WLR 480.
48 Rice M. Emergency department patients leaving against medical advice. *Foresight* 1994;**29**:1–8.
49 Over D, Finch M. The development of new documentation for use in cases of major trauma. *Injury* 1991;**22**:139–45.
50 Wallace S, Gullan R, Byrne P, Bennett J, Perez-Avila C. Use of proforma for head injuries in accident and emergency departments—the way forward. *Journal of Accident and Emergency Medicine* 1994;**11**:33–42.
51 Guly H. Missed diagnosis in an accident and emergency department. *Injury* 1984;**15**:403–6.
52 Rickett A, Finlay D, Jagger C. The importance of clinical details when reporting accident and emergency radiographs. *Injury* 1992;**23**:458–60.
53 Sherry M, Edmunds S, Touquet R. The reliability of patients in delivering the letter from the hospital accident and emergency department to their general practitioner. *Arch Emerg Med* 1985;**2**:165–9.
54 Egleston C, Kelly H, Cope A. Use of telephone advice lines in an accident and emergency department. *BMJ* 1994;**308**:31.
55 Commission of the Provision of Surgical Services. *Report of the working party on head injuries.* London: Royal College of Surgeons of England, 1986.
56 Group of Neurosurgeons. Guidelines for the initial management of head injury. *BMJ* 1984;**288**:983–5.
57 Saetta J, Quinton D, Dacruz D, Barnes M. Delay in thrombolytic treatment in acute myocardial infarction: the role of the accident and emergency department. *Arch Emerg Med* 1990;**7**:206–11.
58 McLay W. *Rape.* Creaton House, Northampton: Association of police surgeons of Great Britain, 1983.
59 Morton R. Fracture clinic referrals: the need for self audit. *Injury* 1988;**19**: 77–8.
60 Morton R, Phillips B. *Accidents and emergencies in children.* Oxford: Oxford University Press, 1992.
61 Ridley S, Wright I, Rogers P. Secondary transport of critically ill patients. *Hospital Update* 1990;**16**:289–98.
62 Jeffries N, Bristow A. Long-distance inter-hospital transfers. *British Journal of Intensive Care* 1991;**1**:197–204.
63 Gentleman D, Dearden M, Midgley S, Maclean D. Guidelines for resuscitation and transfer of patients with serious head injury. *BMJ* 1993;**307**:547–52.
64 Lambert S, Willett K. Transfer of multiply injured patients for neurosurgical opinion: a study of the adequacy of assessment and resuscitation. *Injury* 1993; **24**:333–6.

65 Gwinnutt C, Wilson A, Driscoll P. Inter-hospital transfer. In: Skinner D, Driscoll P, Earlam R, eds. *ABC of major trauma*. 2nd ed. London: BMJ Publishing Group 1995 (in press).
66 Wilkins P, Beckett M. Audit of unexpected return visits to an accident and emergency department. *Arch Emerg Med* 1992;**9**:352–6.
67 O'Dwyer F, Bodiwala G. Unscheduled return visits by patients to the accident and emergency department. *Arch Emerg Med* 1991;**8**:196–200.
68 Pierce J, Kellerman A, Oster C. "Bounces": an analysis of short-term return visits to a public hospital emergency department. *Ann Emerg Med* 1990;**19**: 752–7.
69 DeLacey G, Barker A, Harper J, Wignall B. An assessment of the clinical effects of reporting accident and emergency radiographs. *Br J Radiol* 1980;**53**:304–9.
70 Mucci B. The selective reporting of x ray films from accident and emergency departments. *Injury* 1983;**14**:343–4.
71 Wardrope J, Chennels P. Should casualty radiographs be reviewed? *BMJ* 1985; **290**:1638–40.
72 Swain A. Radiological audit-changes in casualty officer performance during tenure of post. *British Journal of Accident and Emergency Medicine* 1986;**1**:5–9.
73 Gleadhill D, Thomson J, Simmons P. Can more efficient use be made of x ray examinations in the accident and emergency department? *BMJ* 1987;**294**: 943–7.
74 Vincent C, Driscoll P, Audley R, Grant D. Accuracy of detection of radiographic abnormalities by junior doctors. *Arch Emerg Med* 1988;**5**:101–9.
75 Thomas H, Mason A, Smith R, Fergusson C. Value of radiographic audit in an accident service department. *Injury* 1992;**23**:47–50.
76 McCallion W, Templeton P, McKinney L, Higginson J. Missed myocardial ischaemia in the accident and emergency department: ECG a need for audit? *Arch Emerg Med* 1991;**8**:102–7.
77 Verdile V. The telephone in emergency practice. *Foresight* 1993;**27**:1–6.
78 Richmond P, Evans R. Complaints and litigation—three years experience at a busy accident and emergency department 1983–85. *Health Trends* 1989;**21**: 42–5.
79 Yates D, Woodford M, Hollis S. Preliminary analysis of the care of injured patients in British hospitals: first report of the United Kingdom major trauma outcome study. *BMJ* 1992;**305**:737–40.
80 Yates D, Bancewicz J, Woodford M, *et al*. Trauma audit—closing the loop. *Injury* 1994;**25**:511–4.
81 Tulloh B. Diagnostic accuracy in head injured patients: an emergency department audit. *Injury* 1994;**25**:231–4.
82 Driscoll P. Audit in A&E departments. *Medical Audit News* 1991;**1**:8–9.

14 Reducing risks in medical practice

GRAHAM NEALE

As to diseases, make a habit of two things—to help, or at least to do no harm (Hippocrates. *Epidemics*, book 1).

The medical profession has been slow to face up to the problems of adverse events in hospital practice. Medicolegal claims have been directed mainly against the so called high risk specialties of obstetrics, surgery, and the management of trauma, in which the effects of medical accidents are usually more immediate and more obvious than during the course of a medical illness. But times have changed and complaints against physicians are increasing steadily as the general public accept less readily, at face value, professional skill and integrity and more readily believe in their right to be compensated for life's misfortunes. Thus there is an urgent need to identify risk prone situations and risk prone doctors to minimise the chance of causing harm. To date there has been no detailed British study of the epidemiology of medical accidents although this was suggested five years ago.[1] Until such a survey is undertaken, one must rely on evidence from small scale studies[2][3] and reports of individual cases.

In this chapter I concentrate primarily on analysing the causes of nearly 200 claims of medical negligence against hospital physicians collected over a period of 10 years. Thus emphasis is on the more serious accidents and the recommendations for reducing risks are directed primarily to clinicians. The description and analysis of cases is complemented by an attempt to define the human factors in the causation of adverse events (see chapter 3) and will, I hope, provide a baseline for more detailed studies.

Classification of medical misadventure

Accidents in medical practice may occur in one or more areas of endeavour—diagnosis, procedures (both diagnostic and therapeutic), drug treatment (including wrong prescription, incorrect administration, failure to monitor side effects, failure to recognise possible drug interactions), and general management (including follow up). There is little published data to quantify the relative likelihood of accidents in each category. In a survey of 100 cases from the United Kingdom, preventible errors were identified in relation to diagnosis (40%), procedures (35%), drug treatment (5%), and general management (20%).[3] The true relative incidence of errors is likely to be very different because in this study there was a bias towards gastroenterology and because it is easier for patients to recognise errors arising from diagnosis and procedure than from management. In 1984 in the United States 38% of claims were against anaesthetists, surgeons, and obstetricians. Of the remainder 39% related to diagnosis, 27% to treatment, and 16% to drugs.[4] The authors comment on the considerable increase in allegations of incorrect diagnosis—recognition of "sins of omission" as well as "sins of commission".

Misdiagnosis

For the hospital physician diagnosis is the key to sound practice. Misdiagnosis may occur as a result of misinterpretation of available evidence (40%), inexperience (25%), sloppy practice (20%), poor reasoning (20%), and unfamiliarity with the condition (20%).[3] Once a working diagnosis has been established it is remarkably difficult to chart a new course. There is a natural tendency to use data to support preconceived ideas rather than to think anew. This is illustrated in the following examples.

Example 1

A 74 year old man had innumerable attacks of altered consciousness and confusion sometimes associated with sweating, often precipitated by exercise, and always in the morning. He had been treated unsuccessfully for epilepsy. After six years he was admitted to hospital and a prolonged fast was carried out to look for hypoglycaemia. The test was poorly conducted and the result misinterpreted. The patient went a further six years before the correct diagnosis of insulinoma was established.

254

This patient had a tumour producing insulin which lowered his blood sugar to dangerous levels especially when fasting. The condition is rare but the clinical pattern is so striking that the diagnosis should not be long delayed. In this case the diagnosis was suspected but the appropriate test was sloppily performed (the patient fasted only 18 hours instead of 24–48 hours). Even so the blood sugar fell to remarkably low concentrations and the overall result of the test was strongly suggestive of an insulin secreting tumour. Unfortunately the case note summary was written by an inexperienced clinician who misintepreted the evidence and stated that the diagnosis of insulinoma had been excluded. This was accepted at face value and the patient continued to have attacks for a further six years until a new clinician decided to reinvestigate.

Example 2

A 27 year old woman complained of feeling tired and of losing weight. She was under considerable stress because her husband was in the army and her child required treatment for disruptive behaviour at school. The doctor diagnosed anorexia nervosa and treated her with tranquillisers. She failed to improve and six months later was admitted to hospital where she was found to have generalised lymphadenopathy secondary to Hodgkin's disease.

This is an example of an inexperienced doctor making a psychiatric diagnosis on inadequate criteria and making the cardinal error of failing to undertake a straightforward clinical examination together with suitable screening tests for a patient who was wasting away.

In only 20% of incorrect diagnoses could the error be ascribed to difficulty in diagnosing a rare condition (for example, carcinoid misdiagnosed as menopausal symptoms; pancreatitis in a child misdiagnosed as gastroenteritis). There was no evidence that "defensive overinvestigation" would have prevented some or even any of the misdiagnoses. The problems occurred either because of failure to make a straightforward differential diagnosis; or failure to undertake simple screening tests (such as those for an inflammatory disorder); or misinterpretation of tests which were performed. In more than one case the clinician raised a question mark against the working diagnosis but failed to get a second opinion, which may be the best way of overcoming the thought block which prevents a clinician from thinking afresh. But it is important that the second opinion starts from scratch. Listening to a case history or reading the opinion of others may condition even the most astute clinician.

Damage as a result of procedures

The first duty of a clinician is to define the patient's condition and explain it to the patient ("doctor" from the latin, docere, to teach). Unfortunately it is easier to carry out a procedure (and easier still to fill in a form requesting someone else to act) than to think and to discuss the problem with the patient. In the reported study, procedures in which the likely benefits were not balanced against the risks led to claims of negligence in 10% of cases.[3] Unfortunately the pressure to do something is reinforced by the rewards of private practice in which taking a detailed history, undertaking a careful examination, and providing a thoughtful discussion are much less well rewarded than undertaking a procedure. And all invasive procedures carry risks, the implications of which may not be explained clearly to the patient.

Example 3

A 52 year old woman presented with recurrent right sided abdominal pain 18 months after a cholecystectomy. The pain was described as similar to that before her gall bladder was removed. Without other investigation the patient was referred for examination by endoscopic retrograde cholangiopancreatography (ERCP). The endoscopist did not see the patient before she arrived in the endoscopy suite. The biliary tree and pancreatic duct appeared normal and sphincterotomy was performed. Twenty four hours later the patient developed severe pancreatitis followed by retroperitoneal infection. After three months of intensive care she recovered but was left partially sighted as a result of candida septicaemia and associated retinitis.

Endoscopic retrograde cholangiopancreatography enables the endoscopist to inject contrast media into the ducts draining the biliary tree and pancreas and to treat obstruction. It is a powerful means of dealing with pathology in an otherwise relatively inaccessible part of the body. The procedure carries several risks of which inflammation of the pancreas is the most serious. Pancreatitis usually settles down spontaneously after a day or two but may lead to life threatening tissue necrosis and subsequent infection. In this case the operator elected to undertake ERCP without a clinical assessment and without explaining the risks to the patient. It was particularly distressing that the patient's symptoms were probably unrelated to either the biliary tree or the pancreas.

Damage caused by drug treatment

In the published study,[3] treatment carried a rather low relative risk for medical misadventure (5%) which is surprising when one considers the list of possibilities (box 1). Doctors are expected to use the right drug, in the right dose, by the right route, in the right frequency, and if given by injection, at the right site without risk of infection. If a doctor is given a drug to inject and error occurs, the doctor is responsible. Doctors are also required to consider contraindications, interactions, side effects, and allergies. The information which a doctor should provide to a patient for whom he is prescribing is not clearly defined. The law requires the provision of material information on risks of treatment. Case law concentrates on defining the word "material" and usually accepts a "professional" rather than a "patient" standard. This means that a doctor is not negligent so long as he provides a level of explanation (disclosure) consistent with the practice of a responsible body of medical opinion. This implies that the doctor "knows best" and

---

Box 1—Risks in providing drug treatment

- Errors in prescribing (including illegibility of script)
- Errors in dispensing (including labelling of container)
- Misunderstanding by a patient
- Side effect of drugs
    Direct damage
    Hypersensitivity
    Drug interactions
- Drug addiction

In American series, over 50% of claims related to drugs involve side effects

---

allows him the privilege not to disclose possible adverse effects of treatment if he thinks that such disclosure would be detrimental to the patient. There are two important exceptions to this rule. Firstly, the doctor must answer fully and truthfully all questions posed by the enquiring patient. Secondly, he must warn if there is a substantial (say 10%) risk of grave hazard. Finally, a doctor must monitor the effects of drug treatment and recognise possible side effects as indicated in the next example.

Example 4

A 20 year old woman developed inflammatory bowel disease and this was treated with mesalazine (1·6 g a day increasing to 3·2 g a day; a high dose which was deemed necessary because the patient was anxious to avoid taking corticosteroids). The next year the patient was found to have a mild microcytic anaemia and iron was prescribed. A year later she was symptom free but had a haemoglobin of 9·6 g/ 100 ml with a mean corpuscular volume (MCV) of 86. Once again, iron was prescribed. Subsequently the patient's health deteriorated and her haemoglobin fell to 7·6 with an MCV of 83. The consultant noted that there was little evidence of active inflammation and expressed surprise at the continuing anaemia despite treatment with iron by mouth. He decided to admit her to hospital for "a whole body iron infusion". During the hospital admission, the patient was found to have proteinuria and a creatinine of 455 um/l which indicated severe renal damage. Subsequently these findings were shown to be due to interstitial nephritis secondary to treatment with mesalazine

In this case the clinician was probably not aware of the possible side effects of mesalazine on the kidney. In fact at that time there were only nine reported cases in the world literature. But mesalazine is one of a group of drugs with a long list of possible side effects. They key to the diagnosis lay in the blood count. The patient was anaemic with red cells of normal size. Thus iron deficiency was an unlikely cause for the anaemia and a search for an alternative cause was indicated. Risks in relation to the use of drugs may be minimised by taking precautions as listed in boxes 2, 3, and 4.

Box 2—Avoiding the risks of prescribing

- Before prescribing, list all drugs given
- Use well designed prescription charts
- Use prescription renewal systems sensibly
- Use flow sheets for long term prescribing
- Give clear information to patients (both oral and written)
- Document the disclosure of risks and side-effects
- Obtain informed consent when necessary
- Always obtain consent for use of experimental drugs
- Aim for use of computerised quality assurance programmes

Box 3—Classes of drugs which most often lead to claims

- Antibiotics: Failure to document allergy
  Inappropriate drug for condition treated

- Glucocorticoids: Incorrect dosage
  Failure to discuss dangers
  Failure to monitor progress

- Narcotics: Inappropriate prescribing
  Failure to monitor progress

- NSAID: Inappropriate prescribing
  Failure to discuss dangers

Mismanagement

Errors in management in hospital practice were identified in 20% of cases. They seem to occur primarily because of a failure

259

Box 4—Avoiding risks in administering drugs parenterally

- Check that the drug is being given to the correct patient

- Check the injection with another qualified member of staff

- Check the dosage and dilution

- Know the correct site and route of injection

- Make sure that the needle or cannula is correctly sited

- Observe the injection site throughout the giving of the drug

---

of teamwork. The need for teamwork has increased perceptibly over the past 30 years. Hardly any aspect of hospital practice involves a clinician working on his own. No longer is it possible for a houseman to provide the final common pathway through whom all decisions pass regarding the management of a group of patients. The hospital doctor must be aware of his dependence on others, must listen and learn, must understand how to create a successful clinical team, and how to adopt techniques for creating openness and confidence. The team may extend across the whole range of health care workers. A good leader encourages team members to accept feedback and to talk about themselves in relation to the job. The aim must be to help them develop and release their own potential. In this way morale in the unit is strengthened. If teamwork fails then patients may suffer, shown in the next example.

Example 5

A 50 year old woman with chronic oedema of the lower limbs developed severe cellulitis. She had a persistent pyrexia and was treated with augmentin for two days, amoxycillin for two days, and finally erythromycin. The case notes were scanty but it would seem that no attempt was made to identify the causative organism. Five days after admission the patient vomited a small amount of blood. A gastroenterologist was called to undertake endoscopic examination of the stomach. This examination showed "blood clot in the stomach" and it was suggested that blood transfusion was required. No one took any note of the steadily rising white cell count, which reached $54 \times 10^9/l$ (indicating very severe sepsis), nor the oliguria with increasing uraemia (indicating renal failure). The patient was transfused four units of blood over 24 hours and was then noted to be breathless with a raised central venous pressure. She died four hours later. The attending house officer asked his consultant what to put on the death certificate and they agreed on "massive gastrointestinal bleeding". The husband requested a necropsy which was not performed.

In this case it seems likely that the patient died of unresolved sepsis, renal failure, and overtransfusion. The diagnosis of massive bleeding was absolutely untenable in the face of a raised central venous pressure. The patient was seen by several junior clinical staff and a consultant gastroenterologist but there seems not to have been a guiding hand covering the whole of the patient's illness. The laboratory staff made no contribution other than sending out the results provided by their analysers. The nursing notes were scanty and there was no evidence of close monitoring of the progress of a very sick patient. The patient was not even examined after her untimely death despite the husband's request for a postmortem examination. One is reminded of Justice Sheen's observations in his summing up of the inquiry into the sinking of the Herald of Free Enterprise—"From top to bottom the body corporate was infected with the disease of sloppiness."

The causes of medical misadventure

In the previous section I have examined the four major areas of hospital medical practice in which errors may occur. Some such errors are inevitable because all human endeavours carry risks. The role of human psychology in the causation of adverse events is explored in this book by James Reason (chapter 3). In this section I provide examples of cases which fit a modification of his classification (box 5) to try to define more clearly factors which need to be considered in formulating plans to reduce the risks of medical practice.

Unforced errors

Simple slips or lapses in memory may have profound consequences. Thus clinicians should be aware of the likelihood of such errors and try to develop fail safe mechanisms.

Box 5—Human causes of adverse medical events

- Unforced errors:
  Simple slips—for example, omissions, misreading, misordering (example 6)
  Lapses of memory—for example, in making a differential diagnosis (example 4)

- Mistakes (by deliberate action):
  Deviation from standard medical practice (examples 3, 4, 7, 11)
  Lack of knowledge (examples 2, 5, 8, 12, 13, 14)

- Violations of the normal code of practice:
  Taking short cuts ("more efficient") (example 3)
  Breaching a protocol ("knows better") (examples 1, 5, 9, 11)
  Inexperience (especially if linked with overconfidence) (examples 10, 11, 14)
  Deliberate action (for example, euthanasia)

Example 6

A 50 year old woman had episodes of colicky abdominal pain and vomiting at roughly fortnightly intervals. After three months she was referred to a gastroenterologist who made a differential diagnosis of: gall stones; intermittent subacute obstruction of the small intestine; atypical ulcer. He arranged for the patient to be admitted to hospital where the investigations were managed by the medical registrar. Endoscopic and ultrasound examination were normal and the medical registrar noted stress factors in the psychosocial history and arrived at a diagnosis "functional—probably stress related". The case notes summary stated that investigations were normal whereas the radiological report of a barium meal and follow through stated ". . . some thickening of folds seen in distal jejunum. Otherwise no abnormality seen. . . . If there are symptoms suggesting a small bowel pathology, intubation of the small bowel suggested. . . ." The patient's symptoms persisted but there was a delay of five months before a tumour was found in the mid-small intestine.

This was an unforced error. It would seem that neither the consultant nor the registrar checked the radiographs or the accompanying report. Regular meetings of clinicians and radiologists in this hospital would not only encourage teamwork but also help in the development of a fail safe system.

Mistakes

Mistakes are more serious in that, uncorrected, they are likely to be repeated. They may be divided into those in which there are: (a) deviations from standard practice (what Reason terms "rule based") such as when a doctor applies a wrong solution to a relatively familiar problem; and (b) defects in knowledge such as when a doctor encounters an unusual situation and uses on line reasoning based on an incorrect model of the problem (or more crudely makes an inspired guess on how best to proceed).[5]

Example 7

A 19 year old man presented to his general practitioner with abdominal pain, diarrhoea, and weight loss. The general practitioner provisionally diagnosed coeliac disease, put the patient on a gluten free diet, and referred him for a consultant opinion. The consultant saw the patient two weeks later, noted that the patient had improved, and accepted the diagnosis of coeliac disease without seeking histological confirmation by obtaining and examining a biopsy of the small intestinal mucosa. Over the next 18 months the patient was never completely well and the need to stick to a gluten free diet was repeatedly reinforced. He then developed a perianal abscess and ultimately the correct diagnosis of Crohn's disease was established.

This was a deviation from standard practice in which the diagnosis of coeliac disease is based on the appearance of biopsies of jejunal mucosa before and after treatment. The clinician "cut corners" and the patient was treated incorrectly. Possibly the progress of the Crohn's disease would have been little different but the patient was not given appropriate treatment to relieve his symptoms over a period of two years.

Knowledge based mistakes may be made not only by inexperienced clinicians but also by consultants who have lost touch with advances in medical practice. The clinician involved in example 2 was inexperienced. He was correct to take account of

263

psychosocial problems but his knowledge base was weak in that anorexia nervosa was an unlikely diagnosis. Moreover, he unwisely made a psychiatric diagnosis without excluding or looking for concomitant organic disease. In example 8 the knowledge based mistake was made by a consultant physician.

Example 8

A 54 year old man who admitted to regular alcohol intake (perhaps 25–30 units a week) presented with heart failure. A general physician diagnosed alcoholic cardiomyopathy and the patient died three weeks later with bleeding from a stress induced duodenal ulcer. At postmortem he was found to have tight stenosis of the aortic valve. The admitting house physician had recorded an aortic systolic murmur without recognising its relevance and echocardiography was not requested.

A fundamental error was made early in the course of management presumably because the clinician was not aware of the need for echocardiography in the assessment of all cases of heart failure of uncertain cause. Alcoholic cardiomyopathy has no specific features; it is essentially a diagnosis made by exclusion in patients known to drink alcohol in very considerable amounts. This patient was holding down a full time job and was not considered to be an alcoholic. Thus there was good reason to check for all causes of heart failure. In some cases, it may be difficult to define whether a mistake is due to a deviation from accepted practice or to a lack of knowledge. Consider case 4. The clinician treated an anaemia without establishing the cause and failed to consider the possibility of drug side effects. We may presume that he did not know that mesalazine could damage the kidneys (which in itself was not unreasonable because at that time the problem had been described only in case reports) but he should have been aware that mesalazine has a number of unpleasant side effects including damage to the formation of blood.

Violation of normal codes of practice

Factors predisposing to poor medical practice have not been well defined. External conditions which may promote violations of normal codes include lack of a safety first culture, poor morale, and perceived licence to "cut corners". Such conditions are especially likely to lead to accidents by the inexperienced and by those who have little natural concern for their patients or a machismo approach to practice.

In example 3 a potentially dangerous procedure (endoscopic retrograde cholangiopancreatography with sphincterotomy) was undertaken without performing simple tests to determine whether such a procedure was indicated; and sphincterotomy was performed even though the ductal systems were radiologically normal. If this was an example of the usual practice of the doctors involved then one may suspect lack of a safety first culture in the institution in which they work. In example 5, junior doctors were left to muddle on as best they could. The consultant failed to take responsibility and allowed junior staff to issue an incorrect death certificate.

Organisational predisposition to adverse events

As far as I am aware, no serious attempt has been made to identify and to determine the relative importance of error producing conditions in NHS hospitals although one may extrapolate from data published in studies from industry.[6] Almost certainly, the relative risks would be different from those reported but the list in box 6 offers a useful starting point.

Unfamiliarity with task

In hospital medicine, doctors carry out a wide range of different tasks. Some situations (such as venepuncture) may be performed daily, others (such as lumbar puncture) once in six months. It is difficult to provide adequate instructions for these many and varied tasks and the old adage "see one, do one, teach one" still holds some force in medical practice.

Example 9

A 58 year old man was found to have unexplained enlargement of the liver and spleen. A registrar with modest experience undertook to teach a senior house officer the procedure of needle liver biopsy. Four attempts were made to obtain tissue without success and the gall bladder was perforated.

It is potentially dangerous to delegate the responsibility for teaching

265

> ## Box 6—Work conditions predisposing to errors in industry
>
> - Unfamiliarity with task ($\times 17$)
> - Shortage of time (high workload) ($\times 11$)
> - Poor human-system interface ($\times 8$)
> - Misperception of risk ($\times 4$)
> - Inexperience (not lack of training) ($\times 3$)
> - Poor instructions ($\times 3$)
> - Inadequate checking ($\times 3$)
> - Poor signal to noise ratio ($\times 10$)
> - Information overload ($\times 6$)
> - Negative transfer between tasks ($\times 5$)
>
> (Selected data from studies in electrical and electronic engineering.[6])

a procedure. Most manuals on ward based procedures suggest that no more than two attempts should be made to obtain tissue by liver biopsy. In this case four attempts were made at too low a level.

Example 10

A registrar with six months' experience was sharing an endoscopy list with his consultant who was working in an adjacent room. He undertook to examine the upper gastrointestinal tract of a 90 year old woman who had lost weight. He spent 20 minutes trying to intubate the oesophagus during which time he perforated the pharynx.

Here, the consultant was unwise to allow a relatively inexperienced operator to pass an endoscope in a frail elderly patient. Moreover, it would seem that the registrar did not know when to ask for help.

266

High workload

Junior hospital doctors work long hours and experience sleep deprivation and sleep disruption. Experiments on non-medical subjects show that both conditions impair mental test performance and by implication, work efficiency. Tasks which are boring and lengthy are more affected by sleep loss than are short tasks; and, hour for hour, intermittent deprivation is more deleterious than total loss of sleep (loss of one hour's sleep in the middle of the night for two nights is roughly equivalent to complete loss of sleep for one night).[7]

The Department of Health has ordered NHS trusts to ensure that no junior doctor is scheduled for more than 72 hours a week of which only 56 hours are to be regarded as "intense". This has been accepted as a major step forward in reducing stress and lessening the risk of adverse events. The objectives will be fulfilled, however, only if there are sufficient staff to cover the gaps and to undertake careful handover. A reduction in working hours does not mean a reduction in workload and, with a move towards shift work and the loss of continuity of care, job satisfaction may decrease.

In an important study of the effects of sleep deprivation on cognitive performance and mood in medical house officers, it was shown that, although loss of sleep and long hours of work have an important effect on test performances, individual differences between house officers are the main source of the variance in results.[8] This study provides objective evidence for a situation well recognised by experienced hospital consultants—an able clinician after 24 hours on call remains better than a weak clinician who has had 24 hours off duty (see examples 2, 12, 14).

Inexperience and misperception of risk

Clinicians who are responsible for emergency admissions know that much of their skill arises from previous experience backed up by concern for the wellbeing of the patient (and perhaps the fear of making a mistake). They recognise the sick patient and the dangerous situation without having to think. In British hospitals, acutely sick patients arriving in the emergency department are initially assessed and managed by junior staff who report to a senior registrar or consultant. This is fine but what happens if junior staff fail to recognise a dangerous situation.

267

Example 11

Late one evening, a 58 year old man was admitted to a large city hospital after passing three melaena stools. His pulse rate was 88 beats per minute, blood pressure 110/60, and haemoglobin 9·8 g/100 ml. He was seen by only one junior doctor and was put to bed for investigation in the morning. He was not given fluid intravenously, his blood was not cross matched, and his condition was not monitored closely. Six hours later he had a large haematemesis and died.

The case notes do not disclose why this happened. The junior doctor may have violated a well defined protocol but the subsequent discharge letter indicated that in this hospital the organisation of care for gastrointestinal haemorrhage was deficient. Correct management would have included blood transfusion to maintain blood volume; careful monitoring of progress, and early endoscopic examination of the stomach and duodenum. If the bleeding could not have been controlled by endoscopic injection then surgical intervention should have been offered. This is the sort of case in which a protocol for management of a well defined medical condition would have minimised the risks which occur when a patient is under the care of inexperienced staff. Moreover it is essential that experienced senior staff monitor the work of their trainees closely (see examples 1, 2, 5, 9, 10, 14).

Thus it is possible to define some features of hospital practice which predispose to medical accidents and which parallel data provided from industrial studies. In addition, in hospital practice there are two important risks which do not appear on the industrial list—the definition of responsibility and the maintenance of continuity of care. Clinicians repeatedly make "on line" decisions regarding medical problems which occur unexpectedly. Often it is difficult to ensure that the nature and effect of such decisions are clearly understood by all staff involved in the clinical care of the patient.

Interactions within the organisation

Clinicians are at the sharp end of medical practice. It is essential, however, that they recognise that they are members of a team of health care workers, that they understand their limitations in interpreting data, and that they consult frequently. Often clinicians take responsibility for interpreting radiographs of acutely ill patients without consulting a radiologist; yet, in a study of the ability of junior doctors to recognise pathology in radiographs, 35% of abnormal signs and 39% of abnormalities which might have had clinically important consequences were missed.[9] These figures suggest that when a radiologist is not available to read radiographs, there is a one in three chance of misinterpretation.

Example 12

A 41 year old woman had a six month history of recurrent dysuria and had been treated repeatedly with antibiotics for presumed pyelonephritis even though no causative organism had been found in repeated examinations of midstream specimens of urine. She was referred as an emergency with severe lower abdominal pain. The senior house officer accepted the diagnosis of pyelonephritis even though he noted that the pain was not felt in the loins and that there was considerable tenderness in the lower abdomen. The clinicians interpreted a radiograph of the abdomen as showing non-specific changes. In fact, the film showed multiple abnormal loops of gas filled small bowel in the centre of the abdomen with probable mucosal thickening (figure 14.1A). The patient was referred to the urological team who had been advising on her care in the outpatient department. A further abdominal radiograph showed progressive pathological changes (figure 14.1B). Neither film was seen by a radiologist. Two days later, the patient died with peritonitis from perforation of the ileum secondary to Crohn's disease.

In this case a "surgical abdomen" (a condition requiring surgical intervention) was not recognised clinically because the junior doctors were unable to think beyond the original diagnosis and radiologically because the hospital did not have a system whereby all emergency radiographs were seen by a radiologist and reported on within 12 hours. In the survey of 100 medicolegal cases, 24 of 56 adverse events (including 19 with serious consequences) were wholly, or in part, due to incorrect management which might have been avoided if the problem had been discussed with a laboratory specialist or a radiologist.[3]

269

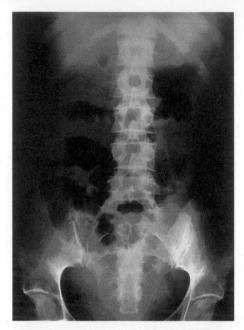

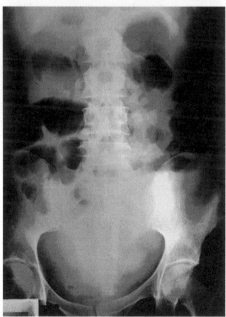

Figure 14.1 (Top) *Abdominal radiograph of patient complaining of severe lower abdominal pain leading to emergency admission to hospital. The film shows multiple abnormal loops of gas filled small intestine but was accepted by the clinicians as unremarkable. (Bottom) 12 hours later, showing progressive abnormality and a diffusely opaque area in the pelvis. Neither film was seen and reported on by a radiologist before the patient died 48 hours later.*

Whose responsibility? Improved training of specialists but the need to maintain the pool of general experience

Recent changes occurring in medical practice may have important effects on risk management. The already declining role of general physicians will be accelerated by new proposals for specialists[10] who will have much less experience of hospital practice outside their own specialty. The present system provides three years of varied experience as a senior house officer or junior registrar (usually in several specialties) and two years as a registrar taking responsibility for acute medical emergencies on a regular rota. The trainee then moves on to three or four years of specialist training as a senior registrar. Under the proposed scheme, experience of general medicine will be telescoped into an, as yet, not clearly defined period of general professional training followed by three or four years of specialty training. In effect, the registrar grade will disappear. These proposals are designed to reduce the duration of postgraduate training and to harmonise specialist qualifications in Europe. Thus, hospital practice in the United Kingdom will have to adapt. It is assumed that specialist care will improve (almost certainly it will be more procedure oriented) but it is important to note that errors due to "unfamiliarity with the task" may be made by specialists as well as generalists. In a survey of 100 medicolegal cases,[3] 12 out of 56 errors were made by specialists, four of whom showed signs of having become "procedure dependent" and in eight cases, the specialists failed to recognise a disease process outside their area of interest. By contrast, seven errors were made by general physicians who were out of their depth with specialist problems and failed to seek advice.

Example 13

At a general practitioner screening examination a 65 year old man with modest hypertension reported lower chest pain. The pain was thought to be due to cardiac angina although it was atypical and not clearly related to exercise. He was referred to a cardiologist who noted tenderness in the right hypochondrium and arranged for barium studies in addition to electrocardiography (ECG) and a stress test. The barium study showed what was thought to be a bulbar duodenal diverticulum and the stress test was stopped with the patient asymptomatic because the ECG showed depression of the ST segment. The patient was treated for angina but a month

271

later died suddenly of a massive bleed from a large duodenal ulcer.

Here the consultant cardiologist allowed his special interest to dominate the assessment of this patient's condition. Abdominal tenderness and an abnormal duodenum on barium examination should have led to further gastrointestinal investigation. Almost certainly a deep ulcer crater was misinterpreted as a diverticulum—an error which could have been corrected by endoscopic examination.

There is insufficient data to determine whether or not changes in the training of hospital consultants or specialists are likely to affect the incidence of adverse events. Certainly, it will be increasingly necessary to include several specialists in the care of complex cases.

Continuity of care: reduction of workload and need for new structures to ensure adequacy of care

In reducing the working hours of hospital doctors, continuity of care and definition of responsibility have not been given sufficient attention.

Example 14

A previously fit 19 year old girl presented to a London teaching hospital with severe sore throat, cough, and blood streaked watery sputum. In addition, she complained of headache and photophobia. She was seen and assessed by an "on call" house officer who made a provisional diagnosis of pulmonary embolism (clots in the lung). After discussion with a registrar, the patient was treated with the anticoagulant heparin pending ventilation-perfusion (V/Q) scanning of the lungs. Over the next three days, the patient was seen by four ward doctors, one of whom recognised the relevance of the headache and photophobia and attempted to obtain a sample of cerebrospinal fluid. He obtained blood stained fluid which he interpreted as a "bloody tap". He did not examine the fluid for evidence of previous bleeding (xanthochromia). The next day a V/Q scan showed a low probability for pulmonary embolism. The patient became increasingly distressed but treatment with anticoagulants was continued until she died 36 h later. At necropsy she was found to have had a subarachnoid haemorrhage and there was no evidence of pulmonary embolism.

This patient was unfortunate to have two diseases. Nevertheless the general practitioner had been treating her correctly for severe tracheobronchitis and it is probable that repeated coughing had led to the intracranial bleed by rupturing a weak blood vessel. Although pulmonary embolism is an important cause of haemoptysis this patient had no risk factors for this condition, and the blood streaked saliva was not what one would expect. There can be no excuse for not centrifuging a sample of blood stained cerebrospinal fluid to look at the supernatant fluid for the telltale yellow discoloration of bleeding in the recent past (xanthochromia). Thus there were major errors in management but the underlying problem was an organisational structure which lacked control by senior staff; with inadequate communication and no clear chain of responsibility. At this hospital senior staff did not routinely see within 24 hours all patients admitted as emergencies.

After recording a verdict of death from natural causes the coroner recommended a review of the management of this patient and it is ironic that he pinpointed the need to "enquire why a houseman was scheduled for 80–90 hours per week covering two hundred beds for the evening". In fact it would seem that this hospital was using a partial shift system to limit the working hours of junior doctors. In the past patients were under the care of a single team (house physician, registrar, and consultant) which some would argue led to a tighter degree of responsibility for the care of the sick patients and as a result less chance of overlooking a major problem.

Conclusion

Claims against hospitals and hospital doctors have led to the definition of high risk specialties such as obstetrics and surgery. In fact the risks of medical misadventure are probably just as great in general medical practice but the results are more easily construed as part of the natural history of the disease and, therefore, are less easily recognisable. In this chapter, I have tried to show where, how, and why things go wrong in medical practice. Box 7 lists some of the ways in which risks in medical practice may be minimised. I have insufficient evidence to indicate the relative

273

Box 7—Reducing risks in hospital medical practice

For all practising hospital doctors

- Build in fail safe mechanisms
  Review all reports from laboratories and imaging units
  Review case records when dictating letters or summaries
  Listen to the patient and all members of the team
  Discuss problems with colleagues (especially radiologists and pathologists)
  If in doubt obtain a second opinion
- Spend time talking with patients and relatives
- Know the risks and explain to patients
  Think before prescribing (see box 3)
- Help maintain morale in the hospital
  Insist on high professional standards
  Meet regularly as a unit
  Attend and participate in interdisciplinary meetings
  If you are a consultant lead from the front and take responsibility
- Know limitations
  Never let pride outweigh judgment
  Maintain interest in and knowledge of medicine as a whole
  Maintain postgraduate educational experience

Directors of units

- Identify what can go wrong in your area of practice
- Analyse degree of risk (how severe, how often, how likely)
- Define changes in practice necessary to limit risk
- Produce clear protocols for the management of defined problems

Medical directors to ensure that

- Consultant staff take full responsibility
  Emergency cases are seen within 24 hours
  Work of trainees is monitored
- Junior staff have
  Reasonable work schedules
  Effective support
  Well organised systems of handover
- Doctors in support services
  Have a proactive role (respond to a problem, not to a request)
  Report promptly
  Liaise with clinicians
- Management understand the relation between risk and resources

importance of the various proposals and I have little doubt that the list is incomplete. Further research into the epidemiology of medical accidents is badly needed[1] to encourage greater care in individual practice and to improve organisational structures.[11]

1 Smith R. The epidemiology of malpractice. *BMJ* 1990;**301**:620–1.
2 Hawkins C, Paterson I. Medico-legal audit in the West Midlands region; analysis of 100 cases. *BMJ* 1987;**295**:1533–6.
3 Neale G. Clinical analysis of 100 medico-legal cases. *BMJ* 1993;**307**:1483–7.
4 Orlikoff JE, Vanagunas AM. Physician-related medical injury. In: *Malpractice prevention and liability control for hospitals*. 2nd ed. Chicago: American Hospital Publishing Incorporated, 1988:39–52.
5 Reason JT. The human factor in medical accidents. In: Vincent C, Ennis M, Audley RJ, eds. *Medical accidents*. Oxford: Oxford University Press, 1993:1–16.
6 Williams J. A data-based method for assessing and reducing human error to improve operational performance. In: Hagen, W, ed. *The 1988 IEEE Fourth conference on human factors and power plants*. New York: Institute of Electrical and Electronic Engineers, 1988:436–47.
7 Home JA, Anderson NR, Wilkinson RT. Effects of sleep deprivation on signal detection measures of vigilance; implications for sleep function. *Sleep* 1983;**6**: 347–58.
8 Deary IA, Tait RM. Effects of sleep disruption on cognitive performance and mood in medical house officers. *BMJ* 1987;**295**:1513–6.
9 Vincent CA, Driscoll PA, Audley RJ, Grant DS. Accuracy of detection of radiographic abnormalities by junior doctors. *Archives of Emergency Medicine* 1988;**5**:101–9.
10 Department of Health. *Hospital doctors; training for the future. The report of the working group in specialist medical training*. London: Department of Health, 1993.
11 Morlock LL, Malitz FE. Do hospital risk management programs make a difference? Relationship between risk management program activities and hospital malpractice claims experience. *Law and Contemporary Problems* 1991; **54**:1–11.

15 Clinical risk management in psychiatry

MAURICE LIPSEDGE

This chapter deals with suicide and violence to others, which constitute the topics of greatest current concern in risk management in the mental health services. Most of the psychiatric claims managed by the Risk Management Foundation of the Harvard Medical Institutions over a 12 year period involved cases in which suicide, attempted suicide, or violence to self or others occurred.[1]

Psychiatric disorder and dangerousness

Psychiatric disorder, especially schizophrenia, is associated with a significant risk of violence before admission to hospital.[2] Patients with schizophrenia in a recent large scale Swedish longitudinal study committed four times as many violent offences as the general population.[3] Among inpatients, those with schizophrenia are also disproportionately more likely to be violent.[4]

Taylor found that the vast majority of the psychotic offenders on remand at Brixton Prison whom she examined had symptoms at the time of the index offence. Schizophrenia is also overrepresented among men remanded for homicide: 11% in Taylor's series.[5] Recent cross sectional surveys show an association between self reported violent behaviour and either a diagnosis of schizophrenia or current psychotic symptoms.[6] Thus violence is most likely to occur when patients have active symptoms of psychosis, and the risk significantly diminishes after treatment.[7] The risk of violence in mental illness is greatest when the patient has delusions and

276

passivity experiences,[8] and there is a well recognised association of violence with delusional belief, as in the "pathologies of passion" such as morbid jealousy and erotomania.[5]

Predicting dangerousness (box 1)

Predicting dangerousness in any individual case is known to be an uncertain exercise, and psychiatrists tend to overestimate the likelihood of violence by patients considered for release from secure institutions.[9]

Methodological problems have vitiated attempts to research the accuracy of psychiatrists' prediction of dangerousness. Difficulties include overinclusive diagnostic groupings (for example, "psychotic"), failure to recognise the importance of the situational context (for example, violence within the family), lack of data on aftercare arrangements and compliance with treatment, and failure

---

Box 1—Factors predicting violence in psychiatric patients: summary

Antecedents: A previous history of violence

Diagnosis: Schizophrenia
Morbid jealousy and erotomania
Illicit drug use or alcohol misuse, or both

Social or domestic factors: Loss of family support and deterioration in personal relationships
Loss of accommodation

Clinical: Patients declared intentions and attitudes to previous and potential victims
Threats of violence
Presence of active symptoms including delusions, especially regarding poisoning and sexual matters, passivity experiences, command hallucinations, jealousy, depression, and angry outbursts
Signs and symptoms of relapse

Management: Loss of contact with mental health services
Poor compliance with medication

Modified from Linford Rees W, Lipsedge M, Ball C, eds. *Textbook of psychiatry*. London: Arnold, 1996.

---

to define violence clearly (for example, arrest rates, conviction rate, or self reported antisocial behaviour.[10] A major problem lies in the design of studies purporting to validate risk assessment, since those patients predicted to behave violently will tend to be admitted to hospital and be given preventive treatment and only those considered *unlikely* to be violent in the near future will be released into the community.[11]

The predictive power of decisions based on actuarial data can be substantially increased by using a more realistic, shorter time frame and by considering the environment into which a patient with a history of violence is to be discharged, since violent acts by psychiatric patients are known to be more likely to occur within a family setting. The confidential enquiry into homicide found that most of the victims were family members or were already acquainted with the attacker.[12] Although the view that the best predictor of future violence is a history of physically aggressive behaviour[13] has become axiomatic, the individual person's mental state is a crucial variable, which, surprisingly, has been omitted from predictive research on violence. Gunn enumerated the important variables involved in predicting dangerous behaviour.[14] He emphasised the importance of those elements which are subject to change, such as family support and personal relationships and the availability of potential victims. A recent prospective study of physical assaults in a psychiatric intensive care unit showed that both a criminal record and previous drug misuse have predictive value, so that a urine test for drugs and attention to forensic and violent history will help to identify those patients who are most likely to become aggressive.[15]

Other critical factors include the patient's declared intentions and attitudes to both previous and potential victims and to caring staff, and his or her mental state, including delusions, command hallucinations, jealousy, depression, and proneness to angry outbursts. Schizophrenic delusions, especially of poisoning or of a sexual nature, are more likely to lead to deliberate personal violence than imperative hallucinations.[2] Detailed discussion should be held with the patient about his or her thoughts and feelings at the time of specific offences, supplemented by documentary evidence on these events from the police depositions and witness statements.

Information about the patient's history, psychiatric condition, likely compliance with treatment, ability for taking responsibility for his or her behaviour, and modes of responding to stress, as well as an assessment of relationships, provide a basis on which to predict those circumstances in which violence might occur[14] and permit interventions designed to modify these situations. A flexible plan might include prescribing antipsychotic drugs for command hallucinations; counselling for substance misuse; marital therapy for potentially explosive domestic relationships; and an anger management programme run on cognitive-behavioural lines or admission to a range of hospital facilities with appropriate levels of supervision or security (from locked wards to regional secure units), or both.

Although clinical judgment adds to predictive accuracy,[14] Gunn warns that predictions about violent behaviour can be safely made only for fairly short periods, hence the need for careful supervision, vigilant monitoring, and the development of supportive therapeutic relationships. Those providing such support require their own supervision and support and an awareness of transference issues.[14] (Transference refers to the way a patient's relationship with mental health professionals is coloured and shaped by their own earlier relationships and by the projection of images derived from the formative experience of close contact with others in the past.)

Managing potentially dangerous psychiatric patients

The Ritchie inquiry into the care of Christopher Clunis, a young man with schizophrenia who killed a stranger in 1992, concluded that this patient's care and treatment "was a catalogue of failure and missed opportunity" over the five years of hospital and community care before he stabbed his victim.[16] The report of the inquiry refers to the fact that many others with severe chronic mental illness in the community, especially in poor inner city areas, are a risk either to themselves or to others. Most mentally abnormal offenders who commit serious offences are already well known to the psychiatric services.[17] Since 1992 there have been further incidents of grave acts of violence committed by patients with severe mental illness.[18]

The inquiry found a significant failure in passing on information between psychiatrists, nurses, general practitioners, social workers, hostel staff, and Christopher Clunis's family. Other deficiencies in care which might have ultimately contributed to the death of his victim Jonathan Zeto included failure to obtain an accurate history and to consider Christopher Clunis's history of violence and to assess his propensity for further violence. Doctors, nurses, and social workers failed to make adequate contemporaneous records of important events, and violent incidents were either minimised or even omitted from records, correspondence, and discharge summaries and were not picked up by clinicians and social workers from the nursing notes.[16]

In considering violent incidents which occurred three years before the fatal stabbing the inquiry concluded that the medical professionals had tended to minimise the gravity of a series of attempts by Christopher Clunis to stab people, on the grounds that little actual physical damage was caused in that particular cluster of incidents: "We feel there is a real danger of looking too much at the consequences of an action without looking at the action itself" (paragraph 26[16]).

The inquiry also disclosed a failure to provide and coordinate adequate aftercare according to section 117 of the Mental Health Act 1983 by both medical and social services and a failure to act on warning signs to prevent a relapse. (Section 117 of the act requires health services and social services to provide aftercare for patients on discharge from hospital after compulsory detention under the mental health act.) Throughout, the report refers to a tendency to overlook or minimise violent incidents and to ignore reports of violence made by members of the public and a failure to ensure continuity of care when the patient had left a particular health district (paragraph 109[16]).

The report of the Independent Panel of Inquiry examining the case of Michael Buchanan, a man with chronic schizophrenia and personality disorder who abused cocaine and who murdered a stranger in 1992, found many failures of care which resembled those in the Clunis case.[18] These included inadequate aftercare planning, failure to allocate a keyworker according to section 117 of the Mental Health Act 1983, lack of recording of numerous violent episodes, failure to assess risk of dangerousness, and premature removal of the patient from the caseload of the community psychiatric nurse. As with Clunis, these failures led to a potentially dangerous patient slipping out of the aftercare system.

To prevent patients with serious mental illness falling through the net of care in this way the Ritchie inquiry reiterates the need for implementation of section 117 of the mental health act and of the care programme approach so that the aftercare needs of each patient are systematically assessed by both health and social services before discharge and an individual plan of care is formulated by the multidisciplinary team.[19] This plan should be discussed with

280

and given to the patient and to all team members. The consultant psychiatrist and the team must assess the risk of the patient harming himself or herself, or others. A keyworker or "care coordinator" has to be appointed and a regular review of the patient arranged. The keyworker should have direct access to the responsible medical officer. There should be contingency plans if the patient fails to engage in treatment and an assertive approach to maintaining patient contact. If a crisis develops and a request is made for an urgent mental health act assessment, this should be carried out within three hours. Non-urgent requests should be met within three working days. The foreword to the revised code of practice emphasises that the mental health act can be used to admit patients not only to prevent harm to self or to others but also to forestall deterioration in a patient's health.[20]

All team members should be aware of the signs of an impending relapse and react promptly. The preliminary report on homicide from the confidential inquiry into homicide and suicide of mentally ill people[12] states that in over half the cases some reduction in attendance for treatment or some failure to take prescribed medication had occurred. Non-compliance with treatment is often an important pointer to relapse.[21] Other circumstances which increase the risk of dangerous behaviour include drug or alcohol misuse in a patient with major mental disorder,[21] as in the case of Michael Buchanan,[18] the occurrence of a potentially dangerous personal situation such as marriage in a patient with a history of morbid jealousy, or disappearance from hostel or bed and breakfast accommodation, as in the case of both Buchanan and Clunis. Identifying all relevant factors in past violent behaviour is essential.[19]

When a patient who is subject to aftercare under section 117 moves out of his or her area, responsibility remains with the multi-disciplinary team until the aftercare has been effectively transferred to a new team. If there is a risk of harm to self or others, all those providing a service to the patient in terms of housing or occupational therapy need to be informed of the risk. Information about any violent or potentially violent incident and a thorough assessment of the risk of dangerousness should be included in the discharge summary. The Ritchie inquiry seems to recommend (paragraph 48) that the need to transmit information about the risk of dangerousness transcends considerations of professional confidentiality.[16] This is supported by the judgment in W versus Egdell and others,[22] which prompted a legal comment that "whenever a doctor perceives a patient to be a serious danger to his family or the public at large, his duty of confidence to that patient will be reduced."[23] The guidelines of the Royal College of Psychiatrists on the aftercare of potentially violent or vulnerable patients indicate that considerations of public safety should give exemption from absolute professional confidentiality, but recommends (paragraph 44) that when such a disclosure occurs the reasons for the decision should be documented.[24] The clinician should also record the steps taken before disclosure, such as attempting to persuade the patient to authorise the disclosure, and advice might be sought from medical colleagues and defence organisations. The guidelines recommend a period of trial leave (paragraph 18) under section 17 of the mental health act to test out uncertainties about the patient's ability to cope in the community and to permit staff to monitor the patient's progress. While on leave the patient's general practitioner should be informed in anticipation of possible problems.[24]

Finally, the Ritchie report recommends (paragraph 3) that when a mentally disordered person charged with an offence is remanded to hospital the consultant psychiatrist should consider whether it is appropriate for the patient to be detained in hospital under the Mental Health Act 1983, "irrespective of the charge and of the ultimate disposal of the case". This includes those cases where the charge is dropped or the verdict is "not guilty".[16]

Assessing risk of suicide

The *Health of the Nation* document on suicide[25] is a model practical manual which provides an effective strategy for preventing suicide. This section draws extensively on its procedures and recommendations.

Suicide accounts for at least 1% of all deaths annually, with a male:female ratio of over 2:1. The highest suicide rates occur in people aged over 75 but, the past decade has seen an alarming increase in the suicide rate among young men.[26] The commonest means of suicide used by men include asphyxiation with car exhaust fumes and hanging whereas self poisoning with drugs is the preferred method of commiting suicide among women.[27]

In addition to age and sex, the socio-demographic and personal factors showing a positive statistical correlation with suicide include divorce; loss of job, unemployment, or retirement; social isolation, recent bereavement; chronic, painful, or terminal illness, a family

282

history of mood disorder, alcoholism, or suicide; loss of a parent in childhood; and being in either social class I or V. In addition, most people who commit suicide have a psychiatric disorder, most commonly depression, schizophrenia, and alcohol addiction.[28]

High risk clinical factors for suicide associated illness include severe insomnia, self neglect, memory impairment, agitation, and panic attacks. In patients with schizophrenia the risk of suicide is known to be greater in young and unemployed men with a history of depression, loss of appetite and weight, recurrent relapses, and a fear of deterioration.[29] A previous history of self harm greatly increases the risk of subsequent suicide, to 30-fold higher than that expected during the 10 years after an episode of deliberate self harm, the first six months being the period of greatest risk. Eventual suicide in such patients is significantly commoner among unemployed men of social class V who misuse alcohol or drugs and who have a history of psychiatric disorder.[30]

In the clinical evaluation of a particular person who might be at risk of suicide, the statistical correlates of suicide enumerated above have low specificity and sensitivity so that screening for at risk cases results in high numbers of both false positives and false negatives.[30] In one study risk factors for suicide combined had a sensitivity of 60% and a specificity of 61%.[31] Although risk factors are not especially helpful in the clinical assessment of short term risk,[30] they can contribute to the overall assessment of risk. Rather than relying too heavily on actuarial risk factors, the evaluation of short term risk should be based on assessing the person's state of mind, recent adverse life events, relationships and degree of available support, which requires a detailed history of the present illness, an assessment of mental state, and a diagnostic formulation.[30 31] Box 2 summarises these factors.

In addition to establishing whether the person has shown evidence of suicidal intent by leaving a note or making a will, the extent of his or her pessimism and anhedonia, despair, and morbid guilt should be elicited since hopelessness and helplessness are known precursors of suicidal behaviour.[32] Has the person considered the possible method of suicide? What circumstances might increase the risk? Is there a risk to others? Information should also be obtained from previous medical and psychiatric records, from relatives, and from other key informants.

The degree of suicidal intent can fluctuate, and apparent improvement may occur in the patient on being removed from a stressful environment, with a risk of relapse on discharge.

Box 2—Factors predicting risk of suicide: summary

- Declared intent

- Preparation, including hoarding of tablets, settling financial affairs or leaving a note, or both

- Past history of deliberate self harm, especially in the previous six months

- Severe depressive illness, schizophrenia, and substance abuse

- Depression in young unemployed men with schizophrenia, with frequent relapses and fear of deterioration

- Pessimism, anhedonia, despair, morbid guilt, insomnia, self neglect, memory impairment, agitation, and panic attacks

- Recent adverse life events and lack of supportive relationships or failure to establish a working alliance with a mental health professional (malignant alienation), or both

- First few weeks after discharge from hospital are particularly risky

Modified from Linford Rees W, Lipsedge M, Ball C, eds. *Textbook of psychiatry.* London: Arnold, 1995.

Furthermore, a gravely suicidal person may deliberately conceal his or her lethal intentions. Others may appear calm and even serene to the interviewer after they have made an undisclosed but firm decision to kill themselves.

Some patients who are at risk of suicide may be cared for in the community. Patients who present a more serious risk will have to be admitted to hospital, either voluntarily or under the Mental Health Act 1983 in those who seem to be at severe and immediate risk of suicide but who refuse admission.

Managing suicidal patients

Community management

The advantages of community care of suicidal patients include avoiding the stigma associated with admission to a mental hospital and maintaining contact with the patient's usual social environment, thus permitting retention of personal autonomy and the deployment of coping skills with the back up of a supportive and understanding therapeutic relationship. The disadvantages include lack of close supervision of the patient's safety and compliance with treatment ambiance, and, at times, imposition of excessive strain on the family or carers.

Community management is not indicated when there is a grave risk of suicide or lack of adequate support, or both, or failure to establish a good working alliance with the patient. The risk is significantly increased by a history of self destructive impulsive behaviour, current substance misuse, and failure to set up a therapeutic rapport. Valuable information can be obtained by a domiciliary visit, which might disclose a cache of medication, evidence of alcohol misuse, or the proximity of a railway line or other hazardous local factors.

Community management requires a care plan that states the type of support and the names of key care staff. The plan should be discussed with and agreed by the patient and the professionals involved. Patients who present a continuing long term risk of suicide should be included on the supervision register (see below). There should be regular systematic reviews of suicide risk, with daily reassessment of mental state in the first instance. These reviews should be recorded and the management plan modified when necessary. Hospital admission may become the only safe option if the patient's condition deteriorates. Communication between general practitioners, carers, and other agencies must be thorough. The patient and carer should be given a contact number to use in emergencies as well as a specific appointment for the next review. Treatment should be prescribed only in limited quantities. The selective serotonin re-uptake inhibitor antidepressants are generally regarded as less toxic if taken in an overdose.[33] Ideally, storage and dispensing of drugs should be delegated to a responsible carer.

Some patients will require long term community support for persistent but relatively mild suicide risk. Patients who can eventually be discharged from follow up require gradual and planned termination of contact rather than an abrupt ending whereas patients whose care is to be transferred to another service should be "handed over" in a measured fashion to allow their familiarisation with the new team.

Hospital management

The period shortly after admission carries a high risk of self harm, and when the suicide risk is particularly high patients are

285

initially nursed in bed, and belongings such as ties, belts, and scissors are removed. The patient should remain continuously visible to the staff and should not be allowed to leave the ward. The staff should carefully supervise smoking and the patient's use of matches and lighters. Patients should be examined as soon as possible after admission by the ward doctor. The treatment plan and the level of observation need to be agreed jointly by medical and nursing staff and recorded and communicated to all ward staff and the patient.

The wards where patients at high risk of suicide are nursed must be physically safe. There should be no access to high windows or staircases, curtain rails should not be able to bear heavy weights, and exit from the ward must be controlled. A guaranteed quota of staff is essential to provide intensive levels of supervision. A keyworker and a deputy should be designated to the patient to try to establish an effective therapeutic rapport, and, in general, the patient should be encouraged to approach staff when feeling distressed and to discuss suicidal ideas freely.

Staff should be aware of the possibility of a misleading shortlived improvement due to respite from a stressful home situation, which will cause a later recrudescence of suicide risk if unresolved. They should also be able to recognise "malignant alienation" which is a potentially lethal distancing of the patient from staff and from carers caused by challenging behaviour or repeated relapses, or both.[34] Another risky clinical situation is the period of recovery of drive and energy in a depressed patient who retains suicidal ideas.

Home leave from the ward presents a period of high risk in recently suicidal inpatients.[35] Patients should be encouraged to return to the ward at any time of the day or night if they feel unable to cope at home. If a patient goes absent without leave the nurse in charge and the resident medical officer should be informed immediately, the hospital and its grounds should be searched, and both the carers and the police should be informed. After an absence without leave or incident of deliberate self harm within the hospital while on leave, the level of observation and the management plan should be reviewed.

An appropriate level of supportive observation is decided after discussion between the medical and nursing staff and may be intensified unilaterally by the nursing staff. It should be reviewed at every change of nursing shift and confirmed by the patient's doctor and also reviewed perodically by the consultant. Intensive supportive observation permits close monitoring of the patient's

---

Box 3—Supportive observation

Constant supportive observation is indicated for patients expressing active suicidal intent or who have recently carried out a self destructive act with serious suicidal intent. The designated nurse remains with the patient at all times throughout 24 hours.

Fifteen minute supportive observation is suitable for a patient who is not actively suicidal but has more risk than the average patient. The designated nurse observes the patient every 15 minutes. The patient is required to inform the nurse of his or her whereabouts, cannot leave the ward without a nurse escort, but can go to the lavatory unaccompanied or talk to visitors for short periods. Visitors should tell the staff when they leave.

"Known place" supportive observation is used during recovery from a suicidal crisis. The designated nurse knows exactly where the patient is at any given time. The patient may go to occupational therapy unaccompanied, but the department is informed when this occurs. The patient may also leave the ward for other purposes for up to 15 minutes.

---

behaviour and mental state. There are three levels of supportive observation: constant, 15 minute, "known place" (box 3).

The first few weeks after discharge represent a period of greatly increased risk of suicide.[36] The risk can be reduced by careful planning for discharge in accordance with the care programme approach[19] by prescribing treatment in safe amounts, by arranging for an early review, and by ensuring that the patient and carers know how to obtain help rapidly if the patient's condition deteriorates.

Successful litigation against hospitals in connection with self harm and suicide has highlighted contributory factors for which the hospital and its staff might be regarded as responsible.[37]

- Unsafe design
- Failure to monitor patient
- Failure to remove dangerous objects
- Failure to use a locked ward
- Failure to supervise staff
- Failure to obtain past records
- Poor communication between staff
- Failure to treat psychiatric disorder adequately
- Negligent discharge.

287

In a survey of litigation claims against hospitals in Australia from 1972 to 1992, in which 20 cases claiming failure to prevent suicidal behaviour were identified,[38] all but one case involved inpatients, and failure to supervise was the leading basis of the claims. Jumping from heights accounted for 13 of the 20 incidents, seven of which were jumping through hospital windows. The basis of the claims was alleged failure to provide a suitable degree of observation and supervision, and most of the claims resulted in settlement in favour of the plaintiffs. The high frequency of jumps has implications for the architectural design of psychiatric units.

Care programme approach and supervision registers

The purpose of the care programme approach[39] is to ensure the support of mentally ill people in the community, thereby minimising the possibility of their losing contact with services and maximising the effect of any therapeutic intervention. The essential elements of the programme include systematic assessment of both health and social care needs, preparing a written care plan agreed between professional staff, the patient, and carers; and allocating a keyworker, who is required to keep in close contact with the patient, to monitor that the programme of care is delivered, and to take immediate action if it is not. Implementation of the care programme approach is ensured by regular review of the patient's progress. This policy emphasises the importance of ensuring continuity of care, with specific guidelines on how to reduce the risk of patients "falling through the net" when they move from one area to another.

The NHS Management Executive's guidance on discharging mentally disordered patients[19] includes invaluable advice on carrying out an assessment of risk in potentially violent patients and emphasises the need to take into account patients' history, their own self reporting, their behaviour and mental state, and any discrepancies between what is reported and what is observed. Effective risk assessment must identify revelant factors involved in previous violent behaviour including the personal and domestic circumstances which might lead to a recurrence.

On 1 October 1994 the Department of Health introduced supervision registers for mentally ill people.[40] The criteria for inclusion include a significant risk of committing serious violence or suicide, or of severe self neglect, as a result of severe and

288

enduring mental illness or severe personality disorder. The Royal College of Psychiatrists has voiced concern that the criteria are too broad, that additional expenditure would be involved, that arrangements for withdrawal from the register are ambiguous, and that the register constitutes a threat to the patient's civil liberties.[41] In addition, the introduction of the register carries the risk of an increase in litigation as failure to include a patient who subsequently commits a serious violent offence might be interpreted as negligent.[42]

Although the register does not bring with it specific additional resources, the new system might provide a suitable framework for community support of potentially violent or self destructive patients. It has been suggested that the register will damage therapeutic relationships, but rather than feeling stigmatised, patients whose names are entered on the register might actually feel more secure and reassured by the knowledge that at times of crisis their needs will be met by a rapid response by the multidisciplinary team. There is a useful emphasis on the prediction of circumstances which might lead to increased risk, such as ceasing to take treatment, loss of a supportive relationship, or loss of accommodation. There is an obligation to convene urgent multidisciplinary reassessments of a patient's status and an emphasis on teamwork and communication with the patient and between professionals and carers. (Staff performing domiciliary visits to potentially dangerous patients should be equipped with emergency call systems and trained in calming and breakaway techniques. Solo visits should not be made to an increasingly unstable patient.[43])

It might be thought that there is an undue reliance on prophylactic antipsychotic treatment but there is well documented evidence that regular neuroleptics greatly reduce the risk of both relapse and violent incidents in mentally disordered offenders.[44]

The Buchanan inquiry concluded that placement on the supervision register might have reduced the risk of Michael Buchanan's offending by making clinicians more "risk aware" and therefore less likely to discharge a potentially dangerous patient after very short periods (two to three weeks after admission under section 37).[18] However, given the lack of semisecure or intensively staffed accommodation in the community, the inquiry concluded that placement on the supervision register would not have completely removed all risk.

289

Why do things go wrong

The concluding points below summarise the factors contributing to the clinical risk in psychiatry.

(1) Professional arrogance combined with a reckless tolerance of deviance can lead to failure by mental health professionals to heed reports by carers and members of the public about disturbed behaviour.[16 45]

(2) Undue emphasis on the civil liberties of psychiatric patients at the expense of tolerating grave suicidal risk and the danger of violent behaviour.

(3) Failure to implement the Mental Health Code of Practice (paragraph 2.6) recommendation that compulsory admission is indicated to prevent deterioration and not just when the patient is regarded as a danger to self or others.

(4) Belief that compulsory admission under the Mental Health Act cannot be implemented "until a patient actually does something dangerous." Formerly a widely held view among mental health professionals, since publication of the Ritchie report they are now prepared to be somewhat more proactive. Mental health professionals have to accept that the practice of psychiatry is essentially a paternalistic activity and that imposing treatment against a patient's will is justified when they believe that the patient's life or health would be at risk if coercion were not applied and the condition were allowed to deteriorate.[46]

(5) A tendency, especially among approved social workers, to take a "snapshot" cross sectional view of the potentially suicidal or violent patient's mental state and behaviour and to ignore both previous episodes and any recent history of deterioration. Social workers routinely take a "longitudinal" view when assessing a case of alleged child abuse, but, paradoxically, often insist on minimising the importance of both past and recent history when making mental health assessments.

(6) Failure to pass on information about potential dangerousness to other professionals, such as hostel staff,[16] for reasons ranging from inertia, inefficiency, or overwork to a misguided overprotective view of the patient at the expense of the safety of potential victims.

(7) Lack of resources, in terms of staff and inpatient facilities. There is a grave shortage of general psychiatric beds and of

290

beds on closed wards. With an increasing awareness of the risk of both suicide and violence within the community, there is a greater demand for admission but the beds tend to be occupied for longer because of staff reluctance to discharge potentially dangerous or suicidal patients into the community, where hostel accommodation and support services are inadequate. The shortage of beds places psychiatric staff in a difficult position if they try to follow the Department of Health's guidance on the discharge of mentally disordered people,[19] which seeks to ensure that psychiatric patients are discharged "only when and if they are ready to leave hospital" and, "any risk to the public or to patients themselves is minimal and is managed effectively. ..."

I thank Dr John Reed, Professor E Murphy, and Dr John Bradley for helpful advice and comments, and Mrs Marcia Andrews for typing the manuscript.

1 Tan MW, McDonough WJ. Risk management in psychiatry. *Psychiat Clin North Am* 1919;13:135–47.
2 Humphreys MS, Johnstone EC, MacMillan JF, Taylor PJ. Dangerous behaviour preceding first admissions for schizophrenia. *Br J Psychiatry* 1992;161:501–5.
3 Lindqvist P, Allcbeck P. Schizophrenia and crime. *Br J Psychiatry* 1990;157: 345–50.
4 Nobel P, Rodger S. Violence by psychiatric inpatients. *Br J Psychiatry* 1989; 155:384–90.
5 Taylor PJ. Motives for offending among violent and psychotic men. *Br J Psychiatry* 1985;147:491–8.
6 Link B, Andrews J, Cullen F. The violent and illegal behaviour of mental patients reconsidered. *American Sociological Review* 1992;57:275–92.
7 Krakowski Jaeger J, Volavka J. Violence and psychopathology: a longitudinal study. *Compr Psychiatry* 1988;29:174–81.
8 Addad M, Benezech M, Bourgeois M, Yesevage J. Criminal acts among schizophrenics in French mental hospitals. *J Nerv Ment Dis* 1981;169: 289–93.
9 Coccozza J, Steadman H. Failure of psychiatric predictions of dangerousness. *Rutgers Law Review* 1976;29:1084–1101.
10 Monahan J. Risk assessment of violence among the mentally disordered: generating useful knowledge. *Int J Law Psychiatry* 1988;11:249–57.
11 Monahan J, Steadman HJ. Toward a rejuvenation of risk assessment research. In: Monahan J, Steadman HJ, eds. *Violence and mental disorder*. Chicago: University of Chicago Press, 1994.
12 Steering Committee of the Confidential Enquiry into Homicides and Suicides by Mentally Ill People. *A preliminary report on homicide*. London, 1994.
13 Scott PD. Assessing dangerousness in criminals. *Br J Psychiatry* 1977;131: 127–42.
14 Gunn J. Dangerousness. In: Gunn J, Taylor PJ, eds. *Forensic psychiatry*. Oxford: Butterworth-Heinemann, 1993:624–45.

15 Walker Z, Seifert R. Violent incidents in a psychiatric intensive care unit. *Br J Psychiatry* 1994;**164**:826–8.
16 Ritchie JH, Dick D, Lingham R. *Report of the inquiry into the care and treatment of Christopher Clunis*. London: HMSO, 1994.
17 Lidz CW, Mulvey EP, Gardner W. The accuracy of predictions of violence to others. *JAMA* 1993;**269**:1007–11.
18 Heginbotham C. *Report of the Independent Panel of Inquiry examining case of Michael Buchanan*. London: North West London NHS Mental Health Trust, 1994.
19 NHS Management Executive. *Guidance on the discharge of mentally disordered people and their continuing care in the community*. Leeds: NHSME, 1994. (HSG (94) (27).)
20 *Revised Code of Practice, Mental Health Act 1993. August 1993*.
21 Swanson JW, Holzer CE, Ganju VK, Jono RT. Violence and psychiatric disorder in the community: evidence from the epidemiological catchment area surveys. *Hosp Community Psychiatry* 1990;**41**:761–70.
22 W v Egdell and others (1988) 2WLR 689.
23 Brahams D. Psychiatrist's duty of confidentiality. *Lancet* 1988;**ii**:1503–4.
24 Royal College of Psychiatrists. *Good medical practice and the aftercare of potentially violent or vulnerable patients discharged from inpatient psychiatric treatment*. London: Royal College of Psychiatrists, 1991. (Council report CR 12.)
25 Morgan HG, Williams R. *Suicide prevention: the challenge confronted*. London: HMSO, 1994.
26 Hawton K. By their own young hand. *BMJ* 1992;**304**:1000.
27 Nordentoft M, Breun L, Monk LK, Nordestgaard AG, et al. High mortality by natural and unnatural causes: a ten year follow up study of patients admitted to a poisoning centre after suicide attempts. *BMJ* 1993;**306**:1637–41.
28 King E. Suicide in the mentally ill: an epidemiological sample and implications for clinicians. *Br J Psychiatry* 1994;**165**:658–63.
29 Drake RE, Gates C, Cotton PG, et al. Suicide among schizophrenics: who is at risk? *J Nerv Ment Dis* 1984;**172**:613–7.
30 Hawton K. Assessment of suicide risk. *Br J Psychiatry* 1987;**150**:145–53.
31 Goldstein RB, Black TW, Nasarallah A, Winokur G. The prediction of suicide. *Arch Gen Psychiatry* 1991;**48**:418–22.
32 Beck AT, Resink HLP, Lettieri D, eds. *The prediction of suicide*. Bowie, Maryland: Charles Press, 1974.
33 Anon. Selective serotonin reuptake inhibitors for depression? *Drug Ther Bull* 1993;**31**:57–8.
34 Watts D, Morgan HG. Malignant alienation. *Br J Psychiatry* 1994;**164**:11–15.
35 Morgan HG, Priest P. Suicide and other unexpected deaths among psychiatric patients. *BMJ* 1991;**158**:308–74.
36 Goldcare M, Seagrott V, Hawton K. Suicide after discharge from psychiatric care. *Lancet* 1993;**342**:283–6.
37 Amchin J, Wettslein RM, Roth LH. *Suicide, ethics and the law*. In: Blumenthal SJ, Kupfer DJ eds. *Suicide over the life cycle*. Washington DC: American Psychiatric Press, 1990:637–63.
38 Cantor CH, McDermott PM. Suicide litigation: an Australian survey. *Aust N Z J Psychiatry* 1994;**28**:426–30.
39 Department of Health Health Circular (90) (23)/Local Authorities Social Services letter (90) (11). London: DOH, 1990.
40 NHS Management Executive. *Introduction of supervision registers for mentally ill people from 1 April 1994*. Leeds: NHSME, 1994. (HSG (94) (5).)
41 Caldicott F. Supervision registers. The college's response. *Psychiatric Bulletin* 1994;**18**:385–6.
42 Harrison G, Bartlett P. Supervision registers for mentally ill people. *BMJ* 1994;**309**:551–2.

43 Taylor P. Forensic psychiatry. In: Paykel ES, Jenkins R, eds. *Prevention in psychiatry*. London: 1994:157–73.
44 Wesley SC, Castle D, Douglas AJ, Taylor PJ. The criminal careers of incident cases of schizophrenia. *Psychol Med* 1994;**24**:483–502.
45 National Schizophrenia Fellowship 1995. "The silent partners" by Gary Hogman.
46 Lipsedge M. Choices in psychiatry. In: Dunstan GR, Sinebourne EA, eds. *Doctors' decisions: ethical conflicts in medical practice*. Oxford: Oxford University Press, 1989.

16 Containing risk in general practice

IDRIS WILLIAMS

General practice is a branch of medicine which is characterised by high levels of uncertainty. Patients present with a wide variety of symptoms and it is the general practitioner's job to organise these into recognisable diagnoses which can form the basis of a sensible management plan. Things are, however, often not that straightforward; grey areas exist where it is impossible to formulate an exact definition of the problem, which might include not only physical but social, psychological, and environmental components. On the other hand patients need clear cut answers to their problems and expectations are growing that these will be forthcoming. When, for various reasons, things do not turn out well, the doctor risks complaints and, increasingly, legal action in the courts. The fear of such action is recognised as one of the principal causes of anxiety and stress among general practitioners. While recognising that there is always an element of risk in general practice it is timely to examine the nature of that risk and outline strategies for reducing it. What follows later in this chapter may seem a counsel of perfection, but each practitioner, in striving to contain risk, will seek to get as close as possible to the ideal. This chapter looks mainly at the professional risks. There are also other forms of risk, which include those of being an employer and personal risks which can be concerned with health and safety; these are discussed at the end of the chapter.

Understanding the legal concept of negligence can assist in its avoidance. Fundamentally, negligence concerns harm or damage which has been inflicted on a person by someone who should be

294

taking care not to have done so. To be successful with a negligence action it is necessary to prove three things: firstly, that there was a duty of care; secondly, that there was a breach in that duty (a negligent act or liability); and thirdly, that harm resulted from the breach (causation). Within each of these three concepts are a range of specific situations and legal technicalities. These are more fully discussed in text books on the subject. A good example is *The general practitioner and the law of negligence.*[1] Some brief accounts of the legal position which relate to general practitioner care follow.

Duty of care

A doctor clearly has a duty of care to a patient and there is usually little difficulty in showing that such a duty of care exists. This also covers contacts by telephone, advice given through a third party (perhaps a deputy), a follow up arrangement, and when giving the results of investigations.

From the point of view of a Family Health Services Authority (FHSA) the patient's own general practitioner is responsible for treatment given by a deputy, unless that deputy is also on the appropriate list of an FHSA. When the general practitioner makes arrangements for a locum or deputy who is not on an FHSA list, for example, with a deputising service, the ultimate responsibility remains with the delegating doctor. It is important that in such circumstances the general practitioner is satisfied that the deputy is competent and available to carry out the delegated duties. It is different in the case of a civil claim, in which the deputy is responsible for his or her own actions. The employing doctor could still be held negligent in the choice of an employee.

The duty of care can extend to others beyond the patient. An example would be when dealing with a case of meningitis to ensure that members of the immediate family and others who have had close contact are protected by appropriate prophylactic treatment.

Family Health Services Authority terms of service

A general practitioner who is a principal on the list of an FHSA is subject to statutory obligations under his or her terms of service. These regulate the standards of care demanded by the FHSA and put him or her under a duty to provide all necessary and appropriate

295

personal medical services of the type usually provided by a general medical practitioner.

The relevant parts of the regulations are as follows:

12 (i) Subject to paragraphs 3, 13 and 44, a doctor shall render to his patients all necessary and appropriate medical services of the type usually provided by general medical practitioners.

   (ii) The services which a doctor is required by sub paragraph (i) to render shall include the following:

      (a) Giving advice where appropriate to a patient in connection with the patient's general health and in particular about the significance of diet, exercise, the use of tobacco, the consumption of alcohol and the misuse of drugs and solvents;

      (b) offering to patients consultations, and where appropriate, physical examinations for the purpose of identifying or reducing the risk of disease or injury;

      (c) offering to patients where appropriate vaccination or immunisation against Measles, Mumps, Rubella, Pertussis, Poliomyelitis, Diphtheria and Tetanus;

      (d) arranging for the referral of patients as appropriate for the provision of any other services under the National Health Service Act 1977;

      (e) giving advice, as appropriate to enable patients to avail themselves of services provided by a local Social Services Authority.

   (iii) Where a decision whether any, and if so what, action is to be taken under these terms of service requires the exercise of professional judgement a doctor shall not in reaching that decision be expected to exercise a higher degree of skill, knowledge, and care than:

      (b) that which General Practitioners as a class may reasonably be expected to exercise.

These regulations are used in practice to cover situations in which a patient complains to the FHSA about the standard of care given by the general practitioner. The decision as to whether there has been a breach in the terms of service is made by a service committee drawn up by the FHSA. The issue is not concerned with negligence itself, but with a breach of the terms of service; the two are, nevertheless, close. Although failure to provide adequate medical services is necessary for a case to be proved, causation is not required. The sanction against the general practitioner is limited to a requirement to comply with terms of service in the future, a warning, or a withholding from fees, or both; the patient does not receive financial recompense.

A report of a review committee on NHS complaints (the Wilson Report)[2] suggests that the present system becomes less adversarial with a two stage system. The Government has recently issued a response to this report—"acting on complaints". A two stage procedure is included, stage I being an in house conciliation procedure, stage II seems to be outside the FHSA with members of the panel drawn from lists maintained by the regional office of the NHS Executive. The whole complaints procedure is overseen by the Health Service Commissioner and there are appeal procedures possible at both stage I and stage II through his office. One has to presume that disciplinary procedures through the medical service committee hearings will remain. The other major change is the proposed time limit of one year for complaints.

Civil courts: breach of duty of care

For a patient to gain recompense it is necessary to take the case to a civil court. Here the test of the standard of care expected by any individual doctor is that of an ordinary skilled man professing to have that particular skill. A refinement of this was established by the Bolam case (1957)[3] when it was held that a doctor is not guilty of negligence if he has acted in accordance with a practice accepted by a responsible body of medical men skilled in that particular art. The implication of this is that it does not have to represent a majority opinion. This often means that a doctor can find a reputable doctor or doctors who will testify in support of the reasonableness of treatment.

Causation

Causation is often a difficult concept for both patients and doctors to understand. Detailed consideration of the subject is beyond the scope of this chapter; some examples may illustrate the variety of situations which can exist.

Often they are situations when a general practitioner is blamed for delay in referral. An example is rectal bleeding, initially diagnosed as

297

due to haemorrhoids, but turning out after the passage of time to be caused by rectal cancer. Causation is concerned with the possibility that the chances of cure were higher, or would have been higher, with prompt referral. If it can be shown that on the balance of probabilities (51% or greater) the chances of cure would have been better with earlier referral then causation is established. Even when negligence can be proved the case will still fail if it cannot be shown that it was the cause of the damage.

There are two other types of case in general practice where causation is important. The first concerns prescribing. If an unduly prolonged course of tablets is given and this results in harm, the initial part of that course might have been perfectly reasonable; the decision about causation will depend on the fine balance at what point did the excess become a material contribution to the harm. Benzodiazepine litigation comes into this category. The second is concerned with the effect of consent on causation. There are an increasing number of cases occurring which involve failure on the part of a doctor to warn a patient about possible harmful side effects of a treatment. It is clearly impossible to mention every side effect of a particular treatment. A liability is usually judged on what a reasonably competent general practitioner would have done. If, however, it can be shown that the patient would have agreed to the treatment even if the side effects had been disclosed then causation would not be proved because the lack of warning would make no difference to the outcome.

It is clearly impossible to inform a patient of every possible side effect. A patient could, quite unnecessarily, be put off the treatment altogether. The judgement as to what to tell is based on seriousness and incidence. Perhaps anything that has less than a 1% chance of occurring can be ignored unless the consequence is clearly serious.

A helpful case in these circumstances is Sidaway v the Board of Governors of Bethlem Royal Hospital and the Maudsley Hospital (1985).[4] It does not concern a general practitioner, but the principle is connected with disclosure of risks of unusual side effects. A neurosurgeon carried out a pain relieving spinal operation, which, because of technical difficulty resulted in damage to the spinal cord, with a resultant disability. The complaint was not of negligent technique, but of failure to warn of the side effect which occurred. The defence showed that there was a responsible body of medical opinion which would not have disclosed the risk and this argument was upheld by the judge. The expert witness for the defence said that the risk of this occurrence was less than 1%.

Limitation

There should be some time limit on when cases can be brought. The Limitation Act of 1980[5] fixed the period to three years. The point, however, is at what stage the three year period starts. This is determined by when the patient knows of the existence of harm and that it could have been caused by the act or treatment which is albeit later alleged to have been negligent. There are certain exempted categories. For children limitation does not start until the age of 18, which in effect means the age of limitation is 21 years. There are also exceptions for the mentally ill. The long term storage of records becomes important in these cases.

Res ipsa loquitur

This is a rule of evidence used by lawyers when it is difficult to prove negligence, but the resultant damage strongly suggests that the treatment must have been negligent (the thing speaks for itself). In general practice this can apply when a physical procedure is undertaken. Rupture of the uterus when inserting a intrauterine device (IUD) might come into this category.

Vicarious liability

In general practice this is to do with the responsibility of a doctor for the negligence of other health workers in the practice. When the health worker is an employee, the doctor has vicarious responsibilities for the actions as long as the person was acting within the course of employment.

The progress of a civil action of negligence

The first indication that a general practitioner has of a case of negligence being brought is a solicitor's letter. This may occur after an FHSA service committee hearing whether the findings have been for or against the doctor. Solicitors are sometimes involved in advising clients even at the stage of a service hearing and there may be a trend developing in which solicitors try a case out at such hearings. A finding against a doctor in a service committee bears heavily against him or her in a civil court, because it seems to suggest that the evidence presented points to the fact of negligence. In any event some action will have gone on before the doctor hears about the complaint and the possibility of a claim being brought. The solicitors will have discussed it with the patient, relatives, and perhaps other witnesses. It is the experience of the defence societies that 60% of claims made result in no action, 35% are settled or fall away, and not more than 5% go to court.

The doctor, on receipt of a letter, will forward this to his or her defence organisation who will handle the case thereafter. Often a considerable period passes before any outcome is determined. This is a time of high stress, as most doctors dread the thought of appearing in a witness box to defend their actions even though it is realised that most cases do not come to this. The solicitor for the plaintiff will obtain the relevant medical records, often from the hospital as well as the general practice. This is known as discovery of documents. Experts will then be consulted and in a general practice case this will be an expert who is usually a practising general practitioner. In general practice the expert is used particularly to comment upon negligence. A consultant in the field of the alleged negligence will often be necessary to comment on causation. After this preliminary assessment a barrister will be consulted and often after a conference with the experts a decision will be made about how to proceed.

If the case is to go on to the courts a statement of claim is written and sent to the defendant's (the doctor's) solicitor. Usually a barrister will draft a defence and may also request further and better particulars of the statement of claim. At this stage a hearing is fixed and documents exchanged. If the case is indefensible there is often an out of court settlement made by the defence societies and the doctor is informed of this possibility; his or her view is taken into account and there is full involvement in the decision. Sometimes out of court settlements are left until the last minute and occur literally in the corridor outside the court room.

The system in the United Kingdom is adversarial, the two sides competing with each other to convince the courts that they are right. It is not, as in criminal cases, dependent on proof being beyond all reasonable doubt which settles the issue, but what is likely to be on the balance of probabilities. Thus if the chances of the negligence causing the damage are assessed at 51% or greater (more likely than not), the case will be proved. The burden of proof is on the plaintiff (the patient); the doctor's position is strengthened if evidence of his reasonable actions can be produced.

Clinical risk areas

Lack of care can have disastrous consequences in any clinical situation. The basis of good practice includes an appropriate response to requests for visits; proper history taking, examination, and investigation; effective problem solving and case management; adequate follow up; effective communication and explanation; and very importantly common courtesy. Observation of these principles goes a long way to containing risk; slips are less likely and an isolated mistake is most likely to be forgiven.

Examples of serious consequences related to two of these aspects are as follows.

The first is related to failure to examine. A young woman who had not had children presented to her general practitioner with painful periods. No pelvic examination was made and analgesics were prescribed. Further prescriptions were given on three further occasions without benefit. Oral contraceptives were then prescribed, again without vaginal examination. The patient subsequently went to the family planning clinic when a large ovarian cyst was found on examination. The patient took legal action against the general practitioner.

The second relates to failure to visit. A young teenager was taken ill with headache, vomiting, and feeling hot while shopping. He was seen by a first aid worker who advised him to return home and call his own general practitioner. The general practitioner refused to visit and made a presumptive diagnosis of viral infection on the telephone. The patient was seen in the morning and admitted with advanced meningitis and died in hospital. The parents took civil action against the general practitioner.

Possible "at risk" situations are now described. The list is by no means comprehensive; it is intended to give an idea about what can go wrong.

Children

The importance of identifying an ill child cannot be overstated; for instance, failure to identify meningitis can lead to grave consequences. Other conditions which need identifying are dehydration from any cause, a blocked ventroperitoneal shunt (a tube which links the brain to the peritoneum to relieve high cerebrospinal fluid pressure in cases of hydrocephalus), appendicitis, and asthma. Most of the complaints associated with

301

these conditions are due to failure to admit the patient to hospital at an early enough stage. This sometimes also applies to rare conditions such as hypernatraemic dehydration (high sodium concentration in the blood) and intussusception (intestinal obstruction caused by one portion of the intestine passing into another). In these situations it is accepted that a general practitioner would not necessarily be expected to make the precise diagnosis; but the child is usually recognisably ill and in need of specialist care and investigation. Children present with many symptoms and all need careful evaluation; especially important are continuous crying, abdominal pain, vomiting, unexplained fever, and a wheeze that does not respond to treatment. In an acute abdomen it is important to look for a strangulated hernia and a torsion of the testis. When a young child presents with febrile convulsions, a watch needs to be kept for the possibility of two pathological situations being present, one being more serious than the other. Another source of complaint against a general practitioner is failure to identify congenital abnormalities at paediatric surveillance clinics. An example would be congenital dislocation of the hip. An important symptom to note is an unexplained limp or gait abnormality in a child of any age; investigation is always required.

Obstetrics and gynaecology

A common cause of difficulty is failure to identify a pregnancy and attribute symptoms to other causes. This sometimes follows sterilisation of either husband or wife; it must always be remembered that vasectomy and tubal ligation operations do have a failure rate although it is small. To overlook a pregnancy may lead to complaints of being deprived of an opportunity to seek termination. Other problems are side effects of oral contraception, difficulties with insertion of an IUD, failing to diagnose early labour usually because of attributing contractions to those of a Braxton Hicks type. Failure to examine is a common complaint in general practice gynaecology, leading to non-identification of pelvic pathology. Failure to diagnose an ectopic pregnancy is also a frequent cause of litigation. When a women of child bearing age presents with lower abdominal pain, consideration of the complications of pregnancy must be made because of their serious consequences. Similarly if a pregnant patient presents with some problem unrelated to the pregnancy the blood pressure and urine should be checked and recorded whatever the presentation.

302

Acute surgical emergencies

Late diagnosis or failure to admit a patient with an acute abdomen, particularly an acute appendicitis, is a common cause of litigation. Another important condition is torsion of the testis. As with an ill child the recognition of an acute abdomen is an important general practitioner skill.

Medical emergencies

Again late diagnosis and delayed admission of acute asthma, a complication of diabetes mellitus, and very importantly myocardial infarction is medicolegally dangerous as well as bad practice. Other conditions such as temporal arteritis, deep venous thrombosis, arterial insufficiency of the lower limbs, sudden loss of vision, need identifying quickly and appropriate treatment and management arranged. Another risk situation is dealing with a "red eye"; great care is needed to exclude glaucoma or iritis. The danger of using steroidal eye drops is well known in exacerbation of infection and dendritic ulcer.

Cancers

Legal actions because of late diagnosis of cancer occur fairly commonly. Examples include breast, skin, parotid gland, and testicular cancers; curiously all visible or palpable. Unexplained symptoms, new lumps, changes in skin lesions, and failure to respond to treatment should raise the suspicion of malignancy. If there is a history of weight loss the actual weight should be recorded in the notes.

Orthopaedics

Missed fractures are obvious pitfalls, but an important condition to pick up early is cauda equina compression as this needs urgent treatment. When a single joint presents with pain and swelling it is important to exclude infection.

Procedures

Any procedure can be a risk situation. Included would be any injection, ear syringing, and wart and cyst removal. Careful attention to technique and record keeping are essential; pathological specimens must always be sent for examination. Infection after

303

injections do occur and cases are brought because of alleged lack of skin cleaning. Although it is common practice to swab the injection site beforehand, it is probably unnecessary.[67] Muscle wasting at the site of a steroid injection is also a common cause of complaint.

Prophylaxis

Two situations are of concern here. The aftercare of an asplenic patient[8] and the need to provide prophylactic antibiotic for the immediate family of a case of meningitis.[9] Other examples are anticoagulation for dysrhythmias and aspirin after infarct.

Referred symptoms

Mistakes are made because of wrongly attributing referred pain, for instance pain in the knee indicating a hip problem.

It must be remembered that a substantial proportion of cases handled by solicitors do not proceed and this would apply to many of the conditions that have been mentioned. Nevertheless they are danger areas.

Methods of containing clinical risk

It is important to develop strategies to reduce risk not only because of the possibility of litigation, but because it is also in the patients' interests to contain as far as possible the risks to which they are exposed. This should not necessarily mean adopting an excessive "defensive medicine" approach, although there is evidence that this practice is increasing. Summerton has shown that the most common practices adopted by general practitioners to avoid the possibility of litigation were increased diagnostic testing, increased referrals, increased follow up and more detailed explanation to patients and note taking.[10] These measures may indeed represent a good standard of practice.

Ideally a general practitioner is equipped with the appropriate level of medical knowledge, a range of relevant skills, and certain professional attitudes. In a medicolegal sense attitudes such as responsibility to the patients, equanimity, and vigilance are important. All these attributes are over a course of a professional life continually being developed and refined. An important skill is risk containment. There are many elements to this skill, each of which is a specific skill in itself. An attempt will be made to set these out; there are bound to be others, but the list should provide a basis for developing a strategy towards clinical risk containment. It is divided fairly arbitrarily into six broad categories. These include clinical skills, clinical knowledge, working with others, personal approach, and arrangements. In all of these the general practitioner must learn to tolerate uncertainty, but eliminate harm from action or inaction.

Clinical skills

Take an appropriate history and do a relevant examination

The importance is self evident and the keywords are "appropriate" and "relevant". In FHSA service committee hearings the phrase "put him or herself in a position to make a diagnosis" is often used. It means turning up then listening and examining; problems arise because doctors do neither. Many cases involve, for instance, the failure of the doctor to undertake a pelvic or rectal examination. To do a vaginal examination and not find the ovarian cyst which is present is one thing; not to examine at all is another.

Communication skills

Good communication is now accepted as vital to effective doctoring and is widely taught in most medical schools and on vocational training courses. Much litigation is the result of poor communication; the complainant is often under a misapprehension or seeking an explanation. To reduce this the skills of listening, effective questioning, reflection, clarification, and explanation need to be linked to problem solving skills.

Problem solving skills

This has probably not been well taught on either undergraduate or vocational training courses. Emphasis tends to be on knowledge, manual skills, and communication skills rather than problem solving. The method of making a diagnosis is classically taught as taking a full history, doing a full examination and any relevant investigations; problems only being defined when all three stages were complete. This is the inductive method of problem solving. It is important, but time consuming and most doctors do not use it except when they are unable to unravel a problem. Most use the hypotheticodeductive method of problem solving in which hypotheses are created and tested; this is often associated with pattern recognition and entails equally careful history taking and examination, but targets these more effectively. A description of these methods is given elsewhere.[11]

"While you are here, doctor"

Being asked to see a second case on a visit can be irritating but should raise alarm bells. There is a natural feeling that seeing one case on a house call has been enough, but sometimes the second case is the more serious and, because of the background resentment, risks being incompletely thought out. I was called to see a student whose complaint was diarrhoea and vomiting: a diagnosis of gastroenteritis was straightforward and I went through the normal routine. As I was leaving the student said: "I have a friend who has the same problems, will the prescription do for her as well?" The temptation was to agree, but alarm bells rang and I reluctantly climbed the stairs to see her. She turned out to have an acute appendicitis and needed urgent hospital admission. The same warnings apply to the patient who when leaving the consulting room blurts out another symptom which may be the real reason for the visit. The symptom often outclasses the earlier complaint in importance and requires much more time to sort out.

Also difficult are patients who turn up again and again with seemingly trivial complaints. One day they will have a real, often urgent problem.

Understand grey areas and use follow up as a tool of management

Earlier in the chapter specific examples have been given of difficult clinical areas. Two examples are chest pain and lower abdominal pain. Either of these may occur and have innocent causes; but they may herald potentially serious problems. Because of this even if there is no immediate evidence of a myocardial infarction or an acute appendicitis a follow up arrangement may be wise from the point of view of both the patient and the doctor. Nevertheless the balance between being overcautious and sensibly cautious is a fine one to achieve. Experience does not always help; but asking the question should I revisit or see again often provides the answer.

Appreciation of severity of illness

A general practitioner is not expected to make inspired diagnoses of uncommon conditions; the practitioner is, however, expected to identify a seriously ill person. This is true of adults, but particularly true of children and infants. It is entirely reasonable to admit an infant as "seriously ill" without a diagnostic label. All general practitioners should understand the significance of such symptoms as persistent vomiting, persistent headache and photophobia, confusion, and the signs of dehydration and meningism in a child.

Clinical knowledge

Expectation of recovery

General practitioners manage many self limiting illnesses in which there is a high expectation of recovery within a foreseeable time. In many cases of this type the general practitioner does not arrange a follow up. Danger lies when the illness does not settle; it can mean an initial wrong diagnosis, a complication of the illness, or a completely new development. The situation in which the illness does not respond to prescribed treatment is similar. In both the general practitioner is likely to be called back and does so probably with some slight irritation; sometimes with still a fixed idea of the diagnosis. Experience shows that these cases need to be carefully re-evaluated; an initial respiratory tract viral infection can develop into a pneumonia. It is helpful to indicate expected recovery times: "I expect you to get better in five days, if not let me know." When faced with no response a handy rule is that if there is no progress by the third visit other action needs taking. Sometimes the side effects of treatment are the cause of delay in recovery. There is also the duty to ensure compliance with treatment; for instance by explaining why the medication is being used and what it does.

Understanding the epidemiology and natural history of illness

Common things are common and in general practice this is very true; but the other aphorism that rare things do actually happen is also true. Rarity is not a successful defence in court when failure to refer is alleged. Identifying the unusual is part of a general practitioner's job and this means actively searching for things which do not fit or make diagnostic sense; in fact having a high index of suspicion is necessary. Early referral is sometimes necessary on purely these grounds; a general practitioner is not expected to make the diagnosis of a rare condition, but is expected to recognise when things do not add up and refer accordingly. Sometimes the

307

referral is in the end unnecessary, but this is the nature of medicine and few consultants would refrain from fully investigating a case where a general practitioner is suspicious.

The general practitioner as a specialist

Some general practitioners work part time as hospital doctors in various roles. Others claim special skills, for instance in minor surgery, hypnosis, etc. Special care is needed to ensure that standards of care and levels of training are commensurate with these additional skills. A general practitioner working in a hospital specialty will be expected to have the knowledge, skills, and attitudes of a reasonably competent doctor working in that grade and specialty.

The risk of side effects and treatment failure

This is becoming an increasingly common medicolegal issue. Examples, apart from side effects of drugs, include the risk of recanalisation after vasectomy, the risk of perforation of the uterus after or during insertion of an IUD. Clearly it is impossible to mention all the side effects of everything; a common sense approach therefore is needed. Important considerations are the seriousness of the side effects and the incidence. As has been mentioned earlier 1% is a useful guide. The style of modern general practice with its emphasis on shared information and decision taking, certainly makes it easier to bring up the subject of possible side effects.

Working with others

Sharing responsibility

Although being a general practitioner can sometimes seem to be a lonely occupation there are usually colleagues around. Faced with uncertainties a shared approach is often helpful. I have never been afraid to share a problem with a partner, even if it looks as though I am indecisive. Patients respect this collaboration; two heads are better than one. I have also been very happy to respond to colleagues in this respect.

Understand the rules of delegation

This particularly applies when a locum is employed and in the case of a practice nurse. It is necessary to check identity, qualifications, registration, adequate training for the job to be done, liability insurance, the accountability lines, and the resources available to the delegatee. If in doubt medical defence organisations can offer help.

Taking over another doctor's case

In partnership practices it is not uncommon for several doctors to be involved in the management of one illness episode over time. This is especially so when out of hours calls are requested. A major pitfall for the second doctor is to accept the first doctor's diagnosis without rethinking the situation. A similar trap is accepting the patient's diagnosis of the problem. It is tempting to accept the patient's explanation of indigestion as the cause for a recurrent chest pain when further questioning would disclose its true anginal nature.

Personal approach

Maintaining a critical approach

Most general practitioners have a high level of suspicion and are not usually prepared to accept situations only at face value. It is helpful also to be self critical. Questions worth asking are: why am I doing this; is there something else I should be thinking about; I wonder if there is something else going on here?

Understanding personal limitations

This develops from the previous point. It is necessary to admit sometimes that one doesn't know what is wrong with the patient or one is unable to carry out a particular procedure. I have never found that patients have been concerned about my inability to solve a problem and would have to refer to a specialist or consult a colleague (or even look at a book!) Indeed they welcome such frankness and think that they are being taken seriously. If a risk is present because of personal limitations that risk should not be taken.

Keeping up to date

This is vital in an ever changing scene. A good example is the prophylactic after care of patients after splenectomy. It is now well known that these patients are at increased risk of severe infection. The infection can spread rapidly leading to fulminant bacteraemia and death. A doctor who, following the

Chief Medical Officer's update[8] has an asplenic patient who develops such an infection without having had appropriate prophylaxis, risks legal action.

Arrangements

Care needs to be taken about general managerial arrangements; these include making appointments with consultants, arranging for admissions after visits, writing down details of follow up calls, checking results of investigations, and informing patients accordingly. It is necessary to look carefully at results to make sure that there are no abnormalities. Failure to follow up an abnormal smear, blood and pus in the urine, or a raised erythrocyte sedimentation rate can cause trouble as the evidence is there for all to see. When on holiday a doctor should make arrangements for his follow up visits and matters arising out of incoming reports to be attended to by one of his colleagues. Health promotion clinics are particularly important in this respect; the onus is very much on the doctor to follow up abnormal test results.

Responding to calls

This is important and has been a regular theme throughout this chapter. Failure to visit or delay in visiting accounts for between 35% and 40% of all FHSA complaints. If in any doubt a doctor should judge the urgency of a case; situations arise when patients merely ring up for advice, but on questioning the case is clearly serious and a visit is appropriate. It is the doctor's duty to make the decision even if the patient or caller is not directly asking for a visit. Availability is also important. Telephone answering machines need to be working and to give an indication of where to get help.

Keep good records

This is of fundamental importance. Legible, clear, comprehensive, contemporaneous records are invaluable in legal situations. This includes the records of nurses, health visitors, and other members of staff, as well as details of requests for visits and possible telephone discussions. The standard of general practice records is not good; some merely state the diagnosis and treatment. There is an unstated convention that only positive findings be recorded, but negative findings are often highly relevant; a finding of no neck stiffness at least proves the test was done. If advice is given out of hours this should be recorded. Justification for not visiting should be written down. If a second call comes in it is wise to respond by doing a visit. Abnormal investigation results need to be kept. When culling notes there needs to be some medical input; information about closed events only should be destroyed. Flow charts of pathological data are helpful.

Consent

This is usually accepted as being implied when a patient seeks medical advice, but it is not necessarily so. When the treatment involves some procedure, even an injection, it is important to check that consent is given. This may also be true of an examination; it is helpful to say something like "I would like to examine you now if I may". Certainly in health promotion clinics the agreement of the patient to an assessment or screening procedure does not necessarily imply an agreement to treat. An example of mine concerned an elderly woman having a health check. In the course of this I discovered a fairly advanced carcinoma of the breast, but was told that she knew what it was, and did not want treatment; furthermore she did not want me to tell the family about it. The converse of this is more usual and patients do expect to have conditions found on screening to be treated. It cannot be too strongly stressed that not to disclose to the patient an adverse finding puts the doctor at real risk. It is also important to make sure about informed consent when giving information about a patient to an insurance company.

Chaperons

The need to obtain consent to an examination has already been mentioned and part of this is to do with the risk of being accused of assault or sexual assault. There is variation in the use of chaperons in general practice, but it is a matter to consider when dealing with risk containment. Judgement is necessary. The need for a chaperon may not only apply when dealing with the opposite sex or only when gynaecological examinations are being carried out. Any situation which involves dealing with the female torso and, for instance, when dim lighting is being used, for example during retinal examinations increases the need for care. It is good practice to explain the reason for the examination as well as to get permission to do it.

311

Confidentiality

This is often breached unthinkingly by practice staff. Careful training of staff is necessary. It is wise not to give the results of an investigation over the telephone unless the member of staff is certain that they know who they are talking to. This is a situation of course that often happens in practice.

Saying sorry

There is the difficult question of whether to say sorry; doctors have been very worried about this for fear of admitting liability. The medical defence organisations advise that if an appropriate apology is given than this does not prejudice their legal position. In effect, saying sorry is for what has happened; not the admission of fault.

Employer risk

Apart from clinical risk a general practitioner faces risks as an employer. The Health and Safety at Work Act (1974)[12] places responsibility for health and safety at work on employers. This applies to general practitioners in health centres and surgery premises. Several aspects need considering.

Equipment has to be safe—for instance, electrical apparatus, gas appliances, and furniture including examination couches. Equipment used in clinical procedures also needs to be safely maintained. This includes apparatus for ear syringing, cryosurgery, and endoscopy. Specific attention needs to be paid to the disposal of clinical waste and sharps. Account needs to be taken of the Environmental Protection Act (1990)[13] and the advice of the committee on substances harmful to health (1988).[14] The storage of hazardous substances as well as clinical waste disposal needs to be watched carefully. An important consideration is that these aspects are not covered by professional indemnity; if general practitioners are subject to action by the Health and Safety Executive legal costs and certainly fines are not covered automatically by the professional indemnity organisation. The medical defence organisations are, however, able to support their members with medicolegal advice. If a conviction under the health and safety legislation leads to an appearance at the General Medical Council then it is likely that members would receive full support in addressing allegations made by the General Medical Council.

312

Certainly all general practitioners should ensure that they have public liability insurance on their premises.

Working areas need to be checked for hazards including obstacles which put patients at risk of falling. Visual display units need checking and members of staff need to be protected against awkward lifting and handling of equipment. Practices also have the responsibility for students and other people visiting the premises. A first aid kit needs to be available and it is advisable for some basic first aid training to be given to staff members and also instructions as to how to respond in the event of a fire. An overall policy on safety within the practice, which is documented together with an accident log incident book, can be helpful if things go wrong.

Everyone in the surgery can be at risk from violent or abusive patients. Again a policy as to how to deal with this situation is helpful. Immunisation state of the practice staff—for instance, against hepatitis B—should be reviewed regularly.

Drugs and prescribing

Prescriptions should be made out accurately and legibly. Overprescribing and polypharmacy should be avoided. There are danger points; warfarin is a common cause of problems, particularly when no dosage is given on discharge from hospital. Even with computers prescribing mistakes can occur; penicillin and penicillamine (both 250 mg) are easily confused. There are strict regulations about certain categories of drugs subject to misuse which are mandatory (the Misuse of Drugs Act (1971).[15] A dangerous drugs register is required and dangerous drugs need to be housed according to the regulations. A bag locked in a car is not sufficient. A doctor may need controlled drugs in some situations, as for example the use of heroin in cases of myocardial infarction; and care should be taken to conform with the regulations. Theft should be guarded against.

The Consumer Protection Act (1987)[16] has relevance to liability when a person is damaged by a defective product. It mostly concerns manufacturers, but dispensing general practitioners should keep careful records of batch numbers and expiry dates. A system to identify the producer or supplier of each drug and the conditions of storage should be in place.[17] The laws and regulations concerning prescribing of drugs can be very complex. When there is any doubt a doctor should contact his defence organisation for advice.

Doctors may be called on to treat drug addicts; this will entail notification to the Home Office, and only prescribing controlled drugs in certain circumstances. It is permissible to prescribe pethidine to a pethidine addict to relieve the pain of renal colic, but not for treatment of the addiction without appropriate notification. In any case it would be better to avoid the addictive drug altogether.

Doctors should minimise the risks of use of controlled drugs by only carrying small quantities in a secure locked container; as has been mentioned, for these purposes a car boot is not a locked container. It is wise to prescribe small quantities, except in terminal care for syringe drivers. Unwanted drugs should be disposed of via an approved person such as an FHSA medical adviser or a policeman. The Misuse of Drugs Act (1971) does include regulations which allow patients to surrender unwanted controlled drugs to a doctor, dentist, or pharmacist. Doctors are not obliged to accept drugs but if they do they are authorised to destroy the drugs without the need to record their destruction or to have it witnessed by an authorised person. This is covered in regulation 26 (6) in the Misuse of Drugs Regulations (1985).[15]

Techniques for management of risk

Formal techniques of risk management in practices have been developed over recent years. They involve three main areas; practice complaints procedures, risk assessment audit, and untoward incident reporting. The medical defence unions have taken the lead in developing all three of these and for each there are helpful publications to aid a practice. These are available from defence organisations and examples are given in the references.[18-20]

A practice complaints procedure allows a problem to be resolved at an early stage by an appropriate explanation and apology, but does not preclude the patient from taking the complaint further if desired.

Untoward incident reporting is a helpful way of detecting deficiencies in the standard of patient care so that that care can be improved. An untoward incident is any occurrence which could have, or which has, harmed a patient, visitor, or member of staff—for example, an overlooked abnormal report, treatment error, or misdiagnosis. This does not mean that there has been a complaint—but there could have been. Untoward incidents can

314

be reported on a standard schedule to the practice manager; discussion then follows with the aim of learning lessons and avoiding future problems.

Risk assessment audit is a system of formal audit of an area of practice work which looks specifically at the risk possibilities and their containment. This is a normal part of a clinical audit programme, but is also particularly relevant to practice management.

Conclusions

The work of a general practitioner is becoming increasingly complicated and difficult. There are many factors which account for this and the trend is likely to continue. Clinical advances have made it possible to treat more diseases effectively and often at home; an increasing proportion of illnesses are now managed completely in primary care. With day surgery, early discharge, and the movement of the continuing care of old people away from the hospital to the community, the trend is for more care to move from the hospital to the home.

Contractual changes mean that general practitioners are having to accept managerial responsibilities, sometimes for a large organisation with a substantial budget, especially so in the case of fundholders. Patients have increasing expectations which, although welcomed in that this leads to improved standards, it puts even greater responsibilities on general practitioners. The problems of society often land up on the general practitioner's doorstep and often there is little that the doctor can realistically and effectively offer. The result is frustration and tension on both sides. This chapter has attempted to relieve some of the uncomfortable effects of that tension.

I acknowledge my reliance on some material in Scott W. *The general practitioner and the law of negligence*, Chartridge: Business and Medical Publications Limited, 1994, and recommend this book for further reading.

I thank Dr Walter Scott, Dr Philip Leech, and Dr Stephen Green for help and advice when writing this chapter.

1 Scott W. *The general practitioner and the law of negligence*. 2nd ed. London: Cavendish Publishing, 1995.
2 Department of Health. *Being heard: the report of a review committee on National Health Service complaints procedure*. London: DOH, 1994 (the Wilson Report).

3 Bolam *v* Friern Hospital Management Committee (1957) 2: Aller 118.
4 Sidaway *v* Board of Governers of Bethlem Royal Hospital and the Mawdsley Hospital (1985) AC 871.
5 *Limitation Act 1980*. London: HMSO, 1980.
6 Aronson JK. Routes of drug administration: intramuscular injection. *Prescribers Journal* 1995;**35**:32–36.
7 Dannte. *Routine skin preparation before injection: unnecessary procedure*. Lancet 1969;**ii**:96–8.
8 Department of Health. Asplenic patients and immunisation. *CMO's update* 1994;**1**:3.
9 Finch R. Bacterial meningitis. *Prescribers Journal* 1989;**29**:2–10.
10 Summerton N. Positive and negative factors in defensive medicine: a questionnaire study of general practitioners. *BMJ* 1995;**310**:27–9.
11 Fraser RC. *Clinical method: a general practice approach*. London: Butterworths, 1987.
12 *Health and Safety at Work Act 1974*. London: HMSO, 1974.
13 *Environmental Protection Act 1990*. London: HMSO, 1990.
14 *Health and Safety: the control of substances hazardous to health regulations 1988. Amendments 1991 and 1992*. London: HMSO, 1988.
15 *The Misuse of Drugs Act 1971 with regulatory amendments in 1973 and 1985*. London: HMSO, 1985.
16 *The Consumer Protection Act 1987*. London: HMSO, 1987.
17 Schutte PK. *Some legal considerations in prescribing*. Prescribers Journal 1991;**31**: 27–33.
18 Beresford D, Green S. *Practice complaints procedure*. London: Medical Defence Union Ltd, 1994.
19 Healthcare Risk Management: *General practitioner practice organisational audit check list*. London: Medical Defence Union Ltd, 1992.
20 Healthcare Risk Management. *Untoward incident report guidelines*. London: Medical Defence Union Ltd, 1995.

17 Risk management in nursing and midwifery

BRIDGIT DIMOND, YVONNE PETERS

The principles of risk management are at the heart of the nursing process. Professional care in nursing initially requires an assessment of the patient's condition, his or her needs, and the objectives to be achieved. Nursing care is then planned on the basis of these needs and how treatment should be supported by nursing care. This process must include an assessment of the risks of harm and how these risks can be eliminated, or, if that is not possible, then how the risks of any harm to or deterioration in the patient's condition can be minimised. Finally, the objectives should be regularly reviewed in relation to the patient's condition, leading to revisions and possibly new objectives being identified. Risk management is therefore an integral part of the nursing care of the patient.

Risk management is also at the heart of any sound policy for health and safety of staff and the general public and some of the elements are considered in relation to specific areas of health and safety which are of particular concern to the nurse. Risk management has also had a higher profile in the thinking of the NHS trusts after the establishment of the internal market as a result of the changes brought about by the NHS and Community Care Act 1990. Part of the corporate responsibility of the executive nurse on the trust board is to highlight areas of risk in relation to nursing and midwifery practice. The agenda is large and the approach variable. Similarly the senior nurses, ward managers, and supervisors of practice in each clinical directorate have a major part to play in ensuring that the principles of risk management are implemented.

317

This is evidenced by the advice from the NHS Management Executive.[1] However, the document does not specifically identify nursing or midwifery issues in risk management, although of course these areas are covered by the general guidance on direct risk in patient care. Issues such as resuscitation, staffing, confidentiality, preservation and storage of records, risks relating to consent to treatment, and risks arising from working beyond one's competence are all central to the role of the nurse and midwife.

The purpose of this chapter is to identify those areas of nursing and midwifery practice in which advances in risk assessment and management have taken place and to identify future developments.

Patient care

Initial assessment

The starting point for any care of the patient must be defining his or her needs, determining the action which must be taken to meet those needs, and identifying any risks which arise in the care and condition of the patient.

Thus the evaluation of the patient's condition and the definition of the treatment plan in the light of the assessed needs is the starting point in all specialties.

For example, in the prevention and management of pressure sores complicated scales have been developed to identify patients at risk and to determine the measures to be taken to prevent those risks arising. Professionals who thought that they knew the risk, based on their experience, have been surprised by the scoring produced by a systematic measurement tool. In the United Kingdom the favoured measures are the Norton pressure sore risk calculator[2] and the Waterloo risk assessment, which has been used in various specialties including neurology.[3] In assessing tissue viability risk assessment must be part of the initial evaluation. Retrospective studies can determine the relation of intrinsic factors such as serum protein concentration and systolic blood pressure, and the presence of or tendency to develop pressure sores can be of value in deciding on more specific and sensitive risk management tools.[4]

The legal implications of pressure sores and recent cases of litigation resulting in significant awards have been examined[5] and the author argues that risk management should become an

318

important feature of the organisation's strategy in avoiding liability and heavy drains against revenue funds (if liability leads to compensation and the present pooling arrangement for covering such claims ends). Risk management envisages a multidisciplinary approach to the identification of the patient's needs and the extent to which they can be met by the resources (including staffing, equipment, and facilities) and environment of the trust.

It is perfectly acceptable to modify existing measurement scales and to add local factors that are relevant such as social issues and the input of carers. The ongoing audit of all measurement tools is an essential component of the quality of the interventions.

Identification of diseases and diagnosis

Research has suggested that there are many areas in which risk assessment in relation to the detection of specific diseases should be incorporated into nursing practice. Thus the basis for cancer risk assessment has been identified[6] and it is recommended that these risk assessments should be incorporated into nursing practice and be used for client education and for motivating changes in lifestyle. The nurse and midwife have a clear part to play in disease prevention, which is identified in recent government and Welsh Office papers.[7] It has been suggested that the assessment of cancer risks can be linked with the prevention and control of financial loss from claims of negligence in relation to cancer nursing.[8] The risks of immunological interactions in cancer nursing through the clinical use of biological response modifiers in the diagnosis and treatment of cancer is also identified. In another field the risk of alterations in sensory perception is recognised.[9]

Defining objectives

Once the risks have been identified in relation to patient care then the next question is the extent to which the risk can be avoided altogether. Thus in some circumstances, the avoidance of any admission to hospital to prevent or reduce the risk of infection might be the agreed path to be taken. This would, however, have to be balanced against any risks arising from failure to admit. Thus in deciding whether day surgery is appropriate for a patient requiring a specific operation, the benefits which flow from not admitting to hospital must be balanced against the possible benefits of inpatient stay and care, taking into account not only the patient's clinical condition and needs but also social and economic circumstances. All this should be recorded.

Control of infection

One area in which some clinicians might argue that the risks can never be avoided but only reduced is that of the control of infection. The current research being undertaken by the Public Health Laboratory Service in 19 hospitals to identify hospital acquired infection should lead to some extremely valuable lessons in terms of prevention of infections. It has already produced some useful results on standards of record keeping and omissions from records of occurrences of infection. The first step must be the recognition of the risk.[10] The awareness of the risk of cross infection was examined by studying the attitudes of nurses and physicians to cleaning of endoscopes.[14] The authors found that 86% of physicians and 30% of nurses were unaware of incidents of cross infection; 83% of nurses or associates and 82% of physicians expressed satisfaction with current cleaning methods.

The nurse dealing with control of infection has a key role in the development and implementation of a cross infection policy. He or she should be the link with nurse and midwifery practitioners, raising their awareness, and influencing decisions such as which patients should be placed in a single room.

The reduction of infections acquired in hospital would obviously benefit patients (the impact on vulnerable patients of such infections is not at present quantifiable), and in addition the savings resulting from the reduction in the number of inpatient days and drug costs are likely to be considerable.

Changes in practice

Day units and units managed by midwifes are just two examples of developments that expand patient and consumer choice and where nurses and midwives are taking on additional skills and responsibility. The risks are managed through appropriate education and training and locally agreed protocols.

Day surgery

The advances made in day surgery and the increase in the number of patients who are able to avoid inpatient stay have only been possible because of three strategic risk assessments: the first at the time of the initial consideration for and referral to day surgery (probably in the outpatient's department); the second when the patient arrives on the day for the day surgery; and the third after the operation when a decision has to be made on whether the patient can be safely allowed home. Other measures can be taken to avoid some risks, such as introducing a telephone service for follow up of patients on their return home.[10] Written information on discharge with expected outcomes of treatment and action in relation to any foreseeable occurrences can also reduce patients' anxiety and increase their level of preparation.

The increase in the use of day surgery has led to a greater awareness of the risks involved and it is clear that the nurse has a major part to play in the identification of the assessment of the suitability of the patient for day surgery and in eliminating or reducing the known risks.

Day surgery has been used as an example of the process of risk assessment but it applies to every field of nursing and midwifery. It is recommended that in every field, the initial risk assessment should be followed by a more structured analysis showing the pros and cons of any planned action. The balancing of risks in favour or against any proposed action is often undertaken without systematic recording of the reasons. It is a skilled task and requires trained and competent practitioners to undertake it.

Units managed by midwives

The report on *changing childbirth*[11] envisaged that in the next five years 30% of women should have a midwife as the lead professional and should be delivered in a maternity unit under the management of that midwife. At least 75% of women should know beforehand through the antenatal care the person who will care for them during their delivery. The individual accountability of each midwife is recognised. Commissioners and providers have been instructed to bring proposals for implementing the recommendations of the report into the NHS agreements. There may well be an increase in the number of midwife managed units, whether within the district general hospital or in the community. The assessment and selection of mothers for this unit will underpin the success of the

321

midwifery care. Clear criteria on those who are unsuitable for such care must be identified and implemented.[12] Close partnerships between midwives, obstetricians, and general practitioners are essential and transfer arrangements must be clearly identified at the various assessment milestones.

Risk management and working within the sphere of competence

Once the risks are identified, an assessment has to be made as to whether they can be completely avoided. Usually the avoidance of some risks means that other risks, hopefully less important, materialise.

The NHS Management Executive recognises that one of the main methods of eliminating or reducing the risk of harm is ensuring that staff work within their sphere of competence. This is the basis for the philosophy behind the United Kingdom Central Council (UKCC) publication on the scope of professional practice.[15]

In 1992 the UKCC for nursing midwifery and health visiting gave its blessing to the development of professional practice in its registered professions on the basis of six key principles. Box 1 shows these principles in summary form.

The concept of the extended role of nurses undertaking tasks normally carried out by doctors, was put aside. Instead the UKCC suggested that "practice must therefore be sensitive, relevant, and responsive to the needs of individual patients and clients and have the capacity to adjust, where and when appropriate, to changing circumstances".[16]

However, this professional development can only take place if the practitioner assesses her competence in relation to the risks of harm to the patient.[17]

The six principles identified by the UKCC as being the foundation of any development of professional practice should minimise the risk of harm occurring to patients and others and ensure that practice can develop safely.

Areas of potential development for nurse practitioners include:

- Acting as first assistant in theatres[18]
- Primary visits in the community
- Minor injury units

322

Box 1—Principles for adjusting the scope of practice

The registered nurse, midwife, or health visitor:

- 1 Must be satisfied that each aspect of practice is directed to meeting the needs and serving the interests of the patient or client

- 2 Must endeavour always to achieve, maintain, and develop knowledge, skill and competence to respond to those needs and interests

- 3 Must honestly acknowledge any limits of personal knowledge and skill and take steps to remedy any relevant deficits in order effectively and appropriately to meet the needs of patients and clients

- 4 Must ensure that any enlargement or adjustment of the scope of personal professional practice be achieved without compromising or fragmenting existing aspects of professional practice and care and that the requirements of the Council's Code of Professional Conduct are satisfied throughout the whole area of practice

- 5 Must recognise and honour the direct or indirect personal accountability borne for all aspects of professional practice

- 6 Must, in serving the interests of patients and clients and the wider interests of society, avoid any inappropriate delegation to others which compromises those interests

---

- Night nurse practitioners
- Nurse prescribing.

The Crown report,[19] the recommendations of which led to the passing of legislation introducing the power of specified nurses to prescribe within a limited range of products came to their conclusions as a result of the balancing of the benefits of enabling nurses to prescribe certain medicinal products against the risks of extending their power. Their main recommendation was that "suitably qualified nurses working in the community should be able, in clearly defined circumstances, to prescribe from a limited list of items and to adjust the timing and dosage of medicines within a set protocol."

The report thus decided against giving the power to community psychiatric nurses to become initial prescribers: "The community psychiatric nurses' dual responsibility to both the general practitioner and the hospital consultant could lead to problems of coordination and communication, and their close relationship with the patients could result in their coming under unacceptable pressure to prescribe".

Initially the power to prescribe has been given only to those holding district nursing or health visiting qualifications in eight pilot areas. After the eight pilot schemes have reported, there may well be an extension of the scheme across the country, leading eventually, if the revenue costs permit, to an increase in those practitioners able to participate and an extension of the types of products which can be prescribed.[20]

Possible risks from this development are minimised by a careful selection of the products which will be permitted to be prescribed by nurses and by clearly defined training. Whether they have the power to prescribe or not, nurses should be aware of the impact of the drugs which they administer.

Many hospital units now have developed protocols enabling nurses to prescribe within the hospital setting. This must be carefully monitored to ensure that there is no infringement of the Medicines Act 1968. Midwives already have the power to prescribe within the limits laid down by this act and by the midwives' rules.

Standard setting and monitoring

The final stage in any risk management programme is the monitoring of care in a quality assurance strategy. Thus the importance of incorporating quality assurance activities into management information systems and linking them to risk management is established.[21] In specific procedures occurrence screening techniques have been used—for example, in intravenous nursing quality assurance and risk management programmes.[22] The author states that although adverse events such as site infection or phlebitis do not automatically indicate that negligence or poor care have occurred, identification of these events provides an early warning of risk and liability exposure. A locally agreed list of occurrences that are to be screened must be developed and a mechanism set up for reporting and acting on information. Sometimes lessons can be learnt from an examination of nursing practice on the basis of case studies.[23] The most effective risk management will be developed through multiprofessional programmes that include setting standards, agreed reporting or screening systems, and continuous audit.

Risk management and patients' rights

Adult mentally competent patients

The mentally competent patient has the right to give or withhold consent to treatment or research. In practice many patients may not be aware of this legal right but publications such as the *patients' charter* are increasing awareness.

Consent is not to the possibility of negligence arising but to an acceptance of the possibility of harm arising through those risks which cannot be eliminated by taking good care. The consent authorises what could otherwise be a trespass to the person. Before consent is given, it is essential that the patient is informed about all the risks of substantial harm.

This does not mean, however, that the consent of the patient allows the registered practitioner to run unnecessary risks. If negligent decisions or actions are taken then this would be regarded as a breach of duty of care: no reasonable professional would have taken that decision. Any risks which are taken must be justified on the basis of reasonableness; therefore, there must be clear reasons for the decision and these must be recorded.

What if the patient wishes to have treatment considered to be particularly risky? What if the patient refuses to have treatment considered to be essential?

The answer to the first question is that the patient cannot necessarily insist on any specific treatment. Resources are finite; there is no absolute right of a patient to claim a specific form of care; treatment, therefore, which is extremely risky or unlikely to benefit the patient can be refused. Difficulties can arise when the patient wishes to have a treatment or procedure which is not yet part of the practitioner's field of competence, or even accepted within traditional medicine. Thus in midwifery for example, a demand by a mother that she should be delivered in water is not currently being met by all NHS providers. Midwives have inquired if they may allow mothers to have a water birth after warning them that they are not, as a result of lack of experience, competent to deliver the baby in such circumstances. Considerable dangers exist for the midwives who agree with a procedure outside their competence. They may also find that they (or their employers) are not protected from liability because of the effect of the Unfair Contract Terms Act 1977.[24]

A patient who is mentally competent can refuse to have any treatment even though it is considered to be life saving.[25] The

325

professional has a duty, however, to ensure that the patient's refusal is valid and that the patient has received all the necessary information to make that decision.[26]

Care of elderly or mentally disordered patients

Risk taking and management in the care of elderly patients or those with learning disabilities is central to ensuring them a reasonable quality of life.[27] Guidelines by *counsel and care* provide model policies and training material on restraint and risk taking in residential care and nursing homes for older people.

Psychiatric care

Risk management in balancing the freedom of the patients against risks of harm to themselves or others is intrinsic to good nursing practice in the care of mentally disordered patients. The statutory powers given to the nurse to prevent an informal patient from leaving are an example of the assessment that the prescribed nurse is required to make. The nurse is required to make the following assessment under section 5(4) of the Mental Health Act 1983, if the patient's doctor is not immediately available: "that the patient is suffering from mental disorder to such a degree that it is necessary for his health or safety or for the protection of others for him to be immediately restrained from leaving the hospital."[28]

Having made this decision and having completed the necessary form for the hospital managers, she can then detain the patient for up to six hours or until the appropriate doctor arrives, whichever is sooner.

Health and safety

In safeguarding the health and safety of staff, the regulations after the European Union directives have made more specific the requirements already legally binding under the Health and Safety at Work Act 1974. Thus the general duty on the employer to ensure so far as is reasonably practicable the health and safety and welfare of all employees[29] is clarified in relation to the arrangements for health and safety, manual handling, visual display units, protective clothing, and safety in the work area. The regulations on the control of substances hazardous to health should also be implemented by all nurses. Occupational health nurses have much

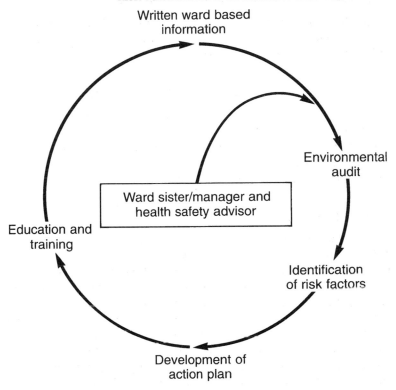

Figure 17.1 *Principles of clinical environment audit.*

wider and clearer responsibilities in relation to risk assessment[30] including that of communicating information on the risks at work.[31] The ward sister or ward manager has a crucial part in ensuring that the environment is safe and that the agreed health and safety policies are implemented (figure 17.1 identifies an approach to clinical environmental audit).

Specific nursing practice issues

The following areas are considered in relation to nursing practice: AIDS/HIV infection control, manual handling, predicting falls, control of substances hazardous to health, and the physical and mental health of staff.

AIDS/HIV infection

The United Kingdom Central Council has made it clear that no registered practitioner is entitled to refuse to nurse a patient who is HIV positive or who has AIDS.[32] However, the employee is entitled to receive all reasonable care from the employer to ensure that she is not infected by a patient. Sim examined risk assessment in relation to AIDS/HIV infections.[33] The factors which lowered or raised the risk were considered and the author concluded that rather than depriving the patient of care, the responsibility is on the management or organisation and each individual nurse and midwife to ensure that the risk is minimised. Risk factors are lowest in the more "predictable" areas of practice such as outpatient clinics but in accident and emergency departments or delivery suites where exposure to potentially infected body fluid is commonplace and often unpredictable the staff are more susceptible to risk. The major factor is the education and training of staff and the use of agreed policies and procedures that protect staff while maintaining the rights and dignity of this patient group.

Manual handling

Back injuries from manual handling affect one out of every five nurses and is the largest factor in sickness absenteeism. Before the regulations on manual handling came into force the prevention of back injuries was recognised as an important aspect for health and safety at work.[34][35] Its importance as a factor in nurses leaving the profession was researched in 1987.[36] The implementation of the regulations in 1992 are therefore an important step in reducing the sickness rates and contributing to a healthier workforce and retaining nurses within the profession. The regulations require the following stages to be implemented:

- Avoid the manual handling, if reasonably possible
- Carry out an assessment of the risks arising from manual handling (this is an absolute duty—it must be carried out, whatever the costs and time it will take and for each episode of handling)
- Avoid or reduce the risk as far as is reasonably practicable
- Review and revise the assessment when necessary.

A prize was awarded to a nurse for developing a lifting risk calculator.[37]

Predicting falls

A 26 item risk assessment tool has been designed to identify the risks of falls. This was based on a literature review and analysis of causative factors of falls that had occurred over a three month period at a 1100 bed acute medical–surgical, psychiatric, and extended care facility in Texas.[38] It was found that only four of the 26 items were statistically related to falls; the risk assessment tool was shortened to the four items and called the RISK (reassessment is safe "kare") tool.

Control of substances hazardous to health

The stages which must be followed in assessing activities under these regulations are similar to those stages in the regulations on manual handling. Certain areas, such as the administration of cytotoxic drugs must be given a high priority. Guidance from the Health and Safety Executive facilitates the implementation of the stages.[39]

Physical and mental health of staff

Since the events at Grantham and Kesteven General Hospital between February and April 1991 which resulted in Beverly Allitt, an enrolled nurse, being convicted of the deaths of four children and causing harm to nine others it is no longer possible for any health professional to argue that such incidents are not foreseeable. There should therefore be in existence in every hospital and community group a policy for dealing with untoward incidents and for assessing their cause and prevention. The recommendations of the independent inquiry into the deaths and injuries caused by Beverly Allitt, which was chaired by Sir Cecil Clothier,[40] should be implemented in relation to the recruitment and selection of staff, the role of the occupational health department, and the procedures to be taken when an unexpected death or untoward event takes place.

Nurses and midwives have a major part to play in the development, management, and monitoring of such policies. The inquiry admitted that even if all the recommendations were to be implemented, "no measures can afford complete protection against a determined miscreant. The main lesson from our Inquiry and our principal recommendation is that the Grantham disaster should serve to heighten awareness in all those caring for children of the possibility of malevolent intervention as a cause of unexplained clinical events."

What is clear is the need for far greater management control over staff, their sickness records, and the knowledge of their present physical and mental health. Practitioners should also be encouraged as the result of the recent freedom of speech circulars[41] to raise their concerns with management without the fear of reprisals or victimisation.

Conclusions

It has been possible to select only some of the major areas for risk assessment from the vast number in which such assessment is essential. Thus topics such as the change in the nurse's role as a result of the reduction in junior doctors' hours and changes in medical practice, paediatrics, accident and emergency, and triage, community care and priority setting, orthopaedics and early mobilisation, ophthalmology, selection of patients for transplantation surgery, neonatal care, and selection of premature babies for survival, have all been omitted.

The basic principles, however, should apply to all specialities and situations. What our research seems to suggest is that there is a lack of a methodological, explicit procedure for the task of risk assessment and management in nursing and midwifery and the necessary record keeping.

The practice of nursing and midwifery will never be reduced to the simple implementation and application of procedures, policies, and codes of practice. Every single sphere of practice demands the exercise of professional discretion, based on experience and education. Each individual patient's care and circumstances must be individually assessed on its own facts. The framework of risk management and assessment provides a structure within which individual care planning can take place and treatment and care provided on the basis of the reasonable standard of care.[42]

We acknowledge the assistance of Rachel Phillips in the literature search for this chapter and Dawn Walters for her helpful comments.

1 NHS Management Executive. *Risk management in the NHS*. London: Department of Health and Social Security 1993.

2 Eagle M. The care of a patient after a caesarian section. *Journal of Wound Care* 1993;2:330–6.
3 Johnson J. Pressure area risk assessment in a neurological setting. *British Journal of Nursing* 1994;3:926–35.
4 Cullum N, Clark M. Intrinsic factors associated with pressure sores in elderly people. *J Adv Nurs* 1992;17:427–31.
5 Dimond BC. Pressure sores: a case to answer. *British Journal of Nursing* 1994; 3:721–7.
6 White LN, Spitz MR. Cancer risk and early detection. *Assessment seminars in oncology nursing*. 1993;9:188–97.
7 Department of Health and Social Security. *Health of the Nations*. London: HMSO 1993; Welsh Office. *Strategic intent and direction and health gain protocols* Wales; 1989–94.
8 Chamorro T, Tarulli D. Strategies for risk management in cancer nursing. *Oncol Nurs Forum* 1990;17:915–20.
9 Wilson LD. Sensory perceptual alteration: diagnosis, prediction, and intervention in the hospitalized adult. *Nurs Clin North Am* 1993;28:747–65.
10 Hawkshaw David A. Day surgery patient telephone survey. *British Journal of Nursing* 1994;3:348–50.
11 *Changing childbirth: report of Expert Maternity Group*. London: HMSO, 1993 (chaired by Baroness Cumberledge).
12 Dimond BC. Midwife managed units. *Modern Midwife* 1994;4:31–3.
13 Kingsley A. First step towards a desired outcome: preventing infection by risk recognition. *Professional Nurse* 1992;7:725–6; 728–9.
14 Foss D, Monagan D. A national survey of physicians' and nurses' attitudes towards endoscope cleaning and the potential of cross-infection. *Gastroenterology Nursing* 1992;15:59–65.
15 United Kingdom Central Council. *Scope of professional practice*. London: UKCC 1992.
16 United Kingdom Central Council. *Scope of professional practice*. London: UKCC 1992:1(paragraph).
17 Hunt G, Wainwright P, eds. *Expanding the role of the nurse* Oxford: Blackwells, 1994.
18 National Association of Theatre Nurses. *The role of the nurse as first assistant in the operating department*. London: NATN, 1993.
19 Department of Health. *Report of the Advisory Group on Nurse Prescribing* London: DHSS, 1989 (chaired by Dr JM Crown).
20 Dimond BC. *The legal aspects of nurse prescribing*. London: Merck Dermatology with Scutari publications 1995.
21 Masso M. The quality assurance dilemma. *Australian Journal of Advanced Nursing* 1989;7:12–22.
22 Tan MW. Occurrence screens: a risk and quality control tool for intravenous nurses. *Journal of Intravenous Nursing* 1990;14:308–11.
23 Lyons YJ. Monitoring practice: an examination of nursing practice in relation to pressure sore prevention and management. *Nursing Times* 1994;20 April: 69–70, 72, 74.
24 Dimond BC. Water births – the legal implications, *Modern Midwife* 1994;4: 12–13.
25 Re C (Refusal of Medical Treatment) 1994 1 FLR 31.
26 Sidaway v Board of Governors of the Bethlem Royal and the Maudsley Hospital (1985) 3 WLR 480.
27 Counsel and Care. The right to take risks. London: April 1993.
28 *Mental Health Act 1983*. London: HMSO 1983 (section 5 (4)).
29 *Health and Safety at Work Act 1974*. London: HMSO 1974 (section 2 (1)).
30 Pastides H. Managing measurable and perceived risk in the occupational setting. *Journal of Ambulatory Care Management* 1994;17:44–52.

31 Kloss D. *Occupational health and the law.* 2nd ed. Blackwells, 1994.
32 Registrar's letter 8/1992 replacing circular PC/89/2 November 1989 United Kingdom Central Council.
33 Sim J. AIDS, Nursing and occupational risk: an ethical analysis. *Journal of Advanced Nursing* 1992;**17**:569–75.
34 Royal College of Nursing working party on back injuries. *Avoiding low back injury among nurses.* London: RCN, 1979.
35 Royal College of Nurses. *An RCN guide for work injured nurses.* London: RCN, 1994.
36 Buckle P. Epidemiological aspects of back pain within the nursing profession. *Int J Nurs Stud* 1987;**23**:319–24.
37 Pilling S, Frank J. Evaluation back up: a lifting risk calculator. *Nursing Standard* 1994;**8**:22–3.
38 Brians LK, Alexander K, Grota P, Chen RWH, Dumas V. The development of the RISK tool for fall prevention. *Rehabilitation Nursing* 1991;**16**:67–9.
39 Health and Safety Executive. *A step by step guide to COSHH assessment.* London: HMSO, 1993.
40 *The Allitt Inquiry.* London: HMSO, 1994 (chaired by Sir Cecil Clothier).
41 Executive letter EL (1993) 51.
42 Bolam v Friern Barnet Hospital Management Committee [1957] 2 All ER 118.

III: Implementation of risk management

18 Essentials of clinical risk management

ROGER V CLEMENTS

Aims of clinical risk management (box 1)

Risk management may broadly be defined as the reduction of harm to an organisation, by identifying and, as far as possible, eliminating risk. The aims of clinical risk management are (*a*) to reduce the frequency of adverse events and harm to patients, (*b*) to reduce the chance of a claim being made, and (*c*) to control the cost of claims that are made. The primary focus is on malpractice, which causes financial losses but also affects the reputation and morale of a trust and its staff. Clinical risk management also involves the continuing care of the injured patients and swift settlements of justified claims. Proper analysis of risk management

---

Box 1—Aims of clinical risk management

- Reducing and, as far as possible, eliminating harm to the patient

- Dealing with the injured patient:
  Continuity of care
  Swift compensation for the justified claimant

- Safeguarding the assets of the organisation:
  Financial
  Reputation
  Staff morale

- Improving the quality of care

---

reporting systems and an audit of clinical complaints also offer invaluable opportunity to improve quality in a way which is securely focused on the welfare of the patient. Improvement of quality must be the highest priority, for only by this means can the exposure to litigation finally be eliminated.

In the new NHS emphasis is rightly on both quality and price. When malpractice results in harm to patients quality is obviously affected, but malpractice also affects the overall cost of care. The provider unit must, firstly, recoup the cost of medical malpractice through its contracts, and therefore successful claims will skew prices. But in a more subtle way poorly handled medical malpractice may damage the reputation of the provider unit, affect the willingness of local practitioners to refer patients, deter patients, and ultimately reduce the size of contracts that are offered. A unit with an effective risk management system, on the other hand, will save money and enhance its reputation. Money is saved not only by improvement of quality but also by early settlement of claims which cannot be resisted, thus keeping money out of the hands of lawyers. The early reporting of adverse events makes possible an economic defence where there is no fault.

Implementing risk management

The principles of industrial and commercial risk management (see Dickson, chapter 2, this volume p. 16) can be applied to the clinical arena:

- Identification
- Analysis
- Control
- Funding.

Funding is at present largely outside the control of individual provider units, though the creation of a central fund (see below) may go some way towards providing the opportunity for prudent management. However, identification and analysis of risks and the steps taken to reduce and control risks are at the heart of clinical risk management.

Several key issues must be considered when a risk management system is established, and these will be discussed in turn:

- Leadership and responsibility
- Developing a risk management team

- Practical issues of implementation
- Cultural changes required
- Continuing care of the injured patient
- Ethical dilemmas
- Support for staff involved in litigation.

Leadership and responsibility: role of the medical director

In most large provider units the broader aspects of risk management (financial aspects, commercial aspects, fire, buildings, etc) will be the responsibility of a steering group led by the finance director. That group is not appropriate to deal with clinical risk, which should have a separate management group which liaises both with the general risk management group and with other quality initiatives within the provider trust.

Risk management must have a high profile in the perspective of the management board. There must be commitment to the concept of clinical risk management at board level, backed up by a written strategy. There must be an executive director of the board charged with personal responsibility for risk management. This will almost certainly be the medical director, whose role is to provide a medical perspective to board decisions, who should be in a position to influence the medical environment both within and outside the provider unit in line with those board decisions. In the NHS Management Executive's document on risk management[2] the medical executive director is not once mentioned. Nevertheless that person can influence complaints monitoring, quality initiatives deriving from complaints, risk management, clinical audit, and claims management. Clinical risk management will therefore primarily be the responsibility of the medical director, although the directors of finance, nursing, and quality will work closely with him or her. Representatives from the clinical directorates may be incorporated in a risk management steering group, although this can make the group rather cumbersome. However the directorates link in with the central department, the role of the clinical director is paramount.

Just as within the trust as a whole the medical director's role is unique and central, so in each directorate the lead clinician must take responsibility for clinical risk management. Otherwise the programme will never carry sufficient weight and acquire the credibility to become effective. Unless the clinical director owns the responsibility for clinical risk management, the directorate will not buy into the process.

337

Developing a risk management team

Two new roles need to be created, that of a claims manager and a risk management coordinator. These roles are very different but in small organisations they may effectively be combined in the same person.

Claims manager

The claims manager is the liaison with the solicitor and the person who effectively instructs solicitors on behalf of the trust. It is the claims manager's responsibility to see that the day to day conduct of legal business suits the trust's agenda. Major decisions about settling or defending claims will be communicated to the solicitors through the claims manager, although he or she will not usually be the person making the decisions. The decision to defend or settle a claim must be a board decision, usually delegated to the medical director. The medical director and claims manager must therefore work closely together in making sure that the solicitors act in the best interest of the trust.

Risk management coordinator

The risk management coordinator has a broader function, including the day to day responsibility for the clinical incident reporting system and collecting data from it. These data must be fed back to the directorates if they are to improve quality. The risk management coordinator should also have a key role in maintaining the standards of the health records. Administration of the complaints procedure might appropriately be delegated to either the claims manager or the risk management coordinator. In most district general hospitals of modest size (£50 m turnover) these roles can conveniently be assumed by one senior manager, directly responsible to the medical director.

Both the claims manager and the risk manager will work most closely with the medical director. This small group would administer the reporting system and would rely on the medical executive director to liaise with each of the clinical directorates and with other board members. Although the clinical director must be responsible for effecting the culture change and for driving the initiative, he or she will depend on his service manager for the day to day running of the reporting system.

338

Practical issues of implementation: reporting system

Central to any clinical risk management system is an adverse outcome reporting system which has the confidence of all members of the organisation. Adverse events are identified from staff reports, although this process may be supplemented by a systematic screening of records. Reports of serious incidents are made before claims are initiated, and while memories are still fresh. The reports are used to create a database to identify common patterns and prevent future incidents. Ideally, patients and relatives are also informed about adverse incidents and action is taken to minimise both the physical and psychological trauma.

Key elements in risk management programmes are educating clinicians about their role in risk management, formalising channels of communication to enable early intervention with patients and their families after adverse incidents, and establishing a strong organisational structure for dealing with the findings of reviews of adverse events. The involvement and personal commitment of senior clinicians are crucial. A first step must therefore be to introduce a reporting system, but alongside must be an educational programme which will secure interest and ultimately ownership. Implementation is best achieved by the following steps.

(1) Identify key risk areas

In any provider unit the key risk areas will usually be self evident. In a district general hospital they are likely to be the accident and emergency department (by volume the biggest risk area); obstetrics, particularly in the labour ward (by quantum the biggest risk area); and the operating theatres.

(2) Take the message to those key areas

The risk management team takes the programme of education to the risk area. For instance, a half day seminar arranged in the accident and emergency department is attended by the key healthcare providers (consultant staff, junior medical staff, senior nursing staff, and main users—for example, orthopaedics, gynaecology, paediatrics, etc). The principles of risk management are explained with due emphasis on the advantages to the quality of care which will accrue.

(3) Allow the healthcare providers to identify trigger events

During the seminar the healthcare providers create their own trigger list of incidents which they think are worth reporting to a

339

risk management system. (If members of the department are to have ownership of the system they must create their own list, then they are likely to respond to it.) They would also be encouraged to modify it with experience so that the list constantly changes. The same process is repeated in the labour ward and in the operating theatres. Box 2 shows the kind of list of trigger events which might result for an average labour ward. Imposition of this list on any labour ward is not intended; it is given only as an example.

Box 2—Trigger events in a labour ward

Apgar score $\leqslant 5$ at 5 minutes
Fetal malformation undiagnosed before birth
Injury to the baby at time of birth
Blood transfusion >3 units
Caesarean section: decision to delivery interval >40 minutes
Third stage or emergency hysterectomy
Failed forceps delivery
Unscheduled return to operating theatre
Stillbirth or neonatal death
Unexpected or late admission to special care baby unit
Third degree tear

---

(4) Institute a reporting system

Having established a list of the trigger events likely to give early warning of patient harm, the risk management department introduces a system of reporting, which above all, must be simple.

For example, one particular hospital uses a double sided printed A4 sheet (see appendix). It avoids large numbers of boxes to tick and it avoids difficult questions, simply requiring the identification of the incident, the carers, and the onlookers, with a small space for free script to allow the reporter the opportunity to describe what happened. The form is constantly under review, has recently been modified, and will continue to be modified. Anyone can use the form. Staff of all grades and of all disciplines from every profession are encouraged to report adverse outcomes. This inevitably leads to much over-reporting of trivial incidents, which is not discouraged. Nobody is dissuaded from making a report.

Non-medical staff quickly see the advantages of the adverse outcome reporting system and seldom need much encouragement to implement it. Without the doctors the risk management programme will not be effective and it is essential that the medical staff should understand what is in it for them. Reporting adverse outcomes or near misses to a risk management reporting system should be associated with reward not punishment.

(5) Monitor and analyse results

The forms are sent initially to the manager at local level—the service manager or equivalent. The service manager has the discretion to decide whether the incident is trivial and of no consequence, when no further action need be taken. If the incident seems to be an important indicator of a quality issue but is unlikely to have harmed a patient on this occasion the manager will take local action but may not forward the form. Only those incidents that relate to harm which might potentially lead to litigation need be sent to the central risk management department. There they are scrutinised again. Some will be rejected as being important to quality but not to the risk of litigation. Only those important for the risk of litigation will be entered on to the database.

The advantages of such a simple system are that it allows:

- The local manager to assess quality issues
- Identification of clusters
- Fuller investigation of the real exposure to litigation.

If the effect on quality is to be maximised the adverse outcome reporting system inherent in any clinical risk management programme must feed in to the other quality initiatives of the trust. Unless the adverse reporting system is an effective part of clinical audit it will not have its maximum effect on quality. Identifying a cluster of adverse outcomes may lead to the correction of a system or the counselling of a staff member. It should not be used for discipline.

(6) Investigate, when appropriate

When an incident is sufficiently important to be entered on to the database a full investigation will take place. The risk management department will require local managers to obtain statements from all healthcare providers involved with the patient. This enables the clinical director and the medical executive director to take an early view on whether an action, if brought by the patient, could be defended. When, months or years later, the "letter before action" arrives, the risk management department can instruct solicitors in an effective and timely manner without the unseemly and usually fruitless search through the archives for members of staff who have long since left not only the trust but usually the country.

Cultural change and difficulties of implementation

A risk management reporting system will inevitably be resisted by doctors. Doctors perceive adverse outcome reporting as a threat to their reputation and their professional integrity. To assure an effective clinical risk management programme a major cultural change will be needed to achieve *acceptance* by clinicians.

Conversely, patients' organisations perceive risk management as a way of covering up when things go wrong. It is therefore important to establish, from the very beginning that risk management:

- Does not concern discipline
- Does not lead to covering up when things go wrong
- Does not encourage "defensive" medicine
- Does not involve creating complex causation arguments to defeat the plaintiff.

Risk management is about avoiding litigation—not about evasion.

To convince clinicians that risk management works, the medical director initially (and subsequently each clinical director) must explain to colleagues the advantages that a risk management programme can bring in quality and price to the organisation. It is essential to eliminate the fear which adverse outcome reporting naturally generates. Doctors need to be reassured that they will not be disciplined for reporting adverse outcomes even if fault is established. They need further to be reassured that one of the main advantages of a satisfactory risk management programme is that their reputations can more effectively be protected when they are not at fault.

Convincing the doctors is not easy; much depends on the individual leadership of clinical directors and the personalities of the senior doctors concerned. For instance, it may be relatively easy in the women's and children's directorate, perhaps because they are already familiar with the threat of litigation and the need to change practice in order to avoid it, and in the accident and emergency department, the high volume part of the industry where errors seem to be more frequent, for a variety of understandable reasons, not least the pressure of work out of hours. Difficulty may be encountered in the directorate of surgery. Part of the mythology

342

of surgery is that the surgeon is in complete control of the operation and therefore completely responsible for everything that happens. Surgeons may feel particularly threatened by the idea that a member of the nursing staff should report an untoward incident—causing them to be brought to account. The pattern of response may vary but, whatever the personalities involved, it is essential that at the beginning key staff in the major areas are targeted and persuaded of the benefits, otherwise the programme will fail.

Continuing care of the injured patient

An injured patient requires more, not less, care than patients with a successful outcome. Paradoxically, it is precisely at the moment when an accident happens that the caring seems to stop. At least that is how the patient perceives it.

Risk management means caring for the patient after the injury. Care includes the following:

- Continuing to treat—or sometimes arranging for alternative care if trust has broken down
- An explanation of what happened
- An explanation of *why* it happened
- Remedial action where possible
- Compensation when appropriate.

Thus the advantages for the patient are clear cut: early investigation of the cause of harm; if no fault, a clear explanation and early settlement.

A good clinical risk management system does not disadvantage a patient with a justified claim. It does of course withhold the payment of damages from those who are not entitled to them. That is only right. But it is also right that those patients should receive a full and early explanation as to *why* they are not entitled to damages. Conversely, the patient who is entitled to damages receives an early settlement without money needlessly passing into the pockets of lawyers.

A good provider unit should establish a reputation for frank explanation and early settlement of cases with fault. A trust with such a policy would quickly gain the reputation for vigorous and successful defence where there was no fault, and the incidence of litigation against it would fall. Litigation is in the interest only of lawyers. The plaintiff wants an early explanation and settlement (when appropriate); good clinical risk management achieves this.

343

Ethical dilemmas

Occasionally, the caring team may become aware that the patient has been injured while the patient continues to believe that he or she has had the best possible care. Under those circumstances the provider unit is obliged to give the patient a full explanation, consistent only with the patient's best interest.

Lord Donaldson has several times drawn attention to the obligation placed on lawyers in such circumstances.[3]

> Both branches of the legal profession have a salutary rule of professional ethics requiring them to advise their client to consult another practitioner if they consider that they may have been in breach of their duty of care and that this breach has led to loss or damage on the part of their client.

He goes on to plead for a similar frankness from doctors.

> The position in relation to the medical profession is, or should be, in many respects the same. The duty of care does not involve the doctor in making a definitive judgement on his own professional conduct and communicating that judgement to the patient. Save in a clear case, he may be less likely than the lawyer to be the person best able to decide. But, in contrast to the position of the lawyer, he has a very special duty of disclosure.

Doctors who find themselves in such a dilemma should find support from their senior managers for a full and honest disclosure to the patient of the unsuspected accident. Caring does not stop when an accident occurs; part of that caring is to make sure that the patient understands what has happened and why.

Support for staff involved in litigation

In return for active participation in risk management, all clinical staff should feel supported and protected by the system; the programme must offer support to the doctor, who often feels vulnerable and isolated when a patient is injured. Few doctors cope well with the knowledge that they have harmed a patient. Practical help should include the following.

- An opportunity to talk through the experience with senior colleagues
- An inquiry process which is supportive, not confrontational
- Readily available legal advice—for example, before appearing in a coroner's court
- Shared experience with those who have had a similar experience.

344

Before crown indemnity, medical staff were used to relying on their medical defence organisations for such support. The defence societies are still available to give informal advice to individual doctors, but they are no longer involved in litigation for hospital doctors and that role should be increasingly subsumed by the risk management department. Similarly nurses and midwives tended to refer to their unions for support in litigation. Although the unions were seldom involved directly in the litigation process, the nurse or midwife often felt protected by the union. A good risk management department should be able to provide just such support for all staff.

The interests of the individual will not necessarily always coincide directly with those of the provider unit. Nor did they in the days when doctors were "protected" by their medical defence organisations. There are countless examples of litigation conducted primarily for the benefit of the medical defence organisation, with doctors coming a poor second in the process, for they were never the first client of the lawyers conducting the action. Doctors tended to assume that the defence societies were exercising their paternalism benignly in the interests of the individual; often, though, the societies were acting either in their own interests or in what they perceived to be the interests of the profession as a whole.

So with individuals and provider units a conflict will occasionally arise. Doctors perceive this conflict most starkly where the trust might be inclined to settle a case which, in their view, can be defended. They would be offended by the admission of liability where they believe none exists. But whose reputation is stained thereby? Doctors need to be reassured that in these days of crown indemnity they are most unlikely to be named in any suit. In any event, in NHS practice an admission of liability is made on behalf of the provider unit, not by an individual. The doctors whose reputation is harmed by malpractice are those whose cases attract publicity. They are doctors who are defended in public—in the courts.

A settlement with or without admission of liability seldom attracts publicity in any personal sense. When doctors' names are published it is because the accusations have been made in open court and, substantiated or not, the accusations can be repeated by the newspapers without redress. The newspapers report the action on the first day of the trial, seldom later. Plaintiff counsel speaks on the first day of the trial cataloguing the misdeeds of the doctor. Even if the doctor is fully exonerated, even if the judge finds on

345

the 14th day of the trial that no blame attaches, even if the decision goes for the defence, nobody gets to know about it because by then the newspapers have lost interest. "Doctor not guilty of negligence" is not news. So to safeguard the reputation of the medical staff, the simple answer is to keep them out of court. Doctors should be reassured that the discreet and early settlement of a case which might attract publicity, whether or not the court found for the plaintiff, may well be in the interest not only of the trust but of the individual doctor whose reputation is thereby protected.

Response to litigation

When a "letter before action" is received, the risk management team, led by the medical director, should determine the response of the trust. It will not always be appropriate to instruct solicitors. In many cases the matter is trivial, the issues are clear cut, and an offer of a very modest settlement may deflect a potentially costly legal action. It is important to remember the common experience of experts and plaintiff solicitors—namely, that often the injured patient seeks only an explanation and an apology and is not *primarily* motivated by money. Nevertheless, most "letters before action" will need to be forwarded to the trust's legal advisers so that the matter may be assessed and an appropriate response formulated. Under no circumstances should doctors ever be allowed to respond personally to a "letter before action." The skill and responsibility of the claims manager, supported by the medical director, does not end with the handing over of the "letter before action": it must include the proper *instruction* of solicitors.

Traditionally, medical malpractice has been handed over by doctors to their medical defence organisations and by health authorities to their legal advisors, with virtually no input thereafter. The matter was run at the speed convenient to the lawyers and the defence organisations with the inevitable result that actions were unnecessarily protracted and costs escalated. That is not in the interest of the provider unit, and it must be a priority of any risk management system to prevent it.

Instruction here carries the ordinary English meaning. The medical executive director should expect from his or her lawyers exactly what any individual instructing solicitor has a right to expect—namely, competent technical advice and compliance with the client's wishes. This means that when an in house investigation has determined that a matter is no longer defensible the lawyers should be instructed to settle it. Expert opinions can often be dispensed with when the in house opinion is clear and decisive. When the matter is to be defended the medical director should ensure that his or her clinical colleagues are involved in the choice of expert and are kept informed, throughout the conduct of the case, so that they can be of maximum help to the legal team. In some respects, this is the most difficult culture change to achieve, for it threatens traditional practices of two professions—the lawyers as well as the doctors! Although it is essential that defensible claims should be vigorously defended, the facts of medicolegal life must be clearly understood.

- Quantum (that is, damages) increases, in absolute terms, with time. The later a claim is settled or lost, the greater quantum is likely to be, leaving aside inflation and the costs of the action
- Failure to settle quickly an indefensible claim can only add further to the anger of the injured patient (or family) and so damage further the reputation of the trust
- Costs accumulate on both sides. If a claim is indefensible the plaintiff will continue to incur costs (ultimately payable by the defendant) assembling evidence to prove liability until that liability is admitted
- The admission of liability at the door of the court almost always represents a massive waste of public money. Seldom have the facts of the case changed; seldom is there any *different* reason for assessing a case as indefensible on the day of settlement than on any of the preceding days, weeks, or months that have passed since the first intimation of a legal action.

Vacillation puts money into the pockets of lawyers. Incidentally, it usually increases, in real terms, the quantum paid to the plaintiff. An effective team of claims manager and medical director should have as their primary objective the prevention of *any* unnecessary costs paid to lawyers on both sides.

When claims should be settled

There will be times when it becomes clear to the medical director that the potential cost of defending an action will greatly exceed any possible quantum. It may be appropriate for him or her to advise the finance director that, even though there may be a chance of defending the action, settlement would be wiser. Settlements at the door of the court occur, mostly, because the defendants took a realistic view of the case only when their minds were finally concentrated by the need to produce evidence in court. The prospect of a lengthy court battle, only to lose, suddenly seems unattractive. Tragically, by the time that moment arrives many thousands of pounds in costs have already been spent by both sides, costs which will have to be borne by the provider unit. Not only that but (except in the Court of Appeal) costs orders against plaintiffs receiving legal aid are not enforced and success after many days in court may prove something of a pyhrric victory if the costs incurred by the defendants exceed the plaintiff's (disappointed) expectations of quantum!

Care is required in these matters. The unit must not get the reputation for being an easy pushover, willing to settle any case where quantum is modest. Some cases have to be defended, if necessary in open court. In making such decisions the medical director and his or her trust board colleagues need to consider how best to preserve their assets, not only financial assets but also reputation and staff morale.

It has been suggested that creating a central fund may reduce the ability of local provider units to make such decisions in their own interests—may insist on cases where there is medical "merit" being defended even though it makes no financial sense to do so. This was strongly hinted at by Brian Marsden, deputy director of finance and corporate information, of the NHS Executive at the conference on prevention and control of clinical negligence at the Royal College of Surgeons in May 1994.

> It is recommended that Trusts should have prime responsibility for handling the majority of claims. They would use solicitors from a nationwide panel approved by the Fund—with the Fund manager being consulted before a claim is settled and having discretion to take over management of any claim considered novel, or likely to create precedent, or to be costly.[4]

Interference, to prevent trusts settling small claims expeditiously and cheaply would be a mistake. Save only for the most exceptional circumstances, such decisions should belong to the local provider unit.

1 Dickson G. Principles of risk management. *Quality in Health Care* 1995;4:75–9.

2 NHS Management Executive. *Risk management in the NHS*. London: Department of Health, 1993.
3 Lord Donaldson. Foreword. In: Clements RV, ed. *Safe practice in obstetrics and gynaecology: a medicolegal handbook*. Edinburgh: Churchill Livingstone, 1994.
4 Marsden B. Funding clinical negligence claims in prevention and control of clinical negligence. *Clinician in Management* 1994;3(suppl 1):4.

19 Implementation of audit and risk management: a protocol

R W BEARD, A M O'CONNOR

In this chapter we have distinguished between audit and risk management. Audit is defined as "an official examination of accounts," and in British medicine to date it has been just that—a review of the process of clinical activity with little attempt to change clinical practice. Risk management, on the other hand, is the introduction of agreed changes in practice, the effectiveness of which is assessed by a decline or otherwise in adverse outcomes. When viewed in this way, audit and risk management are interdependent with audit showing the way to risk management, which in turn may alter the results of audit.

Review of audit and risk management in the maternity services

National concern about the high mortality among pregnant women in 1928 of 440 deaths per 100 000 births resulted in a confidential enquiry into individual maternal deaths occurring during 1930–2. In 1952, agreement was reached between the Royal College of Obstetricians and Gynaecologists and the then Ministry of Health to start a triennial series of confidential enquiries into all maternal deaths in England and Wales. This now covers all such deaths in the United Kingdom. At the same time, national perinatal mortality surveys were done in 1946, 1958, and 1972.

In recent years, surveys have been done within regional health authorities, (most of which have a population of 2–4 million) as part of programmes to systematise maternity care and improve the provision of specialist services such as neonatal intensive care.[1-3] Commenting on these surveys Paterson et al wrote that "Admirable though this process of review at all levels may be, one has to ask how effective it has been in improving practice."[4] A true measure of the effectiveness of these surveys in this respect is difficult to obtain because of the inexorable downward trend of maternal and perinatal mortality throughout the western world regardless of whether or not national inquiries have been done. In Britain there is a long history of local audit in maternity units, usually in the form of regular perinatal mortality meetings and the publication of annual reports. Unfortunately, there is evidence that often little is achieved from this activity. Banfield, who surveyed the audit practice in 15 maternity units, commented that "Perinatal mortality meetings, as currently arranged, do not satisfy modern conditions of clinical audit in practice as well as in theory."[5] He goes on to suggest that the process could only become effective by introducing a formal comparison of the performance of individual units with other units leading to the development of norms.

There is little doubt that the steady increase in medical litigation in recent years has been an incentive to make audit more effective. It is necessary, however, to question the use of aggregated data alone as a means of effective audit. Lomas et al reported that the introduction of nationally endorsed guidelines in Canada designed to reduce the caesarean section rate and based on sound aggregated hospital data in Ontario, had no significant effect on clinical practice.[6] Brennan et al, reporting on the results of the Harvard Medical Practice Study, commented that a substantial amount of injury to patients occurs as a result of medical mismanagement.[7] Few of these injuries are documented in the routine collection of data. In the United States, it has been recognised for several years that if medical litigation is to be effectively reduced, obstetric risk factors must be controlled by what is now known as risk management. Localio et al showed that the higher the caesarean section rate the greater the number of malpractice claims that were made.[8] In 1985 the Medical Malpractice Insurance (MMI) Companies Inc, presumably out of concern for the escalating costs of litigation in obstetrics, introduced a risk management programme into 220 participating hospitals that had a maternity unit.[9] The programme, which had been developed in collaboration with the

351

medical profession, was designed to improve patient care and reduce obstetric malpractice claims. Guidelines were drawn up which reflected prevailing professional standards, such as a maximum time of 30 minutes from the moment a decision is taken to deliver by emergency caesarean section to time of skin incision, and, in time, this became part of the agreed practice of participating hospitals. In addition to regular consultations to help hospitals meet agreed objectives, it was recognised that for the guidelines to become a part of routine practice, it was essential to continually focus attention on the success or otherwise of their implementation. This was achieved by regular data collection and feedback to

Table 19.1 *Frequency of clinical activity and outcome, and medicolegal activity from the start of MMI risk modification programme in 1985 and 1992*

	1985	1988	1992
Baseline fetal monitoring (%)	42	90	95
Fetal monitoring used with oxytocin infusion (%)	—	82	99
Neonatal deaths/1000	—	2·0	1·3
Three year average of successful claims/10 000 deliveries	4·0	2·2	0·6

Modified from Knox, 1994[9]

participating clinicians. Table 19.1 shows the changes in some clinical outcomes and the cost of litigation over the eight years when the programme was operative. Three important changes indicative of the success of the programme are apparent from these figures: (*a*) adherence to the protocol for fetal monitoring was virtually 100% by 1992; (*b*) neonatal mortality, which is a good indicator of quality outcome, fell by 46%, (*c*) the number of malpractice claims fell by 61%. The MMI initiative can be viewed as an interesting example of how effective local initiatives can be and support our view that locally based risk management is likely to be the only way of altering clinical practice.

Vincent and Clements[10] summarised the apparent success of risk management when they stated that "At the heart of most programmes are methods of early identification of adverse events. ... Reports of serious incidents are made before claims are initiated and while memories still fresh. ... Ideally patients and relatives are also informed about adverse incidents and action is taken to minimize both physical and psychological trauma." They highlighted the key elements of an effective programme, such as the education of clinicians about the objectives and application of risk management, early contact with patients and their families after

352

an adverse outcome, and the importance of having an organisational structure that ensures the application of lessons learnt from adverse events. Morlock and Malitz make the critical point that the system will not work without the collaboration and personal commitment of senior clinicians.[11]

A risk management programme that relies solely on reporting adverse events without attention to the way in which care is being provided is unlikely to lead to much change in practice. Risk management needs the back up of an effective review of the existing service, when many defects can be found. In most maternity services, little attention is paid to the disposition of staff so that they can be employed where they are most needed. Communication between staff about important clinical events, interpretation of these events, and accompanying investigations are often assumed to be adequate but experience has shown repeated dangerous inconsistencies in these functions. Behind the performance of these routine activities lies an assumption that trainee doctors and midwives are learning key skills. The British method of training doctors, which is historically an apprentice based system, lacks the formal components that are so necessary with the increasing complexities of modern obstetric practice. If, to this problem is added insufficient staff to cope with the workload, sleeplessness, and a confident belief among the junior staff that one has to "learn from one's mistakes", it is not surprising that, despite well intentioned efforts to audit practice, disasters involving mothers or their babies continue to recur.

Organisational risk in a maternity unit

The first step in achieving a consensus view on how to reduce risk in the St Mary's maternity unit was to set up a medicolegal group. This was established because of our apparent failure to prevent obstetric disasters despite having the same pattern of events, and many of which we considered were avoidable. The group was given a brief by the obstetric consultants and senior midwives "to identify and assess the risks existing within the practice of the unit and to recommend practical steps to reduce these risks thereby leading to an improvement in care." The membership of the group was the clinical director, a senior obstetrician (RWB), a paediatrician, an obstetric anaesthetist, the labour ward manager, a hospital administrator, and a solicitor experienced in medicolegal claims. A senior registrar was both a member and secretary to the group. Eighteen months later, the group reported to the Maternity Services Liaison Committee and after discussion, agreement was reached on the recommendations. After publication of the report, the hospital trust set up a separate risk management group and it was this body that eventually agreed to the appointment of a maternity risk manager (AO'C) with the specific purpose of assessing the development of clinical risk management in other specialties.

The major areas of risk considered by the medicolegal group are presented next.

(1) Competence of staff

Competence can be generally defined as an ability to treat a patient effectively in most circumstances. It was recognised from the outset that risk in the care of the pregnant woman mostly stems from inappropriate decisions being taken by medical or midwifery staff due to lack of knowledge or experience.

It is usually assumed in British hospital practice that appropriately qualified and experienced doctors or midwives can function competently as soon as they take up a new post. Such a view fails to take into account the time taken to adapt to local practices and a new organisational structure. Good examples of this are the use of protocols and the operation of the team system of care. How a newly appointed individual practitioner acquires sufficient competence in new surroundings to treat patients needs to be resolved. This is a particular problem for the locum doctor and agency midwife. Often, without prior experience, they may be placed in a post with considerable clinical responsibility with little or no assessment of their competence or supervision of their work. At previous audit meetings within the unit, this problem has often been identified as a major factor leading to an adverse outcome.

Recommendations

● Newly appointed doctors and midwives to the permanent staff should attend a one day orientation course at which they will be introduced to the clinical practice (protocols) and management procedures of the unit. These staff will be supervised by the regular staff until they are deemed to be competent. Competence will be assessed by observing the performance of agreed practical procedures and a multiple choice questionnaire

354

- The employment of locums will be reduced to a minimum by the use of internal cover. Such a system should not be used if it results in any doctor having to work more than the statutory number of working hours per week or if sessional time allotted for educational activities is eroded. If a locum or agency midwife is appointed by the clinical director or director of midwifery, the activity of that person must be fully supervised by a member of the regular staff, and at no time should that person be allowed to practise independently until judged to be competent by a senior member of staff

- Special attention needs to be paid to defining the criteria which should be applied to the transfer of responsibility of care from the midwife to the doctor of a patient who may develop a complication of pregnancy, after having previously been regarded as normal. Experience has shown that risk is increased if a midwife retains care for too long, or if a doctor, out of ignorance or faulty decision making, fails to accept responsibility for such a case.

(2) Organisation of the service

It is essential that each maternity unit should review the way in which care is provided. This varies widely between units so that inevitably in many units best use is not made of available staff. More seriously, adequate provision of staff may not be made for risk areas such as the labour ward. The introduction of organised team care in the unit has undoubtedly improved the personal contact of midwives and doctors with patients but has resulted in shortages of midwifery staff, particularly on the postnatal ward. Timetables of junior and senior medical staff, which have developed over the years, were sometimes found to be inappropriate for modern obstetric care. For example, it was common to find staff working in a clinic or in an operating theatre when they were also on call for the labour ward, which resulted in a less than acceptable service being available for either activity. There is a need to ensure that senior medical staff are always available for obstetric emergencies and the Royal College of Obstetricians and Gynaecologists have recommended that consultants should have two designated labour ward sessions per week in their contracts.[12] If this is to be fully implemented, it has to be recognised that labour ward practice is a 24 hour activity. Hospital trusts must make provision for doctors to have time off to compensate for duties out of hours. The inevitable conclusion must be that to provide effective cover, more medical staff are required. This is less of a problem for the midwives whose working hours are already limited by statute to a $37\frac{1}{2}$ hour working week.

Practice protocols to aid the organisation of routine maternity care have been used effectively to improve practice for many years. However, they need regular review to keep up with advances in practice recommendations made as a result of audit within the unit, and to remind all staff of what had been agreed in the past.

Recommendations

- The labour ward should be staffed at all times by a registrar and a senior house officer who have no other designated duties. When on duty, consultants should visit the labour ward at least once a day and should always be 20 minutes or less from the unit.[13]
- The clinical director of the maternity unit is responsible for ensuring that at all times the most effective use of staff is made. With the reduction of hours for junior doctors and the time required for more formal teaching of junior staff, care must be taken to ensure that the demands on staff do not become excessive. Resolution of the problem may only occur with the acceptance by the Department of Health that, in some specialties, more staff will have to be employed.
- A senior member of staff should be designated as responsible for ensuring that all practice protocols are applied effectively and are updated at regular intervals.

(3) Communication and consent to treatment

Experience has shown that there is often a pronounced discrepancy between a woman's perception and expectation of the care she will receive in pregnancy and the realistic limits of what is possible for the maternity services to provide. This is partly due to a change in attitude among patients from one of total acceptance of care in the health service to a much more questioning approach, encouraged by the *patients' charter* and *changing childbirth*.[14] These sometimes unrealistic expectations of service provision and a repetitive cycle of adverse events followed by insufficient explanation for these events has increasingly led patients and their families to resort to litigation as the only means of obtaining satisfaction.

In recent years, there has been an increasing acknowledgement by obstetricians and midwives that patients and their partners should be involved in decisions which may influence their pregnancies. For example, delivery by caesarean section may be fully justified, but, because the surgical procedure carries a small but definite risk to the mother, she is entitled to an explanation of the rationale for the intervention. This being so, for what procedures should it be necessary to obtain consent? In general, a useful guideline is that consent should be obtained for any procedure which is an intervention. At present, an intervention is not always accompanied by an explanation as to why it is necessary and undoubtedly, on occasions, patients are none the wiser for the explanation they do receive. It would be helpful to consider providing a written explanation for some of the more common procedures to reinforce what the individual clinician will have said. Attendant risks of the procedure should be included as part of the description. It is recognised that to give meaningful information to women before *any* emergency intervention in labour is an almost insuperable problem.

Recommendations

- On the first visit to a maternity unit for booking, all women should be given a general account of pregnancy such as is contained in the *Pregnancy Book* distributed by the Health Education Authority.[15] The contents of this book should serve as the basis for antenatal classes to describe the service provided by the maternity unit. The opportunity should be taken during these classes to explain how this knowledge will enable patients to be involved in the management of their pregnancies
- Particular care should be taken to ensure that a patient is given a full explanation of any intervention during a pregnancy that is associated with risk to the patient of an adverse outcome. This may be the result of the condition for which the intervention is being recommended or as a consequence of the procedure itself. Examples of procedures requiring an explanation and consent are:

  - Investigations to detect fetal anomalies such as chorion villus sampling, amniocentesis, cordiocentesis, and including investigations that are non-invasive but which may lead to an offer of termination of pregnancy, such as the triple test and fetal anomaly scanning
  - Termination of pregnancy
  - Management of preterm labour, including fetal therapy
  - Elective and emergency caesarean section

357

- Any other procedure which carries risk to the mother and/or baby such as external cephalic version, or induction of labour
- Prescription of any drug.

(4) Communication between members of the care team

Failure of staff to communicate important information about a patient to each other is potentially a major source of risk leading to an adverse outcome. The effective functioning of the team system of care is dependent on a free exchange of information so that the advice of more senior members of the team can be sought. This, in turn, relies on the ready availability of members of the team which brings into question the appropriateness of duty rotas relative to existing timetables and the effectiveness of existing communication systems used for medical emergencies. At any time of the day, difficulty in contacting staff may arise when they are outside the hospital or involved in other activities in the hospital. Examples of this are on call staff, whether an obstetrician or anaesthetist, who are involved in an operation elsewhere or who experience difficulty in responding immediately to a bleep call—for example, if they are caught in heavy traffic. It is recognised that such delay, even a few minutes, may lead to junior staff taking decisions beyond their competence.

Recommendations

- Ready recourse to consultation with more experienced members of the team needs to be repeatedly emphasised to junior doctors and midwives as a routine part of the process for dealing with any but the most straightforward of problems. Communication can also be improved by regular formal rounds on the labour ward and all staff being instantly contactable when on duty. Senior staff who have to leave the hospital when on duty, should be supplied with a portable telephone by the unit.

(5) Patient records and information

Records are a means of assisting the clinician in the management of a patient by providing a record of preceding events. Although clinical records are not written primarily for medicolegal purposes, they must, for both clinical and medicolegal reasons, be a bona fide account of all clinical events, decisions, and relevant discussions with the patient and between colleagues. As such they must be easy to read and clearly attributable. Handwritten notes rarely conform to these standards and a random survey of maternity records in this unit recently showed that in 60% of cases it was not possible to determine who had written the note.

Investigations that are essential to patient care are sometimes mislaid or filed without being shown to the doctor who has requested them. The result is that an appropriate decision may not be taken on the future management of the patient. This particularly applies to fetal cardiotocograph records, which are difficult to store and are rarely accompanied by a management decision before filing in the records.

Recommendations

- All events relevant to the clinical condition of the patient, including discussions held with her about any aspect of care and outcome, must be recorded in her records
- Notes must always be legible, timed and dated, and attributable to the person who wrote them by means of his or her name written in capitals or printed with a stamp
- The results of all investigations must be signed as having been read by the person who ordered them, and a note made in the clinical record as to whether or not action was taken and what type of action this was. It is suggested that fetal cardiotocographs are stored by attaching them sequentially to adhesive strip on backing paper used for pathology reports. A stamp should be provided in the antenatal clinic, wards, and labour ward with details of information required from the interpretation of traces and subsequent management.

(6) Audit at unit level

A review of medical audit and education within the maternity unit showed that: (1) regular case presentations of major adverse events, usually perinatal deaths, took place every two weeks. Attendance of both obstetric and paediatric staff at these meetings was good but conclusions from the case presentations were limited by the fact that it was rare for there to have been prior discussion so that there was an agreed view about the case among staff involved in the case before the meeting. If a consensus is reached no way exists for applying the lessons learnt. (2) The St Mary's Maternity Information System (SMMIS) provides an excellent source of validated data for comparison of obstetric outcomes between the unit and other units in the region. The system has proved invaluable for documentation and communication, but a mechanism has yet to be agreed for using the data to change local practice. (3) Caesarean section meetings, held weekly to try and limit the seemingly inexorable rise in the caesarean section rate, have served as a useful forum for discussion among junior doctors and midwives. Unfortunately, although the meetings improved the liaison between medical and midwifery staff, they have had no significant effect on reducing the caesarean section rate. (4) Efforts to provide in service education for all medical staff have also been relatively ineffective. Attendance was poor despite a regular programme of seminars and lectures by outside speakers accompanied by encouragement, rearrangement of timetables, and agreement from junior medical staff that educational content is apposite to their needs. The conclusions drawn from this experience is that the present system has failed, not because junior staff do not recognise the need for this type of education, but because they are so busy that they either cannot attend because of inflexibility of timetables or because they need the time for relaxation. Senior staff have become disillusioned by the poor attendance, and there is general agreement that the in service education initiative has failed in its present form. (5) Table 19.2 shows that the potential cost of outstanding claims against the unit up to 1993 was a major cause for concern.

Table 19.2 *Number and estimated cost of likely claims from a maternity unit delivering about 2400 women per year*

Details of ongoing obstetric claims:	
Number of claims	24 (four proceedings served)
Period covered when claim filed	1987–93
Estimated cost of claims (£)	
Range	20 000–500 000
Total	4 769 000

Recommendations

- A programme of in service education and evaluation (annex 1) should be introduced. Time for these activities should be created within the existing clinical timetable, and in future junior staff should be required in their contract to attend the programme of seminars and lectures
- A risk management board should be formed which would be responsible for considering all adverse events listed in annex 2 and making recommendations on ways of reducing them.

- A risk manager should be appointed who would be responsible for the following activities:

  - Coordinating the daily quality and risk management activities of the maternity directorate
  - Fostering a cooperative and trustful relationship with all health care personnel working in the maternity directorate
  - Organising and writing of minutes and agendas of the risk management board
  - Ensuring that recommendations made by the board are implemented
  - Presenting to the risk management board all cases with an adverse outcome and, in detail, those cases where substandard practice has been identified
  - Presentation, at regular intervals, to all members of the unit, data on adverse outcomes and comparative data of activity in other hospitals collated from SMMIS
  - Organising the in service education programme for the maternity directorate with a designated senior obstetrician and midwife.

The risk manager

The medicolegal committee recognised from the outset the need to create a new post because of the varied duties of the post. Many difficulties would face the new risk manager because of the developmental nature of the post. Not only would the activities laid down in the job description require justification but it was likely that many professional staff would initially regard the whole process of risk management as threatening. For this reason, emphasis was placed on the need to select a person who was not only dedicated to the work but who would be acceptable to all members of staff. In practice, what was required was an experienced and personable midwife with knowledge of how to handle data (use of computer, understanding of statistics, a postgraduate degree). The person would be expected to develop risk management in such a way that all staff would accept and apply recommended changes in practice. It was made clear from the outset what the activities would be and to whom the appointee would be responsible. It was suggested that the risk manager should collect activity data daily from the labour ward and neonatal unit on adverse events (annex 2) involving any patient or her baby.

361

Table 19.3 *Audit of nine months' experience of adverse events at St Mary's Hospital maternity unit*

| Total deliveries during period | No of patients affected | Adverse events | | | | |
		Numbers	Maternal	Fetal/ neonatal	Severe	Less severe
2307	211 (9·1%)	366	286	80	14	197

Information would also be obtained from the computer, labour ward delivery book, the notes, laboratory reports, and by talking to staff.

Table 19.3 gives a summary of information on adverse events collected over the first five months after the appointment of a risk manager (AO'C). This shows how often such events occur, and provides a yardstick to judge whether recommended changes in clinical practice are proving to be effective. All serious events such as perinatal or maternal deaths and "near misses" are now investigated in detail. Once the investigation has been initiated, the procedure shown in figure 19.1 is followed. The risk manager is responsible for organising the investigation and ensuring that the specified timetable is adhered to. The consultant responsible for the care of the patient heads the enquiry. It is essential that within 24 hours of a perinatal death, the patient and her partner are seen by the consultant obstetrician and if relevant, the consultant paediatrician who presents an account of events that led to the death, previously agreed with both care teams. After consultation with all staff involved in the event, the consultant writes a report that provides a basis for discussion with the patient and her family at the postnatal visit and also any counselling considered to be necessary for staff involved in the case. Within eight weeks of the event, the report is considered by the risk management board when the case will be presented at a unit audit meeting with relevant recommendations.

Risk management board

The purpose of the risk management board is to consider all cases with a defined major adverse event (see annex 2), to determine whether substandard care was involved, and to make recommendations to the clinical director arising from such cases.

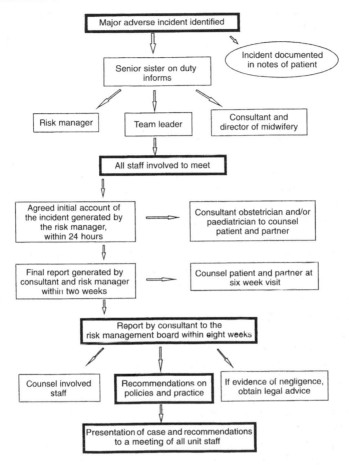

Figure 19.1   *Risk management process.*

The board is chaired by a senior obstetrician and has a senior midwifery, paediatric, and anaesthetic representative, and a member of the junior medical staff. It meets every two to four weeks with an agenda agreed by the chairman and risk manager. The effectiveness of this body is heavily dependent on the provision of reports being freely given within the time frame described in fig. 19.1.

The first objective of an investigation of a major adverse event is to establish this procedure so that staff recognise the benefits of achieving a consensus view of events as soon as possible after the event has occurred. The concern that is often expressed is that in

363

the event of legal proceedings being instituted, written reports are available under law to the plaintiff. This concern can be overcome by confining the permanent written report to a factual account of events as they took place without adding value judgements. These reports are not filed with the case notes. As yet, no final decision has been taken on whether the proceedings of the board which involve substandard care should be included in the minutes of any meeting. This is an important issue because the knowledge that a permanent record will be made may well discourage staff involved in a case from providing a full and honest account of events leading up to an adverse outcome. In British law, unlike the law of many of the states in the United States, all documents relating to a case that goes to litigation have to be surrendered to the plaintiff's solicitors.

To date the risk management board have met on six occasions and the following recommendations have been implemented:

- Introduction of a system for the education and supervision of junior staff
- Supervision of new medical and midwifery staff, and locums that fulfills the recommendations of the medicolegal committee
- Development of an agreed system for preparing reports and counselling staff and patients with their partners (figure 19.1)
- A more systematic approach to the counselling of patients
- Advice to medical and/or midwifery staff involved in cases considered to have avoidable events
- Acceptance by the trust of the need for a safer means by which patients enter the maternity unit at night
- Provision of adequate facilities to use a labour ward as an operating theatre in an emergency

It is recognised by the risk management board that, if clinical practice is to be improved, it will be necessary to introduce a system for ensuring that clinical protocols are adhered to. The fact that adverse events are now continuously and reliably recorded should provide a useful yardstick as to whether protocols are an effective means of improving practice.

Conclusion

The audit of our present maternity service has identified many organisational defects that are a potential source of substandard practice. The recommendations to improve the service that were made by the medicolegal committee have been accepted by the maternity directorate and are gradually being implemented. As a result of this process there is now a general acceptance that the proposed changes are the responsibility of the directorate. This is of particular relevance in the light of the continuing reduction in junior doctor hours of work and the reduction in their actual number when the proposals of the Calman Report are implemented. The effectiveness of the risk management process we have described in reducing adverse events still has to be demonstrated. However, the experience of what is a new initiative in this unit, has been enlightening. Once the trust accepted that clinical risk, with its medical and financial implications, was a problem that had to be contained, the appointment of a risk manager was agreed. In our brief experience of nine months, risk management has been well accepted by both midwives and doctors in the unit as a necessary activity which previously was not being dealt with adequately. In NHS maternity units, doctors and midwives do not have the time or facilities to systematically collect information, to counsel patients, or to ensure that recommended improvements in practice are implemented. The whole concept of risk management is new to the maternity services in Britain, but with more than 30% of the medicolegal costs within the NHS arising from 3% of the medical workforce,[16] it is an initiative that should be considered by all hospital trusts with a maternity service.

1 Northern Regional Health Authority (NRHA) Coordinating Group. Perinatal mortality: a continuing collaborative regional survey. *BMJ* 1984;**299**:1717–20.
2 Mersey Region Working Party on Perinatal Mortality. Confidential inquiry into perinatal deaths in the Mersey Region. *Lancet* 1982;**i**:491–4.
3 North West Thames Regional Health Authority Perinatal Working Party, The Obstetric Survey 1978–1979. Report analysis of data and recommendations. In: *House of Commons, second report from the Social Services Committee, Session 1979–80. Perinatal and neonatal mortality.* Vol 5. London: HMSO, (Appendices 299–323.)
4 Paterson CM, Chapple JC, Beard RW, Joffe M, Steer PJ, Wright CSW. Evaluating the quality of maternity services—a discussion paper. *Br J Obstet Gynaecol* 1991;**98**:1073–8.
5 Banfield PJ. *The role of the feedback of clinical data in the alteration of clinical practice and the development of a working model for clinical audit in maternity care* [MD thesis]. London: University of London, 1994.
6 Lomas J, Anderson GM, Domnick-Pierre K, Vayda E, Enkin MW, Hannah WJ. Do practice guidelines guide practice? *N Engl J Med* 1989;**321**:1306–11.
7 Brennan TA, Leape LL, Laird NM, Hebert L, Localio AR, Lawthers AG, *et al.* Incidence of adverse events and negligence in hospitalised patients. Results of the Harvard Medical Practice Study I. *N Engl J Med* 1991;**324**:370–6.

8 Localio AR, Lawthers AG, Bengtson JM, Hebert LE, Weaver SL, Brennan TA, et al. Relationship between malpractice claims and caesarean delivery. *JAMA* 1993;**269**:366–73.

9 Knox GE (1994). Obstetrical clinical risk modification: are medical malpractice law suits inevitable? *Forum. Risk Management Foundation*. Harvard: Harvard Medical Institutions Inc, 1994;**15**:7–9.

10 Vincent CA, Clements RV. Clinical risk management—why do we need it? *Clinical Risk* 1995;**1**:1–4.

11 Morlock L, Malitz FE. Do hospital risk management programs make a difference? Relationships between risk management program activities and hospital malpractice claims experience. *Law and Contemporary Problems* 1991; **54**:1.

12 House of Commons Health Committee. Supplementary memorandum on intrapartum care submitted by the Royal College of Obstetricians and Gynaecologists to the Maternity Services Committee. *Minutes of Evidence 12 June 1991*. London: HMSO, 1991.

13 Royal College of Obstetricians and Gynaecologists. Deriving standards from the maternal mortality reports. In: *Recommendations of the Audit Committee of the RCOG, 26 January 1994*. London: RCOG, 1994.

14 Department of Health. *Changing childbirth. Report of the Expert Maternity Group:* London: HMSO, 1993 (Chaired by Baroness Cumberlege).

15 Health Education Council. *Pregnancy book. A guide to becoming pregnant, being pregnant and caring for your newborn baby*. London: Health Education Council, 1993.

16 Acheson A. Are obstetrics and midwifery doomed? A report of the William Power Memorial Lecture, December 1990. *Midwives Chronicle* 1991;**104**: 158–66.

Annex 1: in service education programme

1. Introductory session

A morning session will be devoted to introduction/orientation for newly appointed SHOs and registrars. This occurs twice a year, first week of February and first week of August. It is proposed that:

(a) the Labour Ward Protocol will be sent to the new appointee with the letter confirming their appointment to this Department.

(b) the contents of this introduction course will include a talk by a senior midwife explaining the general working of the labour ward, a talk by an ex-SHO introducing the working methods of the wards, clinics, etc., a talk on monitoring women in labour and, finally, a talk by a senior member (an SR or a consultant) on medico-legal aspects and the process of feedback and evaluation of staff performance.

(c) a neonatology session with a consultant paediatrician.

2. Assessment of competence

No new SHO or registrar will be allowed to practise independently on the labour ward until they have demonstrated competence in the following activities:

- interpretation of fetal cardiotocographs and acid base values (by MCO).
- a working knowledge of the labour ward protocol (by MCP)
- repair of episiotomies and tears
- ultrasound scanning for fetal/placental localisation
- low forceps/ventouse
- manual removal of placenta
- rotation forceps (registrars only)
- Caesarean section (registrars only)

3. Organised and structured labour room rounds

Every morning labour room round is conducted by a consultant accompanied by the SR, registrar, SHO, medical students and midwives. It is proposed that the registrar or senior registrar in consultation with the midwives would identify cases of interest which had been dealt with in the previous 24 hours and keep a record. These cases can then be discussed on the Thursday afternoon meeting.

An afternoon labour ward round is conducted by the registrar and an SHO accompanied by the midwife. Similarly, a working ward round should be conducted at night by the registrar and an SHO so as to identify any potential problems and to plan their management with the consultant's input, if required.

4. Teaching sessions and meetings

(a) Monday morning meeting alternating between the Samaritan and St Mary's
(b) Thursday lunchtime meeting
(c) Aleck Bourne lecture series: in spring and autumn every year lectures start at 5.15 pm and last for about an hour
(d) Half day clinical meetings to be held every two weeks
(e) Friday lunchtime research and progress meeting.

Objectives for learning

The first six months

Obstetric skills

During this period the SHO will learn and competently carry out:

General antenatal care

Including risk assessment, general, abdominal and pelvic examination and obstetrical assessment of the pelvis and uterus. Use of the St Mary's Maternity Information system including analysis of data.

Fetal heart rate monitoring, real time ultrasound examination, tocolysis.

Understanding of the application of fetal and maternal physiology to the management of pregnancy, labour and the puerperium.

Management of labour

Clinical assessment of labour and progress, recognition of normal labour and causes, understand and appropriately apply:

– Relaxation and support techniques
– Techniques of analgesia
– Active management of labour
– Partogram
– Induction of labour
– An understanding of the physiology of the fetal circulation and of acid-base balance
– Indications for forceps and Caesarean section.

Management of delivery

Local anaesthesia, pudendal block and use of nitrous oxide and epidurals and preparation for general anaesthesia:

– Episiotomy
– Repair of vaginal and first and second degree perineal tears
– The use of ventouse and forceps
– Perform manual removal of placenta.

Post-natal care

– Indications for continued observation on the labour ward after delivery
– Care and management of normal and abnormal puerperium
– Advice on breastfeeding
– Contraceptive advice.

Neonatal care

– Assessment of the condition of the baby at birth
– Neonatal resuscitation
– Indications for transfer to SCBU
– Examination of the normal neonate.

Contraception

– Competence in contraceptive counselling and techniques.

Objectives for learning

Second six months

Obstetric skills

Competence in the management of obstetric complications including pre-eclampsia and eclampsia, antepartum bleeding, premature rupture of membranes and premature labour.

He/she will achieve skills and techniques including amniocentesis.

Competence (under supervision) in the management of difficult labour, including occipito transverse and posterior positions, breech and twin delivery. Skills will be demonstrated in post partum uterine exploration and repair of third degree tears.

Perform, with assistance, uncomplicated Caesarean sections.

Self evaluation/feedback questionnaire

During your 12 weeks of obstetrics or gynaecology rotation, please comment on the following aspects of the teaching that you received (please circle appropriate answers):

1. **Tutorials**
   (a) Number   Too many/Adequate/Too few
   (b) In general: Helpful/Not helpful

2. **Ward round teaching by:**
   (a) Consultant: Plentiful/Adequate/Inadequate/None
   (b) Senior registrar: Plentiful/Adequate/Inadequate/None
   (c) Registrar: Plentiful/Adequate/Inadequate/None

3. From whom did you get the **most useful teaching**?
   Consultants/Senior Registrars/Registrars/Midwives

4. (a) Did you have an opportunity to attend gynaecology clinics?
   Several/Sufficient/Inadequate/None

   (b) Did you have an opportunity to examine and evaluate patients?
   Several/Sufficient/Inadequate/None

5. Did you get ample opportunity to attend theatre sessions?
   Too many/Adequate/Too few

6. Did you get any opportunity to perform gynaecological surgery?
   Several/Sufficient/Inadequate/None

   Procedure: Done Yourself/Assisted

7. (a) Did you have an opportunity to attend antenatal outpatient clinics?
   Several/Sufficient/Inadequate/None

   (b) Did you have an opportunity to examine and evaluate antenatal patients?
   Several/Sufficient/Inadequate/None

   (c) Were the midwives helpful?
   Very helpful/Reasonable/Unhelpful

8. (i) How many normal deliveries did you conduct?
   (ii) Did you manage and participate in:

   (a) Breech delivery   Done yourself/Assisted
   (b) Twin delivery   Done yourself/Assisted

(c) Caesarean section   Done yourself/Assisted
(d) Kiellands forceps   Done yourself/Assisted
(e) Ventouse   Done yourself/Assisted
(f) Outlet forceps   Done yourself/Assisted

9. (a) During your rotation were you advised of your progress?
YES/NO

    (b) Did you have a formal final clinical assessment?
YES/NO

10. What "on call" rota did you participate in?
1:2 1:3 1:4 1:5 Other:

    Was the amount of "on call" duty:
Too much/Adequate/Too little

11. How would you rate your obs or gynae rotation:
Excellent/Very good/Good/Average/Poor

12. Which obs and gynae text books did you use during your attachment?

13. Research Projects (if any):

14. Goals set for next rotation:

15. Do you have any suggestions/comments regarding how the rotation could be improved?:

EVALUATIONS FORMS FOR JUNIOR STAFF

To be filled in at the end of every rotation by the supervising Consultant.

Name ....Date.......................................

Period of rotation ....Specialty..............................
Please score Grade 1 to 5 as follows:

1 = Not Satisfactory; 2 = Below Average; 3 = Average;
4 = Above Average; 5 = Excellent; DK = Don't know or cannot assess

GRADE

1. **Medical knowledge**
   Knowledge of Basic Sciences
   Theoretical knowledge of surgery
   Ability to apply the same

2. **Clinical knowledge**
   Ability to demonstrate clinical signs
   Diagnostic skills

3. **Technical skills acquired**
   In basic ward procedures and surgical procedures
   in O.R.

4. **Patient management**
   Ability to order correct investigations
   Independent patient management

5. **Punctuality and public relations**
   Attitude towards time, hard work and unusual
   demands
   Relationship with nurses, colleagues and patients'
   relatives

6. **Presentation and teaching**
   Degree of analytical skills
   Ability to present material, ward rounds and
   seminars
   Ability for instructions to junior colleagues,
   students, nurses

7. **Current topics**
   Abreast with current literature and personal
   publications for research

8. **Comments:**
   General assessment
   Special skills
   Specific recommendations.

Annex 2: agreed list of "adverse events" recorded by the risk manager

Mother

*Death
 Convulsion
*Transfer to intensive care unit
 Major anaesthetic complication
 Major postpartum haemorrhage (>1000 ml)
 Postnatal haemoglobin <8·0 g/dl
 Any blood transfusion
 Prolonged postnatal stay in hospital
   (after vaginal delivery >5 days, caesarean section >10 days)
 Errors of drug administration
 Any serious soft tissue injury such as 3° tear, ruptured uterus, bladder injury
 Any complication requiring transfer to the operating theatre after completion of the third stage

Baby

*Seizures within first 48 hours, coma/shock
 Apgar score ≤3 at five minutes
 Meconium aspiration syndrome
 Unanticipated admission to special care baby unit
*Stillbirth/neonatal death (babies of ≥24 weeks gestation unassociated with lethal congenital anomaly)
 Major congenital abnormality first detected at birth
 Fractured skull, clavicle, long bone
 Subdural haematoma or tear of falx cerebri
*Any paralysis
 Iatrogenic injury up to one week after birth

*Major adverse event. This will include any "near miss" involving mother and/or baby regardless of eventual outcome.

20 Incident reporting systems: early warnings for the prevention and control of clinical negligence

ORLEY LINDGREN,
JONATHAN SECKER-WALKER

Evidence from North America shows that prompt incident reporting by medical professionals can serve a useful "early warning" function in identifying future clinical negligence claims and providing information for risk prevention and quality improvement.[1] Pilot studies started during 1994 are now beginning to establish the feasibility of applying these early warning systems in NHS trust hospitals. Such systems should improve the prevention and control of clinical negligence as well as contributing information to quality assurance programmes. The early warning, positive claims management approaches pioneered by Professional Risk Management (PRM) and adopted by the teaching hospitals in California are presently being piloted in several large teaching hospitals in the United Kingdom by the PRM affiliated organisations Quality and Risk Management Ltd and Merrett Health Risk Management Ltd.[2] Much of the work reported in this chapter was initially developed by these organisations.

An empirical study by Lindgren et al was undertaken to confirm or deny the philosophy that early warning based on incident reports or occurrence reports could improve claims management and outcomes.[1] The results showed that clinical negligence claims

375

established on the basis of early warning incident reports involve the full range of severity, identify claims warranting substantial indemnity payments, facilitate the opening and closing of claims more quickly, and produce substantial savings in legal expenses. Qualitatively, risk and claims managers believe that these benefits accrue because of greater availability of better information on the claims.

Traditional incident reports: advantages and limitations

Reporting of incidents in hospitals involving visitors and staff, as opposed to adverse events involving patients, has been required in both North American and European Hospitals for many years. Created as administrative reporting systems, these reports typically identify mishaps that were the result of non-doctor actions or hospital physical plant problems.[3] These reports ordinarily provide a brief written description of the hospital acquired mishap, sometimes compiled on a standard check list by nurses or hospital and health service employees other than doctors.

These traditional incident reports have proved useful for prompting changes in hospital physical plant layout or equipment and changes in nursing practices.[3] They have been of some value also to risk and insurance personnel in identifying problems of general liability and employer's liability, but have had little utility for identification of medical professional liability. Insurance companies responsible for hospital and physician malpractice claims management have in the past made little use of traditional incident reports to prompt their investigations or establish claims files; rather, when incident reports were forwarded to them, they simply filed them and awaited a legal claim. With the introduction of early warning systems this situation is changing.[1]

Traditional incident reports often do not define the incidents clearly, and describe errors that were corrected or had no consequential impact on patient care. Moreover, the reports rarely consider serious injuries stemming from medical or surgical care which are the focus of subsequent clinical negligence claims and awards. These reports are also of little use in pinpointing patient injuries or areas of risk that may generate claims or litigation resulting in large financial losses for hospitals.[4 5] Because physicians rarely participate and because many fear subsequent discovery of the information through legal process, most serious hospital acquired mishaps typically go unreported. Of thousands of traditional incident reports filed, only a few were related to valid claims. Most clinical negligence claims are only noticed after a formal legal complaint is filed. Estimates as to what percentage of clinical negligence actions begin with an incident report vary. In the United States these percentages range from 5% to 30%, although the estimates are often not clear as to the type of reporting systems being measured.[67] Based on in depth reviews of thousands of recent clinical negligence claims and incident reports in the United Kingdom, it seems that 0% to about 2% of clinical negligence claims are first "noticed" through a traditional incident report (D Bowden, personal communication).

From the perspective of risk and claims managers this is discouraging. Thus instead of sifting through incident reports, claims managers have traditionally not set up claim files and begun investigating and resolving claims until after they receive legal notice—in the form of a letter of complaint and demand for compensation, a letter of intent to sue or "letter before action", or some other legal notice of an impending litigation.

Creating systems to improve on traditional incident reports

The need for improved detection of adverse events proceeding to clinical negligence claims has long been clear. "Generic screening", which originated in the California insurance feasibility study,[8] provided a tool for systematically screening patient medical records for instances of preventable adverse events occurring in hospitals, some of which would be liable for compensation under a then proposed medical malpractice liability compensation scheme.[10] This system proved useful for research purposes, and subsequently has been successfully applied in similar studies in New York[9] and elsewhere. Although this approach has been applied as an operational tool for risk management, medical audit, and quality assessment quality assurance,[45] it has been shown to be relatively inefficient because of its multi-tiered review system, high rates of errors and false positives, and lack of relation with quality of patient care.[10] As an alternative for operational use in risk management and quality assurance, Mills and colleagues developed a method of identifying adverse patient outcomes observable in clinical settings

377

through prospective reporting according to specific reporting categories.[11] This system was widely used for quality assurance purposes, but had limited application for clinical negligence claims and insurance purposes at the time.

During the period 1975–7, through the joint efforts of Los Angeles County's Department of Health Services and the Professional Risk Management Group in California, a system was developed whereby both nurses and doctors reported based on both broad criteria and specific criteria and the incidents were classified in a one stage reporting system. Independent professional claims personnel decided which incidents needed investigation or intervention. This approach provided the basis for the early warning system for medical malpractice which has been widely adopted by teaching hospitals and healthcare systems in California. This system was the subject of the research described here; it is also the model for similar systems presently being implemented in several pilot projects in NHS trust hospitals in the United Kingdom.

Philosophy of proactive claims management

The basic philosophy of risk and claims management is that medical care providers should observe and immediately report deviations from expected outcomes and any hospital acquired patient injury with liability potential. This in turn triggers immediate investigation in cases with the potential for liability or further patient injury, and active intervention to assist the patient; it reduces liability potential and yields information for purposes of preventing future mishaps.

The early warning concept that is a fundamental element of this philosophy is that adverse events are detected and reported at the time of or soon after their occurrence. In the California institutions in which this philosophy has been operational, the physicians and surgeons are employees of the multihospital system and as such are covered under the institution's self insurance programme for both hospital liability and clinical negligence. These can be considered "enterprise liability" systems in the sense that the liability is the responsibility of the organisation, rather than being apportioned separately against the hospital and the doctors. It resembles the situation that now exists in the United Kingdom NHS hospitals with the new central negligence scheme for trusts. Doctors and nurses are actively involved in designing and improving the early warning system, and have become actively involved in reporting. Higher levels of participation on the part of clinical staff have been accomplished by (a) making the process of reporting easier; (b) requiring that the reports trigger subsequent investigation rather than being assumed to have face validity; (c) being used in a positive manner to identify and solve problems and not used punitively; and (d) by feeding back the beneficial impacts of the system in helping injured patients, aiding legal defence, and resolving valid claims efficiently.

Participating medical and nursing staff are encouraged to report by telephone or face to face with independent, external PRM "account executives" who function as risk and claims managers, selected in part for their interpersonal skills. In California, communications to the account executives are protected under confidentiality provisions. Both verbal and written reports are collected on standard forms which are coded and entered into dedicated computer systems. The account executives carry out investigations on site and consult with hospital risk managers and staff. The account executives also man a 24 hour hot line which facilitates incident reporting and best practices with respect to incidence response. In the United Kingdom it is more likely that reports will be made in the first instance to an internal risk manager although other, external, organisations may take part in the later stages of an investigation.

These early warning systems flag potential clinical negligence claims and trigger active claims and management of patient injury. The account executives work in close coordination with the hospital's own risk manager to reduce the physical and legal damages stemming from the incident. Patients are often provided prompt diagnosis and treatment of their hospital acquired injuries. Care providers are encouraged to inform patients and their families of problems with their care and to maintain close communication. When necessary to preserve communication, the account executive and hospital risk manager may meet directly with the patient and family (and their solicitor if any) in an attempt to clarify the problem and to resolve it without resort to litigation.

Claims which are identified early and handled proactively sometimes cannot be resolved or otherwise prevented from being filed as a legal claim. In the United States, even when this occurs, the account executive stays in an active role in managing the claim, whereas independent defence counsel is often retained on behalf of its institutional clients to handle required legal motions and necessary formal discovery and court proceedings. Information developed by the account executive as part of the proactive investigation is organised and fed into the litigation process sooner than it would otherwise be available—thereby facilitating early resolution or optimum defence of the cases.

Information from the investigation and management of clinical negligence claims is used to prevent injury to subsequent patients and to help educate and motivate clinical staff to report future injuries. With early warning systems in place, this information is available much sooner and with greater precision than information from clinical negligence claims files established in the conventional manner.

Research results

Research carried out by Lindgren et al[1] was based on analysis of nearly 8000 clinical negligence claims and 50 000 oral and written incident reports from more than 30 health service facilities in California covering a period of 13 years to the end of June 1989. The health service facilities included teaching hospitals in urban and suburban areas, high risk women's hospitals, and various outpatient and public health clinics. These facilities employ more than 3000 doctors and tens of thousands of other healthcare workers, all of whom are included under the health service's institutional liability coverage. The claims were all medical professional and hospital liability claims. Those characterised as early warning claims were first noticed by an incident report, oral or written. Claims described as legal notice claims were established on the basis of the first notice being written notice of intent to file a claim, or "letter before action" service of process of a lawsuit. Not included in the analysis were premises or general liability, employer's liability, car accident liability, etc. A claim involving an injured party was counted as one claim regardless of the number of claimants or the number of defendants named.

Performance of the early warning systems

Incident reports (written and verbal) were found to provide warning of claims in less than 30 days after the adverse event in 95% of the claims so identified. Of the total claims opened during the study period, 42% were identified through incident reporting. Verbal incident reports, although few in number, identified 32%

of the claims established from all forms of notice, whereas written incident reports, far more voluminous, identified about 10% of the claims files. Of claims identified through legal notice, only 1% were within 30 days; most arrived more than a year after the adverse event.

Early warning provided by incident reports were also shown to speed claims investigation and resolution—thereby avoiding many of the costs and problems associated with the traditional "long tail" of clinical negligence claims. On average the early warning claims were opened with a delay of just over six months from the date of incident, but the legal notice claims were on average not opened until more than a year after the incident—and about 6% of these were not yet opened at the end of three years.

Once the claim file had been established, the early warning claims were closed on average in about six months, whereas the legal notice claims required more than a year and a half to close. Claims prompted by incident reports average just over a year from incident to closure, whereas legal notice claims average nearly three years to closure. Although most early warning claims are resolved within less than a year from patient injury to payment or other closure, only about 15% of the legal notice claims closed this quickly.

Early warning claims close more quickly despite having more severe injuries and higher financial severity or "claims spending"

Clinical negligence claims for more severe injuries usually take longer to resolve than claims for minor injuries. (Severity of injury was defined in this study as the extent to which an injury caused pain and suffering and either was life threatening or required treatment to be corrected.) In a substudy of nearly 1000 recent claims, early warning claims were found to involve injuries that were just as severe and permanent as legally initiated claims, yet they were opened and resolved much more quickly than were the legally initiated claims. Verbally reported claims were generally about more severe injuries than written incident report claims, yet a similar pattern of speed of resolution was also found for them. Among the benefits of speed in investigating and resolving claims is that information for quality improvement is recent and can be applied more promptly.

381

Early warning claims were also found to involve equal or higher financial severity. This is defined as total claims spending (or indemnity expense plus allocated expense). Verbal incident reports identify claims with significantly higher total claims spending than either legal notice claims or written incident report claims. The higher financial severity of the verbal incident reports no doubt reflects in part the greater severity of injury reported in these claims.

Allocated expenses are lower for incident report claims

Transaction costs of the legal system have often been cited as being a disgraceful waste of money which should otherwise be paid to injured parties and used to prevent injury from occurring in the first place.[12-14] Payment in "overheads" or "administrative costs" of clinical negligence is the money spent attributable to the management of an individual claim on lawyers (solicitors and barristers), expert witnesses, court costs, copying records, and other related costs for those who are not claimants (the injured party and family). Technically called "allocated costs" or "allocated loss" adjustment expenses, these typically, in North America, run to half or more of the "total loss dollar" of claims; in the United Kingdom costs for both defence and plaintiff overheads are said to run twice to three times that paid to claimants in indemnity (Lord Chancellor's Office, personal communication). Unallocated costs are those costs not readily attributable to an individual claim, including the administrative overheads of the third party administrator or insurance company.

The allocated expenses for incident report claims were found to be significantly lower than those for legal claims. This holds true for overall claims—a result which would be expected from a claims management policy which is to monitor and control outside defence lawyers' costs and to require account executives to actively control and settle all meritorious cases that can be settled at a reasonable value. Allocated expenses ratios for incident report claims are even lower for only claims in which indemnity was paid—14% compared with 32% for legal notice claims. These percentages are lower than published industry standards in that they reflect systematic management of settlement, avoiding and controlling lawyers where possible, settling with less protracted litigation, and otherwise holding down costs. Savings in costs of managing liability claims should mean more funds available for patient care and for improving the quality of care.[1]

382

Early warning and litigation outcomes favourable to the defence

As expected from a proactive claims management programme emphasising settlement of meritorious claims, more than 90% of the nearly 8000 claims in the study were settled, with or without payment of indemnity. From the perspective of health service risk and claims management, the results from the few cases that went all the way through trial were very successful: 84% were defence verdicts. Of the 16% that were deemed to be plaintiff verdicts, only 6% were for monetary awards higher than the pretrial defence settlement offers, and no verdicts exceeded $1 million. Interestingly, most cases tried to verdict were the high injury severity/high financial severity claims first reported by early warning, particularly the verbal incident reports. These cases are sent to trial by PRM and the associated hospitals because they are believed to either be non-meritorious or that a mutually agreeable settlement value cannot be achieved. These early warning claims may be more defensible than legal notice claims because of the collection of more complete and accurate factual information while it is still fresh, and the retention of key pieces of evidence, including the interviewing and tracking of key defence witnesses. These same factors should also contribute to obtaining relatively better information for quality assessment and quality assurance from the early warning claims process.

Variations in reporting and opportunities for improvement

The percentage of clinical negligence claims identified through incident reports *versus* legal notice varied considerably among the 30 facilities, among medical specialties, and across study years. Such variation shows that there is room for improvement and points the way toward how these improvements can be achieved.

Facilities specialising in high risk obstetrics and acute gynaecology and paediatrics report a significantly higher percentage of their claims through early warning (68%) than other specialties combined (just under 50%). Specialties with the highest incident report claims ratios included anaesthesia, obstetrics, gynaecology, and paediatrics. These results are not surprising in that these specialties had sustained the highest malpractice/clinical negligence rates and insurance premiums in past years. This resulted in intense educational efforts to promote prevention and control of claims through clinical risk management activities including voluntary

383

incident reporting and early warning, introduction of clinical guidelines, increased awareness of liability and patient injury problems, the promotion of safe practices, and voluntary reporting of adverse events. Apparently these efforts have produced results which include increased voluntary reporting of potential liability claims through the existing early warning systems.

Conclusion of the research

In summary the results from 14 years of application of early warning risk management in 30 health service institutions suggest that incident reports, especially those which are provided verbally via telephone and face to face provide early warning of a large proportion of liability cases. This in turn produces quicker movement of the claims investigation and resolution process, and is associated with a lowering of non-indemnity expenses compared with legal notice claims. These beneficial results occur across a broad range of clinical negligence claims, from those which involve slight injury to serious injury, occurring in many different types of facilities and involving several medical specialities. Clearly more is to be learned about how these systems work, how they can be improved, and how they can be successfully applied in other settings.

Education, evaluation, and pilot projects underway in the United Kingdom

The extent to which clinical negligence claims are prompted by incident reports was one focus of major reviews of clinical negligence claims undertaken on a regionwide basis across two NHS regional health authorities. In a detailed review of nearly 2000 outstanding clinical negligence claims against NHS units, fewer than 1% were found to have been set up on the basis of an oral or written incident report. Of those that were, most were from a recent period within a district where early reporting and early investigation of potential claims was emphasised. The recommendations of the review to the NHS districts and regions were that incident reporting and early warning systems be established, and this is well under way in several larger trust hospitals in at least one of the regions studied.[15]

Work in London in establishing hospitalwide clinical audit has included initial efforts to establish similar hospitalwide reporting of adverse medical events.[15] The project has involved key trust doctors and nurses in redesigning the previous incident form and reporting procedures, and in working out how to facilitate reporting, cooperation with verification procedures, and feedback of results both for management of risk, claims, and quality. Results should be forthcoming in 1996–7.

In the United Kingdom allegations of improper management of labour and delivery in cases involving cerebral palsy in the child have become the most frequent and costly of all clinical negligence claims. Obtaining early warning of these claims is difficult, however, because cerebral palsy is rare, occurring in less than five per 1000 births, and only about 10% of the cases of cerebral palsy are likely to be associated with factors of labour and delivery. One of the ways in which early warning of adverse obstetric events and potential claims is achieved is through the use of a "perinatal outcomes analyst"—a nurse who is qualified both in obstetrics and neonatology and who is responsible for encouraging early reporting by unit nurses and doctors, for investigating those reports, and for incorporating the verified information into specific prevention and quality improvements as well as making it available for risk and claims management.[16]

Establishing early warning systems in United Kingdom trust hospitals

Establishing early warning systems is not easy. Successful systems have been accomplished elsewhere by bringing in an experienced outside contractor who will work with managers and medical and nursing staff leaders to design and implement the system. Among the issues to be considered are:

- Building on existing incident-reporting system
- Maintaining confidentiality/security of all systems
- Participation of key doctors, nurses, and managers
- Verifying incident report data before they are used
- Ensuring that incident report data are not misused
- Integrating early warning data with other relevant data
- Obtaining information for risk prevention and quality improvement
- Obtaining information for proactive risk and claims management.

The day to day operations of the system can be carried out by the trust staff or as a joint activity of staff and a contractor.

Implementation of the early warning system and a proactive risk and claims management programme requires a major cultural change for a trust. Until 1990 medical negligence claims were managed, and paid for, by medical defence organisations, from which the only input into the hospital for future improvement in practice was exhortation. Hospitals therefore entered the 1990s with little or no experience of proactive risk and claims management.

Drawing on the American experience of 15 years or more of claims and risk management and adapting it to the British culture suggests that the following steps are necessary to implement a successful incident reporting system.

(1) Provide in depth briefing for trust board or executive

For staff to feel comfortable about reporting accidents and near misses to patients, the threat of the use of the disciplinary procedures for reporting such incidents needs to be lifted. This requires a trust board commitment from the chairman, chief executive, and medical director downwards. Clearly there are exceptions when incident reporting is malicious or the incident reported is criminal or constitutes gross misconduct.

(2) Produce necessary documentation including policy statements, objectives, organisational structure, information management systems, functional descriptions, and job descriptions

A decision to proceed with risk management should, of necessity, involve most staff and clarity as to the policies and procedures involved is essential.

(3) Decide on the composition and responsibility of the risk management committee

The risk management committee should be composed of senior staff who have the ability to effect change within the organisation, and ideally should have the medical director and the director of nursing as members. This committee should also have the responsibility of ensuring that staff are not disciplined for reporting accidents.

(4) Organise procedural changes consequent to the appointment of the risk manager

A risk manager is required to be responsible for coordinating the risk management process. This involves the collection of data and production of reports, investigation of adverse incidents, collection of notes, radiographs, and witness statements where appropriate, advice and support in the handling of clinical complaints, interaction with legal advisors, support to the risk management committee, and obtaining early expert opinion when required.

(5) Interview each clinical director

Without the support and understanding of clinical directors, a clinical risk management programme is unlikely to be successful.

(6) Gain the commitment of senior clinical staff to reporting specific "indicators"

There are some events that occur within medicine and surgery that indicate that something in the disease process or the treatment has caused damage to the patient that was not expected, such as cardiac arrest or development of paraplegia after surgery. These events are usually not related to negligence but may be so viewed by the patient or their relatives. To keep track of these events or indicators, it is important that clinical staff recognise the need for themselves, their junior staff, or nursing colleagues to report them to the risk manager.

(7) Provide a comprehensive education programme for all staff

All staff in the trust need to be educated about the purpose and benefits of the risk management programme. This needs to be carried out at the same time that the incident reporting procedures and forms are promulgated. In addition, risk management needs to form a part of induction programmes.

387

(8) Introduce adverse incident report forms

The adverse incident form needs to be compatible with a suitable computer software system. It needs to be simple and quick for staff to use and yet needs to collect relevant information for risk identification and management purposes.

(9) Acquire a customised incident reporting database for the trust

The database needs to be compatible with the incident form. It must be simple for a secretary to input the data and must produce reports that are relevant to the risk management committee.

(10) The risk manager requires support when appointed

There are not many health service personnel with the required background and experience from the United States to perform the functions of a risk manager without training and although external consultancies are not currently encouraged by the NHS executive, this is an example when they can be of great use and of immediate economic benefit.

(11) Provide regular adverse incident reports for the risk management committee

The adverse incident reporting system must produce reports that are timely and informative for the risk management committee. The system should identify areas where certain adverse incidents are occurring with a frequency that suggests some abnormality in process.

(12) Teach the risk manager how to investigate adverse incidents relevant to prevention and control of clinical negligence

If the risk manager comes with a clinical training this will require less support than someone from other backgrounds. Significant adverse incidents need to be followed up and investigated, notes and witness statements collected, and a decision taken as to the degree of substandard care and how to deal with the patient. This requires training.

(13) Teach the risk manager to reduce legal costs

After identification of a serious adverse incident or receipt of a letter before action, adequate collection and preparation of patient notes, CTGs (cardiotocographs: fetal heart traces), radiographs, witness statements, and addresses of staff who have left, together with an early assessment as to liability by taking expert opinion sooner rather than later, should substantially reduce the need for the trust to require its solicitors to undertake these functions at considerable expense.

(14) Reinforce the programme by regular feedback to the staff

The experience of most hospital staff is that incident forms depart for a black box, never to be seen again. Rapid feedback from the risk manager to staff following up adverse incident reports is an important method of positive reinforcement for the programme as staff notice that action follows their use of the form.

Often with outside technical support, a trust can establish a well working risk management programme within a short time to produce the following advantages:

- Early identification of risks
- Early communication with injured patients (and with staff to reduce the likelihood of subsequent injuries)
- Improved handling of clinical complaints
- Reduction of solicitors' bills
- Potential for reduced premiums if subscribing to the central fund or other insurance
- Using a concurrent claims database, more accurate projections of future likely liability
- And last, but not least, identifiable improvements in the quality of clinical care.

Conclusion

Since the mid-1970s, early warning systems have been developed and applied for improved management of risks, claims, and quality in health care provider organisations in California. Since the beginning of the 1990s, early warning systems have been discussed in the United Kingdom. By the mid-1990s such systems are beginning to be developed in pilot and demonstration projects in

NHS hospital trusts. Within the next year or so we would expect that there will be sufficient experience with these systems in the United Kingdom to determine if indeed that they can be adapted and found to work in this environment. Although these systems were originally adopted mainly for purposes of improving the management of clinical negligence claims, they have considerable potential to augment information for quality improvement as well.

1 Lindgren OH, Christensen R, Mills DH. Medical malpractice risk management early warning systems, *Law and Contemporary Problems*, 1991;54:22–41.
2 Lindgren O, Haywood R, von Bolschwing GE. Managing clinical claims and risks – papers 3, 4, and 5. In: Lindgren O, ed. *Prevention and control of clinical negligence. Clinician in Management*. London: Churchill Livingstone, 1994; 3(suppl No 5):11–14.
3 Mills DH, von Bolschwing G. *Clinical risk management: experiences from the United States* Chapter 1, this volume, 1995.
4 Orlikoff JE, Fifer WR, Greeley HP. *Malpractice prevention and liability control for hospitals*. 2nd ed. Chicago: American Hospitals Association, 1988:34–5.
5 Orlikoff JE, Vanagunas AM. *Malpractice prevention and liability control for hospitals*. 2nd ed. Chicago: American Hospitals Association, 1988:55–57.
6 American College of Surgeons/Bader and Associates Inc. *Patient safety manual: a guide for hospitals and physicians to a systematic approach to quality assurance and risk management*. 2nd ed. Cambridge, Massachusetts: American College of Surgeons, 1985:51–4, 70–2.
7 US General Accounting Office. *Initiatives in hospital risk management*. Washington DC: Government Printing Office, 1989:15–16, 23. (GAO/HRD-89-79.)
8 Mills DH, ed. *California Medical Association and California Hospital Association report on the medical insurance feasibility study*. San Francisco: Sutter Publications, 1977. Mills DH, Medical insurance feasibility study: a technical summary. *West J Med* 1970;128:360–5.
9 Brennan TA, Localio AR, Leape LL, Laird N, Peeterson L, Hiatt H. Identification of adverse events occurring during hospitalization. *Ann Intern Med* 1990;112:221–6.
10 Sanazaro P, Mills DH. A critique of the use of generic screening in quality assessment, *JAMA* 1991;265:1977–81.
11 California Hospital Association. *Notification system/quality assurance*. Sacramento: California Hospital Association Assurance Insurance Service, 1979 (cited in Sanazaro and Mills[10]).
12 Danzon PM. *Medical malpractice: theory, evidence and public policy*. Harvard: Harvard University Press, 1985:121.
13 Wadlington WJ. Legal responses to patient industry: a future agenda for research and reform. In: Bovberg RR, Metzloff B, eds. *The medical malpractice system and emergency reform. Law and Contemporary Problems*; 1991;54(2):199
14 US Department of Health and Human Services. *Report of the Task Force on Medical Liability and Malpractice*. Washington DC: DHSS, 1987.
15 Walker JS. Risk management and clinical care. Postgraduate medical education and training, University of Oxford and region. *Auditorium* 1994;2:17–20.
16 Lindgren OH, Haywood R, Bowden D. The perinatal outcome analyst: a lesson from America. *Health Services Journal* 1994;(suppl: managing risk):1–2.

21 Accident investigation: discovering why things go wrong

CHARLES VINCENT, PIPPA BARK

The formal investigation of adverse events in medicine is a relatively new phenomenon. Clinicians have always privately discussed, and often agonised, over mistakes and poor outcomes. Serious incidents may be discussed with supportive colleagues or in departmental meetings.[1][2] However, few studies or reports of such meetings are published, making it difficult for staff to learn from others' mistakes or to develop a method of systematically investigating such incidents.

Incidents that lead to litigation are investigated intensively, albeit long after the event. Cases of medical negligence focus primarily on the analysis of the medical records to determine (*a*) whether there was substandard care and (*b*) whether it caused identifiable injury. There is usually no attempt to understand *why* care was substandard. The doctor or nurse concerned may have been undertrained, exhausted, badly supervised, inadequately equipped, or in the throes of a major family crisis—but this is generally irrelevant to the case. In addition, the event is usually reconstructed from medical records some years later, backed by the understandably hazy memories of those staff who can be traced. One great strength of adverse incident reporting is that information is collected soon after the event and a fuller, more accurate account obtained. This, however, is only the first step in understanding the complex web of circumstances involved in most serious incidents.

391

This chapter describes our experience of developing a method of investigation. We hope to show that a systematic and detailed analysis of a few cases can pay rich dividends. Although this kind of analysis is too detailed for frequent use it could certainly be carried out at intervals by risk managers and others. We emphasise that, with a few exceptions,[34] this type of study is in its infancy.

In the first part of the chapter we describe some essential background to the investigation of accidents. We review different research methods and consider their respective strengths and limitations and how far they can be applied within individual departments. The second part describes the investigation of a serious adverse event and offers some practical guidance as to the form the investigations might take. The chapter is best read in conjunction with the chapters in the book that concern risk in obstetrics, by James Drife and the analysis of accidents in other areas, by James Reason. The chapter on developing risk management protocols in obstetrics by Richard Beard and Anne O'Connor has a special relevance as the method described here is an extension of the auditing methods they describe.

Methods of studying adverse events

Anyone concerned with adverse events, whether from a management, clinical, or research perspective, needs to consider which method of study is optimal for them. At one extreme are broad brush epidemiological analyses such as the Harvard medical practice study[56] and large scale audits of serious incidents, such as the confidential enquiries into maternal deaths, perinatal deaths, and deaths after surgery.[7-9] At the other extreme, individual case studies provide a picture of the evolution of an accident (see Vincent[10] for a more detailed discussion of the different methods).

Screening of medical records for adverse events, such as in the Harvard study, provides invaluable information on the nature and frequency of adverse events. Such large scale studies are, however, immensely time consuming and expensive and only feasible in a research context. It may be useful though for a risk manager to screen classes of records for specific problems previously identified by staff (for example, Sharples 1990[11]).

An analysis of closed claims from records and other documentation might seem an obvious first step for a new risk manager. There may not be a sufficient number of similar claims for patterns to emerge, however, and there may not be sufficient information to reconstruct events. Considerable problems may also exist in identifying inadequate behaviour or a specific mechanism of injury.[12] It is almost impossible to discover the reasoning behind decisions or the contributory factors that led to a course of action from such information.

Both adverse event screening and closed claims analyses rely on the quality of medical records, records that were not designed expressly for this purpose. Audits of medical records have disclosed persistent and sometimes alarming deficiencies.[13] Poor, sketchy, or disorganised records are not a good foundation for any record based audit.

These methods provide some information about the causes of adverse events. They tell us little about the genesis of accidents, however, or the full range of factors that may be implicated. An alternative approach is to look in detail at specific incidents in which a patient was harmed, or narrowly avoided harm. The critical incident technique is a common sense method for retrospectively analysing a series of such incidents, and much closer to the approach a risk manager might take.

Reports of accidents and near misses are obtained from those involved, and then analysed for common themes. For instance, Cooper and his colleagues[14] reviewed 1089 potentially dangerous incidents in anaesthesia including breathing circuit disconnections, drug syringe swaps, gas flow control errors, and losses of gas supply. In the intensive therapy unit critical incident studies have found that inexperience with equipment and shortage of trained staff often contribute to such incidents.[1]

The critical incident technique is advantageous as near misses are analysed as well as bad outcomes; it monitors all aspects of care; it focuses on the prevention of incidents and can, to some extent, monitor the effects of any preventive strategy.[15] The principal problem has always been maintaining the interest and enthusiasm of the staff involved, and fostering a climate in which incidents are reliably reported and analysed. Reports may not be sufficiently detailed to permit a full analysis of all the factors involved.

If there is an effective incident reporting system a risk manager may be able to interview staff while memories are fresh, rather than rely on necessarily brief incident reports. Interviews can provide much richer information, and it is also possible to enquire about the reasoning behind staff actions as well as simply noting

393

what they did. As with critical incident analysis this approach cannot provide general estimates of risk or frequency of adverse events and relies on data from participants rather than objective observers.[12] However, if interviews and reports are collated soon after the accident there is more chance of a relatively objective assessment. The greatest strengths of interview are that, unlike other methods, the evolution of an accident can be studied including the reasoning behind the participants' actions.

Essential background to the investigation of accidents

Before we describe the analysis of an incident, it is necessary to set the scene with some remarks about the nature of accidents.

Complexity

Analyses of medical accidents typically show a series of errors combined with a set of unusual circumstances leading to a catastrophic outcome. Very seldom is a single person responsible for such an outcome. In depth investigation will invariably expose various errors and human factors acting in conjunction with external risk factors.

Active and latent failures

Human decisions and actions play a major part in nearly all accidents both through active and latent failures.[16]

Active failures are unsafe acts committed by those at the "sharp end" of a system (such as pilots, surgeons, nurses), whose actions have immediate consequences. Unsafe acts or omissions include memory lapses, slips during actions, and mistakes due to ignorance or misreading a situation. In medicine most attention has been paid to the active failures. Legal arguments in medical negligence claims usually focus on the actions of the staff involved rather than on background conditions such as inadequate staffing levels.

Latent failures arise from fallible decisions often taken by people not directly concerned in the workplace. Their damaging consequences may lie dormant for a long time becoming evident only when they combine with local triggering factors (for example, unusual events). These latent failures provide the condition in which unsafe acts occur (Reason, chapter 3).

394

Errors and hindsight

With hindsight it may be easy to recognise an error. However, one should be wary of being critical of apparently obvious errors. People reviewing cases are always presented with a simplified version with the result that they do not face the complexity and uncertainty of the situation experienced by the participants at the time.

Judgements about errors are also influenced by knowledge about the outcome. Two groups of anaesthetists were asked to evaluate human performance in sets of cases with the same descriptive facts, but in which the outcomes were randomly assigned to either bad or neutral. The anaesthetists consistently rated the care in cases with bad outcomes as substandard and the care with neutral outcomes as up to standard, even though the care described was identical.[17]

Blame

When adverse events are discussed in morbidity and mortality meetings or in audit sessions, discussion tends inexorably to drift towards identifying the person primarily responsible for any errors.[1] Such meetings can be dreaded by junior staff, even in the most supportive of departments.

The culture of blame is usually both unfair and unhelpful. Because many accidents are precipitated by latent failures it is unreasonable to blame those at the "sharp end" who are in a sense victims of other people's prior decisions. It also discourages the reporting of adverse events and causes unnecessary distress to staff who are probably already disturbed by the loss or injury of a patient. The true causes of the incident are unlikely to emerge in an atmosphere of blame and suspicion. Such discussion may deepen divisions between staff rather than repairing any disruption of relationships and paths of communication.

That said, it is inescapably true that litigation does involve the imputation of blame, in that individuals are usually named as having provided substandard care in proceedings. There may also, on occasions, be evidence not of isolated errors but of consistent violations or neglect of responsibilities. Then of course blame, and probably disciplinary action, would be appropriate. It is, therefore, not possible or desirable to avoid blame altogether.

Interviewing after adverse events

In the remainder of the paper we report the investigation of an incident in a maternity unit. It is not, strictly speaking, an adverse event as no harm ultimately came either to the mother or the baby. However, it was undoubtedly a "near miss" being a narrow escape for both. It is one in a series of cases we have examined to construct a format that could contribute to effecting change in any department. Our series of interviews was conducted as a research study, but the basic method can be followed by any risk manager or interested clinician.

Identification of an incident

There is no need to restrict interviews to cases that might lead to a claim. In our study staff in an obstetrics department were asked to consider any recent case which had caused concern. Any "near miss" or worrying incident can provide a wealth of valuable information and staff may be more open where litigation is not a threat. When cases had already been examined in audit sessions there was a tendency to bias the narrative towards a greater emphasis on rationalisation and justification of actions.

Interview participants

All those involved were listed, including the mother and attending friends and relatives, obstetric, midwifery, paediatric, and anaesthetic staff, and porters and technicians. Those not routinely at audit and morbidity meetings, such as operating department assistants and porters, often have a great deal to contribute, as do the patients and their relatives.

Interview structure

Each person was interviewed on a one to one basis without reference to the case records (see below) for between 30 and 45 minutes.

Staff were asked to provide a detailed description of the sequence of events with particular reference to their own role and anyone they came into contact with. Typically the interview would begin by asking the person to "tell me everything you can remember about what happened starting from the first time you heard about this patient." Key features of the description were noted and examined in greater detail when the speaker had completed their description of the sequence of events. The most telling details came from establishing the reasoning behind each action. Asking why each procedure was done often uncovered previously unquestioned assumptions.

Inaccuracies in events or contradictions between speakers were not commented on, although contradictions within one story were pointed out and clarified. Finally, interviewees were asked if there was anything that they would have done differently with the benefit of hindsight and how they considered that the department could be improved in the light of this experience. A summary of the interview was typed and given to the interviewee a few days later to amend if necessary. The interviewer followed up omissions and the interviewee added any additional information. Amendments were usually minor alterations of factual details or involved rephrasing a sentence to be less critical. For example, in one interview concerning a haemorrhage, a nurse who had originally stated that "everyone was out of control" later amended this to "the blood loss was out of control."

The case records: a distraction during interviews

The case records are clearly a vital source of information in the investigation of any incident. Litigation may be decided entirely on the basis of the account given in the medical records. In mortality and morbidity meetings the case notes are seen as fundamental to understanding what occurred. In pilot interviews, however, the case notes proved to be a distraction. People tended to bury themselves in the notes confirming detail such as choice of drug, dose level, timing of procedures. The case notes prevented them from forming a coherent narrative of events or from describing the thinking behind actions at the time. We therefore asked people not to use the notes and to reply on their memories. Interviewees were offered a list of the staff involved as a prompt and were told that they could confirm details from the notes after the interview.

Accuracy of recall

Although many apologised for being rusty on details, all could remember the event when provided with the patient's name, diagnosis, and date. There was general agreement about the principal events and whereas perspectives varied, each interview produced an impressive amount of detail. Estimates of time did

Box 1—The process of interviewing and feedback

1 Set up the interview
Find a private room. Ensure discussion is relaxed and informal
Encourage the interviewee to avoid interruptions (to get cover
for their duties and to take the bleep for them)

2 Give basic information about the case
Patient's name, date, and diagnosis; list of those involved
Explain that case notes are not used but offer them the chance
to validate details later if they wish

3 Obtain description of events
Ask interviewees to describe in detail everything they can
remember
Encourage them to give a sequential account, prompting when
necessary
Follow up each stage with the reasons behind it (Why did you
do that procedure? Why did you wait two hours? Why did the
doctor shout?)
Ask them to explain each procedure in detail

4 Follow up references to
Emotions (surprise, confusion, shock, anger)
Change in pace (delays, inactivity, sudden accelerations)

5 Ask if there was anything that they would have done differently
In ideal circumstances
With the benefit of hindsight

6 What improvements would they suggest?

7 Round up the interview
Reassure about strict confidentiality
Ask how the interview went and if they have any questions
Arrange a follow up time for amending script

tend to be unreliable and it was useful to confirm these with the
case notes afterwards. In one case, estimates of the duration of an
operation varied from 15 minutes to three hours. People often had
trouble remembering who they worked with, especially if they were
not in their specialty or were of lower status.

Experience of being interviewed

Although finding an uninterrupted half hour was difficult for
some, once the interview had begun, speakers quickly became

Box 2—Practical points

It helps to:

- Ensure confidentiality
- Ensure privacy while interviewing
- Establish the time the interview will take
- Explain the aim of the interview
- Explain that purpose of the interview is not disciplinary
- Ask open questions

The interview is hindered by:

- Taking the case notes
- Asking leading questions
- Referring to other people's accounts
- Praising or blaming
- Validating opinions
- The interviewer giving their own interpretation of events
- Discussing the individual comments with anyone else

involved in reliving the experience. Some interviewees commented on the cathartic nature of the interview and said that, although they would not usually have talked about the case in such depth, they found the process illuminating. The interview enabled participants to clarify their thoughts and one commented that, after identifying the key issues, she now felt able to discuss the case with the consultant. Staff often returned voluntarily to consider the implications of what they had said and to add extra comments. When shown the typed version of events, there was general surprise at how much information they had volunteered.

The investigation of an adverse obstetric event

The example concerns a healthy teenage mother in the late stages of labour. The staff involved were three experienced midwives and a student midwife on eight hour shifts, a registrar on his first week in the department, an on call senior registrar, a locum senior registrar, and a consultant who was also new to the department. The team members were not accustomed to working together.

The description is based on interviews with five of the staff involved. (A description of fetal monitoring techniques can be found in chapter 8.)

12 midnight

A teenage single mother at term arrived at the labour ward with spontaneous rupture of her membranes and with her cervix 3 cm dilated. Pethidine was given for pain relief because she refused an epidural. The fetal heart was monitored and midwife A noted decelerations on the cardiotocograph (CTG) trace, a possible indication of fetal distress. The contractions were strong and the baby's head was visible. The registrar made two attempts at obtaining a fetal blood sample, but experienced difficulties as the mother was tense with painful contractions. As a result the amount of blood obtained was insufficient to establish oxygen and carbon dioxide concentrations. A pH level was obtained, which was borderline, but the registrar and midwife A agreed that the reading could be unreliable. The CTG trace improved after the procedure.

4 00 am

The mother had progressed to 7 cm dilatation, but the head had not descended; it seemed a tight fit in the pelvis. Contractions were irregular and the number of decelerations of the heart rate had increased. Midwife A contacted the registrar who confirmed her findings. The mother was becoming increasingly distressed and was pulling off the monitoring equipment.

6 00 am

Midwife A and the registrar were concerned that the labour was not progressing so they decided to use syntocinon to augment the labour. With the increase in uterine activity that followed the CTG trace became abnormal, so the syntocinon was reduced. The registrar phoned the senior registrar (on call at home) who said to carry out a caesarean section if there was no progress by 9 00 am.

7 00 am

The morning shift arrived. There were still decelerations and the labour had progressed little. Midwife A suspected an obstruction due to cephalopelvic disproportion (the head was too big for the pelvis) and relayed her fears to midwife B at the handover.

8 00 am

Midwife B changed the monitor because she feared it was faulty as the trace was unclear. Monitoring was still difficult with the second machine, because of the mother's distress, but it seemed that there were decelerations and tachycardia (rapid heart rate). The registrar carried out a vaginal examination and found evidence of likely obstructed labour with a swollen cervix and blood staining of the urine. Both the midwife and the registrar considered that a caesarean section should be done. The midwife stopped the syntocinon and prepared the mother for theatre.

9 00 am

The consultant arrived on the ward, disagreed with the registrar's interpretation of the fetal heart trace saying that the decelerations were not significant and that there was no obstruction. The consultant thought that the mother's distress was affecting the staff's judgement and wanted to give the mother a chance of a natural birth, avoiding the risks of a caesarean section. The consultant instructed the staff to recommence the syntocinon.

The registrar went off duty after handing over to the attending locum senior registrar. The senior registrar agreed with the midwife's and registrar's assessments but said he could not challenge a consultant's decision. He was obviously worried and spent much of the morning sitting with the mother.

10 30 am

On restarting the syntocinon, the contractions once again became very strong and the mother became distressed. After agreeing to have an epidural she became a little calmer. Both the registrar and the midwife were reluctant to increase the dosage of syntocinon because it induced strong contractions. They alternately increased and decreased the syntocinon. The baby was showing evidence of fetal distress with tachycardia and decelerations.

12 00 noon

Concerned by the decelerations and blood in the mother's urine, the senior registrar examined the mother again and found the cervix more swollen and not dilating. The contractions were getting

401

weaker. The senior registrar and midwife B continued to believe labour was obstructed. The consultant disagreed and instructed the staff to increase the syntocinon.

Shortly afterwards, the fetal heart trace deteriorated further. The normal protocol would be to turn the syntocinon off immediately, but because the midwife felt intimidated by the consultant this was not done. She went to the operating theatre to ask the senior registrar for advice and he said to turn it off. He was very concerned but still did not feel able to override the consultant.

1 00 pm

A student midwife took over care from midwife B and immediately expressed her concern to the sister in charge. The sister recognised the crisis and saw that she must arrange a caesarean section without obviously overruling the consultant's decision. She sent the student midwife to have a break. While the midwife was away, the sister deliberately increased the syntocinon to induce more pronounced abnormalities on the CTG trace.

The sister then reduced the syntocinon and called the locum senior registrar. They decided that the increase in decelerations when the syntocinon infusion was increased was enough to justify delivery by caesarean section.

4 00 am

After further delays and prevarication the mother was taken for a caesarean section without the consultant being informed. The baby was born at 4 00 pm in a poor condition with an Apgar score of 2 at one minute, 4 at five minutes, and 6 at 10 minutes. The baby was not breathing and was covered in meconium, an indication of severe distress. He was transferred to special care and recovered quickly with no immediate signs of neurological damage. The baby has since proved to be healthy. Cephalopelvic disproportion was recorded in the medical notes as the indication for the caesarean section.

Staff reactions after the incident

With hindsight, there was unanimous agreement that the caesarean section should have been performed earlier with delays at various points. Staff agreed that the decision to operate would have taken even longer to reach had the sister not intervened. The senior registrar took her advice because he trusted her judgement after many years of working together. The sister commented that the caesarean section would not have been done if she had not been there, suggesting a lack of confidence in the team she was in.

The midwives were disturbed by the case and discussed it with "everyone under the sun" (except the consultant). The registrar felt undermined because his judgement had been challenged and did not speak to any of his colleagues about the case. The midwives asked to discuss the case with the consultant, but three months after the event the consultant had cancelled several meetings and despite repeated requests for rescheduling a time, they had been unsuccessful. Nothing had been done to deal with the emerging concerns: the differences in CTG trace interpretation were not discussed, nor were conflicting ideas of care management, unreliable equipment, or deviations from protocols.

The analysis

Many different approaches could be taken to establish the various contributory causes of this "near miss." We will briefly describe some of the main unsafe acts and latent failures that this analysis has shown. It is of course the staff themselves who have disclosed these problems; the investigator's task is to make their understanding explicit and extract the key features.

Active failures: unsafe acts

All the staff were taking decisions that were, to them, reasonable at the time given the constraints they were under. However, it is clear, of course only in retrospect, that many of them constituted "unsafe acts" in Reason's terms.[16] Some of the main ones, in chronological order, were:

(1) The importance of the decelerations on the CTG trace were not given sufficient weight, partly because there is a high rate of false positives.

(2) The midwives, whose role is to care for women in normal labour, were initially disbelieved when they reported that labour had become abnormal, and hence should be the responsibility of the duty doctors.

(3) The youth of the mother was not recognised as an important factor leading to an obstructed labour. It was also not recognised

403

when the decision was made to continue efforts to achieve a vaginal delivery in someone who was already frightened and emotionally exhausted.

(4) The midwife did not follow the midwifery protocol in that she did not turn down the syntocinon as soon as she saw the deteriorating trace.

(5) The consultant overrode the decision of the team without giving due weight to their reasons for considering that a caesarean section was urgently needed. The decision not to proceed with a caesarean section was probably influenced by the lack of confidence and ability of junior staff to present their case for intervention.

(6) The senior registrar, registrar, and midwives felt forced to act against their own judgement.

(7) The syntocinon was not given correctly. The senior registrar and the midwives were reluctant to use the syntocinon when they judged there was an obstruction. In response they alternately increased and decreased the syntocinon, neither stopping it nor allowing the dose to increase to an effective level.

(8) The sister felt forced to induce more evident signs of fetal distress to impress the doctors of the gravity of the condition of the baby.

Latent failures

Several latent failures contributed to the problems in handling this case.

(1) There was inadequate training for CTG trace intepretation. There was no formal course for junior doctors on arrival in the department, and although advanced courses were advertised, staff did not think the department could afford them. In this case, where interpretation was contradictory, there was no follow up discussion.

(2) When decelerations were seen the tendency was to assume something was wrong with the machine rather than with the mother. The response of the midwives was simply to fiddle with the machine and see if the reading changed. If this did not work, they would change the machine. They apparently did not try to confirm the CTG findings by intermittent counting of the fetal heart rate with a Pinard stethoscope.

(3) There was inadequate training and information about a new fetal blood sampling machine. Staff were given one demonstration, but were unable to interpret error messages. The manufacturer attributed errors in sampling to air getting into the samples, but the staff disagreed. This issue was unresolved and staff were unsure whether to trust the findings.

(4) There was a general acceptance of equipment being faulty as the norm, with a lax system for reporting faulty results. Staff provided each other with inadequate information about prior problems with equipment, each one using equipment that had been found faulty by another. If a monitor was judged faulty, it was wheeled out but not signed to indicate a fault; therefore other staff would then use it.

(5) No one person was responsible for induction programmes, which were inadequate. Both the registrar and consultant were attempting to get to grips with a new job and a high workload after a very brief induction period. They were expected to assume full responsibilities before being integrated into the team.

(6) Shift rotas did not take new staff into account, or the need to have at least one experienced member of staff in the duty team. A registrar in his first week was working with a new consultant and a locum senior registrar.

(7) Each grade monitored and observed the mothers before calling in their superior. This led to huge duplication of effort and time loss, with individual persons within the hierarchy needing to reassure themselves of the state of affairs before making a management decision. In this case, with a mother who was highly distressed and at times out of control, the repeated examinations, tests, and monitoring in addition to the contradictory information added to her fear.

(8) There was no system within the unit to learn from cases like this one by discussion among the staff. Mistakes were repeatedly compounded and lost confidence was not restored. There was also no mechanism for dealing with the potential dangerous conflict that had arisen in this case between the consultant and the rest of the team.

(9) Discussion of this case indicated that much of the monitoring could have been done "the old fashioned way" without the use of the CTG monitor; indeed the more experienced midwives said

they would have preferred to do it that way, especially as the CTG monitoring was distressing the mother. The key point is perhaps that there was no agreement within the unit as to what monitoring systems should be used in which circumstances.

(10) The outstanding deficiency in the management of this case was the lack of definition of who was responsible for what and the lack of an agreed line of communication. When the consultant insisted on further augmenting labour, thereby increasing the risk to the fetus, the normal lines of communication broke down. No system existed to deal with such an eventuality, leading to a highly questionable desperate decision by the sister to induce fetal distress.

Instituting change

The case was made anonymous and presented to the unit for discussion. An overall account of the main features of the case was described, followed by a summary of staff concerns and recommendations for change. The audience rated each suggestion on a scale of agreement or disagreement before discussing the implications of the case. Staff commented on the thoroughness of the analysis and were surprised at the amount of useful information and number of recommendations that had been extracted from a single case. Box 3 summarises the key recommendations.

Box 3—Departmental agreement (%) with recommendations made by individual subjects

Training:	Doctor	Midwives
Formal CTG training should be available for all staff	100	100
CTG updates should be compulsory for all	90	100
Midwives and doctors should be given CTG training together	60	100
There should be follow up sessions on all cases where there has been disagreement in interpreting a CTG trace	90	100
All new staff should have an induction period (of a week or two) when they can become established into the system without beginning clinics etc	70	95

Box 3—*continued*

Training:	Doctor	Midwives
There should be more emphasis on showing the correct way of doing things rather than criticising when a mistake has been made	100	100

Protocols:

	Doctor	Midwives
Variations between consultants should be made explicit	90	100
Midwives and doctors should have matching protocols	100	100
There need to be specific protocols for very young mothers	40	25

Staff communication:

	Doctor	Midwives
Assertiveness training would help many juniors when approaching senior staff	67	75
On call senior staff should follow up calls for advice or help	100	100
Doctors should attend midwives' calls without sifting them	56	100
General practitioner trainees and obstetrician trainees should be taken account of on the rota	100	100
Team building would improve staff communication and reduce risks	78	100

Patient communication

	Doctor	Midwives
Patients should be followed up after a distressing labour	90	100
Potential complainants or litigants should be approached by the staff rather than waiting for the patient to make the first move	100	100

Supervision:

	Doctor	Midwives
There should be more senior staff at night	67	50

Equipment:

	Doctor	Midwives
Monitors need to be more reliable	33	75
Training is needed to familiarise staff with different fetal blood sample machines	70	75
Staff should have the option of delivering without monitors when appropriate	44	100

The level of agreement with most suggestions was high, but some disagreement did arise between grades and between specialties. For example, the failure of a senior registrar to contradict a consultant was considered understandable by junior staff who found some consultants intimidating and unlikely to listen, but was met with surprise by senior doctors who believed they were accessible to juniors.

Box 3 shows some interesting divergences of opinion between doctors and midwives. For instance, midwives were strongly in favour of joint CTG training with doctors, whereas some junior doctors were against this. Presumably joint training sessions would enable a more systematic approach to the use and interpretation of CTG traces and a greater awareness and agreement about when responsibility for a labour should be transferred from the midwives to a doctor. In this team responsibilities were not clearly defined leading to duplication of effort, inconsistent decision making, and no clear line of responsibility during a crisis. The importance of clear demarcation of roles and responsibilities, together with other issues raised in this analysis, are discussed further by Beard and O'Connor (chapter 19). Their risk management protocol was generated after a comprehensive review of risk areas. One way of generating a list of potential risk areas and solutions might be the detailed analysis of a series of potentially worrying cases.

Conclusion

This kind of analysis has the potential to disclose deep rooted unsafe features of organisations that are both inefficient and potentially dangerous. By understanding the root causes, changes can be implemented to reduce risk to patients. The most striking finding is that, in this case at least, the problems were not strictly medical but concerned more with the fallibility of decision making, poor communication, social pressures, and various staffing and equipment problems.

Inadequacies in fetal monitoring procedures and interpretation of results, lack of protocols, lack of team cohesion, and so on could all be shown by systematic audit. An audit of each topic, however, will be time consuming and expensive. The detailed examination of a single case, whether or not litigation is involved, can show a host of weaknesses in care, both within and between specialties and encompassing all grades of staff. Particularly worrying findings can then be followed up with systematic audits where necessary. Cases such as the one described are of course often discussed in morbidity and mortality meetings or in audit sessions. Several cases are usually discussed in the course of an hour, and so there is usually only time to decide whether care was substandard in any way and, if so, to identify the main deficiencies—the active failures as we have described them. Time will not be available to consider the deeper causes of the errors, the latent failures, or to begin to generate ideas for implementing change. We suggest that a more systematised approach dealing with fewer cases in more depth is likely to yield greater dividends than the "many" cases currently analysed briefly and hence less effectively.

We thank Richard Beard, Roger Clements, and Anne O'Connor for the considerable time and effort they devoted to clarifying the clinical issues and expanding our own analysis in several ways.

1 Wright D, MacKenzie SJ, Buchan I, *et al*. Critical incidents in the intensive therapy unit. *Lancet* 1991;**338**:676–8.
2 Wu AW, Folkman S, McPhee SJ, *et al*. Do House officers learn from their mistakes? *JAMA* 1991;**365**:2089–94.
3 Gaba DM, Maxwell M, DeAnda A. Anaesthetic mishaps: breaking the chain of accident evolution. *Anaesthesiology* 1987;**66**:670–6.
4 Cook RI, Woods DD, McDonald JS. *Human performance in anesthesia – a corpus of cases*. Columbus: Ohio State University, 1991.
5 Hiatt HH, Barnes BA, Brennan TA, Laird NM, Lawthers AG, Leape LL, *et al*. A study of medical injury and medical malpractice: an overview. *N Engl J Med* 1989;**321**:480–4.
6 Leape LL, Brennan TA, Laird N, Lawthers AG, Hiatt H. *Adverse events and negligence in hospitalized patients*. *Iatrogenics* 1991;**1**:17–21.
7 Department of Health and Social Security. *Report on confidential enquiry into maternal deaths in England and Wales*. London: HMSO, 1989.
8 Buck N, Devlin HB, Lunn JN. *Confidential enquiry into perioperative deaths*. London: Nuffield Provincial Hospitals Trust, 1987.
9 Campling EA, Devlin HB, Hoile RW, Lunn JN. Report of the confidential enquiry into perioperative deaths. London: Nuffield Provincial Hospitals Trust/ Kings' Fund, 1992.
10 Vincent CA. The study of errors and accident in medicine. In: Vincent CA, Ennis M, Audley RJ, eds. *Medical accidents*. Oxford: Oxford University Press, 1993:17–33.
11 Sharples PM, Storey A, Aynsley-Green A, *et al*. Avoidable factors contributing to death of children with head injury. *BMJ* 1990;**300**:87–91.
12 Caplan RA, Posner KL, Ward RJ, *et al*. Adverse Respiratory Events in Anaethesia: A Closed Claims Analysis. Anaesthesiology 1990;**72**:828–33.
13 Galletly DC, Rowe WL, Henderson RS. The anaesthetic record: a confidential survey on data omission or modification. *Anaesthesia and Intensive Care* 1991; **19**:74–8.

14 Cooper JB, Newbower RS, Kitz RJ. An analysis of major errors and equipment failures in anesthesia management: considerations for prevention and detection. *Anaesthesiology* 1984;**60**:34–42.
15 Williamson J. Critical incident reporting in anaesthesia. *Anaesthesia and Intensive Care* 1988;**16**:101–3.
16 Reason JT. The human factor in medical accidents. In: Vincent CA, Ennis M, Audley RJ, eds. *Medical accidents*. Oxford: Oxford University Press, 1993;1–16.
17 Cook RI, Woods DD. Operating at the sharp end: the complexities of human error. In Bogner MS ed. *Human error in medicine*, Hove: LEA, 1994:255–310.

22 Dealing with clinical complaints

JUDITH ALLSOP, LINDA MULCAHY

Complaints about the NHS can be viewed as an irritating intrusion. Existing complaints systems are time consuming and stressful. Complaints cause extra work, may provide no visible reward, and can lead to disciplinary action. At worst, they can lead to protracted court actions for negligence against a trust or health agency. Yet, *Being heard*, the review of complaints systems in the NHS commissioned by the Department of Health[1]; discussion documents published by the Complaints' Task Force[2]; and a growing body of management literature suggest that complaints can provide opportunities for risk managers and quality managers as well as threats.[3] Moreover, the case for including complaints in risk management programmes has been increased by health service reforms, which have left hospital trusts responsible for financing claims made against them and accountable to purchasers for the way in which they handle complaints. In the United Kingdom the NHS Executive has made reference to complaints as one of several indicators of risk due to adverse events.[4]

Complaints can be used positively in several ways. They can provide an opportunity for providers to see themselves and their service as others see them and to identify the issues which concern users. Most importantly, complaints can allow for rectifying a past mistake and enable services to be put right for the future. A well handled complaint can increase a patient's trust in doctors, nurses, other health care staff, and managers. Finally, complaints can allow the identification of adverse events which might otherwise go undetected, and they act as an early warning system for

411

legal claims. Lessons can be learnt from individual complaints, and—if properly categorised, contextualised, recorded, and analysed—complaints can identify areas for action.

But how far are these messages applicable to dealing with clinical complaints in healthcare settings? Are there aspects of doing clinical work—that is, any expert work on the body—which pose special problems? Even if there are, can clinical complaints be used more effectively for clinical risk management programmes?

This paper begins with a brief discussion of the present complaints system and changes proposed in the Wilson report, which form the basis for the government's response, *Acting on Complaints*.[5] It examines the barriers to effective handling of complaints and what complainants and the organisation want from the system. The final section examines the key factors in developing good practice in handling complaints. The focus is on mechanisms internal to the trust or general practice. Whatever the final shape of guidelines developed by the Department of Health, chief executives, clinicians, and managers will need to develop their own approach. We suggest that this will bring benefits for patient care as well as for risk management.

Handling complaints: current system

A "complaint" may be taken as an expression of dissatisfaction which can be made orally or in writing. The dissatisfaction may be about the patient's own care or that received by someone else—a relative or a close friend. Two main complaints procedures operate in the NHS, one which relates to hospitals and community services, the other to general practitioners.

In the hospital sector the Hospital Complaints (Procedure) Act 1985 obliges hospitals to respond to complaints according to a set of national procedures. Overall responsibility for the handling of complaints lies with hospital managers, who are required to arrange for investigation and monitoring. However, an arrangement made between the British Medical Association and the Department of Health allows for complaints about clinical treatment to be referred to the consultant responsible. When complainants are not satisfied with the response received they can ask to meet with the relevant clinician and, at the discretion of the regional director of public health, can have the case referred to a peer review panel, known as an independent professional review. Complainants who are still

Table 22.1   *Complaints from the public received by statutory bodies, England*

	1981–2	1985–6	1991–2	1992–3
Complaints received by Health Service Commissioner*	586	807	972	1041
Complaints regarding conduct of doctors**	646	748	1301	1615
Hospital clinical complaints†	7005	10 014	17 991	20 647
Community	331	1419	1419	1246
	7336	10 624	19 410	21 893
Complaints about general services††	706	1287	1608	1891

*Health service commissioner's annual reports.
**General Medical Council's annual reports.
†*NHS Complaints Review (1994):* appendix and written complaints by or on behalf of patients, England: financial year 1992–3, Department of Health.
††NHS Executive.

dissatisfied at this stage may be able to refer the matter to the health service commissioner or the courts.

Complaints about general practitioners may be made through the Family Health Services Authority (FHSA), which is responsible for administering the contract between the Department of Health and these practitioners. An attempt to resolve complaints may be made through offering the services of a lay conciliator. If complaints suggest a breach in the general practitioners' contract of employment with the NHS they may be adjudicated by a service committee panel with professional and lay members and a lay chair. In essence, the contract requires the doctor to provide a reasonable standard of care for registered patients at their home or in the surgery, referring them for specialist care if necessary. Complainants dissatisfied with the above procedures may also refer the matter on to the health service commissioner or the courts.

The incidence of complaints

Table 22.1 shows that complaints about health care have been rising; complaints about clinical care have risen faster than those about non-clinical matters. Medicolegal claims are also increasing. Payments to victims of medical negligence have risen by a staggering 56% in the past two years and are currently costing the NHS £125 m.[6]

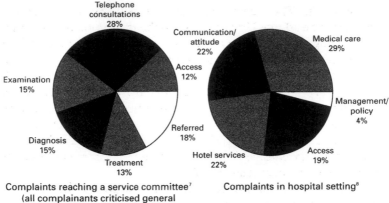

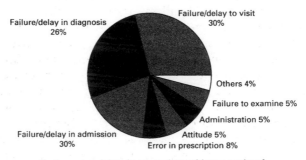

Figure 22.1   *Substance of complaints: findings of three studies*

The subject of complaints varies according to the service being complained about and the jurisdiction of the particular system. Figure 22.1 shows the allegations made in three studies of complaints in healthcare settings.[7–9]

Need for change

During the 1990s criticisms of existing complaints procedures mounted, and in 1993 the Wilson committee was set up to review current arrangements. Reporting in 1994, it proposed a simplified two stage structure for trusts and general practices. At stage one, complaints could be handled in several ways—informally by front line staff or, if the complainant remained dissatisfied, by a complaints officer, manager or senior clinician, and, finally, the chief executive. Conciliators could also be asked to mediate in certain cases. The committee was not prescriptive about the structure to be adopted but emphasised the importance of listening, investigating, and resolving the complaint to the satisfaction of the complainant. It suggested that responsibility for all complaints, including those relating to clinical matters, should rest with management. To encourage an ethos that did not apportion blame the committee recommended that disciplinary action should be separated from complaints procedures. A second stage was proposed for complainants who remained dissatisfied, whereby a panel with a lay chair and a majority of lay members could be set up to review the complaint afresh.

Although the Department of Health's proposals have not yet been implemented, many trusts and general practices have begun to develop new systems. It is in their interest to do so. The case is increasingly strong for identifying and dealing with dissatisfaction early in order to prevent complaints escalating. The resources needed to handle complaints formally are high, although the exact costs have proved difficult to calculate.[1] Even if complaints do not proceed to litigation—and very few do—the costs of investigations and meetings in terms of time and staff can be considerable. In FHSAs, where formal procedures involve lay panels, one study showed that complaints can take on average between 18 months to two years from the receipt of the complaint to a service committee decision.[7] Independent professional reviews may take even longer.[7 10]

The 1990 health service reforms in the United Kingdom brought further incentives for change. Trusts and general practices now have greater financial autonomy and more competition exists between them. Additionally, the loss of crown indemnity has made trusts financially responsible for meeting the costs of legal claims. Maintaining good standards of care and managing risk more efficiently is therefore even more important. Finally, the government's citizen's charter initiative has led to widespread discussion of the use of complaints throughout the public sector. In 1993 the Complaints Task Force, set up by the Charter Unit, published a list of principles to guide the operation of complaints systems (box 1).[11]

Barriers to effective handling of complaints

To be sure they are providing good care, health providers need to know what patients and their relatives think of services and,

---

Box 1—Principles for operating complaints systems

Complaints systems should:
Be easily *accessible* and well publicised

Be *simple* to understand and use

Allow *speedy* handling, with established time limits for action, and keep people informed of progress

Ensure a full and *fair* investigation

Respect people's desire for *confidentiality*

Address all the points at issue and provide an *effective* response and appropriate redress

Provide *information* to management so that services can be improved

---

particularly, what causes dissatisfaction and can lead to complaints. Patients and their relatives have a unique view of their medical care. For example, only they may know the intensity of a pain or that there is a mistake in a prescription. Yet there are several barriers to people expressing their concerns. The Wilson committee commented: "Complainants can face an uphill struggle when using NHS complaints procedures. Firstly, in making their views known and, secondly, in receiving the sort of response they would wish for."[1]

Why people don't complain

Despite the rising incidence of complaints much of the dissatisfaction experienced does not result in a complaint because the level of knowledge of how to complain remains low[12] and people find the various systems confusing. The Wilson committee identified at least nine separate procedures for handling complaints in the NHS. In a study of 1640 householders by Mulcahy and Tritter in 1993, 60% of those who said they were dissatisfied did not discuss their dissatisfaction outside their immediate network of family and friends, and 18% of these blamed their failure to complain on a lack of knowledge.[13] Low expectations, feelings of gratitude, fear of retribution, and deference to health professionals also cause dissatisfaction to remain unvoiced; however, personal circumstances, life events at the time, and general attitudes were

416

also given as reasons for not taking the matter further. Box 2 gives examples of people's reasons for not complaining despite being dissatisfied.

Box 2—Reasons for non-complaint*

My mother did not want me to complain because she felt that she would be victimised and it would affect her treatment

If you take them on, you may suddenly find you cannot get a doctor locally

I don't see any point. You'll never prove anything against doctors. They just club together. I just moan

When I came out [of hospital] I was glad to be alive. It seemed trivial. It was just a relief I hadn't got cancer, I thought that was enough

I just thought I'd try to keep clear of NHS people—I dreaded the fact I may get old and may have to use them more frequently

I'm afraid of making a fool of myself

And you're not going to complain about the nurses because you know they're under pressure

*Quotations taken from the following:
L Mulcahy, J Tritter; Dissatisfaction, Grievances and Complaints in the NHS, a report to the Department of Health, 1993.
A May, J Cayle, J Allsop; High Hopes, Complaints and Charters, report for Riverside Community Health Council, 1993.

Complainants' views of complaints process

If people do decide to raise their concerns research suggests that staff are not always willing or able to help them and that people often feel "fobbed off."[14] Some who want to make complaints over the telephone report a lack of response and follow up to their calls. Indeed, some trusts will not accept complaints over the telephone. Written responses can also fail to satisfy a complainant. Here there are several common concerns. Letters of reply are too brusque and impersonal, the process is too slow; people are not kept informed of progress; and when an investigation does take place and the complainant receives a response he or she may feel this is inadequate. All these factors can increase the anger and frustration

417

of a dissatisfied person. In certain cases it may harden the complainant's resolve to pursue the complaint and change what he or she wants as an outcome. Box 3 gives some examples of complainants' comments about the complaints process.

Box 3—What is wrong with complaints process*

Difficulty in getting information about how to complain
A lot of people in the public service are not trained to deal with the public. You have to say things in a calm manner and try to calm the person down. It is the front line staff who should be most helpful. They should be able to tell you who to complain to in writing, or give you the address, to save you going to someone else which gets you more irate

Difficulty in making complaints over the telephone
"We'll look into it." Then you ring again and hear the same thing

Lack of personal response
Instead of a written letter you get something duplicated. It's senseless

Length of time taken to respond initially
They could give a time even if it's on a postcard saying we will deal with this in one month, that would keep you going

If people keep you informed, that's fine, it means that people are listening to you

I think the thing should be speeded up . . . if you can do it when its fresh in your mind, you might get upset about it, but its clean and fresh . . . if it's looming in the background, you've got to start reliving it again. It stops you grieving

Length of time to investigate and report back
The main problem was the length of time it all took . . . [to about what anaesthetics were used]. The actual date I received that information was the 6 August, which seemed a very long time indeed, from May until August, just to find out what to me seem the answers to an easy question

Inadequate responses
What shook me most of all, by the sort of terseness of the reply . . . I suppose I wanted to feel a sense of apology and I didn't get it

*Quotations taken from the following:
A May, J Coyle, J Allsop; High Hopes, Complaints and Charters, report for Riverside Community Health Council, 1993.
Market Opinion and Research Institute.[14]

Responses of those handling complaints: attitudinal and organisational barriers to learning

The survey by Mulcahy and Tritter found that when people did voice a complaint, it tended to be to the person they held to be responsible for their care—that is, doctors and nurses.[13] This suggests that clinicians' responses are critical in the process of establishing the nature of, and responding to, the grievance. Despite this, a recent Market Opinion and Research Institute (MORI) survey of public attitudes to complaints systems indicated that many NHS users perceived medical staff to be hostile to complaints and to fear recrimination.[14]

It is in the interest of patients, hospitals, and general practitioners to create an ethos in which dissatisfactions can be raised. If a complaint is made then it should be dealt with efficiently and fairly. The case study (box 4) illustrates concerns which were not adequately considered at the time. A complaint was made, but matters were not finally resolved until nine months later.

Health professionals are commonly perceived to be defensive. This may arise from the uncertainties of medical knowledge and the uncertainties of the course of an illness for a particular person. Yet, having made a decision, a clinician must proceed with certainty, on the basis of probabilities. Adverse outcomes are endemic. Also, a gap may exist between what is theoretically possible in terms of treatment, given ample resources, and what is possible in the circumstances.

If complaints about clinical care are taken as an attack on the professional judgement and the personal integrity of a clinician then it is not surprising that strong feelings are aroused. As a consequence, defensive strategies, such as denial or even a counter attack, may be adopted, rather than a more detached attempt to discover the complainant's problem. Another reason for defensiveness is the costs to the person concerned if a complaint escalates. This may lead to enquiries by senior colleagues and the possibility of disciplinary action, both of which threaten reputation, promotion, and livelihood. However, although it is important to understand the reasons for these responses, they cannot justify overtly defensive reactions to complaints.[15]

Negative responses tend to exacerbate complaints rather than resolve them. One study of general practitioners showed that if after a complaint a general practitioner removed a patient from the practice list, showed a lack of sympathy, or was hostile, or

---

Box 4—Case study

A 48 year old woman had a hysterectomy but subsequently experienced two adverse events. A student nurse cut a vein when removing a catheter, which caused heavy bleeding. The vein was stitched but there was a setback in her recovery. Two days later, a heavy metal box placed on a side cupboard had fallen; in avoiding it, the patient had moved quickly, pulling on the wound. The events caused considerable distress to the patient and her relatives. At the time they were not acknowledged by the staff, let alone discussed with the patient. Indeed, her daughter later said: "the staff involved stayed away from mum . . . and she said there was a lack of eye contact and they weren't dealing with it any more."

On discharge, the patient was very weak, and months afterwards she had failed to recover. She had a deep pain in her side and could walk only slowly with the aid of a stick. She could not take paid work. Her daughter, who lived with her, was distressed with her poor health, blamed the hospital but did not know what to do about it. They found the GP unhelpful and unwilling to arrange a further appointment. Eventually, an appointment was made for a hospital check up eight months ahead.

The patient's daughter became unemployed and also became increasingly depressed. She blamed herself for not being able to pay for better care for her mother. Months after her mother's discharge, on a visit to the town hall, she began talking to a woman at a health stall about her mother and said she had wished to complain. She was given the address of the Community Health Council, which gave her support. An exchange of letters with the hospital ensued. Eventually, at an interview with a senior consultant the patient and her daughter related the events. The consultant had no idea what had occurred. As the incidents had not been recorded at the time the investigation was considerably prolonged. However, a resolution was finally reached. The hospital appointment was brought forward and physiotherapy offered.

---

failed to address the issues raised, these then became issues in the dispute.[7] Similarly, an analysis of letters of response to hospital complaints showed that incomplete explanations, dismissive letters, "pseudo-apologies," technical language, and defensive responses played a part in hardening the complainants' attitudes.[16] The length of time taken to deal with a complaint, a lack of openness and not informing the complainant of progress, and an unwillingness to take action when incompetence has been disclosed can also induce disillusionment and a determination to pursue the complaint.[7]

Managerial responses to complaints

The responses of managers to complaints can also be unsatisfactory. Mulcahy and Lloyd-Bostock found that in some trusts managers tended to act merely as clinicians' agents whereas in others they failed to involve clinicians at all.[17] Sometimes, although they began an inquiry process, managers did not undertake a systematic investigation but simply copied the complainant's letter to the people concerned and asked for a response. In other instances, little attempt was made to translate technical or defensive material taken from medical statements into simpler language. Significantly, investigating officers did not always ask the complainant for additional details of their criticism, despite the fact that many accounts were insufficiently detailed to be useful for either investigative or risk management purposes.

Desired outcomes of complaints

Failure to respond to people's expectations when they complain brings with it the risk of continuing dissatisfaction. Studies suggest a variety of motives for complaining. A complaint may be an end in itself, or complainants may want an apology or an answer to a question. Many complainants say they want to prevent a recurrence of an event for the sake of others. They may want a decision or procedure reversed; something done more quickly; a loss made good or something put right; a waiver or reduction in a fee; the payment of monies due; the restoration of possessions; or remedial treatment. A few want compensation or someone punished.[7 15 18 19] Particularly if something has gone wrong, many patients and families want a full and clear explanation. Vincent *et al* showed that in surgical accidents poor communication about what went on may increase distress.[20] If several agencies and people are involved in care, no single person may have responsibility for giving information in a way which is understood to the lay person. Box 5 illustrates what people interviewed in the course of these research studies wanted.

Verifying the accounts may be necessary in order to give a full explanation. An investigation may suggest that there is a difference between a complainant's account and the information collected from those concerned with the patient's care. In this case a meeting

Box 5—What people want to happen as a result of complaining*

An apology
There is a lack of being able to say I'm sorry, we've done it wrong, we will get it right next time

An explanation or answer to a question
First of all I wanted answers to questions concerning things going wrong. Up to this point there seemed to be nothing in the way of information coming forward

Accountability
I wanted some form of justice that this sort of man can't treat people like this . . . some form of authority should know how he behaved and stop him behaving like that in the future

Prevention of the same thing in others
Because you should not let anyone be in such pain . . . Because I don't know how many people before this has happened to and nobody has done anything about it. That's why I decided to complain

Immediate or additional treatment or an admission of error, or both
I wanted some form of physiotherapy and I wanted her to be thoroughly checked and most of all I wanted them to admit that, yes, that something had gone wrong on their side

Punishment for the person responsible
I wanted him struck off

Something to change as a result of the complaint
If something is wrong then you want to complain about it, and if they get more complaints then they might do something about it.

*Quotations taken from the following:
A May, J Coyle, J Allsop; High Hopes, Complaints and Charters, report for Riverside Community Health Council, 1993.
Market Opinion and Research Institute.[14]

is advisable, at the patient's home or at another neutral place or at the hospital or surgery, in an attempt to clarify issues further. In their interviews with complainants Mulcahy and Lloyd-Bostock found that the criticisms people made in conversation were sometimes appreciably different from those they had made in writing. When this happened more serious allegations of clinical mismanagement were made at interview. This may be due to the difficulties which lay people have in expressing their real concerns in writing.

Complaints and feedback

We have argued above that lessons can be learnt from complaints, but in order to do so, the limitations must also be recognised. Identifying the aspects of complaints which are of use for quality and risk management is not always straightforward.[21]

Firstly, the relationship between dissatisfaction, making a complaint, and adverse events is complex. Adverse events that occur may never become the basis for a complaint either because the patient or carer is unaware of them or because they have been explained by staff and are not considered "complaint worthy." The Harvard study of medical records showed that there were more adverse events than were ever reported through complaints or claims.[22] Conversely, claims were made when no adverse event had occurred.

Secondly, complaints tend to arise in a particular context which needs to be analysed and understood to be useful for risk managers and quality managers. They can provide useful and unique pointers to problems as perceived by patients and their carers. However, the complexity of delivery systems; the variety of tasks to be accomplished for a single patient; the number of care givers involved and their inter-relationships need to be carefully traced. Studies of adverse events show that these are rarely a "one off" event but the result of several small errors by various people.[20] In general practitioner settings complaints were less commonly about a single event and more often arose in the course of several interactions during an episode of longer illness.[7] When there are changes in patterns of healthcare delivery or resources are scarce there may be an absence of clear lines of responsibility, which obstructs good patient care.

Thirdly, both Allsop and Lloyd-Bostock concluded that complaints often tend to be embedded in a narrative account which may contain much information which is not strictly relevant to the healthcare provider.[7 16] Typically, several allegations are made, which relate to both past experiences as well as present care. Accounts tend to focus on the behaviour of healthcare staff and on the outcomes of illness episodes. Moreover, the strength of the emotions felt may get in the way of a precise "naming" of a grievance unless complainants have had help in talking through their complaint. As lay people, patients and their carers see events from a particular perspective. They may not know precisely what has gone wrong. They tend to have an incomplete picture of certain aspects of care. If they are the patient, they may not be aware of all the stages of treatment. If they are the carer, they may not have been present at all. We do not suggest that this limits the value of cases, but rather it indicates that those investigating should aim to clarify the complainants' account.

Fourthly, the issue of who has ownership of the grievance is also more complex than it might seem. In healthcare settings a significant proportion of complaints, particularly about clinical care, are made not by patients but by family members.[7 16 18] They may be expressing their own dissatisfaction as well as acting on behalf of a patient for whom they have a caring responsibility. Those dealing with clinical complaints need to be sensitive to the fact that criticisms about care do not always come from patients themselves and they should tailor their investigations accordingly. Letters of response should also be written with this in mind, and meetings should offer to include family members or others.

Summary

In summary the way complaints are handled under current NHS procedures has several weaknesses which stem from the nature of complaints; the ambiguities about what they represent; a lack of knowledge about the dynamics of complaints on the part of managers and clinicians; a lack of skill in investigating complaints; and, for the purposes of risk management, the absence of methods for recording, categorising, and analysing complaints so that they can identify user concerns and predict areas of risk. Ideally, to be of use to the organisation, dissatisfactions and complaints need to be noted, recorded, and investigated thoroughly. The outcomes of investigations and feedback are important not only for patients in resolving a complaint for them but also for staff and the organisation concerned.

Key aspects of handling complaints effectively

There are several ways in which effective handling of complaints can be achieved and can contribute to risk management programmes, depending on the ethos of the trust or general practice.

424

Central to this is accepting that complaints reflect users' views, and that a low level of complaints does not necessarily indicate good care nor a high level, poor care.

Attitude and motivation: a positive approach

Taking complaints seriously is more critical than having particular structural arrangements. A coherent corporate approach should be developed and the complaints system assessed against three evaluation criteria. Does the system promote good practice and deter poor practice? Are those who use it satisfied? Can the insights gained be used for feedback? The interest, commitment, and cooperation of the chief executive and those in clinical leadership positions are essential to any programme (box 6).

Box 6—Developing a coherent corporate approach

- An ethos of taking complaints seriously
- Commitment of senior managers and clinicians to a multidisciplinary approach
- Clear delineation of staff responsibilities
- Standards for processing and recording complaints
- Assessment of the complaints system against evaluation criteria

---

Paradoxically, when there is a strong lead from the centre front line staff initially receiving the complaints are able to take responsibility for trying to resolve problems as they arise and exploring what the complaint is about. Given that complaints typically entail a chain of events and several people from different specialties, this requires trust and cooperation between colleagues, which is characteristic of well functioning cross disciplinary teams (box 7). The circumstances in which complaints should be referred on for further investigation should be made clear.

Welcoming comments and complaints

Patients have made several suggestions about how complaints procedures could be improved. Box 8 illustrates some of these.

> ## Box 7—Training, support, and publicity
>
> - Staff knowledgeable about complaints systems
> - Procedures publicised
> - Training for frontline staff
> - Ease of access to information
> - Sensitivity to the needs of minority groups
> - Support for complainants

Because a complaint may be made to anyone within a hospital or community trust it is important that everyone knows about the complaints system and is able to give inquirers the name of a contact person or a contact number. Leaflets with this information should be widely displayed. Nurses, receptionists, hospital volunteers, and others in daily contact with patients should have priority for receiving suitable training. Details of how to make a complaint should be part of standard patient information packs and made available to hospital outpatients as well as inpatients. Information about the trust, including its complaints system, should also be made widely available through the community health council, general practitioner surgeries, and other local

---

Box 8—Patients' suggestions for improvements to complaints procedures*

Some sort of advertising like leaflets: if you can see a sign saying complaints department, you will go there. You don't need anyone else to tell you

They could put up a sticker, saying: complaints, contact such and such

The person you contact should deal with your problem all the way through

*Quotations taken from the following:
A May, J Coyle, J Allsop; High Hopes, Complaints and Charters, report for Riverside Community Health Council, 1993
Market Opinion and Research Institute.[14]

---

organisations. Some hospitals use the local press and radio for this purpose.

Research suggests that many people like to convey their dissatisfaction by telephone and indeed some hospitals have freephone lines for complaints. However, take up varies widely, for unknown reasons. Chief executives may need to encourage experimentation to find the right approach for their community. In a large hospital calls may come in at several points, and if the response to the caller is inappropriate or callers are referred repeatedly this can add to anger and frustration. One patient commented: "They say he's tied up, they keep saying that. I say, will you untie him please and bring him to the phone." However, not all callers are so assertive, and for some the cost of "hanging on" is prohibitive.[14]

Lessons can also be learnt from comments about what people see as good practice. When asked about the experience of a service committee procedure, one complainant commented: "I can quite honestly say, having gone right the way through from beginning to end, that I can't think of any way it could be improved. They responded immediately. I remember that day I left a call for X and immediately they gave me the right number to call and he called back in 20 minutes. People had enough time to listen and that helped enormously ... but I think it [the complaints procedure] should be better known."*

In relation to access, the question of whether special efforts should be made to reach particular groups in the population is important. Although systematic evidence is lacking, qualitative research suggests that people in certain social positions—for example, those with a low income or from certain ethnic minority groups and some elderly people feel themselves to be in a weak position in making a complaint. There are also groups whose expectations of services are low. Again, there is some evidence that members of ethnic minorities are reluctant to complain.[14] Health providers can help through translating leaflets into languages relevant to their local community. They should be able to tell people where to get support, to provide help to those making

*Quotations taken from the following:
L Mulcahy, J Tritter. Dissatisfaction, Grievances and Complaints in the NHS, a report to the Department of Health, 1993.
A May, J Coyle, J Allsop. High Hopes, Complaints and Charters, report for Riverside Community Health Council, 1993.

complaints, and to be sensitive to the differing expectations of patients.

Once someone has decided to complain, he or she may need support to continue. Some hospitals have funded a patient's advocate post, which can also be used as a first point of access. Other trusts and general practices have found it helpful to consult with user groups about how their handling of complaints is perceived and to survey complainants. Pietroni and Uray-Ura described the establishment of a user group in their general practice and its use in dealing with complaints.[23]

Eliciting comments, listening, and investigation (box 9)

Some trusts and general practices have found eliciting comments helpful as a way of identifying and dealing with problems early. This may be done spontaneously as part of patient care. For example, in one trust, a sister in the eye clinic routinely asked patients how long they had been waiting. Patients were given the option of continuing to wait or of seeing another doctor. Patient's advocates may also help in finding out patients' views.[24]

Once a complaint has been made, the likelihood of resolution is greater if it can be dealt with at the time by the person receiving the complaint. This means making sure that he or she understands what the complaint is about and what the concerns of the complainant are. As indicated above, this may not be straightforward. It may be necessary to inquire into the circumstances which gave rise to the complaint or to refer the

---

Box 9—Responsive handlers of complaints should:

- Elicit comments
- Understand what a complaint is about
- Find out what the complainant wants
- Be investigative not adversarial
- Acknowledge the complainant's feelings
- Address *all* concerns
- Act on the issues raised

---

complaint to a senior clinician, a manager, or a complaints' officer. It is important to inform the complainant of what has been done and what the next steps are.

Perhaps the most crucial skills are listening to what the complainant has to say, clarifying the issues, finding out what the person wants, and attempting to find a solution. In healthcare settings complainants lack knowledge and, above all, may fear a rebuff. They may find it difficult to raise their concerns; they often feel frightened and unwell and do not know what to expect. If all staff members are to respond appropriately then training is essential. Some trusts have introduced focus group discussions which involve patients or user groups, or both, in training sessions. In this way, the staff of the trusts are able to see themselves as others see them. Ideally, the informal complaints made to first line staff should be recorded or reported so that they can be used for feedback and to identify trends in a way which fits with work routines, such as at a weekly staff meeting, a case conference, or in the notes made when shifts change.

For some complaints a fuller investigation will be necessary. This should involve a senior clinician or a complaints' officer, or both. Those undertaking investigations should be trained and follow similar procedures. The objective should be seen as establishing what happened rather than attributing fault. An offer to meet at the complainant's home or another location of his or her choice may be helpful. Box 10 shows the general principles of investigation.

Box 10—Principles of investigation

The person investigating should:

- Not have a direct interest in the complaint
- Keep notes on the information collected and from whom
- Identify conflicts in accounts and attempt to resolve them, if this is not possible, state why not
- Be open about the information collected and what has been said
- Reach a view and have reasons for that view
- Report the findings to a senior person who is responsible for action

---

Responses to complaints, whatever form they take, should recognise the complainant's concerns and outline the process of any investigation, the main findings, what action has been taken, and what further steps will be taken. For example, a letter might begin by acknowledging the complainant's feelings by saying: "I was very sorry to hear of the unhappiness caused when. . . ." It should then address *all* the issues raised by the complainant. In some trusts the standard practice is to thank the person for bringing matters to light and to say what lessons have been learnt and what changes will be made as a result of the complaint. This type of response acknowledges that many people find it difficult to complain and do so because they want to improve the service for others.

Most trusts have a specialised complaints department. This can set standards for handling complaints—for procedures, time limits, data collection, and analysis of complaints—and carry out surveys to assess satisfaction with process. Some trusts have found it useful to set up audits of complaint procedures which involve user groups. In one trust, for example, response letters are discussed with the Community Health Council and other user groups.

If complaints are to be encouraged then it is important for team leaders to support staff who raise issues and who have tried to resolve complaints. It is also essential not to attribute blame before investigation. If people have made mistakes accident analysis suggests that these are rarely due to a single event. In most situations joint responsibility should be assumed. The tension between supporting staff when an honest error has occurred and dealing with poor performance and incompetence is a challenge for leaders in all organisations. Occasionally action must be taken in the interests of the service as a whole, but only after a full inquiry.

Outcomes of complaints

The outcome of complaints can be seen at two levels, firstly, for the complainant and, secondly, for the organisation. Firstly, if investigations show that things have gone wrong some form of redress may be needed. The general purpose of redress is to put things right if possible. It can also reinforce an entitlement to a service or can be used to restore a person to the position he or she would have been had the problem not arisen. It may also compensate people for inconvenience or suffering. As mentioned, complainants may have various concerns, and each should be identified and responded to. Secondly, for an organisation to learn from complaints there should be clear leadership from senior management. This means not only having systems in place to set standards and check on their maintenance but also encouraging an ethos of reflection on the results of investigations. In 1995 the Health Service Commissioner commented on the lack of learning from complaints, that he was ". . . getting rather fed up with seeing the same mistakes made again and again and the trend of handling local complaints getting worse."[25] Ultimately, it is the responsibility of the chief executive to see that this does not occur.

Conclusion

We have argued that dealing with clinical complaints in an open and sympathetic way is part of good patient care. It is also part of risk management. Through reflecting on individual complaints, health providers can see their service as patients and their carers see it. If something untoward has occurred there is a chance to reflect on the chain of events which led to that poor care and to take the necessary action to address problem areas. Because the frequency with which untoward events occur is also significant, it is necessary to look at trends over time to identify where a more detailed review may be necessary. The Wilson committee and the government's response set the framework for change; implementation of the recommendations will depend on the commitment of individual clinicians and managers. A positive response could lead to stronger partnership between patients, their carers, and health providers. Not only will chief executives need to set up new systems, they will also need to evaluate their implementation.

1 NHS Executive. *Being heard—report of the Review Committee on NHS Complaints Procedure.* Leeds: NHSE, 1994.
2 Complaints Task Force. *Access, speed and simplicity, fairness, information, attitude and motivation. Redress.* London: HMSO, 1994. (Discussion papers, 1–6.) Mean report, *Putting things right.* London: HMSO, 1995.
3 Seelos L, Adamson C. Redefining NHS complaint handling—the real challenge. *International Journal of Health Care Quality Assurance,* 1994;7:26–31.
4 NHS Executive. *Risk management in the NHS.* London: Department of Health, 1994.
5 Department of Health. *Acting on complaints: the government's proposals.* London: DOH, 1995.

6 House of Commons, Parliamentary Answers, 7 March 1995. Reported in *Guardian*, 8 March, 1995.

7 Allsop J. Two sides to every story: complainants' and doctors' perspective in disputes about medical care in a general practice setting. *Law and Policy* 1994; **16**:149–84.

8 Owen C. Formal complaints against general practitioners: a study of a thousand cases. *Br J Gen Practice* 1991;**41**:113–5.

9 Lloyd-Bostock S, Mulcahy L. The social psychology of making and responding to hospital complaints: and account model of complaint processes. *Law and Policy* 1994;**16**:123–47.

10 Donaldson L, Cavanagh J. Clinical complaints and their handling: a time for a change. *Quality in Health Care* 1992;**1**:21–5.

11 Complaints Task Force. *Effective complaint handling: principles and check list.* London: Citizen's Charter Unit, HMSO, 1993.

12 Prescott Clarke P, Brooks T, Machray C. *Focus on health care: surveying the public in four health districts.* Vol. 1. London: Social and Community Planning Research and Royal Institute of Public Administration, 1988.

13 Mulcahy L, Tritter J. Hidden Depths. *Health Services Journal* 1994;Jul:24–6.

14 MORI. Complaint handling in the public sector. London: HMSO, 1995. (Citizen's Charter Complaints Task Force.)

15 Donaldson L. Doctors with problems in the NHS workforce. *BMJ* 1994;**308**: 1277–82.

16 Lloyd-Bostock S. Attributions of cause and responsibility as social phenomena. In: Jaspars LJ, Fincham LF, Hewstone LM, eds. *Attribution theory and research: conceptual developmental and social dimensions.* New York: Academic Press, 1993: 261–10.

17 Mulcahy L, Lloyd-Bostock S. Managers as third party dispute handlers in complaints about hospitals. *Law and Policy* 1994;**16**:185–208.

18 Vincent C, Young M, Phillips A. Why do people sue doctors? A study of patients and relatives taking legal action. *Lancet* 1994;**343**:1609–13.

19 Bark P, Vincent C, Jones A, Savory J. Clinical complaints: a means to improving the quality of care. *Quality in Health Care* 1994;**3**:123–32.

20 Vincent CA, Pincus T, Scurr JH. Patients' experience of surgical accidents. *Quality in Health Care* 1993;**2**:77–82.

21 Mulcahy L, Lloyd-Bostock S. Complaining—what's the use. In: Dingwall R, Fenn P, eds. *Quality and regulation in health care.* London: Routledge, 1992: 51–68.

22 Brennan TA, Leape LI, Laird NM, Hebert L, Localio AR, Hawthers AR, *et al.* Incidence of adverse events and negligence in hospitalised patients: the results of the Harvard medical practice study. 1. *N Engl J Med* 1991;**324**:370–6.

23 Pietroni P, de Uray-Ura. Informal complaints procedure in general practice: first year's experience. *BMJ* 1994;**308**:1546–8.

24 Audit Commission. *What seems to be the matter: communication between doctors and patients.* London: HMSO, 1993.

25 Select Committee on the Parliamentary Commissioner for Admininstration. *6th Report 1994/5 session.* London: HMSO, 1994.

23 Caring for patients harmed by treatment

CHARLES VINCENT

I felt as though the medical authorities were clamming up as soon as I expressed my concern over the way I looked. . . . So much evidence has come to light (after seeing a solicitor). . . . If nothing else comes from all this, I have the satisfaction of knowing that it wasn't just my imagination or me simply making a fuss.

The lawyer has just sent me a negative report which may terminate any possible case but this kind of careful and detailed report could have avoided many years of anguish if supplied soon after my reaction to the news of my daughter's damage.[1]

Patients and relatives may suffer in two ways from injuries due to treatment. Firstly, from the injury itself and, secondly, from the way the incident is handled afterwards. Many people harmed by their treatment suffer further trauma through the incident being handled insensitively and inadequately. Conversely, when staff come forward, acknowledge the damage, and take the necessary action the overall trauma can be greatly reduced.

Many people dealing with injured patients are not directly involved in clinical work. It is not easy to appreciate in, say, the quiet of a barrister's chambers, just what a lifetime of chronic pain means. Those acting for hospitals may never even meet the patients involved, except in court. Staff involved in the original incident may not be those involved in rehabilitation and later treatment. The experience of injured patients therefore tends not to be fully appreciated, especially when they become tarred as litigants.

Although there is evidence that some injured patients are harmed further by subsequent clinical mismanagement,[2] I will assume here

433

that, for the most part, medical treatment is adequate once the problem is recognised. The same cannot be said for the attention given to patients' psychological and social problems, which are complex, fluctuating, and not well understood.

Psychological reactions to injury

The speed and extent of recovery from any injury depends on many different factors. The nature and extent of the injury, the degree of pain, and the degree of subsequent disability are crucial. The personality of the affected patients, the history of previous trauma and loss in their lives and their financial security and employment prospects may also influence subsequent adjustment. Although reactions vary greatly certain constellations of symptoms recur.

Traumatic and life threatening events produce various symptoms, over and above any physical injury. Anxiety, intrusive memories, emotional numbing, and flashbacks are all common sequelae and important components of post-traumatic stress disorder.[3 4] Sudden, intense, dangerous, or uncontrollable events are particularly likely to lead to such problems, especially if accompanied by illness, fatigue, or mood disturbances.[5] Awareness under anaesthesia is an example of such an event.

Most accidents, and most medical accidents, do not produce post-traumatic stress disorder in its pure form. The long term consequences of the event, in terms of pain, disability, and effect on family relationships and ability to work, will be much more important than the initial incident, and depression is a more usual response. Whether people actually become depressed and to what degree will depend on the severity of their injury; the support they have from family, friends, and health professionals; and various other factors.[6 7]

Studies of people involved in serious accidents (for example, road accidents) suggest that 20–30% have long term psychological impairment.[3 8 9] Accidental injury during treatment, although little researched, also seems to produce serious psychological symptoms. Vincent et al reported a study of patients who had received damage to organs and nerves, perforations, and other injuries during surgery.[1] The overall effect of these injuries on the patient's lives, as judged by themselves, was considerable including increased pain, disability, psychological trauma, and effects on their work and social lives. The patients frequently experienced disturbing memories, depression, and anxiety.

434

When a patient dies

Any bereavement entails multiple losses: a widow or widower loses companionship, a confidant, and a sexual relationship and may experience a loss of identity. Many bereaved people describe the loss in almost physical terms—as having part of them torn away.[8] Bereavement may be particularly severe if the loss is untimely or unexpected[9] or when the bereaved has had little forewarning about the loss.[10] A bereavement that follows a sudden, accidental death may be exceptionally severe. Lehman et al[11 12] carried out a study on people four to seven years after they had lost a spouse or child in an accident. Many continued to ruminate about the accident and what could have been done to prevent it; they seemed unable to accept, resolve, or find any meaning in the loss.

Relatives of patients whose death was sudden or unexpected may find the loss particularly difficult to bear. If the loss was avoidable in the sense that poor treatment played a part in the death, their relatives may face an unusually traumatic and prolonged bereavement. They may ruminate endlessly on the death and find it hard to accept the loss.

After the incident: pathways to litigation

Many patients and relatives involved in litigation consider that substandard care extended well beyond the original mishap. They are disturbed by the absence of explanations, a lack of honesty, the reluctance to apologise, and being treated as neurotic. When explanations are given they are often thought to be unclear, insufficiently informative, and unsympathetic.[1]

The lack of explanation and other factors play a part in the decision to take legal action. There seem to be four main reasons for litigation. In order of importance they are: standards of care—both patients and relatives want to prevent similar incidents in the future; explanation—to know how it happened and why; compensation—for financial losses, pain and suffering, or to provide care in the future for an injured person; and, finally, accountability—considering that an individual or organisation should be held responsible. In some cases, of course, the need for compensation will be the overriding reason for litigation. If a child is seriously injured, for instance, the financial burden for a lifetime is colossal. Box 1 gives some examples of patients' and relatives' comments about their experiences.

435

Box 1—Patients' and relatives' experiences after the incident

I wrote (to hospital) expressing shock and asking that measures be taken to prevent recurrence. It was not even acknowledged. I know it was received. It was in the file.

When I asked my solicitor to ask for a written apology they said "No way". They have admitted negligence, they have offered compensation, they want to make amends—they won't give me an apology—"Yes, we did do it but we're not sorry" sums up their attitude.

I do feel it is extremely important for a professional counselling service to be offered to victims right after the incident occurs not only for one's physical, but also mental condition. . . .

I feel strongly that a professional separate body should be set up to decide levels of compensation payable . . . fair compensation should be decided by an independent body without incurring the high costs and emotional stress involved by having to take legal action yourselves.

I am sure if I had been told honestly at the time I could have faced it much better . . .

I hope . . . when there is a medical accident the incident is discussed and not ignored because it won't go away, it will surface sometime in the future and by then more bitterness and anger will result.

The lack of compassion shown by all concerned at the time of my (son's) death and the complete lack of information since has caused us great distress.

Taken from Vincent et al[1]

These findings again point to the importance of communication, not just in the sense of having a pleasant manner but in the deeper sense of appreciating the patient's emotional state and understanding the needs of distressed or traumatised people. Communication assumes a special importance when things have gone wrong. Patients often blame doctors not so much for the original mistakes, as for a lack of openness or willingness to explain after the event. They believe that to err is human but not to acknowledge errors is reprehensible. However, this is not to say that justified litigation for a serious injury can, or should, be deflected and smoothed over by a few friendly discussions.

Litigation may also stem, in part, from an initially poor relationship between doctor and patient. Two recent American studies examined the malpractice history of Florida obstetricians. No relation was found between quality of care and claims history. However, patients of clinicians with a high rate of claims made against them in the past were more likely to report feeling rushed, feeling ignored, receiving inadequate explanations or advice, and they spent less time during routine visits with their doctor.[13][14]

Compensation neurosis and the stress of litigation

A person who decides to take legal action must be extremely determined. The process is expensive, protracted, frustrating, and stressful for all concerned, functions as a continual reminder of the original incident, and may interfere with a return to a more normal life. As against that a successful action may, as well as bringing financial benefits, validate the patient's beliefs about the incident, and this may come as a considerable relief.

It is sometimes suggested that if litigation is underway symptoms may be prolonged, exaggerated, or sometimes invented to obtain compensation. If this is a conscious and deliberate deceit, it is referred to as malingering. More commonly the suggestion is that the patient is unaware of doing this and has a "compensation neurosis". Views such as these can lead to a patient's distress being taken less seriously than it should be and it is worth briefly considering the validity of this notion.

Research on the impact of litigation offers little support for the notion of compensation neurosis. There is scant evidence that patients typically resume employment when litigation after industrial and automobile injuries is settled.[15][16] Dworkin et al[16] found that employment status, not compensation and litigation, predicted long term outcome in patients with chronic pain. They concluded that "it would be valuable to redirect attention away from the deleterious effects of compensation neurosis and towards the role of activity and employment in the treatment and rehabilitation of chronic pain patients." There is as yet no research examining recovery from medical accidents. However, these studies suggest that compensation and litigation should probably not be considered as primary determinants of the recovery process. Litigation is certainly stressful but compensation neurosis, in the sense of unconsciously exaggerated symptoms that delay recovery, is rare.

Experiences of injured patients and their relatives

Reports of studies help us to understand the main effects of injury to patients, but it is still difficult to grasp the full extent of the trauma that patients sometimes face. The following case histories are an attempt to flesh out the dry statistics and lists of symptoms. Risk managers, clinicians, and lawyers dealing with injured patients need to understand these experiences if they are to provide the necessary help and minimise the trauma to patients and relatives. Providing this help should also reduce the chances of litigation and, where a case does ensue, reduce the damages for pain and suffering.

The stories described were all gathered in the course of interviews for reports. All the patients were involved in legal action, although not necessarily for large sums of money. Substandard treatment was evident in all cases. None of the people involved had any history of psychological problems of any importance or of serious physical illness. The trauma they described was attributable to their treatment, or that of their relative. The quotations are the patient's or relative's own words taken from the interviews. Names and other identifying details have been changed to protect the anonymity of those involved.

Surgery and obstetrics are, unfairly, overrepresented in these examples because they are among the specialties most at risk for litigation and, in financial terms, pose some of the worst problems. There is no suggestion however that surgeons or obstetricians are more or less likely to provide negligent care than other health professionals.

Case 1—Perforation of the colon: effect on the patient

Mrs Long underwent a ventrosuspension, the fixation of a displaced uterus to the abdominal wall. After the operation she awoke with a terrible pain in her lower abdomen, which became steadily worse over the next four days. She was very frightened and repeatedly told both doctors and nurses, but they dismissed the pain as "wind." On the fifth day the pain reached a crescendo and she felt a "ripping sensation" inside her abdomen. The surgeon (surgeon A) was called, dismissed the pain, and said she could go home the next day. That evening the wound opened and the contents of her bowel began to seep through the dressings. Even then no one seemed concerned. When surgeon A arrived to examine her "his face was a picture—as he finally realised something was wrong." Her bowel had been perforated.

A temporary colostomy was carried out by surgeon B and, a few days later, a further operation was performed to close the wound before she was discharged. The hospital promised that a nurse would attend twice daily at her home, to help her with the colostomy. No one came.

Surgeon B, whom the patient liked and trusted, was away when the time came for the colostomy to be reversed a few months later. The next operation, by surgeon C, was "another fiasco." After a few days there was a discharge of faecal matter from the scar, the wound became infected, and the pain was excruciating. For two weeks she was "crying with the pain, really panicking—I just couldn't take any more."

A final operation to repair the bowel was successful but left her exhausted and depressed. She only began to recover her strength after a year of convalescence. Three years later she was still constantly tired, irritable, low in spirits, and "I don't enjoy anything any more." She no longer welcomes affection or comfort, in fact she prefers to be on her own. She feels that she is going downhill, becoming more gloomy and preoccupied. "I feel that I was strong at the time of the operation but now I'm just crumbling."

Mrs Long's scars are still painful. Her stomach is "deformed" and she feels much less confident and attractive as a result. Three years later the trauma of her time in hospital is still very much alive. She still has nightmares about her time in hospital and is unable to talk about it without breaking into tears. She feels very angry and bitter that no one ever apologised to her or admitted that a mistake has been made.

Traumatic experiences, chronic pain, and physical weakness combined to produce a serious depression which lasted several years. It is remarkable how many patients injured during treatment report that at first they were not believed when they described their excessive pain. This series of errors and mishaps seems to have been partly due to the fact that three different surgeons were

439

involved. The lack of communication between them and the lack of coordination in her care heightened Mrs Long's anxiety. She felt all along that no one person really knew what was wrong with her or had full responsibility for her treatment.

Case 2—Asphyxia during labour: the effect on the mother

Mrs Farr's daughter Polly, now six, has severe cerebral palsy after an injury at birth. Polly's intellectual abilities do not seem to be seriously impaired, but she is severely physically handicapped.

After the birth Mrs Farr was told that Polly had sustained an injury to her brain, but at first she could not really take in this information or comprehend the full implications—"we were just in total shock." After Polly returned from intensive care it took a long time to convince Mrs Farr that Polly was actually her child. At home she hid herself away and pretended everything was alright. It was some weeks before she telephoned a friend and told her "Polly's brain damaged." She said that this was one of the worst things that she had to do.

For the first eight months of Polly's life Mr and Mrs Farr had very little professional help. They had the usual paediatric check ups, seeing registrars who "didn't want to know about Polly" and an "absolutely hopeless" health visitor. They desperately wanted more information and to talk to other people who had children with similar disabilities. They had no idea what to expect or what kind of future Polly might have. After eight months Mrs Farr joined a small support group of mothers and children with similar problems run by a physiotherapist who "became my lifeline." Otherwise she was extremely isolated, apart from nightly phone calls to her mother.

In the first years of Polly's life Mrs Farr cried constantly and blamed herself for everything. She felt that "they'd taken away the baby I should have had and I'd been given Polly." It seemed to her that her real baby had died and she was grieving for the child she never had. She felt that Polly would be better off dead and on many occasions threatened to kill both herself and Polly. Mr Farr would leave the house each morning knowing that they both might be dead when he returned. The physical demands of caring for Polly coupled with the anguish and threats of suicide all but destroyed the marriage. There was no improvement in her mood for three years until she became pregnant again and Polly started school. Until then Polly needed 24 hour attention and she felt "totally trapped."

Mrs Farr copes remarkably well with the enormous physical and emotional demands of caring for Polly. However, she is constantly on edge and cannot relax. "Always in the back of my mind there's something I have to do. I dream about this—I'm always in a panic, always disorganised and out of control." She does everything possible to make Polly's life as good as it can be, but "even now I don't really feel bonded to Polly—I just care for her."

After five years the hospital finally admitted liability. Although no one ever suggested Mrs Farr was to blame, she felt intensely ashamed and guilty before that. Finding out that Polly was injured during the labour has eased some of these feelings and, for the first time, offered some prospect of compensation and help for Polly.

Most of Mrs Farr's problems face all mothers of seriously handicapped children. The grief at the loss of the child that was expected combined with the grinding responsibility of 24 hour care can break the strongest person. It is remarkable then that almost none of the various professionals involved with Polly thought to ask how Mrs Farr was; a few brief questions would have quickly elicited the fact that she was actively suicidal.

If more resources were available, awards would not need to be made for a lifetime's care in the private sector. Services are not adequate, which is one of the reasons for the massive awards made when negligence is shown. However, an admission of liability need not have taken five years; even then, no help was offered. The solicitors then entered another battle for interim payments to provide some basic facilities for Polly. The hospital's duty of care to Mrs Farr seems to have ended, as far as they were concerned, once litigation began. An early offer of compensation, probably in the form of a structured settlement, would have been comparatively cheap for the trust concerned to institute. Polly's needs could then have been reviewed and payments adjusted accordingly, to the benefit of everyone concerned.[17]

Case 3—Damage to the uterus: effect on the husband

Mr Parry's wife underwent a termination of pregnancy because of fears for the viability of the fetus. During the operation her uterus was perforated and the small bowel was damaged. She spent

441

one week in the intensive care unit and only recovered slowly after the operation.

On the morning after the termination Mr Parry was woken at 5 30 am by the police. He found his wife unconscious and heavily sedated in the intensive therapy unit. A doctor explained that the bowel had been damaged and a hysterectomy performed to control the bleeding. Until she regained consciousness, he was in a state of intense and unremitting anxiety.

"When I saw her, it just blew my mind. I was absolutely terrified. I can still see her lying there. I was in tears, thinking she might die. She was deeply unconscious, just like a baby, and then it was as if she was very old. I remember preparing myself for the fact that she might die. It wasn't for four days until she began to wake."

Mr Parry cared for his wife at home. Mrs Parry was in pain, physically extremely weak, and felt tearful and vulnerable. She gradually recovered, but Mr Parry was sleeping badly and in a state of almost continual exhaustion. He did not even begin to recover his strength until a year later by which time his wife was relatively well.

Mr Parry experienced various anxiety related symptoms. Every day he would have flashbacks in which he would re-experience his first sight of his wife in the intensive therapy unit. These experiences always provoked anxiety. Tears would well up and he would feel both angry and distraught that she almost died. At the same time he found it hard to blame the people who were caring for her, as many of them seemed near to exhaustion themselves. He was often on edge, his concentration was poor, and he had many uncharacteristic memory lapses.

The exhaustion and anxiety culminated in a collapse while on a business trip. After returning home he spent some weeks recovering, sleeping a great deal, and unable to cope with any source of stress. Two years later he still has flashbacks, although these are now fairly rare. He is now overly protective of his family and becomes extremely apprehensive if his wife goes out. He is preoccupied by the possibility of an accident and worries all the time until she returns.

This example shows clearly that the patient who is injured may not be the worst affected. The attention of the staff was, rightly, concentrated on Mrs Parry. Once she began to recover their job seemed to be over. Only much later, after his collapse, did Mr

Parry's general practitioner realise that in the long term he had been more seriously affected than his wife. His symptoms were characteristic of post-traumatic stress disorder, although he did not experience the full syndrome. Mr Parry was, like the staff, much more worried about his wife than himself. When she had the injury, it would have been very difficult for him to put himself forward as needing help. Nevertheless, if he had been asked, medication and supportive treatment might have averted the later collapse and prolonged convalescence.

Case 4—Neonatal death: effect on the father

Mr Carter's son, Jamie, sustained injuries at birth causing irreparable spinal cord injury. He died when he was two months old without regaining consciousness.

Late in the labour Mr Carter saw that the midwife had become "rather flustered—I should have realised then that something was wrong." When Jamie was delivered "the cord was round his neck. He wasn't in a good state—even I could see that. If he had died then it would have been much easier for us." Three days after the birth a paediatrician confirmed that their son was, as they suspected, severely handicapped. He had fits and was partially sighted. He never cried or made any sounds because his vocal cords had been damaged. Despite these injuries he continued to grow and put on weight. Two weeks after Jamie's birth Jamie's parents were told that he would not live. They then spent a terrible two months, mostly at the hospital, waiting for him to die.

Mr and Mrs Carter had several meetings with hospital staff but Mr Carter never felt that he had received a full explanation. He remembers being told that "it was just one of those things—that really sent me sky rocketing. No one said it was a mistake, that's what wound me up. Till this day I've got many questions. No one acted quickly enough. No doctor came at all until the paediatrician."

Mr Carter's reaction to Jamie's death was intense, violent, and prolonged. He became quiet, withdrawn, and remote even from his wife, feeling "empty and hopeless." He was tormented by disturbing images and memories of Jamie, of the birth, of his slow death, and particularly of his small, shrunken skull toward the end. Images of Jamie's birth "popped into my head at the most unexpected times. Very vivid, just looking in on it. It just grabs you round the throat. . . ." His sleep was interrupted by violent nightmares of a kind he had never previously experienced. "There was all this blood and gore, fantasy-like stuff." During the day violent images, sometimes of killing people, would come into his head, which absolutely horrified him. Although Mr Carter had always been a relaxed and easy going person he was now easily angered. Confrontations at work sometimes led to fights. "I was really angry all the time, so aggressive—I wanted to hurt people, and I'm not like that at all. I felt that I had to blame someone all the time for everything."

About a year later Mrs Carter became pregnant again. Mr Carter was very anxious during the pregnancy but his symptoms began to subside after their daughter was born. Two years later he still breaks down and cries occasionally, and is generally a sadder and quieter person. When he passes the cemetery where his son is buried he still becomes angry, but now his feelings subside.

Many of the symptoms and experiences reported by Mr Carter are common in any bereavement. Depression, distressing memories, feelings of anger, and dreams of the person who has died are not unusual. However, the intensity, character, and duration of Mr Carter's reaction indicate that this was far from an ordinary bereavement. Anger of that intensity and violent daydreams are not usual, and show that he was experiencing post-traumatic stress disorder. The staff of the paediatric unit clearly tried to help Mr and Mrs Carter, although he still felt that the full story was being hidden from him. Later reports suggested that he was right. Even if Jamie's death had been unavoidable it would probably still have been very difficult for Mr Carter to accept an explanation given the severity of his emotional reaction. The staff did not seem to realise what he was suffering. They did not ask and he did not tell them.

What to do?

All injured patients have their own particular problems and needs. Some require a great deal of additional help, others prefer to rely on their family and friends. Some will primarily require remedial medical treatment, whereas in others the psychological effects will be to the fore. Nevertheless, several basic considerations will help in dealing with anyone who has been injured or seriously distressed by their treatment, whether or not negligence or litigation is involved. These suggestions are derived from patients, their relatives, researchers, and from other writers on this topic.[18-20]

(1) Believe people who say that their treatment has harmed them

Patients who consider that they have been injured during their treatment should in the first instance be believed. In many cases they may have had unrealistic expectations of their treatment, or have not fully understood the risks involved. In a few cases they may be malingering or hypochondriacal. However, if 4% of admissions result in some kind of injury to the patient[21] then a report of such an injury should at least be seen as credible. It should certainly not be automatically seen as evidence of personality problems, or of being "difficult," or even as necessarily being threatening to the staff involved. Being believed is extremely important for accident victims and, conversely, not being believed is always frustrating and can be intensely disturbing.

(2) Give an early explanation

Many studies have shown that patients are generally dissatisfied with the information that they are given in the ordinary course of treatment.[22] The lack of a clear and convincing explanation is especially distressing when something has gone wrong. When patients think that information is being concealed from them, or that they are being dismissed as trouble makers, it is much more difficult for them to cope with the injury. A poor explanation fuels their anger, may affect the course of a bereavement, and may lead patients to distrust the staff caring for them. They may then avoid having further treatment—which in most cases they very much need.

When something has gone wrong a senior doctor needs to give a thorough and clear account of what exactly happened. At the first interview, junior staff involved with the patient may also be present. The patient and their relatives need to have time to reflect on what was said and to be able to return and ask further questions. Several meetings may be needed over the course of weeks or months. Similar considerations of course apply when doctors are breaking bad news of any kind.[23]

(3) Continuity of care or referral?

A patient harmed by treatment poses acute and painful dilemmas for the staff involved. It is natural to avoid that pain by avoiding

445

the patient, yet the staff's response is crucial to the patient's recovery.

> The awful sinking feeling that comes with the realisation of a clinical error, particularly one whose consequences for the patient may be serious, must be familiar to all experienced practitioners.... Sharing with the patient the realisation of that error, admitting that it has occurred, and facing squarely the responsibility for it requires courage. Nevertheless such an approach is appreciated by the patient....[17]

Clements discusses this issue with sensitivity and clarity. In essence he suggests that where the explanation is innocent and accepted by the patient treatment can simply continue. When nothing has in fact gone wrong, but the patient believes it has, a referral to another doctor may be the only course. A much more difficult situation arises when care has been substandard. Clearly the patient must be offered a referral elsewhere if that is what they wish but:

> Our experience is that, even under such circumstances, the patient will often choose to continue under the care of the same doctor. Paradoxically her faith in that doctor may well have been enhanced.[17]

(4) Maintaining the therapeutic relationship

Injured patients may receive support, comfort, and practical help from many sources. It may come from their spouse, family, friends, colleagues, doctors, or community organisations. An especially important source of support will be the doctors and other health professionals who are involved in their treatment.

Both patients and doctors may change their attitudes to each other after medical accidents. Patients often have less trust both in their doctor's competence and in them personally. The reaction of staff varies considerably. Some become more attentive and caring, but many injured patients find that staff attitudes change for the worse. Typical comments are that the staff were more withdrawn and distant and gave them less information.[7]

Patients who have been injured during their treatment may need more time and support than other patients. An honest explanation and a promise to continue treatment may enhance the patient's trust and strengthen the relationship. After an initial mistake it is extremely reassuring for a patient to be overseen by a single senior doctor who undertakes to monitor all aspects of their treatment, even if it involves several different specialties.

Even the best and most sympathetic care can lead to unexpected difficulties. After one avoidable stillbirth a full explanation was offered and the parents were given extensive support. In a final interview the parents expressed their gratitude to the staff. However, the mother was left with a sense of emptiness and frustration:

> I sometimes think it would have been better if I had had somebody to hate. As it was everybody said how sorry they were and I couldn't even get angry even though my baby had died.

Clements comments:

> The doctors and midwives in sharing their grief with the parents had effectively neutralised their justifiable anger at the unnecessary loss. Perhaps we went too far and in expressing our own grief put an unreasonable burden on the parents, allowing them to feel sympathy for us. It is not easy to get it right. The care of the injured or bereaved patient ... should at all times remain balanced and not take advantage of the injured patient's vulnerability to attract sympathy. It is after all their loss, not ours.[17]

(5) Ask specific questions about emotional trauma

A common theme of interviews with injured patients is that none of the professionals involved in their care appreciated the depth of their distress. In many cases outright psychiatric disorders were missed. Risk managers, clinicians, and others involved with these patients can ask basic questions without fear of "making things worse." The case histories illustrate some of the most common reactions and experiences of people with depression and post-traumatic stress disorder. Other crucial areas of enquiry are feelings of anger, humiliation, betrayal, and loss of trust—all often experienced by injured patients.

Box 2 shows a simple questionnaire (used in conjunction with standard psychological tests) that I use as a screening device and to guide a later interview. It is not to be used as a substitute for asking questions but does offer guidance as to the kind of areas one should enquire about. Most injured patients referred for reports will circle at least half of the items.

(6) Consider counselling or psychotherapy

A proportion of patients are probably sufficiently anxious or depressed to warrant formal psychological or psychiatric treatment. Although it is important that a consultant is involved in giving explanations and monitoring remedial treatment it is unrealistic to

Box 2—Checklist of symptoms and problems

Please circle any of the topics listed below that are areas of particular difficulty and which you feel we should discuss during the interview.

A feeling of losing control

Anxiety or panic

Appetite or weight changes

Changes in family relationships

Changes in your social life

Checking things over and over again

Depression

Difficulty making decisions

Difficulty working or studying

Disability

Distressing memories

Disturbing dreams

Feeling less attractive

Feeling hopeless about the future

Feeling you have changed as a person

Financial problems

Finding it hard to concentrate

Getting less pleasure out of life

Guilt

Increased alcohol consumption

Increased smoking

Increased use of drugs

Losing touch with family or friends

Memory problems

Nervousness when travelling or away from home

Pain

Problems with your children

Problems with your spouse or partner

Reduced mobility

Sadness

Sexual problems

Tension

Thoughts that won't leave your mind

Tiredness

Worrying a lot

Please note any other important problems not listed above:

....

....

....

expect the staff of say, a surgical unit, to shoulder the burden of formal counselling. They have neither the time nor the necessary training to deal with the more serious reactions.

A referral to a psychologist or psychiatrist may be clearly indicated, but must be carefully handled. Injured patients are understandably very wary of their problems being seen as "psychological" or "all in the mind." This may be especially true of referrals to a psychiatrist who may (however unfairly) be seen as dealing with mental illness rather than simply offering support and treatment. In a large trust a specialist counsellor may be warranted. This would benefit both injured and traumatised patients and the staff who care for them. Whoever the therapist, it is fundamental that he or she accepts the reality of the patient's injury and does not attempt to explain the patient's reaction away on the basis of past psychological problems. Some patients report that their therapist found it extremely difficult to talk straightforwardly about injuries caused by treatment.

In some circumstances a therapist or counsellor not connected with the trust or practice concerned may be better. Clearly this is necessary if the patient no longer trusts the staff who cared for him or her but it may be helpful even where the staff are continuing to care for the patient. As the example of the stillbirth shows, a patient may be unable to disclose the anger they feel when the staff are also distressed. One of the great values of an outside therapist, not involved with the incident, is that the patient can safely rage, break down, and admit to violent and irrational feelings—provided that the therapist has the necessary qualities of equanimity and acceptance.

(7) Inform patients of changes

Patients' and relatives' wishes to prevent future incidents can be seen both as a genuine desire to safeguard others and as an attempt to find some way of coping with their own pain or loss. The pain may be ameliorated if they believe that, because changes were made, then at least some good came of their experiences. Relatives of patients who have died may express their motives for litigation in terms of an obligation to the dead person to make sure that a similar accident never happens again, so that some good comes of their death.

If changes have been made as a result of the error, it is very much worth informing the patients concerned. They can also be informed about retraining of staff or disciplinary action. Whereas some may regret that the changes were made too late for them, most will appreciate the fact that their experience was understood and acted on. It is, however, clear that letters from administrators not involved in clinical work stating simply that "the necessary steps have been taken to prevent a recurrence" do not convince and may fuel people's anger.[24]

(8) Consider an independent expert report

If a patient proceeds beyond the initial stages of litigation their case is reviewed by a truly independent expert instructed by their solicitor. Unlike the complaints procedures the patient sees the clinical report, has access to the notes, and may be able to discuss the case with the expert. All of these things are very much appreciated. Many patients, after reading such reports, experience relief that their suspicions were confirmed and that they were correct to persist in their complaints. Equally, when they have misunderstood some aspects of the clinical process, an independent expert may be able to clarify matters for them. Unfortunately this clarification usually comes years after the event.

If a claim is made a trust's solicitors will, in due course, commission their own expert reports. An independent report could be commissioned at a much earlier stage though, in addition to internal investigations, if the case is sufficiently serious. The patient would probably need independent legal advice to assure them that the expert was truly independent. If there has been negligence, nothing will have been lost as far as the trust is concerned and the case can be resolved more quickly. If there has not, then the patient can perhaps be deflected from pointless and costly litigation and other help can be offered.

(9) Consider mediation

The legal process may, in various ways, exacerbate the problems facing both patients and staff. It is in everyone's interests, except a certain type of lawyer, that disputes should be settled without recourse to litigation or, at the very least, at an early stage in the legal process. Mediation and alternative dispute resolution are not a panacea, and it is vital that the mediator is skilful and appropriately trained. Nevertheless, this option should always be considered if the matter is sufficiently serious and especially if litigation appears likely (for a full discussion see Brown and Simanowitz[25]).

(10) Offer compensation

Injured patients need help immediately. They need medical treatment, counselling, explanations but they often need money as well. They may need to support their family while they are recovering, pay for specialist treatment, facilities to cope with disability, and so on.

Mrs Farr's life would have been immeasurably improved with an early, properly structured, settlement providing her with facilities to care for her daughter and with respite care. In less serious cases a few thousand pounds early on to provide private therapy, alterations to the home, or additional nursing may make an enormous difference to the patient both practically and in their attitude to the hospital. Clearly ethical reasons exist for offering compensation when a patient has been injured; it should be seen as part of continuing care. There are also sound financial ones; help someone at an early stage and the trust or general practitioner will face lower legal bills and much smaller claims for pain and suffering.

(11) Consider the wider implications

The stories described in this chapter, although serious, are comparatively rare. It might seem that they are one offs, which do not reflect the overall quality of care. A theme that runs throughout this book though is that the study of individual adverse events can often disclose wider problems.[26] Similarly the way that the staff react to serious incidents may show a more general pattern of good or bad communication, and a greater or lesser awareness of patients' experiences. If patients injured by treatment consistently claim that they had to fight to get a proper explanation it may be that other patients in the unit or practice are also struggling to get the information they need.

I thank the people who gave permission for their stories to be used and Roger Clements, Fiona Moss, Angela Phillips, and Arnold Simanowitz for their comments.

1 Vincent C, Young M, Phillips A. Why do people sue doctors? A study of patients and relatives taking legal action. *Lancet* 1994;**343**:1609–13.
2 Harper Mills D, Von Bolschwing GE. *Clinical risk management: experiences from the USA*. 1995. Chapter 1, this volume.

3 Landsman IS, Baum CG, Arnkoff DB, *et al.* The psychological consequences of traumatic injury. *J Behav Med* 1990;**13**:561–81.
4 Davidson JRT, Foa EB. Diagnostic issues in post-traumatic stress disorder: considerations for DSM-IV. *J Abnorm Psychol* 1991;**100**:346–55.
5 Rachman S. Emotional processing. *Behav Res Ther* 1980;**18**:51–60.
6 Brown GW, Harris T. *Social origins of depression.* London: Tavistock Publications, 1978.
7 Vincent CA, Pincus T, Scurr JH. Patients' experience of surgical accidents. *Quality in Health Care* 1993;**2**:77–82.
8 Parkes CM, ed. *Bereavement: studies of grief in adult life.* London: Penguin, 1988.
9 Vachon MLS, Rogers J, Lyall A, Lancee WJ, Sheldon AR, Freeman SJJ. Predictors and correlates of adaption to conjugal bereavement. *Am J Psychiatry* 1982;**139**:998–1002.
10 Lundin T. Morbidity following sudden and unexpected bereavement. *Br J Psychiatry* 1984;**144**:84–8.
11 Lehman DR, Wortman CB, Williams AF. Long-term effects of losing a spouse or child in a motor vehicle crash. *J Pers Soc Psychol* 1987;**52**:218–31.
12 Lehman DR, Lang EL, Wortman CB, Sorenson SB. Long-term effects of sudden bereavement: Marital and parent-child relationships and children's reactions. *Journal of Family Psychology* 1989;**2**:344–67.
13 Entman SS, Glass CA, Hickson GB, *et al.* The relationship between malpractice claims history and subsequent obstetric care. *JAMA* 1994;**272**:1588–91.
14 Hickson GB, Clayton EW, Entman SS, *et al.* Obstetricians' prior malpractice experience and patients' satisfaction with care. *JAMA* 1994;**272**:1583–7.
15 Mendelson G. Follow-up studies of personal injury litigants. *International Journal of Law and Psychiatry* 1984;**7**:179–88.
16 Dworkin RH, Handlin DS, Richlin DN, Brand L, Vannucci C. Unravelling the effects of compensation, litigation and employment on treatment response in chronic pain. *Pain* 1985;**23**:49–59.
17 Clements R. The continuing care of the injured patient. In: Clements R, Huntingford P, eds. *Safe practice in obstetrics and gynaecology.* London: Churchill Livingstone, 1994:425–7.
18 Simanowitz A. Standards, attitudes and accountability in the medical profession. *Lancet* 1985:546–7.
19 Bennet G. After an accident around childbirth. In: Clements R, Huntingford P, eds. *Safe practice in obstetrics and gynaecology.* London: Churchill Livingstone, 1994:417–24.
20 Clements R, Huntingford P, eds. *Safe practice in obstetrics and gynaecology.* London: Churchill Livingstone, 1994.
21 Hiatt HH, Barnes BA, Brennan TA, *et al.* A study of medical injury and medical malpractice: an overview. *N Engl J Med* 1989;**321**:480–4.
22 Ley P. Improving patients' understanding, recall, satisfaction and compliance. In: Broome AK, ed. *Health psychology: processes and applications.* London: Chapman and Hall, 1989:74–102.
23 Finlay I, Dallimore D. Your child is dead. *BMJ* 1991;**302**:1524–5.
24 Bark P, Vincent CA, Jones A, Savory J. Clinical complaints: a means of improving quality of care. *Quality in Health Care* 1994;**3**:123–32.
25 Brown H, Simanowitz A. *Alternative dispute resolution and mediation.* 1995. Chapter 25, this volume.
26 Reason J. *Understanding adverse events: the human factor.* 1995. Chapter 3, this volume.

24 Supporting staff involved in litigation

HAZEL GENN

This chapter focuses on the litigation process from the point of view of doctors and considers the kind of education, preparation, and support that are necessary to help health care professionals to understand and contend with negligence claims. It draws on data gathered during a large scale research project[1] designed to investigate how the compensation system operates in practice. The research includes the perspectives of those involved in cases, or directly affected by them—the medical profession (including hospital doctors and general practitioners), patients, lawyers handling claims, and such bodies as the medical defence organisations, health authorities, and the Association for Victims of Medical Accidents.

The chapter stresses the extent to which legal procedures may exacerbate the problems for both sides in medical negligence litigation and attempts to highlight the fact that questions of "blame" are central to the process of obtaining compensation. Differences between doctors' and lawyers' assumptions about patients' objectives in suing for negligence are considered, before a discussion of doctors' experiences of being the subject of a negligence claim. The chapter concludes with suggestions about the type of education and support that is needed to reduce the damaging effects of negligence claims on doctors, while working toward safer procedures and effective reporting systems that will help to avoid accidents in the future.

Liability for medical negligence

Medical negligence claims are a particular and difficult category of personal injury litigation. The negligence action provides the

453

means by which a person injured in a medical accident can attempt to secure compensation for their losses. Since the 19th century the law of negligence has drawn a clear distinction between those accident victims who could prove that they had been injured by someone else's fault, and those who could not. The law recognises that in the first instance the losses that are suffered as the result of an accident must be borne by the victim, and that they should remain with the victim unless there is a justifiable reason for shifting the loss to another. The most important justification for shifting the loss from the victim is the negligence of another, and according to the law of negligence such a finding will lead to the compulsory shifting of loss from the victim to the person whose negligent behaviour caused the injury.[2] For the purposes of this chapter the linkage in the legal rules between compensation and blameworthy conduct is crucial. In simple terms, compensation depends on fault and the only way that an injured victim can achieve compensation for lost earnings, the cost of care, and other extra costs resulting from injury is to succeed in an action for negligence. Whatever the patient's feelings about a doctor, their entitlement to compensation depends on establishing negligence, and it is important that this connection should be emphasised in order to understand allegations of negligence against doctors in their proper context.

The adversarial nature of the legal process

To succeed with an action for negligence the patient must prove that the damage was "caused" by the negligent behaviour of the doctor. Whether or not the plaintiff succeeds with a claim depends not on whether in terms of some *objective truth* the doctor behaved negligently, but whether on the basis of the records of treatment and other documentary evidence and in the opinion of medical experts, the action of the doctor failed to be "in accordance with the practice accepted by a responsible body of medical men skilled in that particular art." [the *Bolam* test[3]]

Decisions about whether a patient's injuries have or have not been caused by negligent treatment are reached by means of the English adversarial process which has a tendency to exaggerate conflict and which comprises byzantine procedures and arcane rules governing the various steps in the litigation process. The result of these procedures is the accumulation of considerable expense by both parties to the litigation, and a degree of misery for all those involved. On the patient's side, it is pointed out that although there has recently been an increase in the number of claims started, some 75% are abandoned without any recovery[4]; that it is very difficult for patients or their families to succeed with an action for negligence against health care professionals; that the legal rules are weighted in favour of doctors and against the injured plaintiff; that medical negligence cases are inordinately complex and lengthy; and that at the end of the day, patients may settle their cases, but may never obtain a satisfactory explanation of what went wrong in the treatment. On the doctor's side it is argued that the availability of the negligence action inhibits the proper investigation of the causes of accidents, while at the same time having positive disadvantages for doctors and for the practice of medicine. The situation has been summed up by one legal commentator as follows:

> Litigation is costly and the legal hurdles often insurmountable. The law protects English doctors more than other systems do. Yet the medical profession seems just as unhappy with it as potential claimants. The concern is not only with the slowly growing tendency to sue doctors rather than to thank them; it is primarily directed at the gladiatorial nature of our law, that seeks to attribute blame and destroy reputations. For unfortunately, a finding of negligence is often felt by doctors to carry with it an imputation of professional incompetence which, of course, it need not do.[5]

Paradoxically, the most blatant instances of negligence are settled very quickly without ever getting anywhere near a court action, and for those who are the subject of such claims the uncertainty is relatively short lived. When the behaviour of a doctor is more doubtful, or when the causal link between the doctor's actions and the patient's condition is not clear, the degree of scrutiny may be greater, and the period over which the claim is investigated may be very long indeed. It is also true that the cost of litigation leads defendant institutions to make commercial decisions. When a plaintiff's claim is of low value, when the question of negligence is not clear, and when the plaintiff has obtained legal aid, the cost of defending the claim and of winning might be very high indeed. The result is that a commercial decision may be taken to settle the claim, which brings uncertainty to an end but which seems to the doctor to be an admission of his negligence.

Evidence suggests that when liability is disputed negligence actions take between four and eight years to be concluded (Fenn P, conference, 1995). During that period the patient suffers the uncertainty about whether any compensation will ever be received, and the doctor has to live with the spectre of a court trial—although there may be long intervals during which there is no activity, after which the case suddenly comes alive again.

Why do patients sue doctors?

Understanding why patients sue doctors is important because it may affect the way that doctors respond to being sued.

Patients' own accounts of their reasons for attempting to claim damages suggest a complicated mixture of motivating factors[6] including concern with standards of care; the need for an explanation of what took place during their treatment; the need for compensation; and concern about the accountability of the medical profession. Patients do not often get what they want. In most cases they do not get compensation and there is often no revelation about the cause of the accident because some of the worst cases of negligence are settled quickly and without public exposure. Doctors and lawyers confirm that the most glaring instances of negligence are the least likely to receive publicity, precisely because they are the cases which will be settled very quickly. It is the grey areas, those where there is a division of opinion about the actions taken, that are likely to be the most strenuously defended.

> The vast majority of those cases where there is something for the plaintiff, the case never gets to court at all and they are some of the very worst ones, where doctors do things that you really wouldn't believe unless you had been hit on the nose. And often the parties don't know about it, because if the party involved is a junior doctor who has since moved on, and it is obviously going to be settled, the defence organisation might never ask them about it. So the person who is actually responsible for perpetrating the injury may never get to hear about it. . . . So he doesn't get the opportunity to learn from the fact that he has damaged somebody for life. This is what you have to take into account when you are talking about the accountability of the profession. [barrister]

An exploration of lawyers' and doctors' beliefs about patients' reasons for bringing negligence claims disclosed some interesting differences in emphasis.

What do doctors believe patients want?

Most of the doctors interviewed during our research felt that patients are motivated more by the desire to obtain an explanation

456

of what exactly occurred during their treatment and why they suffered physical damage, than by the desire for money. For example:

> I think patients sue because of lack of communication, lack of courtesy, lack of empathy and sympathy by the doctor. I think that if as a doctor you are sympathetic to an individual patient, it is very unlikely that that patient will feel aggrieved, no matter what happens.

> There are two reasons in my experience. One is that they want an explanation for what happened and they haven't had it, and the second is that they are convinced that the hospital isn't telling them the truth. They are not telling them anything at all or they are telling them things people don't believe are true. Sometimes in the course of interviewing a potential plaintiff, you explain what happened and why it happened, and they are happy. Well, not happy—but they are content that they don't have a case and they don't have to go further because they have had an explanation.

Among those expressing this point of view there was an acknowledgement that doctors are not always good at explaining what has gone wrong, if something has gone wrong, and not always prepared to say they are sorry if they feel that they are responsible for injury, or that they are sorry the outcome to the treatment has not been good. It is often difficult to apologise in ordinary life, but it is even more difficult when the results of treatment are clearly causing suffering:

> Usually they want somebody to say they are sorry. For the most part the reason people sue is not through wanting to sue, but it's through feeling that they have been treated badly and the best was not done by them and that an honest mistake was not owned up to ... It's a big thing to say I'm sorry. If somebody comes out a vegetable and you have the feeling that maybe it's your fault there was something that you could have done, it's a very big thing to say "My God it's my fault. I am terribly terribly sorry." Most people are very bad at saying sorry.

In addition to the normal inhibitions on apologising, there was also a perception among some doctors that the potential for becoming involved in a negligence suit can act as a restraint on frankness. This is a well recognised effect of fear of litigation which operates not only in the field of medical negligence, but in most other situations in which a mistake may lead to an allegation of negligence.

Doctors therefore tended to view litigation as a response to lack of sympathy, or an inability on the part of the medical profession to say sorry or to communicate effectively with the patient about what happened during the course of the treatment or intervention.

In some cases that reasoning may well be true: but it is not the whole story. Whereas it is important to consider how to deal with patients once it is clear that something has gone wrong or that there has been an unexpectedly adverse outcome to treatment, it is equally important to review procedures, actions, and decision making which leads to avoidable accidents.

What do lawyers believe patients want?

Lawyers' perceptions of patients' reasons for claiming shows the same sort of mix as has been suggested by previous research.[6] The reasons include the desire for an explanation of what went wrong; the desire for an apology; concern to prevent the same thing happening to another person; and the desire for compensation. The most important motivating factor for any particular patient varies from case to case, depending on needs and circumstances.

Among defence solicitors, most thought that the desire for a thorough investigation of the accident was often an important factor in patients' decisions to sue. Just under half thought that this was often achieved and just over half thought that it was not often achieved. All plaintiffs' solicitors thought that a desire for a proper investigation was important and that these objectives were often achieved through the legal claim.

Solicitors' and barristers' views differ from those of doctors on the question of the importance of compensation to the decision to bring an action for negligence. Lawyers tended on the whole to rate the desire for compensation somewhat higher than doctors, who believe that more openness and willingness to make an apology might be likely to deflect legal action. Lawyers tended to feel that although many patients do want an explanation when they seek legal advice about claiming, they also want money. Sometimes patients want money to care for a permanently injured patient; sometimes money is required to replace lost earnings; and sometimes patients want money just as a recognition of their suffering. In addition, patients' motives may change. The primary reason that leads an injured patient or a bereaved relative to the door of a solicitor may bear little relation to their motivation for continuing with a difficult and traumatic legal case several years later. The following quotations from barristers and solicitors suggest that the view of many of the doctors whom we interviewed takes insufficient account of the desire and indeed the *need* for compensation among victims of medical accidents:

A lot of plaintiffs tell me, and tell other people that I read about in correspondence, that what they really want is to know what happened. If only they were told what had happened, and why it is they are in the condition they are in now, or their relative dies or whatever, they would be happy. But however often this is said to me, I don't believe it. Because in those cases where people have been told in truthful terms what happened, they are still not satisfied. Indeed, in cases where there has been a monumental blunder, being told that there has been a monumental blunder does not necessarily assuage your sense of grievance! . . . They will always tell you that if they had received a polite explanation as to what occurred at the time rather than what they perceive to be a wall of secrecy, they would have been satisfied. But I don't believe that. I suspect that they really want the money. And as much as they can possibly get. [barrister]

I am not a great believer in the idea that people don't want financial compensation. I think the majority, if they have been badly damaged, feel that they deserve some compensation for the way they have been treated, for the pain, or something. There are a few, and I think they are in the minority who simply say "I am not interested in the financial rewards, I simply want an explanation as to what went wrong." A lot of people want an explanation, but the majority want an explanation and some damages as well. [barrister]

Personally I don't actually believe what is often said that patients only want an apology or an explanation. I think that may well be true when they are dealing with a complaint under the clinical complaints procedure . . . I think it very unusual for a patient to have gone to solicitors asking them to look into something, for them still to only be after an explanation or an apology. Then they want money . . . I think I know this is a fact, because often my first letter, on instructions from my client is to say Well we are very sorry this happened. But . . . But that doesn't stop the claims coming, so I think "sorry" isn't sufficient. An explanation is insufficient. [defence solicitors]

The last view which distinguishes between complaints and legal claims, is supported by recent research suggesting that negligence claims cannot accurately be viewed as unresolved complaints (Mulcahy L, conference, 1995). Although a proportion of claims begin as complaints, the more common pattern for negligence claims is for the patient or the patient's relative to go directly to a solicitor to obtain legal advice about the possibility of bringing a claim for negligence. Negligence claims thus often take a different course from complaints, and the first intimation that a hospital may receive about a patient's dissatisfaction or concern with their treatment by a doctor is a letter from solicitors advising of a potential claim.

It is necessary for those in the health services to recognise the fact that in some cases good procedures, quick action, and sensitive behaviour toward a patient who has had an adverse outcome may avert a legal claim. In other cases, however, when the treatment has resulted in death or serious injury, an apology, good communication, and excellent claims procedures *will not*, and *should not*, avert an allegation of negligence, because the patient's prime objective in suing is the hope of recovering compensation for financial losses, for extra costs, and for suffering.

The effects of claims on doctors

Allegations of negligence are common against car drivers, employers, occupiers of premises, and professionals who advise and carry out services in a wide range of situations. This is the inevitable result of a system which provides compensation for injury and economic loss according to notions of fault. Despite the pervasiveness of the negligence allegation, its impact is experienced differently among different classes of those subjected to such allegations. The difference is well illustrated by a case reported in a London newspaper some time ago. An article headed *I feel no guilt says death crash driver* concerned the case of a mother seeking compensation for her son killed in a road accident and recounted the fact that the driver who killed the woman's son did not even attend the court hearing of the case. The driver was reported to have said: "I feel no guilt. Why should I? I didn't even know the case was on until I read about it in the [newspaper]. The argument is between her and the insurance company. I am sorry for what happened, but it was just an accident, no more than that."

This story highlights the disparity in the position of drivers who accidentally kill or maim and those of doctors who accidentally kill or maim. In both situations, unless the negligence has been gross, no criminal liability attaches to their actions. Although in both cases it will be held that the actions of the driver or of the doctor directly led to the injuries, the personal impact may be very different. For a road driver, a finding of liability will call into question the driver's skill as a motorist, but may have few other implications. The driver will not necessarily be disqualified from driving, and may not even receive points on his licence; he will not be required to pay any money directly to the injured plaintiff or a deceased person's family, although he may find that his insurance premium increases in the future. For a doctor the result is similar, but a finding of liability that calls into question his skill

460

as a doctor may be seen as an attack on his professional competence that can shake the foundations of his confidence as a medical practitioner.

The results of research from the United States[7] suggest that common responses to being involved in a medical negligence action is a feeling that the claim was unjustified, and that settling cases is like an admission of guilt. As a result of being sued respondents have reported a tendency to keep more meticulous records, to order diagnostic tests for "protection" even though not strictly necessary, to refrain from seeing certain kinds of patients, and to refrain from performing certain high risk procedures. As far as the emotional impact of claims is concerned, research has disclosed reports of inability to concentrate and indecisiveness among doctors, suggesting a temporary (and in some cases prolonged) impact on the physician's ability to practise. There is also clear evidence of loss of self confidence, as well as reports of symptoms of depressive disorders and anger.[8] Importantly, high proportions of doctors who have been the subject of negligence litigation mention feelings of aloneness" in their efforts to vindicate themselves, but only a few seek moral support from their peers. It is suggested that suppression and silence are typical coping mechanisms within the medical profession.

An important piece of research conducted in New York hospitals found that 1% of patients discharged from New York hospitals had been injured through some negligent medical management, but that the proportion of those who sued was no more than one in eight and that only half of those succeeded in obtaining any damages. The study also found that although physicians perceived the risk of being sued as three times greater than the actual risk, they viewed the effect of the tort system as a psychological distraction rather than a factor which influenced the way that they practised medicine. Doctors reported that claims made against them caused great distress, worry, anger, and frustration and the most severe reactions came from doctors whose cases had gone to a full trial, or had been reported in the media. Many considered that the publicity given to cases that went to trial represented a punishment and that this punishment was unfair because malpractice claims arose largely from circumstances beyond their control.[9]

Research in this country on the impact of negligence claims has focused rather more narrowly on the extent to which the experience of being involved in litigation, or fear of becoming involved in

461

litigation, causes doctors to adopt unjustified and defensive medical practices.[10][11] Such evidence suggests that doctors do adopt defensive medical practices, if only occasionally, to avoid claims of negligence, and that in some circumstances this is accompanied by a misunderstanding of the legal standard of care as it applies to doctors.[12]

Our interviews, conducted primarily with hospital consultants in different specialties, sought to explore differing responses to being the subject of a negligence action. The interviews suggest that doctors do not take litigation in their stride and it may not be desirable that they should. There are, however, important questions to be asked about the long term effects of a protracted negligence action and the effects of fear of litigation (whether accurate or exaggerated) on the practice of medicine.

All of the doctors interviewed who had experienced being the subject of a medical negligence action found the experience to some extent distressing at the time. It is, however, important to distinguish the different ways in which litigation causes or exacerbates existing distress. Doctors may experience concern or distress when an action which is not perceived as mistaken causes an adverse outcome. Doctors also talked about the distress that is experienced as a result of having caused suffering by an action deemed to be a mistake. Thus doctors may realise either immediately or after some time that, despite doing their best for a patient they have made a mistake which has caused an adverse outcome. In these situations litigation simply reinforces and prolongs the distress that is already being felt. In other cases it is the litigation itself that is the primary cause of distress. Being sued is therefore distressing because it prolongs and exacerbates existing distress, and because it involves an allegation that an occurrence which is already causing distress to the doctor is also blameworthy.

Often, the fact that a misjudgment has been made, or that something has gone wrong with a procedure, may be immediately apparent and immediately acknowledged by a doctor. A vivid example was provided by a consultant who had caused a spinal injury during a delicate operation. Despite his best efforts, and working in a highly risky area, the procedure resulted in paralysis for the patient. In such a situation litigation prolongs and reinforces guilt and remorse over several years:

> I didn't think I had been negligent. I think it was just one of those things. I knew it was a dangerous area, you were fairly close and the thing just went forwards into the backbone. I felt at the time and I still

462

feel very sorry for the woman who was injured. I knew that I had done it. I didn't think I had been negligent, but she was obviously damaged by me, and so you felt sorry for her. The Medical Defence Union had to ask some rather unpleasant, pretty straight questions about the incident which was fairly painful at the time ... you would have an interview or two, and then the thing would go fallow for several months at a time, and then it would rear up again, and that in itself was unsettling. I didn't feel at the time that it was an attack on my professional competence, but the trial went on for something like four days, and I obviously didn't like the judgment ... It is very painful to the person at the time, because somebody is casting a slur on your professional capabilities. I still feel desperately sorry that I did damage to somebody, most of us don't go into medicine with that intention. I don't know how much it really did get to me, because I used to bottle up emotions but not long after the case, I had a depression ... I don't think it was the cause of my depression. I think there were probably other factors, but I wouldn't like to say categorically that it wasn't one of the factors. I think that had I thought that I might have been negligent, I would have found it incredibly difficult. I suppose because you are a perfectionist, I would have found it very difficult to live with the fact that I had actually done somebody some harm by something that I should have avoided. [consultant, orthopaedics]

There are also circumstances when the adverse outcome results not from the slip of a wrist but from what turns out to be a misjudgment even though the doctor thought that the decision was the correct one at the time. In these situations doctors often compare their decision making not with car drivers, who make thousands of rapid and potentially lethal decisions on every car journey, but with other professional advisers. They view the decision making process as similar but the potential ramifications of their decisions as far more serious both for their patients and for their own peace of mind. For example:

There is this guilt. If you are sued because you did a survey on somebody's house and they have to have £20 000 of work done as a result of your poor survey of their roof, it is an economic consideration. That's fine. They get the roof done, you are informed. You carry insurance to cover that and now and again you get sued so that the insurance pays for their roof. With medicine it is guilt. Having a paraplegic baby on your conscience is a terrible thing. And being sued for it hurts, because you keep being taken on to the rack again. Think about it. Up to the Medical Defence Union, more letters come back, appearances in court, put off, come back in, all that sort of stuff. So it isn't just the financial thing because we are insured. It is the guilt, the feeling of responsibility that you have done it. [consultant, cardiology]

In this way the effect of negligence claims may be to stigmatise actions which doctors do not see as blameworthy despite the fact

463

that they acknowledge that their action has, indeed, caused damage.

Sometimes litigation simply causes anger and anxiety where there is no existing distress and no perception on the part of the doctor of any mistake or unexpected outcome to treatment.

> If you have been slaving for years, doing what you are trained to do, good for mankind, then mankind turns and slaps you in the face ... you do get upset. Your whole world collapses. You either get upset and get depressed or you get bloody angry ... Some people take it as a personal attack ... Architects on the whole do not hold the power of life and death in their hands unless the design of the leaning tower of Pisa crashes down and kills half the residents of Pisa. Accountants may bankrupt you, but they won't kill you. [consultant, orthopaedics]

> On one case I felt no guilt at all, I just felt a bit hacked off actually, that I had given a huge amount of time to that family, I had actually taken the trouble to make an occasion possible where I could explain things and despite all this they still complained. [consultant, cardiology]

The protracted period over which litigation tends to run exacerbates these problems. A common theme that recurred in interviews was the sheer duration of litigation. Medical negligence litigation, when liability is being denied, characteristically takes four years or more from the first intimation of the claim to settlement or trial. In many cases it can be considerably longer. This time factor is important because it means that the anxiety, guilt, and unhappiness that may be suffered by a doctor extends over many years with the consequent effect on morale and self confidence.

> A very long time ago as a senior house officer allegations were made about my treatment at an inquest, and that was followed up by the beginning stages of litigation ... it actually came to nothing but I reckon I had about five or six years of unhappiness over that in which I would occasionally wake up at night worried about it, in which I would dwell on it ... so that it actually affected me badly even though I wasn't sued, merely the faintest hint of it. So I think it is devastating to anybody, and it shouldn't be but it is ... It is an appalling experience for the plaintiffs I agree, but I think it is an appalling experience for the defendants as well and one of the reasons why it is appalling is that the whole blasted thing takes so long and it hangs over you, year after year, without resolution, which I think is terrible for both sides. [consultant, paediatrics]

There was also a strong sense that the litigation process works a particular sort of unfairness. Lengthy litigation, almost by definition, exposes, questions and condemns publicly decision making or behaviour that is at worst questionable. This is because

464

the grossest incidents of negligence will be unlikely to be defended vigorously by health authorities or defence societies.

> A really good doctor will be slagged off in court and at the end of the day have a hell of a time, whereas the bloody awful doctor will get away from it all because his case will be settled because he is bloody awful! [consultant gynaecologist]

> If it was really horrendous it would be settled and it would probably never hit the papers . . . I think that is one of the tortures. [consultant, paediatrics]

Evidence from interviews thus suggests that the emotional impact on doctors of being involved in litigation is substantial, particularly in cases which result in serious injury, when the doctor acknowledges that something went wrong, but does not consider that his actions were in any way blameworthy. Interview transcripts provide graphic evidence of the strain imposed on doctors and "torture" metaphors are often used in describing the experience of litigation over several years.

Conclusion

Benefits and disadvantages of the litigation system

Medical negligence litigation is a fact of life. The number of claims brought against doctors has been steadily increasing over the past five years and there is little likelihood that this trend will alter. The increase in claims may be due to several factors, not least an increased awareness among the public of the possibility of securing compensation through the legal system, and a growing number of solicitors specialising in medical negligence litigation who are expert in their field. Other proposed changes in the legal system—for example, the introduction of conditional fees (the method by which solicitors take on a legal case on a speculative basis and only receive payment if the action is successful. This is the fee system that operates for legal claims in Scotland)—may well lead to a further increase in the volume of claims.

Litigation can have both beneficial and harmful results. On the benefits side, concern about the costs of compensating accidents can result in greater emphasis on risk management, on accident prevention, and on the development of safe procedures, and can provide the stimulus for investment in up to date equipment. If the spectre of litigation produces these results it may be regarded as operating in the interests of patients and doctors, and in the development of medicine.

> I think the thought of being sued if you get it wrong does concentrate the mind very appropriately on standards of care ... there have been some very good spin offs from litigation, the best example being in the States with anaesthetics. Some years ago the anaesthetists headed the league table for awards of damages against them, and the insurers in the States said we are not going to cover you unless every patient who is under general anaesthetic is continuously electronically monitored ... Now that seems to me to be an excellent result from litigation ... Every patient when under a general anaesthetic, not only the States but in this country too, has a continuous cardiac monitor. Well I would want that if I was a patient, and I think that must be a positive outcome from litigation. [consultant anaesthetist]

> I do think [litigation] has influenced the amount of monitoring equipment we use routinely, and entirely for the better. Five years ago we didn't have oxygen saturation monitoring—now I never put a patient to sleep without an oximeter ... I have of course made lots of mistakes, some of them negligent, but it seems to me to be largely a matter of chance if patients sue or not, and if they do so whether they get anything out of it. [consultant anaesthetist]

In addition to such positive benefits, however, the experience of litigation and the fear of litigation may have harmful results by causing stress and unhappiness among doctors who are being sued and by the tendency for doctors to carry out unnecessary procedures which may have harmful side effects, or to refrain from carrying out potentially beneficial procedures that carry a high risk.

To minimise the harmful effects that fear of litigation and involvement in negligence litigation may produce, doctors and other health care professionals require education about medical law and they require support of different kinds.

Education about medical law

There is currently a regrettable lack of knowledge among health care professionals about the law relating to their professional activities. Medical law rarely features prominently in medical school curricula. If present at all, it tends to be subsumed in medical ethics courses which may be compulsory, may be optional, and are rarely included in the assessment of student learning. The result is that such matters are regarded as optional or unimportant "add ons" to curricula that are already bursting with the quantity of clinical knowledge to be digested. Lack of knowledge about the basics of medical law means that those involved in the treatment

466

and care of patients may misunderstand what the law requires of them, leading to unrealistic overestimates or underestimates of their legal duties. Matters that should be regarded as a fundamental part of the education of health care professionals include an appreciation of the standard of care required by law; responsibilities relating to confidentiality; principles regarding consent to treatment; issues concerning decisions to treat, decisions not to treat, and decisions concerning withdrawal of treatment. There are also important issues concerning the conduct of medical research which raise legal as well as ethical questions. These issues need to be incorporated into the curriculum at an early stage so that health care professionals are educated to know their legal obligations and to recognise the legal and ethical issues involved in even the most mundane day to day decision making concerning the treatment of patients under their care.

Supporting junior staff

Constructive support of junior staff is necessary throughout their training but it is crucial when mistakes have occurred. In these situations support is necessary to avoid or mitigate damage if possible; for others to learn from the error; as an opportunity to reflect on the processes that led to the mistake; and to prevent the mistake from getting out of proportion in the mind of the doctor. Unless junior doctors feel able to discuss mistakes and near misses with their senior supervisors the opportunity to avert disaster may be lost and doctors will continue to feel isolated. The early years of doctors' training are fraught with difficulty. They are required to work under considerable pressure, often at the outer limits of their competence. The importance of support in these circumstances was shown by the case of one junior doctor who recounted an incident in which he had failed to give proper instructions regarding the use of anticoagulant drugs when discharging cardiac patients. The failure came to light subsequently and although no serious damage had been done, the doctor was called by his consultant and given a severe "ticking off". His response to the event, however, was very much influenced by the nature of the support that he received from his consultant. He said:

> I was very sorry that I had done that. But the consultant gave me the impression that he hadn't disowned me because of that. The circumstances were bad, and it should not have happened, but he stood by me on that one. Not to fob off the person, but he spoke to the

467

person as the representative of the team. It was a frightening episode.
[junior doctor]

The importance of supporting junior members of the team was
acknowledged by some of the consultants whom we interviewed.
For example:

> I feel very strongly that the head of a department should take
> responsibility for other staff. The law doesn't see it that way. I think
> the leader of the team is responsible for what happens, even if not
> directly responsible. [consultant, obstetrics and gynaecology]

> The man who is climbing up the ladder and training to be a surgeon
> and makes a mistake ... in those cases, it is extremely important if
> someone like me takes the chap aside and stops it from affecting his
> career. If he is just left to his own devices, that will be a disaster because
> he might even give up surgery in a major case. [consultant, orthopaedics]

> My concern is that often junior staff have to deal through hospital
> lawyers with any claims against them without consultant help. There
> ought to be consultant help. Recently I had to help in a case where
> complications occurred. The plaintiff's lawyers claimed that the junior
> had been negligent—which was not the case—but the hospital lawyers
> would have accepted this. [consultant anaesthetist]

Supporting senior staff

For those who are involved directly in litigation, there is a need
to consider how support from peers or others can be provided over
the protracted course of litigation. Evidence from previous research
as well as the current project indicate the tendency for those
involved in negligence claims to feel isolated and to remain silent
about the effect of the claim on them. This tendency affects senior
staff as much as junior staff. The potential difficulties that face
senior staff who are the subject of claims and the possible impact
on their confidence and sense of wellbeing needs to be considered.
Support from colleagues, support from management, and the
availability of counselling are relatively simple measures that would
help to reduce the impact of claims.

The need for support and counselling is illustrated by the
following extracts from interviews with hospital consultants:

> I've had complaints brought against me with solicitors' letters and ...
> my experience of dealing with other people's makes it much easier for
> me not to be particularly distressed and to look on it quite objectively
> ... I find that the defence organisations are really very good ... but
> what they need to develop is more expertise and some positive support
> and counselling for the doctors who are less experienced than me and

get very worried and distressed when this happens. I have seen senior colleagues really become desperately anxious about these things. [consultant, paediatrics]

There is a sense that the patient's family is being believed and there is little support from senior colleagues. A sense of failure without being helped to put the case into perspective.

There is a clear role for management in considering the issue of how best to provide support for staff. There is also an important need for management to develop procedures that will guide behaviour after an adverse outcome. Interviews indicated doubt about how doctors were expected to respond when treatment of a patient led to a poor outcome. Whereas some doctors considered that it was important to discuss the situation openly with patients others felt constrained from doing so in case this might prejudice their position should the patient decide to take legal action. What is clear from interviews is that there is often uncertainty about *how* medical staff should act in these difficult situations. This uncertainty and fear of litigation may well be what leads medical staff to seem uncommunicative, unhelpful, and lacking in sympathy for the patient's situation. Thus in some circumstances, fear of litigation itself may ironically create the conditions in which litigation becomes more likely because the patient feels unable to obtain a proper explanation of why their treatment has failed or led to an unexpected outcome.

The need to establish clear guidance for staff and to consider the difficult legal and ethical issues in these situations was expressed by a trust medical director as follows:

What I am concerned about is the harm to patients and how we deal with that. There are all sorts of issues around like what you do when you have injured a patient and the patient doesn't know that he has been injured . . . There has been no focus on that in the past . . . People have been somewhat ambivalent about that. The defence organisations used to say "Oh yes. Of course you should explain when something has gone wrong but you mustn't admit liability." And of course that has left doctors not really knowing what they are to do. Of course you don't admit liability when you knock someone over in the road, but there is nothing to stop you saying an accident has happened. It is not for us to say whether it was our fault or not, but we can say "If you are concerned about it you should seek an independent opinion." That seems to me to be a perfectly honourable thing to say and allows you to go on caring for your patient, which if you close the shutters you can't do any more, because the patient either goes away or gets a very rough deal. [trust medical director]

The effect of silence after adverse outcomes and the need for greater openness were similarly expressed by hospital doctors and general practitioners:

> Hospitals bring suspicion on themselves by advising staff to say nothing and refusing to release notes to aggrieved patients or their legal representatives. Notes seem to go "missing" when requested. [general practitioner]

> It is hard for junior hospital doctors to give a frank explanation when a potential problem is brewing for fear that this is not backed up by seniors if the problem escalates, but a simple explanation early on is the most likely way of defusing situations. I feel that I often did stick my neck out, but this is not rewarded in any way (except maybe that I have never had to defend a claim) and it has caused minor remonstrations that I overstepped the mark once or twice. I feel juniors should be told the unit's policy when they join, and if they are not to speak directly to relatives or the patient etc then whoever is authorised should make a commitment to come and talk then if practical including evenings and weekends.

Changing attitudes

There may also be a need to educate doctors about the realities of litigation, and to reflect on whether there is a need for a modification of the culture within which doctors feel unable to acknowledge and discuss their mistakes, and within which those who are the subject of litigation may feel isolated and unsupported. It is important that the medical profession acknowledges that negligence actions are a likely consequence of practising medicine, and there must be education about the realities of negligence claims. Health care professionals must understand the basis on which claims can be commenced, but equally importantly they must be educated about some of the practicalities of litigation procedures and must be prepared for the long period over which a claim for negligence may run. Many doctors act as experts in negligence cases and therefore have considerable experience of the litigation process. Through their examination of material relating to negligence claims they have knowledge about the kinds of actions that lead to allegations of negligence in their particular specialty and therefore represent an important educative resource for their peers and for their junior staff. Through their experience of litigation procedures they can communicate practical information about what happens in the course of a negligence action.

470

Those doctors whom we interviewed and who often act as expert witnesses claimed that reading numerous case files in order to give an expert opinion had made a considerable impact on them, especially in terms of note taking. They remarked on the failure of many doctors to keep detailed notes of decisions and reasons for decisions, and said that they were now much more careful themselves about documenting their decisions in cases and that this was passed on to juniors in their training.

The need for a change of attitude toward negligence litigation was expressed forcefully by one consultant who was experienced in acting as a medicolegal expert:

> There are two principal reasons for the doctors' reactions to being sued. One is that doctors generally find it very difficult to move out of the Victorian status of being demigods and knowing things which the patient can't know and being omnipotent and generally being good to their patients and being respected for it. Once you are challenged that what you have done is negligent, it then destroys the whole edifice of the doctor as God. That's one very powerful thing which is very difficult to address, because nobody actually admits it, but people in very exalted positions who are accused of negligence behave in the most extraordinarily paranoid way because of it, since they think their status is going to be interfered with if they make a mistake. The second reason is that nobody has ever said to doctors in the way that they say to lawyers, "Look we all make mistakes, you are going to make a mistake from time to time. You are no different from anybody else. Come clean, tell your clients that you have made a mistake. We all have our off days, we all forget things, we are all thinking about something else, not concentrating, making mistakes which any reasonable doctor should not make in the circumstances." There is nothing particularly disgraceful or reprehensible about it, as long as you don't make a habit of it. We are all human. [consultant, cardiology]

To limit the more destructive effects of negligence litigation on doctors' self confidence and work, it is important to encourage greater openness among doctors, to provide support for those facing protracted litigation, to learn from the events that give rise to litigation, and, importantly, to see allegations of negligence in their proper context. The inescapable link between the availability of compensation for injured victims and proof of fault on the part of doctors will continue unless and until a different compensation system is introduced. The resulting difficulties for both patients and doctors in the current system were captured in the following extract from an interview with a Queen's Counsel specialising in medical negligence. In an action for damages for brain damage

471

suffered by a baby the Queen's Counsel acted for a consultant accused of negligence. He recalled:

[The consultant] was very brave throughout, gave her evidence very well and in due course she was found not to be negligent. About three days later I got a letter from her, telling me for the first time that if she had been found negligent she did not think that she would have been able to continue in practice. And I believe that. That just illustrates how much it meant to her, if after all these years she had been found to have contributed to this little girl's brain damage she just would not have been able to carry on as a doctor and that was her whole life ... On the other hand it would be completely wrong to say that because doctors feel that way a seriously injured plaintiff who has suffered as a result of their negligence shouldn't get proper compensation. [barrister QC]

1 Genn H, Lloyd Bostock S. Medical negligence – major new research project in progress. *Journal of the Medical Defence Union* 1990;**42**. The analysis of data is continuing and is funded by the Nuffield Foundation.

2 Harris D. Evaluating the goals of personal injury law. In: Cane P, Stapleton J, eds. *Essays for Patrick Atiyah*, Oxford: Clarendon Press, 1991:289–308.

3 Bolam v Friern Hospital Management Committee (1957) 2 All ER 118;(1957) 1 WLR 582.

4 Fenn P, Whelan C. Medical litigation: trends, causes, consequences. In: Dingwall R ed. *Socio-legal aspects of medical practice*. London: Royal College of Physicians of London, 1989:5–19.

5 Markesinis BS, Deakin SF. *Tort law*, 3rd ed. Oxford: Oxford University Press, 1994:265.

6 Vincent C, Young M, Phillips A. Why do people sue doctors? A study of patients and relatives taking legal action, *Lancet* 1994;**343**:1609–13.

7 Ennis M, Vincent C. The effects of medical accidents and litigation on doctors and patients. *Law and Policy* 1994;**16**:97–121.

8 Charles C, Wilbert JR, Kennedy C. Physicians' self-reports of reactions to malpractice litigation, *Am J Psychiatry* 1984;**141**:563–5.

9 *Patients, doctors and lawyers: medical injury, malpractice litigation, and patient compensation in New York*. Report of the Harvard Medical Practice Study to the State of New York, Cambridge: HMPS, 1990.

10 Stallworthy J. *The influence of litigation on medical practice*. London: Academic Press, 1977.

11 Jones MA, Morris AE. Defensive medicine: myths and facts. *Journal of the Medical Defence Union* 1989;40–42.

12 Tribe D, Korgaonkar G. The impact of litigation on patient care: an enquiry into defensive medical practices. *Professional Negligence*, 1991;**2**:2–6.

25 Alternative dispute resolution and mediation

HENRY BROWN, ARNOLD SIMANOWITZ

Doctors and patients are not natural enemies. On the contrary, there is commonly a special relationship between them, with vulnerability and trust on one side and caring and professional expertise on the other.

A medical dispute can create turmoil of that relationship, particularly if it is conducted in the traditional adversarial procedure. Depending on how it develops, the patient may see the practitioner as uncaring and evasive and the practitioner may see the patient as threatening and ungrateful. Legal considerations, the requirements and strategies of indemnifiers, and the language and approach of litigation all serve to fuel antagonism on both sides. Any experience of hospitals or practitioners closing ranks to prevent access to "the truth" may heighten suspicion and hostility.

Currently, most medical disputes follow an adversarial path. This entails pursuing a formal claim for damages, through the courts by way of litigation if necessary. The initiation of litigation serves various functions: it signals a serious intention to prosecute a claim; it leads to the use of procedures enabling fact gathering and eventual verification to take place; it is a vehicle for providing an outlet to anger, frustration, and other feelings; it interrupts the limitation period; and, incidentally, it provides a potential framework within which settlement negotiations can eventually take place.

However, litigation also has shortcomings, both for patients and practitioners. For patients, the public perception is that the most serious failings are cost and delay. With the reduction in availability of legal aid very few ordinary families can afford to undertake medical negligence litigation. Although the move towards conditional fees, which is a form of "no win, no fee," may seem superficially attractive, it will have little effect in medical negligence while the plaintiff remains at risk of paying the huge costs of the defendants in the event of the action failing. Furthermore, solicitors are likely to undertake only cases with high probabilities of success, which are very difficult to identify in medical negligence cases. Although delay, unlike cost, may not actually deny justice to patients, it causes immense distress and hardship. The average time before a medical negligence case is resolved is about four years. Meanwhile the patient and any dependants may suffer considerable privation, and expensive care which may be urgently needed could be denied. For practitioners the years of delay while an allegation of negligence, often unjustified, hangs over them can cause untold distress.

As serious an issue for patients is the need to prove negligence and the difficulty in doing so. Not only does this involve finding a medical expert prepared to criticise a colleague robustly but the burden of proof is so difficult to discharge that only a minority of medical negligence claims succeed at trial.

The more important shortcomings for patients and practitioners, and indirectly for health authorities and trusts and their managers are, however, that the wrong issues are addressed because everything has to be reduced to pounds and pence and that the adversarial procedure turns patients into enemies of the healthcare providers. Although financial compensation may be important to claimants, that is by no means universal. The financial claim may often have little more than symbolic value for people seeking accountability—who, for example, wants £7500 or indeed any sum when they have lost a young child?

Accordingly, in common with other fields of activity, there have been moves to seek alternatives to litigation for medical disputes by using processes which effectively serve many of the functions of litigation but with the opportunity to avoid some of its negative consequences, and with the additional dynamic of constructive neutral intervention (see, for example, Kellett,[1] Leone,[2] and Reeves[3]).

Alternative dispute resolution (ADR) processes

This paper examines alternative dispute resolution processes with particular reference to the medical context. These processes

474

have a common thread—namely, the use of a neutral who impartially helps the parties to resolve their dispute. There are two fundamentally different ways in which the neutral can do so: by *adjudication*, in which the neutral makes a decision which is binding on both sides, and through various forms of *non-adjudicatory alternative dispute resolution*, in which the neutral has no authority to make any binding decision but instead helps the parties to arrive at their own binding agreement as to the terms of resolution.

Adjudicatory forms of alternative dispute resolution in the medical context are primarily arbitration or expert determination, though any other process involving decision making that was binding would fall into this category—for example, the way of dealing with disputes within the health standards inspectorate proposed by Action for Victims of Medical Accidents (AVMA) and the Association of Community Health Councils in England and Wales (ACHCEW). There is a view that adjudicatory processes should not be classed as alternative dispute resolution but in this paper they will be viewed as such.

Non-adjudicatory alternative dispute resolution processes entail the neutral using various skills in facilitating a settlement of the dispute by agreement between the parties. Some of these processes may entail an examination of the merits of the dispute and an attempt to provide a non-binding opinion to help guide the parties in their settlement attempts, but because of the non-binding element these processes remain non-adjudicatory. Others do not consider the merits of the dispute, leaving the parties and their professional advisers to place their own weight on the factors relevant to settlement. In the absence of agreement the parties reserve the right to have the issues resolved by adjudication, whether by litigation or by an adjudicatory form of alternative dispute resolution. These non-adjudicatory, or consensual, forms include mediation, the mini-trial, and neutral fact finding experts.

This paper will focus primarily on mediation, as the form of non-adjudicatory alternative dispute resolution most widely used or considered by various authorities, as it can be used without any need for legislation or formalisation, and also as it addresses more than the formal allegations by the patient and therefore seems to be more suited to disputes between doctor and patient.

In several countries outside the United Kingdom, some forms of alternative dispute resolution are available through the courts as an alternative to the strict litigation process, known as "court attached" processes (for example, court attached arbitration, court attached mediation, judicial settlement conferences, and settlement weeks, also the concept of a "multi-door courthouse" used in the United States, under which cases are screened by an appointed court official to help decide which kind of process to use; see Brown and Marriott[4]). Although some of these processes are under consideration in the United Kingdom, they are not yet in effect and will not be mentioned further.

Adjudication of medical disputes

Several alternatives to litigation exist where adjudication is required, as follows.

Arbitration

Arbitration is a privately arranged and confidential process by which a third party neutral, selected by the parties or through some agreed selection procedure, hears and determines the issues, and whose decision is binding. The arbitrator's approach may be judicial in its quality, but the procedures and rules of evidence may be simplified from the traditional court process, and special rules may be applied by agreement. So, for example, the arbitrator may be helped by an expert medical assessor; the way in which expert medical evidence is adduced can be specified; and extensive oral submissions can be largely replaced by written submissions. Arbitration in the United Kingdom is regulated by a statutory regimen, which provides a framework, with some freedom to move outside it.

Towards the end of 1991 the Department of Health issued a consultation paper on proposals for the arbitration of medical negligence claims.[5] Based on ideas first put forward by Lord Griffiths at a conference of Action for Victims of Medical Accidents in June 1991, its main proposals were for adjudication by a lawyer and two doctors with evidence restricted to documents and with no cross examination of witnesses. In early 1995 no decision had been made by the department on the proposals nor had the comments of the consultees been published. It is known, however, that there was little enthusiasm for the proposals from patients' or practitioners' representatives and it is unlikely that the proposals will be taken any further.

Arbitration services are available for medical claims (for example, the Chartered Institute of Arbitrators has developed an arbitration scheme for medical negligence claims within the National Health Service), but as arbitration is seen by many patients' groups as a watered down version of litigation which, save perhaps for cost and speed, is less fair to patients it is not generally considered an attractive proposition.

Expert determination

Expert determination differs from arbitration in that the expert's functions and authority arise from the contract of appointment, subject to which a determination binding upon the parties is generally required to be made. There is no statutory framework (for an overview of the use of expert determination see Kendall[6-8] and cases of Campbell versus Edwards,[9] Nikko Hotels versus MEPC plc,[10] and Jones versus Sherwood[11]). Provided that there is no fraud or collusion and the expert makes a decision within the terms of his or her brief, which may not necessarily involve hearing oral or written submissions, there is not usually any basis for reviewing or appealing the decision.

There may be circumstances in which an expert determination is appropriate, but many disputants may prefer, if they seek an adjudication, to have the benefit of court procedures and appeal and review possibilities.

Medical inspectorate

As mentioned, the idea of dealing with disputes between patients and doctors within the context of a health standards inspectorate has been proposed by Action for Victims of Medical Accidents and the Association of Community Health Councils in England and Wales. There would be four separate commissions to deal with claims, complaints, disciplinary matters, and administrative problems. The advantage for patients would be that all issues would be addressed by one body whose different sections would be interconnected and thus able to share information. Practitioners would benefit because not only would considerable time be saved but once the issues were dealt with by the inspectorate, this would be finally conclusive as between practitioner and patient.

Claims would be investigated formally by the inspectors and most would be dealt with administratively. When disputes did arise a tribunal under the High Court would adjudicate, using the inquisitorial approach of the inspector for establishing the facts but allowing the parties or their representatives to challenge them.

Although the proposals do not specifically include arrangements for mediation, the framework would readily allow for referral to mediation. The proposals are under continuing discussion and the idea of an inspectorate has been taken up by some of those concerned with the issue of risk management.

Ombudsman

An ombudsman is usually an independent person whose role is to deal with public complaints against administrative injustice and maladministration and who has the power to investigate, criticise, and make issues public, and in some instances to make compensatory awards (see Mills[12]). As these functions comprise the examination and resolution of grievances outside the judicial system (see Birkinshaw[13]), and may include investigation and mediation, many alternative dispute resolution organisations view the ombudsman as properly coming under the broad heading of alternative dispute resolution.

Health service commissioners have been appointed for England and Wales pursuant to the National Health Service Act 1977 and the Health Services Act 1980. They may investigate complaints relating to alleged failures by health authorities or trusts to provide services or complaints of injustice or hardship suffered as a result of action taken by a health authority or trust. However, the limitations of their investigative powers do not give them significant relevance to individual medical negligence disputes. For example, they may not investigate complaints in which the person has a right of appeal or review to a tribunal or a remedy by way of court proceedings, nor in which the action of the health authority or trust was taken in connection with diagnosis, care, or treatment of a patient solely in consequence of the exercise of clinical judgment.

Mediation and other non-adjudicatory processes

Shared attributes

Non-adjudicatory alternative dispute resolution processes including mediation share several characteristics. They are generally all conducted on a confidential and evidentially privileged basis, with the right reserved to go to trial (or to some other form of adjudication) if agreement cannot be reached. Compared with adjudication, they are generally relatively low risk, low cost, and expeditious. They tend to heal rather than exacerbate differences; and their success rate in most fields is relatively high. On the other hand, these processes do not constitute a panacea; there are situations in which their use would be inappropriate and in which a third party adjudication is necessary and proper; and they need to be handled with care and skill.

In risk management terms, these consensual processes are obviously more effective than litigation and other forms of adjudication. This is because in adjudication significant decisions are taken out of the hands of the parties, who become dependent on lawyers, expert witnesses, and an adjudicator. However, in non-adjudicatory alternative dispute resolution such as mediation, all decision making remains in the hands of the parties (and with the managers of health authorities or trusts when there is an obligation to indemnify) and there can be no outcome which is unacceptable to them (apart from reverting to adjudication). Inevitably, this is the most effective way to try to manage the risk of a dispute. Another significant factor is that these processes offer a forum in which parties can communicate more freely and can express concerns and offer explanations, and even apologies, if appropriate. They afford the opportunity for patients to understand the considerations that may have made a clinical decision more problematical and for practitioners to understand the feelings and concerns of the patient.

Traditional lawyers and negotiators sometimes query the value of impartial intercession, pointing out that they are capable of conducting a case and negotiating a settlement without this process. This view certainly has some validity. When constructive discussions and negotiations result in parties arriving at an agreed settlement there is no need for neutral intervention as offered by alternative dispute resolution processes. Unfortunately, in a significant majority of cases this is not the reality, at least until a very late stage, when time has passed, costs and risks have escalated, and both sides have had to experience much anxiety and emotional distress. Mediation and other forms of alternative dispute resolution can bring a new dynamic into the situation at any stage, with established procedures and skilled practitioners to help in those cases which cannot easily be settled by way of ordinary bilateral negotiations.

Mediation (conciliation)

Mediation may be defined as a process by which disputing parties voluntarily engage the help of an impartial mediator, who has no

479

authority to make any decisions for them but who uses certain skills to help them to resolve their dispute by negotiated agreement without adjudication (for details of the mediation process see Brown and Marriott,[4] Acland,[14] and Bevan[15]).

The term "mediation" is sometimes understood to be more proactive than "conciliation," entailing a higher level of mediator intervention, but sometimes the reverse usage is used. There is no consistency, but increasingly the trend is to regard these terms as interchangeable. Mediation is used here to include conciliation. This is not, however, to be confused with the conciliation which forms part of the present family health services authority complaints procedure. Although this form of conciliation is often helpful in many cases it does not address all the issues worrying the patient and specifically does not deal with compensation. The patient may "resolve" the complaint without being aware of all the facts and implications. That can mean that the matter is not finally laid to rest.

There is a broad framework for all kinds of mediation, but within this there is no single universal model that applies to all situations. Various factors may influence the way in which the mediation is conducted, as follows.

(1) Different alternative dispute resolution organisations may follow different rules or codes of practice. Generally, these provide practical and ethical ground rules, and there is likely to be a broadly consistent approach.

(2) Mediation may be *interest based* or *facilitative*, in which the parties are helped to explore their mutual interests and to try to arrive at a settlement which is in their respective best interests. Alternatively it may be *rights based* or *evaluative* in which event the mediator, personally or with other professionals or experts, may help the parties to assess their respective strengths and weaknesses with a view to their agreeing a resolution which has due regard to their respective rights, so far as these can be evaluated. Some mediators will work in a facilitative mode, regarding evaluation as having no place in mediation; but even those who will work evaluatively are likely to do so only after exploring mutual interests facilitatively, because once a mediator evaluates, his or her impartiality may be regarded as suspect by one side or the other. If mediation is to be developed for medical disputes and be beneficial for risk management and to patients, an interest based model may

need to prevail. Although a rights based process may be of interest and may have some relevance, there is a risk that this approach could perpetuate some of the problems and the attitudes of practitioners, managers, and patients that are inherent in litigation. It is unlikely that continued emphasis on rights would be capable of resolving all the issues between the parties. To take just one example, a patient may wish to continue to be treated in the same hospital or it may clearly be to his or her benefit for that to happen: whereas an interest based process could make this feasible, that may not be the case where the focus is on rights.

(3) Management styles and practice and levels of intervention will vary from one mediator and model to another. Some mediators may adopt a minimal intervention approach, providing a forum and facilitating communications and negotiations between the parties. At the other end of the range mediators may tend towards greater intervention and directiveness; but in no case are parties compelled to accept a mediator's views. Most mediators fall somewhere in between, using their skills and management authority to help the parties towards resolution without imposing any personal preferences.

(4) Although many models of mediation involve a mediator working alone, there is also a model of co-mediation in which two mediators work together as a team. Although this may be more costly than sole mediation, it does offer various advantages including the possibility of having mediators from different disciplines—for example, a doctor and lawyer—working together.

Mediation applicable to medical disputes might proceed as follows.

Stage 1

Once appointed by both parties, the mediator (or the mediation organisation concerned) liaises with the parties (or, if desired, their solicitors) in order to arrange a meeting and a timetable for the delivery and exchange of documents. The period to be set aside for the mediation meeting would depend on the complexity of the matter, but two days would not be an unreasonable initial estimate in many cases. If more time was found to be needed it could by agreement be extended beyond the initial period. The mediation venue would, if possible, be neutral, and two separate rooms should be available if required.

481

Stage 2

Within an agreed period the parties' lawyers provide preliminary details of the dispute to the mediator and to one another, in the form of written submissions and a bundle of documents, which would be likely to include medical reports and other relevant documents available to both parties, including those relevant to quantum. If legal proceedings have started copy pleadings are also furnished. Mediation cannot be started too early once proceedings have started. There is a view that mediation should await the close of pleadings and the conclusion of discovery, but most practitioners of alternative dispute resolution would probably regard that delay as unnecessary as the machinery for the definition and clarification of the issues and for the furnishing of relevant documents can be framed within the mediation process itself.

Stage 3

Where the issues are complex the mediator may have a preliminary meeting with the parties or their respective lawyers to agree the timetable and ground rules for the mediation.

Stage 4

The substantive mediation meeting is then held. The mediator is likely to meet together with the parties and their solicitors, with counsel if required, to discuss and explain the process. Each party (or more usually, though not necessarily, their lawyer) will then be given the opportunity to make an oral presentation of their case. Witnesses are not usually called, though the presentation might outline the broad nature of the evidence to be adduced if the matter were to go to trial. However, there is no reason why parties should not be able to agree with the mediator for expert witnesses to outline certain aspects in support of a presentation if this is considered helpful. There is no cross examination, but if the mediator approves, questions to clarify aspects may be asked.

Stage 5

After the parties have met in joint session and respectively presented their cases negotiations then take place, facilitated by the mediator, either continuing in joint session, chaired by the mediator, or, more usually, in a series of separate meetings (called "caucuses") which the mediator has with each party. By assuring each party as to the confidentiality of matters discussed in the caucuses, except as the party may agree to have disclosed; by using the overview gained by this process; by shuttling from one side to another; and by using various skills and techniques the mediator helps the parties to narrow and resolve their differences and to arrive at mutually acceptable settlement terms.

Stage 6

The mediator may during this process use any other strategy which he or she may consider helpful. For example, the mediator may wish to see the parties together without their lawyers, or vice versa; or may allow an opportunity for explanations or discussion if appropriate; or discuss the matter with respective experts, either separately or, if so agreed, together; or seek additional information; or adjourn the mediation to enable the experts to consider certain aspects or for any other reason. The mediator is responsible for managing the process, which may be done in consultation with the parties; but the parties remain responsible for agreeing the outcome (subject to the parameters stipulated by the defence organisations, insurers, or indemnifying authorities when relevant).

Stage 7

If a settlement is reached it will usually be recorded immediately as a binding agreement or, when court proceedings are pending, as a consent order.

Defence organisations, insurers or indemnifying authorities (or the Central Fund if and when applicable) will need to give authority for the mediation to be conducted and for a binding settlement to be recorded. (In March 1994 the National Health Service Executive issued a consultation document *Clinical negligence: proposed creation of a central fund in England.* Under the accepted proposal, a fund would be established to which affiliated trusts would make contributions from which the larger compensation payments would be made. The fund would be administered by a special health authority; and the proposal specifically provides that "fund managers should be consulted before a claim is settled and should seek to dissuade trusts from settling at an early stage cases which properly could be defended" and that they may at their discretion take over the management of any claim.) As when authorising settlement negotiations, they may provide parameters for acceptable levels of settlement. Their representative may attend the mediation meeting or may make alternative arrangements for the settlement terms to be confirmed while the mediation is under way. It is not usually acceptable to conduct a mediation, with its preparation and perhaps some days of meetings, if either side does not have the authority to record a binding settlement if it is reached.

The qualities, skills, qualifications, and attributes needed for effective mediation of medical disputes are considered below.

Mini-trial

The mini-trial is not a "trial" at all, but rather another kind of assisted negotiation: it may be seen as a form of evaluative mediation (see Brown and Marriott,[4] Green,[16 17] and Wilkinson[18]). In the mini-trial the parties have the case presented to them by their respective lawyers on an abbreviated non-binding basis, to enable them to assess the strengths, weaknesses, and prospects of the case. In effect, the parties themselves become a tribunal informally hearing the case (resulting in the Centre for Dispute Resolution in the United Kingdom calling this process the "executive tribunal"). With the benefit of these insights the parties with their legal representatives have an opportunity to enter into settlement discussions on a realistic basis.

A key figure in this process is a neutral adviser, who is usually someone with authority in the field of the dispute, and who may chair and manage the process, asking questions of the presenters and clarifying points for the parties. If required, the neutral adviser may give a non-binding opinion on the case. The adviser may also adopt a facilitative or mediatory role in any settlement discussions which may follow.

The case is usually presented in accordance with an agreed procedure and timetable. Ordinarily no witnesses are called, but expert witnesses might explain technical aspects or key witnesses may explain parts of the case. Other devices may be used to illustrate the case, such as charts, photographs, or films. The neutral adviser helps the parties to understand and form their own views on the case before they rejoin their respective lawyers to consider and discuss what they have observed and learnt.

Other forms of alternative dispute resolution

The various other alternative dispute resolution processes include, for example, the *neutral fact finding expert*, in which the parties jointly appoint a neutral expert to investigate facts and form a legal or technical view either about certain specified issues or about all issues generally and to make a non-binding report to the parties which helps to inform any settlement discussions that may then take place. "*Med-arb*" is a process in which the neutral attempts to help the parties to settle their dispute through mediation; but if this is unsuccessful, he or she then makes a binding determination as arbitrator. "*Med-arb*" has dangers as well as advantages and needs to be selectively and carefully chosen and applied; it would not seem to be appropriate in the ordinary course of medical dispute. Goldberg et al[19] quote Professor Lon Fuller as questioning whether if the same person acts as mediator and then as arbitrator, in addition to damaging his efficacy as a mediator, he would not have "fatally compromised the integrity of his adjudicative role." Alternatives have been devised in the United States—for example, allowing parties the options of either proceeding with the arbitration if the mediation fails or of opting out of it (Goldberg et al[20]) or treating the mediator as an advisory arbitrator whose opinion is authoritative but non-binding.

Another alternative dispute resolution neutral role that has been successful in the United States is the *early neutral evaluator*, who is appointed by the court at an early stage. He or she considers the documents, meets the parties and hears oral presentations, and then expresses a non-binding view on an off the record and evidentially privileged basis. This is followed by helping the parties to consider how to conduct the litigation more expeditiously and economically, devising plans for conducting the discovery of documents, sharing material data and expediting procedures, and helping the parties to explore settlement possibilities and alternative dispute resolution processes which might be suitable for the resolution of the issues (see Levine[21 22]).

No fault compensation

No fault compensation is not usually regarded as an alternative dispute resolution process, but it needs to be mentioned because many see it as an attractive alternative to adversarial litigation (see Spastics Society[23] and Royal College of Physicians[24]). Its basic premise is that when a medical "accident" takes place the patient is entitled to compensation without having to prove negligence. In many of the more straightforward cases this is an enormous advantage and leads to many claims being settled quickly and without lawyers. The major problems with such a procedure are, firstly, that the definition of an accident remains with practitioners;

485

secondly, the potentially high cost of compensating all accidents; and, thirdly, the fact that other issues such as accountability are not dealt with.

Sweden, Denmark, and Finland operate compensation systems which purport to be of this type; however they are not truly "no fault" systems. In effect, as the accident must not have been foreseeable, they are fault based, and the arbitrary selection of accidents which merit compensation is wholly unsatisfactory. In New Zealand a no fault system existed for many years, covering all accidents, including medical accidents. A major drawback from the patients' viewpoint, and indeed risk management generally, was that accountability was ignored. In 1994 because of the cost the government totally emasculated the system, leaving many claimants without remedy as the right to go to court had long since been abolished.

Mediator's role, attributes, skills, and qualifications

Role and functions

Mediators combine several roles and functions, which may overlap. These include the mediator as manager of the process, with responsibility for maintaining order and regulating the proceedings; as information gatherer, receiving information both directly through open and confidential proceedings and also by watching for non-verbal signals and by getting data from third parties; as reality tester and evaluator, helping parties to appreciate whether their ideas, perceptions, or proposals are realistic; as scribe, if required, helping the parties to record any settlement terms; and as settlement supervisor, if required, ensuring that terms of settlement are properly implemented and resolving any issues arising during the course of implementation.

Attributes

Attributes, the inherent personal qualities and traits, rather than learned skills and techniques, required of mediators include the following.

● Sensitive understanding of issues and a respect for parties' concerns

- Sound and judicious judgment
- A creative and constructive response to problems
- Integrity and trustworthiness
- Flexibility and an ability to cope with changing circumstances
- An empathetic approach
- Authority to manage the process and an ability to work autonomously.

Skills

Skills may be learned or intuitive, and those of mediators include the following.

- Communication skills, which include listening to the parties and appreciating their views; observing non-verbal communications; helping the parties to hear and understand one another; asking questions effectively; reframing when necessary, by changing a frame of reference to give events a different yet correct meaning or perspective; and summarising properly
- Managing conflict and allowing the opportunity for parties to ventilate their emotions without damaging the prospects of negotiating an effective outcome
- Encouraging negotiation and developing a problem solving mode
- Managing the process in a firm, sensitive, impartial manner
- Facilitation of communications, discussions, and negotiations with a view to achieving an agreed outcome
- When working in an evaluative mode, expressing personal views without undue pressure and enhancing rather than damaging the prospect of agreed resolution.

Qualifications

There are no formal qualifications to act as a mediator, but it is generally accepted that special training is necessary and this is provided by several alternative dispute resolution organisations, most of which will provide mediator accreditation and some of which may maintain a panel of approved neutrals.

Mediators bring into the process their personal attributes and skills; their specialised training; their experience as neutrals; and, of course, their own individual professional, business, or personal backgrounds. There are mediators from a wide range of occupational backgrounds, including law, medicine, accountancy, management, industry, social and community work, and counselling and other mental health fields.

Two kinds of expertise can be brought into the mediation process: one is substance expertise, which is the specialist knowledge of the subject matter of the dispute, and the other is process expertise, which is proficiency in and understanding of the mediation process itself. Given the choice, process expertise must be the more important in choosing a mediator as a competent expert in mediation can generally adapt to dealing with different kinds of disputes; but if a mediator has both process and substance expertise, that might be an ideal combination.

Conclusion

The present response to a patient's misgivings about any particular treatment or an assertion of professional error, as well as the whole system of managing and resolving any disputes that may then arise, require a fundamental re-examination. This system lends itself to an adversarial and potentially hostile confrontation.

There are several contributory reasons, as shown in box 1. These and other factors all combine to create a situation in which the mere hint of "negligence" may lead to a knee jerk reaction of determined defence.

This situation could be reviewed at different levels. At a fundamental level the whole question of negligence and causation could be re-examined. This has already been mooted with the notion of no fault compensation and the proposals of Action for Victims of Medical Accidents and Association of Community Health Councils in England and Wales for a health standards inspectorate; and the last word may not yet have been spoken on these basic issues. At another level the adversarial procedure could be re-evaluated and new procedures developed to improve the conduct of medical disagreements and claims, from their inception to their conclusion. There is no reason why representatives of medical groups, patients' groups, and other interested groups should not be able to consult with one another and devise improved procedures to replace or supplement existing ones. To some extent this is already happening. This could widen and enhance resources for resolving issues constructively while respecting the concerns of all parties and preserving all existing safeguards, such as the right to trial where other options fail.

Box 1—Reasons for adversarial nature of disputes

Need to establish negligence by the practitioner transforms a clinical occurrence with negative implications into a compensatable claim.

Claims may be asserted, or be perceived as being made, in a contentious way.

Professional culture does not prepare practitioners for the possibility of lapse or error or how to respond.

Finding of negligence could have adverse professional implications for practitioners.

No opportunity to consider the clinical event in an impartial and objective way.

Economics often control the strategy of litigation, which commonly requires the claimant to overcome many obstacles to establishing a case.

Lawyers have established strongly partisan approaches and are grouped into those supporting claimants and those defending practitioners, with little room for middle ground.

Often medical experts too develop strongly partisan approaches.

The language and approach of litigation have an effect of spiralling mutual antagonism upwards.

Emotions may understandably run high on both sides.

Meanwhile, practitioners, patients, and managers do not need to wait for fundamental organisational changes before they start implementing ways of widening their resources for dealing with medical disputes. As indicated here, processes already exist and are available in appropriate cases to allow parties to try to resolve their differences without proceeding to litigation or to supplement an adjudication with a parallel procedure for mediation, dispute management, or other third party assistance (box 2).

Mediation and other alternative dispute resolution processes are not intended to replace litigation, which continues under the present system to have an important role when a third party adjudication is necessary. They do, however, provide a much wider range of alternative processes than mere confrontation. It has been said of litigation that, "If the only tool you provide a person with

---

Box 2—Some alternative dispute resolution organisations and practitioners

The Chartered Institute of Arbitrators, International Arbitration Centre, 24 Angel Gate, City Road, London EC1V 2RS (tel 0171 837 4483) offers an arbitration scheme with a mediation option.

The Centre for Dispute (CEDR), 100 Fetter Lane, London EC4A 1DD (tel 0171 430 1852) has a specialist medical sector working party for medical negligence and other healthcare disputes.

ADR Group, Equity and Law Building, 36–38 Baldwin Street, Bristol BS1 1NR (tel 01179 252 090), network of lawyers mediators in the UK, provides mediators for various kinds of disputes, including medical negligence.

The British Academy of Experts, 90 Bedford Mansions, Bedford Avenue, London WC1B 3AE (tel 0171 637 0333) maintains a register of mediators.

Mediation UK, 82a Gloucester Road, Bishopston, Bristol BS7 8BN (tel 01179 241234) is an umbrella organisation whose members cover a wide range of mediation activities.

---

is a hammer, you should not be surprised if all he can see are nails." Alternative dispute resolution offers a toolkit which preserves all established options but allows other possibilities to be introduced into the resolution of disputes. In medical disputes, in particular, it allows for the possibility of incorporating into agreed ground rules any permutation of fact finding, explanation and dialogue, facilitation with communications, assisted negotiation, neutral expert settlement guidance, accountability, and any other factor that parties might consider to be important. Settlement terms can, and sometimes need to, include not only financial aspects but also a form of words that parties find mutually acceptable, in a way that conventional litigation cannot achieve.

1 Kellett AJRN. Healing angry wounds: the roles of apology and mediation between physicians and patients. *Journal of Dispute Resolution (Missouri)* 1987: 1.
2 Leone A, Jr. Is ADR the Rx for malpractice? *Dispute Resolution Journal of the American Arbitration Association* 1994;49:7.

3 Reeves JW. ADR relieves pain of health care disputes. *Dispute Resolution Journal of the American Arbitration Association* 1994;**49**:14.
4 Brown H, Marriott A. *ADR principles and practice*. London: Sweet and Maxwell, 1993.
5 Department of Health. *Arbitration in respect of claims for medical negligence against the National Health Service*. London: DOH, 1991.
6 Kendall J. Expert judgment. *Solicitors Journal* 1990;**134**:1430–1.
7 Kendall J. Let the experts decide. *Abritration and Dispute Resolution Law Journal* 1993;**210**:210–4.
8 Kendall J. *Dispute Resolution: expert determination*. London: Longman, 1992.
9 Campbell v Edwards [1976] 1 WLR 403.
10 Nikko Hotels (UK) Ltd v MEPC plc [1991] 28 EG 86.
11 Jones v Sherwood [1992] 2 All ER 170.
12 Mills MP. Mediation is ombudsmanry. In: *Beyond borders. Proceedings of the 19th annual conference of the US Society of Professionals in Dispute Resolution*, Washington, DC: 1991:98.
13 Birkinshaw P. Complaints mechanisms in administrative law: recent developments. In: Mackie K, ed. *A handbook of dispute resolution*. London: Routledge, Sweet and Maxwell, 1991:43.
14 Ackland AF. *A sudden outbreak of common sense: managing conflict through mediation*. Hutchinson, 1990.
15 Bevan A. *Alternative dispute resolution*. London: Waterlow, 1992.
16 Green E. Growth of the mini-trial. *(US) 9 Litigations 12*. 1982.
17 Green E. *Mini-trial handbook*. New York: Center for Public Resources, 1981.
18 Wilkinson JH. A primer on mini-trials. In: *Donovan Leisure Newton and Irvine ADR practice book*. New York: Wiley, 1990:171–80.
19 Goldberg SB, Green ED, Sander FEA. *Dispute resolution*. Boston: 1985.
20 Goldberg SB, Green ED, Sander FEA. *Dispute resolution*. Boston: 1987.
21 Levine DI. Early neutral evaluation: a follow-up report. *Judicature* 1987;**70**:236.
22 Levine DI. Early neutral evaluation: the second phase. *Journal of Dispute Resolution* 1989;1.
23 Spastics Society. *Paying for disability: no fault compensation – panacea or Pandora's box?* London: Spastics Society, 1992.
24 Royal College of Physicians. *Compensation for adverse consequence of medical intervention. Report*. London: RCP, 1990.

26 Claims management: a guide for hospital claims managers

ISABEL M SANDERSON

This chapter on hospital claims management is intended as a practical guide to those in hospitals who have the responsibility for the management of medical negligence claims. In the future, many trusts will choose to join the Clinical Negligence Scheme for Trusts, and in due course, specific guidance for members of the scheme will be available. Some information on the legal procedures and definitions of some legal terms are included, but these are not comprehensive, and those who require more information should consult appropriate textbooks or journals.

What is a claim?

A claim may be defined as any demand by a patient for financial compensation, which puts the hospital in the position of possibly having to make a financial settlement. The claim may be indicated by a personal letter from the patient, requesting recompense. It may be covertly suggested by a solicitor's letter requesting disclosure of records, or by a specific letter before action making allegations of negligence, or by a writ which should be accompanied by the particulars of the claim.

There are two types of claim to be considered—the personal injury claim, and the medical negligence claim. Most requests for disclosure of hospital records relate to potential personal injury

492

claims. Many of these will be claims against an insurance company, where the potential plaintiff is a car driver, passenger, or pedestrian injured in a road traffic accident. In most hospitals, these requests will massively outnumber the requests for disclosure of records required by solicitors contemplating medical negligence actions. It is important not to forget that some personal injury claims will be highly relevant to the hospital—namely, claims by staff for injury occurring on the premises or as a result of their occupation. Examples of staff injury include the catering assistant who received severe burns to the arm after an electric shock from an electrically unsafe heated food trolley, and nurses' back injuries resulting from inappropriate lifting techniques. This chapter principally concerns itself with medical negligence.

What a plaintiff must prove

To succeed with a claim in medical negligence, the plaintiff must (a) establish a duty of care, (b) show that there was a breach of that duty (liability), (c) show that the breach of duty gave rise to an injury (causation). In addition, a plaintiff will have to show that the injury arising from the breach of duty was reasonably foreseeable.

The duty of care

The patient who sues a doctor will usually have little difficulty in establishing the duty of care, because the nature of the relationship between the patient and the doctor is such that the doctor owes a duty of care to the patient when advising or giving treatment. Under the law of tort, a person who can reasonably foresee that his conduct may cause harm to another person has a duty expressed as the duty of care. A hospital undertaking to provide NHS services, and the people employed in that hospital, are clearly in a position to cause harm to the patients who use the hospital's medical and other services. The hospital, as the employer of the professionals, is vicariously liable for its servants or agents (its employees). Thus the hospital has an institutional duty of care and its employees have an individual professional duty of care, but the plaintiff will usually sue the hospital which employs the professionals. In private practice, a patient will have an individual contract with the professional, and also with the hospital. As the doctor in private practice (and the general practitioner in the health service) is an

493

independent contractor, the patient may use the doctor individually in negligence under the law of tort and under the law of contract. It is important to remember that, as well as negligent action, negligent omissions may also give rise to liability. Although the duty of care may be an easy one to establish for the plaintiff, the issues of liability and causation are more complex.

Liability

To establish that the trust or individual practitioner is liable to pay compensation, a plaintiff must show that the standard of care fell below that of the ordinary reasonably skilled and experienced person in that particular professional group. The test for the defendant doctor or nurse will be against that in his or her particular professional group.

In an obstetric case, for example, when a patient is admitted to a general practitioner unit and looked after by a midwife and the general practitioner, the test will be against the standards of such units, and not against the standard expected of a consultant unit. In a case where staff are employees of the hospital, the trust will have vicarious liability and will accept financial and legal responsibility for the acts and omissions of its employees.

Standard of care

The leading case on the standard of care is Bolam v Friern Barnet Hospital Management Committee [1957] 1.WLR: 2 All ER 118.

Mr Bolam received electroconvulsive therapy for severe depression, and during the convulsion he fell off the trolley and was injured, receiving several fractures. He alleged that he should have been warned of the risks, that he should have been given relaxant drugs and, that if no relaxant drugs were given, he should have been provided with adequate physical restraint.

His case failed, and in considering the issue of the physical restraints, the evidence adduced at trial was that some doctors would have thought them necessary, but many others did not. In finding the doctor not guilty of negligence, the judge found that he had acted "in accordance with a practice accepted as proper by a responsible body of medical men skilled in that particular area." In other words, if the doctor's actions can be supported by an expert or experts of suitable stature in his or her own field, there is a probability that the defence will succeed, even though another

494

expert of equal stature may aver that the doctor should have acted differently.

In practical terms, it is up to the judge to decide whose evidence he prefers, and there is always a risk that he will prefer the evidence of the plaintiff's experts. In the civil courts, the case is decided on the balance of probabilities (as opposed to the test of "beyond reasonable doubt" in the criminal courts). This means that if there is a greater than 50% chance that the injury arose from a doctor's negligence, the plaintiff will win, if less than 50%, the defence will succeed.

Practical considerations

In personal injury cases, there is usually not much difficulty for the plaintiff to establish liability, but causation and the assessment of quantum (amount of compensation) may be more of a problem. In medical negligence, liability is more difficult to establish. There are some situations in which liability is clear, such as the postoperatively retained swab in the abdomen. All hospitals have checking procedures for swabs, and if a swab is retained, either the operator or assistant was negligent, or the procedures were negligently lax. When delay in the recognition of abnormalities occurs—for example, the signs of postoperative haemorrhage or delay in the diagnosis of say, fractures—liability may also be reasonably easy to decide, but in cases when something unexpected occurs, such as a patient developing a neurological abnormality after an uneventful operation, it may require a great deal of work, with the instruction of several experts, to determine the issues.

Causation

To succeed with his case, the plaintiff must show that not only was the doctor or nurse negligent, but that it was the negligent act or omission which gave rise to the injury for which compensation is sought. For example, if a patient injured an elbow in a fall off a bicycle, and the outcome was a stiff and deformed elbow joint, this could be due to the nature of the injury. If the plaintiff alleged that a delay in the diagnosis was the cause of the disability, it would have to be proved that, on the balance of probability, proper treatment given at the time the plaintiff alleges the diagnosis should have been made would have prevented the disability. If the defendant can show that the disability is a direct result of the

495

injury, and that delay made no difference to the outcome, the plaintiff's claim will not succeed. In this case, both sides will require suitable expert advice (see paragraph on experts).

If the patient is able to prove that the injury experienced arose from a negligent breach of the doctor's duty of care, then there will be entitlement to compensation (damages) for the injury caused. In England, damages were divided into *general damages*, which compensate the person for the "pain and suffering, and loss of amenity" arising as a direct result of the injury, and *special damages*, which will compensate for the economic losses associated with the injury. In expensive claims (those over £100 000) the general damages are usually modest in comparison with the total claim. The size of a claim will have a direct relation to the patient's personal circumstances—that is, the nature of his or her occupation and whether he or she will be able to continue work, whether there are dependants for whom the patient is financially responsible, and whether specific care, such as extra nursing or physiotherapy, will be required together with changes to the surroundings (for example, extending the ground floor of a house) to enable the patient to continue living in his or her own home. The special damages are intended to maintain the plaintiff at the standard of living enjoyed before the injury. It therefore follows that a plaintiff who has enjoyed a high salary, an expensive lifestyle, and with several dependants, is likely to be awarded substantially greater damages than a plaintiff who is, say, unemployed, or retired, with no dependants, even though the injury may be similar.

Box 1—To succeed with a claim

A plaintiff must:

1 Establish a duty of care

2 Prove that there was a breach of that duty

                           LIABILITY

3 Show that the breach of duty gave rise to injury

                           CAUSATION

4 Show that the injury was reasonably FORESEEABLE

5 $1+2+3+4 \rightarrow$ payment of   DAMAGES

Damages

Assessment of quantum in simple cases can be done by negotiation yourselves with the patient's representative. In complex cases you will need the help of your solicitor and a specialised barrister.

Box 2—Examples of general damages and special damages

General damages

Unnecessary laparotomy £3500

Brain damage, cerebral palsy £100 000–£120 000

Quadriplegia with awareness, RTA up to £130 000

Under the Fatal Accident Act, bereavement £7500 (+ about £1500 funeral expenses)

Special damages

Laparotomy	might include an economic loss relating to delay in returning to work
Cerebral Palsy	might include the costs of care, the purchase of special equipment, and the cost of conversion of a house, etc
Death of a breadwinner	if there are dependants, this could entail a substantial economic loss

---

Provisional damages

However good your experts are in assessing the patient's current condition and prognosis, it is inevitable that there is an element of guesswork in the calculations. If the plaintiff has received advice that although, on the basis of the current condition, he or she may well continue that way, but there is a risk of a serious deterioration in the future, a provisional award at trial may be sought, with leave to apply again to the court should the condition later deteriorate.

Anatomy of a claim

A claim for medical negligence may be commenced in the high court or the county court. The procedure for claims which are commenced in the high court is governed by the Supreme Court

Act 1981, and the Rules of the Supreme Court (RSC). County court matters are determined in accordance with the County Court Act 1984 and the County Court Rules (CCR). If an action is raised in one court, there are provisions within the regulations for the case to be transferred, either from the County Court to the High Court, or vice versa. Changes in the rules aimed at speeding up the litigation mean that any case that is provisionally valued at £50 000 or less is likely to be raised in the County Court. The time span for a County Court action.

It is clear from box 3 that the opportunity to investigate and

---

Box 3—Anatomy of a claim

Time span

1 Incident—injury
2 Investigation   } Immediate

3 Complaint   3 years
4 Reply   } Six weeks   "knowledge"

5 Letter before action
   Request for disclosure of   "knowledge"
      records

6 Writ/summons issued
                     } 4 months
7 Served

8 Acknowledgement   } 14 days

9 Defence   } 14 days
   requests for further and better particulars   County Court
   Interrogatories   (Automatic
                                                  directions) 15/12
10 Directions—list of documents
   Exchange of expert evidence on
      liability and causation
   Exchange of expert evidence on
      current condition and prognosis
   Exchange of witness reports

11 Setting down for trial

---

analyse the claim is greatest in the early stages, before the writ or summons is issued. It is helpful to think of the claim in three stages: stage 1, from the time of the incident to the receipt of a letter from a solicitor; stage 2, from the time the solicitor's letter is received until the issuing of the writ or summons; and stage 3, from the issue of the writ or summons until the claim is settled or set down for trial.

Box 4—Stage 1—Incident to the letter from lawyer

Investigating the incident

1 If you think a claim is likely, make up a litigation file

2 Investigation

- Identify all personnel involved

- If the staff member was a locum or from an agency, or has left the hospital, tag their personnel records, and obtain a forwarding address

3 Obtain factual statements from all relevant witnesses.

4 Secure the evidence

- Identify the patient's records and ensure that all records are located

- Mark the records in some identifiable way to indicate that they may be required for legal action, and ensure that they are retained in their original form, and not shredded, microfilmed, or destroyed

- Make a list of documents

5 If the incident involves defective equipment, withdraw the item from use immediately, and preserve it

6 Value the likely claim

7 Assess defensibility

- Obtain expert comment

- Consider making an ex gratia payment at this stage

8 Notify the compensation recovery unit if the value is greater than £2500

9 Formulate an action plan

499

Stage 1: investigation of an incident

If your hospital has an effective incident reporting system, and as a result of the investigation of the incident you think that a claim is likely, it is important at that stage to make up a litigation file. If a letter of complaint has been received, a letter of explanation should be written ensuring that every detail of the complaint is answered. If crucial aspects of the complaint are not answered, or "fudged" in the reply, there is a possibility that the patient will think that you are "covering up" or "lying", and once a patient feels that a proper explanation has not been given, the likelihood is that he or she will become more determined to pursue the complaint, and this may provoke a consultation with a solicitor.

The letter of response to the complaint should be drafted in a sympathetic and conciliatory manner, and if appropriate, should include an apology. It is important that the apology does not constitute an admission of liability, particularly where expert evidence has not been sought, and more so, where the individual practitioners have not been asked for their comments. All such letters should be checked by the consultant in charge of the case to be certain that clinical error has not slipped in under the guise of misdrafting.

Identifying staff

It is essential that *all* staff involved in the care of the patient should be identified as early as possible. The records should be scrutinised and every entry, nursing, medical and other (pharmacist, physicist, occupational therapist, physiotherapist, etc) identified, and each person so identified, asked for a personal factual statement.

The more serious the incident, the more scrupulous should be the identification of staff. Obtain the help of the consultant in charge and the nurse in charge of the ward.

The witness statement

The statement should be a first hand account of the person's own involvement, written in the active form, and include the actions taken (I took a history (*give details*), examined the patient

500

(*give details*)), the timed observations ("At 10 00 am I noticed that the patient was breathing heavily, and was sweaty,, so I called the house doctor who was with the patient in the next cubicle"), and observations on actions of others ("I noted that Dr X arrived within two minutes and carried out an examination of the cardiovascular system, and then asked me to hand her the prescription chart, and ordered drug Y to be given by injection. I obtained the drug (*name*) from ward stocks, and noted that the doctor gave the injection at 10 10 am," *not* "It was noted that the patient was sweaty and the doctor was called and the patient was given drug Y").

You may find that when you have received all the statements from staff, there are gaps in the narrative. For example, in the case of a child with an extravasated intravenous drip, an individual witness may have "skated over" the details, and avoided a crucial issue. You can sometimes pick this up when the person changes the statement from the active to the passive voice—from "I saw" to "it was noted". It is *much* more difficult to work out the facts of the case when the statement is made in the passive voice, and all doctors and nurses should be asked to draft their statements in the first or third person active voice "I saw/I did", "I saw that he did ..." *not* "it was noted/done". Any gap in the narrative should be further investigated. You may find that in the case, for example, of a child with damage from an extravasated drip, the gap in the narrative demonstrates the vulnerable point in the claim. The gap may indicate that, for a critical period, there was no one observing or supervising the child and the intravenous line. Gaps in the narrative may also indicate that you have "missed out" a witness, and this person should be identified as soon as possible.

Creating a file

When an incident is likely to become a claim, or a letter is received indicating that the plaintiff is seeking compensation, you will open a litigation file. Over the course of a complicated claim, a litigation file can become several centimetres thick, and include many hundreds of pieces of information. As this information may be obtained gradually over a long period, and as the claims handler is likely to be involved in many other claims, it is very easy to forget stages of the claim. It makes working on the file very much easier if essential information is contained in the front of the file.

You may wish to create a "working document" with four sheets at the front. The first sheet will contain essential information (box 6), including a summary of the allegations, the identification of the staff involved, the names of the experts instructed, the preliminary view on liability and causation, and the value, together with the likely date of payment, and the information about the compensation recovery unit.

The second sheet should have a detailed medical chronology, and it may be helpful, in the right hand margin, to put the name of the relevant witnesses against each detail in the chronology. For claims in which lawyers have become involved, and the case is becoming complex, it is helpful to have a legal chronology on sheet 3.

The fourth and subsequent sheets at the front of your file should contain your worksheets, which should be dated, and comprise a summary of the work carried out on any particular date, together with your action plan.

Clearly it is important to have a means of bringing forward your file for review, and this is greatly facilitated if your claims handling data is computerised.

Box 5—Your litigation file

Four sheets at front:

1 Essential information

2 Medical chronology

3 Legal chronology and information

4 Work sheet—dated—entries of work done, to include action plan

---

Box 6—Example of a worksheet action plan

4 March 1994—Write to witnesses

Action plan—Review file in six weeks (date). Chase up witnesses if no reply received

Box 7—Claim file front sheet

Patient name   M/F   Date (of opening file)
address   Date of birth
                              Date of incident
                              Date of death
                              LBA—date
                              Patient's solicitors
                              Proceedings: Y/N Date:
Incident reported: Y/N   Hospital
Complaint: Y/N   Department
                              Principal specialty: O + G
Allegations: 1   Other: Anaes
            2   A&E
            3

Staff involved	Status	Report requested	Received
1 Dr A Bloggs	Consultant physician		
2 Dr J Oblogski	Consultant anaesthetist		
3 Dr I L Gas	Anaesthetic registrar		
4 Sister E Jones	Sister in charge ICU		
5 S/N S W	S/N nights ICU		

Outside advisers instructed
Internal advisers

Experts	Specialty	Report requested	Received	Total score
1				
2				

Preliminary view: Liability   Causation

Solicitors
instructed—date
Date to committee   Decision

Day 1 value   Revised
                             value

Likely date of payment   Payments
                             made

CRU
Informed—date
CTB certificate

Stage 2: solicitor's letter to issuing of writ or summons

A patient who thinks that he or she is entitled to compensation will usually consult a solicitor, who will obtain a statement from the client at the initial interview. The solicitor will then write to the potential defendant, setting out the details of the allegations. It is important, at this stage, to recognise that the claim, as alleged, is not a figment of the fertile imagination of the solicitor, but is likely to be a fairly deadpan summary of the story told to the solicitor by the potential plaintiff. The letter before action is likely to include a request for medical records. For medical records made on or after 1 November 1991, the Access to Health Records Act 1990 gives a right to the plaintiff to obtain copies of his or her medical records. A solicitor writing on behalf of a patient will usually enclose the potential plaintiff's signed consent.

When such letters are received by the hospital, it is essential that there is a system of dealing with the requests, which includes the records being checked by the treating clinician. Only in rare circumstances would the release of the records not be authorised, but the receipt of a letter before action with a request for disclosure is a warning to the hospital that there is at least the possibility of a medical negligence action. Although most requests for disclosure of records do not relate to medical negligence claims against the hospital, but are more usually a request for disclosure in relation to personal injury claims against insurance companies, for example, after a road traffic accident, nevertheless, these requests should be carefully reviewed to ensure that there is no risk of a claim by the patient against the hospital. If in doubt, the claims handler should be notified by the medical records department, and a letter written to the solicitors with a polite enquiry as to the intention of their client. When medical records are disclosed, the person responsible for disclosure should ensure: (*a*) that the patient has provided a signed letter of authority, (*b*) that the clinician in charge of the case has also agreed to disclosure, (*c*) that the claims handlers for the trusts are notified in any case where it is thought that litigation is likely, (*d*) that the pages are photocopied clearly and completely—it is very helpful if copied records can be annotated at this stage. If radiography or other special investigations are to be disclosed, it is essential that clear instructions are given for their return.

504

Box 8—Stage 2

Letter before action→Writ
Is the patient legally aided?

1 Give disclosure of records—make sure photocopies are legible

2 Identify all documents in your possession relevant to the claim

3 Ask for reciprocal disclosure if relevant

4 Obtain outside assistance in identifying issue

5 Expert advice—liability and causation

6 Assess defensibility

7 Review contingent liability

8 Consider negotiating settlement

9 Action plan

10 Notify Compensation Recovery Unit (if not already done)

Privilege

The content of the communication between a lawyer and her client is "privileged" which means that it is confidential and its disclosure may not be forced. The communication between a doctor and patient is confidential, but in certain circumstances its disclosure may be forced—for example, by order of a court. Documents created by a hospital as a result of internal inquiries are not privileged, and if a plaintiff's solicitor applies to the court for access to such documents, the court, having established that those documents are relevant to the plaintiff's case, is likely to order disclosure. The consequence of this for hospital risk and claims managers is that statements created for the purpose of investigation (of a clinical complaint) may be disclosable. When creating a file for litigation, you should therefore explain to your witnesses that you require their statements solely for the purposes of litigation and for subsequent onward transmission to your solicitors. These statements are likely, therefore, to be considered privileged.

Preaction discovery

In a medical negligence action, discovery of documents happens twice. Preaction discovery may be granted by virtue of section 33 of the Supreme Court Act 1981. By virtue of this legislation, the

505

Box 9—Action points for medical records staff

1 Does the letter from the solicitor say for whom he is acting?
   If he does not specifically state that he is acting for the patient, is there a signed consent from the patient for the disclosure of the records?
   A signed letter of consent is essential if the letter does *not* indicate that the solicitor is acting for the patient. If you disclose information without consent, you are breaching the patient's right to confidentiality.

2 Is the letter definitely from a solicitor?
   Although it is very unusual, patients and "others" have been known to try to obtain records by underhand methods—if you are at all uncertain, take advice from your solicitors.

3 Does the letter indicate the nature of the patient's claim?
   Most sensible plaintiffs' solicitors will summarise briefly the nature of their enquiry—for example, indicate that their client is making a claim against an insurance company after a road traffic accident. If not, you are entitled to enquire the purpose of the request, and whether they intend a claim against the hospital.

4 Have you checked with the consultant in charge of the case?
   If there is a possibility that the case *could* become a medical negligence one, it is useful to know as soon as possible, so that you can investigate it, even if the patient's declared aim is a personal injury or a medical negligence claim against another defendant.

5 Have you marked the patient's file to show that records have been requested?
   When litigation is threatened, it is essential that *all* the patient's records are maintained in their original form, and not shredded, microfilmed, or destroyed.

6 Have you made a double set of photocopies?
   Have you numbered the photocopies and kept a record of the numbering?
   Are the photocopies clear, legible, and with intact margins?
   If not, you will undoubtedly be asked to go through the exercise again. It is best to get it right first time.

---

court has the power to order the discovery of documents, provided certain conditions are satisfied, and for any records that predate November 1991, it is likely that a solicitor will invoke this section of the Supreme Court Act. The conditions for such disclosure are: (*a*) the person making the application is likely to be a party in the proceedings, (*b*) a claim for personal injury or death is likely to be made, (*c*) the person against whom the order is sought is likely to be party to such proceedings—such person seems likely to have had in his or her possession, custody or power, documents relevant to the proposed action.

At this stage, it may be relevant to seek reciprocal disclosure of records. For example, it may be clear from the correspondence that a claim is intended against the hospital, and there may be information in the medical records that suggests that the patient has had relevant treatment elsewhere. It is useful, at this stage, to make analysis of the case easier, to ask for disclosure of other relevant records, through the plaintiff's solicitors. At this stage, it is wise to obtain your own expert advice on liability and causation. In the first instance you may wish to obtain internal advice from one of your consultants, but if the claim is a large one, you may wish to instruct an outside expert. To instruct your own expert to give a medical opinion on liability and causation, you should provide your expert with an indexed, and preferably paginated bundle of documents, which would include the medical records, the statements from all relevant witnesses, and any incident reports obtained. It is also helpful to ask the expert to comment on causation. If, at this stage, you have either sufficient information without expert advice, or have sought expert advice, you may be in a position to label your file "defend" or "settle".

How to obtain expert advice

Consider asking your own in house "experts". It may be helpful at this stage to consider the usual sources of risk in medicine which give rise to claims, and put specific questions to your expert to help him or her to give you proper advice. Were any of the origins of clinical risk ("all in the 'I's"; box 10) relevant in this case? Ask your local expert for comment.

An example

A senior house officer in accident and emergency sent away from casualty a woman who was complaining of chest pain. The patient died at home two hours after discharge. The patient was an outpatient attender of the local cardiologist. The nursing admission notes to casualty suggested a cardiac problem. The senior house

---

Box 10—The origins of clinical risk: "all the 'I's"

Intervention—Surgery/vascular access/etc

Ignorance

                  new senior house officer

Inexperience

Inadequate training

Inappropriate delegation   locums?

Inadequate supervision

Inadequate protocols/procedures—Any department

Inadequate communications—Consent forms
                             —Medical records: were they available?

Indolence/inertia   —Telephone requests for 2nd opinions?
                             —Did the registrar avoid coming to see
                                 the patient?

Incompetence

---

officer's note suggested musculoskeletal pain. He diagnosed the electrocardiogram as "within normal limits"—it was subtly abnormal and significantly different from the old electrocardiogram in the outpatient records.

On liability:

(1) Was the senior house officer negligent in sending the patient home?
(2) Was the hospital negligent in not providing the services that could properly be expected of an accident and emergency department, even if the senior house officer's actions were reasonable?

Further questions to ask:

- Did the senior house officer read the nurse's note?
- If not, why not?
- Were the "old notes" available in the middle of the night?
- Did the doctor see them?
- If not, would it have made a difference?

- Had the doctor had proper training in reading electrocardiograms?
- If not, should he have called a more experienced doctor?
- Did he contact another doctor? Did he receive telephone advice?
- Was there a more experienced doctor available?
- Was there a guideline or protocol for this young unsupervised doctor to follow?

In this case, in the first instance, it would be the right thing to ask your consultant in accident and emergency for an overview, and perhaps then ask your consultant cardiologist for a view on causation: "Would it have made any difference if she had been admitted to hospital?"

This analysis is helpful to the claims handler in deciding whether it is likely to defend or settle a claim, and to determine the percentage likelihood. If the claim is pursued outside expert help will be needed, as internal advice, however well intended, cannot avoid a degree of bias.

To choose experts, you will need one on liability. Choose an expert in the discipline against which the claim is made. The same expert *may* be able to give you a view on causation, but in cases such as the one identified here, an expert from a different specialty—in this case, cardiology—is required.

How to decide whether to defend or settle

It is a helpful aid to the management of a claim to have a simple system whereby you place your case in the defend area of the range, the doubtful area of the range, or the settle area of the range. If a case is clearly a settler, then the hospital should hasten to settle in order to contain costs, because the longer any case goes on, the more expensive it will be to settle it, particularly in relation to costs. If, on the other hand, on your initial assessment of the case, there seems to be no liability, and the allegations made by the patient about the doctor's action or omission are not considered causative of the injury, then you may wish to defend the case. In medical negligence, however, a substantial proportion of the cases are not clearcut, and if your case comes in the middle category, it requires intensive investigation. The scoring system in box 11 is a simple way of deciding, at any point in the case, how you should proceed. To score your case, however, you may need some basic help on the medical issues from your in house medical adviser or an external medicolegal adviser.

Box 11—How to decide whether to defend or settle

Liability	Causation
Definitely not liable—1	Not causative—1
Probably not liable—2	Unlikely—2
Doubtful—requires investigation—3	Uncertain—3
Probably some liability—4	May be causative—4
Definitely liable—5	Definite causation link—5

Score out of 10

4 or less: mark the file defensible (provided you have done your spadework)

5 or more: requires intensive investigation—expert reports to see if defensible

8+: make *haste* to settle to contain costs

When to decide

Keep under constant review. No decision to defend or settle is ever "writ in stone". At any point in the case, more information can come to light which will alter your view of the case, and it is important to bear this in mind. Therefore, at every stage, a review of your decision should be undertaken.

Instructing your medical expert

(1) Choose an expert who has been recommended to you, in the specialty against which the allegations are made, to advise on liability.
(2) Ask the expert in a preliminary letter whether he or she is able to oblige. It is a discourtesy to send 5 kg of papers to an expert who has many other demands on his time without first seeking his agreement.

Box 12—When to decide: Keep under constant review

1 At time of incident

2 On receipt of letter before action

3 On receipt of writ/summons

4 After receipt of expert advice on allegations in particulars of claim

5 After exchange of expert evidence

6 After exchange of witness statements

7 Up to the door of the court and beyond

---

(3) Establish whether the expert will be able to report within a "reasonable" time—say six to eight weeks. If there is a specific reason for urgency, *explain* this in your covering letter, and invite the expert to respond by telephone or fax, so that you do not induce further delay before seeking another expert if the first choice cannot oblige you.

(4) ● Provide an outline of the case
   ● Identify the issues
   ● Provide full witness statements
   ● Provide full copies of all relevant records
   ● Provide copies of the legal proceedings. If these have not been served, provide a copy of the letter before action
   ● Ask the expert if any other papers or documents are required.

The compensation recovery scheme

The compensation recovery scheme is run by the Compensation Recovery Unit (CRU). The scheme applies to any accident or injury which occurred on or after 1 January 1989, and for which compensation was paid on or after 3 September 1990. Claims for compensation must be notified to the CRU within 14 days of their receipt by the potential compensator (the hospital). The claim should be notified on form CRU1, which is available from the CRU (The Compensation Recovery Unit Benefits Agency, Reyrolle Building, Hebburn, Tyne and Wear NE31 1XB). The onus is on the compensator to complete this form, and it is essential that the claims handler should have procedures set up to ensure that the

511

notification procedures are adhered to. On receipt of a valid CRU1 form, the CRU will inform the compensator that they have no interest in the case, and that it may be settled without further reference to themselves, or they will issue a CRU4, which indicates that settlement may not be achieved without first obtaining a certificate of total benefit (CTB) from the CRU. The CTB will show an amount of money that should be withheld from the compensation payment, and paid instead to the Department of Social Security. If you fail to withhold the designated sum from the compensation, you will remain liable to pay the sum identified in the CTB. It is therefore in your financial interests to be sure that you have complied with the regulations relating to the CRU scheme.

Negotiating a settlement

If a case is straightforward or of low value, it may be cost effective to the trust for the claims handler to negotiate a settlement at this stage. If, however, there is likely to be an appreciable economic loss, the probability is that you will require advice through your solicitors on a proper assessment of quantum. In a very high value case it would be inappropriate to consider settlement without the issuing of proceedings and the service of a schedule of damages. In such a case you will have instructed solicitors and they will take advice on quantum from a barrister who specialises in the field of medical negligence.

Sources of information on quantum

1 The Judicial Studies Board. *Guidelines for assessment of general damage in personal injury cases.* London: Blackstone Press, 1994.

2 Kemp, Kemp. *The quantum of damages.* 3 volumes. London: Sweet and Maxwell, 1995.

3 *Medical Law Reports.* BMP Ltd, Saxeway, Chartridge, Buckinghamshire HP5 2SH. (monthly).

4 *Personal and Medical Injuries Law Letter.* The Legal Studies Publishing Ltd, Mortimer House, 37–41 Mortimer Street, London W1N 7RS (ten times a year).

Stage 3: issue of writ or summons to settlement or trial

On receipt of a writ or a summons, it is essential, at this stage, to instruct solicitors, if this has not already been done. By this stage, you should have a complete file, including full witness statements, copies of all relevant records, and probably expert advice on your position. It makes it much easier for your solicitors if they are provided with full documentation at the time of instruction.

Box 13—Stage 3—Receipt of writ (high court) or summons (county court)→trial

Costs escalate:

1 Instruct solicitors

2 Statement/particulars of claim—further investigation

3 When defence due, counsel will be instructed

4 Reinstruct outside advisers/experts

5 Review defensibility

6 Conference with counsel to rehearse issues

7 Assess quantum

Action point for claims handlers

If the first hint of a claim is when a writ or summons is issued, you should undertake the same exercise as in stage 1 or 2. If the matter is more than three years from the date of injury, there may be a case for requesting your legal advisers to strike out the action, but you may not assume that the courts will strike out the action, even if the action seems to be time barred. At this stage, it is important to trace former employees, who may be crucial witnesses to the case.

Limitation period and "knowledge"

Various statutes of limitation have been enacted over the years, with the purpose of limiting the time in which individuals can engage in litigation. As time passes, memory diminishes, and

513

evidence may be lost which will hamper, particularly, the defendant, in a claim. In medical negligence cases, the limitation period is three years, which means that that is the period in which the writ must be issued. This, however, may prejudice a plaintiff if the knowledge that he or she has a case in negligence does not arise until more than three years later. There have, for example, been cases where swabs or surgical instruments have been left behind in the abdomen unrecognised for long periods of time. The patient clearly could not have this knowledge until the true facts were discovered by subsequent investigation. This is a very simple example, but illustrates the point that, although from the defendant's point of view, it would be conveniennt to be able to close a file three years after the incident giving rise to a potential claim, it may not be possible to do so. In practical terms, the three years runs from the time the patient knows that he has a case. It is sensible to make a fairly generous allowance for the time in which the patient acquires his "knowledge".

Striking out

If there has been dilatoriness on the part of the plaintiff or his legal advisers, it may be possible to strike out the action.

Box 14—Action for case handlers

- In cases when the facts are more than three years old, seek advice from your solicitors about "striking out"

- Do not assume that the court will automatically strike out. If it is clear that the patient's "knowledge" was less than three years previously, it is unlikely to be struck out

- If you believe you will suffer prejudice (for instance, witnesses lost, ill, deceased), obtain as much information as possible to support your case.

Instructing lawyers

Choose competent solicitors who are experienced in dealing with the complexities of medical negligence. Give them specific instructions and ask for feedback—it is important that the solicitor keeps everyone involved in the case aware of all developments.

Ask for specific advice on the merits of the case at specific stages, and for information on the solicitors' action plan. Do the spade work yourself to make it easy for the lawyers and reduce your costs. In a "doubtful" expensive case, consider the merits of an early conference with counsel who is likely to take the case to court.

Choosing a solicitor

The trust will have requirements for a wide variety of legal advice relating to its many activities, and whereas it may be convenient to instruct a single firm of solicitors, it may not always be wise, especially in relation to the management of medical negligence claims, which require considerable expertise. The average district general hospital may have in the region of 35 new medical negligence cases a year, few of which will be of high value. If the trust is the only client providing medical negligence cases, it is unlikely that the solicitors will have the necessary expertise to deal with the cases, particularly those of high value. Consideration should be given, therefore, to instructing a firm with special experience and expertise in this field. In due course, the SHA regulating the clinical negligence scheme for trusts may set up a panel of approved solicitors, and trusts who are members of the scheme will be able to take advantage of the listed firms.

Instructing a solicitor

In most cases the trust will be able to deal with the early stages of the litigation process (disclosures of records, obtaining statements, etc) without recourse to its solicitors. Where there is an experienced legal services manager, claims of modest value may also be settled without needing to involve the solicitors.

It is important to remember that the trust is the client and the solicitors may only proceed with the client's agreement. It is therefore important, in order to maintain control of the situation, to give clear instructions to your solicitors about what is required.

If your first intimation of the claim is the service of a writ, you should send the original without delay to your solicitor, so that he may take the necessary steps on your behalf in the court. In most cases, however, you will have had the opportunity to investigate the claim and make some assessment of its defensibility. Box 15 summarises the instructions to your solicitor.

Box 15—Instructing your solicitor: make it easy for him and save your own costs

1 Provide a detailed chronology of the medical facts

2 Identify all the witnesses and provide factual statements

3 Provide copies of *all* correspondence concerning the case

4 Provide full copies of the medical records

5 Identify any other relevant documents

6 Provide an in house "expert" overview

7 Provide expert reports where possible

8 Send the *original* writ

9 Make a note in your own file to check progress

10 Make sure you receive copies of all the legal documentation

---

After the service of the statement or particulars of claim, there are 14 days in which to acknowledge service to the court. It is vital, therefore, that if you have not already instructed them your solicitors are now instructed as a matter of urgency. There is then an obligation to serve the defence within a specific time limit. There may be further pleadings, such as a request for further particulars of the statement of claim or of the defence, together with a reply to those requests, and the service of interrogatories, usually by the plaintiff.

Each of these activities has a time constraint, and when seeking further information from your staff—for example, to obtain their comments on a "request for further and better particulars" of a statement made in the hospital's defence, or to obtain answers to the "interrogatories"—it is essential to make sure that your staff understand the urgency of your request. In complex cases when your professional staff have already met your solicitors, it may be easier if the solicitors communicate directly with your staff. As the claims handler representing the trust you should, however, be sure that you are kept informed of these activities.

Once the pleadings are closed, a summons for directions is issued. This sets out the timetable to take the case up to trial. The matters that are dealt with at this stage of the case include the service by the plaintiff on the defendant, and vice versa, of a list of documents in

516

the plaintiff's possession, inspection of the documents, disclosure of expert reports, firstly on condition and prognosis, and subsequently on liability and causation. If the expert proposes to rely on textbook articles or published items, a list and photocopies of such documents must also be served on the other party. There is also the provision for a meeting of medical experts. At this stage, if a conference with counsel has not already been held, it is likely that such a conference will be called, to rehearse the medical and legal issues.

Reasons why claims cannot be defended

Very often cases which seem straightforwardly defensible when viewed initially become difficult to defend, and might be considered "non-negligent losers".

Box 16—Reasons why claims cannot be defended

1 The claim is indefensible

2 Res ipsa loquitur—your staff or experts cannot think of a non-negligent *explanation* of the injury

3 Individual actions considered defensible, but overall care looks second rate

4 "Evidence" lost (records/radiographs, cardiotachograph traces)

5 Witnesses "lost": overseas/deceased/not identified

6 Crucial witnesses are "bad" witnesses

7 Witnesses are unwilling to co-operate, especially if no longer your employees

8 Your expert "collapses" at the last minute

9 It is very cheap to settle and no important principle rests on it

---

Res ipsa loquitur

The doctrine of "Res ipsa loquitur", "the thing speaks for itself" may be used by a plaintiff in circumstances where an unexpected and apparently unrelated outcome occurs. When a plaintiff introduces this doctrine, for the matter to be defensible it is essential that the professional witness or the expert instructed is able to produce a plausible "non-negligent" explanation.

517

A patient goes into hospital able to walk, has an operation on the abdomen, and wakes up from the anaesthetic unable to walk. She is found to have a femoral neuropathy. The solicitor for the patient is likely to allege that this untoward development resulted from negligence by the operator. To rebut the allegation, the surgeon or the expert needs to have a non-negligent explanation for the injury. The tendency of doctors to say "it's just one of those things" is unlikely to be a sufficient explanation in these circumstances.

Assessing quantum and budgeting

It is helpful to your hospital's budget and financial planning to quantify the case and assess the likely date of settlement.

(1) When assessing quantum, always bear in mind the worst case value, but check the details of your case to see whether the circumstances make it a less expensive one than "the worst case".
(2) The smaller the claim, the sooner it can and should be settled.
(3) In assessing the figures for damages you should also include a sum for plaintiff's and defendant's costs.

If the case is valued at less than £10 000, it is useful to include a figure of 40% for plaintiff's costs, and for defendant's costs if solicitors have been instructed. Above that figure, allow 10%. These are only crude suggestions to enable you to make an educated guess. In any given case, you may find that the complexity of the issues has led to a higher percentage being spent on costs, and smaller value cases are always disproportionately heavy on costs. Indeed you may occasionally find that the plaintiff's costs exceed the settlement figure.
(4) Always have in mind the likely date of settlement or trial. Generally, the longer the matter is left unresolved, the higher the costs, so it is vital that the claims handlers keep a degree of control on the way the case is progressing.

If, at any stage, the likelihood of success of an otherwise defensible claim seems to be diminishing, it is worth considering whether the case can be compromised. It may be necessary to consider making an admission of liability, and at this stage, quantum should be assessed by counsel, who may recommend a payment into court.

518

Payment into court

If a suitable payment in is made, it is likely to make it difficult for the plaintiff to continue to trial. The aim of a payment in is twofold: firstly, to prevent a trial and the substantial increase in costs incurred in going to trial, and secondly, if the patient does not accept the payment in, and does not succeed at trial, or if he or she does succeed, and does not beat the payment in, then the plaintiff will be at risk and may be ordered to pay the defendant's costs. Making a payment in in a doubtful case therefore offers a degree of protection against costs.

Preparing for trial

In the weeks before trial, the activity is stepped up. It is essential that the trust claims handler retains control at this stage. There is the likelihood of a conference with counsel to discuss the details of the case. It is preferable for the claims handler to attend the conference to be fully conversant with the strengths and weaknesses of the case, and to be in a position to take urgent action (for example, obtaining agreement to settle and facilitating the issuing of a cheque), if required.

At this stage of the case, it is important that all the witnesses are fully informed of developments. Once a trial date is notified, all witnesses should be informed, to ensure that they are available. Claims handlers should attend conferences with counsel and expert witnesses, so that they are in a position to advise the trust on the trust's position. If the plaintiff accepts a settlement or a payment into court, as a courtesy, it is important to inform all witnesses immediately.

The trial itself is the most expensive part of a case. Barristers are paid a brief fee plus daily "refreshers". If the case is an expensive one, (a brain or spinally injured plaintiff, for example), the likelihood is that a Queen's Counsel will have been instructed in addition to the junior counsel who would have advised on the earlier stages of the claim, thus substantially increasing your costs. If, as often happens, the plaintiff is legally aided, you will be responsible for your own costs, even if you win the case.

During the trial itself, it is advisable to have a trust representative present throughout. If the consultant whose team is being sued can spare the time to be present in court, it can be enormously helpful to the trust's case, as he or she may be able to clarify issues that arise.

Finally, when the case is over, either side may apply for taxation of costs. A fee is payable to the Taxing Master for the exercise, but considerable savings can sometimes be made if the other side have been ineffectual, or charged excessively. Your lawyers will advise you whether an application for taxation is appropriate.

Conclusion

I hope that this brief chapter will provide helpful pointers to claims handlers, particularly those who do not have a large case load. It is important to remember that the more positive action you take in managing the claim the more likely you are to obtain a cost effective outcome. Medical negligence is a fascinating field and with the help of your medicolegal advisers, medical experts, and medical negligence specialist lawyers you will obtain much professional satisfaction in obtaining the optimum result for plaintiff and defendant.

Appendix I

JOHN HICKEY

Risk management and the Clinical Negligence Scheme for Trusts

The Clinical Negligence Scheme for Trusts (CNST) became operational on 1 April 1995. The CNST is a mutual pooling arrangement, the objectives of which are to:

- Protect NHS Trusts in England from the financial consequences of clinical negligence
- Promote good risk and claims management
- Improve the quality of patient care.

Risk management in the United Kingdom seems to have been somewhat unfocused in the past with different trusts adopting different approaches, with varying degrees of success. The CNST strategy is to set certain minimum standards for risk management practice and to provide a financial incentive through discounted contributions to those Trusts which meet these standards. The minimum standards set in the first year of the CNST are listed below; there is no doubt that they will evolve over a period of time, both in depth and breadth. For example, standards more applicable to community and ambulance Trusts are under development. The implementation of a risk management programme requires the development of accord between clinicians and managers and, in many respects, a change in attitudes by some clinicians. As many claims of negligence are brought solely as a result of failures of communication, risk management also requires trust and open communication between health care workers and patients. Equally, a risk management system will not work properly if clinicians are constantly in fear that disciplinary action will result from, for example, the reporting of untoward incidents.

The CNST will assess the progress each NHS Trust has made in its risk management processes by on site visits. Given that large acute Trusts may in future be paying as much as £1m per year (at 1995 prices) in contributions to the CNST, then a risk management discount of as much as 25% represents a considerable sum of money. In a closed pool such as the CNST, if one trust pays less then clearly another Trust must pay more. It is therefore of the utmost importance that the assessments upon which the levels of discount are based are truly objective.

The CNST risk management standards will be developed over a period of time. At the time of writing, the broad standards are being translated into detailed standards which will be published to all members of the CNST. The detailed standards will be weighted according to importance and members of the CNST will be expected to meet these standards in order to achieve the full discount on contributions to the CNST.

The other point worthy of note is that the standards will change as risk management develops generally. The current standards should therefore be regarded only as a starting point. Furthermore, it is likely that in future years the score which Trusts have to achieve to obtain the maximum discount will increase thus building in a "ratchet" effect.

Two types of standard are proposed:

- Minimum standards which must be attained
- Optional standards to which Trusts should aspire as they will promote good risk management.

Minimum standards

(1) *The Board has a written and formally agreed risk management strategy*

The Board is committed to effectively managing clinical risk throughout the Trust. This is achieved by having a written risk management strategy which is agreed by managers and endorsed in policy and practice throughout the organisation.

(2) *An Executive Director of the Board is charged with responsibility for clinical risk management throughout the Trust*

The person appointed seeks advice and support from the

Clinical Directors and other functional managers. A formal risk management forum is set up in which risk-related issues are discussed. Policy is implemented through the general management arrangements of the Trust.

(3) *There is a Risk Manager*

A part of full time Risk Manager is in post with day to day responsibility for the management of clinical and other risks. The Risk Manager is accountable to the Executive Director with responsibility for risk.

(4) *A clinical risk management system is in place*

The Trust can show that a clear approach has been taken to clinical risk management. A clinical risk assessment has been made with an action plan for reducing the key risks identified for urgent attention. There is a system for ensuring that the results of risk assessment findings are routinely incorporated into policy and procedure.

(5) *A Clinical Incident Reporting System is operated in all medical specialties and clinical support departments*

An incident may be defined as any unexpected event occurring during treatment, or unexpected result of treatment, which may, or does, cause harm to the patient. It is essential that such incidents are:

- Recorded to form a database
- Investigated in a timely way

and that appropriate action is taken to:

- Limit damage as in standard 6
- Prevent recurrence

This will be achieved by:

- Reviewing practices and procedures
- Providing feedback to staff.

(6) *Senior managers and clinicians operate a system for rapid follow up of serious incidents*

The Trust has a policy statement which states that when a serious incident or death occurs, the effects on the patient, relatives, professional staff, and the Trust are minimised without delay. Everything possible is done to give a sympathetic account of the event to the patient and relatives. Appropriate counselling and support is offered to anyone affected.

(7) *An agreed system of managing complaints is in place*

While many complaints have no significant clinical content, those that do are identified and dealt with via the risk management or general management routes.

(8) *Appropriate information is provided to patients on the risks and benefits of the proposed treatment or investigation before a signature on Consent Form is sought*

The Trust is able to confirm that it is using the NHS Executive recommended Consent Form and that the risks and benefits are explained to patients. Ideally this explanation should be made by the person proposing to undertake the procedure.

(9) *A comprehensive system for the completion, use, storage and retrieval of medical records is in place. Record keeping standards are monitored through the clinical audit process*

Clear records are kept of all clinical events (including x-rays and CTG traces). They are securely stored and easily retrieved.

(10) *There is a clear documented system for management and communication throughout the key stages of maternity care*

All staff with clinical responsibility for an aspect of maternity care are familiar with the systems and operate them routinely.

(11) *There is an induction/orientation programme for all new clinical staff*

All personnel when joining the Trust, or moving to new jobs within the Trust, are given sufficient training to enable them to perform safely the basic tasks of the post. Junior medical staff are provided with a comprehensive staff handbook which includes key policies and procedures.

The Trust has an agreed routine for briefing locum medical/ agency clinical staff before they are allowed to commence their duties.

Optional standards

(1) *In each specialty there is a continuing programme of education for all doctors in training, nurses, and other health professionals. All consultant staff meet the requirements for continuing medical education*

Staff in clinical practice are well trained in their basic discipline, and kept up to date with developments in their specialty.

(2) *All protocols, procedures, and policies in common use meet the standards set by the Scheme*

The protocols, procedures, and policies in use will reflect the best practice noted by the Scheme during compliance visits. These will be promulgated to members from time to time.

(3) *There are standard operational procedures in regular use which permit staff involved in serious clinical incidents to be identified and traced*

The Trust maintains a record of specimen signatures of all clinical staff. Where a member of staff has been involved in a serious incident which may give rise to a claim, their name is recorded. They are advised of the importance of being able to be contacted at some point in the future. A procedure is in place to set up a "contact address" in the United Kingdom for future use. This contact address is updated at regular intervals.

Although the CNST risk management proposals are as yet imperfect, they represent a major step forward in ensuring that clinical risk management in England advances from being a topic which is often under discussion within Trusts to one which is accepted as being an integral part of a Trust's activities. After all, Trusts exist to provide quality care for patients and risk management is, ultimately, a mechanism for improving the quality of care. By its very nature medicine in particular and health care in general is associated with risk. Providers of health care (and indeed purchasers) should therefore make every effort to reduce those risks in order to achieve their objectives of providing the highest quality care.

Appendix II

Acting on complaints: the Government's proposals in response to *Being heard*, the report of a review committee on NHS complaints procedures

The report of the Review Committee chaired by Professor Alan Wilson on NHS complaints *Being heard* was published for consultation in May 1994. The main conclusions of the report are discussed by Judith Allsopp and Linda Mulcahy (chapter 22).

The Government has now considered the report in the light of consultation. Its decisions were published in March 1995 and are set out below. Complaints procedures will now therefore be expected to adhere to these guidelines.

The target date for implementation is 1 April 1996, to coincide with the creation of unified health authorities taking over the roles of district health authorities and family health service authorities.

New NHS complaints procedure

I. There will be a new simplified and fairer NHS complaints procedure, embodying the principles recommended by the Review Committee: responsiveness, quality enhancement, cost effectiveness, accessibility, impartiality, simplicity, speed, confidentiality and accountability.

The new complaints procedure will focus on satisfying complainants' concerns while being fair to practitioners and staff. It will have the minimum number of different features necessary to reflect different contractual arrangements, the need for professional advice, etc.

II.   We will ensure that greater publicity is given to the new complaints procedure.

Our aim will be to build on the progress already made through the Patient's Charter and to ensure that there is readily available information on how to complain for all NHS service users.

III.   The new complaints procedure will be concerned only with resolving complaints, and not with disciplinary matters.

We will review, in consultation with the professional representative organisations and other interested parties, the existing disciplinary procedures for family practitioners in order to separate them from complaints procedures and to remove the identified shortcomings. The hospital complaints procedure is already separate from discipline.

If a complaint raises such serious issues as to warrant it, we will ensure that any relevant information from complaints handling procedures is passed on quickly to management and/ or professional regulatory bodies so that they may consider what other steps may be necessary.

Two stage NHS procedure

IV.   We accept the recommendation of the Review Committee for a two stage complaints procedure within the NHS, overseen by the Health Service Commissioner (Ombudsman).

Stage I

V.   In the first stage those providing services to patients should try to resolve the complaint as quickly as possible.

At Stage I the following options would be available for resolving the complaint:

an immediate, often oral, first line response;

investigation/conciliation;

action by an officer of the health authority for family health services or by the chief executive for trusts.

These would not be sequential procedures which a complainant had to go through in turn. The kind of response would depend on the nature of the complaint and the wishes of the complainant. There will need to be well publicised access for all complainants to a named person such as a complaints officer.

VI. The current Patient's Charter right to receive a full and prompt written reply from the chief executive to any formal complaint against a trust will be retained.

The Review Committee did not think it appropriate for Chief Executives to provide written replies to all complaints given the emphasis on a rapid first line response. The Select Committee on the Parliamentary Commissioner for Administration, however, felt* that it was important to retain this right. We agree with the Select Committee that the chief executive should continue to sign all written respones to complaints in order that he or she should maintain oversight over all complaints, while ensuring that complaints receive as quick a response as possible.

* In their sixth report, 1993–94 session. HC 42, paragraph 63.

VII. Practice-based complaints procedures will be developed in all family health services.

We will be discussing with the professional representative organisations and others how to develop practice-based complaints procedures in family health services.

Stage II

VIII. If complaints cannot be resolved by service providers, complainants will have the option of asking for a further review which may include the establishment of a panel to reconsider the complaint. Such panels will have a lay chair and a majority of members totally independent from the provider of the service. Independent clinical assessors will provide advice in appropriate cases.

In relation to hospital services the decision on whether to convene a panel will be taken by a non-executive director of the relevant NHS trust (the "convener"). In relation to primary care services, the convener will be a non-executive member of the relevant health authority. In making this decision, the convener will act in consultation with the independent lay chairman who would chair the panel if one were to be convened. In England, the independent chairman will be drawn from a list maintained by the regional office of the NHS Executive.

In deciding whether to establish a panel, the convener and independent lay chairman will consider:

- whether the trust or practice can take any further action short of establishing a panel to satisfy the complainant;
- whether the trust or practice has already taken all practicable action and therefore establishing a panel would add no further value to the process.

If this consideration leads them to conclude that a panel should not be established, the complainant can, of course, put their case direct to the Health Service Commissioner (Ombudsman). This is an important safeguard.

Panels will be composed as follows:

- in relation to a non-clinical complaint about hospital services, the independent lay chairman, the convener and, in most cases, a non-executive from the relevant health authority. Where appropriate, the health authority would also consult the relevant GP fundholder to take their views. If the fundholder agrees, he or she might represent the purchaser interest on the panel;
- in relation to primary care complaints, the independent chairman, the convener and another independent lay person drawn from the regional list;
- panels wholly or partly related to clinical matters (whether in hospital or primary care cases) would also be advised by two independent clinical assessors.

Reports by complaints panels will routinely be made available to the complainant and the relevant trust and purchaser or, in the case of family health services, the relevant health authority and family practitioner.

Detailed guidance on the criteria for convening panels, their membership, how best to ensure the input of independent professional advice in appropriate cases, and on their operation will be developed based on discussion with interested parties.

Training and support

IX. We will consult the professional regulatory and educational bodies on incorporating communications skills in training programmes. A new training package will be produced, in consultation with interested parties, to improve complaints handling at all levels within trusts.

The need for good communications skills among health service professionals is already recognised among professional and training bodies. The proposed new training package for trusts will take on board the recommendations of the Review Committee on improvements in the way complaints are handled: eg rapid first line response; making early personal contact with patients; making conciliation more widely available (where it meets the complainant's wishes); improving communications skills; meeting the particular needs of community service staff; ensuring efficient handling of complaints involving more than one organisation, etc. We will also address the skills and support needed to enable family health services' practice based procedures to meet the recommendations of the Review Committee on best practice in dealing with complaints.

X. Community health councils will continue to carry out their role in supporting complainants. We will also discuss with interested parties how to ensure that practitioners and staff are aware of the support available when a complaint is made against them.

Community health councils (CHCs) already play a major role in supporting individual complainants, in addition to providing a consumer input into strategic decision-making about services at the local level. The Government expects this role to continue.

The Review Committee recommended that special attention should be paid to the needs of vulnerable groups for support and representation in making complaints. CHCs have an

531

important role to play here, but the Government also welcomes the initiative of NHS trusts who have set up their own patient advocacy/patient friend schemes to encourage and support patients in pursuing complaints and making suggestions about services.

Advice, support and representation should also be available for practitioners and staff subject to complaint both from management and representative associations.

Application to other organisations

XI. We will develop, in consultation with interested parties, guidance for complaints against purchasers, ensuring as much commonality as possible with the approach outlined above for family health services and trusts. We will also consult interested parties on how to ensure that complaints procedures are dealt with effectively in contracts between purchasers and non-NHS providers.

XII. We will continue to encourage local authority social services departments and health authorities to work closely together on complaints which have both health and social care aspects and to explain to the public how systems work through local community care charters.

Time limits and response times

XIII. We propose that there should be a time limit of one year after the event being complained about for a complaint to be made, with the discretion for the complaints officer or convener to waive this in appropriate cases.

The publicity given to the new procedures will stress the importance of making a complaint as early as possible in order for it to be successfully resolved. Nevertheless, we consider that the current time limit for complaints against family health service practitioners of 13 weeks is too short to enable some legitimate complaints to be dealt with. We do, however, consider that in fairness to practitioners and staff there should be a time limit of one year for complaints, but that there should be flexibility for this to be waived where reasonable. This would mirror the current procedure for complaints to the Health Service Commissioner (Ombudsman). We will need to discuss with the professional representative bodies the implications for disciplinary procedures in primary care.

XIV. We will set challenging but achievable standards for response times.

It is important to set tough deadlines for responses to complaints. The consultation responses, however, indicate that the deadlines recommended by the Review Committee may not always be realistic if a thorough investigation of a complaint needs to be made. We believe that a deadline of two working days for an initial response and four weeks for a full response, following investigation/conciliation at stage one, are realistic but challenging targets. It is not possible at this stage to set deadlines for the completion of the stage two process, particularly those cases which will involve the need to seek professional advice. A sensible deadline will need to be worked out during the implementation period, in discussion with interested parties.

Role of the Health Service Commissioner (Ombudsman)

XV. The Government will seek legislative time to extend the jurisdiction of the Health Service Commissioner to all complaints by, or on behalf of, NHS patients.

Currently the Health Service Commissioner's jurisdiction covers hospital complaints (excluding those concerning the exercise of clinical judgement), and complaints against family health service authorities, but not against family health service practitioners. As recommended by the Review Committee and by the Select Committee on the Parliamentary Commissioner for Administration, we propose that his jurisdiction be extended to cover clinical complaints against all NHS staff and all complaints against family health service practitioners and their staff. The Commissioner will need access to appropriate professional advice in undertaking these new responsibilities. Complainants would not be able ordinarily to take the complaint to the Commissioner before they had exhausted the internal complaints system. The current exclusion from matters which the Commissioner can investigate, of action taken in respect of disciplinary or other personnel or contractual matters, shall continue.

We agree with the Select Committee on the Parliamentary Commissioner for Administration that there should be no change in the Commissioner's current jurisdiction over complaints against purchasing. He can and does investigate complaints where there appears to have been specific harm or injustice caused to an individual as a result of a decision by a purchaser.

Filing, recording, and monitoring

XVI. We will review the systems for filing, recording and monitoring complaints in the light of the recommendations of the Review Committee and of the Select Committee on the Parliamentary Commissioner for Administration.

The principles we will follow in looking at these systems are to ensure that the right kind of information is collected in the right way at each level to ensure confidentiality; to enable the complaints procedure to run smoothly; to help management identify areas for improvement in quality of service generally; and to keep any additional administrative burdens to a minimum.

Implementation

XVII. Implementation in England will be managed by the NHS Executive, calling on advice and consulting as necessary. The NHS Executive will consider how complaints handling should be monitored both at the centre and by purchasers. The target date for implementation is April 1996.

Our aim will be to set up efficient mechanisms for implementing the changes described above, while avoiding the creation of a whole new complaints bureaucracy. We will leave as much flexibility as possible for individual organisations to meet the specific needs of their patients, practitioners and staff, while ensuring that the

534

essential features of the new system outlined above are available to all patients, practitioners and staff throughout the country.

Performance management arrangements in the NHS will take account of performance in implementing the new procedures and achieving satisfactory resolution of complaints.

Appendix III

Job descriptions for clinical risk managers

Risk managers may have a variety of different responsibilities depending on the priorities of the unit or hospital, the extent to which they are involved in the management of claims, and the extent to which they concern themselves with day to day clinical events.

The following two sample job descriptions have contrasting approaches. The first post has hospitalwide responsibilities and a much stronger emphasis on legal and insurance aspects. The second is for a risk manager on a unit, whose responsibilities have a much stronger clinical emphasis and a greater involvement in research and audit.

The purpose of presenting the job descriptions is not to suggest a "correct" way of assigning responsibilities, but to show the wide range of work that may be involved and to show that there are very different ways of conceptualising the post, according to the needs of the trust or unit.

CLINICAL RISK MANAGEMENT NHS TRUST

Job Title: Clinical Risk Manager

Grade and Salary: Senior management contract related supplement

Responsible to: Medical Director of the Trust

Responsible for: Part time secretary

Liaise with: All clinical staff within the hospital, clinical audit, consumer affairs department and other members of the risk management group, representatives, litigants, insurance brokers, claimants, and finance department staff.

Job purpose: To establish a systematic approach to the analysis, evaluation and minimisation of clinical risk within the Trust. To oversee the management of legal claims against the Trust and insurance matters.

Main Duties and Responsibilities:

1   To work with all Clinical Directors in planning and implementing a proactive policy of risk management.

2   In conjunction with the designated group of clinicians, to make recommendations designed to reduce or eliminate risks identified.

3   To develop and implement reporting systems on adverse clinical incidents in liaison with clinical audit, the consumer affairs manager, and department of quality.

4   To design and deliver training programmes on risk management to all levels of clinical staff.

5   To present summaries or reports on specific incidents as necessary to the relevant clinical audit groups and risk management group.

6   To ensure early post event meetings involving all relevant clinical staff following any serious adverse incident.

7   To produce a quarterly risk management report.

8   To advise the Clinical Audit Committee of issues benefiting from further study arising from risk management reporting systems.

9   To analyse trends and specific untoward incidents arising from patient complaints.

10 To oversee the processing of all insurance claims for losses and damage under the terms of the Trust's insurance policies.

11 To manage the renegotiation and contacting of insurance cover with the Trust's insurance brokers.

12 To evaluate and monitor the Trust's insurance brokers performance and to oversee the market testing of brokers' services as appropriate.

Person specification

1 Educated to degree level, with post graduate professional qualifications in either medicine, nursing, paramedical services, or the law.

2 At least four years' experience of risk management in a related field or management of a clinical team or handling of legal cases in health related field of activity.

3 Highly developed influencing and organisational skills.

4 Ability to rapidly grasp related financial management matters.

CLINICAL RISK MANAGER: MATERNITY UNIT

1 General information

Job title: Risk management, Audit and Education Manager

Department: Maternity Unit

Grade: Midwifery Grade G

2 Line relationships

Responsible to: Clinical Director

Accountable to: Head of Midwifery Services

Liaise with: Other staff in the department and throughout the hospital as well as other health care agencies

3 Job summary

3.1 To develop and coordinate risk management in the Maternity Directorate.

3.2 To report regularly and liaise with the clinical director, and members of the obstetric, midwifery and neonatal staff on developments in risk management, audit, and in-service education.

3.3 To keep a record of all activities undertaken in the first year and to report regularly to Hospital Risk Management Group.

3.4 To make effective use of the computerised Maternity Information System to improve the quality of care through effective risk management and audit.

3.5 To foster a cooperative relationship between doctors, midwives, and health care professionals.

4 Main duties and responsibilities

4.1 Risk Management

To work with the Clinical Director, the Head of Midwifery Service, and a designated representative of the hospital insurance company to plan and implement a policy of "risk management" for the Maternity Unit. This will involve:—

4.1.1 Daily screening of records of all mothers and babies delivered in the previous 24 hours to abstract pregnancy and labour adverse events and develop a system to document these events.

4.1.2 Reporting adverse and untoward clinical events to a Committee responsible for considering and commenting on those events to the clinical Director of Maternity. The composition of this Committee and the action deemed necessary when individual case histories have been considered by the members will be the responsibility of the Clinical Director.

4.1.3 Develop a system to record all adverse and untoward events affecting patients, visitors and staff. These will be reported directly to the Clinical Director.

4.1.4 Make regular reports to the Trust Risk Management Committee on the Maternity Unit's Quality Risk Management (QRM) Programme.

4.1.5 Present to the staff of the Maternity Unit relevant case histories (after discussion by the Committee) and summarised data on QRM as a part of the audit programme.

4.1.6 Ensure that in the events of any serious adverse outcome or untoward event, the relevant clinicians (obstetricians, midwives, and neonatologists etc) come together at the earliest possible opportunity to discuss the case and counsel the parents.

4.2 Maternity and Neonatal Audit

4.2.1 Become sufficiently familiar with the Maternity Information System so that relevant data can be abstracted after simple analysis.

4.2.2 Develop audited data, involving a list of appropriate outcome indicators of clinical performance, and present this data to the staff of the Maternity Unit.

4.2.3 Working in conjunction with a designated group of clinicians, use audited and QRM data, to make recommendations designed to reduce or eliminate risk.

4.3 In Service Education

4.3.1   To work with the consultant designated a responsible for an agreed programme of in-service education.

4.3.2   To assist in the organisation of the introductory course or new medical and midwifery staff and the completion of log books by new medical staff.

4.3.3   To develop a system for ensuring that medical and midwifery staff attend a required number of in-service educational events.

4.3.4   Ensure that all clinical protocols are distributed and implemented by medical and midwifery staff working in the Maternity Unit. Also to be responsible for adding new items once agreed to the protocol.

Appendix IV

Incident report form

The form shown on the following two pages is intended only as a sample report form. As Roger Clements makes clear in chapter 18, such forms develop with experience and changing needs, although a core of basic information is always required. The nature and severity of the incidents to be reported should always be generated and agreed by staff on the unit in question and may also change with time as different problems come to the fore.

DEPARTMENT OF RISK MANAGEMENT

REPORTING OF ADVERSE OUTCOME/RISK OCCURRENCE

CATEGORY [Please tick as appropriate]	
001	MEDICAL
002	SURGICAL
003	PAEDIATRICS
004	PATHOLOGY
005	ANAESTHETICS
006	DIAGNOSTIC IMAGING
007	CASUALTY
008	OUT PATIENTS DEPT
009	GYNAECOLOGY
010	OBSTETRICS/MIDWIFERY
011	PHARMACY
012	PHYSIOTHERAPY
013	OTHER
	[Please specify]

GROUP [Please tick]	
101	PATIENT
102	MEMBER OF STAFF
103	VISITOR
104	OTHERS

GRADE OF INCIDENT [Please estimate]	
201	SERIOUS
202	ROUTINE
203	SLIGHT

THIS SECTION FOR GROUP 101 [PATIENTS] ONLY

TYPE OF INCIDENT ....
[From Directorate specific list]

NAME OF CONSULTANT........................... HOSPITAL NO ....

****

NAME...................................WARD/LOCATION...............................
[For ALL Groups]   [Where incident occurred]

****

SYNOPSIS OF ADVERSE OUTCOME/RISK OCCURENCE:-
[For ALL Groups]

_____

_____

_____

_____

_____

_____

_____

please continue overleaf

PLEASE GIVE THE FOLLOWING INFORMATION AS APPROPRIATE:-
[PLEASE PRINT]

Name[s] and addresses of any witnesses

[1]_____[2]_____

_____

_____

_____

_____

Name[s] of other nursing and medical staff involved in the management or present at the time

[1]_____[2]_____

[3]_____[4]_____

[5]_____[6]_____

[7]_____[8]_____

****

REPORTED BY   **DATE AND TIME**   **SIGNATURE**
[PLEASE PRINT]   [Where incident occurred]

_____

****

SIGNED BY DEPARTMENT MANAGER   **DATE**

_____   _____

****

THIS FORM SHOULD BE COMPLETED, SIGNED AND DATED AS SOON AS
POSSIBLE FOLLOWING THE INCIDENT. IT SHOULD BE PASSED TO YOUR
MANAGER FOR CHECKING AND COUNTER-SIGNATURE.

THE DEPARTMENT MANAGER SHOULD RETAIN A COPY OF THIS FORM AS
A RECORD. THE ORIGINAL SHOULD BE SENT TO MALCOLM FRANCIS,
DIRECTOR OF ADMINISTRATIVE SERVICES, IMMEDIATELY.

AN ANALYSIS OF COMPLAINTS RECEIVED INDICATES THAT THEY RARELY
LEAD TO LITIGATION WHEN HANDLED PROPERLY AND QUICKLY

REVISED MARCH 1993

Appendix V

Risk management organisations

The following organisations offer a range of clinical risk management services including safety reviews, advice on risk management strategies, claims management, and training. The services vary from one organisation to another and no particular recommendations are implied. They are simply the main organisations known to the editor at the time of publication.

Commercial organisations

Healthcare Risk Solutions,
Kennedy House,
115 Hammersmith Road,
London W14 0QH, UK

Telephone   0171 602 7700
Fax   0171 602 8833

Merret Health Risk Management,
60 West Street,
Brighton
BN1 2RB, UK

Telephone   01273 747272
Fax   01273 206450

QRM Healthcare Ltd,
Hitching Court,
Blacklands Way,
Abingdon,
Oxfordshire OX14 1RG

544

Telephone   01235 544820
Fax   01235 544876

St Paul International Insurance Company,
St Paul House,
61–63 London Road,
Redhill,
Surrey RH1 1NA, UK

Telephone   01737 787 787
Fax   01737 787 172

St Paul's offers free risk management services to organisations who insure with them, but do not offer risk management advice otherwise.

MCMS,
Medical Protection Society,
50 Hallam Street,
London W1N 6DE, UK

Telephone   0171 637 0541
Fax   0171 636 0690

Medirisk,
Medical Defence Union,
192 Altringham Road,
Sharston,
Manchester M22 4RZ, UK

Telephone   0161 428 1234
Fax   0161 491 3301

Professional associations

ALARM,
Association of Litigation and Risk Managers,
General Accident Building,
77/83 Upper Richmond Road,
London SW15 2TT, UK

Telephone   0181 780 2211
Fax   0181 780 1141

ALARM holds regular meetings and seminars for mutual support and exchange of information.

Institute of Risk Management,
Lloyd's Avenue House,
6 Lloyd's Avenue,
London EC3N 3AX, UK

Telephone   0171 709 9808
Fax   0171 709 0716

The Institute does not at present offer specific advice about clinical risk management but provides training and information about all other aspects of risk management.

Appendix VI

Reproduced with permission of the Law Society.

Application on behalf of a patient for hospital medical records for use when court proceedings are contemplated

Difficulties in obtaining a full and legible set of medical records are a constant source of delay and frustration in both medical negligence and personal injury litigation.

This application form and response forms have been prepared by a working party of the Law Society's Civil Litigation Committee and approved by the Department of Health for use in NHS and trust hospitals. This version was released in July 1995.

The purpose of the forms is to standardise and streamline the disclosure of medical records to a patient's solicitors, who are investigating or already pursuing a personal injury claim against a third party, or a medical negligence claim against the hospital to which the application is addressed and/or other hospitals of general practitioners.

Use of the forms is entirely voluntary and does not prejudice any party's right under the access to Health Records Act 1990, the Data Protection Act 1984, or ss. 33 and 34 of the Supreme Court Act 1981. The aim is to save time and costs for all concerned for the benefit of the patient and the hospital and in the interests of justice. Use of the forms should make it unnecessary in most cases for there to be exchanges of letters or other enquiries. If there is any unusual matter not covered by the form, the patient's solicitor may write a separate letter at the outset.

APPLICATION ON BEHALF OF A PATIENT
FOR HOSPITAL MEDICAL RECORDS
FOR USE WHEN COURT
PROCEEDINGS ARE CONTEMPLATED

This should be completed as fully as possible

Insert Hospital Name and Address

> *To: Medical Records Officer*
>
> *Hospital*

1 (a)	Full name of patient (including previous surnames)	
(b)	Address now	
(c)	Address at start of treatment	
(d)	Date of birth	
(e)	Hospital ref no if available	
(f)	N.I. number, if available	
2	This application is made because I am considering:	
(a)	a claim against your hospital as detailed in para. 7 overleaf	YES/NO
(b)	pursuing an action against someone else	YES/NO

3	Department(s) where treatment was received	
4	Name(s) of Consultant(s) at your hospital in charge of the treatment	
5	Whether treatment at your hospital was private or NHS, wholly or in part	
6	A description of the treatment received, with approximate dates	
7	If the answer to Q2(A) is 'Yes', details of the likely nature, and grounds for, such a claim, and approximate dates of the events involved	
8	If the answer to Q2(B) is 'Yes', insert: (i) the names of the proposed defendants	
	(ii) whether action yet begun	YES/NO
	(iii) if appropriate, details of Court and action number	
9	We confirm we will pay (i) reasonable copying charges (ii) a reasonable administration fee	YES/NO YES/NO

10	We request prior details of: (i) photocopying and administration charges for medical records (ii) number of, and cost of copying, x-ray and scan films	YES/NO YES/NO
11	Any other relevant information, particular requirements, or any particular documents <u>not</u> required (eg copies of computerised records)	
	Signature of Solicitor	
	Name	
	Address	
	Ref	
	Telephone Number	
	Fax Number	
		Please print name beneath each signature. Signature by child over 12 but under 18 years also requires signature by parent
	Signature of patient:	
	Signature of parent or next friend if appropriate:	
	Signature of personal representative where patient has died:	

Signature of solicitor	
Name	
Address	
Ref	
Telephone number	
Fax number	
Signature of patient:	*Please print name beneath each signature. Signature by child over 12 but under 18 years also requires a signature by parent*
Signature of parent or next friend if appropriate:	
Signature of personal representative where patient has died:	

FIRST RESPONSE TO APPLICATION
FOR HOSPITAL RECORDS

Insert Name and Address of Hospital here

	NAME OF PATIENT Our ref: Your ref:	
1.	Date of receipt of patient's application	
2.	We intend that copy medical records will be despatched within 6 weeks of that date	YES/NO
3.	We require pre-payment of photocopying charges	YES/NO
4.	If estimate of photocopying charges requested or pre-payment required, the amount will be	£ /notified to you
5.	The cost of x-ray and scan films will be	£ /notified to you
6.	If there is any problem, we will write to you within those 6 weeks	YES/NO
7.	Any other information	
	Please address further correspondence to:	
	Signed:	
	Direct telephone number:	
	Direct fax number:	
	Dated:	

SECOND RESPONSE ENCLOSING
PATIENT'S HOSPITAL MEDICAL RECORDS

Address: Our ref:

                                     Your ref:

	NAME OF PATIENT:	
1.	We confirm that the enclosed copy medical records are all those within the control of this hospital, relevant to the application which you have made to the best of our knowledge and belief, subject to paras 2–5 below	YES/NO
2.	Details of any other documents which have not yet been located	
3.	Date by when it is expected that these will be supplied	
4.	Details of any records which we are not producing	
5.	The reasons for not doing so	
6.	An invoice for copying and administration charges is attached	YES/NO
	Signed	
	Date	

Index

Related titles

QUALITY AND SAFETY IN ANAESTHESIA

Edited by Jonathan Secker-Walker

With contributions from leading figures in anaesthetic audit, this concise book addresses the quality and management of risk; critical incidents and human factors in anaesthesia; standards for routine monitoring; standards in training; managing a department; resource management; and computers.

Readership: anaesthetists, hospital managers

OUTCOMES INTO CLINICAL PRACTICE

Edited by Tony Delamothe

Outcomes research, the new buzz word in health care, refers to the generation, collection, and analysis of the results of medical care. Such information offers the opportunities to improve clinical effectiveness and set standards for good practice. Based on a ground breaking conference held by the *BMJ*, BMA, and UK Clearing House, *Outcomes into Clinical Practice* discusses the issues involved and gives real examples of how outcomes research works best.

Readership: all members of clinical teams, both in hospitals and general practice, health care purchasers, clinical audit officers

RATIONING IN ACTION

Most doctors accept that rationing of health care is inevitable. But how should available resources be distributed? In this book doctors, managers, politicians, and philosophers discuss the inevitability of rationing and what it means both to the health providers and their patients.

Readership: doctors, hospital managers, politicians, ethicists

For further details contact your local bookseller, or in case of difficulty, contact Books Division, BMJ Publishing Group, BMA House, Tavistock Square, London WC1H 9JR, UK (Tel +44(0) 171-383-6245; Fax: +44(0) 171-383 6662)